PET

SINC

Under

The Under Fire™ Series

General Editor: Jeffrey A. Schaler

VOLUME 1

Szasz Under Fire: The Psychiatric Abolitionist Faces His Critics

VOLUME 2

Howard Gardner Under Fire: The Rebel Psychologist Faces His Critics

VOLUME 3

Peter Singer Under Fire: The Moral Iconoclast Faces His Critics

To Sonia Schaler Haynes

And the people asked him, saying, What shall we do then?

—Luke 3:10

BILLY: Tolstoy asked the same question. He wrote a book with that title. He got so upset about the poverty in Moscow that he went one night into the poorest section and just gave away all his money. You could do that now. Five American dollars would be a fortune to one of these people.

GUY: Wouldn't do any good, just be a drop in the ocean.

BILLY: Ahh, that's the same conclusion Tolstoy came to. I disagree.

GUY: Oh, what's your solution?

BILLY: Well, I support the view that you just don't think about the major issues. You do whatever you can about the misery that's in front of you. Add your light to the sum of light. You think that's naive, don't you?

GUY: Yep.

BILLY: It's all right, most journalists do.

GUY: We can't afford to get involved.

—C.J. Koch, *The Year of Living Dangerously* (1978)

PETER SINGER
Under Fire

The Moral Iconoclast
Faces His Critics

EDITED BY

JEFFREY A. SCHALER

CLACKAMAS COMMUNITY COLLEGE LIBRARY PROPERTY

OPEN COURT
Chicago and La Salle, Illinois

Volume 3 in the series, Under Fire™
General Editor: Jeffrey A. Schaler

Cover photograph by Derek Goodwin, www.derekgoodwin.com

To order books from Open Court, call toll-free 1-800-815-2280, or visit our website at www.opencourtbooks.com.

Open Court Publishing Company is a division of Carus Publishing Company.

Copyright © 2009 by Carus Publishing Company

First printing 2009

All rights reserved. No part of this publication may be reproduced, stored in a retrieval system, or transmitted, in any form or by any means, electronic, mechanical, photocopying, recording, or otherwise, without the prior written permission of the publisher, Open Court Publishing Company, a division of Carus Publishing Company, 315 Fifth Street, P.O. Box 300, Peru, Illinois 61354-0300.

Printed and bound in the United States of America.

Library of Congress Cataloging-in-Publication Data

Peter Singer under fire : the moral iconoclast faces his critics / edited by Jeffrey A. Schaler.
     p. cm. — (The under fire series ; v. 3)
     Includes bibliographical references and index.
     ISBN 978-0-8126-9618-9 (trade paper : alk. paper)
   1. Singer, Peter, 1946- I. Schaler, Jeffrey A.
     B5704.S554.P48 2009
     170.92—dc22

                                     2009007274

Contents

About the Authors   xi

Acknowledgments   xvi

Singer's Burden: Suffering and the Man
JEFFREY A. SCHALER   xvii

An Intellectual Autobiography
PETER SINGER   1

I.   THE MORAL STATUS OF ANIMALS   75

1.   The Human Prejudice
BERNARD WILLIAMS   77
Reply by Peter Singer   97

2.   Justifying Animal Use
R.G. FREY   103
Reply by Peter Singer   123

II.   THE SANCTITY OF LIFE   131

3.   Singer on Abortion and Infanticide
DON MARQUIS   133
Reply by Peter Singer   153

4.   Singer's Unsanctity of Human Life: A Critique
HARRY J. GENSLER   163
Reply by Peter Singer   185

5. Unspeakable Conversations, or,
    How I Spent One Day as a Token Cripple
    at Princeton University
    HARRIET MᶜBRYDE JOHNSON   195
    Reply by Peter Singer   206

6. Not Dead Yet!
    STEPHEN DRAKE   213
    Reply by Peter Singer   221

III. GLOBAL ETHICS   227

7. Famine, Affluence, and Psychology
    JUDITH LICHTENBERG   229
    Reply by Peter Singer   259

8. What Do We Owe to Distant Needy
    Strangers?
    RICHARD J. ARNESON   267
    Reply by Peter Singer   294

9. Should Peter Singer Favor Massive
    Redistribution or Economic Growth?
    TYLER COWEN   301
    Reply by Peter Singer   320

10. The Ethics of Assistance: What's the Good
     of It?
     DAVID FAGELSON   329
     Reply by Peter Singer   351

IV. ETHICAL THEORY   357

11. Singer's Unstable Meta-Ethics
     MICHAEL HUEMER   359
     Reply by Peter Singer   380

12. Philosophical Presuppositions of *Practical Ethics*
     MARCUS DÜWELL   395
     Reply by Peter Singer   419

13. Separateness, Suffering, and Moral Theory
     DAVID SCHMIDTZ   429
     Reply by Peter Singer   455

14. Singer on Moral Theory
     JAN NARVESON   463
     Reply by Peter Singer   488

15. Animal Liberationist Bites Dog
     BERYL LIEFF BENDERLY   499
     Reply by Peter Singer   504

Peter Singer Bibliography   507

Index   559

About the Authors

RICHARD J. ARNESON is a professor in the Department of Philosophy at the University of California, San Diego, and Institute for Law and Philosophy, School of Law, University of San Diego. He has written several essays that aim to integrate an appropriate account of personal responsibility and sensible notions of individual well-being into an egalitarian theory of distributive justice. He also writes about the strengths and weaknesses of act consequentialism as compared to rival doctrines. He has published close to one hundred essays on topics in moral and political philosophy.

BERYL LIEFF BENDERLY is a prize-winning journalist and author. Her hundreds of articles have appeared in national magazines ranging from *Glamour* to *Scientific American*, in newspapers including the *New York Times* and *Washington Post,* and on major websites. She is also the author or co-author of eight adult trade books.

TYLER COWEN is Holbert C. Harris Professor of Economics at George Mason University. He is author of eight books and numerous articles, in the fields of both economics and philosophy. His pieces have appeared in numerous journals including *American Economic Review, Journal of Political Economy, Ethics,* and *Philosophy and Public Affairs.* He co-writes a blog at www.marginalrevolution.com and he is currently researching a book on the foundations of a free society.

STEPHEN DRAKE is a person with "invisible" disabilities that are related to a brain injury he experienced at birth and is a survivor of a doctor's recommendation of passive euthanasia. Prior to working with Not Dead Yet (NDY), he worked with the Facilitated Communication Institute and Center on Human Policy at Syracuse University. He has been active in

Not Dead Yet since 1996, and in 1999 started work as NDY's research analyst. He's a frequent contributor to national disability magazines and has been honored by national TASH and the Arc of Illinois, for his work on behalf on NDY. Describing himself as a "recovering academic," he has published articles in peer-reviewed journals as well as national newspapers and disability publications. In 1999 he helped to organize a large protest at Princeton University over the hiring of Peter Singer. He writes commentary on the NDY blog at notdeadyetnewscommentary .blogspot.com.

MARCUS DÜWELL holds a chair in philosophical ethics at the Department of Philosophy at Utrecht University. He is research director of the Ethics Institute of Utrecht University, director of the Netherlands Research School for Practical Philosophy and director of the Leiden-Utrecht Research Institute, ZENO. From 1993 until 2001 he was academic coordinator of the Interdepartmental Center for Ethics in the Sciences and Humanities at the University of Tübingen. His research interests include bioethics (especially the ethics of genetics and environmental ethics) and basic questions of moral philosophy (foundations of individual rights and human dignity) and the relation between ethics and aesthetics. He is Editor-in-Chief of the book series, "Ethics and Applied Philosophy."

DAVID RUSSELL FAGELSON is an associate professor of law and society at American University's School of Public Affairs in Washington, D.C. He is the author of *Justice As Integrity: Tolerance and the Moral Momentum of Law* (2005). Before he joined the faculty at American University, Fagelson was a Research Associate and Director for Law and Governance at the IRIS Center, University of Maryland, where he advised US, multilateral, and foreign government officials and members of nascent civil society in former-Communist countries making the transition to market oriented and constitutional democracies, where his work focused on the enforcement of rights.

R. G. FREY is Professor of Philosophy at Bowling Green State University in Ohio and Senior Research Fellow in the Social Philosophy and Policy Center there. He is the author and editor of numerous books and articles in normative and applied ethics, including animal ethics.

HARRY J. GENSLER, S.J., is Professor of Philosophy at John Carroll University, Cleveland. He has strong interests in logic, ethics, and where these two areas come together. His authored books in logic include *Introduction to Logic*; *Historical Dictionary of Logic*; and *Gödel's Theorem Simplified*. His authored books in ethics are *Formal Ethics*; *Ethics: A Contemporary Introduction*; and *Historical Dictionary of Ethics*. He also co-edited, with James C. Swindal, *The Sheed and Ward Anthology of Catholic Philosophy*. His personal Web site at jcu.edu/philosophy/gensler reveals strong interests in computers and in backpacking.

MICHAEL HUEMER received his Ph.D. from Rutgers University in 1998 and is presently associate professor of philosophy at the University of Colorado at Boulder. He is the author of *Skepticism and the Veil of Perception* and *Ethical Intuitionism*, as well as numerous academic articles in ethics, epistemology, and other areas.

HARRIET MCBRYDE JOHNSON practiced law in Charleston, South Carolina, for twenty years. Her solo practice emphasized benefits and civil rights claims of poor and working people with disabilities. She was active in the disability rights movement for thirty years. Her memoir, *Too Late to Die Young: Nearly True Tales from a Life*, was published in 2005. In 2006, she published *Accidents of Nature*, a novel about growing up with disabilities. Johnson drew national attention for her opposition to "the charity mentality" and the "pity-based tactics" of the annual Jerry Lewis muscular dystrophy telethon. She protested the Jerry Lewis telethon for nearly twenty years. South Carolina State Supreme Court Chief Justice Jean Toal stated that Johnson was "a fierce advocate for the disabled, a nationally revered attorney and a titanic figure in state legal history." Johnson died on June 4th, 2008.

JUDITH LICHTENBERG is Professor of Philosophy at Georgetown University. Before moving to Georgetown in 2007, she taught at the University of Maryland for twenty-five years. She is co-author, with Robert K. Fullinwider, of *Leveling the Playing Field: Justice, Politics, and College Admissions* (2004); editor of *Democracy and the Mass Media* (1990); and author of many articles. She is currently writing a book entitled *Charity, Its Scope and Limits*.

DON MARQUIS is Professor of Philosophy at the University of Kansas. His essay "Why Abortion Is Immoral" appeared in the *Journal of Philosophy* in 1989, has been reprinted seventy-six times, and has generated an extensive critical literature. He has also written about the ethics of adultery, the legalization of physician-assisted suicide and the ethics of randomized clinical trials in medicine. During the 2007–2008 academic year he was Laurance S. Rockefeller Visiting Professor for Distinguished Teaching at the Center for Human Values at Princeton University.

JAN NARVESON is now Professor Emeritus of Philosophy at the University of Waterloo in Ontario, after teaching there for four decades. He is the author of more than two hundred papers in philosophical periodicals and anthologies, mainly on ethical theory and practice, and of five published books: *Morality and Utility* (1967), *The Libertarian Idea* (1989); *Moral Matters* (1993, second edition, 1999); *Respecting Persons in Theory and Practice* (2002); and, with Marilyn Friedman, *Political Correctness* (1995). He is also the editor of *Moral Issues* (1983); *For and Against the State* (with John T. Sanders, 1996), and *Liberalism: New Essays on Liberal Themes* (with Susan Dimock, 2000). He is or has been on the editorial boards of many philosophical journals; he was also elected a Fellow of the Royal Society of Canada, and sat on its Joint Committee on Health and Safety. He is a frequent guest at colloquia and conferences around North America and in the U.K. and Europe. In 2002, he was appointed an Officer of the Order of Canada, Canada's next-to-top civilian distinction.

JEFFREY A. SCHALER is a psychologist and assistant professor at American University's School of Public Affairs in Washington, D.C., where he teaches courses on justice, morality, law, psychiatry, and drug policy. An existential analyst in private practice since 1974, Schaler is the author of *Addiction Is a Choice* (2000). *Peter Singer Under Fire* is his fifth edited volume. He is the Executive Editor of *Current Psychology*, a quarterly, international publication on diverse areas in psychology, now in its twenty-eighth year. Schaler is currently writing a book about the relationship between science and public policy, particularly how psychiatry has become an extension of law, and why professors are discouraged from teaching their students how to think about mental illness and addiction.

PETER SINGER is the Ira W. DeCamp Professor of Bioethics, University Center for Human Values at Princeton University, and Laureate Professor at the Centre for Applied Philosophy and Public Ethics, University of Melbourne. He is the author of many articles and books. His most recent book is entitled *The Life You Can Save* (2009). His website is princeton.edu/~psinger.

DAVID SCHMIDTZ is Kendrick Professor of Philosophy, joint Professor of Economics, and Director of the Center for Philosophy of Freedom at the University of Arizona. He is author of *Rational Choice and Moral Agency*, *Elements of Justice*, and *Person, Polis, Planet*. He and Jason Brennan currently are working on a book on the history of liberty for Blackwell's *Brief History* series.

BERNARD WILLIAMS was Knightbridge Professor of Philosophy at Cambridge University, Monroe Deutsch Professor of Philosophy at the University of California at Berkeley, and White's Professor of Moral Philosophy at Oxford University. He was a Fellow of All Souls College, Oxford, until his death in 2003. He wrote many articles and books on moral and political philosophy, the history of philosophy, and the ancient world.

Acknowledgments

A heartfelt thanks to all the contributors to this volume for their extraordinary patience; to Peter Singer for trusting me; to David Ramsay Steele for his continued editorial guidance and friendship; and to the following persons for their help in various ways over the years: Ernest H. Bradley, Daniel Dreisbach, Herbert Fingarette, Kathryn C. Ryan, Thomas Szasz, and Richard E. Vatz.

Sir Bernard Williams's essay entitled "Human Prejudice" first appeared in *Philosophy as a Humanistic Discipline* by Bernard Williams, copyright Princeton University Press, Princeton, 2006, and is reprinted here by permission of Princeton University Press and Patricia Williams. Harriet McBryde Johnson's essay entitled "Unspeakable Conversations, or, How I Spent One Day as a Token Cripple at Princeton University," is from the *New York Times* (February 16th, 2003), copyright by Harriet McBryde Johnson and reprinted by permission of Harriet McBryde Johnson. The excerpt from "Unspeakable Conversations," is reprinted with permission from Henry Holt and Company and Harriet McBryde Johnson.

Singer's Burden: Suffering and the Man

JEFFREY A. SCHALER

> Do not free the camel of the burden of his hump; you may be freeing him from being a camel.
>
> —G.K. Chesterton

Some people call Peter Singer one of the most outstanding contemporary philosophical minds. Others have called him the most dangerous person in the world today. He could be both. What this book provides is a kaleidoscope of perspectives on issues that are at the heart of Singer's writing and his worldview.

Why is Peter Singer important? In part because he puts his finger on moral or ethical issues that many of us consider vital, but shy away from confronting and discussing—issues such as how best to live, who should live and who should die, the relative importance of humans and other animals, including humans of limited abilities, and the obligations we have to people we have never met, especially the millions of desperately poor people in the third world.

Singer's writing and ideas make us think about important problems in the world—the problem of pain and suffering, for example, experienced by all living beings capable of suffering, or the problem of world poverty. Some of the ways he suggests for solving these existential and economic problems are controversial, to be sure, from euthanasia, the deliberate killing—sometimes called 'mercy killing'—of some human beings to liberating animals mistreated and killed for diverse reasons. Few people are indifferent to Peter Singer, and people often react strongly to his ideas, sometimes accusing him of proposing that we identify and dispose of lives unworthy of life, the way that Nazi doctors once did. As several discussions in this book show, Singer's readers have often misunderstood and misrepresented what he has said. Singer knows that his ideas are complicated and easily misinterpreted. He asks that we at least consider them.

Singer's contention that we in the affluent world have a moral obligation to donate the majority of our income to help the poverty-stricken millions in the less-developed countries has found few supporters, though also few prepared to say exactly where the error in his moral reasoning lies. His efforts to persuade people to boycott factory farming have been somewhat more successful in winning approval, though most people continue to consume the products of factory farming, apparently with an untroubled conscience. (I suspect their attitudes towards killing animals might change if they personally had to kill the animals they eat.)

If we could name one central issue that Singer is most concerned with, I believe it should be the problem of suffering. While many people share his concern about suffering, where people disagree with him is often in terms of how he proposes that we might reduce suffering. The contributors to this volume were each asked to focus their writing on certain areas of Singer's work. These include whether or not we have an obligation to reduce the disparity between the rich and the poor, whether human life is sacred, and whether we should radically transform our way of life to avoid the mistreatment of animals.

Should we, for example, allow the killing, at the request of their parents, of newborn babies, up to a month of age, who have such severe birth defects that they are incapable of experiencing life in ways that we normally identify as human? Are they not yet persons? Why or why not? What does it mean to be a *person*, compared to a *thing*, for example? What of those babies, such as those who have hemophilia or Down's syndrome, who could live fulfilling albeit somewhat curtailed lives, but whose rearing would put their parents to a lot of trouble and expense?

Singer agrees with those opponents of abortion who say that if abortion is permitted then there can be no reason always to rule out infanticide. But Singer draws the opposite conclusion: abortion can be morally acceptable, and therefore so can infanticide. What Singer proposes here is legally permitting the termination of the lives of newborns whose lives (and that of their parents) will be burdened by suffering or disability. Many people—probably most people—would permit a woman to dispose of the fetus she is carrying if that fetus has Down's syndrome, but would balk at the same woman killing her Down's syndrome baby shortly after birth. Singer maintains that, judged by such criteria as consciousness and self-awareness, there is no bright line separating an unborn from a newborn human, and that therefore infanticide carried out by the mother or at her request should not, in all circumstances, be a crime.

The thrust of Singer's argument is to take practices that are actually going on now, and make them more consistent, more open, more humane, and more subject to the decisions of parents. There are many common medical practices, informal yet effective, where doctors withhold life support from severely disabled newborns. And yet, in cases where medical intervention is withheld, or in cases where the disability will lead to death within a few months regardless of intervention, babies may be kept alive in continual severe pain, although their parents may wish to hasten the process and eliminate the pain.

Singer also proposes acceptance of deliberately ending life at the other end of the life cycle, though in this case the euthanasia would usually have to be voluntary. Older persons with incurable physical disabilities or in extreme pain may wish to terminate their lives, and are (outside of a few European countries) generally prevented by law from having their wishes carried out. In some cases terminal patients in extreme pain on a daily basis want their physicians to give them the means to die—drugs, for example, that would end their pain and their life. In other cases, such patients may no longer be mentally able to decide one way or another, but at an earlier stage, when they were sharp and clear-headed, may have expressed a definite desire to have their lives ended under certain circumstances, which have now arisen. All the many thousands of people living out their final days in agony, who wish to die or who earlier recorded (in a 'living will') their wish to die if such circumstances should arise, should be allowed to get their way, according to Singer, subject to various legal restrictions. Here again we see that what motivates Singer is compassion and concern to reduce suffering, but reduction of suffering is allied with respect for personal autonomy. For my part, I draw a distinction between suicide and so-called 'physician-assisted suicide'. In my view, a person has a right to commit suicide, but physicians don't have the right to kill any of their patients, even at the patients' invitation.

Who is to say whether a person's life is worth living or not? Singer's answer is clear and unequivocal: wherever possible, that person themselves. The decision to terminate a person's life, in Singer's view, is not properly a decision for the state nor even primarily for the physician assisting in the death, but for the person whose life is to be terminated. At the same time, Singer holds that some organisms which are zoologically members of the species *Homo sapiens* do not qualify as persons, because they lack self-consciousness and reason. These include, according to Singer, newborn babies and such examples of long-term coma as Terri Schiavo.

Many people countenance ending the lives of permanently comatose or vegetative individuals by invoking the concept of 'brain death'. Singer, however, will not afford them this quantum of solace. Brain-death, he maintains, is a deceptive fiction. So-called brain-dead individuals are in point of fact not dead but alive. Killing or allowing 'brain-dead' individuals to die is therefore not compatible with the sanctity of human life, and Singer therefore argues for the abandonment of this principle: according to him, human life is not inherently sacred.

Essential to Singer's approach to ethical decisions is consequentialism. In Singer's view, if I act in some way and the foreseeable result is someone's death, then I am responsible for that death. In other words, Singer rejects the traditional view that the distinction between killing and letting die, between an act and an omission, is of immense moral significance. In Singer's view, to let someone die when you could keep them alive is indeed tantamount to killing them, whether the individual who dies is a newborn baby, an old person with Alzheimer's, a child drowning in a pond, or a starving peasant in Bangladesh who could have been saved by our donation of food aid.

Let's take a look at some of the implications of Singer's other ideas, ideas he defends and qualifies in this book. Do animals capable of suffering have 'rights'? Peter Singer speaks of "liberating" animals, liberating them from human captivity, liberating them from being killed for food and clothing. While he does not like to speak of animal rights, he is concerned about the suffering that we create in animals. As Hercule Poirot 'disapproved of murder', Singer disapproves of suffering, whether human or non-human.

We accept that the coercion of animals, like the coercion of children, is morally and legally acceptable when it comes to medical treatment. Children do not have the cognitive capacity to comprehend the consequences of refusing medical treatment—they might die, for example, if they had their way in deciding whether to undergo a painful course of injections. Animals are similar to children in this respect. We coerce children to receive medical treatment when they refuse because we are responsible for them as their guardians. Are we similarly responsible for the animals that we domesticate or own? Are animals simply property that we can do anything we like with? We're obligated to care for our children and if we fail in our duty to care for them, the state intervenes via *parens patriae* and takes care of the child by placing him or her in a foster home. (For a powerful description of the ethical problems with viewing animals as disposable property, read Dostoevsky's famous scene of a horse being beaten to death in *Crime and Punishment*.)

Most of us would agree that there is a difference between an animal, say a dog, and a child. What is it that makes us human? Is it just a human body? When someone is born with limbs missing, or two heads, we still regard the organism as human, and legally as a person (or two persons), despite the most severe disabilities or defects. Is it that we have a conscience, a sense of right and wrong, that makes us human? Many people would agree with some such criterion.

In the realm of institutional psychiatry and the law, a person diagnosed or labeled as a sociopathic killer, with a severe narcissistic-borderline personality disorder, is often described as having no conscience, no sense of right and wrong. We sometimes loosely say that someone like Jeffrey Dahmer or Ted Bundy is not fully human. They have no conscience, no sense of regard for others. Regard for others becomes a criteria of humanness.

Dog owners know that many dogs easily betray their own guilt when their owners come home to find they've been in the garbage, defecated on a fine oriental rug, or eaten the casserole that was to be the family dinner. Dogs often look guilty when they or the other dog at home has 'done something wrong'. They do a very poor job of hiding their sense of shame. The owner will quickly say "Okay, what did you do wrong?" Their conscience seems to betray their guilt. If dogs express more conscience than a serial killer, is the dog more 'human' than the human?

Questions about what it means to be human seem to stimulate more questions, than answers. How we define and describe 'human' has a lot to do with how we explain behavior, and what our various policies in relation to humans will be. A person's behavior can deviate from the norm, but he or she does not cease to be human just because his or her behavior deviates from the norm.

We can explain behavior from a religious or spiritual point of view; from a psychological point of view; a biological or neurological point of view; and from a sociocultural point of view. And finally what we do or don't do about a person or persons we are allegedly concerned about is based on how we explain what we define or describe, assume, as human. From a policy point of view, we may or may not hold a person responsible for his behavior based on various ways we explain his behavior. We may or may not grant him certain rights, natural or otherwise, because of how he behaves and how we explain his behavior. We may try to change or influence his behavior through drugs or some other means if he is truly sick, but then again we must agree on what it means to be sick. We must agree on the meaning of disease and health. And we may rely on the government as a means of controlling certain persons—or we may use relational forms of control that are informal. Where the state is not involved, we can encourage or discourage behavior by approving or disapproving of what a person does or doesn't do.

Much of what we choose to do or not to do in relation to others has everything to do with how we define or describe what it means to be human. There must be some agreement on what it means to be human before we can even consider answering Peter Singer's important and provocative questions, let alone act on persons with Singer's ideas as our premises. In fact, his questions take us back to defining what it means to be human, let alone what we consider humane.

When we think about Peter Singer's ideas concerning killing members of the human species we have to ask not only whether this policy is morally and ethically right, but whether the state is to be involved in sanctioning killing or not. History has taught us something about what happens when the state gets into the business of killing its citizens. When the state kills people whose lives are considered not worthy of living, and justifies such killing on grounds like 'compelling state interest', we open up very dangerous possibilities for killing to become a means of social and political control, not just a means of decreasing suffering. Peter Singer has never countenanced any such policies, though he has often been assailed with 'slippery slope' arguments about where toleration of euthanasia and infanticide might lead.

From my own point of view, there is no one I would trust with the power to make decisions about ending a person's life. This is why I have always opposed "physician-assisted suicide," or "assisted suicide," such as that committed by Jack Kevorkian. I agree with the right to commit suicide: a person takes his life into his own hands. When it becomes acceptable for another party to legally take a person's life, with or without that person's consent, I believe the possibility of political killing could increase exponentially.

Naturally, Singer has frequently addressed the slippery slope kind of argument against euthanasia. He has two main replies. First, he maintains that the notorious example of Nazi Germany did not, in fact, follow any such course. Nazi policies of disposing of unwanted categories of individuals did not evolve out of policies of toleration of euthanasia or assisted suicide, but arose from a different impetus, as indicated by the fact that these policies were secret, and that privileged categories of the population were exempt from them. Second, he points to many cultures in human history, including ancient Greece, Rome, and China, where (for example) infanticide of newborns was tolerated—or even compulsory—and where laws against killing of adults were still vigorously enforced.

As you can see, just one of Peter's ideas, involving an appeal to the notion that some human lives are not as worthwhile as others, creates and stimulates very important considerations. Assisted suicide has already become legal in three US states—Oregon, Washington, and Montana— and in some other countries. In this area, if not yet in others, Singer appears to be on the winning side.

Another of his ideas concerning the liberation of animals, the awareness and concern about suffering in animals, can lead us to think about and become clearer about what it means to be human. Peter Singer is a vegetarian for moral rather than health reasons. I share his interest in and practice of vegetarianism. We both would likely prefer that others become vegetarian because we share a concern about reducing the suffering of animals. Raising animals to eat their flesh is both unnecessary and cruel, in our opinion.

Singer has also been associated with opposition to the use of animals in scientific experiments. One of my cousins is a pharmacologist who makes medicines for serious autoimmune diseases. When I told her that my book on Singer was coming out this year she said to me "I wish I had known. I would have liked you to ask him a question for me: Does he use any medicines that were developed through the use of animals that were later destroyed?" The question probably betrays a misunderstanding of Singer's views. He has made it clear that, in cases where killing or inflicting pain on animals actually leads to substantial reductions in suffering through medical advances—including the calculations of suffering experienced by animals, which must count the same as if it were a similar quantity of human suffering—the animal experiments are morally justified. If experimenting on animals is necessary to save human lives, then experimenting on animals might even be morally obligatory. Singer has been denounced by more extreme animal welfare proponents for his acceptance of this principle. He does claim, however, as a matter of fact, that many animal experiments now performed cannot be defended in this way.

When a person decides for himself or herself to refuse to eat meat or fish, this is an individual matter, an individual decision, based on an individual's morality and values. At the same time, the animal is an 'other', a conscious individual capable of suffering. If I had my way, I suppose it would be against the law to raise and kill calves for veal, and perpetrate similar non-essential cruelties. And yet I am troubled when it comes to imposing my values on others, and even more troubled, when the state tries to dictate or legislate individual moral behavior which poses no threat to other humans. Singer conducts most of his discussions at the level of moral guidelines for individual behavior, and we can't always tell what implications he would draw for government policy.

I admire Peter's courage to stand by his ideas and principles in the face of criticism, particularly when he was hired by Princeton and received so much criticism on the occasion of his joining the faculty there. The level of vituperation Peter has had to endure is not unlike what Socrates had to go through. It might have been easy for him to become arrogant and callous as a result. But he seems to have retained his humanness in a good way. I found him personally to be a very decent and sensitive person, certainly concerned with my own well-being.

With each volume in Open Court's *Under Fire* series—*Peter Singer Under Fire* is the third in this series—we present a picture of our subject, the 'target', as a person in action, parrying multiple attacks by diverse opponents, people who agree and disagree with the subject's ideas and values in various ways and to different degrees.

In the case of Peter Singer, I did not want to confine the critics to academics. The active and eloquent crusader for rights of the disabled, Harriet McBryde Johnson, died on June 4th, 2008. She agreed to contribute an essay to this volume on condition that the book also include an additional essay by someone else from the organization Not Dead Yet. After consulting with the publisher, I agreed to this condition. She gave me Stephen Drake's name. Stephen is a founder of Not Dead Yet. I am pleased at the outcome and at securing Peter Singer's first published responses to Harriet McBryde Johnson and Stephen Drake, though I am saddened that Harriet did not live to see these provocative and illuminating exchanges in print.

Harriet and Stephen are more than just critics of Peter's. Harriet was and Stephen is vehemently opposed to Peter's ideas about killing disabled or defective newborns, and his judgment that fully whole and healthy individuals can somehow expect to have more valuable lives. As Johnson said in the *New York Times Magazine* in February 2003, "The presence or absence of a disability doesn't predict quality of life." People in the disabled rights movement sometimes refer to the majority of adults who do not currently suffer any disability as "the temporarily able-bodied."

There seem to be two ways in which people justify pain and suffering as existential necessities: 1. Some people see it as payment for sin, wrongdoing, or some evil a person has committed. 2. Others view pain as preparation for salvation, merging with God, a cleansing. I reject both of these views. I see no purpose in pain if it can be avoided. In this I believe I agree with Peter Singer.

Peter Singer's views on suffering are important, as are the views of those who take issue with him. If they can help us to ask and answer our own questions about these and related issues, well then, that's good enough. In order to effectively reduce pain and suffering, we must first become aware of some of the ethical issues involved, and there is no better preparation for this awareness than a critical look at the thought of Peter Singer.

An Intellectual Autobiography

PETER SINGER

Origins

It is strange to think how easily our lives could have followed entirely different paths. If my sister had fallen in love with a different man, or I had had a different adviser when I enrolled at Melbourne University, I might never have become a philosopher. If I had not started a conversation with a Canadian graduate student after a class at Oxford, I might have been a very different, probably much less significant, philosopher. But I should begin at the beginning.

I am a baby boomer, born in 1946 in Melbourne, Australia's second largest city, and the capital of the state of Victoria. My parents came to Australia in 1938, fleeing Vienna after the Nazi takeover of Austria. My father had been a coffee salesman. On arriving in Australia, he was told that he could not make a living selling coffee, because Australians drank tea. My mother was a graduate of the University of Vienna's medical school. After she passed the tough exam that stopped many graduates of foreign institutions from practicing medicine in Australia, her earnings provided a reliable income for the family until my father's perseverance with coffee was eventually rewarded. Having a working mother was unusual, then, and probably predisposed me to an egalitarian view of men and women. (My mother's assumption that she would have a career, I later realized, came from her mother, one of the first female graduates of the University of Vienna, who had also worked after her marriage.) To help look after the home and take care of me and my older sister, Joan, my parents employed a full-time housekeeper.

My father and mother were of Jewish descent, but neither of them was religious. When I was young my father occasionally went to synagogue on the high holydays, but my mother never did, and eventually my father stopped going. My maternal grandmother—the only one of my four grandparents to survive the Holocaust—lived with us until her death in 1955. She fasted on the Day of Atonement and avoided pork. But our family was eager to assimilate into an Australian way of life, and we ate what we liked and received presents on Christmas Day. (To help us become true Australians, my parents spoke only English to Joan and me—something I have always regretted, because I had to learn German the hard way, in school.) As I approached thirteen, my parents asked me if I wanted to have a bar-mitzvah. Other Jewish boys of my age were talking excitedly about the presents they would receive on that occasion, but I didn't like the idea of giving up Sunday mornings for several months to learn enough Hebrew to read a passage of the Torah in synagogue, and the ceremony didn't mean anything to me. So I said that I didn't want one. My mother seemed pleased. My father was ambivalent, but he didn't try to persuade me to change my mind.

Our home had an atmosphere of European culture and learning. My father had an interest in European history, and read widely, especially on Austria-Hungary, though he also had a fascination with Napoleon. My mother had a connection with psychology that derived from her father, David Oppenheim, who had been a member of Freud's circle and later was a close associate of Alfred Adler.[1]

I went to a progressive private primary school called Preshil, which happened to be in walking distance of our home. We had few set lessons, but were encouraged to be creative, and work together on projects. If you didn't want to go to a class, you were permitted to wander around the playground instead. Few of us ever did—it was more fun to be inside with your friends and the teacher. Preshil gave me a happy and positive start to learning, but more significantly, it encouraged an independent spirit. Australians in general are said to be more egalitarian and less deferential to their "superiors" than Britons or Americans, but Preshil carried this further than most—we called the teachers by their nicknames and were encouraged to treat them as our equals.

Preshil only went up to Grade 6 then, so when it was time for me to move to secondary school, my parents, wanting the best for me, sent me to Scotch College, an expensive Presbyterian boys' school. Every morning the entire school assembled to hear a reading from the bible, sing a hymn, and recite the Lord's Prayer. We also had Religious Studies once

---

[1] I grew up with stories of how Freud, for all his genius, was an intolerant authoritarian; Adler was viewed much more favorably. See Peter Singer, *Pushing Time Away: My Grandfather and the Tragedy of Jewish Vienna* (New York: Ecco, 2003).

a week, and a chapel service once a term. This exposure to Christianity had an effect on me that was the opposite of what the school's founders presumably intended. During morning assembly I would browse the bible that we each had in front of us, and find passages that seemed difficult to reconcile with the idea that this was a truthful account of the doings of a benevolent and omnipotent being. It was here that I came across the extraordinary story of the fig tree, which Jesus curses because it has no fruit. Later the disciples pass the spot again, and notice that the tree has withered and died. When I asked our Religious Studies teacher why Jesus made the tree die, he told me that it was to show that what is barren is not good. But Mark says the tree had no figs because it wasn't the season for figs, so that answer didn't satisfy me.[2] I also read the passage in which Jesus tells the rich man to give all he has to the poor, and adds that it is as hard for a rich man to go to heaven as for a camel to go through the eye of a needle. I wondered how that squared with the fact that the most expensive car in the school parking area was the chaplain's shiny black Mercedes.

Entering the second-last year of high school we had to choose between sciences and humanities. I was good at maths and science, but nevertheless opted for the humanities, perhaps because I was thinking of following my sister into law, or maybe because, like my father, I enjoyed history, and didn't want to give that up. It was not then possible to study philosophy at high school in Australia. I first heard of philosophy, as an academic discipline, around 1961, when Joan was going out with John Dwyer, who she subsequently married. John had studied law, but he took some philosophy subjects afterwards, and then did a Master of Arts in philosophy, writing his thesis on issues about the role of intention that were relevant to law as well as ethics. It was probably John who suggested that I might enjoy reading Bertrand Russell's *History of Western Philosophy,* the first philosophy book I read.

As I neared the end of high school, I considered my career options. Going into my father's business would have been an easy choice. But I had worked there during summer vacations and I didn't find the work really interesting in itself. Following my sister seemed more stimulating, and I liked the idea of arguing cases in court, so I applied to do law at the University of Melbourne. (Australia follows the British educational model—law and medicine are undergraduate courses.) As an incoming student, I saw a course adviser who told me that, since I had

---

[2] The Gospel According to Mark, 11:11–21.

done well in subjects like history and literature, I might find the study of law a little dry. He suggested I do a combined Arts/Law degree. This would take six years, rather than the usual four-year law course, but would give me a much broader education, something more like students receive in the United States when they do a Bachelor of Arts before studying law. I had not thought previously of doing an Arts degree, but I accepted the suggestion. That meant another decision: in what Arts subjects would I major? History was an obvious one, but the little philosophy I had read intrigued me, so I took it together with history.

Undergraduate Studies

I found myself in a large first-year philosophy class taken by Professor Sandy Boyce-Gibson, the chair of the department. It was the only subject first-year students in philosophy could take, and the syllabus, for most of the academic year—courses then lasted the full year, not just a semester—was a study of Plato's *Republic*. Boyce-Gibson was due to retire at the end of the year. He may have been a good lecturer once, but he had been giving these lectures for a long time. I might have dropped philosophy, were it not for the fact that I was living in a residential college that offered additional discussion groups for first-year students. The discussion group on philosophy was taken by John Alexander, a humane and learned man who was able to bring out the deep questions about ethics underlying Plato's often one-sided dialogue. In the discussions he guided, I began to see that Plato was asking important questions to which I did not have satisfactory answers. From then on, it was always ethics and political philosophy that interested me most. It was here, I thought, that the real world rubbed up against philosophy in the most direct way.

In second year, I took an ethics course with H.J. McCloskey, who was to become my first philosophical mentor. At that time many members of the University of Melbourne philosophy department were heavily influenced by followers of Wittgenstein, particularly the Wittgenstein of the *Philosophical Investigations,* and by J.L. Austin. In their view what had traditionally been thought of as big philosophical problems were really linguistic confusions, to be explained away by carefully examining the meaning of the words. For example, philosophers have worried about how we can have free will, when everything in the universe has a cause. The Wittgensteinians asked, what does it mean, to say of someone that he acted of his own free will? Consider a bridgegroom, smiling happily as he stands by his chosen bride at the altar. What would lead us to deny that he is acting from his own free will? The revelation that the bride is pregnant and her father forced the groom, at the point of a gun, to marry her, would do it. But in the absence of some such story, this is a paradigm case of someone acting from their own free will. Hence to argue that, because everything has a cause, the groom could not be acting from his own free will, is simply to misuse language.

In keeping with this general approach to philosophy, it was thought that there was nothing philosophical to be done in ethics except to examine the meanings of words like "good" and "right." One of the most influential works in ethics at that time was C.L. Stevenson's *Ethics and Language,* the thesis of which is that when I say "X is good" I am not saying anything that could be true or false. Instead I am expressing my favorable attitude to X, and urging you to adopt a similar attitude of approval to X. On this view of philosophy, the study of ethics could not lead to any conclusions about what we should do. Our judgment about that would depend on our attitudes, which were based in our emotions rather than our reason or reflection. As for political philosophy, it was widely thought to be dead.

McCloskey greatest philosophical virtue was his immunity to fashion, whether sartorial or philosophical. In ethics he was a follower of W.D. Ross, an intuitionist who had dominated moral philosophy at Oxford in the 1920s, and held that we have direct intuitive awareness of objective moral facts.[3] But more important for me was the fact that McCloskey thought there are substantive questions in ethics and political philosophy and the role of philosophers is to produce arguments that can resolve these questions.

McCloskey saw utilitarianism as the major rival to his own intuitionist ethic. But utilitarianism, he argued, has unacceptable implications. He asked us to imagine that in a small town in the South of the United States, a black man has raped a white woman. The woman is unable to identify her attacker. A white mob seizes six black men and gets ready to lynch them. The sheriff wants to prevent the murder of the six men, but if he simply tells the mob to stop, they will ignore him. The only way he can save the six is by pretending that he knows who the rapist is. The mob will then lynch only that person, and five innocent lives will be saved. A utilitarian, McCloskey urged, must think that, as long as the deception can be kept secret, this is what the sheriff ought to

---

[3] See H.J. McCloskey, *Meta-ethics and Normative Ethics* (The Hague: Nijhoff, 1969).

do. But that, McCloskey insisted, would clearly be wrong. Hence utilitarianism cannot be the right ethical theory.

This was my first exposure to what is probably the commonest form of anti-utilitarian argument, one that was raised already against Jeremy Bentham, and is still used today—indeed, similar examples can be found in two of the critical essays in this volume. But I wasn't as certain about my intuitions in this case as McCloskey seemed to be. If framing one innocent man really was the only possible way of preventing the deaths of six innocent men, and there would be no other bad consequences from the frame-up, maybe that really was what the sheriff ought to do?

Those doubts led me to question other aspects of McCloskey's case against utilitarianism. By the end of the year, I thought that utilitarianism was as promising a normative theory as any. As time passed and no more convincing objections to utilitarianism turned up, my support for it gradually became less tentative.

In addition to my studies, some of my student activities had an impact on my philosophical development. There was an ongoing campus debate about the existence of God. On one side there was the Evangelical Union and the Newman Society, representing Protestants and Catholics, respectively, and on the other side, the Rationalist Society. Members of the philosophy department took an active role in these debates. One of them, Vernon Rice, was a Catholic and tried to persuade us of the validity of his own version of the ontological argument for the existence of God, but most of them were atheists who delighted in refuting whatever arguments the Christians could put up. Here substantive philosophical arguments were in play, and since belief in God often makes a difference to how people live, the arguments mattered. That attracted me, and I became a member of the Rationalist Society. I was soon familiar with the fallacies in all the usual arguments for the existence of God, and with the weakness of attempting to dispense with argument by saying that God is beyond reason, and can only be known through faith.

The real clincher, however, was the argument from evil. How could the kind of god the Christians described—omnipotent, omniscient, and omnibenevolent—have allowed something like the Holocaust to take place? To this some Christians responded that God gave us free will, and this is so great a good that it outweighs all the evil that humans bring about. That was, I thought, a dubious ethical judgment, but in any case it failed to account for suffering that had nothing to do with the exercise of free will—people drowning in floods, being crushed in earthquakes, or dying of starvation in a drought. Wouldn't an omnipotent and omnibenevolent god have at least given us a less erratic climate, and a more stable surface to build on? While one might have doubts about the existence or non-existence of different gods, variously defined, for me the fact of evil removed any reasonable possibility that the world could have been created by the kind of god Christians worship.

In 1965 the Australian government committed troops to fight alongside American forces in Vietnam. Conscription had already been introduced. I opposed both the war and conscription, and took part in several demonstrations against the war. Eventually I became president of an organization called Melbourne University Campaign Against Conscription. I also worked on the student newspaper, *Farrago,* and for a time edited—and largely wrote—the newsletter of the Melbourne University Labour Club.

Abortion was then illegal in Australia, although women who knew where to go and had the money to pay for it could still get abortions. Through a report on this situation that I did for *Farrago,* I became convinced of the need for legal and safe abortion, and for a time served as treasurer of the Abortion Law Reform Association of Victoria. The debates about the ethics of abortion in which I was then involved were my first forays into the field that was later to become known as bioethics. One moment still sticks in my memory. At a public meeting I was arguing that abortion cannot be considered the equivalent of murder, because the fetus is mentally so much less developed than we are. Someone made the obvious response that if mental development is so important, then killing a newborn baby should not be considered murder either. The thought popped into my head that perhaps killing a newborn baby really is not as bad as killing an older person. The question made me think about how difficult it is to draw a sharp line at birth and say that before it, the fetus may be killed merely because the woman does not want to have a child, but immediately after it, the child has the same right to life as anyone else.

In my third year at university I began going out with Renata Diamond, whom I had met the previous year in a class on Renaissance history. She was much more of an intellectual than I was—better read, and more familiar with theater, film, and a broad range of ideas of all kinds. Suddenly the concerns of Melbourne University's philosophy and history departments seemed narrow. It was only after I got to know Renata that the idea of pursuing ideas as a way of life began to form as a serious alternative to the career I had been contemplating as a lawyer.

Choosing Philosophy

The plan for the combined arts/law course enabled me to complete the degree of Bachelor of Arts with Honours in the usual time for that degree—four years—and would have left me two years of full-time law to complete that degree. When I finished the B.A. at the end of 1967, I learned I had done well enough to be offered a scholarship to do a Master of Arts. After checking with the law school that I could resume my law studies if I wished to do so, I decided to take the scholarship. That still left another difficult decision. As a student with a graduate scholarship, I would have been welcome in either the philosophy or the history departments. McCloskey was keen for me to work on a topic in ethics under his supervision, but I had become fascinated with the history of Europe in the twentieth century, especially the rise of fascism. So my initial choice was history. But once I started thinking about my history thesis topic, a problem soon emerged. The history department wanted its graduate students to write a thesis based on original documents on a topic that had not yet been dealt with by other historians. There were no archives of original documents relating to Nazism in Australia, and overseas travel was expensive, and not supported by my scholarship. I wasn't entirely averse to writing on a topic in Australian history, but most of the interesting topics seemed, from my undoubtedly limited perspective, to have already been written about, and so were not eligible as thesis topics. I was eventually persuaded to study some political thinkers and agitators on the fringes of Australian politics in the 1930s. Here there were plenty of original documents, but they related largely to people no one had ever heard of. Within three months, I found myself the world's greatest expert on a topic in which few people had any interest. I had wanted to deal with the big issues of the history and politics of the twentieth century, something that could explain how we got to where we are, and perhaps provide some clues about how we could do better in future. This wasn't it.

I talked to McCloskey about switching to philosophy. I already had a topic in mind. Suppose that one accepts that something is the right thing to do. It seemed to me possible to ask why one should do it. To some philosophers this is nonsense—once you accept that something is the right thing to do, they hold, it is not possible to ask any further questions about why one should do it, because that is already implied in saying it is the right thing to do. I wasn't satisfied with this response. McCloskey was doubtful that I would find much to say on this topic, but he was willing to supervise it. I dropped my history research and began to write a thesis entitled *Why Should I Be Moral?* The topic became a lifelong interest—the final chapter of *Practical Ethics* contains some of the views I developed in my thesis, and *How Are We to Live?* is another attempt to address the same problem.

As a graduate student in philosophy, I was appointed a part-time tutor, teaching groups of about a dozen first year philosophy students. They were also attending lectures, so my role was go over any points in the lectures that they did not understand, and give them an opportunity to express their own views and learn to discuss philosophical questions. The idea of teaching philosophy was at first daunting, but it was also stimulating, and I found it generally wasn't difficult to get a discussion going. The most important thing was to put the conflicting ideas clearly and in a way that showed what was at stake. That was a lesson that later was to prove valuable in my writing as well.

Changing to philosophy was one of two momentous decisions I made around this time that set the path for my future. The other was that, at the end of 1968, Renata and I married.

Early in 1969 I was accepted by the University of Oxford to study for the postgraduate degree of Bachelor of Philosophy, and received a scholarship from the University of Melbourne for that purpose. This was heady stuff. Oxford was then the pinnacle of the contemporary philosophical world. A.J. Ayer, Stuart Hampshire, and P.F. Strawson were dominant figures in logic and metaphysics, while those working more specifically in ethics and political philosophy at Oxford included R.M. Hare, H.L.A. Hart, Philippa Foot, Sir Isaiah Berlin, John Plamenatz, and Anthony Quinton.

Every Oxford student is attached to a college. I chose University College because, in memory of G.A. Paul, an influential University College philosopher who had taught at the University of Melbourne, it offered a bursary for Australian students. That added, if I recall correctly, one hundred pounds per year to the modest allowance provided by my scholarship. University College did, in fact, have among its dons a distinguished trio of philosophers—John Mackie, John McDowell, and Gareth Evans—but since I was a graduate student, I would not be taught through my college anyway, so that was not a factor in my decision.

I count myself fortunate to have been one of the last for whom it was possible to have an academic career without getting a doctorate. In the U.S. that time had already passed, but Australia was lagging a few years behind, and the advice I received from the Department of Philosophy at Melbourne was that the Bachelor of Philosophy was actually a better qualification than a doctorate for a teaching career, because it offered a broader grounding in philosophy. To gain a doctorate in Britain or Australia, you simply wrote a thesis, usually 80–100,000 words. There were no course requirements. For the B.Phil.—at the time, a uniquely Oxford degree— you had to pass exams in three subjects, one of them a "chosen authority"—that is, a study of one of the great philosophers—and write a short thesis, of about 30,000 words. Another advantage of the B.Phil. was that it was only a two-year degree. So everything seemed to point to that option, and I suffered no disadvantage from not having a Ph.D.

Philosophy at Oxford

Renata and I arrived in Oxford in October 1969. The sub-faculty of philosophy approved my request to take exams in ethics, political philosophy (including questions on the philosophy of law and the philosophy of history), and, as my chosen authority, Hegel and Marx. The latter choice was unusual because it consisted of two philosophers, rather than just one, and because Marx was not generally among the canon studied in philosophy departments at English-speaking universities. But there had been a resurgence of philosophical interest in Marx. John Plamenatz, professor of political theory at Oxford, had written on him and so too had G.A. Cohen, at the time a rising young scholar who now holds the chair that Plamenatz then occupied. Robert Tucker's seminal *Philosophy and Myth in Karl Marx* had generated discussion, about the extent to which Marx's later work should be understood as a kind of transformed Hegelian philosophy, so the combination made sense.

Plamenatz was appointed my supervisor and we began by working on topics in political philosophy. Each week I sent him a short paper on a topic he had suggested, and we met and discussed it. Before going to Oxford I had heard stories of students being humiliated as, over a full hour, their papers were mercilessly torn apart. Fortunately Plamenatz was on the whole positive about my work. The most alarming aspect of our sessions was that the reading he recommended included works in French and German. He asked about my German—in which I had some competence—but just seemed to assume that every educated person reads French. I had to confess that my high school French had not equipped me to understand Hyppolite's lectures on Hegel.

Plamenatz was encouraging and knowledgeable, but not exciting. I found more stimulation in the smorgasbord of lectures and seminars offered by Oxford's many philosophers. You could attend whatever lectures you wished, for they were not tied to any course. So I had the chance to hear all of the great figures I have already mentioned, as well as some younger philosophers of whom I had not heard until I came to Oxford, but whose work had a freshness that made it especially exciting.

Ronald Dworkin, an American whose immaculate light-colored suits and bright ties stood out amongst the well-worn tweed jackets and drab sweaters favored by most Oxford academics, had just taken over the chair of jurisprudence from H.L.A. Hart. In a lively series of lectures he argued—against the positivist view of law Hart had put forward in *The Concept of Law*—that judges cannot and should not avoid drawing on moral values in order to determine what the law is. I wasn't persuaded— his arguments seemed to me better suited to the American legal tradition, grounded on the broad ethical statements of the American Bill of Rights, than to British law.

The most unusual classes I attended were on Hegel, given by J.L.H. Thomas, a junior fellow at All Souls College. His name was completely unknown to me then, and will be unknown to most readers today, because when his seven-year fellowship came to end, so did his academic career. Held in a splendid seminar room at All Souls, its ancient barrel-vaulted ceiling decorated with coats of arms, these classes were attended by no more than a dozen students. Thomas began by handing us copies of his own translation of a passage about twenty pages long from Hegel's *Phenomenology of Spirit*—one year it was the introduction, and following year, the famous master-slave dialectic. No other reading was recommended—we were supposed to respond directly to the text in front of us. Thomas began the first class by asking one of us what the first sentence meant. He then showed that the student's answer was not entirely satisfactory, and asked someone else. This went on, until we all felt we could understand the sentence. Only then would we go on to the next sentence. Since Hegel's meaning cannot be understood without some awareness of the philosophical problems with which he was dealing, a single sentence might take us most of the ninety-minute class to unravel. At other times we would make more rapid progress, but it soon became clear that, even though we were to meet twice-weekly for eight weeks, a total of twenty-four intensive hours of discussion, we would be pushing to complete our reading of the twenty-page passage. It may seem tedious to spend so long on a short text, but all the time we were thinking for ourselves about an approach to philosophy that was very different from that of the British tradition in which most of us had been educated. Without Thomas's classes I doubt that I would have ever learned to read Hegel with any real understanding, and I would certainly never have dared to write even a short introductory book on him.

The most stimulating classes I attended, however, were a series of seminars given by Derek Parfit, Jonathan Glover, and James Griffin on what we would now call applied ethics. Each week, one of them would give a talk that initiated a lively discussion. When I arrived in Oxford Parfit was, like Thomas, a relatively unknown junior fellow at All Souls. He outlined what was to me an entirely new issue—although it had been noticed, a century earlier, by Henry Sidgwick, and Jan Narveson, a Canadian philosopher, had recently published an article on it. When a choice we make has no impact on the size of the future population, a decision that increases the total utility of the resulting population will also increase the average utility of the population. But this is not necessarily the case if the decision will affect the size of the future population—for example, a government decision to offer tax concessions to parents. Should we then judge the decision by its impact on the total utility, or the average utility, of the resulting population? Perplexingly, Parfit demonstrated that both options have strongly counter-intuitive implications. Attending the seminar were most of Oxford's brightest philosophers, dons and graduate students, and several of them suggested approaches that they thought would deal satisfactorily with the problem. When that happened, Parfit would outline a new situation in which the proffered solution led to conclusions no one would want to defend. Parfit would then suggest variations on the solution that might be thought to circumvent those conclusions, and then show why these variations also would not do.[4]

Whether listening to others trying to meet Parfit's arguments, or trying to contribute to the discussion myself, I had the sense that I was watching a philosophical grandmaster who already knew all the moves that could be made, and had effective responses for each of them. I have met other philosophers who I am sure are cleverer than I am, but with no one else have I had so clear a sense of the inferiority of my philosophical abilities.

Though not as philosophically dazzling as Parfit, Jonathan Glover always found intriguing philosophical issues in serious practical problems. Some of them later appeared in his fine book *Causing Death and Saving Live.*[5] His work blazed a trail that I was to follow into applied ethics.

---

[4] For Parfit's later elaboration of this theme, see his *Reasons and Persons* (Oxford: Clarendon Press, 1984), part IV.

[5] Jonathan Glover, *Causing Death and Saving Lives* (Harmondsworth: Penguin, 1977).

R.M. Hare

Important as all these lectures and seminars were, the Oxford philosopher from whom I learned the most was R.M. Hare, who held the White's Chair of Moral Philosophy. In an honours course in ethics during my final undergraduate year, I had read Hare's books, *The Language of Morals* and *Freedom and Reason*. What excited many philosophers about Hare's work is summed up in the title of the second of these books. Emotivists like C.L. Stevenson gave a prominent place to our freedom to make moral judgments based on our own attitudes. If they were right, no one could tell us that we had simply failed to see some moral truth that a person of sharper moral insight knew to be true, for there were no such truths, only emotions or feelings to be expressed. This liberating view seemed firmly grounded in G.E. Moore's famous argument against the "naturalistic fallacy" which involves defining morality in terms of natural properties (like happiness, for example), and in the evident oddity of the claim that we can just "intuit" non-natural moral truths. But emotivism is open to the obvious objection, that if morality is simply a matter of emotions or feelings, then your own view is no better than that of anyone else. In saying that Nazism is wrong, we want to say something more than "Boo to the Nazis!" But the emotivist has eliminated all other possible meanings that the condemnation of Nazism might have.

Hare agreed with the emotivists that moral judgments are not descriptions, and hence cannot be straightforwardly true or false. He argued that they are prescriptions, that is, judgments that entail imperatives, but like imperatives, they are subject to logical rules. For example, I cannot intelligibly say, at the same time say: "Close all the windows" and "Leave the center window open." This made it possible for reason to play a role in moral argument. Hare further widened that role by claiming that moral judgments are distinguished from other imperatives because they are "universalizable." The idea underlying Hare's notion of universalizability can be found in many ethical traditions, but Hare gave it a logical precision that earlier forms had lacked. His account of universalizability is essentially that a moral judgment cannot be based on individual properties, such as proper names or personal pronouns. If I think that it is wrong for you to cheat on your taxes, then I must also hold that if I am in similar circumstances, it would be wrong for me to cheat on my taxes. I cannot claim that because it is I who benefit when I cheat on my taxes, the cases are different. "I" here refers to an individual, not to a universal property.

In *Freedom and Reason* Hare concluded with a practical example of how universalizability can help us to see what is wrong with some purported moral positions. He shows how difficult it is to be a racist, if one does not distort the facts, and is prepared to universalize one's belief. For racists must themselves be prepared to join the victims of their oppression, if it should turn out that they are, contrary to their present beliefs, members of the oppressed race. And while this may be so improbable that it can easily be disregarded as a factual possibility, universalizability applies even to hypothetical situations. Hence racists must be prepared to apply their principles even in those hypothetical situations in which they discover that their biological parents are not who they believe they are, but are members of the allegedly inferior race. As Hare said in *Freedom and Reason*, while a very few racists may be so fanatical that they can sincerely accept their principles in these hypothetical circumstances, we can be quite sure that the overwhelming majority of them are not. They are racists only because they belong to the race to which they are giving special status and privileges, and they are not putting themselves in the position of those they are oppressing. Thus a correct understanding of the logic of moral reasoning can show why everyone who is not a fanatic—a term Hare used in a special sense to refer to someone who holds moral ideals that are not based on a consideration of the interests of those affected—must regard racism as morally wrong.

Hare was a lofty and intimidating figure with a reputation for dealing severely with those he considered muddled—and that, I had been warned, meant everyone who disagreed with him. Nevertheless half-way through my first year in Oxford, I worked up the nerve to send him an essay, written while I was still in Australia, that was critical of his combination of prescriptivity and universalizability. My argument was, in essence, that if morality is necessarily prescriptive, then it can't also be necessarily universalizable—for what are we to say if someone acts on prescriptions that are based on non-universalizable principles such as: "I shall always do whatever is in my own interests"? Either we say that such a principle is a moral principle, in which case moral principles need not be universalizable, or we acknowledge that, even though such people can continue to talk about what actions might or might not be justifiable in universal terms, morality is not, for them, prescriptive.

Hare invited me to discuss my essay with him. I went to his office with some trepidation, but to my relief, his response was not hostile at all. He did point me to some passages in *Freedom and Reason* that I had misunderstood, in particular those accepting the possibility of the amoralist who refuses to use moral language except in an "inverted commas" sense. He had, in other words, already anticipated what I thought was a damaging objection. Nevertheless, he must have thought that the essay had some merit, because he encouraged me to correct the misinterpretation, but develop the underlying points into a more substantial paper for publication. He also offered to supervise me when the time came for me to study topics for the paper in moral philosophy. I accepted, of course, and Hare was my supervisor for most of the remainder of my time at Oxford, a period that covered not only work in moral philosophy, but also the writing of my thesis. Knowing that my writing would be subjected to his meticulous point-by-point criticism was a powerful incentive to strive for the highest standards of clarity and rigor.

The war in Vietnam was still continuing, along with a fierce debate among the war's opponents about how far we were justified in going to stop it. Civil disobedience was widely used, which raised the question whether, in a democratic country, there is an obligation to obey the law, even when the country is fighting an unjust war. I wanted to write my thesis on this topic, but Oxford had a reputation for being conservative in its understanding of moral philosophy, and there was still no such field as "applied ethics." I asked Hare whether such a topic would be acceptable. He encouraged me to go ahead, and so I began to examine arguments for an obligation to obey the law, with particular attention to relevant differences between democracies and other political systems. I also considered the arguments of those who defended a right to disobey the law, including not only philosophers, but also activists who favored civil disobedience.

Animals and Ethics

Philosophers like Hare, Parfit, and Glover undoubtedly were major influences on me during my Oxford years. Yet the encounter that really changed my life was with a fellow graduate student. In the autumn of 1970 I attended a series of lectures by Jonathan Glover on free will, determinism, and moral responsibility. After one lecture I began talking to one of the other students, a Canadian named Richard Keshen, about some of the issues that had been raised in the discussion. He suggested we continue the conversation over lunch at his college, Balliol. That day there was a choice between spaghetti with some kind of reddish-brown sauce over it, or a salad plate. Richard asked if the sauce had meat in it, and when told that it did, took the salad plate. I took the spaghetti, and when our discussion of free will and determinism had run its course, I asked Richard why he avoided meat.

I had met very few vegetarians up to that time, and those I had met thought meat was bad for their health, had religious grounds for avoiding it, or were pacifists, holding that killing is always wrong. I wasn't religious, or a pacifist, and I didn't believe meat, in moderate quantities, was unhealthy. Richard's answer was more challenging. He told me that he didn't think we had a right to treat animals in the way that the animals that had become the meat I was eating were treated. That made me ask about how the animals were treated, and started me thinking about how we ought to treat animals. We talked for a while, and then Richard suggested that I should meet Stanley and Roslind Godlovitch, two other Canadians in Oxford who had been responsible for Richard and his wife, Mary, becoming vegetarians. Stan Godlovitch was doing a Ph.D. in philosophy of biology, with an interest in how biologists understand animal behavior, while Roslind was thinking and writing about the ethics of how we treat animals, though she was not then enrolled as a student. They had come to see our treatment of nonhuman animals as analogous to the brutal exploitation of other races by whites in earlier centuries, and as a result, about a year earlier, had become vegetarians.

Naturally, I also talked to Renata about this disturbing challenge to the way we ate. Neither of us were "animal lovers." We did not have any pets, and had never even discussed having one. That we were opposed to cruelty, however, went without saying. On Roslind's recommendation, we both read Ruth Harrison's *Animal Machines,* the first book to reveal—and document, with photographs and ample citations from farming journals—what modern farming methods do to animals. That looked like cruelty to us.

Over the next month, I had several conversations with Roslind about the ethics of how we treat animals. She had recently published an article on that topic in *Philosophy,* and was in the process of revising it for a book that she, Stan, and John Harris[6] were editing. Ros was a little unsure about the revisions she was making, and I spent a lot of time trying to help her clarify and strengthen her arguments. In the end, she went her own way, and I don't think any of my suggestions were incorporated into the version of the article that appeared in the book, *Animals, Men and Morals.*[7]

---

[6] This is not the John Harris who went on to become a professor of bioethics at the University of Manchester. Confusingly, there were two John Harrises studying philosphy at Oxford at that time.

[7] Roslind Godlovitch, Stanley Godlovitch, and John Harris, eds., *Animals, Men, and Morals: An Enquiry into the Mal-Treatment of Nonhumans* (London: Gollancz, 1971).

In the process of putting her arguments in what seemed to me the strongest possible form, however, I convinced myself that the case for vegetarianism, at least for people situated as we were, with plenty of nourishing alternatives to meat, was overwhelming.

Renata and I agreed that we could not justify continuing to eat meat. As I have already mentioned, in discussing my Master of Arts thesis, on one view of what is involved in making a moral judgment, understanding that you ought not to do something is equivalent to a deciding not to do it. You may, through weakness of will, fail to carry out your resolution, but as far as the process of practical reasoning is concerned, you have come to the end and there is nothing more to be said. It wasn't like that for me. Self-interest—as I perceived it at the time, anyway—pulled strongly against turning vegetarian. Meat was the centerpiece of almost every dinner I had ever eaten, and most lunches too. My reluctance to abandon something that I enjoyed was boosted by my anxiety over what others would say when told of my new diet. Vegetarians were very rare then, and most people thought them decidedly odd. I had always prided myself on not having hangups about certain kinds of food. In Australia, Renata and I had tried rabbit, and kangaroo, both meats that Australians rarely eat, and when we were with Jewish friends who followed a kosher diet, we were always glad that we didn't have to fuss about whether the pea soup was made with a ham bone. Now, it seemed, if we were to follow through on our ethical conclusions, we would have to become very fussy ourselves. Family, friends, fellow-students and teachers would surely think we had become cranks.

While talking with Renata about what we were going to do, I came up with an objection to the view that once we knew what we ought to do, we had to just go ahead and do it. The objection was that those of us who have money to spend on luxuries know, in our heart of hearts, that we ought to be doing far more to help the world's poor than we actually do, but we still don't do it. We ourselves, I suggested to Renata, were in that position. If we can live with the knowledge that we are not doing what we ought to be doing about starvation in India, why can't we live with the knowledge that we are not doing the right thing about eating animals?

I'm not proud of having put forward this line of thought. Fortunately, Renata gave it short shrift. The implication of my objection, she said, is that we should become vegetarians and start giving a significant part of our income to an organization that helps those in desperate need. I couldn't disagree with that. Before then, by the standards of ordinary morality, Renata and I were not bad people, but we had never made a conscious decision to live ethically. Now we made that choice. It was something we wanted to do, perhaps because we were living in idealistic times, perhaps in order to maintain our self-esteem. (Richard Keshen would have liked that explanation, because his doctoral thesis was about the importance of self-esteem.[8]) It seemed especially contradictory to take a theoretical interest in ethics and yet push its conclusions to one side when they became difficult to act upon.

As we put these decisions into practice, ethics became a much more central part of our everyday lives. I've subsequently found that we were not unique in moving from an interest in following a vegetarian diet to a broader decision to live a more ethical life. Perhaps that is because it is easy to follow a conventional ethic without much thought, but once you depart from the conventional view on something as basic as food, it is impossible to avoid thinking and talking about ethics on that and many other questions as well.

Our change of diet began with a decision not to buy anything that came from a factory farm. We cut out chicken, veal, and all pig products. We found a nearby farm that sold free range eggs. We could see the hens out on pasture, and we didn't have any qualms about eating their eggs. Beef, lamb, and dairy products remained in, but instead of eating more of them, we replaced the animal products we had eliminated with vegetarian alternatives. Cooking and eating the new vegetarian dishes proved to be fun. Previously Renata had done almost all the cooking in our home, but her repertoire was European. Our new friends had lent us a vegetarian cookbook with separate chapters on vegetarian dishes in cuisines we had never attempted to cook, like Indian, Middle Eastern, Japanese, and Chinese. Since Renata's expertise with some of these cuisines was no greater than mine, I became the specialty chef for Asian cooking.

As our enjoyment of vegetarian food increased, so did our conviction that there was really no need for us to continue to eat meat at all. Even if the animals we were eating were not living in factory farms, we knew they suffered in other ways, especially in transport and slaughter. So within a few weeks we became more or less vegetarian. I say "more or less" because our concern was with animals capable of suffering, and nothing that I could discover about bivalves like oysters, scallops, clams, and mussels suggested that they were conscious. We continued to eat them, occasionally, when we dined out and there were no good vegetarian choices on the menu.

---

[8] Richard Keshen, *Reasonable Self-Esteem* (Montreal: McGill-Queens University Press, 1996).

At the same time, we began investigating how we could best assist those who were unable to feed themselves and their families. Since Oxford was the seat of Oxfam, one of the best-known non-government development agencies, we began by visiting their offices and collecting information about the kind of projects they funded. We liked their approach to the problems, working with local grass-roots organizations in developing countries. They also told us that we could earmark a donation for a specific project, so that we would not, for example, be contributing to a project that exploited animals. We were living comfortably enough, on Renata's salary as a schoolteacher and my scholarship. We started giving ten percent of our gross income to Oxfam—a percentage that we have gradually increased over the years.

Through the Keshens and the Godlovitches, we got to know a remarkable "Oxford Group" of ethical vegetarians. Among them were other graduate students and contributors to *Animals, Men, and Morals*, like David Wood, who was interested in continental European philosophy, and Michael Peters, a Marxist with a structuralist twist. Richard Ryder, who had coined the term "speciesism" and was contributing an essay on animal experimentation to the same volume, was a clinical psychologist at the Warneford Hospital. He convinced me that there are serious problems in the use of animals for research, though I could not accept his ethical position that we are never justified in inflicting pain or suffering on one being for the benefit of another. He was later to publish *Victims of Science*, a pioneering critique of experiments on animals.[9]

I was not only more utilitarian in my thinking than Ryder or any of the others, but also more in the mainstream of Anglo-American ethics. (Richard Keshen was studying Spinoza, while Stan Godlovitch refused to work in ethics at all.) Andrew Linzey and Stephen Clark, both of whom later wrote books about the treatment of animals, were also in Oxford at the time, but I do not recall meeting either of them until after I had left Oxford.

An Academic Post

These life-changing events occurred towards the end of 1970 and early in 1971. In June 1971 I completed my thesis and took my final exams for the Bachelor of Philosophy. When the results came out, I learned only that I had passed—no other grades were posted. Soon after John

---

[9] Richard Ryder, *Victims of Science* (London: Davis-Poynter, 1975).

Mackie, the senior philosopher at University College, asked me to come to see him. I then discovered that I had tied with one other student for the highest overall grade of those taking the course that year. Mackie also told me that one of the examiners of my thesis was H.L.A. Hart, who was also a member of the governing body of Oxford University Press, and that Hart thought the press might be interested in publishing a revised version of the thesis as a book. On top of this, Mackie mentioned that he had been awarded a Radcliffe fellowship that would give him more time for research by providing funds for a person to take over his college teaching for the next two years. The College was seeking to fill this position, and Mackie told me that if I wished to be considered for it, I would be a strong candidate.

We had been planning an adventurous return trip to Australia, traveling overland as far as Singapore. I had no job offer there, but the academic job market was then not as tight as it subsequently became, and I thought that I would probably be able to get something. Renata was enjoying her teaching, however, and the prospect of staying longer in Oxford was attractive, so I told Mackie that I was interested. I don't think the position was ever advertised, and I was never interviewed for it but some time later I was offered a Radcliffe Lectureship at University College.

Despite the position's title it involved no lecturing, only college tutoring. Undergraduates at Oxford then had a weekly tutorial, which was usually a one-on-one, one hour meeting with their tutor, although growing pressure on academic staff meant that some tutorials involved two students. Like graduates, the undergraduates wrote something each week to give their tutor. Some tutors asked the students to read it aloud at the beginning of the tutorial, but I preferred to have it handed in the day before, as I found that I couldn't always grasp the argument well unless I read it. I tutored moral and political philosophy, twelve to fourteen tutorials per week, which was a heavy load when preparation and reading of the papers is included. In compensation, the teaching year at Oxford was only three terms of eight weeks each, so I had time for research and writing during the remainder of the year.

Even though Oxford was a difficult university to get into, I found the students varied greatly in their ability to think philosophically. Many were a real pleasure to teach; some were hard going. Among the brightest was Andrew Reeve, now a professor at the University of Warwick. Among those with the deepest interest in living an ethical life was Alan Lewis, who subsequently changed his name to Alan Human, and has had to cope with periods of severe mental illness and homelessness. He still contacts me from time to time, and now has a self-portrait on the web.[10]

Around this time I began to submit articles for publication in philosophical journals. Derek Parfit, who had heard me give a seminar paper rebutting an objection to utilitarianism put forward by D.H. Hodgson in his book *Consequences of Utilitarianism,* suggested to *The Philosophical Review* that they consider publishing a revised version of that paper in the form of a critical review of Hodgson's book. They did so, and that became my first significant publication in a philosophical journal.[11]

Another early publication, entitled, perhaps with an element of provocation, "Moral Experts," was a brief assertion of the claims of moral philosophers to contribute to public debates about practical ethical issues.[12] Its significance lies not so much in the argument it contains, which now seems entirely obvious, but in the fact that it challenged what was then a prevailing orthodoxy. I began by citing some statements by leading philosophers like C.D. Broad and A.J. Ayer to the effect that it is a mistake to "look to the moral philosopher for guidance." I then suggested that familiarity with moral concepts and experience in detecting fallacies in argument might be helpful in working out what to do, and that therefore moral philosophers did possess at least a degree of expertise in resolving difficult moral questions. I suspect that such obvious points had not been made previously because, with a few notable exceptions, most senior academic philosophers *wanted* to remove themselves from life outside the universities and focus on topics far removed from the interest of the general public. "Moral Experts" is, as much as anything, a manifesto for a new generation of philosophers taking a different view.

If "Moral Experts" gave reasons for believing that practical ethics could be a fruitful field of philosophical activity, my next publication, "Famine, Affluence, and Morality," made a contribution to that field. It was an attempt to state philosophically the view I'd expressed to Renata, when we were considering becoming vegetarian: how can we be justified in spending money on things we didn't really need, when that money could save the lives of others in desperate poverty? The issue was dramatized by the unfolding crisis in what was then East Pakistan and is now Bangladesh, where in response to atrocities

---

[10] http://www.oxfordmuse.com/selfportrait/portrait4.htm.
[11] "Is Act-Utilitarianism Self-Defeating?" *Philosophical Review* 81 (January 1972), pp. 94–104.
[12] "Moral Experts," *Analysis* 32 (March 1972), pp. 115–17.

committed by the Pakistani army, millions of refugees had poured across the Indian border and were in danger of starvation. The amount of aid being given to India by the West was a small fraction of what was needed to feed the refugees. The newly-established journal, *Philosophy and Public Affairs,* was the perfect place for such an article. "Famine, Affluence, and Morality" has since become the most widely reprinted of all my writings.[13]

I also sent off for publication the paper that had developed out of my early essay critical of Hare's views.[14] Now my target was much broader than Hare's work. I argued that the debate then dominating moral philosophy, between naturalists and their non-cognitivist opponents over how to define morality, was essentially trivial. The naturalists defined morality, and the moral "ought" in terms of their content. Moral terms, on their view, had to refer to important goods or evils, like avoiding harm to others, or else they were not being used in their proper moral sense. On the other hand the non-cognitivists asserted that a person's morality is constituted by whatever principles he or she approves of, or prescribes, or takes as overriding. But in this debate, the real issue was being overlooked. Both sides agreed that it is desirable for people to act in certain ways, for example not harming others. The underlying question therefore is what kind of reasons or arguments can be offered to persuade people to act in these ways. The naturalists were disturbed by the non-cognitivist view that anything at all could be a moral principle, and thought that this undermined our efforts to get people to do what is right. Instead, they wanted to be able to hold that morality requires us to act in certain ways, and claimed that anyone who denies this is misusing moral language. The non-cognitivists pointed out that if the moral terms were defined by reference to a specific content, it was open to anyone to say "If that is what it means to say that I ought, morally, to do something, then I don't care about morality." They saw it as crucial to link morality with each person's own preferences or reasons for action.

In contrast to both these positions, I argued that the gap that really matters is not between "is" and "ought" but between a desirable morality and reasons for action. The naturalists sought to close this gap by tying morality to a particular content, and the non-cognitivists sought to close it by tying morality to our reasons for action. But that was like try-

---

[13] "Famine, Affluence, and Morality," *Philosophy and Public Affairs* 1 (Spring 1972), pp. 229–243.
[14] "The Triviality of the Debate over 'Is-Ought' and the Definition of 'Moral'," *American Philosophical Quarterly* 10 (January 1973), pp. 51–56.

ing to close a gap in a fence by linking some extra fencing just to one side or the other of the gap. I now saw Hare as trying to hook the extra fencing up to both ends, using the requirement that moral judgments be prescriptive to tie morality to our reasons for action, and the requirement that moral judgments be universalizable to tie it to a desirable morality. But this allowed gaps at both ends: for the amoralist could still decline to care about universalizability, and the person Hare called "the fanatic" could universalize appalling moral principles. (Hare subsequently came to believe that he could deal with the fanatic, but admitted that amoralism is possible and not necessarily irrational.[15])

At Mackie's suggestion, I went to see Hart about the possible publication of my thesis. He advised me to submit it to Oxford University Press, along with a letter indicating that I was willing to develop some sections further. My proposal was accepted, and the amplified thesis was published under the title *Democracy and Disobedience* in 1973. At the time I was, of course, thrilled to have a book published by such a distinguished press. Looking back on it now, I cringe at the excessively "Oxford" flavor of the discussion of a dispute in an academic common room that I use as a model for political argument. The major arguments for a *prima facie* obligation to obey the law in a democracy would benefit from a more explicit statement of their moral premises. It isn't clear to what extent these arguments are compatible with utilitarianism, and if not, what other moral premises they require. Although the arguments may still be defensible, I do not think of *Democracy and Disobedience* as part of my core contribution to ethical thinking.

Perhaps this is the place to mention a significant event in ethics and political philosophy: the publication, in 1971, of John Rawls's long-awaited *A Theory of Justice.* When I read it, I was puzzled about all the praise the book received. It seemed then—and still seems to me now—an excessively long and often tedious work with a gaping hole at its very core, the claim that people in the original position would choose the two principles of justice rather than a form of utilitarianism. Curiously, few people take much notice of the arguments Rawls offers for this claim, but those who do can hardly fail to notice how weak they are.[16]

The esteem in which the book was held, I concluded, must be a result of something other than the strength of its arguments: perhaps the

---

[15] See R.M. Hare, *Moral Thinking: Its Method, Levels and Point* (Oxford: Clarendon, 1981).

[16] See John Rawls, *A Theory of Justice* (Oxford: Clarendon, 1972), sections 26–29.

author's eminence and connections, or the desire of so many people in the field for an alternative to utilitarianism. But at least *A Theory of Justice* accelerated the revival of political philosophy (a revival that had started six years earlier, with the publication of Brian Barry's *Political Argument*).[17]

I wanted to do philosophy in a way that reached beyond the bounds of the academy, so when I learned of a meeting in London to consider forming an association for "Radical Philosophy," I decided to go. Expecting a format that invited participation from all those present— this was a period when progressives were all talking about "participatory democracy"—I was disappointed when the meeting began with one of the organizers giving a long presentation of his analysis of our present condition and the role British academic philosophy was playing in propping up the system. After this had gone on for a while, I broke in to say that if we were going to be radical, we might try to get beyond the idea of one person lecturing at length to everyone else. This interruption was evidently regarded by some of those present as discourteous, but it did at least lead to a discussion of the different possibilities that could be covered by the idea of making philosophy radical. For the remainder of my time in England I was involved with the Oxford branch of the Radical Philosophy Association that was formed at the London meeting, but I lost interest when it became clear that there was nothing really radical about the manner in which those who were running the Association did philosophy. They were not addressing practical ethical issues, nor reaching out to a wider audience. Instead they favored Marxist and continental philosophers whose work was less accessible to most people than the British philosophers on which the current curriculum was based. I couldn't see that anything would be gained from the changes they sought in the way philosophy is done.

Animal Liberation

I wanted to make philosophy radical by linking it more closely to practice. Eating ethically and giving to help the poor are important elements in this. Once I was committed to a new way of thinking about animals, I wanted to spread the idea. Together with the Godlovitches and Keshens, I booked a space next to the thousand-year old tower of St Michael's Church on the Cornmarket, Oxford's busiest shopping street. With assistance from Compassion in World Farming, then a tiny organ-

---

[17] Brian Barry, *Political Argument* (London: Routledge, 1965).

ization run by its founder, Peter Roberts, we had a display of a veal calf in a wooden stall, and hens in battery cages, showing passers-by how these animals were kept on factory farms. The calf was made of felt and the hens were *papier-mâché*, but one short-sighted passerby upbraided us for our cruelty in keeping hens in such small wire cages. Others, however, were surprised and supportive, and at the end of the day we thought we had achieved something.

Animals, Men, and Morals, edited by the Godlovitches and John Harris, was published in Britain in 1971. We had great hopes that it would trigger widespread discussion, and perhaps even protests against the forms of animal exploitation that some of its chapters described. Instead, the major newspapers and magazines ignored it completely. The topic of animals was, their editors seemed to think, not worth taking seriously. It was a deep disappointment to us all. A few months later, Ros told me that there was to be an American edition of the book. That started me thinking about a way to draw attention to the American edition so that it would not suffer the same fate as the British one. I had been wanting to write about why we needed to change our attitude to animals, but since so many of my ideas on this topic had come from others, especially from Ros, who was planning to write a book on the topic, I felt I should allow her to publish a fuller version of her position first. Now I thought of a way to satisfy my own desire to write about the issue and at the same time help my friends' book get the attention it deserved. I wrote to the editors of *The New York Review of Books* describing *Animals, Men, and Morals* and saying why it was a pioneering book that merited discussion in the pages of what was then indisputably the leading English-language forum for radical and leftish ideas. I offered to review the book myself, and outlined the kind of review I would write. Since I had had no previous contact with the editors I didn't know what kind of answer I would get. Robert Silvers's reply was guardedly encouraging. He would like to see the article, although he could not promise to publish it. In a burst of creative energy released by the feeling that I had an opportunity to do something significant against a great wrong, I set to work, and wrote a review-essay that I headed "Animal Liberation." I was elated when Silvers accepted it, but then had to wait impatiently for several months—until April 1973—to see it in print.[18]

I soon received enthusiastic letters from people who had similar feelings about our exploitation of animals, but had never put them into a

---

[18] "Animal Liberation," *New York Review of Books* (April 5th, 1973).

coherent philosophical framework. The first philosopher to write to me about "Animal Liberation" was James Rachels, the editor of *Moral Problems,* a pioneering anthology of articles in applied ethics. Rachels said he had long wondered what it was that justified the way we treat animals. After reading my review, he now saw that nothing justified it. That boosted my confidence that I was on the right track.

Another letter was from an editor at Simon and Schuster suggesting that I develop the ideas sketched in my essay into a book. There was, obviously, room for a book that offered a more systematic approach to the topic than the collection of disparate views that made up *Animals, Men, and Morals.* There was also a need for factual research on factory farming and the use of animals for research in the U.S., since the data in both *Animal Machines* and *Animals, Men, and Morals* was largely British. My two-year Radcliffe lectureship was drawing to a close, and I had accepted the offer of a visiting position at New York University, so I knew that I would be well-placed to do the research. Finally, it was now two and a half years since I had first discussed animals and ethics with Ros, enough time, I thought, for her to get her own work well under way, if she was ever going to complete it. She had, however, made little progress with it.[19] So during our last summer in Oxford—while also preparing for the birth of our first child—I began work on *Animal Liberation.*

Renata and I arrived in New York in September with our month-old daughter, Ruth. I had with me an outline of the planned book, and drafts of what were to become the first chapter, which contains the core of the ethical argument, and the historical chapter, which outlines the development of speciesism in Western thought. But the editor who had encouraged me to write the book had left Simon and Schuster, and they were no longer interested in it. Shortly after I received this rejection, Robert Silvers invited me to lunch, to discuss whether I might be interested in writing another article for *The New York Review.* I told him I would be happy to do so, and subsequently wrote several review-essays for him; but I also took advantage of the occasion to ask him to recommend a publisher, or perhaps an agent, for a book based on the "Animal Liberation" article. Instead of doing so, he expressed interest in publishing it himself. (*The New York Review* had published one or two other books that had grown out of articles.) Before long, I had a contract with *The New York Review* for the publication of *Animal Liberation.*

---

[19] Roslind Godlovitch enrolled as a student at Oxford and began to write a doctoral thesis, under Hare's supervision, on ethics and animals, but she did not complete it, and never published her own projected work on animals.

My appointment at New York University was for one year, with an expectation of renewal for up to three years. Soon after I arrived, I learned that the university was in dire financial straits, and had had to sell its Bronx campus in order to stave off bankruptcy. Staff were being cut, and there was not going to be any renewal of my appointment. Around this time, however, I received a letter from Brian Ellis, the head of the Philosophy Department at La Trobe University, a new university in one of Melbourne's suburbs. He asked if I would be interested in an appointment. I was, because we had always intended to return to Australia eventually, and now that we had a child, we were particularly keen to be near our parents and extended family. I was offered a Senior Lecturership, a flattering offer considering how junior I then was. My NYU appointment ended in June 1974, but it suited La Trobe University for me to begin in January 1975, since the Australian academic year begins at the end of the southern summer. That suited me too, because it gave me six months to work full-time on *Animal Liberation*.

For several weeks I became a regular at the New York Public Library, reading farming magazines to discover the confinement methods then in use, and what producers were saying about them. The emphasis always was on what methods were most profitable, never on what best met the needs of the animals. More weeks were spent in the offices of United Action for Animals, going through the organization's extensive files on animal experimentation. Eleanor Seiling, the strong-willed head of the organization, had employed researchers to comb the scientific journals and summarize experiments that inflicted substantial suffering on animals. Often the experiment caused excruciating pain to the animals, yet achieved nothing to advance knowledge in any significant way. I read dozens of such experiments for every one that I used in the book. Before I used any experiment, I always checked the summary against the researchers' original published paper. Reading these reports was a harrowing and emotionally draining experience. I was kept going by an overwhelming sense of the importance of getting this material to the public in a form that would enable everyone to see just how wrong such treatment of animals was, and demand that it end. That made the writing flow easily—it was a relief to be able to put down on the page what was building up inside my head.

Teaching at New York University in 1973–74 gave me my chance to design my own lecture course, and I taught the first of many courses I have taught in applied ethics, covering not only the usual philosophical questions about the nature of ethics, but also the issues I had been writing about, like the ethics of how we treat animals, and our obligations to the poor. The students were excited by the material, but compared to even the weaker Oxford students, many of them wrote very poorly.

When my one-year appointment at New York University came to an end, the university's Department of Continuing Education invited me to teach an evening course for adult students, so in the fall of 1974 I offered a course based on the draft materials for *Animal Liberation*. It attracted about fifteen students. One student stood out from the others because of his rumpled clothes, his New York working-class accent, and his blunt way of expressing himself. Henry Spira had been a merchant seaman, a civil rights activist, a union reformer and a high school teacher. He had read about animal liberation in the leftwing American magazine *The Guardian*. That article mocked *The New York Review* and its trendy liberal editors for publishing an article on something as absurd as animal liberation. Despite the ridicule, Spira, who had spent his life opposing exploitation of the powerless, but had never thought of animals as an exploited group, grasped that there might really be something worth reading in my article. He got it and was persuaded by it. At the end of the New York University course, he invited those who were interested in moving from theory to action to meet in his apartment to discuss what could be done about the issues we had been discussing. I couldn't attend that meeting, as I was about to go to Australia, but out of the small group of those who did attend came the first American campaign ever to succeed in stopping a series of experiments on animals. Spira himself became the most successful American animal rights campaigner of the 1970s and 1980s.[20]

I had first met Tom Regan when he took a group of students to Oxford in the summer of 1973, after my *New York Review* essay had appeared. He was interested in Gandhi and pacifism, and that had led him to vegetarianism. After I came to the United States he invited me to give a lecture at North Carolina State University at Raleigh, where he was teaching. While I was there, we agreed to edit a collection of writings on ethics and animals, eventually published under the title *Animal Rights and Human Obligations*.

In December 1974, just before Renata and I left New York for Australia, I handed Bob Silvers the typescript of *Animal Liberation*. It was published nine months later to some good reviews, including a very positive one in *The New York Times Book Review,* but sales remained

---

[20] See Peter Singer, *Ethics into Action: Henry Spira and the Animal Rights Movement* (Lanham: Rowman and Littlefield, 1998).

modest for the first year or two. That began to change in 1978, when the American animal rights movement was starting to grow and the book went into paperback. *Animal Liberation* never became a bestseller, but has remained in print for more than thirty years and has now sold more than six hundred thousand copies in twenty languages.

Back to Australia: La Trobe University

In 1975 La Trobe University had the largest philosophy department in Australia, with about twenty-seven philosophers on the staff. This unusual size was the result of the department's success in attracting a large first-year enrolment, at a time when Australian universities were rapidly expanding. My former teacher, H.J. McCloskey had been appointed to one of two chairs of philosophy there, along with Brian Ellis. McCloskey and I talked quite a lot, but our philosophical conversations soon became repetitive, for neither of us changed our positions. J.J.C. Smart, one of Australia's most eminent philosophers, was also there. Ethics was not Smart's main interest, but he had recently revised his classic brief defense of utilitarianism, and I appreciated the support he gave to my approach to ethics.[21]

I liked his evident enjoyment of life in general, and of philosophy in particular. (In this, as in his approach to ethics, he was a contrast to McCloskey, who despite getting a chair felt unappreciated and often spoke bitterly about other philosophers.) One of Smart's endearing characteristics was that when a speaker presented a paper at one of the department's seminars, he would fall asleep and snore loudly. When the speaker finished, he would wake up and ask a question—astonishingly, always an apt one.

The department also had some outstanding younger philosophers. I always learned from Frank Jackson's clarity and logical argument. Like Smart, most of his research was in fields other than ethics, but he was a shining exemplar of the now-abandoned ideal that each member of a philosophy department should keep up with all the major areas of philosophy. Robert Young shared my interests in applied ethics and political philosophy. We co-taught a popular course on social philosophy, covering topics like global justice and foreign aid, the moral status of animals, abortion and euthanasia. He was not a utilitarian, for he thought justice is an independent value, but we agreed on many practical issues.

---

[21] J.J.C. Smart and Bernard Williams, *Utilitarianism: For and Against* (Cambridge: Cambridge University Press, 1973).

At La Trobe I also taught a course with someone with whom I was in profound disagreement. Moshe Kroy had been appointed to the department on the basis of his work in logic, but when he arrived he announced that his interests had changed and he wanted to teach ethics. The reason for this change was that he had become an enthusiastic advocate of Ayn Rand's defense of a morality based on advancing one's own interests, as exemplified in her novel *Atlas Shrugged*. The department feared that Kroy's proposed course on ethics would be a one-sided Randian polemic, and asked me to share it with him, to ensure that alternative views were fairly presented. Although Kroy offered as intelligent a defense of Rand as anyone could make, he could not succeed in making her position palatable to most of the students.

After attending the seminars presented by Derek Parfit during my early years in Oxford, I had not stopped thinking about how a utilitarian might approach decisions that have an impact on the size of the future population of the universe. Now, in response to an invitation from Michael Bayles to contribute to a volume on the subject, I attempted to develop a distinct approach that would give priority to the interests of those who would exist anyway, independently of the decision made. When I sent off my essay, my solution seemed convincing. In his response in the same volume, however, Parfit found objections to which I had no answer, and I had to abandon my approach.[22]

Thirty years later, despite having supervised the work of some very bright graduate students who were also interested in the issue, I still do not know how to resolve the problem.

In 1976 I was asked by Jeremy Mynott, an editor with Cambridge University Press, to write a textbook in applied ethics. I responded that since I had been teaching a course in that area with Robert Young, I would like to co-author the book with him. After some correspondence, Cambridge rejected this idea. They wanted a work presenting one approach to the issues covered. I accepted their decision reluctantly, because I knew that in writing the book I would be drawing on the course that Robert and I had developed together. But the subsequent popularity of *Practical Ethics* as a textbook in applied ethics courses suggests that Cambridge may have been right.

Our second daughter, Marion, was born in June 1975, so life became busier at home. I had expected to be at La Trobe for many years, but when

---

[22] "A Utilitarian Population Policy" in M. Bayles, ed., *Ethics and Population* (Cambridge, Massachusetts: Schenkman, 1976); see also Derek Parfit, "On Doing the Best for Our Children" in the same volume.

Monash—another relatively new university in a different Melbourne sub-urb—advertised a chair in philosophy, McCloskey encouraged me to apply. Australian universities, following the British model, have a strict-ly limited number of chairs, or full professorships, usually only one or two per department, so it was an opportunity that might not come again for several years, at least not in Melbourne, where there were then only three universities. I applied and was subsequently interviewed by the selection committee, which consisted of about a dozen senior professors from different departments, most of them not philosophers, plus a couple of departmental representatives, some members of the university's gov-erning body, and John Passmore of the Australian National University as an outside adviser. I recall being asked if I planned to continue writing books. I answered that since under the sabbatical system I would have one year's leave in every seven, I thought that should be enough to enable me to complete a book. The committee seemed to think that a book every seven years was a high rate of publication—as indeed it was, at the time. When I was offered the chair, I had just turned thirty.

Monash University

I moved to Monash at the beginning of 1977. At Monash, this was still the era of the "god-professor" because the head of the department, who had to be a professor, was an autocrat with no obligation to take any notice of the views of other members of staff. I didn't want to wield that kind of authority over a department whose academic staff was mostly more senior that I was, so I told them I would put contentious issues to a vote and accept the majority view. One of the first things we decided to do was to revise our course offerings to attract more stu-dents. We changed the year-long first-year introductory course in phi-losophy, so that students could choose from several options for the first semester. Among these was an option in Contemporary Moral Issues, which I taught. For the first time I found myself lecturing to more than two hundred students. I also taught a second year ethics course, deal-ing with both meta-ethical and normative issues in ethics, and a fourth year course on issues in applied ethics. For the Bachelor of Arts degree in Australia, only students seeking a degree with honors—usually, those interested in going on to graduate studies—do a fourth year. The others graduate in three years. Our fourth year courses were therefore small seminars with high-quality students. Graduate students some-times sat in, but they were not required to take any courses, only to write a thesis.

The new courses increased enrolments in philosophy, and helped clinch our case for filling a second chair. The appointment of Frank Jackson made Monash one of the strongest philosophy departments in Australia. It was a department with several hardworking able philosophers, but also one or two older members who did very little. (One of them had a drinking problem, and I was discretely advised not to give him classes after lunch.)

Among many good colleagues with whom I had discussions on a variety of issues, I should particularly mention Chin Liew Ten and Aubrey Townsend. With Ten, who was later to write a fine book on John Stuart Mill's views on liberty, I talked often about issues in ethics and political philosophy, especially the question of how far the state could legitimately go in interfering with people for their own good. I had been interested in road safety since my days working on *Farrago,* when I had reviewed Ralph Nader's pioneering exposéé of American cars, *Unsafe at Any Speed,* and written a feature article on safety problems in cars popular in Australia. In 1970 Victoria had become the first jurisdiction in the world to require the use of seatbelts in cars, and within three years, all other Australian states and territories had passed similar laws. Deaths on the road, which had been rising steadily up to that date, began to fall, and have, by and large, continued to fall ever since.[23]

It is hard for a utilitarian to deny that the benefits of saving so many lives and preventing so many serious injuries outweigh the minor restriction on individual liberty that the law involves. Ten, however, defended Mill's principle that "the only purpose for which power can be rightfully exercised over any member of a civilised community, against his will, is to prevent harm to others" and that the individual's own physical or moral good does not justify the state in restricting what individuals may do. Mill justified this view, in part, by his claim that "Each is the proper guardian of his own health, whether bodily, or mental, or spiritual."[24]

But prior efforts to persuade Australians to wear seat belts had had limited success, despite the clear evidence that it is in their interests to do so. Hence I was skeptical of Mill's claim, and thought that a modest amount of coercion might be justified, if the benefits were clear. On the other hand, I have to admit that Mill's principle is a useful argument in other contexts, for example against laws prohibiting voluntary euthana-

---

[23] Australian Bureau of Statistics, *2001 Yearbook Australia* (Canberra: Commonwealth of Australia, 2001), pp. 854–57.
[24] J.S. Mill, *On Liberty*, Chapter 1; see also Mill's *Principles of Political Economy,* Book 1, Chapter 11.

sia and physician-assisted suicide, or restricting sexual activities between consenting adults. I was attracted to H.L.A. Hart's view that Mill was right to object to legal moralism, that is to state enforcement of morals where there is no harm to anyone, but wrong to object to the state paternalistically protecting those who, for one reason or another, were liable to harm themselves unnecessarily.[25]

But for a utilitarian, there is in any case a conceptual problem about the idea of immoral acts that cause no harm. Why should such acts be considered immoral at all? Rather than object to legal moralism, the utilitarian is on stronger ground when arguing that the moral views that condemn such acts are mistaken.[26]

Aubrey Townsend was an outstanding philosopher with few publications, but a broad range of interests, and a strong commitment to teaching philosophy well. When he thought people were wrong, or not doing what they should do, he did not hesitate to tell them so, often quite bluntly. For that reason not everyone liked him. But he was never unfair, and since he worked much harder than most—and largely for the benefit of his students, or the department, never for his own career interests—I did not resent his criticisms.

Before I came to Monash, Townsend had published an early critique of my views about animals.[27] It was, and remains, one of the better defenses of recognizing human beings as having a higher moral status than animals. Townsend holds that we ought to protect animals from pain, since they are sentient beings—and so factory farming is wrong. But we owe human beings more than simply protection from pain. They differ from nonhuman animals because they are autonomous beings with beliefs and intentions. We therefore ought to respect the autonomy of normal human being, whereas with animals there is no autonomy to respect—and hence no reason against painless killing. That left the familiar question of human beings whose intellectual capacities are inferior to those of nonhuman animals. Townsend's argument here is simply that there may be pragmatic reasons for drawing a clear line around those beings who cannot be killed, and—since it is difficult to determine which humans do and which do not have the requisite capacity for

---

[25] H.L.A. Hart, *Law, Liberty, and Morality.* (Oxford: Oxford University Press, 1968).

[26] See my "Mill's Revelance Today: A Personal View," in Georgios Varouxakis and Paul Kelly, eds., *John Stuart Mill: Thought and Influence—A Bicentennial Appraisal* (London: Routledge, forthcoming).

[27] A.V. Townsend, "Radical Vegetarians," *Australasian Journal of Philosophy* 57 (1976), pp. 85–93.

autonomy—the best way to do this is to treat all humans as having rights that animals lack. The extent of my disagreement with this position will become clearer when I turn to the development of my views about the sanctity of human life.

New Fields

One advantage of my move to Monash was that, unlike La Trobe, it had a medical school. In response to an invitation from John Ladd, a philosopher at Brown University, I had contributed to a book called *Ethical Issues in Life and Death*.[28] That essay, "Unsanctifying Human Life," elaborated on a few remarks about killing animals that I had made in the first chapter of *Animal Liberation* and is the first version of my subsequently notorious rejection of the sanctity of human life. The argument itself follows straightforwardly from the rejection of speciesism. If species membership is not morally crucial, I argued, there are only three possibilities:

- We should extend to nonhuman animals the protection we now give to human life;

- We should regard the killing of humans as no more serious than we now regard the killing of animals;

- We should develop a view of the wrongness of killing that depends on some characteristics of particular beings, rather than their species membership.

I favored the third position. But what characteristics are relevant to the wrongness of killing? If the characteristic were, say, consciousness, this would lead to a less permissive stance about killing animals. If it were a high-level rationality or autonomy that no nonhuman animal could meet, it would lead to a more permissive attitude to killing some humans, since not all humans would meet such a requirement. More plausible, I suggested, was some intermediate position according to which the lives of some animals, with higher cognitive capacities, should be regarded more seriously than we do at present, while taking the lives of some human beings, lacking in such capacities, should be seen more permissively.

A different reason for taking an interest in the field that was just beginning to be called "bioethics" emerged soon after my appointment at

---

[28] J. Ladd, ed., *Ethical Issues Relating to Life and Death* (New York: Oxford University Press, 1978).

Monash, when I attended a lecture by Bill Walters, of the university's Department of Obstetrics and Gynecology. He described research at Monash and in England, aimed at assisting infertile couples to have a child. This research would, he told us, lead to the fertilization of a viable embryo in a test-tube, or more precisely, in a laboratory dish. Walters acknowledged that his medical training did not properly equip him to deal with the new ethical, social, and legal issues this would raise. After the lecture I introduced myself and suggested we meet to consider how best to address the ethical issues about which he had spoken. Walters brought John Swan, the Dean of Science and a man of broad interests, into our discussion, and that was the germ of what later became the Monash University Centre for Human Bioethics. But that was still some years ahead.

On Leave, 1978–79

When I was appointed, Monash had agreed to recognize my sabbatical leave entitlements from La Trobe University. That meant that I was soon eligible for six months' sabbatical leave and six months leave without pay. In July 1978 we left for Oxford, where our third daughter, Esther, was born in December. While I renewed contact with Oxford philosophers, I worked on completing *Practical Ethics*. The book was aimed at undergraduate students, so I did not try to give a definitive answer to each question I discussed. But I also did not seek to write in a neutral way. Instead I focused on presenting a consistent preference-utilitarian approach to each of the issues I discussed, while at the same time indicating other possible approaches and the major objections to my views. Some people have suggested that I wrote in a deliberately provocative manner, quoting sentences like "Killing a snail or a day-old infant does not thwart any desires [about one's future] because snails and newborns are incapable of having such desires."[29]

The choice of a snail for the comparison does look like it was intended to provoke. But comparing the mental level of a newborn infant, *in respect of the capacity to have desires about one's own future,* with a nonhuman organism was a way of making more vivid the lack of this capacity in a newborn infant. The comparison requires an animal that everyone would agree is incapable of having desires for the future. For that reason I could not choose a dog or a cat, let alone a chimpanzee. I wrote plainly and bluntly, and I did want to challenge my

---

[29] *Practical Ethics*, second edition, p. 90.

readers to re-examine their preconceptions, but I did not set out to provoke protests.

I had planned to spend part of my leave as a guest scholar at the Hastings Center, the first bioethics center in the world, then formally known as the Institute for Society, Ethics, and the Life Sciences. But I had been invited to apply for a fellowship at the Woodrow Wilson International Center for Scholars, in Washington, DC. The application process required the nomination of a project, and I had an idea that I wanted to work on. In 1975 E.O. Wilson had urged, in his controversial *Sociobiology: The New Synthesis* that we study human social behavior, including morality, from the perspective of evolutionary biology. Although some on the left rejected the idea because it smacked of genetic determinism, human beings, like other animals, have evolved through natural selection, and some of our social behavior must reflect this fact. Yet when Wilson actually ventured into the biological explanation of morality, he committed the common fallacy of deducing an "ought" from an "is"—in other words, drawing values from descriptive statements. I therefore sent the Woodrow Wilson Center a proposal to study the significance for ethics of the emerging field then known as sociobiology (now called evolutionary psychology). When I was offered a fellowship, Monash extended my leave without pay to the end of 1979, which made it possible for me to spend two months at the Hastings Center, and eight in Washington DC.

At the Hastings Center there was a sense of excitement about exploring new issues. Adding to the fact that bioethics was still a relatively new field was the sensational news that Bill Walters had predicted: the birth in England of Louise Brown, the first baby to have been conceived outside the human body. The ensuing debate on the ethics of *in vitro* fertilization was dominated by religious figures, many of whom condemned the procedures that had brought Louise Brown into existence. Since Britain and many of the other countries in which this debate raged were largely secular societies, I thought it would be a good thing if non-religious bioethical thinkers were more widely available for public comment and if the media knew where to find them. That was one factor that led me to become more seriously involved in bioethics in the coming years. Another factor also resulted from my stay at the Hastings Center. I got to know and like Dan Callahan, the Center's director, and Art Caplan, whose talent for clever soundbites later made him a sought-after bioethics commentator with the media, but I was unimpressed by the standard of discussion in the Center's workshops and publications. Few people in the field were used to the kind of rigorous critical scrutiny that had become standard in English-language philosophy. That was something I thought I could bring to this new field.

My own research and writing while at Hastings was not in bioethics. Oxford University Press had asked me to write a volume in a new series called Past Masters, consisting of very short introductory volumes on great thinkers of the past.[30]

They probably expected I would want to write on Bentham or Mill, but instead I offered to do one on Marx, because I had never written up the ideas I had formulated as a graduate student at Oxford. I had then concluded that Marx—not only the young Marx, but in all his work—is best understood neither as an economist, nor as someone with a new scientific approach to human history, but as a philosopher working within a Hegelian framework. I expected to be told that someone much more expert than me had already been commissioned to write the Marx volume; instead, to my surprise, my offer was accepted. I wrote *Marx* in two months early in 1979. The book's success—among other Past Masters only *Jesus* sold a comparable number of copies—led, a year or so later, to a commission to write a similar volume on an even more surprising figure: Hegel. Presumably all the genuine Hegel scholars had balked at the absurdity of writing an introduction to this difficult thinker in no more than a hundred pages. I, on the other hand, would not have wanted to write a big book on Hegel, because I preferred working on current problems. But I enjoyed the challenge, and *Hegel* does enable complete novices to grasp the gist of the philosopher's work in a single evening's reading. I knew that the book couldn't be too much of an oversimplification of Hegel's thought when I received a complimentary note about it from my former Hegel teacher, J.L.H. Thomas.

I was at the Woodrow Wilson International Center from the beginning of May until the end of the 1979. During this time I wrote a draft of *The Expanding Circle: Ethics and Sociobiology*. The title came from a quotation by W.E.H. Lecky: "At one time the benevolent affections embrace merely the family, soon the circle expanding includes first a class, then a nation, then a coalition of nations, then all humanity, and finally, its influence is felt in the dealings of man with the animal world."[31]

My aim was to correct some misconceptions about what would follow from greater knowledge of the biological basis of our moral sense,

---

[30] The series has since been merged into a different series, called *Very Short Introductions*.

[31] W.E.H. Lecky, *The History of European Morals from Augustus to Charlemagne* (London: Longmans Green, 1869).

and to set out a philosophically adequate conception of ethics as an evolved form of human social behavior. It was then common to assume that morality is entirely a product of culture, and so varies from one culture to another. There are, of course, significant differences in the moral views of different cultures, but I argued that some significant features of morality are common to all or virtually all human societies, especially the norms of obligations to kin, and of reciprocity. These are just the norms that one might expect to have evolved among social mammals able to recognize other individuals, and to remember who has done them favors and who has harmed them.

People sometimes assume that showing an ethical principle to be universal is a way of showing it to be valid. But if the explanation for universality lies in our evolutionary history, I argued, then showing that an ethical principle is universally held may be a way of debunking it, rather than giving it support. An evolutionary explanation of a universally-held ethical principle suggests that for most of our history as humans, or perhaps even further back, accepting the principle enhanced reproductive fitness. This does little to indicate whether the principle is a desirable one today, when circumstances may be very different, and it tends to weaken any claim that the principle is rationally-based principle, or self-evident, or a truth discovered by a special faculty of moral intuition.

The existence of genuine altruism is a puzzle for evolutionary psychology, since it would seem that any inheritable tendency towards it would be disadvantageous for the altruistic individual, and so would be eliminated from the gene pool. Some evolutionary theorists therefore deny that genuine altruism really exists, but this is difficult to reconcile with observed human behavior. I argued that it may be our capacity to reason that enables us to appreciate the needs of strangers, and to respond to those needs even when we do not feel emotional affinity, and the response involves some cost to ourselves. No doubt our ability to reason developed because it conferred advantages on us, but reason is like an escalator, in the sense that once you step on it, it carries you onwards, whether or not you wish to go to the end. Some elements of our ethics—especially ideas of impartiality and equality—may therefore be the outcome of our reasoning capacities and hence less directly under the influence of our genes than more emotional or intuitive responses.

I sent a draft of the book to E.O. Wilson. I had been quite critical of his attempts to deduce normative conclusions from factual premises, and so I was pleasantly surprised to receive a warm letter inviting me to see him when next I was near Harvard. I did so, and he gave me back the draft with detailed marginal annotations. We then had a long discussion about the book, in which he acknowledged that he had been wrong to suggest that one day it would be possible to deduce ethical principles from an understanding of the nature of the human brain.

The Expanding Circle was published by Farrar, Straus, and Giroux, a trade book publisher, one of whose editors had expressed an interest in publishing something of mine. It was well-reviewed but sold only modestly, and remains one of my less well-known books. Nevertheless it is one that I'm particularly pleased to have written. It contains suggestions that were speculative when the book appeared, but have since been supported by further work in evolutionary psychology.[32]

For me, the book has served as a kind of long-term research program, further outputs of which are *A Darwinian Left,* and my recent article "Ethics and Intuitions."[33]

During this period of leave, I also worked with Jim Mason on the text of *Animal Factories,* a book intended to tell the American public about factory farming. I had known Jim since 1974, when I was writing *Animal Liberation* and Jim, who had a farming background but was working for a group called Friends of Animals, had accompanied me on visits to factory farms in upstate New York and New England. For *Animal Factories* he traveled around the United States with a photographer who took remarkable black and white photographs that showed what factory farming was like. I then worked with Jim on a text that gave a short history of factory farming and described its impact on animals and the environment. *Animal Factories* was published by Crown in 1980 and went into a revised edition ten years later. It was, however, ahead of its time, at least for the United States. It was not until after 2002 that factory farming started to receive serious attention there, culminating with a remarkable victory in 2008, when Californian voters approved an initiative to prohibit confining farm animals so closely that they cannot turn around and stretch their limbs freely. That vote will transform the living conditions of nineteen million battery hens.

The Centre for Human Bioethics

In June 1980, six months after I returned to Melbourne, Candice Reed, Australia's first baby—and the world's third—to be conceived *in vitro,* was born. Her successful conception was the work of a joint Monash University–Melbourne University team that included Carl Wood,

---

[32] See for example Robert Wright, *The Moral Animal* (New York: Pantheon, 1994).

[33] "Ethics and Intuitions," *Journal of Ethics* 9: 3–4 (October 2005), pp. 331–352

Monash's professor of obstetrics and gynecology, and Alan Trounson, an embryologist in his department. The birth received an immense amount of media attention. The Roman Catholic Church and anti-abortion groups attacked IVF, as the process soon became known, largely because it involved research on embryos that destroyed some of them. Later some feminists joined in the attack, arguing that the desires of infertile couples to have children are part of a socially constructed and oppressive image of women that leaves them feeling incomplete if they do not reproduce. These feminists saw IVF as giving more power over women to a predominantly male medical profession.[34] IVF was also questioned on the grounds of its cost and the long odds against success. Others asked if, in a world in which there are children in need of adoption, we should go to such lengths in trying to assist infertile couples to have their own children.

John Swan, the Monash University Dean of Science who had joined the discussions I had had with Bill Walters before going on leave, correctly judged that the time was right to set up a centre that would bring together scientists, lawyers, philosophers, and social scientists to discuss the issues raised by the new reproductive technology. We invited Louis Waller, an eminent professor of law, to join us and put a proposal to the university to set up the centre. Swan suggested the name "Centre for Human Bioethics" as a way of fending off potential opposition from those who may have feared that a centre in which I was involved would object to research on animals. The Centre for Human Bioethics, the first non-religious bioethics center in Australia, aimed to promote the study of the ethical, social, and legal problems arising out of medical and biological research, to carry out research in the area, to provide an advisory and resource centre for government, professional, educational and community groups, and to stimulate the development of educational programs in human bioethics for professionals and the public.

It took another two years before the university could be persuaded to put in sufficient funds for me to become half-time director of the Centre, while continuing half-time in the Philosophy Department. In the meantime, however, the Centre had been given a very modest amount of money in order to enable it to offer a position as a research fellow to Helga Kuhse. I first met Helga when she took my course in Advanced Ethics. She was a mature-age student who had come to Australia from

---

[34] See for example Rita Arditti, Renate Duelli Klein, and Shelley Minden, eds., *Test Tube Women: What Future for Motherhood?* (Boston: Pandora, 1984).

Germany and at the time was doing a B.A. with honors in politics. Though she had little training in analytic philosophy, her essays were more thorough and better argued than those of other students. After graduating she began to write a Ph.D. under my supervision on issues related to the traditional doctrine of the sanctity of human life. She was invaluable in getting the new Centre started, and soon became a major figure in bioethics in her own right. Our collaboration was to be a long and fruitful one.

"Test Tube Babies"

At first the Centre focused on the hot topic of the day, the new reproductive technology. Together with Bill Walters, I collected some early work on the topic in *Test-Tube Babies: A Guide to Moral Questions, Present Techniques, and Future Possibilities*, published in Australia in 1982. That book included the first work I co-authored with Helga, a short essay on the moral status of embryos. We imagined a situation in which a laboratory is disposing of an unwanted egg and some sperm by flushing them down a sink. Is it really possible to believe, we asked, that there is no moral problem with doing that as long as they are separate, but if somehow the sink became blocked long enough for a sperm to penetrate the egg, one would then be required to "rescue" the zygote and try to enable it to become a child? Someone who believes in the sanctity of human life from the moment of conception presumably has to answer affirmatively, but that seems an implausible claim. Why should there be such a sharp difference between these two scenarios?

The Centre's first significant research grant was for research on ethical issues raised by in vitro fertilization and future possible developments, including embryo donation, surrogate motherhood, ectogenesis, cloning, and genetic selection. I employed Deane Wells, then a part-time tutor in philosophy, as a research assistant. Sometimes an assistant may do little more than find books and other materials, or administer a questionnaire. But my best research assistants have had valuable ideas about the research, and have drafted articles or chapters of books. In that situation, co-authorship seems the only proper way of recognizing their contribution, and Deane was deservedly a co-author of the book that presented the results of our research, *The Reproduction Revolution,* published in the U.K. and Australia in 1984, and in the U.S. the following year, under the sexier title *Making Babies*. Deane was a bright and entertaining person to have around the Centre, but he had political ambitions, and moved to Queensland where he rightly judged his prospects of winning Labor pre-selection for a seat in parliament were better. (He has subsequently had a successful political career, serving as Attorney-General, Minister for the Environment, and Minister for Education, in Queensland state governments.)

The Reproduction Revolution was among the first serious philosophical books on the issues raised by the new reproductive technology. Today some sections have become dated, while others are still relevant or even futuristic. We spent many pages defending the ethical legitimacy of in vitro fertilization for infertile couples, something that hardly anyone outside the Roman Catholic Church disputes today. On the other hand the chapters on cloning and genetic selection have greater relevance than ever, since human cloning and genetic selection to enhance our offspring are closer than they were when the book was published. The opposite has happened with the chapter on ectogenesis, because less progress than we expected has been made towards rearing embryos entirely outside the body.

On some points Deane could not accept what I had originally drafted. What we ended up writing on the possibility of growing fetuses outside the body for spare parts, for example, was a compromise between two different views, and I'm not sure that it is really defensible.[35] On the other hand, for someone who was hoping for a political career, Deane was willing to put his name to positions that many politicians would never dare state as unambiguously as we did. When I saw him again while working on this autobiography, I asked him if the book had been a handicap in his political career. He laughed and said no, it had probably helped him.

The Treatment of Disabled Infants

In 1982 a couple in Bloomington, Indiana, refused permission for a life-saving operation on their newborn infant, who had Down syndrome. The hospital took them to court, but the Supreme Court of Indiana sided with the parents and "Baby Doe," as the infant became known, died before the U.S. Supreme Court could hear the case. The Reagan administration responded to an outcry from the religious right and introduced new regulations to compel doctors to operate in such cases. I had already written on euthanasia for severely disabled infants in *Practical Ethics*. I now

---

[35] Peter Singer and Deane Wells, *The Reproduction Revolution: New Ways of Making Babies* (Oxford: Oxford University Press, 1984), pp. 148–49.

wrote an invited commentary on the issue for the American journal *Pediatrics,* and Helga Kuhse and I wrote about the issue in *The New York Review of Books.*[36] Helga also published an article in the *Journal of Applied Philosophy* on the British trial of Dr Leonard Arthur, who had been charged with murder after a Down syndrome baby in his care died.[37]

In Australia, specialists in neonatal intensive care invited us to discuss the decisions they had to make regarding the treatment of infants with severe disabilities. The treatment of babies with spina bifida, in particular, put doctors in an ethical quandary. This condition involves an opening in the spine that often leads to paralysis below the waist. It is much less common now than it was in the 1980s, both because we now know that it can be prevented by giving women folic acid during pregnancy, and because the few remaining cases can be detected prenatally, and abortion usually follows. In the 1970s and early 1980s, however, doctors saw a significant number of these children. For the more severely affected, there was no treatment that, in their opinion and that of at least some of the parents, could lead to a satisfactory quality of life. Following the lead of John Lorber, a British physician, some doctors operated only on the less severely affected infants. The others would usually develop an infection through the open, untreated wound on their backs. These babies would be allowed to die by witholding treatment. Death sometimes took place in a few days, often in a few weeks, but occasionally only after several months. During this period, the babies were likely to be ill and suffering from infections and medical complications. Both they and their parents had a miserable time.

This was an ethically indefensible way of treating these unfortunate infants, for two reasons. First, the whole point of non-treatment, as Lorber had admitted in print, was that the babies should die. Death was thought to be kinder to the infants, and to the families, than continued life. But why, then, allow the infants to die such lingering deaths? Second, many doctors made the decision to treat or not treat the infant without consulting the parents. They might tell the parents that "nature was taking its course," without indicating that they had assessed the baby's condition and made a decision not to treat the baby. These

---

[36] Peter Singer, "Sanctity of Life or Quality of Life?" *Pediatrics* 72 (1983), pp. 128–29; Helga Kuhse and Peter Singer, "The Future of Baby Doe," *New York Review of Books* (March 1st, 1984), pp. 17–22.

[37] Helga Kuhse, "A Modern Myth: That Letting Die Is Not the Intentional Causation of Death—Some Reflections on the Trial and Acquittal of Dr. Leonard Arthur," *Journal of Applied Philosophy* 1:1 (1984), pp. 21–38.

doctors thought that they were protecting the parents from the terrible responsibility of deciding on the death of their own child. We thought that, difficult as it might be, the decision affected the parents more than anyone else other than the baby itself, and they should be consulted.

Helga was working on a detailed critique of the traditional doctrine of the sanctity of human life, including a discussion of the distinction between killing and letting die, and here was a practical situation in which that distinction was being invoked. Some infants were born with such a hopeless prognosis that no one, not even religious conservatives, wanted them to receive life-support. But surely letting them die slowly could not be the best thing to do. We decided to write a book together on the topic. *Should the Baby Live?* is the fullest elaboration of my position on the issue that, of all the issues I have discussed, has caused the most heated protests. Even some who agree with my views on this issue have told me that it was a mistake to write about it, because the resulting controversy makes people less likely to listen to me on other, more important topics like the treatment of animals and our obligations to the poor.[38]

The central conclusion of our book is that parents should have a greater role in life-and-death decisions about their child. We believe that in these extremely difficult situations, this procedure will lead, in most cases, to more humane outcomes. But in writing the book we were also interested in showing that the simplistic idea that all innocent human life is of equal value, and should not be directly taken, was not being applied—and could not reasonably be applied—to current medical practice in this area.

In researching the issue, we interviewed some of the leading physicians, both in Australia and overseas, who deal with newborn infants with conditions like spina bifida. On a visit to England, I went to Sheffield to talk to John Lorber, and to R.B. Zachary, a physician who strongly disagreed with Lorber's practice. We also spoke to parents of children with disabilities, including Helen Harrison, author of *The Premature Baby Book,* and the mother of a prematurely-born and severely disabled boy. At that time, the opposition to both active euthanasia and nontreatment of severely disabled infants came almost entirely from religious and anti-abortion groups. The same was true of opposition to abortion following prenatal diagnosis when a serious disability was detected. We knew of no one who was opposed to that standard practice,

---

[38] See Harry Gensler's essay in this volume, which makes a similar point, although without agreeing with my views on the treatment of disabled infants; and see also my response.

but not opposed to abortion in general. The militant disability movement, which claimed that both termination following prenatal diagnosis, and the non-treatment or active euthanasia of infants with severe disabilities, stemmed from prejudice that led to an overly pessimistic view of the lives of people with disabilities, was still in the future. There was also little empirical work about the quality of life of people with disabilities. I can now see that we were not sufficiently sensitive to the existence of that prejudice—in the community in general and in the medical profession, perhaps even in ourselves—against people with disabilities and did not give sufficient attention to this issue of the quality of life possible for people with disabilities. But even when there is no prejudice, the question of what makes for a good quality of life is a difficult issue on which to come to a solidly-based conclusion.[39]

I completed the draft of *Should the Baby Live?* during a six-month appointment as a visiting professor at the University of Colorado, Boulder, in 1984. The visit enabled me to spend time with Dale Jamieson, then a professor there, who became a close friend. Dale was already concerned about the impact of greenhouse gas emissions on our planet's climate. He started me thinking about this issue, although it didn't appear in my writings until a decade later. I also taught Lori Gruen, then a graduate student interested in ethics and animals, with whom I was to work in later years. A significant change in my way of working also happened in Boulder: I began writing on a computer.

Directing the Centre for Human Bioethics

After *Should the Baby Live?*, eight years were to pass before I published another book that I regard as a significant contribution to philosophy or bioethics. Several factors probably contributed to this hiatus. Family life with three young children and a working spouse was one of them. Another was my involvement in the animal movement. Directing the Centre for Human Bioethics kept me busy too. We organized conferences, and answered queries from the media and the public. Helga and I were frequently in the newspapers or on television, so the Centre was doing well in raising the university's public profile. Since getting research grants was seen as another sign of the Centre's success, and brought the university government funding, we needed to keep applying for grants in order to ensure that the university would keep supporting

---

[39] See Harriet Johnson's and Stephen Drake's essays in this volume, and my responses.

the Centre. This was, and remains, a stupid and wasteful system for assessing excellence. Some of the things that would have been most interesting to do didn't really need much money. They needed time for Helga and myself to read, think, talk, and write. But you couldn't get a research grant for that. So we had to devise projects that required a research assistant, for example, surveying doctors' attitudes to voluntary euthanasia. The pressure to get grants thus distorted our research priorities. It also soaked up a lot of time, for writing the applications was a time-consuming process and there was no guarantee of success. Fortunately, by 1987 the Centre had done well enough for the university to allow me to become its full-time director. Now I had no formal undergraduate teaching duties, although I sometimes gave lectures in Philosophy Department courses. I continued to supervise graduate students, and was fortunate to have some exceptionally good ones. In addition to Helga, I supervised the Ph.D.s of Julian Savulescu and Udo Schuklenk, both of whom have gone on to have distinguished careers in bioethics.

Although I wasn't writing any books that contributed to the development of my core ideas, I did have a role in several other books: I edited *In Defense of Animals,* a collection of writings by philosophers and activists in the animal movement, and *Applied Ethics,* a selection of my favorite writings in that field. *A Companion to Ethics,* another edited volume, consists of specially commissioned essays covering the field of ethics. To make the book more readable, I persuaded the publisher to break from the standard "Companion" format of brief entries in alphabetical order. Instead, a detailed index makes it possible to use the book as a work of reference. *Embryo Experimentation* is the product of a major research project on the ethics, law, and science of experimenting on human embryos. Helga Kuhse and I directed the project, while Stephen Buckle, Karen Dawson, and Pascal Kasimba worked as researchers specializing in, respectively, philosophy, the biological sciences, and law. All five of us co-edited, and largely wrote, the book. *Ethical and Legal Issues in Guardianship Options for Intellectually Disadvantaged People,*is a booklength report into exactly what the title says. I wrote the section on ethics while Terry Carney, an academic at Monash's law school, wrote the more substantial legal sections.

During this period I was also involved in two books that were aimed at a wide popular audience. With Lori Gruen I wrote *Animal Liberation: A Graphic Guide.* The book was intended to be an illustrated introduction to the ideas of animal liberation, but we did not like the illustrator's heavy-handed style, and apparently the public didn't either, for the book flopped. *Save the Animals!* was an Australian version of a similar book done in the United States by Ingrid Newkirk, founder of People for the Ethical Treatment of Animals. It suggested 101 things people could do to help animals. Barbara Dover, a friend from the Australian animal advocacy organization Animal Liberation, worked with me on the Australian edition.

From 1987 until 1999, Helga and I had another responsibility. After the appearance of *In Defense of Animals,* René Olivieri, my editor at Blackwell, the book's publisher, asked me if I was interested in editing an academic journal about ethics and animals. The idea didn't appeal to me, partly because I thought that generating more academic articles was not the highest priority for the animal movement, and partly because I doubted that there would be enough good articles submitted to fill a high-quality academic journal. But for some years I had felt the lack of a journal in bioethics, that would apply the same rigorous selection standards as good philosophy journals. The existing journals, of which the *Hastings Center Report* was probably the best-known, published many articles that would never have got past the referees of academic journals like *Philosophy and Public Affairs* or *Ethics.* The other problem with most of the journals then was that they were American and largely ignored what happened anywhere else. So I offered to co-edit, with Helga, a journal of bioethics that would be both more rigorous, and more international in outlook, than any journal that was being published at the time. Olivieri agreed, and so we founded *Bioethics.* At first it wasn't easy to get articles of the quality we wanted, but gradually both the quantity and quality of submissions picked up. The journal is still thriving, under different editors. One measure of the journal's achievement is that other journals have lifted their standards, and become more internationally-minded.

The "Singer Affair" in Germany

In 1989 I was invited to speak at a symposium on "Bioengineering, Ethics, and Mental Disability," organized jointly by Lebenshilfe, the major German organization for parents of intellectually disabled infants, to be held in Marburg.[40]

I accepted the invitation; and since I was going to be in Germany anyway, I also accepted an invitation from Professor Christoph Anstötz,

---

[40] The passage that follows draws on my fuller discussion in "On Being Silenced in Germany," *New York Review of Books* 38:14 (August 15th, 1991).

professor of special education at the University of Dortmund, to give a lecture a few days later on the subject "Do severely disabled newborn infants have a right to life?" Just a day or two before I was due to leave for Germany, my invitation to speak at the Marburg conference was abruptly withdrawn. The reason given was that, by agreeing to lecture at the University of Dortmund, I had allowed opponents of my views to argue that Lebenshilfe was providing the means for me to promote my views on euthanasia in Germany. The letter withdrawing the invitation drew a distinction between my discussing these views "behind closed doors with critical scientists who want to convince you that your attitude infringes human rights" and my promoting my position "in public." A postscript added that several organizations of handicapped persons were planning protest demonstrations in Marburg and Dortmund against me, and against Lebenshilfe for having invited me—which may have been the real reason for the withdrawal of the invitation. The protesters were distributing leaflets and press releases quoting some sentences about euthanasia for disabled infants from *Practical Ethics* which had been published in German five years earlier. The protests soon found their way into the popular press, where it became known as the "Singer Affair".

Although I was no longer participating in the conference, the protesters continued their opposition to what they were now calling the "Euthanasia Congress." Shortly before the symposium was due to open, Lebenshilfe canceled the entire event. Soon after, the Faculty of Special Education at the University of Dortmund decided not to proceed with my scheduled lecture there. (Instead, I had an unpublicized meeting with some of Anstötz's students.)

Since I was already in Europe—I had been giving some lectures in Italy—Georg Meggle, professor of philosophy at the University of Saarbrücken, invited me to lecture at his university in order to show that it was possible to discuss the ethics of euthanasia rationally in Germany. When I rose to speak I was greeted by a chorus of whistles and shouts from a minority of the audience determined to prevent me from speaking. Professor Meggle offered the protesters the opportunity to state why they thought I should not speak. Their comments showed how completely they had misunderstood my position. Many believed that I was politically on the far right. They were taken aback when I told them that I was the child of Austrian-Jewish refugees, and that three of my grandparents had been murdered by the Nazis. Some seemed to think that I was opposed to all measures that would advance the position of the disabled in society, whereas it follows from my general utilitarian view that once a life has been allowed to develop, then we should do what we can, subject to the inevitable constraints on our resources, to make that life as satisfying and rich as possible. Someone else came to the platform and said that he agreed that it was not necessary to use intensive care medicine to prolong every life, but allowing an infant to die was different from taking active steps to end the infant's life. That led to further discussion, and so in the end we had a genuine debate.

For the next few years, these events continued to reverberate, in German-speaking countries. Philosophy courses in which *Practical Ethics* was assigned as a text were disrupted, and at least one course had to be abandoned midway through the semester. The fifteenth International Wittgenstein Conference, which had been planned for 1991 in Kirchberg, Austria, on the theme "Applied Ethics" led to protests against three of the invited speakers: Professor Georg Meggle, Professor R.M. Hare, and myself. After a dispute between the president of the Austrian Wittgenstein society, who wanted the invitations withdrawn, and the organizing committee, which declined to withdraw them, the conference was abandoned.

The protests went a stage further in May 1991, when I was invited by the Zoological Institute of the University of Zurich to give a lecture on "Animal Rights." When I rose to speak, a section of the audience—perhaps a quarter or a third—began to chant: "Singer *raus*! Singer *raus*!" As I heard this chanted, in German, by people so lacking in respect for the tradition of reasoned debate that they were unwilling even to allow me to be heard, I had an overwhelming feeling that this was what it must have been like to attempt to reason against the rising tide of Nazism in the declining days of the Weimar Republic. An overhead projector was still functioning, and I began to write on it, to point out this parallel that I was feeling so strongly. At that point one of the protesters came up behind me and tore my glasses from my face, throwing them on the floor and stamping on them so that they shattered. My host wisely decided to abandon the lecture.

As this indicates, these protests did not come exclusively from conservative or religious circles, or from those with disabilities. The more militant, if less numerous, elements of the protests were generally from the left. Feminist organizations were also prominent among the protesters, because of their opposition to "eugenics." Since the right to abortion is one of their basic beliefs, however, the issue of prenatal diagnosis caused them some difficulty. The position most of them took was that a woman should have the right to abort her fetus for any reason at all, *except* because the child will have a serious disability. (Not all feminists were opposed to my views. The magazine *Emma,* headed by Alice Schwarzer, was sympathetic to my work on animals, and perhaps for that reason had a better understanding of my views on other issues as well. Nor did it lack the courage to criticize those who tried to stop me speaking.)

As a philosopher with controversial views I was, of course, used to debate and to criticism, sometimes heated, of my views. But until 1989, no one had actually protested against my views or sought to deny me a platform from which to state them. I'm generally a calm person, but it was extremely frustrating to have people trying to stop me speaking when they clearly knew very little about what I was saying. Given my family background, the attempt to link me with Nazi ideas was especially offensive. But as a philosopher, I was more troubled by the fact that my opponents brushed aside the difficult questions that face anyone who really wants to maintain that all human life is of equal value. These questions are discussed later in this volume.

Naturally, these events sharpened my interest in the issue of freedom of speech. I re-read Mill's *On Liberty* with increased appreciation. The most common reason given for preventing me challenging the belief that all human life is of equal value was exactly that discussed by Mill when he writes, in *On Liberty,* of those who would deny the right to challenge a belief, not because they are certain the belief is true, but because the belief is "indispensable to well-being" and "none but bad men would desire to weaken these salutary beliefs." To this Mill's response seems to me devastating:

> This mode of thinking makes the justification of restraints on discussion not a question of the truth of doctrines, but of their usefulness; and flatters itself by that means to escape the responsibility of claiming to be an infallible judge of opinions. But those who thus satisfy themselves, do not perceive that the assumption of infallibility is merely shifted from one point to another. The usefulness of an opinion is itself a matter of opinion: as disputable, as open to discussion and requiring discussion as much, as the opinion itself.[41]

On only one point does my experience not entirely support what Mill writes. He asserts: "And it will not do to say that the heretic may be allowed to maintain the utility or harmlessness of his opinion, though forbidden to maintain its truth. The truth of an opinion is part of its utility." That is no doubt correct, if we are concerned with opinions about

---

[41] Mill, *On Liberty,* Chapter 2.

something that can be true or false. But, arguably, that is not the case with moral opinions. My German opponents seemed divided on this question. The conservative Christians thought that I was denying a moral truth about the sanctity of all human life. To this group Mill's point would apply. Others, however, were from the left, and regarded morality and politics as simply a power struggle. They saw themselves as on the side of the oppressed, whereas my views were part of a capitalist-fascist attempt to eliminate all who are not productive workers. It was precisely because they saw ethics as relative to economic interests that they rejected the idea of debate and discussion as a way of reaching truth. This position is immune to refutation by Mill's arguments, but it undercuts itself, because those who take it must also acknowledge that they cannot claim truth for their own views. If reason plays no role in ethics, there is nothing left but a power struggle.

One happy outcome of these distressing events is that they revealed how, in a society with a reasonably free press, attempts to suppress ideas only ensure that the ideas gain a wider audience. Germany's leading liberal weekly newspaper, *Die Zeit*, published two articles that gave a fair account of the arguments for euthanasia, and also discussed the taboo that had prevented open discussion of the topic in Germany. For this courageous piece of journalism, *Die Zeit* also became the target of protests. From this point the euthanasia debate was picked up by both German and Austrian television. The outcome was that instead of a few hundred people hearing my views at lectures in Marburg and Dortmund, several million read about them or listened to them on television. In German academic circles, both philosophical and those around special education, there was soon a growing discussion of applied ethics in general, and euthanasia in particular. The protests dramatically increased the previously modest sales of the German edition of *Practical Ethics*—it sold more copies in the year after June 1989 than it had in all the five years it had previously been available in Germany.

The publicity also led to a German translation of *Should the Baby Live?* although there was a twist to that story. An editor at Rowohlt, one of Germany's biggest publishers, expressed interest in publishing a German edition. A contract was signed, the text was translated into German, and Rowohlt announced its forthcoming publication. Then the protests began, including a threat to bomb Rowohlt's offices. Rowohlt took fright, and abandoned publication. Fortunately the book was picked up by a tiny but more courageous publisher, Harald Fischer, and eventually appeared in German in 1993. But it was not until 2004 that I was again able to give, without disruption, a publicly advertised talk in Germany.

The International Association of Bioethics

In the early 1990s the "Singer Affair" seemed to be part of a larger hostility, in German-speaking countries, to bioethics as a field, and perhaps even to the broader field of applied ethics. In the state of Baden-Württemberg, Social Democrats urged that the government formally declare the thought of "Anglo-Saxon institutes such as the Kennedy Institute of Ethics, the Hastings Center, or the Center for Human Bioethics" to be "incompatible with the norms of the Constitution." Several German scholars found themselves under pressure, and stopped teaching bioethics. Yet during this period German academics in general, and philosophers in particular, remained largely silent. The exceptions were mostly from the minority of German philosophers who worked in the analytic tradition.[42]

As a result of these events, Helga Kuhse and I wrote an editorial in *Bioethics* in which we suggested the creation of an international association of bioethics, both as a professional association and, when the occasion required, to provide some international pressure in defense of those who seek to teach or discuss issues in bioethics, when they come under attack, whether from protests like those I had experienced in Germany, or from governments controlled by religious fundamentalists, like that in Iran.[43] The editorial led to many positive responses, including one from Dan Wikler, a philosopher and bioethicist then working at the University of Madison, Wisconsin. Dan had been thinking of a similar idea, and his contacts were particularly valuable in gaining broader support.

We also had support for the idea from bioethicists in the Netherlands, and as a result received a generous offer from the Health Council of the Netherlands to host the First World Congress of the International Association of Bioethics. The Congress took place in Amsterdam in October 1992. The meeting accepted, with relatively minor amendments, the statement of aims and the constitution I had drafted. I was elected to the Board of Directors, and the Board subsequently elected me President, a position that the constitution specified could be held for only one two-year term. As a member of the Board, I served three terms, the maximum the constitution permitted. By the end of that time, it was clear that the International Association of Bioethics would survive. It has continued to host international congresses every two years, and has

---

[42] See Eric Brown, "The Dilemmas of German Bioethics," *The New Atlantis* (Spring 2004).
[43] Editorial, *Bioethics* (January 1990).

been of some value in linking up bioethicists around the world, especially those outside North America and Europe. Although there have been one or two occasions on which it has opposed restrictions on bioethics and bioethicists, its value in this regard has, fortunately, not been seriously tested.

In 1992, I felt that it was time for the Centre for Human Bioethics to have a fresh director, so Helga took over that role, and I stepped down to the position of deputy director.

The Great Ape Project

Paola Cavalieri, an Italian animal activist, edited an occasional magazine called *Etica e Animali* (*Ethics and Animals*) and had organized several talks in Italy for me. In 1991 she asked me if I would be willing to write an essay for a special issue of *Etica e Animali* urging that, in view of the demonstrated intelligence, self-awareness, and rich emotional lives of chimpanzees, they should be given the same basic rights that we grant to all human beings. As Paola and I discussed the idea, we became excited at the possibilities it offered. Since chimpanzees had demonstrated self-awareness, rationality, strong emotional attachments, and even the ability to communicate by means of abstract symbols, they were clearly at a cognitive level comparable to, and in some respects surpassing, that of a two-year old child. Nothing except blatant speciesism could ground a denial of basic rights to such beings. Yet thousands of chimpanzees were being used essentially as research tools for human benefit, confined in laboratories in barren cages, and experimented on in painful and often lethal ways that no one would defend if they were done to human beings. Many other chimpanzees were in zoos and circuses, again often in appalling conditions, while we knew that chimpanzees in their natural habitat in Africa were threatened by logging and forest clearance.

Concerned as we were to help chimpanzees, part of our excitement about what we were planning came from our expectation that the benefits of gaining rights for chimpanzees would extend to other animals. Our thinking about animals is distorted by the fact that we use the single term, "animal" for such a diverse range of beings—and we use it to separate them from ourselves. Yet chimpanzees are much closer to us than they are to most other animals. Genetically they are even closer to us than they are to gorillas. Moreover because they have faces in which we can read emotions, we empathize with them more than we do with many other animals. Hence Paola and I saw chimpanzees as a way of bridging the gap between "us" and "them." If chimpanzees were to be granted basic rights, could gorillas and orangutans be far behind? And then other animals might follow.

We discussed who else might contribute to the issue. Jane Goodall was an obvious choice, and there were other scientists who had studied chimpanzees, either in their natural habitat or in captivity and seemed to have great empathy with their subjects. We also wanted philosophers, lawyers, and social scientists. But would they write for a small Italian journal? At some point in the discussion, I suggested that the idea was too big for *Etica e Animali*: instead, we should turn it into a book and edit it together. Paola agreed and we began to write to people who might contribute to what we were then calling "The Chimpanzee Project." One of the first to get a letter of invitation from us was the evolutionary biologist Richard Dawkins. He responded enthusiastically, adding the suggestion that since gorillas are also self-aware, can use symbolic language, and have rich emotional lives, we should include them, perhaps calling it "The African Ape Project." We liked the idea, but wondered, then, on what basis we could exclude orangutans. Although more distant from us genetically, they too have cognitive abilities similar to chimpanzees. In the end, we decided to include them, and so we had "The Great Ape Project," a name that had the advantage of abbreviating to GAP, which was a reference to the separation between humans and animals that we were trying to bridge.[44]

The Great Ape Project: Equality beyond Humanity was published in 1993. The contributors included Jane Goodall, Douglas Adams, author of *A Hitchhiker's Guide to the Galaxy,* Jared Diamond, Richard Dawkins, and Marc Bekoff. Most of the philosophers well-known for their work on animals and ethics sent us an essay, including Stephen Clark, Bernard Rollins, Stephen Sapontzis, Tom Regan, James Rachels, Ingmar Persson, Dale Jamieson, and Colin McGinn. We had researchers who had taught great apes to use sign language: Roger and Deborah Fouts, who had worked with chimpanzees, Francine Patterson, with gorillas, and Lynn White Miles, with an orangutan. Gary Francione wrote on the legal situation of great apes. Christoph Anstötz, the professor of special education who had been attacked by many of his colleagues for inviting me to speak at the University of Dortmund, wrote a courageous essay comparing profoundly intellectually disabled humans with the great apes.

---

[44] We did not consider bonobos separately, because at this time they were usually known as "pygmy chimpanzees" and considered a subspecies of chimpanzees.

All of the contributors signed a "Declaration on Great Apes" that began with a demand for "the extension of the community of equals" to the great apes. The phrase was Paola's, and we explained it as referring to "the moral community within which we accept certain basic moral principles or rights as enforceable at law and governing our relationships with each other." These rights were specified as including, but not necessarily limited to, a right to life, to liberty, and to prohibition from torture.

The Great Ape Project had little trouble in gaining publicity, but building an international organization proved difficult. Without significant funds, beyond the royalties from the book, it was difficult to employ someone to run an office, and relying on volunteers was not satisfactory. Nevertheless, the Great Ape Project has had some impact. In 1999, as a result of the efforts of the New Zealand branch, legislation was passed in that country recognizing the special status of great apes, and prohibiting experiments on them except for their own benefit either as individuals or as a species. In Britain, the government said it would no longer license experiments on great apes, and gradually other European countries also changed their policies, and the use of great apes for medical research in Europe ceased. In the United States, although medical research using chimpanzees continues, government agencies funding it now require that healthy chimpanzees may not be killed at the end of an experiment, but must be sent to a sanctuary. Unfortunately Congress has not provided sufficient funds for sanctuaries, and so some chimpanzees still languish in their miserable barren cages after they have been "retired" from research.

The Spanish branch of the Great Ape Project has been among the most active, and it was no doubt for that reason that the biggest breakthrough to date occurred in Spain in 2008, when a parliamentary commission declared its support for the Great Ape Project and called on the government to adopt, within a year, legislation to prohibit potentially harmful experiments on great apes that are not in their interests. Additionally, it recommended that Spain take steps in international forums and organizations to ensure that great apes are protected from maltreatment, slavery, torture, being killed, and being made extinct. The use of the term "slavery" in respect of something that it is wrong to do to animals is especially significant, for until now it has been assumed that animals are *rightly* our slaves, to use as we wish, whether to pull our carts, be models of human diseases for research, or produce eggs, milk or flesh for us to eat. Recognition by a government that it can be wrong to enslave animals is a significant breach in the wall of exclusive moral significance we have built around our own species. At the time of writing (January 2009) the Spanish government has indicated that it will comply with the commission's request, and legislation is being drawn up under which keeping great apes in captivity will be allowed only for purposes of conservation, and then only under optimal conditions for the apes.

Writing for a Wider Audience

My next book was the direct result of an approach by Diana Gribble, a publisher who had, with Hilary McPhee, set up Australia's first successful feminist press, and was now involved in a new publishing venture, Text. She had read *Practical Ethics* and thought that the last chapter—on why we should act morally—raised a question that every reflective person thought about, and so could be the basis for a widely-read book. I found the idea intriguing. By this time I had done quite a lot of writing for popular newspapers and magazines. It is important that philosophy, and especially ethics, should reach out beyond the academy and show the public as a whole that it has something significant to say. Yet since *Animal Liberation*, none of my books had reached a broad audience. The topic Gribble suggested was one that had interested me ever since I wrote my Master's thesis on it, but I still wasn't really happy with the conclusion I had reached there, or in *Practical Ethics*. Perhaps it was time to revisit the question.

Gribble's invitation came at the end of the 1980s, the "decade of greed" in which the investor Ivan Boesky had famously proclaimed that "Greed is good." Boesky's subsequent conviction and imprisonment for insider trading—based on actions he had taken after he already had legitimately acquired a fortune of over $100 million—suggested an absurdly narrow understanding of self-interest, one that would benefit from some of the wisdom of ancient philosophers. Because I had, on recent visits to Japan to give talks, been intrigued by the cultural differences between Japan and the west, I included a chapter on Japanese attitudes to self-interest. Writing for the general public, I felt freer to speculate on issues like the psychology of happiness and fulfillment that fall outside my academic expertise. I made the best argument I could for the view that committing ourselves to an ethical life is the best way to further our own enlightened self-interest, because we are likely to find it a more worthwhile and fulfilling life than other options.

How Are We to Live? was a popular success in Australia, and did well in several other countries too. Roger Crisp, an Oxford philosopher, gave it the best compliment any author could receive when he wrote, in his review in *Ethics*: "Imagine that you could choose a book that everyone in the world would read. My choice would be this book." After that, I may seem churlish if I say that I am not really satisfied with the book. But I worry that my defense of a link between living an ethical life and living a fulfilling one contains an element of wishful thinking. The objection that concerns me most is that, since I myself don't do everything that I think I ought to do, it seems that even the author was not entirely convinced of the book's argument. In addition, I may not have given sufficient weight to variations in individual temperaments. Since an ethical life is, at least as I conceive it, a demanding one, it can be burdensome rather than fulfilling. Similarly, some people may enjoy a life dedicated to amassing wealth, since there are always new ladders to climb. Or perhaps there is some middle position, a moderately ethical life that includes "time off" from the demands of ethics, and is likely to be both enjoyable and fulfilling for many people.

Although Gribble commissioned *How Are We to Live?* and discussed the broad outlines with me, once I started writing it, I worked more closely with a young editor named Michael Heyward, who later became head of Text's book publishing arm. He was keen for me to do another book, similarly aimed at an intelligent general readership. Since my experiences in Germany, I had continued to think about issues relating to life and death, including the concept of "brain death," the new definition of death that had begun to spread in the 1970s, and was now almost universally accepted. One might think that those who defended the doctrine of the sanctity of human life would be shocked at the idea of surgeons cutting the organs out of patients whose hearts were still beating and giving them to strangers. Instead, the simple device of redefining these patients as dead, on the basis that their brains had irreversibly ceased to function, was supposed to make this procedure compatible with respect for the sanctity of human life. It was, as an examination of the history of the change showed, a matter of the advantages of the new definition clearly outweighing the disadvantages. Yet the change in the definition of death seemed to me to be unstable—once we accept brain death, why should we not also accept the death of the cortex, that is, the part of the brain required for consciousness, as the death of the person?

To the discussion of this issue, I added an updated account of my views on abortion, life and death decisions for disabled infants, the claims of animals like great apes to a right to life, and an account of recent developments in the Netherlands, where voluntary euthanasia was being openly practiced. The core of the book is the argument that although we continue to pay lip service to the traditional ethic of the sanctity of life, and disguise our departures from it in various ways, when we look at all of these things together, we can see we have effectively abandoned it—and for good reason.

I wrote *Rethinking Life and Death* in about four months, during a period of study leave that, in contrast to previous ones, I took mostly at home. I worked long days, sustained by the excitement of knowing that I had something important to say—a feeling that I had not had so intensely since writing *Animal Liberation.* The book was very successful, winning the National Book Council of Australia's Banjo Award for the best nonfiction book published in 1995. It remains one of the four books—along with *Animal Liberation, Practical Ethics,* and my most recent work, *The Life You Can Save*—that I think best expresses my views on issues in applied ethics.

A Foray into Politics

After my return to Australia in 1974, Renata and I joined the Australian Labor Party, but as it moved more to the center, I gradually became disenchanted with its policies until, during the Labor government led by Bob Hawke, I resigned my membership. I had watched the growth of green parties in Europe with interest, and supported the campaign led by Tasmanian parliamentarian Bob Brown to stop the building of a dam on the Franklin River in Tasmania's southwest wilderness. In 1992 Brown began working with green groups throughout the country to create a political party, to be known as the Australian Greens. I attended a meeting to set up a Victorian branch, and became one of its foundation members. I hadn't intended to be particularly active, but in 1994, my local federal parliamentary representative resigned, causing a by-election. I was living in a safe Liberal Party seat (the Liberal Party is the conservative party in Australian politics), so safe that the Australian Labor Party, the other major political party, announced that it would not field a candidate. The Greens decided that this was a chance to raise their profile. Since I lived in the electorate, and was probably their best-known member, they asked me to be their candidate. Why not? I thought. There seemed nothing to lose, and new experiences to be gained. After a short campaign, I received a surprising twenty-eight percent of the vote, the highest ever received by a Green candidate in an Australian federal election. That led to the Greens selecting me as their lead Victorian candidate for the Australian Senate in the next election, due in 1996. This was still mainly a profile-raising exercise, but because the Australian Senate is elected by proportional representation, it was not completely out of the question that I could be elected. Had that happened, I would have served at least one six-year term.

As part of my contribution to raising the profile of the Greens, Bob Brown and I wrote a short book introducing the Australian Greens and their policies. Text Publishing gave us an advance that helped the party's campaign funds. Unfortunately the Prime Minister called the election earlier than anyone had expected, and as a result Text had only six weeks to sell the book before the election. The campaign was far more demanding, and nastier, than the one I had fought in my local electorate. The university granted me six weeks leave without pay for the period, and I worked full-time to make the Greens' policies better known. In sharp contrast to the earlier by-election, this contest was dominated by the two major parties, and getting any media coverage at all for the Greens was always a struggle, while getting fair coverage of our policies was nearly impossible. The behavior of Cheryl Kernot, the leader of the other minor party, the Australian Democrats, gave me a taste of political realities. Her rhetoric was about breaking the "two party duopoly" of Australian politics, but her actions showed that her real concern was to keep out the Greens, who she saw as her party's real rival.

I received three percent of the vote, not nearly enough to get elected. Though I had never really expected any other outcome, I went back to academic life with mixed feelings. I was turning fifty, and had been writing on issues in bioethics for nearly twenty years. Were there other things to do before I got too old?

Two Biographies

My mother and her sister, my aunt Doris, had often told me how their father, David Oppenheim, had been a member of Freud's "Wednesday Circle," a small group that, in early twentieth-century Vienna, met with Freud in his apartment to explore the new field of psychoanalysis. My grandfather had even co-authored a paper with Freud, on "Dreams in Folklore." He had also written a book and many other papers, mostly after he left Freud's group to work with Alfred Adler. My mother and my aunt had many letters, some written by my grandfather to my grandmother early in the twentieth century, before they were married, and some written by my grandparents after the Nazi takeover of Austria, from 1938 to 1941, when they were still in Vienna and my parents had gone to Australia. I had long wanted to know more about my grandfather's ideas, and to understand why my grandparents had not joined my parents in Australia when they still had a chance to do so. Of all my grandfather's work only the article co-authored with Freud had been translated into English. I read German more slowly than English, and the handwritten material was more difficult still. I thought that I might like to write something about my grandfather, but I didn't know whether the material would be of much interest beyond the extended family. Since this would take some time, and was far from bioethics, I negotiated with Monash University to go part-time so that I would have the time to do it.

Before I got properly started on reading my grandfather's work, however, I received a distressing phone call from Henry Spira in New York. Over the years since he had attended my adult education course on "Animal Liberation," we had become close friends. He phoned me regularly to discuss tactics for his remarkably successful campaigns, and I stayed in his Upper West Side apartment whenever I visited New York. He had even come out to Australia once, and stayed with us. I had told him that one day I wanted to write a book about him and his campaign strategies, so that other activists, whether campaigning for animals or for other causes, could learn how one person, without a lot of money or a big organization, could make a difference. Now he called to tell me that if I wanted to write that book, I had better do it soon, because he had terminal cancer. I dropped everything else and was in New York six days later.

Henry lived longer than his doctors predicted, and I had time to visit him more than once, to interview those who knew him well, and to go through the files he kept on all his campaigns. As well as writing the book, I brought in a film-maker, John Swindells, and we co-produced a video called *Henry: One Man's Way,* which was shown on Australian television.[45] Getting the book published proved more difficult—publishers were not interested in a biography of someone whose name was not a household word, and my proposal was rejected by at least twenty publishers. I persisted largely because I believed the book really would help future activists, and also because I knew the book, with its promise that his strategic ideas would not be lost, meant a lot to Henry. (Today I might have achieved the same objectives just by posting it on a website, but the web was not yet widely used for such purposes.) At last I received a positive response from Rowman and Littlefield, and Henry lived long enough to see *Ethics into Action: Henry Spira and the*

---

[45] *Henry: One Man's Way,* available from Animal Rights International, www.ari-online.org

Animal Rights Movement, in print. His death was a great personal loss to me, and a loss to the animal movement, but he lives on through the video and the book. *Ethics into Action* has not been a big seller, but many activists have told me how useful they have found it. That's what Henry would have wanted.

When the book on Henry was done, I returned to working on my grandfather's papers. I had found, in my aunt's flat, over a hundred very personal letters that my grandfather had written to my grandmother before they were married. These letters made it possible for me to know what my grandfather was like when he was in his twenties, and once I had read them, I knew that I had to write a book about him. The material relating to his work with Freud was also fascinating, although it was hard for me to take the paper he had co-authored with Freud seriously—parts of it read like a parody of Freudian psychoanalysis applied to folk tales. The book and papers my grandfather wrote when he was a member of Adler's group were also, on the whole, a little disappointing, in that they rather mechanically applied Adler's famous "inferiority complex" to different works of literature. On the other hand the correspondence between my grandparents and my parents from 1938 to 1941 was another rich source of information, though about a truly tragic story.

By 1999 I had a draft of a book on my grandfather running to more than 160,000 words. I hadn't been quite sure how to write it, because I was aware of the problem I had had with the book on Henry—would anyone publish a biography of a man no-one had heard of? But meanwhile, an important change was taking place in my life, and ultimately it made a difference to the publication of this book as well.

An Offer from Princeton

In 1997 I received a letter from George Kateb, acting director of the Center for Human Values at Princeton University, asking if I would be willing to be considered for a new chair in bioethics that had been created in the Center. The term "bioethics" was being interpreted broadly, to include issues relating to animals and the environment. I had had other offers from other American universities before, but this was an attractive and well-timed invitation. Our daughters had finished school and left home. Renata's parents, and my father, had died. My mother was, sadly, suffering from dementia and no longer knew who I was. Joan and I had arranged care for her, and Joan was, when I raised the possibility of our going away, willing to continue to do this on her own. I was feeling stale at Monash, and government-imposed cuts on Australian university budgets made them less enjoyable places to work than they had been previously. For several years, Renata had been Oxfam Australia's Publications Officer, and although she enjoyed the work, she too was ready for a change. She was not willing to leave Melbourne to live in a small college town, but Princeton has the great advantage of being close to New York. It is also an outstanding university, and promised stimulating colleagues, excellent students, and a light teaching load. Renata and I talked it over and agreed that I should say that I was willing to be considered.

I was, in any case, due to visit Princeton the following year, since I had been invited to respond to one of J.M. Coetzee's Tanner Lectures—the lectures later reprinted, with the commentators' responses, as *The Lives of Animals,* and also as part of the novel *Elizabeth Costello.* As the visit grew closer, Kateb wrote that I was at the top of the selection committee's list, and it would be good to talk when I visited Princeton. Renata therefore came with me, and attended the Tanner lectures and the various events associated with them. They were an intellectual treat, with lively discussions continuing over several meals. I liked my potential future colleagues, especially Kateb and Amy Gutmann, the founding director of the Center for Human Values. Although the position was in the Center, the appointee would be an associate of the department of his or her discipline. In the Princeton philosophy department, I already knew David Lewis, since he was a frequent visitor to Melbourne, and I had met Gil Harman before. Now I met several others. It was an outstanding department, generally ranked first in the country, but it was not strong in ethics, and had no one doing applied ethics. Though no one ever said it explicitly, I also came to understand that some of those involved with the appointment felt that Princeton was a little stuffy and conservative, and would be enlivened by the appointment of someone with views outside the usual consensus.

Several months later, after all the due procedures had been followed, I was offered the position. I told the Center for Human Values that I would join them in July 1999.

From Monash to Princeton

As my time at Monash drew to a close, the issue in bioethics about which I was thinking hardest was the difficult topic of allocating scarce resources in health care. If it costs $500,000 to save the life of an extremely premature infant, and that sum could pay for hip replacement operations in one hundred elderly patients immobilized by an arthritic hip, which is the better use of the money? This question was becoming increasingly important, because although the Australian health care system provided free health care for all, rising costs meant that it could not afford to pay for every possibly beneficial medical treatment that a doctor might recommend. (Nor, indeed, can any other health care system, although in the United States, the myth that major health insurance schemes do pay for every medically beneficial treatment still prevails.) Together with Helga Kuhse and Jeff Richardson, Director of the Centre for Health Economics at Monash, and with the research assistance of John McKie, at the Centre for Human Bioethics, I published some papers on this topic investigating and defending what is known as the QALY approach to evaluating the benefits of health care procedures. The term stands for "quality-adjusted life-year," a method that takes account of the number of years by which the procedure extends life, or improves the quality of life. It is broadly consistent with utilitarianism, except that it measures only the benefits conferred by health care, rather than wider benefits or losses, such as the impact of losing a parent on a family with young children. The QALY approach has been heavily criticized, and we tried to sort out which criticisms were justified and which were not. We co-authored a book entitled *The Allocation of Health Care Resources: An Ethical Evaluation of the "QALY" Approach*, but we couldn't claim to have solved the difficult problems we were tackling.

My short book *A Darwinian Left* attracted more attention. It is an extended version of a lecture I gave at the London School of Economics, for a program there called Darwin@LSE that aimed to show the relevance of an evolutionary approach to the understanding of human nature and, consequently, to social issues. Since LSE had been founded by the Fabian socialists Beatrice and Sidney Webb, and had a proud tradition of leftist thinking, promoting Darwinian thinking there was a novel idea. I used the lecture to argue that the left had made a mistake in thinking that an evolutionary approach to human nature is part of a right-wing ideology that is hostile to its vision of a good society. The left has to be open to the evidence, and it is now clear that Marx and his followers were wrong to believe that if we change the economic basis of society, we will transform human nature as well. Human nature has been formed by the way in which we have evolved, and anyone interested in changing society must draw on that understanding of human nature in order to plan the reforms that will work best. *A Darwinian Left* contributed to an ongoing debate about the extent to which the left is committed to holding that human nature is malleable rather than shaped by our biological inheritance.

I had an inkling that my appointment at Princeton was not going to pass unnoticed when someone forwarded me a message that Margaret Tighe, a leader of the Australian anti-abortion movement, had sent to anti-abortion groups in the U.S. Tighe told her U.S. friends about my views, and suggested that they might like to give me "a warm welcome." They did. Even before I arrived, anti-abortion groups and an organization of people with disabilities called Not Dead Yet demonstrated at the university, calling for my appointment to be rescinded. Steve Forbes, a Princeton trustee and a candidate for the 2000 Republican presidential nomination, vowed that as long as I was at Princeton, he would not donate to the university. *The New York Times* put the story on the front page, calling it the biggest commotion over an academic appointment since Bertrand Russell's appointment to the City University of New York in 1940.[46] (Russell's offense was his support for "free love," that is, sex between people who are not married.) On my first day of classes, hundreds of protesters, some of whom had come from as far away as Chicago, descended on Nassau Hall, the center of the university's administration. Several members of Not Dead Yet chained their wheelchairs to the doors of the building, blocking the entrances for two hours before they were removed by police. (My own class was undisturbed, thanks to a security cordon around the building in which it was held.) The protest made good television, and was widely covered.

Harold Shapiro, the university's president, was unflinching in his support for my appointment and for the general principle of academic freedom. The protests never had any support from students or faculty at Princeton University, and the university's Board of Trustees firmly repudiated Steve Forbes's position as a violation of academic freedom. The worst aspect of the publicity was that both Shapiro and I received death threats. Since American "pro-life" activists have murdered doctors who carried out abortions, the threats had to be taken seriously.

On the positive side, as in Germany, the protests drew attention to my views. I was deluged with media requests for interviews, and did as many as I had time for. Some were very hostile, but most gave me a chance to explain my position. When I was asked to write an article for *The New York Times Sunday Magazine*, I used the opportunity to restate the argument I had first made in "Famine, Affluence, and Morality"

---

[46] Sylvia Nasar, "Princeton's New Philosopher Draws a Stir," *New York Times* (April 10th, 1999).

about the obligation of the wealthy to contribute to organizations helping the world's poorest people.[47]

The article included telephone numbers readers could call to donate
to UNICEF or Oxfam America. It received a huge response, with the
Times getting some 800 letters about it. More significantly, UNICEF
and Oxfam later told me that they had received, in the month following
the article, a total of about $600,000 more than they usually took in
through the phone numbers I had given. Some of those donors have continued to give substantial amounts in subsequent years, so the total that
can be attributed to the article must be in the millions. That began a
fruitful collaboration with Oxfam America in which Renata, who
became the organizer of Oxfam's New York supporters' group, has also
been involved.

Another positive outcome of the protests was my next book. Dan
Halpern, who heads the publishing imprint Ecco, a division of
HarperCollins, had discussed the controversy with friends on several
occasions, and found that while they all had strong opinions about my
appointment, these views were based on second-hand summaries or out-
of-context quotes. Halpern therefore invited me to compile a collection
of my writings that would present, in a single volume, my most important ideas, with sufficient context to enable readers to understand why I
reached the conclusions that many of them found shocking. *Writings on
an Ethical Life* fits with my general aim of reaching beyond professional
circles in order to encourage a public debate on important ethical questions. I want to change people's views, and their actions, on issues like
the obligations of the rich to the poor, or what we eat, but I also expect
that learning to think rigorously and critically will bring more general
benefits.

Too many of my colleagues write only for other philosophers. That's
understandable, because it is the opinions of other philosophers that will
determine whether they get jobs, or tenure, or promotion. But it's also
regrettable, because it means that most intelligent, educated people who
pick up a philosophy book or journal will get little from it. Often, even
if they understand the words on the page, they will not understand what
the issue being discussed is, or why it matters. The book or article will
be responding to what other philosophers have said, and they in turn will
be responding to others. Somewhere, if you can get beyond these layers
of argument and counter-argument, there will be a major philosophical

---

[47] "The Singer Solution to World Poverty," *New York Times Sunday Magazine*
(September 5th, 1999), pp. 60–63.

issue, perhaps whether ethical judgments can be said to be true or false, or what it is for us to be responsible for our choices. But because professional philosophers write for their colleagues, they often fail to keep the big issues in the foreground. Their readers will know, they assume, why what they are writing is relevant to those issues. That makes their writing unintelligible to anyone unfamiliar with the philosophical literature it presupposes.

Not everyone reads books, so writing for newspapers and appearing on radio and television programs is essential for reaching a wider audience. Time permitting, I accept most opportunities to discuss my views in the media, as long as I believe they will be fairly presented. For the same reason, in 2005 I agreed to write a monthly column on "The Ethics of Life" for Project Syndicate, a non-profit organization that seeks to bring a range of opinion to quality newspapers around the world. The column goes to more than three hundred newspapers in 132 countries, although not all of them choose to print it each month. It is also available on Project Syndicate's website in English, Spanish, Russian, French, German, Czech, Chinese, and Arabic.[48]

Teaching is another way in which the virtues of philosophical thinking are spread beyond academia. Coming to Princeton meant a return to undergraduate teaching, which I had not done at Monash since 1987. Teaching undergraduates at Princeton is rewarding because the university offers an exemplary liberal arts education. Many of the students are bright, hard-working, and keen to make the most of their time at one of the world's great universities. Whether they plan to study medicine or law, to go into investment banking or work for a nonprofit organization, they realize that they have four years in which to learn and to be challenged to think differently. That seems to lead many of them to enroll in my course in Practical Ethics. It's pleasing, too, that students from conservative and religious backgrounds take the course, and are willing to hear the arguments I put forward to defend positions that they find, at least initially, abhorrent. By the end of the course, a few of these students have changed their minds; all gain, at least, a better understanding of why others take a view that is different to their own.

Teaching should not be advocacy, but I do not claim that my teaching is morally neutral. That would imply that careful reasoning and critical scrutiny of arguments do nothing to show that one ethical stance is more defensible than another. That is contrary to what I

---

[48] See http://www.project-syndicate.org/series/31/description.

believe, and would raise a question about whether practical ethics is worth teaching at all. I do, however, require my students to read arguments for views that are contrary to mine—I do not set my own books as the required texts—and I do my best to present positions opposed to my own as fully and fairly as possible. Students often come into my class with their own ethical views about, say, abortion, but also believing that when people differ on such a topic, all they can do is agree to respect each other's opinion. I show them that you can demand reasons for the ethical positions people take, and then examine those reasons. If you do that, some views will turn out to be defensible and others will not. That helps us get clear about the basis for our own values and can even lead us to change our opinions on issues that we would never have thought we would change our minds about. In other cases, like our obligations to contribute to reducing world poverty, my classes may challenge people to live up to values that they already accept. I find it quite moving to see how a philosophical discussion can lead someone to change their diet, or—as happened in the case of two students in one of my classes a few years ago—to set up a student organization promoting the work of UNICEF, the United Nations Children's Fund.

Ethics and Globalization

Not long after coming to Princeton I was invited to give the Terry Lectures at Yale, a series of four lectures, the text of which was to be to submitted to Yale University Press for publication as a book. As my theme I took the impact of globalization on our ethical obligations. It was a new topic for me, though it drew in part upon my long-standing interest in the obligation of the rich to assist the poor. My choice of topic was a direct result both of events at the time, and of what I was hearing at Princeton and elsewhere.

In December 1999 the World Trade Organization attempted to hold its regular ministerial meeting in Seattle. Animal welfare and environmental groups protested against WTO decisions that struck down national laws protecting animals and the environment—for example, the WTO struck down, as an illegal restraint of trade, U.S. prohibitions on the sale of shrimp from nations that did not require their fishing fleets to be fitted with devices that prevented them killing sea turtles. Other protesters saw the WTO as a means of advancing the domination of the U.S., the European Union, Canada and Japan over the global economy, and objected to the widening gap between rich and poor nations. The American labor movement was in Seattle too, to protest against the export of jobs to countries with sweatshop conditions in which workers had no right to form a union.

Many commentators dismissed the protesters as Luddites. This response was everywhere: in newspaper articles, in comments from colleagues at Princeton, and at a meeting of the World Economic Forum that I attended in Davos, a month after the Seattle protests. Isn't it obvious, they were saying, that free trade is good for everyone, especially the poor? And that the WTO is not hostile to environmental protection, just pro-free trade? Conversely, the anti-globalization movement didn't seem to be interested in providing a forum for a debate either. At an anti-globalization forum I attended in New York, every speaker was opposed to globalization, and no time was permitted for questions or discussion—although some of the perspectives taken at least seemed to be at odds with each other, such as the suggestions that U.S. jobs were being exported to poor countries, and that globalization was designed to benefit only the rich nations. At least in the first months after Seattle, it seemed that the protests would lead only to the two sides talking past each other. This was a situation in which not only different views of the facts, but also different values were clashing. I thought it would be worth looking more carefully at the arguments, and trying to sort out both the facts and the value issues at stake.

There were other issues that I wanted to bring under the umbrella of globalization. One of the benefits of being at Princeton is that there is a stream of academics, policy analysts, and government officials giving seminars on current problems of the day. I had been surprised at how dismissive most of them were of international institutions, such as the United Nations and the (then only projected) International Criminal Court. The case for strengthening, rather than undermining, global institutions needed to be made. Speakers addressing climate change were even worse. They spoke about economic aspects of the U.S. signing the Kyoto Protocol, and whether we could expect any political leader to advocate doing so, but they never seemed to realize that climate change is—as Dale Jamieson had been arguing for more than a decade—fundamentally an ethical issue, and one on which the U.S. and Australia were both clearly behaving very badly indeed. I wanted to remind my audience at Yale that sharing the atmosphere is very much like dividing up a cake, and some basic principles of justice apply. I brought the number of topics up to four by including a lecture that commented on some relevant new writing on our obligations to aid the poor.

I gave the lectures in November 2000, and wrote up the book version the following year. I was still polishing my manuscript when the events of September 11th 2001 showed a darker side of globalization: no country, no matter how strong, is immune to having its cities attacked. *One World: Ethics and Globalization* was published by Yale University Press in 2002. The reviews suggested that I had succeeded in crossing the usual party lines, for the book was appreciated not only by those who usually like my work, but also by several who don't. Gregg Easterbrook, for example, wrote in the *Washington Monthly* that although the author of the book is "that Peter Singer" who is "generally a hero to the loony left" this book "struggles with the issues of globalization in a rigorously hard-headed manner rarely seen on this topic."[49]

Pushing Time Away

I came to Princeton with a draft of the book about my grandfather, unsure if anyone would want to publish it. I spoke about it to Sylvia Nasar, the journalist who had written the *New York Times* story on my appointment, and was also the author of *A Beautiful Mind,* the best-selling biography of the Princeton mathematician John Nash. She suggested I try her literary agent, Kathy Robbins. Kathy read the draft and agreed to try to find a publisher for it, but only after I cut it substantially. The problem was that whenever I discovered something about my grandfather, I wanted to put it in, since otherwise the information would be lost—no one else was likely to read these sources again. Reluctantly I pruned my 160,000 word draft back to 100,000 words and Kathy submitted it to Dan Halpern at Ecco, who agreed to publish it. There was still a lot of back and forth between me, Julia Serebrinsky, my editor at Ecco, and Kathy about how best to shape the book. Should the book be a straightforward biography, or should my own story, and my desire to get to know my grandfather, figure in the book? Ecco thought I should remain a prominent character, but wanted still more cuts.

As a title, I had wanted to use a pseudonym that my grandfather took when writing for a collection of articles published by Freud's circle: *unus multorum,* "one of the multitude." I liked it because one of my aims in writing the book was to bring back to life, as a distinctive individual, "one of the multitude" who had died in the Holocaust. But Kathy, Dan and Julia were appalled at the idea—a book with a Latin title would, they

---

[49] Gregg Easterbrook, "Greatest Good for the Greatest Number," *Washington Monthly,* (November 2002), http://www.washingtonmonthly.com/features/2001/0211.easterbrook .html.

told me, probably sell about a hundred copies. An alternative came to me because Julia was getting married. In editing the book she had been struck by a phrase in one of my grandfather's letters to my grandmother. In trying to persuade his parents to accept the idea that he wanted to marry an older woman, he had told them that "What binds us, pushes time away." Julia asked me if she could use it as part of what would be said at her own wedding. In warmly encouraging her to do so, it occurred to me that the phrase could also refer to what I was trying to do in the book, in getting to know my grandfather. *Pushing Time Away* appeared in 2003 to generally positive reviews and sold reasonably well, but with this book, what meant more to me than the sales was the appreciation of David's other grandchildren—my sister and my cousin—and the moving letters I got from many others from similar backgrounds, telling me the stories of their families.

The Ethics of George W. Bush

On August 9th 2001 President George W. Bush told the nation that he would not permit federal funds to be used for research on new stem cell lines grown from embryos destroyed after that date. The televised speech set out a case for protecting human embryos from destruction. I used it in my teaching that fall, setting it as reading for my students, and asking them to assess the president's reasoning.

Barely a month after Bush's speech on stem cells, that topic faded into the background as the nation fixed its attention on the terrorist attack of September 11th 2001 and America's likely response, the bombing or invasion of Afghanistan, where Al Qaeda had training camps. I was disturbed by the lack of debate on campus about the looming war. Perhaps because of my family background, I saw a parallel between Bush's demands on the Taliban regime, and Austria-Hungary's ultimatum to Serbia, after the assassination of Archduke Franz Ferdinand in Sarajevo, which most historians saw as an aggressive act that triggered World War I. So I organized a seminar to discuss whether the U.S. would be justified in attacking Afghanistan. To ensure, as I thought, a range of opinion on the issue, I invited four speakers, including Richard Falk and Michael Walzer, both of whom are generally considered to be on the left. (Noam Chomsky had been my first choice but was unable to speak.) By the time the event took place, the bombing had begun. The lecture theater was crammed to overflowing, and we had to transfer to a larger theater. To my surprise, all four speakers supported the war—even Falk, who said it was the first time he had supported America going to war.

As chair, I had not intended to speak, but after hearing all the speakers I thought it was necessary to provide a broader range of views, and made a brief statement of the case against the war, stressing that the Taliban's offers to negotiate had been brushed aside, so war was not, as the conventional "just war" doctrine requires, the last resort.

Bush often used moral language to defend his policies—including his tax cuts, and even his rejection of the Kyoto protocol on global warming. The "war on terror" further increased that tendency. In January 2002 he gave his famous speech naming Iraq, Iran, and North Korea as the "axis of evil" and later that year, began the buildup that was to lead to the war on Iraq. During this period the mainstream media seemed to think it unpatriotic to criticize the president. That left the field of criticism to people like Al Franken who ridiculed Bush, calling him stupid and a liar. But no one was taking what Bush said seriously, and scrutinizing his claims to be acting on sound moral principles. Perhaps an ethicist could have something to contribute to this national debate. After three years at Princeton I was due for six month's sabbatical leave, and could take a full year on half pay, so I could get a book done in time for publication early in 2004, when Bush would face re-election. I spoke to Kathy about it, and she liked the idea. Dan Halpern didn't, so she took it to other publishers and found several interested—it eventually went to Dutton. By the time the book appeared, in March 2004, however, it was already evident that the war in Iraq was not going to be the swift success that its advocates had predicted, and the previously deferential attitude to Bush had evaporated. *The President of Good and Evil: The Ethics of George W. Bush* had to compete with several books critical of Bush and his administration by better-known authors like Richard Clarke, former head of counter-terrorism, and ex-Watergate conspirator John Dean. Some reviews noticed that my book was attempting something distinctive, but it sold only modestly—and did nothing to hinder Bush's re-election.

Recent Projects

While working on *The President of Good and Evil* I was also involved in editing two books. One was *In Defense of Animals: The Second Wave,* an anthology that retained the structure of the earlier *In Defence of Animals,* but changed almost all of the essays in order to allow the current generation of theorists and activists to be heard. The other was *The Moral of the Story: An Anthology of Ethics through Literature,* jointly edited with Renata. The idea was to illustrate a broad range of moral issues by using works of literature: short stories, poems, and extracts from novels and plays. Renata's wide reading complemented my greater expertise in philosophical ethics, and we both enjoyed working on the project.

A group of Australian community organizations asked me to write a short book assessing Australia's record as a global citizen, to come out before the 2004 Australian federal elections. Since the Australian Prime Minister, John Howard, shared with George W. Bush the ignominy of being the only leaders of industrialized nations to refuse to sign the Kyoto Protocol, and had also behaved appallingly in keeping out people seeking political asylum in Australia, I agreed to write the book, provided I was given some research assistance. Tom Gregg was appointed to provide that assistance, and we ended up writing *How Ethical is Australia?*, which was published as part of a series of public interest books. Again, however, it failed in its key objective: Howard was re-elected.

My next book grew out of a suggestion from Jim Mason that we should think about a new edition of *Animal Factories*. That evolved into a proposal for a different book, with a working title *The Ethics of What We Eat*. To structure the book, we found three different families: one eating a standard American diet, one "conscientious omnivores" who seek out organic and humanely produced foods, and the third keeping to a strictly vegan diet. We described what each family ate and how their food was produced. Then we assessed the ethical issues raised by their choices. The book is aimed at a broad readership, and much of it is concerned to present factual information, rather than philosophical argument, but the ethical issues discussed include animal welfare, environmental sustainability, organic farming methods, genetic modification, and fair trade. It has now been published under three different English titles: Rodale, the American publisher, thought that our working title was "too academic" and after much discussion, called it *The Way We Eat: Why Our Food Choices Matter.* In Australia, Text were happy with *The Ethics of What We Eat,* whereas Arrow, the British publisher preferred *Eating: What We Eat and Why It Matters.* After the book did considerably better in Australia than in the U.S., Rodale switched to the original working title for their paperback edition.

In 2007 I gave two series of lectures: the Dasan Memorial Lectures in Korea, and the Uehiro Lectures in Practical Ethics at Oxford University. The Dasan lectures set out the main themes of my work, with one lecture on the nature of ethics, and others on global ethical issues, animals, and life and death decisions in medicine. There was extensive media coverage of my visit to Korea, and it was encouraging to see that my work is being widely read there. Korea seems more sympathetic to a utilitarian approach than many other countries, including the United States. The lectures were published in Korea, in English and with a Korean translation.[50]

In the Uehiro lectures at Oxford, I returned to the theme of what those of us living in affluent nations ought to be doing to help people living in extreme poverty in developing nations. I had decided the time was right for a book on this topic, and chose Random House as the publisher, largely because of the expectation of working with Tim Bartlett, who had a reputation as an editor who gave authors detailed critical comments and suggestions for improvements. I was not disappointed. Not since I worked with Robert Silvers on *Animal Liberation* had I had an editor who pressed me so relentlessly to produce the best book I was capable of writing, one that would be widely read and, more importantly, likely to move many of its readers to action. *The Life You Can Save: Acting Now to End World Poverty* was published in 2009. I traveled widely to promote the book in Australia, the U.S., Canada, the United Kingdom, and Sweden. Events at which I spoke about it were attended by large and enthusiastic crowds, and the book received largely good reviews. What was particularly encouraging was the number of reviewers and readers who told me that the book had led them to increase their own giving. Within a month, more than 2,500 people went to a website associated with the book, www.thelifeyoucansave.com, and pledged to give according to a scale I had proposed, that starts at one percent of income and increases as income rises.

In Conclusion

I have written about the nature of ethics, and plan to write more in that area in the future. The general direction in which I hope this work will proceed can be discerned in "Ethics and Intuitions," an article published in 2005, in which I consider the relevance to ethics of recent work in psychology and the neurosciences.[51] (I refer to these ideas in my response to Michael Huemer in this book.) Nevertheless, it is clear that my most important contributions to philosophy are in applied ethics, and

---

[50] *Living Ethically in the Twenty First Century: Contemporary Society and Practical Ethics.* The Tenth Dasan Memorial Lectures in Philosophy (Seoul: Chulhakkwahyunsilsa, 2008). In Korean and English.

[51] "Ethics and Intuitions," *Journal of Ethics* 9 (October 2005), pp. 331–352.

more specifically, on the moral status of animals, on the obligations of those who are comfortably off to those in great need, and on life and death decisions in medicine. When people ask me why I continue to defend views that are so shocking or abhorrent, I tell them that it is the absence of good reasons for holding any alternative position. I do not take our conventional moral judgments, or our common moral intuitions, as authoritative, but apart from that, there is nothing extraordinary about the thinking that has led me to the views I hold. They are grounded on quite simple premises that are difficult to deny. In the introduction to *Writings on an Ethical Life,* I set out four premises, three of them moral, and one factual, from which most of my views follow. The factual premise is that humans are not the only beings capable of feeling pain, or of suffering. Though Descartes famously denied this, and some twentieth-century behaviorists said such claims are "unscientific," today most people, including scientists who study animal behavior, accept it. The moral premises are as follows:

1. Pain is bad, and similar amounts of pain are equally bad, no matter whose pain it might be.

2. The seriousness of taking a life depends, not on the race, sex, or species of the being killed, but on its individual characteristics, such as its own desires about continuing to live or the kind of life it is capable of leading.

3. We should consider ourselves responsible both for what we do, and for what we refrain from doing.

This is probably the most concise statement possible of the basis of my views. In some respects it is too concise, but it can serve as a starting point for discussion. In the essays that follow, these moral premises are challenged, implicitly or explicitly. I welcome the attention that so many distinguished authors have given to my work, for philosophy thrives on criticism. The beauty of the format of this series is that you, the reader, hear from both the author and the critics, and then get to make up your own mind on the issues.

I

THE MORAL STATUS
OF ANIMALS

1

The Human Prejudice

BERNARD WILLIAMS

Once upon a time there was an outlook called "humanism." In one sense there still is: it is a name given these days to a movement of organized, sometimes militant, opposition to religious belief, in particular to Christianity. What was more or less the same movement used to go under a name equally inherited from the past of philosophy, which was "Rationalism." In Britain, atheist organizations under these different names have existed at the same time, and I believe that one man, who wrote indefatigably to the newspapers, may once have been secretary of them both.

It is not "humanism" in any such sense that I shall be concerned with, but I will make one point about it, because it is relevant to questions about our ethical outlook and the role played in it by the idea of humanity, which are the questions that I do want to discuss. Humanism in the sense of militant atheism encounters an immediate and very obvious paradox. Its speciality lies not just in being atheist—there all sorts of ways of being that—but in its faith in humanity to flourish without religion; moreover, in the idea that religion itself is peculiarly the enemy of human flourishing. The general idea is that if the last remnants of religion could be abolished, mankind would be set free and would do a great deal better. But the outlook is stuck with the fact that on its own submission this evil, corrupting and pervasive thing, religion, is itself a *human* invention: it certainly did not come from anywhere else. So humanists in this atheist sense should ask themselves: if humanity has

77

invented something as awful as they take religion to be, what should that tell them about humanity? In particular, can humanity really be expected to do much better without it?

However, that is not the subject. When I said that once upon a time there was an outlook called "humanism," I meant rather the time of the Renaissance. The term applied in the first place to new schemes of education, emphasizing the Latin classics and a tradition of rhetoric, but came to apply more broadly to a variety of philosophical movements. There was an increased and intensified interest in human nature.[1] One form of this was a new tradition inaugurated by Petrarch, of writings about the dignity and excellence of human beings (or, as the tradition inevitably put it, of man). These ideas were certainly not original with the Renaissance. Many of the arguments were already familiar, for instance the Christian argument that the superiority of man was shown by the choice of a human being to be the vehicle of the Incarnation; or the older idea, which goes back at least to Protagoras as he is presented by Plato, that humans have fewer natural advantages—fewer defenses, for instance—than other animals, but that they are more than compensated for this by the gift of reason and cognition.

Others of course took a gloomier view of human powers and potentialities. Montaigne wondered how peculiar human beings were, and was a lot less enthusiastic about the peculiarities they had. But whether the views were positive and celebratory, or more skeptical or pessimistic, there was one characteristic that almost all the views shared with each other. They shared it, too, with traditional Christianity, and this was hardly surprising, since virtually everyone in the Renaissance influenced by humanism was some sort of Christian. For a start, almost everyone believed that human beings were literally at the center of the universe (with the exceptions perhaps of Nicolas of Cusa and Giordano Bruno, who thought that there was no center to the universe). Besides that purely topographical belief, however, there was a more basic assumption, that in cosmic terms human beings had a definite measure of importance. In most of these outlooks, the assumption was that the measure was high, that humans were particularly important in relation to the scheme of things. This is most obviously true of the more celebratory versions of humanism, according to which human beings are the most perfect beings in creation. But it is also present in outlooks that assign human beings a wretched and imperfect condition—Luther's vision, for

---

[1] I am indebted here to Jill Kraye, "Moral Philosophy," in *The Cambridge History of Renaissance Philosophy* (Cambridge University Press, 1988), esp. pp. 306–316.

instance, in which man is hideously fallen and can do nothing about it simply by his own efforts. The assumption is still there—indeed, it is hardly an assumption, but a central belief in the structure—that that fact itself is of absolute importance. The cosmos may not be looking at human beings, in their fallen state, with much admiration, but it is certainly looking at them. The human condition is a central concern to God, so central, in fact, that it led to the Incarnation, which in the Reformation context too plays its traditional role as signaling man's special role in the scheme of things. If man's fate is a very special concern to God, there is nothing more absolute than that: it is a central concern, period.

Overtly anthropocentric views of the cosmos are certainly less common today than they were then. Leaving aside the distribution of concerns on earth itself, which I shall come back to, people for a long time now have been impressed by the mere topographical rearrangement of the universe, by which we are not in the center of anything interesting: our location in the galaxy, just for starters, seems almost extravagantly non-committal. Moreover, many people suppose that there are other living creatures on planets in this galaxy, in other galaxies, perhaps in other universes. It seems hubristic or merely silly to suppose that this enterprise has any special interest in us. Even Christians, or many of them, are less impressed by the idea that God must be *more* concerned with human beings than he is with any other creature (I'm afraid I don't know what the current state of thought is about the Incarnation). The idea of the absolute importance of human beings seems firmly dead or at least well on the way out.

However, we need to go a little carefully here. The assumption I am considering, as I put it, is that in cosmic terms human beings have a definite measure of importance. The most common application of that assumption, naturally enough, has been that they have a high degree of importance; and I have suggested that that itself can take two different forms: the Petrarchan or celebratory form, in which man is splendidly important, and what we may call the Lutheran form, that what is of ultimate significance is the fact that man is wretchedly fallen. But there is another and less obvious application of the same assumption: that human beings do have a definite measure of importance in the scheme of things, but that it is very low. On this view, there is a significance of human beings to the cosmos, but it is vanishingly small. This may not be a very exciting truth about the cosmos, as contrasted with those other outlooks I mentioned, but it is still meant to be a truth about the cosmos; moreover, it is meant to be an exciting, or at least significant, truth about human beings. I think that this may have been what Bertrand Russell was thinking when, for instance in an essay significantly called *A Free Man's Worship*, he went on about the transitoriness of human beings, the tinyness of the earth, the vast and pitiless expanses of the universe, and so on, in a style of self-pitying and at the same time self-glorifying rhetoric that made Frank Ramsey remark that he himself was much less impressed than some of his friends were by the size of the universe, perhaps because he weighed 240 lb.

This outlook can make people feel that human activities are absurd, because we invest them with an importance which they do not really possess. If someone feels about human activities in this way, there is never much point, it must be said, in telling him that his feelings involve a muddle: the feelings probably come from some place which that comment will not reach. All the same, they do involve a muddle. It is a muddle between thinking that our activities fail some test of cosmic significance, and (as contrasted with that) recognizing that there is no such test. If there is no such thing as the cosmic point of view, if the idea of absolute importance in the scheme of things is an illusion, a relic of a world not yet thoroughly disenchanted, then there is no other point of view except ours in which our activities can have or lack a significance. Perhaps, in a way, that is what Russell wanted to say, but his journey through the pathos of loneliness and insignificance as experienced from a non-existent point of view could only generate the kind of muddle that is called sentimentality. Nietzsche by contrast got it right when he said that once upon a time there was a star in a corner of the universe, and a planet circling that star, and on it some clever creatures who invented knowledge; and then they died, and the star went out, and it was as though nothing had happened.[2]

Of course, there is in principle a third possibility, between a cosmic point of view and our point of view, a possibility familiar from science fiction: that one day, we encountered other creatures who would have a point of view on our activities—a point of view which, it is quite vital to add, we could respect. Perhaps science fiction has not made very interesting use of this fantasy, but there may be something to learn from it, and I shall come back to it at the end of these remarks.

Suppose we accept that there is no question of human beings and their activities being important or failing to be so from a cosmic point of view. That does not mean that there is no point of view from which they are important. There is certainly one point of view from which they are

---

[2] "On Truth and Lies in a Nonmoral Sense," opening paragraph.

important, namely ours: unsurprisingly so, since the "we" in question, the "we" who raise this question and discuss with others who we hope will listen and reply, are indeed human beings. It is just as unsurprising that this "we" often shows up within the *content* of our values. Whether a creature is a human being or not makes a large difference, a lot of the time, to the ways in which we treat that creature or at least think that we should treat it. Let us leave aside for the moment distinctions of this kind that are strongly contested by some people, such as the matter of what we are prepared to eat. Less contentiously, we speak, for instance, of "human rights," and that means rights that are possessed by certain creatures because they are human beings, in virtue of their being human. We speak of "human values." Indeed, at Princeton there is a Center for Human Values. Of course, that phrase could mean no more than that the values in question are possessed by human beings, but in that purely possessive sense the term would hardly be adding much, since on this planet at least there isn't any other creature that has any values, or, certainly, a Center to study and promote them. Human values are not just values that we have, but values that express our humanity, and to study them is to study what we value inasmuch as we are what we are, that is to say, human beings.

Now there are some people who suppose that if in any way we privilege human beings in our ethical thought, if we think that what happens to human beings is more important than what happens to other creatures, if we think that human beings as such have a claim on our attention and care in all sorts of situations in which other animals have less or no claim on us, we are implicitly reverting to a belief in the absolute importance of human beings. They suppose that we are in effect saying, when we exercise these distinctions between human beings and other creatures, that human beings are more important, period, than those other creatures. That objection is simply a mistake. We do not have to be saying anything of that sort at all. These actions and attitudes need express no more than the fact that human beings are more important *to us*, a fact which is hardly surprising.

That, mistaken, objection takes the form of claiming that in privileging human beings in our ethical thought we are saying *more* than we should: we are claiming their absolute importance. There is a different objection, which might be put by claiming that we are saying *less* than we need to say: that we need a reason for these preferences. Without a reason, the objection goes, the preference will just be a prejudice. If we have given any reason at all so far for these preferences, it is simply the one we express by saying "it's a human being" or "they're human" or "she's one of us," and that, the objectors say, is not a reason. They will remind us of the paradigm prejudices, racism and sexism. "Because he's white," "because he's male," are no good in themselves as reasons, though they can be relevant in very special circumstances (gender in the case of employing a bathroom attendant, for example, though even that might be thought in some circles to involve a further prejudice). If the supposed reasons of race or gender are offered without support, the answer they elicit is *What's that got to do with it?* Those supposed reasons are equally of the form "he's one of us," for a narrower "us." The human privilege is itself just another prejudice, these objectors say, and they have a suitably unlovely name for it, "speciesism."

How good is this objection? How exactly does it work? It will take a little while to answer those questions, because they require us to try to get a bit clearer about the relations between our humanity on the one hand and our giving and understanding reasons on the other, and the route to that involves several stops. A good place to start, I think, is this: not many racists or sexists have actually supposed that a bare appeal to race or gender—merely saying "he's black" or "she's a woman"—did constitute a reason. They were, so to speak, at a stage either earlier or later than that. It was earlier if they simply had a barely articulated practice of discrimination: they just went on like that, and did not need to say anything to their like-minded companions in the way of justification of the practice. The day came when they did have to say something in justification: to those discriminated against, if they could not simply tell them to shut up, to outsiders or to radicals, or to themselves in those moments when they wondered how defensible it might be, and *then* they had to say *more*. Mere references to race or gender would not meet what was by then the need; equally, references to supernatural sources which said the same thing would not hold up for long. Something which at least seemed relevant to the matter at hand—job opportunities, the franchise or whatever it might be—would then be brought out, about the supposed intellectual and moral weakness of blacks or women. These were reasons in the sense that they were at least to some degree of the right shape to be reasons, though they were of course very bad reasons, both because they were untrue and because they were the products of false consciousness, working to hold up the system, and it did not need any very elaborate social or psychological theory to show that they were.[3]

---

[3] For a theoretically unambitious version of a "critical theory" test which applies to such situations, see *Truth and Truthfulness* (Princeton University Press, 2002), Chapter 9, sections 4 and 5.

With the case of the supposed human prejudice, it does not seem to be quite like this. On the one hand, it is not simply a matter of inarticulate or unexpressed discrimination: there is no secret that we are in favor of human rights, for instance. On the other hand, "It's a human being" does seem to operate as a reason, but it does not seem to be helped out by some further reach of supposedly more relevant reasons, of the kind which in the other cases of prejudice turned out to be rationalizations. We are all aware of some notable differences between human beings and other creatures on earth, but there is a whole range of cases in which we cite or rely on the fact that a certain creature is a human being, but where those differences do not seem to figure in our thought as *justifications* for going on as we do. In fact, in many cases it is hard to see how they could. Uniquely on earth, human beings use highly articulated languages; they have developed to an unparalleled extent non-genetic learning through culture, possess literatures and historically cumulative technologies, and so on. There is of course a lot of dispute about the exact nature and extent of these differences between our own and other species. There are discussions, for instance, of how far some other primates transmit learned skills, and whether they have local traditions in this. But this is not the point: there is, on any showing, a sharp and spectacular behavioral gap between ourselves and our nearest primate relatives. This is no doubt because other hominid species have disappeared, doubtless with our assistance. But why should considerations about these differences, true as they are, play any role in an argument about vegetarianism, for instance? What has all that got to do with human beings eating some other animals, but not human beings? It is hard to see any argument in that direction which will not turn out to say something like this, that it is *simply better* that culture, intelligence, technology should flourish—as opposed, presumably, to all those other amazing things that are done by other species which are on the menu. Or consider, not the case of meat-eating, but of insecticides: if we have reason to use them, must we claim that it is simply better that we should flourish at the expense of the insects? If any evolutionary development is spectacular and amazing, it is the proliferation and diversification of insects. Some of them are harmful to human beings, their food, or their artifacts; but they are truly wonderful.[4] What these last points show is that even if we could get hold of the idea that it was *just better* that one sort of animal should flourish rather than another, it is not in the least clear why it should be us. But the basic point, of

---

[4] Cf. in this connection the late Stephen J. Gould's point about the false impression of "progress" given by the standard old representation of the evolutionary tree.

course, is that we can't get hold of that idea at all. This is simply another recurrence of the notion we saw off a while ago, absolute importance, that last relic of the still enchanted world. Of course, we can say, rightly, that we are in favor of cultural development and so on, and think it very important; but that itself is just another expression of the human prejudice we are supposed to be wrestling with.

So there is something obscure about the relations between the moral consideration "it's a human being," and the characteristics that distinguish human beings from other creatures. If there is a human prejudice, it is structurally different from those other prejudices, racism and sexism. This doesn't necessarily show that it isn't a prejudice. Some critics will say, on the contrary, that it shows what a deep prejudice it is, to the extent that we cannot even articulate reasons that are supposed to underlie it. And if, as I said, we seem very ready to profess it, the critic will say that this shows how shamelessly prejudiced we are, or that we can profess it because, very significantly, there is no-one we have to justify it to, except a few reformers who are fellow human beings. That is certainly significant. Other animals are good at many things, but not at asking for or understanding justifications. Oppressed human groups come of age in the search for emancipation when they speak for themselves, and no longer through reforming members of the oppressive group, but the other animals will never come of age: human beings will always act as their trustees. This is connected to the point, which I shall come back to, that in relation to them the only moral question for us is how we should *treat* them.

Someone who speaks vigorously against speciesism and the human prejudice is of course Professor Peter Singer. (Incidentally, he holds his chair at the Center for Human Values at Princeton, which I have already mentioned, and I have wondered what he makes of that name. In the purely possessive, limp, sense of the expression it is presumably all right, but in the richer sense which must surely be its intention, I should have thought it would have sounded to him rather like a Center for Aryan Values.) Whatever exactly may be the structure of the human prejudice, if it is a prejudice, Singer's work has brought out clearly some consequences of rejecting it as a prejudice, consequences which he has been prepared to advocate in a very robust style.

A central idea involved in the supposed human prejudice is that there are certain respects in which creatures are treated in one way rather than another simply because they belong to a certain category, the human species. We do not, at this basic initial level, need to know any more about them. Told that there are human beings trapped in a burning building, on the strength of that fact alone we mobilize as many resources as we can to rescue them. When the human prejudice is rejected, two things follow, as Singer has made clear. One is that some more substantial set of properties, supposedly better fitted to give a reason, are substituted. The second is that the criteria based on these properties, the criteria which determine what you can properly do to a creature, are applied to examples one at a time: it is always a question whether this particular individual satisfies the criteria.

Consider the question, not of protecting, but of killing. Singer thinks that our reasons for being less ready to kill human beings than we are to kill other animals—the "greater seriousness" of killing them, as he puts it—are based on our superior mental powers—our self-awareness, our rationality, our moral sense, our autonomy, or some combination of these. They are the kinds of thing, we are inclined to say, which make us 'uniquely human'. To be more precise, they are the kind of thing that make us persons.[5]

Elsewhere, he cites with approval Michael Tooley's definition of persons as "those beings who are capable of seeing themselves as continuing selves—that is, as self-aware beings existing over time."[6] It is these characteristics that we should refer to, when we are deciding what to do, and in principle we should refer to them on a case by case basis. "If we are considering whether it is wrong to destroy something, surely we must look at its actual characteristics, not just the species to which it belongs", and "actual" here is taken in a way that leaves no room for potentiality. You can't say that an embryo gets special protection because it is potentially a person; it is not yet a person, and therefore it is a nonperson, just as (in Tooley's terminology) someone suffering from acute senile dementia is an ex-person.[7]

As I have said, Singer brings out very clearly these two consequences of his view, and relies on them in arriving at various controversial conclusions. I am concerned with the view itself, the rejection of the human prejudice, rather than particular details of Singer's own position, but there is one point I should mention in order to make clear what is at issue. What Singer rejects is not quite the form of the human prejudice to which I and many other people are attached. Singer considers the following familiar syllogism:

---

[5] Peter Singer, *Unsanctifying Human Life* (Oxford: Blackwell, 2002), p. 193.

[6] p. 239.

[7] p. 194. For potentiality, see Peter Singer and Karen Dawson, "IVF Technology and the Argument from Potential," *Unsanctifying Human Life*, pp. 199–214.

Every human being has a right to life.

A human embryo is a human being.

Therefore the human embryo has a right to life.[8]

We had all better agree that the conclusion follows from the premises. Those who oppose abortion and destructive embryo research typically think that both the premisses are true. Those who, under certain circumstances, support these things must reject the argument, and they typically deny the second premiss. Singer denies the first. More strictly, he thinks that the first is correct only if "human being" is taken to mean "person," but in *that* sense the second premiss is false, because the embryo is not yet a person. There is a sense in which the second premiss is true (the embryo belongs to the species) but in that sense of "human being" it is not true that every human being has a right to life. I mention this because it distinguishes Singer from those, such as most moderate pro-choice campaigners, who accept, obviously enough, that the embryo is human in the sense that it is *a human embryo*, but do not accept that it is yet a human being, any more than a bovine embryo is a cow. Jonathan Glover once caused nearly terminal fury in a distinguished "pro-life" advocate by what seemed to me the entirely reasonable remark that if this gentleman had been promised a chicken dinner, and was served with an omelet made of fertilized eggs, he would have a complaint. The point is an important one. The standard view, the view which Singer attacks, is that "human being" is a morally relevant notion, where "human being" indeed means an animal belonging to a particular species, our species; but those who hold this view are not committed to thinking that a fertilized ovum is already such an animal, any more so than in the case of other species.

I think that this and some other peculiarities of Singer's position come in part from his concern with one kind of controversy: he is trying to combat conservative policies based on a particular notion, the sanctity of human life. This helps to explain why his position on abortion and infanticide is the same as the pro-life position, but the other way up: he and the pro-lifers both argue "if abortion, then infanticide," but they take it as an objection, and he takes it as an encouragement. Against this, it is very important to say that one can believe that the notion of a human being is central to our moral thought without being committed to the

---

[8] p. 192.

entire set of traditional rules that go under the label "the sanctity of human life."[9]

The most basic question, however, is that raised by the general structure of Singer's position, and it is the same kind of question that we have encountered already. *Why* are the fancy properties which are grouped under the label of personhood "morally relevant" to issues of destroying a certain kind of animal, while the property of being a human being is not? One answer might be: we favor and esteem these properties, we encourage their development, and we hate and resent it if they are frustrated, and this is hardly surprising, since our whole life, and not only our values but our having any values at all, involve our having these properties ourselves. Fine answer, but it doesn't answer this question, since we also, and in complex relation to all that, use the idea of a human being in our moral thought, and draw a line round the class of human beings with regard to various things that we are ethically prepared to do. A different answer would be that it is *simply better* that the world should instantiate the fancy properties of personhood, and not *simply better* that human beings as such should flourish. But that is once more our now familiar friend, absolute importance, that survivor from the enchanted world, bringing with it the equally familiar and encouraging thought that the properties we possess— well, most of us, not counting the infants, the Alzheimer patients and some others—are being cheered on by the universe.

I should say at once that this is not Singer's own answer to the question. He is a Utilitarian, and he thinks (very roughly speaking) that the only thing that ultimately matters is how much suffering there is. To the extent that we should give special attention to persons, this is supposedly explained by the fact that persons are capable of suffering in some special ways. I do not want to argue over the familiar territory of whether that is a reasonable or helpful explanation of all the things we care about in relation to persons. I want to ask something else, which leads us back to my central question of our moral conception of ourselves as human beings living among other creatures. My question is not: does the Utilitarian view make sense of our other concerns in terms of our concern with suffering? My question is rather: how far does their view make sense of our concern with suffering itself?

Many Utilitarians, including Singer, are happy to use the model of an Ideal or Impartial Observer. A philosopher proposing one version of

---

[9] Ronald Dworkin, in *Life's Dominion: An Argument about Abortion, Euthanasia, and Individual Freedom* (Random House, 1993), tries to recruit "life is sacred" in favor of radical policies. I doubt that this works any better.

such a model fifty years ago memorably described this figure as "omnis-cient, disinterested, dispassionate, but otherwise normal."[10] The model comes in various versions, in many of which the figure is not exactly dispassionate: rather, he is benevolent. This can mean several different things, in terms of there being a positive value to preference-satisfac-tion, and so on, but let us concentrate on the simplest application of the idea—that the Ideal Observer [IO] is against suffering, and wants there to be as little of it as possible. With his omniscience and impartiality he, so to speak, *takes on* all suffering, however exactly we are to conceive of that, and takes it all on equally. He does look, of course, a lot like a slimmed-down surrogate of the Christian God, and this may well suggest that he represents yet another re-enactment of the cosmic point of view: suffering or its absence are what have absolute importance. But I assume that Utilitarians such as Singer hope that the model can be spelled out in more disenchanted terms.

They deploy the model against what they see as prejudice, in partic-ular the human prejudice, and the idea behind this is that there is a sen-timent or disposition or conviction which we do have, namely compas-sion or sympathy or the belief that suffering is a bad thing, but we express these sentiments in an irrationally restricted way: in ways gov-erned by the notorious inverse square law, where the distances involved can be of all kinds, spatial, familial, national, racial, or governed by species-membership. The model of the IO is supposed to be a corrective; if we could take on all suffering as he does, we would not be liable to these parochial biases and would feel and act in better ways. No doubt the history of the device does lie in fact in a kind of secularized *Imitatio Christi*, and I suspect that some of the sentiments it mobilizes are con-nected with that, but the Utilitarians hope to present it as independent of that, as a device expressing an extensive rational correction of some-thing we indeed feel.

So I want to take the model seriously: perhaps more seriously, from a certain point of view, than those who use it. I have two problems with it. One is very familiar, and concerns the relations between the model and human action. Even if we thought that the IO's outlook were a reli-able guide to what would be a *better state of affairs*, how is that con-nected to what we—each of us—should be trying to do? With regard to animal suffering, a form of the problem (a form that goes back to the nineteenth century) is the question of policing nature. Even though

---

[10] Roderick Firth: "Ethical Absolutism and the Ideal Observer," *Philosophy and Phenomenological Research* 12 (1952), pp. 317–345.

much suffering to animals is caused, directly or indirectly, by human beings, a lot of it is caused by other animals. This must form a significant part of what is on the IO's screen. We are certainly in the business of reducing the harm caused by other animals to ourselves; we seek in some degree to reduce the harm we cause to other animals. The question arises, whether we should not be in the business of reducing the harm that other animals cause each other, and generally the suffering that goes on in nature. Utilitarians do offer some arguments to suggest that we should not bother with that, arguments which invoke the most efficient use of our time and energies and so on, but I find it hard to avoid the feeling that those answers are pallid and unconvincing rationalizations of a more basic reaction, that there is something altogether crazy about the idea, that it misrepresents our relations to nature. Some environmentalists of course think that we should not try to improve nature in this respect because nature is sacred and we should interfere with it as little as possible anyway, but they, certainly, are not governed simply by the model of the IO and his concern for suffering.

This leads to a second and more fundamental point. Those who see our selective sympathies as a biased and prejudiced filtering of the suffering in the world; who think in terms of our shadowing, so far as we can, the consciousness of the IO, and guiding our actions by reflection on what the IO takes on: I wonder whether they ever consider what it would really be like to take on what the IO supposedly takes on. Whatever exactly "takes on" may mean, it is supposed to imply this— that the sufferings of other people and of all other creatures should be as vividly present to us, in some sense, as closely connected with our reasons for action, as our own sufferings or those of people we care for or who are immediately at hand. This is how the model is supposed to correct for bias. But what would it conceivably be like for this to be so, even for a few seconds? What would it be like to take on every piece of suffering that at a given moment any creature is undergoing? It would be an ultimate horror, an unendurable nightmare. And what would the connection of that nightmare to our actions be? In the model, the IO is supposed just to be an Observer: he can't do anything. But our actions, the idea is, are supposed to shadow or be guided by reflection on what he in his omniscience and impartiality is taking on, and if for a moment we got anything like an adequate idea of what that is, and we really guided our actions by it, then surely we would annihilate the planet, if we could; and if other planets containing conscious creatures are similar to ours in the suffering they contain, we would annihilate them as well.

The model has things entirely inside out. We indeed have reasons to listen to our sympathies and extend them, not only to wider groups of human beings, but into a concern for other animals, so far as they are in our power. This is already a human disposition. The OED definition of the word "humane" reads:

> Marked by sympathy with and consideration for the needs and distresses of others; feeling or showing compassion and tenderness towards human beings and the lower animals . . .

We can act intelligibly from these concerns only if we see them as aspects of human life. It is not an accident or a limitation or a prejudice that we cannot care equally about all the suffering in the world: it is a condition of our existence and our sanity. Equally, it is not that the demands of the moral consciousness require us to leave human life altogether and then come back to regulate the distribution of concerns, including our own, by criteria derived from nowhere. We are surrounded by a world which we can regard with a very large range of reactions: wonder, joy, sympathy, disgust, horror. We can, being as we are, reflect on these reactions and modify them to some extent. We can think about how this human estate or settlement should be run, and about its impact on its surroundings. But it is a total illusion to think that this enterprise can be licensed in some respects and condemned in others by credentials that come from another source, a source that is not already involved in the peculiarities of the human enterprise. It is an irony that this illusion, even when it takes the form of rejecting so-called speciesism and the human prejudice, actually shares a structure with older illusions about there being a cosmic scale of importance in terms of which human beings should understand themselves.

If we look at it in the light of those old illusions, this outlook—namely, the opposition to the human prejudice—will be closer in spirit to what I called the Lutheran version rather than the celebratory versions, in virtue of its insistence that human beings are twisted by their selfishness. It is unlike the Lutheran outlook, of course, precisely in its anti-humanism: Luther thought that it did matter to the universe what happened to mankind, but this view thinks that all that matters to the universe is, roughly speaking, how much suffering it contains. But there is another difference as well. Luther thought that human beings could not redeem themselves unaided, but the opponents of the human prejudice typically think that with the help of rationality and these theories, they may be able to do so. (Here there is a resemblance to the so-called "humanists" with whom I started with at the very beginning of this lecture, the strangely optimistic advocates of atheism.)

I have said that it is itself part of a human, or humane, outlook to be concerned with how animals should be treated, and there is nothing in what I have said to suggest that we should not be concerned with that. But I do want to repeat something that I have said elsewhere, that, very significantly, the only question for us is how those animals should be treated.[11] This is not true of our relations to other human beings, and this already shows that we are not dealing with a prejudice like racism or sexism. Some white male who thinks that the only question about the relations between "us," as he puts it, and other human beings such as women or people of color is how "we" should treat "them" is already prejudiced, but in the case of other animals that is the only question there could be.

That is how it is here, on this planet, now; it is a consequence of the fact I mentioned earlier, that in terms of a range of abilities that control action, we happen to live on an evolutionary plateau. Human beings do not have to deal with any creature that in terms of argument, principle, world-view or whatever, can answer back. But it might be otherwise; and it may be helpful, in closing, to imagine something different. Suppose that, in the well-known way of science fiction, creatures arrive with whom to some extent we can communicate, who are intelligent and technologically advanced (they got here, after all), have relations with each other that are mediated by understood rules, and so on and so forth. Now there is an altogether new sort of question for the human prejudice. If these culturally ordered creatures arrived, a human being who thought that it was just a question of how *we* should treat *them* has seriously underestimated the problem, both ethically and, probably, prudentially.

The late Robert Nozick once gave it as an argument for vegetarianism that if we claimed the right to eat animals less smart than ourselves, we would have to concede the right to such visitors to eat us, if they were smarter than us to the degree that we are smarter than the animals we eat.[12] In fact, I don't think that it is an argument for vegetarianism, but rather an objection to one argument for meat-eating, and I am not too sure how good it is even in that role (because the point of the meat-eater

---

[11] *Ethics and the Limits of Philosophy* (Fontana, 1985), pp. 118–19.

[12] Williams here referenced Nozick's *Philosophical Explanations*, though no passage in that book says this. Nozick's *Anarchy, State, and Utopia*, pp. 45–47 is closer, though the sense does not exactly fit Williams's wording. —Ed.

may not be the distance of the animals from our level of understanding, but the absolute level of the animals' understanding). But the main point is that if they proposed to eat us, it would be quite crazy to debate their *rights* at all. The nineteenth-century egoist philosopher Max Stirner said "The tiger that assails me is in the right, and I who strike him down am also in the right. I defend against him not my *right*, but *myself*."[13]

But Stirner's remark concerns a tiger, and it is a matter of life and death. Much science fiction, such as the puerile movie *Independence Day*, defines the issue in those terms from the beginning, and so makes the issues fairly easy. It is fairly easy, too, if the aliens are just here to help, in terms that we can recognize as help. The standard codings of science fiction, particularly in movies, are designed to make such questions simple. The hostile and nasty tend to be either slimy and disgusting, or rigid and metallic (in one brilliant literary example, Wells's *War of the Worlds*, they are both). The nice and co-operative are furry like the co-pilot in *Star Wars*, or cute like ET, or ethereal fairies like those little things in the bright light at the end of *Close Encounters of the Third Kind*. However, we can imagine situations in which things would be harder. The arrivals might be very disgusting indeed: their faces, for instance, if those are faces, are seething with what seem to be worms, but if we wait long enough to find out what they are at, we may gather that they are quite benevolent. They just want to live with us—rather closely with us. What should we make of that proposal? Some philosophers may be at hand to remind us about distinguishing between moral and non-moral values, and to tell us that their benevolence and helpfulness are morally significant whereas the fact that they are unforgettably disgusting is not. But suppose their aim, in their unaggressive way, is to make the world more, as we would put it, disgusting? And what if their disgustingness is really, truly, unforgettable?

Or turn things round in a different direction. The aliens are, in terms of our preferences, moderately good-looking, and they are, again, extremely benevolent and reasonable; but they have had much more successful experience than we have in running peaceable societies, and they have found that they do need to *run* them, and that too much species-self-assertion or indeed cultural autonomy prove destabilizing and destructive. So, painlessly, they will rid us, certainly of our prejudices, and to the required extent, of some of our cultural and other peculiari-

---

[13] *Der Einziger und sein Eigenthum*, translated by S.T. Byington as *The Ego and His Own* (Sun City: West World Press, 1982), p. 128.

ties. What should we make of that? Would the opponents of speciesism want us to join them—join them, indeed, not on the ground that we could not beat them (which might be sensible if not very heroic), but on principle?

The situation that this fantasy presents is in some ways familiar. It is like that of a human group defending its cultural, possibly ethnic, identity against some other human group which claims to dominate or assimilate them: with this very large difference, however, that since we are dealing here with another and indeed extra-terrestrial species, there is no question of cultural or ethnic variation being eroded by sexual fusion. (From the perspective of sex, it must be said, the idea that so-called speciesism, racism, and yet again gender prejudice, are all alike, already looks very peculiar.)

Anyway, the fantasy situation with the aliens will resemble the familiar political situation in some ways. For one thing, there may well be a disagreement among the threatened group, in part an ethical disagreement, between those we may call the collaborators, and others who are resisters. (It looks as though the Utilitarians will join the collaborators.) In the fantasy case, the resisters will be organizing under the banner "Defend humanity" or "Stand up for human beings." This is an ethical appeal in an ethical dispute. Of course this does not make "human being" into an ethical concept, any more than the cause of Basque separatism—an ethical cause, as Basque separatists see it—makes "Basque" into an ethical concept. The relevant ethical concept is something like: loyalty to, or identity with, one's ethnic or cultural grouping, and in the fantasy case, the ethical concept is: loyalty to, or identity with, one's species. Moreover—and this is the main lesson of this fantasy—this is an ethical concept we already have. This is the ethical concept that is at work when, to the puzzlement of the critics, we afford special consideration to human beings because they are human beings. The fact that we implicitly use this concept all the time explains why there is not some other set of criteria which we apply to individuals one by one. It is merely that as things are in actual life we have no call to spell this concept out, because there is no other creature in our life who could use or be motivated by the same consideration but with a different application: that is to say, no creature belonging to some other species can articulate, reflect on, or be motivated by reasons appealing to their species membership.

So the idea of there being an ethical concept that appeals to our species membership is entirely coherent. Of course, there may be ethical arguments about the merits or value of any concept that appeals to something like loyalty to group membership or identity with it. Some people, in the spirit of those who would be principled collaborators in the fantasy case, are against such ideas. In the political morality of the present time, the standing of such attitudes is strikingly ambiguous. Many people, perhaps most people of a critical disposition, seem to be opposed to such attitudes in dominant groups and in favor of them, up to a point, for subordinate groups. (It is a good question, why this is so, but I shall not try to pursue it here.) Others, again, may be respectful of the energizing power of such conceptions, and of the sense they can give of a life that has a rich and particular character, as contrasted, at the extreme, with the Utilitarian ideal of the itinerant welfare-worker who, with his bad line to the IO, goes round turning on and off the taps of benevolence. At the same time, however, those who respect these conceptions of loyalty and identity may be rightly skeptical about the coercive rhetoric, the lies about differences, and the sheer violence that are often associated with such ideas and with the movements that express them. Some of these objections carry over to the ways in which we express species identity as things are, and that is why the opponents of so-called speciesism and the human prejudice quite often have a point about particular policies towards other animals, even though they are mistaken about the framework of ideas within which such things should be condemned.

It is a good question whether the human prejudice, if one wants to call it that, must for us be ultimately inescapable. Let us go back once more to the fantasy of the arrival of the benevolent managerial aliens, and the consequent debate among human beings between the collaborators and the resisters. In that debate, even the collaborators have to use a humanly intelligible discourse, arguments which their fellow human beings can recognize. But does that imply that their arguments would have to be *peculiar* to human beings? If so, their situation would indeed be paradoxical. It would be as though, in the similar political discussions about, say, the cultural identity of the Basques, even the assimilationists had to use only arguments peculiar to Basque culture. So let us suppose that it does not imply this. The relevant alternative in the fantasy case will be that collaborators use arguments which they share not only with their fellow human beings but with the aliens. These arguments presumably provide the basis of their collaboration.

Some moral philosophers think that the correct moral principles are ones that could be shared with any rational and reflective agents, whatever they were otherwise like. But even if this were so, it is important that it would not necessarily favor the collaborators. This is because those principles would not necessarily tell us and the aliens how to share a life together.[14] Maybe we and they would be too different in other respects for that to be possible—remember the disgusting aliens—and the best we could do is to establish a non-aggression pact and co-exist at a distance. That would leave our peculiarities—our prejudices, if that is what they are—where they were. But suppose we are to live together. There is no reason to suppose that the universal principles we share with the aliens will justify our prejudices. We cannot even be sure that they will justify our being allowed to have our prejudices, as a matter of toleration; as I said in setting up the fantasy, the long experience and benevolent understanding of the aliens may enable them to see that tolerating our kinds of prejudice leads to instability and injustice, and they will want to usher our prejudices out, and on these assumptions we should agree. The collaborators must then be right, because the moral conceptions they share with the aliens transcend the local peculiarities.

But if this is so, doesn't something stronger follow? I said, in setting up these fantasies, that the *Independence Day* scenario, in which the aliens are manifestly hostile and want to destroy us is, for us, an ethically easy case: we try to defend ourselves. But should we? Perhaps this is just another irrational, visceral, human reaction. The benevolent and and fair-minded and far-sighted aliens may know a great deal about us and our history, and understand that our prejudices are unreformable: that things will never be better in this part of the universe until we are removed. I am not saying that this is necessarily what the informed and benevolent aliens would think. Even if they did think it, I am not saying that the universal moralists, the potential collaborators, would have to agree with them. But they might agree with them, and if they were reluctant to do so, I do not see how they could be sure that they were not the victims of what in their terms would be just another self-serving prejudice. This, it seems to me, is a place at which the project of trying to transcend altogether the ways in which human beings understand themselves and make sense of their practices could end up. And at this point there seems to be only one question left to ask: Which side are you on?

In many, more limited, connections hopes for self-improvement can lie dangerously close to the risk of self-hatred. When the hope is to improve humanity to the point at which every aspect of its hold on the

---

[14] Perhaps we might consider in this perspective the fact that Kant, despite his central emphasis on the application of the moral law to rational agents as such, expresses the third formulation of the Categorical Imperative in terms of how we must always treat *humanity*.

world can be justified before a higher court, the result is likely to be either self-deception if you think you have succeeded or self-hatred and self-contempt when you recognize that you will always fail. The self-hatred, in this case, is a hatred of humanity. Personally I think that there are many things to loathe about human beings, but their sense of their ethical identity as a species is not one of them.

Reply to Bernard Williams

PETER SINGER

A Rare Defense of Speciesism

Speciesism is the prejudice that lies at the core of our attitudes to non-human animals, and hence underlies the way in which humans treat tens of billions of animals every year. Yet it is not easy to find a secular philosopher prepared to defend it. Even Ray Frey, who has long been regarded as one of the leading philosophical opponents of the position I advocate, and whose essay follows this one, rejects speciesism. Hence a defense of speciesism by a philosopher as skilled and eloquent as Bernard Williams is significant and will prove instructive.

Williams begins with a discussion of different possible views of the place of human beings in the universe. He rejects religious and anthropocentric views according to which the universe revolves around us, either literally or metaphorically. But the problem with such views, he says, is not merely that we overestimate our significance from the cosmic point of view, but that we assume that there is such a thing as a "cosmic point of view" at all. Hence the claim that we have some, but perhaps relatively little, significance, is rejected as a muddle. Instead Williams prefers the Nietzschean view that "once upon a time there was a star in a corner of the universe, and a planet circling that star, and on it some clever creatures who invented knowledge; and then they died, and the star went out, and it was as though nothing had happened."

It may be that human existence, or even all sentient life on this planet, will one day come to an end, and it will be "as though nothing had happened," but in fact something will have happened. Given that at least some of the sentient beings living on that planet were happy ones, there is no muddle involved in thinking that the history of the universe would have been worse if that had not been the case, and instead were full of unredeemed and endless misery. Just *how much* of a difference this will make in any judgment of the history of the universe will depend on something we do not know: the proportion of sentient life in the universe as a whole that is to be found on this planet. In the unlikely event that the Earth is the only place in the universe where sentient beings ever exist, then our judgment of how well the universe has gone should depend entirely on how well the existence of sentient beings on Earth has gone. But if our planet is only one among billions of planets each of which at some time has billions of sentient beings, then how well sentient existence on our planet goes is a very minor factor in any judgment of how well the universe goes.

Taking an Impartial Perspective

To say this does not involve the quasi-religious claim that the universe actually has a purpose or a point of view. The denial of a purposeful universe does not compel us to accept that the only sense in which our existence matters is that it matters to us. We can still maintain that our lives, and the satisfaction or frustration of our preferences, matter objectively. Nothing Nietzsche or Williams says refutes this possibility. All that is needed is the ability to imagine an impartial observer who puts herself in the position of all of the sentient beings involved, and considers which of various possible universes she would prefer, if she were to live all those lives. There is no need for this imaginary observer to be actual.

Williams takes as "the simplest application" of the ideal observer, one who "is against suffering, and wants there to be as little of it as possible." He then has no trouble in dismissing the inner life of this ideal observer as "an ultimate horror, an unendurable nightmare" that, if it led to any action at all, would lead us to "annihilate the planet" and any similar planets as well. But who ever said that the ideal observer would have the one fixed idea of being against suffering? Williams's ideal observer would seem designed for use by a negative utilitarian—that is, one who holds that we should minimize suffering, but not that we should maximize happiness. Since Williams mentions "Utilitarians such as Singer" in connection with this model, he appears to assume that it is the kind of model I would use. But I have never been a negative utilitarian. It is true that in my applied writings, whether about the treatment of animals, global poverty, or euthanasia, I have focused on the reduction of suffering. I do so because there is so much needless suffering in these areas that a greater increase in utility is likely to result from attempts to reduce this suffering than from attempts to increase pleasure or happiness in other areas. In *Practical Ethics* and at all other times when I set out the foundations of my ethical position, I write of doing what "has the best consequences, on balance, for all affected" or "furthers the interests of those affected."[15] That obviously includes the pleasures and satisfactions that those affected can experience, as well as the pain and unsatisfied desires. One would have to be an extreme pessimist to assume that considering this would lead an ideal observer to desire to annihilate the planet.

Williams's purpose in arguing against the idea of a cosmic point of view, or even an ideal observer, is to suggest that all our values are necessarily "human values." In one sense, of course, they are. Since we have yet to encounter any nonhumans who articulate, reflect upon and discuss their values, all the values up for discussions are human, in the sense that they have been formulated and articulated by human beings. (Williams' comment that the word "human" in the name of Princeton University's Center for Human Values is either superfluous or expressive of some kind of human chauvinism to which I must object, is based on this point. He overlooks a third possibility: many people, especially many Americans, believe all values come from God. The Center's title suggests a different view, and one that I wholeheartedly support.)

The fact that our values are human in this sense does not exclude the possibility that our distinctively human nature includes an ability to develop values that would be accepted by any rational being capable of empathy with other beings. Nor—and this is the most important point—does the human nature of our values tell us anything about what our values can or should be, and in particular, whether we should value the pains, pleasures and lives of nonhuman animals less highly than we value our own pains, pleasures and lives. Williams, to his credit, does not attempt to argue that because our values are human values, concern for animals is somehow misguided. On the contrary, he acknowledges that "it is itself part of a human, or humane, outlook to be concerned with how animals should be treated, and there is nothing in what I have said to suggest that we should not be concerned with that." Instead Williams's argument is directed to the idea that we do not have to justify having a bias or prejudice in favor of human beings over other animals. Speciesism is not like racism or sexism, and is not morally objectionable.

Is Speciesism Like Racism and Sexism?

I use the term "speciesism" to suggest a parallel with racism and sexism. In each of these forms of prejudice, a dominant group develops an

---

[15] *Practical Ethics*, second edition (Cambridge University Press, 1993), pp. 13, 14.

ideology that justifies disregarding or discounting the interests of out-siders so that they can be used in ways that benefit those who are domi-nant. The analogy is useful, in part because it leads us to see that domi-nance exists not only within the human species, but between our own species and others. Moreover, the parallel between speciesism, racism and sexism raises questions about the use of mere biological differences as the justification for differences in how much consideration we give to others.

Nevertheless, it is true that the parallel between racism, sexism and speciesism is inexact. Williams gives some of the reasons why this is so. The differences between normal humans and, say, kangaroos, are vastly greater than the differences between people of different races, or between men and women. I said as much myself in *Animal Liberation*: "There are many matters in which the superior mental powers of normal adult humans make a difference: anticipation, more detailed memory, greater knowledge of what is happening, and so on."[16] The claim that speciesism is morally objectionable is not affected by such arguments, because speciesism is defined as discrimination on the basis of species, not discrimination on the basis of superior mental powers, even if those superior mental powers typically are possessed by members of our species and not by members of other species.

The most curious aspect of Williams's discussion of speciesism is that he never discusses the cases in which this discrimination is most evident—cases involving human beings who are accorded the same superior moral status as other humans even though they do *not* have mental powers that are superior to those of a dog or a pig. Consider the fact that we are prepared to subject chimpanzees, monkeys, pigs and dogs to painful and lethal experiments, but we regard it as a violation of human rights to do this to humans who, perhaps because of a genetic abnormality, or an accident at birth, never have had, nor will have, intel-lectual abilities comparable to these animals. Does this not show a prej-udice in favor of humans that has nothing to do with mental abilities or any of the other features that Williams discusses in distinguishing humans from nonhuman animals?

"Which Side Are You On?"

When it comes to the crunch, however, Williams's last resort in defense of "the human prejudice" is surprisingly crude. It is encapsulated in his

---

[16] *Animal Liberation* (A New York Review Book, second edition, 1990), p. 16.

question: "Which side are you on?" That question is put in the hypothetical scenario in which our planet has been colonized by benevolent, fair-minded and far-sighted aliens who, no doubt fair-mindedly and on the basis of full information, judge it necessary to remove us.

It's odd that Williams should first deny the analogy between racism and speciesism, and then resort to "which side are you on" as the ultimate bulwark of his argument. We have heard that question before. In times of war, or racial, ethnic, religious or ideological conflict, "which side are you on?" is used to imply that any questioning of the struggle is treason. McCarthyists asked it of those who opposed their methods of fighting communism. During the administration of President George W. Bush, it was used to suggest that critics of the administrations's policies were giving support to terrorists. The question divides the world into "us" and "them" and demands that the mere fact of this division transcend the very different question: "What is the right thing to do?"

In these circumstances, the right thing to do, and the courageous thing to do, is not to side with the tribal instincts that prompt us to say "My tribe (country, race, ethnic group, religion, and so forth) right or wrong" but to say: "I'm on the side that does what is right." Although it is fantastic to imagine that a fair-minded, well-informed, far-sighted judge could ever decide that there was no alternative to the "removal" of our species in order to avoid much greater injustice and misery, if this really were the case, we should reject the tribal—or species—instinct, and answer Williams's question in the same way.

Just eight years after the publication of *Animal Liberation*, Robert Nozick argued that we can't infer much from the fact that we do not yet have a theory of the moral importance of species membership, because the issue had not, until recently, seemed pressing, and so no one had spent much time trying to formulate such a theory.[17] Since 1983, however, many philosophers have given a great deal of attention to the issue of the moral importance, or otherwise, of species membership. None of them has succeeded in saying anything at all convincing. Nozick's comment therefore has taken on a different significance. If a philosopher of Bernard Williams's undoubted caliber has also failed in his attempt to justify speciesism, it seems increasingly likely that it cannot be justified.

---

[17] Robert Nozick, "About Mammals and People," *New York Times Book Review* (November 27th, 1983), p. 11.

2

Justifying Animal Use

R. G. FREY

Over the years, but especially since my return from England in 1986, I have received a torrent of material to do with animal issues, especially to do with the use of animals in factory farming and their use in medical and scientific experimentation. This flood of material has far outstripped my ability to keep abreast of it, at least if I am to continue with my other interests in philosophy. Much to my amazement, papers arrive from all over the world, from people in different walks of life, and from high-school students and even those in junior high school. Book typescripts come in, as do all manner of journal articles, articles for popular magazines, and discussion notes. Questionnaires arrive wanting my opinions on certain animal issues, and I regularly receive invitations to give talks upon and write about "animal rights." In my case, since I do comparatively little writing for the popular press, I suppose all the reprinted pieces that have found their way into anthologies explain the flood. But it is truly remarkable, I think, that a subject that was virtually moribund thirty years ago should come to occupy such a prominent place in ethical discussion. To be sure, the growth of applied or practical ethics has ensured that some subjects, such as medical ethics, gain attention, but no one could doubt that issues to do with animals, as it were, may even be said today to form such a subject.

Virtually all of this material refers to Peter Singer and discusses some particular one of his views at length. Where it compares and contrasts philosophers, Singer is always one of those cited, and his views are picked over carefully by all who purport to be concerned with animal welfare. It is hard to think of another area of philosophy so closely identified with a single individual, though it is well not to forget others who have significantly contributed to the discussion of animal issues. Of course, *Animal Liberation* (1975) is the book that spurred discussion, but *Practical Ethics* (1983) should be mentioned in this regard as well. These two books anchor the public's perception of Singer's discussion of animals. Alas, the two works are often run together, in a way that gives a misleading impression of *Animal Liberation*.

I. Utilitarianism and Animals' Pain

Before I turn to my main subject, since I have in the recent past had my say about Singer's views on *Animal Liberation* (to do with speciesism, with pain as a moral-bearing characteristic, with pain as a way of including animals within the moral community), it might be as well to note several points of difference between *Animal Liberation* and *Practical Ethics*.[1] Two central points matter. First, there really is no ethical theory—certainly, no utilitarian ethical theory—in *Animal Liberation*. Indeed, I doubt that any book could do as well as that one has done and be filled with moral philosophy. What happened is that the utilitarianism that is most definitely part of the latter book is read over into the former, and the focus upon pain in that former work makes it easier to see the utilitarianism fitting nicely as the overlay to the factual discussions of factory farming.

The beauty of the first book lies in its economy of argument, in how pain does all the work. Pain is a moral-bearing characteristic, so it is the ability to feel pain that gets animals into the moral community, that gives them moral standing, that makes it wrong to overlook what is done to them in course of raising them for food and in raising and preparing them for experimentation. The most striking charge of the book is speciesism, where this simply amounts to treating the painful experience of humans in a way that we do not treat similar painful experience of animals. Most especially, whereas it might be thought that some complicated story was required in order to include animals within the moral community, pain is a sufficient condition for their inclusion. This economy of argument—that pain or sentiency is the

---

[1] See *Interests and Rights* (Oxford: Clarendon, 1980) and *Rights, Killing, and Suffering* (Oxford: Blackwell, 1983) for book treatments of issues relevant to Singer's views in *Animal Liberation*.

lynch pin of *Animal Liberation*—seemingly cuts the ground from under those who would oppose Singer's line of argument. Either one denies that animals do indeed feel pain, or at least feel it in some morally relevant sense, or one denies that factory farming techniques are as painful as Singer maintains. While some have gone down the former path (Peter Carruthers is among the more prominent), not many have done so. Whereas down the other path lies a whole array of empirical data to do with fast food improvements in the way animals are bred and slaughtered, tighter regulations, for example, upon how veal calves are raised, tighten restrictions upon debeaking in chickens, and so on. Down this path is rather slow, step-by-step reform, often real reform, but reform at a pace too slow to satisfy those who demand change once and for all now. In fact, fast food distributors have made differences in the treatment of animals over the last ten years or so, as many of the more egregious practices have been altered, drastically changed, or eliminated.

Of all this material I have received, then, Singer is the darling of the crowd and the charge of speciesism—the crucial charge of *Animal Liberation*—has been the central fault of those who mistreat animals. The moral use of pain in this way—to confer moral standing, to make the pains of animals morally relevant to what we do to them, to anchor a charge of speciesism against those who fail to take seriously the pains of animals—makes *Animal Liberation* a captivating book, one that the lay reader can come away from with an understanding of what factory farming is about and what through pain is wrong with it. I do not know of another work of advocacy of a cause by a philosopher that has had anything like the effect of *Animal Liberation*.

It is rather remarkable, then, that in all this material I have received, and in all the other material on animal welfare issues with which I am familiar, it is comparatively unusual to find someone who is actually, so to speak, a Singerite. For what has happened, of course, is that the individuals in question have gone on to read *Practical Ethics*, where many of the same views about animals are presented but where they are encumbered with thoughts to do with utilitarianism. Utilitarianism as a moral philosophy is in decline: Singer and I may hold on to versions of it, but not all that many people any longer give evidence of doing so. Three thoughts come out of *Practical Ethics* that intersect dramatically with the position on animals that comes out of *Animal Liberation* and pose sources of worry.

First, there is the thought that something might justify the infliction of the pain in question. Empathy will get us, as feeling creatures, to put ourselves into the positions of other feeling creatures, to the fullest extent we can. But how do we get from there to the claim that inflicting pain in this case is wrong? What seems required here is a claim that nothing at all could ever justify the infliction of pain, at least in the case of a creature that does not want it, but this seems precisely to be what is at issue in the case of the vivisectionist and the factory farmer. After all, the vivisectionist need not claim that some animal does not feel pain, or that the animal wants the pain that is to be inflicted, or that feeling creatures may not empathize with other feeling creatures. The vivisectionist's question is whether the infliction of that pain can be justified, and the appeal to empathy with other feeling creatures does not seem to address that point. Mere pain or merely empathizing with the pains of others does not deal with this point.

Second, can something offset or compensate for the pain involved? The very mention of utilitarianism typically leads one to suspect that trade-offs are in the air. Indeed, at bottom, I cannot see what meat-eating is except the manifestation of a very strong preference on the part of humans for animal flesh, and it is that preference that impinges upon the degree of suffering that animals undergo. If one can obtain the flesh in question by means of less painful practices, there is no inbuilt reason not to prefer such means. But the whole point of trade-offs is what utilitarianism is about—what benefit is derived at what cost. That pain is involved in some practice does not show that no benefit is derived from that practice.

Third, and perhaps foremost, there is the fact that we are dealing with lives, and this raises the obvious worry, common to all forms of non-utilitarian ethical theory, of how stern will be the utilitarian resistance to trading-off lives. A very strong right to life has in the recent literature been thought a firmer guarantee to life than has the utilitarian assurance that we utilitarians retain a very lusty preference for life. Worries about pain give no assurance on this point.

Strange as it may seem, then, while Singer is the modern founding father and patron saint of the animal lobby, it is quite difficult to find actual Singerites. He is a man identified with a subject, yet very few of those who take up a position on the subject take up his position. This has produced a very odd result: the use of "animal rights" talk, that is, the conferring on animals of moral rights, has in no small measure been the result of the fact that Singer's utilitarianism features no obvious set of moral rights that all creatures possess, including a right to life. To be sure, one can put schemes of rights into utilitarianism on utilitarian grounds, but Singer quite noticeably, and rightly to my mind, does not place such a scheme of rights into his utilitarianism. So, we reach an odd result: the recent father of *Animal Liberation* is someone from whom many animal rightists work to protect themselves.

II. Our Use of Animals

On many issues, I agree with Singer. I think (the "higher") animals have moral standing, I think that what we do to animals matters morally and that they, therefore, are members of the moral community, and I agree that we must reject speciesism. I will say a bit about these things below, but what I essentially want to do is to try to describe why it is that pain is not the central focus of such a discussion about animals. To some extent, of course, this sounds fatuous: of course pain is relevant to animals and the morality of what is done to them. But it is not, I want to suggest, the central focus of such a discussion, in the way it is made to be in *Animal Liberation*.

It is easy to illustrate my point. Suppose one undertakes some medical experiment upon an animal that is entirely painless: is it wrong to undertake that experiment? If so, the infliction of pain will not establish the point. Indeed, I suspect that a great many experiments involving animals are either not painful or have the pain mitigated by analgesics: yet, the lives of the animals in question are used up by us. What entitles us to this use? Notice that the issue is not what entitles us to the painful use of animals; it is the question of what entitles us to the use of animal lives at all. Asking this question does not require us to ignore animal pain, but it could still be asked even if there were no pain present at all on the particular occasion. What entitles us to use up animal lives, even in a painless way? Of course, *Animal Liberation* is about factory farming, and there, it might be claimed, pain is certainly an issue. And so it is; anyone who thinks that factory farming can be done without pain has not looked closely at the issue. But is not the issue of use still present? What entitles us to farm animals, whether painfully or not? To object to their painful farming is not as such to object to their farming, and this is what seems to be at issue, when we speak of using up animal lives.

What Singer has done, and done effectively, is to focus upon the painful use of animals, without having addressed, so far as I can see, the more general question of their use in the first place. And the reason this more general question has not been addressed is that *Animal Liberation* does not really contain a discussion of the value of animal lives. This is the great issue that seems to lie at the center of the debate about animals and, I think, explains a good deal of the human response to that debate.[2]

As I write, there is widespread worry about the spread of avian flu to humans; as a result, there has taken place a mass culling of birds, geese, ducks, and so on. I will not comment on the barbaric manner in which these birds are often seized and killed; but what their killing seems to represent in human terms is that their lives, at the very least so far as the value of human lives is concerned, count for very little. During my many years in England, I gained evidence that the English truly were a nation of dog lovers; yet, the response to mad cow disease, on more than one occasion, has been a massive culling of herds, with roaring fires upon the downs with which to consume their bodies. One may or may not accept human health as the motivating factor behind this extensive killing; but there is no evidence that what humans think in the matter is that lives of value are being taken. The compensation promised farmers is for their financial losses, not the losses in valuable lives assessed in some non-commercial manner. It is this matter of the value of a life that really intrudes in the animal debates. Today, many billions of chickens are bred for food each year, and I do not think very many people attach value to the life of any particular chicken. To debeak them in a particular way can be very painful and should be stopped; but this does not show that humans are wrong to think that chickens' lives have little value.

It is not the painful use of animals that centrally is at issue but the use of their lives at all, and what most who reflect on the matter give as their rationale for using these lives turns upon their conception of how valuable those lives are. This strikes me as the central issue, for it encapsulates why we think we can use animals in the first place. To be sure, we think we can benefit from using them either as research subjects or as food; but the argument from benefit is connected to the comparative value of lives. I have set out my line of argument here in a

---

[2] See "Vivisection, Medicine, and Morals," *Journal of Medical Ethics* 9 (1983), pp. 94–104; "The Ethics of the Search for Benefits: Animal Experimentation in Medicine," in R. Gillon, ed., *Principles of Health Care Ethics* (New York: Wiley, 1993), pp. 1067–075; "The Ethics of Using Animals for Human Benefit," in T.B. Mepham, G.A. Tucker, J. Wiseman, eds., *Issues in Agricultural Ethics* (Nottingham: Nottingham University Press, 1995), pp. 335–344; "Medicine, Animal Experimentation, and the Moral Problem of Unfortunate Humans," in Ellen Frankel Paul, Fred D. Miller, Jr., Jeffrey Paul, eds., *Scientific Innovation, Philosophy, and Public Policy* (Cambridge: Cambridge University Press, 1996), pp. 181–211; "Justifying Animal Experimentation: The Starting Point," in Ellen Frankel Paul, Jeffrey Paul, eds., *Why Animal Experimentation Matters* (Newark: Transaction, 2001), pp. 197–214.

number of other places, so I shall be brief. I shall use medical research as my example, though I shall say something further about factory farming as well.

In my view, moral standing turns upon whether a creature is an experiential subject, with an unfolding series of experiences that, depending upon their quality, can make that creature's life go well or badly. Such a creature has a welfare that can be positively or negatively affected, depending upon what we do to it. With a welfare that can be enhanced or diminished, a creature has a quality of life. Few deny that Alzheimer's patients and the severely mentally-enfeebled are such creatures and so are beings with a quality of life that can be positively or negatively affected by what we do to them. Equally, however, few informed people today would deny that rodents, dogs, and chimps are such creatures. They are experiential subjects with a welfare and quality of life that our actions can push up or down, and this is so whether or not they are held to be moral agents.

I do not think, then, that the moral community is shaped by who or what is a moral agent. It is shaped by who or what is an experiential subject and so is a creature with a welfare and a quality of life that can be affected by what we do to it. Such creatures have biographical lives that consist in the unfolding of experiences. While there can be cases where I am uncertain whether a creature is an experiential one (for example, mere adaptation to environment will not suffice, since plants can do this), I do not think the usual experimental subjects are doubtful ones. Thus, I think that animals have moral standing and so are part of the moral community, and on exactly the same basis that we are.

What is it about animals that is supposed not to count, morally? The two most obvious candidates are their pains and sufferings and their lives. On my view, pain is pain, as much an evil for a chimp as for a child, and the pains of both chimp and child count, morally. I can see no moral difference between pouring scalding water on a dog and pouring it on a child: if it is wrong to do this in the case of the child, and most people would agree it is wrong just because of the pain the child feels (and not because of the relationship the child may bear to one), I can see no reason why it is not wrong to do this to the dog. Where pain is concerned, species makes no difference; what matters is that both are experiential creatures and that pain typically represents an evil in the lives of all such creatures, if not intrinsically, then certainly instrumentally, with respect to the quality of life. Of course, it may be true that adult humans suffer in more and different ways than animals, but that does not affect the point that animal pains are morally significant features of the world that we need to take into account in deciding how we are to act. I am not, therefore, a speciesist.

If, however, the pains and sufferings of animals count morally, it is hard to see why their lives do not. For one of the things that so concerns us about pain and suffering is how these things can seriously blight a life and diminish its quality, and this possibility exists in the cases of all those who can experience these things. Neither in ourselves nor in the "higher" animals do we take unabated agony to be an indication, all other things being equal, of a high or desirable quality of life. Living creatures with experiential lives are things with a welfare and a quality of life and so their lives have some value. The deliberate destruction of things of (some) value must be justified. This is what the appeal to benefit (actual and potential) is supposed to provide.

Animal life has some value, but it does not have the same value as normal adult human life. I accept a quality of life view of the value of a life, in which it is not life, but quality of life, that determines a life's value. Such views are a commonplace today, figuring as they do in virtually all of the literature out of medical and social ethics to do with the human condition. Experiential creatures generally, however, have a welfare and a quality of life, which can be increased or diminished by the quality of their experiences, including those which ensue as a result of our treatment of them. Their lives can go well or badly. It is not just humans of whom these things are true. So I think a quality of life view determines the value not only of human but also of animal life.

I think that the value of a life is a function of its quality, its quality of its richness, and its richness of its capacities or scope for enrichment. Richness of content, in other words, determines a life's quality and value, and a creature's capacities or scope for enrichment determines richness of content. Much more work in the animal case remains to be done. For a commitment to a quality of life view of the value of a life requires that we have access to the subjective experiences or inner lives of animals, that we be able, in terms appropriate to the species of animal in question, to determine to a reasonable degree how well or badly their lives are going. That we do this all the time, at least at some level, is clear. But if quality of life judgments are sometimes difficult in the human case, even though a good deal of the time they seem unproblematic at least in broad measure, it stands to reason that they can be difficult in the animal case.

I accept that the dog has subjective experiences, that those experiences determine its quality of life, and that the quality of its life determines that life's value. We use behavior and behavioral studies to give us access to the inner lives of animals, of course, and what we use in a rough and ready way to begin with we can come to use with more assurance as empirical studies of animals make more information available to us. Perhaps I will never know exactly what it would be like to be a dog, but I can come to know more and more in this regard, as we learn more about them and their responses to their environments.

If the value of a life depends upon its quality, and the quality of two animal lives can vary substantially, then those two lives will have a different value. This can be true even of animals of the same species, for example, two bears. But the really crucial point here is that most of us do not think animal life is as valuable as human life, and I think we are right to think this. The richness of normal adult human life vastly exceeds that of animals, and our capacities for enrichment, in all their variety and extent, vastly exceed anything that we know or associate with them. While it is true that the bear has a more acute sense of smell than we do, what we should need to think, in order to think the quality and value of its life approached the quality and value of ours, is that the bear's sense of smell confers on its life a quality that approximates the quality that all of our capacities for enrichment, along multi-dimensions that appear unavailable to the bear, confer on our lives. Some activities we share with the bear, but there are dimensions of enrichment in our lives—music, literature, science, reflection generally—that do not appear present in the lives of bears.

It can, of course, be objected that animal lives are every bit as rich as the lives of normal adult humans, that, for example, the differences in capacities and, therefore, in the depth, extent, and variety of experiences between a normal adult human and a rodent, dog, or chimp do not convey varying degrees of richness upon the respective lives. It can be hard to see what this claim of equal richness can be based upon. In the case of chimps, I am quite prepared to be convinced by more and more evidence that their similarities to ourselves run deeply and in ways reflected in their experiential lives. If this turns out to be true, and in creatures whose DNA is ninety-nine percent the same as our own it may well, claims of equal richness will be appropriate, and my view would then regard chimps the way it regards normal adult humans.

But what about rodents, rabbits, and chickens? In these cases, where as best we can tell there are wide discrepancies in capacities (and so experiences) with normal adult humans, we need something to anchor the claim of equal richness. That anchor is not provided by the claim that the present life is the only life that that animal or normal adult human has, so that the present life is as valuable to the animal as its present life is to the human. This only shows that a creature has to be alive in order to have a quality of life; it shows nothing about the quality of life a creature has.

My view, then, is that animals are members of the moral community because they are experiential creatures with a welfare or well-being that can be affected by what we do to them. They have moral standing. But they do not have the same moral standing as normal adult humans, because the value of the lives of the latter far exceed the value of the lives of the former. The truth is that not all creatures who have moral standing have the same moral standing.[3]

Obviously, much more needs to be said on these matters, even to begin to fill in a quality of life view of the value of a life. But the point with respect to Singer is, I think, made. What *Animal Liberation* is about is the evils of speciesism, but the position I am beginning to describe here is not speciesist though it allows animal experimentation. The reason normal adult human lives are more valuable than animal lives is not because of species but because of richness and scope for enrichment. I am not guilty, therefore, of discriminating in favor of humans because they are human. Indeed, my view plainly allows that the quality and therefore value of some human lives can fall well below that of some animal lives.

The position also permits meat-eating, at least if the argument from benefit can extend to that practice. But exactly what benefit, other than convenience and ease of access to protein, is at issue? Given that we do not need to eat meat in order to live, I think what drives the practice, if we leave aside all questions of ritual, religion, and the like, is the strong preference for the taste of meat. Notice, now, how important the issue of value of life can appear. For is it my view that the strong preference for the taste of meat, as it were, trumps the chicken's life? Singer's discussion of pain and cruelty does not impact this issue in the right way; for even though a certain practice of debeaking is cruel and ought to be stopped, nothing has been said as a result about the ordinary person's thought that the chicken's life is of little value. Is the person wrong to

---

[3] See note 2 and also "Moral Standing, The Value of Lives, and Speciesism," in H. LaFollette, ed., *Ethics in Practice* (Oxford: Blackwell, 1997), pp. 139–152; "Ethics, Animals, and Scientific Inquiry," in J.P. Gluck, T. DiPasquale, F. Barbara Orlans, eds., *Applied Ethics in Animal Research: Philosophy, Regulation, and Laboratory Applications* (West Lafayette: Purdue University Press, 2002), pp. 113–124; "On the Ethics of Using Animals for Human Transplants," in R. Sherlock, J.D. Morey, eds., *Ethical Issues in Biotechnology* (Lanham: Roman and Littlefield, 2002), pp. 291–96. See also my "Autonomy, Diminished Life, and the Threshold for Use," in J.S. Taylor, ed., *Personal Autonomy* (Cambridge: Cambridge University Press, 2004), pp. 183–200.

think this? What is the comparative value of, say, human and animal life? What are we to look at in the chicken's case to give us an accurate assessment as to the quality and value of its life? It is this issue of the comparative value of lives that is, I think, the central issue of the animal debates. Pain is, of course, relevant to this issue, for, as I say, it can blight and diminish a life; but it is by no means the only item. The very economy of argument in *Animal Liberation* through the focus on pain fails to engage the items that would enable us to grapple with the comparative value of animal life.[4]

If I am right, *Animal Liberation* is a treatise on the evils of speciesism. I agree that speciesism is to be rejected, together with, in Singer's famous expression, racism and sexism. But rejecting speciesism does not mean an end to all animal experimentation and meat-eating, which is what *Animal Liberation* has been taken to imply.

III. Preferences and Quality of Life

Without an account of quality and value of life, then, we cannot grapple with the comparative question. But to fuse welfarist, mental state, and preference satisfaction accounts of value, as Singer appears to do in *Practical Ethics*, leaves us not only with the problem of gaining access to the inner lives of animals but also that of understanding quality in terms of preferences and of trade-offs. There is a subjective-objective issue here over welfare.[4]

The discussion of Quality-Adjusted Life-Years (QALYs) can be thought to provide us, at least provisionally, with one way of going about this task. It is a way that many think utilitarians should find especially congenial, incorporating, as it does, (1) the idea of trade-offs not only between lives and segments of lives but also between lives and enhanced lives; (2) the idea of injecting scales or measures into discussions of quality of life; and (3) the idea of maximizing QALYs as the goal of efficient health-care expenditure.

In order that we may understand exactly what is meant by talk of quality-adjusting a life-year, discussion of QALYs takes place against a background of talk of quality of life, and one view of the quality of life is that it just is a matter of preference-satisfaction. In other words, at any particular moment, the quality of one's life is determined by the satisfaction of

---

[4] For an overview of how I think this debate goes, see my "Animals," in H. LaFollette, ed., *Oxford Handbook of Practical Ethics* (New York: Oxford University Press, 2003), pp. 151–186.

some preference set, though it is allowed that that set can vary in the course of time; so the claim is not that there is a unique preference set that constitutes one's quality of life eternally but rather that the satisfaction of some set or other of one's preferences constitutes one's quality of life.

This way of putting the matter at once gives rise to two obvious problems. First, if there is no unique set of preferences that constitutes one's quality of life throughout one's life, then one must indicate which preferences are to form the requisite set at any particular moment of one's life. This set cannot be the set of all preferences, since we arguably never find ourselves in a situation or condition in which absolutely all of our preferences are satisfied. Besides, some preferences are fleeting while others seem in no way connected so centrally with my life as to be ones in terms of which that life's quality is to be judged (for example, a preference for black socks). Second, if the preferences in terms of which the quality of my life is to be judged can vary in the course of my life, then the problem of isolating which preferences the satisfaction of which determines the quality of my life can be compounded by the fact that ones that previously were used to determine quality need not be the ones now to be used to determine quality. The mere fact that some preferences persist cannot be taken in and of itself to indicate which preferences are to form the set that matters, since a comparatively new preference can now come to form a central part of the set in question.

If the requisite set is not the set of all actual preferences, neither is it the set of all future preferences, and for the same reason. But there is also another problem that surfaces here, namely, that the formation of many QALY scales requires that people now indicate what their preferences would be (or what they would prefer in the future) if they had some illness or complaint that they do not now have. But even in the abstract we can see that, if the set of all my actual or future preferences is not the requisite set, then I need to provide, in addition to saying how on some scale I might quality rank my life in the future based on some preference or other I do not now have but will have, some indication of how I know that this preference I will have is one that is going to form part of the requisite set. If I cannot do this, then I cannot know now that the quality of my life will be affected in future through the satisfaction or frustration of the preference in question.

A shift to informed or corrected preferences does not help here, and for two reasons. First, suppose we agree that only informed preferences will comprise the requisite set that determines quality of life: must I satisfy the whole set of my informed preferences at any moment in order for the quality of my life to be determined or can it be determined from the satisfaction of just any one of them? The former seems entirely unrealistic: I rarely am in circumstances where I can satisfy all of my informed preferences, yet I often claim in other circumstances that my life is going well. The latter, however, seems false; that is, there seem to be all kinds of circumstances in which one of my informed desires is satisfied but where I claim that my life is going badly.

Thus, I can read Tolstoy and satisfy my informed preference for his novels over those of Mickey Spillane but claim the quality of my life is abysmally low, just as I can satisfy my informed preference to give up alcohol yet claim that the quality of my life is still abysmally low. Second, a shift to informed preferences works only if we suppose that, when I, as it were, correct my actual preferences in the required ways (for example, taking into account certain factual information, achieving a certain kind of detachment from the impulses of the moment), my informed preferences then become my actual preferences. That is, what the switch from actual to informed preferences is supposed to achieve is this: I use the demands of full information, detachment, rationality, and so forth, as filtering devices on my actual preferences in order to tell which ones I am to satisfy. My informed preferences become my actual preferences; they represent, when all the filtering has taken place, what I then come actually to prefer. This must be so; otherwise, the switch to informed preferences achieves nothing, since there would be no reason to believe a priori that I will actually prefer what informed preferences would tell me to prefer. Thus, even if we take informed preferences to form all or part of the set of preferences that will determine quality of life, it is informed preferences actualized that will be claimed to determine quality of life.

Not all informed preferences are actualized. I can have an informed preference to give up heroin but lack the willpower to give it up; here, too, a kind of weakness of will characterizes us. But then in this case what do we say about my life's quality? It might be judged negatively, because I cannot actualize my informed preference; yet I might judge my life subjectively to be very positive. How the animal case adjusts to this fact needs to be explained.

This brings us to what Parfit has called an objective list view: it might be that there are certain "objective" things true of me (for example, heroin is slowly impairing my judgment about how to satisfy as many of my most powerful desires as I can) that would seem a more reliable guide to my quality of life than either my subjective impression or my tallying up how many of my actualized informed desires are satisfied. Consider caloric intake: I might have a rosy view of my quality of life even though my caloric intake placed me on a rapidly declining slope of ill health and death. Whatever the truth of the objective list view, whatever the possibility of some element of it being reconciled with a preference view of the quality of life is not to the point here. For the preference theorist that is at issue is one who can only accommodate elements of the objective list view through the list helping him come to a realization of which are his informed preferences; that is, the list becomes something which goes into the filtering device of full information. Again, the theorist that concerns me is the one who maintains, now with the list helping to inform preferences, that quality of life is determined by some set of actualized preferences.

The above, then, I take to be obvious: if quality of life is to be determined by preferences, one is obliged to say which preferences form the requisite set. If it is some subset of all our actual preferences, then one must say both which preferences form that subset and in virtue of what those particular preferences form that subset. How does the fact of experiencing pain intersect with this discussion? Does it stand as an objective feature of life that always negatively affects the quality of life? Or can it be that a subjective account of welfare enables me to prefer a life with this amount of pain to a life with that amount of whatever?

A digression here may be of interest. John Harris has suggested that the plausibility of the notion of a QALY stems from the fact that, if a person could choose, they "would prefer a shorter healthier life to a longer period of survival in a state of severe discomfort and disability. The idea that any rational person would endorse this preference provides the moral and political force behind the QALY." Harris has his doubts about this notion, and so do I.

With QALYs, we are asked as individuals to quality rank lives and segments of lives with various disabilities and discomforts. As I indicated above, we are asked questions of a kind that inquire of us now what our preferences would be (or what we would prefer now for the future) if we had some illness or complaint that we presently do not have. Or, if we have the illness or complaint, we are asked about what sort of trade-off we would accept in return for the assurance that we would be cured or made well. In terms of Harris's question, we are asked how much shorter a healthy life we would prefer to a longer life with the illness or complaint in question, how many people with the illness or complaint would have to be saved to be preferred to saving a smaller number of healthy people, and so on.

What we are being asked, in other words, is for our preference now with respect to disability or discomfort states, on the assumption that we can say now how that disability or discomfort state would affect the quality of our lives. But unless we can specify which of our preferences form (or will form) the requisite set for determining quality of life, then we do not know now what to say about the effect of that disability or discomfort state on our quality of life or, indeed, whether our preference with respect to that state vis-à-vis healthy life will even be part of the set that determines quality of life. The point is not that a healthy person could not say here and now that, all other things being equal, they would prefer a shorter healthy life to a longer life with some disability; they could say this, but it is only a remark about their present preferences, given their present view of what the state of disability would be like. Put differently, I can rank some state of disability now with respect to my present preferences vis-à-vis healthy life, and I can report that I would think myself to be worse off (at least in broad terms) with the disability I would regard myself as having in the future, if my present preferences remained the same. Yet, it is precisely this, namely, the sameness of preference, that I cannot assume, since, if I actually have the disability state, it is unlikely that I will be using my preference for not having it as the touchstone of ranking.

The point: though one can know now that disability states are serious and generally affect adversely the lives which have them, that is not the same thing as knowing what one would trade-off in order to avoid having or being in that state. To know only that something generally affects lives adversely is not yet to be able to make trade-offs, since one does not know how much of one thing one will trade off for some amount of the other. Indeed, it is not even to know that one would trade off in the case in question for a healthier life. An analogy might be this: I might well not give up my home for any number of chocolate bars, but I might well give it up for an ocean cruise. To know that chocolate bars generally induce people to trade-offs is not to know that one will be so induced in the case in question. Similarly, to know that a certain disability state generally induces trade offs vis-à-vis a shorter, healthier life is not to know in any particular case that one will be so induced. Surely this applies to the fact that pain is part of a life?

When we quality rank different disability states, even if we use the same scale or measure for plotting the strength of our preferences for this state of healthy life versus that state of disability, we know that there are likely to be problems of interpersonal comparisons. For when you give your preference over immobility a ranking of 5 and I give mine a ranking of 5, and 5 indicates on the scale a state that which we wish strongly to avoid, there is no reason to conclude from similar rankings that the strengths of our preferences over immobility are identical. Put this way, though, it is clear why there has been a major effort at refining QALY scales; for the interpersonal problem can look like a matter of refinement of scale, a matter of being able to fine tune a scale that enables us more deftly to correlate position on the scale with actual strength of preference. Then, by plotting the responses of a great many people who are asked to quality rank lives with certain disabilities, one can hope to treat position on the scale as if were something more than merely compiled subjective responses of the state of each individual's own strength of preference with respect to the trade-off at issue.

The assumption that underlies the interpersonal case is that the intrapersonal case is possible; that is, we are supposed to proceed from the intrapersonal to the interpersonal, from how we would rank health states according to our own preferences to how they are ranked by other, rational persons. But the intrapersonal case is not all that settled. For in order to deal with the fact that I am concerned with my actual preferences now, so that I can rank my preference now for healthy life versus some state of disability, the best I can tell you now is what I think the effect on my life would be if I had the disability state; I can only tell you now what I would give up now in order to avoid that state. For me to say anything about the future, I must be able to project myself into the future and envisage what my preferences will be, but in circumstances now in which I cannot tell what I would be prepared to trade-off then. I try to see myself as a continuous self and so see some connection between myself now and my preferences and myself then and my preferences, but in circumstances in which I cannot tell now that the continuity of preference will be such so as to preserve intact then the trade-offs I would be prepared to make now.

Is this saying something other than that I cannot know now what I should be prepared to trade-off between healthy and disabled life until I come to have the disability in question? It is. I do not need to know what I would be prepared to trade-off to avoid a certain disability, in order to know now, say, that that disability adversely affects lives. For me to know what I would be prepared to trade off now I need to be able to see how much the one state positively enhances my quality of life and how much the other state negatively detracts from my quality of life. For me to know what I would be prepared to trade off in the future in this case I need to know (1) whether my preferences in the future remain as they are now and (2) whether the effect on my quality of life of the two states is the same then as it is now. But I need to know these things in circumstances in which I do not know what the subset of my preferences are or will be that determines quality of life. So what I have to do is to project myself into the future, imagine my preferences to be of a certain order (the same as or different from those at present), and suppose I can rank them in such a way that I can tell how much of one I would trade off for the other. The mere experiencing of pain does not show how this is to be done.

Intrapersonal comparisons involve different time-slices of the same individual. Which preferences go to make up a person's quality of life cannot be assumed to remain unchanging throughout all time-slices; indeed, it is obvious in all our cases that this is not true. Some things come to matter to us later in life; some things we come to appreciate more; some things we come to desire or want more because we see them as important to our lives. In all these cases, the preferences that go into forming the subset that determines quality of life have changed, and we need in different time-slices of ourselves to be aware of these changes, if we are to enhance the quality of our lives. What enhances the quality of our lives in one time-slice may not be what enhances the quality of our lives in another time-slice; what negatively impacts a life in one time-slice may not do so in another. Again, how does the mere experiencing of pain intersect the discussion?

To be asked, then, to rank preferences over different time-slices, in circumstances in which I do not know now what the subset of preferences will be that determine quality of life; to be asked to rank them by their differing effects on quality of life; it seems impossible to perform these tasks. I can only perform them if at least one item in the equation remains the same: if I can assume my preferences will be the same over the different time-slices, or if I can assume I know over both time-slices which subset of my preferences will be the ones that determine quality of life, then I can rank my preferences. Where both items are in doubt I cannot rank them in any way other than the general way I indicated, namely, by saying simply that generally, usually, a disability state adversely affects a life. But this does not permit the trade-offs that QALYs imply. It neither shows that I will trade off in this case nor indicates how much of one thing I will accept for the other. The reason I cannot answer the "how much" question is that I cannot tell, merely from the fact that a certain disability state adversely affects a life, that it will adversely affect my quality of life to a degree sufficient to generate a trade off in me, if it is unclear what subset of preferences determines quality of life and thereby unclear what effect preference-frustration will have on a life.

What has gone wrong? It is to assume that I can compare over two different time-slices of myself my preferences and their strength over health and certain disability states vis-à-vis their effect on the quality of my life, in circumstances where I can be sure neither that the preferences in one time slice will be those in the other nor that the subset of preferences that determines quality of life can be identified in either set. How then I can do intrapersonally what everyone agrees I have trouble doing interpersonally is unclear. Merely citing how a life looks does not solve the problem.

A preference theorist who makes quality of life out to be a matter of preference-satisfaction and who allows that our preferences can change over time and so allows that the subset of preferences which determine quality of life need not be the same throughout all time-slices of the person needs to indicate what exactly it is that makes intrapersonal comparisons between different time-slices what will constitute my quality of life? Unless my preferences remain the same, how can I know this? But we know our preferences do not remain the same. So how do I know this? Intrapersonal problems arise even without considering interpersonal ones, and even assuming, for the sake of argument, that some or all animals are persons.

IV. Vegetarianism as Protest

Finally, as I have said, the economy of argument of *Animal Liberation* is one of its most impressive features. The very power of the book is in part tied to this economy of argument and its focus upon animal pain. In part, also, however, the power of the book is tied to the alleged simplicity of remedy for the pains of animals that factory farming inflicts. If I understand matters correctly, there has been a change on Singer's part on this score. Specifically, I gather now that vegetarianism is held out as a form of protest against the ills that beset factory farming. Certainly, too, there is a form of dirty-hands argument that may be available to one here: if I abstain from meat, I do not dirty my hands with the particular practices that form the basis of my protest about the production of meat. More could be said. But there is a way in all this that vegetarianism appears to be optional, as something I might very well decide to adopt in order to register a protest but that I might decide not to adopt it as well.

This is not the picture that *Animal Liberation* conveys, I think, where a view of vegetarianism as protest seems to undercut the forcefulness of the case being made against factory farming. The picture there seems to be that giving up meat is the single, most causally efficacious thing one could do to affect breeding and killing methods. Notice that, with a protest, there is no claim that one is doing something that will be causally efficacious in stopping the practices to which one objects; in a sense, it does not matter whether one's protest is efficacious or not. One's abstention from meat or one's putting up a sign in one's window is still a protest. What makes *Animal Liberation* in part so powerful is that it seems to present the reader not only with the diagnosis of a great ill but also the most efficacious means of doing something about that ill. That means lies within one's grasp: abstain from eating meat (or, at least, factory-farmed meat). To be told that what one is now doing is protesting is not quite cohesive with this picture, since, as I say, protest and efficaciousness need not go hand in glove.

The claim that I can know now that my act of giving up meat will affect breeding and killing methods is not believable, either here on in the case of any very large market, where the preferences of millions of people are registered and work their way through the economic system. No single act, no single person's series of such acts, seem likely to have any affect in a market so large. This is so, I think, even if we concede that there are thresholds in these sorts of cases and that one's act of abstaining from meat is at or very near the threshold, since it seems unlikely a single act, rather than a substantial series of similar acts, are required to exceed the threshold and to bring on harmful threshold effects. I have discussed these sorts of problems elsewhere and will not pursue them here.

The really crucial point is the one about protest and effectiveness. A lot of people put a lot of time into trying to induce the fast food chains that, for example, buy chickens to change certain practices in the way chickens are bred for market. Change has begun to occur. Practices that used to characterize the breeding of veal calves have begun to change. Animal welfare legislation, especially in Britain, has begun to address not just the use of the great apes in scientific research but also the practices that characterize great feed lots. Environmental concerns have begun to put restrictions upon large factory farms that in part force them to change certain kinds of practices of disposing of waste products or of dissipating foul odors, and as this legislation begins to affect the economic condition of such farms the fact that we will take steps that impair that condition gets established.

Now the claim is not that everything is rosy; it is that change is occurring without vegetarianism having been required of us. But will it not help that some of us are vegetarians? Perhaps so. But this is not the forcefulness behind the causal efficacious point sketched above.

I cannot leave off the discussion of factory farming without noting the staggering number of animals involved (tens of billions), even compared to ten years ago, and the way markets have expanded. Not long ago, it was fashionable to write about emerging nations being in a position to make the following choice: they could choose to disperse the grain that they would need to import to feed animals to poor humans in their society. This is not the place to discuss famine and affluence, on which Singer has written powerfully, but I am not familiar with a single nation that has chosen this grain picture over the importation or raising of meat. Globally, the meat market, and the agri-business lobby generally, is today simply gigantic, and the picture of a man in the privacy of his study deciding to forego meat and thinking thereby that he was going to have an effect on this market is even less plausible than it was.

I do not have space here to address vivisection and the issues involved in trying to work the argument from benefit over the use of animals in medical and scientific research. I have written about these issues in a number of other places. But I have often wondered whether, if Singer were about to start over, he would choose factory farming as his target. For most of the literature that has occurred on factory farming since Singer wrote has been simply a record of more of the same, without the interesting variation in philosophical issue that seems to arise in the case of animal experimentation. And I am far from clear that the focus on pain would have begun to address this variation.

One final but crucial point, to do with the relationship of utilitarianism and vegetarianism. Today, I think it would be fair to say, Singer maintains that vegetarianism is by way of being a protest to the rearing and killing of animals for food. There are different ways of protesting something: one might put a sign in one's front lawn, or lobby strenuously for animal welfare legislation, or press fast food purveyors for changes in their rearing methods, or abstain from eating meat. One may, of course, do all of these things. But the impression that *Animal Liberation* leaves is that vegetarianism is required of one, precisely because it is causally the most effective means one can adopt to change rearing and killing methods. It is not morally optional but morally required, and the power of the book strikes me as very much tied to this point. But this causal point does not obtain, nor does it in any large market, where the causal efficacy of any particular act (of abstaining from meat) is simply too small to have the effect of changing methods. Nor is it likely to have this effect, even if one assumes that there are thresholds involved and that one's act of abstaining is at the very threshold; a number of other acts seem required at the threshold to produce this effect. One does not, it will be said, make matters worse. But the claim of *Animal Liberation*, I think, is that one can know now, by abstaining from meat, that one is taking the most effective step one can to reduce the horrors of factory farming that the book describes. This is not the same thing as registering a protest.

Reply to R.G. Frey

PETER SINGER

Beyond Speciesism and Absolutism

Ray Frey is not a speciesist. He agrees that speciesism is to be rejected, along with racism and sexism. But he believes that "rejecting speciesism does not mean an end to all animal experimentation and meat-eating, which is what *Animal Liberation* has been taken to imply." As we shall see, in this Frey is correct, as long as we place sufficient emphasis on the word "all" which precedes "animal experimentation and meat-eating."

Frey begins by observing that although members of the public interested in issues of ethics and animals frequently identify the animal movement with my work, and especially with *Animal Liberation,* most of the animal movement's supporters are not "Singerites." Since I know of no surveys on this matter, I do not know on what basis Frey would rest his claim that this is true of "most" of the animal movement's supporters. What I share with the animal movement is opposition to speciesism. But it is certainly true that some of the animal movement supporters, while radical about animals, are more conventional about human rights. They hold that all humans have the same inviolable rights, irrespective of their intellectual abilities or quality of life. So when these animal advocates become persuaded that we should not discriminate against nonhuman animals solely because they are not members of our species, they simply include animals under the protection of the same set of rights that they believe humans have. They therefore regard animals as having rights that we are not justified in violating, even for the sake of overwhelming benefits. Accordingly, they reject all painful or lethal experiments on animals. Even if, hypothetically, an experiment on a hundred monkeys would enable us to find a cure for a major disease like HIV/AIDS, saving millions of lives and preventing untold suffering and distress, they would not consider it justifiable to perform the experiment.

This is not my position. Some years ago, Frey had a brave exchange with Sir William Paton, a prominent animal experimenter. Frey defended experiments on animals because of the benefits he believes they bring, but added that he could not conceive of any way of making such a defense consistent, except to allow that, at least in principle, experiments on severely intellectually disabled human beings with a quality of life no higher than that of nonhuman animals can also be justified.[5] His honesty in saying this probably cost Frey many well-paid speaking invitations at conferences in the biomedical sciences. Frey's line here is similar to that which I defended in *Animal Liberation,* when I wrote that "in extreme circumstances, such absolutist answers always break down" and added that "if a single experiment could cure a disease like leukemia, that experiment would be justifiable." I went on to suggest that a test for whether a proposed experiment on animals is justifiable, on nonspeciesist grounds, is whether the experimenter would be prepared to carry out the experiment on human beings at a similar mental level—say, those born with irreversible brain damage. There might be cases, I added, in which it is right to do such an experiment, but, as the extensive accounts of experiments performed on animals in *Animal Liberation* made clear, such cases would be a very small proportion of the experiments that are performed on animals.[6] Taken as a whole, the institutional practice of treating animals as mere tools for research is not defensible.

In a 2006 British television documentary called "Monkeys, Rats and Me: Animal Testing," I upset some animal rights advocates by a comment I made about some experiments on monkeys. Tipu Aziz, an Oxford neurosurgeon who conducts experiments on monkeys, told me that his experiments, and that of others in his group, had involved about a hundred monkeys, and had led to significant improvements for forty thousand people with Parkinson's Disease. I responded that, if this was true, and there was no other way of achieving those results, the research could be justifiable. The exchange was widely publicized in the British press, under headlines like "Father of Animal Activism Backs Monkey Testing" and as a result I received a lot of critical or puzzled emails

---

[5] R.G. Frey and Sir William Paton, "Vivisection, Morals, and Medicine: An Exchange," *Journal of Medical Ethics* 9:2, pp. 94–97, reprinted in Tom Regan and Peter Singer, *Animal Rights and Human Obligations* (Englewood Cliffs: Prentice-Hall, 1989), pp. 223–236.

[6] *Animal Liberation* (New York: A New York Review Book, 1990), p. 85.

from people in the animal movement.[7] One British animal group decided that it no longer wished me to be its patron. But my statements were consistent with what I had written many years earlier in *Animal Liberation.*

Of course, it is possible to dispute the claims Aziz made. Some animal advocates assert that nothing of benefit to humans is ever learned through animal experimentation. This would make the case against animal experimentation much easier, but put in such an unqualified form, it strikes me as wishful thinking. It is true that there are differences between humans and other animals, and there are many instances in which drugs that work safely and effectively on other animals prove harmful to humans, and vice versa. But since we are animals, and our bodies show this in numerous ways, it is plausible to suppose that we can learn some things about how our bodies work by experimenting on animals.

When it comes to eating animals, rather than experimenting on them, the dilemma is less acute because—at least for those of us living in developed societies with a wide choice of foods to eat—eating animals does not save lives or relieve great suffering. But again, as a utilitarian, I cannot hold that being a vegetarian or vegan is a moral absolute. As Jim Mason and I indicated in *The Ethics of What We Eat*, there are circumstances in which eating meat does no harm to animals. Dumpster diving—retrieving food that has been thrown out by supermarkets, even though it has not spoiled or been contaminated in any way—is one option, because eating food that will otherwise end up as landfill has no impact on encouraging further production of that food.[8] Eating fresh roadkill is another example.

Why We Should Be Vegetarian

Frey suggests that I have changed my position on vegetarianism:

> If I understand matters correctly, there has been a change on Singer's part on this score. Specifically, I gather now that vegetarianism is held out as a form of protest against the ills that beset factory farming. . . . This is not the

---

[7] Gareth Walsh, "Father of Animal Activism Backs Monkey Testing," *Sunday Times* (November 26th, 2006); see also "Animal Guru Gives Tests His Blessing," *Observer* (November 26th, 2006).

[8] Peter Singer and Jim Mason, *The Ethics of What We Eat* (New York: Rodale, 2007). This book was first published in the US under the title *The Way We Eat: Why Our Food Choices Matter.*

picture that *Animal Liberation* conveys, I think, where a view of vegetarianism as protest seems to undercut the forcefulness of the case being made against factory farming. The picture there seems to be that giving up meat is the single, most causally efficacious thing one could do to affect breeding and killing methods. Notice that, with a protest, there is no claim that one is doing something that will be causally efficacious in stopping the practices to which one objects; in a sense, it does not matter whether one's protest is efficacious or not.

There has been no change in my views here. Consider the following passage from *Animal Liberation* in which I argue for vegetarianism:

> Becoming a vegetarian is the most practical and effective step one can take toward ending both the killing of nonhuman animals and the infliction of suffering upon them. . . . The purchase of the corpses of the animals they rear is the only support the factory farmers ask from the public. They will use intensive methods as long as they continue to receive this support; they will have the resources needed to fight reform politically; and they will be able to defend themselves against criticism with the reply that they are only providing the public with what it wants.
>
> Hence the need for each one of us to stop buying the products of modern animal farming—even if we are not convinced that it would be wrong to eat animals that have lived pleasantly and died painlessly. Vegetarianism is a form of boycott.[9]

Since a boycott is usually a form of protest, I don't see any difference between this passage and the view that Frey thinks I "now" hold, that "vegetarianism is held out as a form of protest against the ills that beset factory farming." Frey must also know that as a utilitarian, it cannot be my view that "it does not matter whether one's protest is efficacious or not." The whole point of protesting, for utilitarians, is to change the conditions against which the protest is directed.

Frey is rosy-eyed when he writes that because of changes made by fast food manufacturers over the last ten years, "many of the more egregious practices have been altered, drastically changed, or eliminated." In fact, the only changes made by fast food corporations in this area in the United States are improvements in humane slaughter for mammals (but not for poultry, numerically by far the largest category), an increase of about twenty-two square inches in the amount of space allocated to laying hens, and a ban on forcing hens to molt by starving them for two

---

[9] *Animal Liberation* (London: Cape, 1976), pp. 173–75. The wording varies slightly in the second edition, but the main point is unchanged.

weeks. Even with more space, laying hens continue to be crowded into cages so small that they could not stretch their wings even if they were alone in the cage—but they must share the cages with four or five other hens. They have the ends of their beaks cut off so that they will not kill each other under these crowded conditions. Pregnant sows and veal calves are still confined in stalls or crates so narrow that they cannot turn around or lie down with their limbs stretched out, and so short that they cannot take even a few paces. (As I was writing this response to Frey, some significant progress in the struggle against "the more egregious practices" did occur: I mention these changes in my response to Harry Gensler. Nevertheless, across most of the United States, and particularly in the states which have the largest numbers of farm animals, very little has changed yet.) Chickens raised for their meat are kept in flocks of more than twenty thousand birds, crowded into huge sheds in an atmosphere heavy with ammonia from their droppings, bred to grow so fast that their legs often collapse under them, leaving them to die from thirst or hunger. The parents of these fast-growing chickens have to be kept permanently hungry, because they have been bred to have such a voracious appetite that, if allowed to eat freely, they would become too obese to breed.

In the European Union, reforms have gone further, and individual crates for veal calves are now banned. Crates for pregnant sows and the standard bare wire cages for laying hens are also being phased out. These changes have come about as a result of political pressure, not through fast food producers. The biggest victory for the American animal movement in many decades, the overwhelming support given by Californian voters in November 2008 to an initiative that requires all farm animals to have room to turn around and stretch their limbs freely, was also the result of hard work by many thousands of animal welfare activists, and had no support from fast food producers.

Frey is, however, right to object that I can't prove that becoming a vegetarian is the *most* effective step one can take to reduce animal suffering. No doubt much depends on your personal position. If you can afford to give a million dollars to a campaign against factory farming, that could be more effective than a personal decision to become a vegetarian or vegan. But why not do both? It's not as if there is any conflict between them. Moreover, since eating is something we often do in company, it is not only the personal impact one may have in reducing the demand for meat that must be taken into account, but also the influence one may have on others. As I have recounted in the autobiographical essay in this volume, it was exactly that form of influence that led me to become a vegetarian. Frey's reference to "a man in the privacy of his study deciding to forego meat" is odd. What matters is not where the man makes the decision to forego meat, but where he carries out that decision. Presumably he is not going to continue to eat, for the rest of his days, in the privacy of his study.

One possible strategy for bringing about an improvement in the lives of animals without becoming a vegetarian or vegan is to become a "conscientious omnivore." Conscientious omnivores boycott the products of factory farming, but eat animal products when they can be obtained from farms that give their animals decent lives and generally treat them well. Jim Mason and I discuss this position in *The Ethics of What We Eat,* and consider a variety of factual questions regarding the likely impact of such a diet on animals and the environment. I will not repeat that material here, beyond quoting our conclusion, which perhaps is not as hard-line about being a vegetarian or vegan as Frey may have expected:

> Where does all this leave the diet of conscientious omnivores? Perhaps it's not, all things considered, the best possible diet, but the moral distance between the food choices made by conscientious omnivores and those made by most of the population is so great that it seems more appropriate to praise the conscientious omnivores for how far they have come, rather than to criticize them for not having gone further.[10]

Frey wonders if, were I starting afresh to write about issues concerning animals, I would have chosen factory farming as my target. I would choose it again today, because of its overwhelming practical importance. Here's one way of grasping the magnitude of animal suffering it involves: the number of animals used in research in the United States each year is approximately the population of Texas. The number of animals raised and killed for food in the United States each year is about one and a half times the population of the world. It may be true that, as Frey suggests, using animals in research raises more philosophically challenging questions; but utilitarian philosophers should be thinking about what will do the most to make the world a better place.

Comparing Utilities

The remaining issue that Frey raises, in his Section III, is that of interpersonal comparisons of utility. This is a problem for all utilitarians,

---

[10] *The Way We Eat*, p. 258.

Frey included, and indeed for anyone, utilitarian or not, who thinks that the impact of our actions on the welfare of others is morally relevant. That must include virtually everyone who thinks about ethics at all, for even those who base their ethics on rules must provide some ethical guidance in circumstances in which we have to choose between options which observe all the relevant ethical rules but have varying impacts on the welfare of different people. Indeed, Frey's point is that even intrapersonal comparisons of utility run into problems when they compare different time slices of the same individual, given that the individual's preferences may have changed between the two time-slices. But we all make comparisons between the ways in which different choices will satisfy our preferences at different times of our lives, so this problem is universal. On the one hand, this makes the problem more difficult still; on the other, it absolves me of the need to give a specific answer, because if my view is in trouble on this point, I'm in good company.

Since this discussion of interpersonal comparisons is a section in an article entitled "Justifying Animal Use" it seems reasonable to suppose that Frey intends it to contribute to the discussion of our uses of animals. It is, however, difficult to see what that contribution might be. Interpersonal comparisons of utility between members of different species are different in degree, but not in kind, to interpersonal comparisons between member of our own species. The problem always is to know what it is like to be another sentient being. If Jack and Jill are one-year-old human infants, and Jack cries more often and more loudly when he falls over than Jill does, does that mean that Jack feels more pain when he falls, or that he expresses his feelings more vigorously? Most parents wish they knew, but it is hard to be sure. Similarly, it is very difficult to know whether a cow whose calf is taken away shortly after birth—as all calves are in the dairy industry—suffers less than a human mother would experience if her child were taken away from her. For one view on that matter, here is a quote from Temple Grandin, a livestock consultant whose work depends on her ability to put herself in the position of animals. The neurologist Oliver Sachs was with Grandin on a farm visit:

> We saw one cow outside the stockade, roaming, looking for her calf, and bellowing. "That's not a happy cow," Temple said. "That's one sad, unhappy, upset cow. She wants her baby. Bellowing for it, hunting for it. She'll forget for a while, then start again. It's like grieving, mourning—not much written about it. People don't like to allow them thoughts or feelings."[11]

---

[11] Oliver Sacks, *An Anthropologist on Mars* (New York: Knopf, 1995), p. 267.

Is Grandin right? How much like human grieving and mourning is the cow's distress? We don't really have any way of answering that question at present. Frey's discussion of the quality-adjusted life-year, or QALY, approach doesn't touch on this problem, for that approach depends on asking people complicated questions about their preferences in hypothetical situations. No one has yet worked out how to ask a cow such questions. Marion Stamp Dawkins and other scientists have, however, developed techniques of "asking" animals what they prefer by giving them choices, and then seeing how hard they will work—for example, by repeatedly pressing a lever, or pecking a disk—in order to get to their preferred option.[12] That is, perhaps, as close as we can get to asking animals the kind of questions that we ask normal human beings in order to assess the quality of their lives.

---

[12] Marian Stamp Dawkins, "The Scientific Basis for Assessing Suffering in Animals," in Peter Singer, ed., *In Defense of Animals: The Second Wave* (Oxford: Blackwell, 2006), pp. 26–39; Marian Stamp Dawkins, *Animal Suffering: The Science of Animal Welfare* (London: Chapman and Hall, 1980).

II

THE SANCTITY
OF LIFE

3

Singer on Abortion and Infanticide

DON MARQUIS

The Sanctity of Human Life

Human beings, such as you and I, possess at least one property that makes killing us *distinctively* wrong or *seriously* wrong. Peter Singer believes that because infants have no such property infanticide is not always wrong. *No* infant is *seriously wronged* by being killed, although if an infant is wanted by others, then infanticide could wrong *others*. Normal infants will almost always be wanted. Some handicapped infants are unwanted. In such cases killing them is morally permissible (*Practical Ethics*, pp. 122–26). This view has engendered great interest and great hostility.[1]

Singer's views on infanticide are implied by his defense of abortion choice. Like infants, no fetus possesses a property that could make killing her seriously wrong (*Practical Ethics*, Chapter 4). This view, when combined with the liberty rights of pregnant women, underwrites abortion choice.

---

[1] Singer's views on these matters can be found in *Practical Ethics* (Cambridge: Cambridge University Press, 1979); *Should the Baby Live?* (with Helga Kuhse, Oxford: Oxford University Press, 1985); "Individuals, Humans and Persons: The Issue of Moral Status" (with Helga Kuhse) and "IVF Technology and the Argument from Potential" (with Karen Dawson) in Peter Singer, Helga Kuhse, Stephen Buckle, Karen Dawson and Pascal Kasimba, eds., *Embryo Experimentation* (Cambridge: Cambridge University Press, 1990); and *Rethinking Life and Death* (New York: St. Martin's Press, 1994).

Singer's views on abortion and infanticide are corollaries of his general account of the wrongness of killing. Singer has devoted many pages to arguments against the doctrine of the sanctity of human life (*Practical Ethics*, pp. 72–78; *Should the Baby Live?*, Chapter 6; *Rethinking Life and Death*). Here is an account of the sanctity of life doctrine that is as plausible as I can make it. Individuals like us have certain fundamental rights, such as the right to life, the right to liberty and the right to have at least a minimal opportunity to flourish. Some have believed that we have these rights in virtue of being male, or in virtue of being Caucasian, or in virtue of belonging (or not belonging) to a certain religion, or in virtue of our ethnicity. In developed countries virtually everyone now thinks that such beliefs about our fundamental rights are incorrect. Instead there is widespread agreement that we possess these fundamental human rights in virtue of our humanity. Thus we call these rights 'human rights' or 'basic human rights'. The most basic human right is the right to life, for without life no other human endeavor is possible. Therefore, unless exceptional circumstances obtain, it is wrong to kill a human being, just because she is human. This doctrine implies that abortion is wrong, for human fetuses are organisms that are human. It also implies that infanticide is wrong.

Peter Singer has rejected this sanctity of human life doctrine for two main reasons. First, he argues that it has implausible consequences. Suppose we hold the view that if humans have the right to life, then dependent human beings also have the right to a reasonable degree of care necessary to sustain their lives. The doctrine of the sanctity of human life plus this reasonable view seems to entail that we have an obligation to provide medical care to preserve the lives of anencephalic newborns (babies born without the neurological capacity for consciousness) and individuals in a persistent vegetative state (humans who have lost irreversibly the neurological capacity for consciousness). These consequences are very implausible. Indeed, they are so implausible that, as Singer has pointed out, even many of those who *affirm* the sanctity of human life doctrine are unwilling to accept them (see *Should the Baby Live?*, Chapter 2, *Rethinking Life and Death*, Chapter 6). Accordingly, the doctrine of the sanctity of human life is vulnerable to clear counterexamples.

Second, Singer argues that the doctrine of the sanctity of human life rests upon a morally irrelevant consideration. Just as we reject sexism because it rests on a biological, but not morally relevant, characteristic, and just as we reject racism because it rests on a biological, but not morally relevant, characteristic, we should reject the doctrine of the sanctity of human life because it rests on a biological, but not obviously morally relevant, characteristic (*Practical Ethics*, pp. 48–57, 76–78). What counts from a moral point of view are characteristics that we often regard as exemplifying being "fully human." These characteristics are mental characteristics that are typically associated with biological humanity. They are not identical to the property of being biologically human. Not all individuals who are biologically human possess these mental characteristics, and, for all we know, not all individuals who possess these mental characteristics are biologically human.

Singer's rejection of the doctrine of the sanctity of human life is clearly correct. I believe that Singer is also correct about three additional issues that many believe important for resolving the abortion issue. First, Singer believes that religious concerns are irrelevant to resolving the abortion debate. If the view that abortion is wrong were based on religious considerations, then there would be no sound basis for the view that abortion is wrong, (*Practical Ethics*, pp. 3–4). Second, Singer believes that the morality of abortion cannot be based solely upon the liberty right of a pregnant woman (*Practical Ethics*, pp. 113–16; *Rethinking Life and Death*, p. 85). If fetuses possess a property in virtue of which it is seriously presumptively wrong to kill them, then a pregnant woman's interests (except, perhaps, in extreme cases) are not sufficient to justify abortion. Third, Singer believes that the views that a human being acquires the right to life at viability or at quickening are unsound (*Practical Ethics*, Chapter 6). Discussion of these issues would only be tedious.

Why Killing Is Wrong

Because the doctrine of the sanctity of human life is clearly false a replacement for it is needed. The general idea behind Singer's account of the wrongness of killing is straightforward. Plainly it is wrong to end the life of a standard human being. Plainly it is not wrong to end the life of a cabbage (*Practical Ethics*, p. 72; *Embryo Experimentation*, p. 70). Singer holds that the kinds of characteristics that seem to justify this difference are what Joseph Fletcher called "indicators of humanhood." These indicators include self-awareness, self-control, a sense of the future, a sense of the past, the capacity to relate to others, concern for others, communication, and curiosity (*Practical Ethics*, p. 75). All these characteristics are mental (*Practical Ethics*, p. 76). Singer wishes to call individuals who possess some or all of these characteristics 'persons'. He believes that the mental characteristics central to being a person are rationality and self-consciousness.

Fetuses are not persons. Accordingly, an account of the wrongness of killing in terms of persons rather than in terms of human beings will underwrite the permissibility of abortion. What Singer needs, as he realizes, is some general account of the wrongness of killing that explains why some mental characteristics are morally significant and non-mental biological characteristics are not. In the absence of such an account, justifying the wrongness of killing in terms of being a person is as arbitrary as a justification in terms of being a human being. Singer has mentioned four accounts of what it is about persons that makes killing them seriously wrong.

Respect for Autonomy

Singer has suggested that the wrongness of killing may be based upon our obligation to respect the autonomy of others. If this is so, then since fetuses lack autonomy, in the absence of some other reason why killing a fetus is wrong, abortion choice is morally permissible.

That Singer should offer this account is odd. The obligation to respect autonomy is rightfully regarded as a Kantian consideration. Kant's antipathy to utilitarianism is well-known. Singer is not a follower of Kant. His sympathies with utilitarianism are well-known (*Practical Ethics*, pp. 2–3).

However, let us waive these oddities. We should judge such an account a success only if the central notion to which it appeals is clear. Kant's own account of autonomy is so much a part of his general moral philosophy that it is hard to endorse Kant's respect for autonomy without endorsing much, at least, of his anti-utilitarian moral philosophy. According to Kant, to respect our autonomy is to respect the moral law within us, which is to respect our free nature. Our free nature is inseparable from our independence of our phenomenal selves. We know this, to the extent that we do, because only if this is true is morality possible. Happily, what Kant meant by autonomy is not important for our purposes. What we want to know is whether or not the wrongness of killing can be based on autonomy as Singer understands it, where we do not fill in any blanks with Kantian doctrine.

According to Singer "By 'autonomy' is meant the capacity to choose, to make and act on one's own decisions" (*Practical Ethics*, p. 83). However, he clearly means that autonomous beings must have the ability to "consider the alternatives open to them" (*Practical Ethics*, p. 83). Furthermore, Singer's discussion makes clear that respecting autonomy means, not only respecting a person's *capacity* to choose, but also respecting the *actual* choices that a person with such capacities makes.

The doctrine of respect for autonomy as Singer articulates it is far too broad. Imagine you are walking your dog. You have some evidence that your dog is under control off leash. Your dog is off leash. Your dog contemplates a squirrel. Your dog decides to chase the squirrel. Your dog's decisions are autonomous by Singer's criteria. Singer's version of the duty to respect autonomy appears to make leash laws immoral. Even taking into account Singer's well-known concern for animals, this clearly won't do.

Can this problem be fixed by limiting our respect for autonomy to our respect for rational choices? Let us waive the difficult question of whether a dog's choices are rational. (Clearly there is some sense of 'rational' in which they are.) The problem is that if we adopt a sense of 'rational' which is such that the dog's choices are not rational, we may have a sense of 'rational' in which the choices of a five year old are not rational. Another difficulty with this move is that often in bioethics respecting autonomy comes to no more than respecting the choices of others even if they are irrational. I shall not explore Singer's autonomy account of the wrongness of killing further. He has not said enough about it so that it can be an adequate basis for the distinctive wrongness of killing persons.

Classical Utilitarianism

Singer's discussion of the classical utilitarian defense of the special wrong of killing persons is somewhat indecisive. A utilitarian might hold that killing an individual is wrong because it deprives that *individual* of future happiness. The trouble with this explanation, as Singer seems to recognize (PE,p. 79), is that it does not explain why killing a person is worse than killing a fetus. Of course, a utilitarian would hold that because killing a person deprives an individual of future happiness, there is less overall happiness in *the world* than there would have been otherwise. That is what, for the classical utilitarian, makes the act of killing wrong in the final analysis. Singer realizes that such utilitarian accounts of the wrongness of killing generate well-known paradoxes. For one thing, if it is wrong to deprive the world of future happiness by killing a person, then presumably it is wrong to deprive the world of future happiness by deliberately abstaining from creating a person. This would make the Old Testament obligation to go forth and multiply more than a quaint saying (*Practical Ethics*, pp. 85–88).

Singer considers a strategy for turning this objection. If I believe that killing persons is morally permissible, then I shall be unhappy, for I shall be worried about being killed myself. Since fetuses cannot worry, abortion will not make them unhappy. Hence, killing persons is especially wrong (*Practical Ethics*, p. 79).

Singer admits that "There is, of course, something odd about objecting to murder, not because of the wrong done to the victim, but because of the effect on others. One has to be a tough-minded classical utilitarian to be untroubled by this oddness" (*Practical Ethics*, p. 79). This suggests that Singer is not intent on going to the wall with this justification for the special wrongness of killing persons. What is wanted is a victim-centered account of this distinctive wrongness.

Preference Utilitarianism

Singer has reasons for favoring a preference utilitarian account of the wrongness of killing persons (*Practical Ethics*, pp. 80–81). Only persons see themselves as entities with a future and therefore, only persons can prefer that they continue to exist. If wrongful action consists in frustrating the preferences of others, then, *ceteris paribus*, it will be wrong to kill persons and not wrong to kill non-persons. Hence (apparently), a preference utilitarian can offer a morally relevant account of why killing persons is wrong, why not creating persons is not wrong, and why a woman's choice to end the life of her fetus is also not wrong.

Singer has noted a problem with this account. Preference utilitarianism seems to entail that ending my existence is not wrong if my preference to continue to exist is outweighed by the preferences of others that I not continue to exist. Not only preference utilitarianism is subject to this difficulty. The difficulty concerns the fact that utilitarianism "does not take seriously the distinction between persons."[2]

Why Persons Have a Right to Life

Nevertheless, the view that a person has the right to life in virtue of her preference for continuing to exist is Singer's favored account of the wrongness of killing. Singer is, like many utilitarians, suspicious of

---

[2] John Rawls, *A Theory of Justice* (Cambridge, Harvard University Press, 1971) Chapter 1, section 5.

rights talk.[3] When Singer says that an individual has a right to life he means no more than it would be seriously wrong, *ceteris paribus,* to kill that individual. Singer has endorsed Michael Tooley's account of this preference-based view (*Should the Baby Live?*, pp. 120–131; *Practical Ethics*, p. 83).[4] The basic idea behind Tooley's view is that, in general, to violate someone's right to something is to frustrate her desire for that thing. To violate someone's right to life is to frustrate her desire to continue to live. One can have a desire for one's continued existence only if one possesses a concept of one's self as a continuing subject of experience. No fetus has a concept of herself as continuing subject of experience. Therefore, no fetus desires to continue to exist. It follows that no fetus has the right to life. Because there is no basis for a fetal right to life that could override a woman's right to control her body, abortion is morally permissible. Singer has noted some apparent difficulties with Tooley's view. Presumably a person who is asleep or temporarily unconscious is not presently contemplating her future existence, much less desiring it (*Practical Ethics*, p. 82). Surely a theory that permits killing sleeping people or temporarily unconscious people is subject to a far greater difficulty than a sanctity of life theory that obligates us to keep alive anencephalics and patients in persistent vegetative state.

However, David Boonin has offered a desire account of the wrongness of killing that appears to deal successfully with these difficulties.[5] When I wake up in the morning, I do not have to learn everything that I believed the day before. I seem to have almost all of the same beliefs, concepts, and desires that I had yesterday. This suggests that these mental items were retained in some form or other while I was asleep. Accordingly when I was asleep I possessed, in some way, the concept of myself as the continuing subject of experience. When I was asleep in some clear sense I desired to live. Boonin calls these desires dispositional, as opposed to occurrent.[6] A similar analysis for temporarily unconscious individuals seems reasonable. Accordingly, the Tooley-Singer account of the right to life can be provided with resources for dealing with sleeping persons and with temporarily unconscious individuals.

---

[3] Famously Jeremy Bentham, *Rights, Representation, and Reform: Nonsense upon Stilts and Other Writings on the French Revolution*, edited by Philip Schofield, Catherine Pease-Watkin, and Cyprian Blamires (Oxford: Clarendon Press, 2002).

[4] Michael Tooley, "Abortion and Infanticide," *Philosophy and Public Affairs* 2:1 (1972), pp. 37–65.

[5] Singer has indicated in personal correspondence that he endorses Boonin's account.

[6] David Boonin, *A Defense of Abortion* (Cambridge: Cambridge University Press, 2003), pp. 64–69.

Infanticide

Singer's defense of abortion has implications for infanticide. An infant, like the fetus it was, lacks any of the properties on which its right to life could be based. In particular, because it lacks a concept of itself as a continuing subject of experience, it lacks the desire to continue to exist. Because spatial location is morally irrelevant, the fact that this human being is no longer located inside its mother lacks moral importance (*Practical Ethics*, pp. 123–26).

Singer has suggested that this view is "much less shocking" than it may seem (*Should the Baby Live?*, p. 135). He points out that women will, in general, have far stronger reasons for having abortions than for killing their infants after they are delivered. Although Singer's discussion here is not entirely clear, his view seems to be that if a pregnant woman does not want her child at all, then she will have an abortion. If she does not want her infant, then this will generally be because the infant is handicapped. If the infant has prospects for a valuable and happy life, then its parents will want to keep it; otherwise, the fetus it was would have been aborted. Hence, in neither case will infanticide occur and the potential of an infant herself can be a reason against killing her. Nevertheless, Singer still holds that no infant has the right to life. And he has suggested that perhaps even two- and three-year-olds may lack the concept necessary for having this right (*Practical Ethics*, p. 124).

On the one hand, it is important to be clear that Singer does not hold the view that it is permissible to kill infants who are wanted, either by their parents, or by others. To kill such a child would be to harm either her parents or others (*Should the Baby Live?*, p. 135). On the other hand, Singer refers, with apparent approval, to societies in which infanticide has been practiced in the past on a rather large scale (*Practical Ethics*, p. 125; *Should the Baby Live?*, Chapter 5). Furthermore, if a society confronted a serious overpopulation problem, it seems reasonable to think that Singer would have difficulty finding reasons for rejecting a social policy of widespread infanticide.

Should Singer's views on infanticide be rejected on the ground that they are so contrary to common moral judgments? In the first place, it is not entirely clear that they *are* contrary to common moral judgments. In some neo-natal intensive care units, parents of very low birth weight newborns have the right to decide whether their children should be kept alive. Singer has argued—persuasively, in my view—that there is no principled way to ban overt infanticide if this right is accepted (*Should the Baby Live?*, Chapter 4). In the second place this question does not have to be answered, for there are other far more compelling considerations that bear on Singer's account of the moral permissibility of ending early human life.

Why the Tooley-Singer Theory Is Unsatisfactory

Some counterexamples to the Tooley-Singer account of the wrongness of killing cannot be got around as easily as the apparent counterexamples already mentioned. Consider some examples that Tooley himself mentioned. Consider the case of a woman suffering from depression who says that she wishes she were dead. Consider the case of an individual who "may permit someone to kill him because he had been convinced that if he allows himself to be sacrificed to the gods he will be gloriously rewarded in a life to come."[7] Apparently, the Tooley-Singer account of the wrongness of killing entails that it is morally permissible to kill any of these individuals. Since it is not morally permissible to kill any of these individuals, the Tooley-Singer account is wrong.

These problems are very serious. The Tooley-Singer account of the wrongness of killing does not account for the wrongness of killing most of the people in this world who are suicidal. Indeed, it does not account for the wrongness of killing the far greater number of people who suffer from depression and who do not desire to go on living, but who, because of their depression, cannot work up the incentive to kill themselves.

The problems with the Tooley-Singer account don't end here. Tooley's account of the wrongness of killing is based upon a more general account of rights in which rights are based on desires. Consider a two year old. Presumably she has a right to be vaccinated even though she does not desire to be vaccinated. Consider a six year old. Presumably she has a right to an education even if she does not desire to go to school. Thus, not only are there counterexamples to an account of the right to life in terms of the desire to continue to exist, but there are problems with a general strategy of accounting for rights in terms of desires. Unless these problems can be fixed, the Tooley-Singer defense of abortion choice and infanticide is unsound.

Strategies for Repairing the Tooley-Singer View

Can the Tooley-Singer view be revised to avoid these difficulties? Let us consider some possible revisions. Tooley repeatedly emphasized how

---

[7] See Tooley, *op. cit.*, pp. 47–48.

the right to life should be understood in terms of having a concept of oneself as a continuing subject of experiences. People who are suicidal and people who wish to be killed for religious reasons have such a concept. It is equally clear that fetuses and infants lack such a concept. Perhaps the relationship between rights and desires in the Singer-Tooley account should be jettisoned in favor of an account of the wrongness of killing based only on the possession of the concept of one's self as a continuing subject of experience.

This revision is unsatisfactory. To drop either the general account of the relation between desires and rights or the particular account of the relation between the desire for continued existence and the right to life in the Tooley-Singer account is to drop the justification for the moral relevance of having the concept of self as a continuing subject of experience (as opposed to some other concept chosen at random). The reason the Tooley-Singer account seems to be an improvement over the sanctity of human life account is that it appeals to a property that involves *valuing* whereas the property of being a human being does not. Accordingly, the price of this modification is too high.

Another possible revision of the Tooley-Singer account involves dropping the appeal to the desire to live and substituting an appeal to preferring to live, or to taking an interest in living, or to caring about living, or to valuing one's future life.[8] All of these gerunds refer to mental states. Thus the account of the right to life in terms of some mental activity that involves valuing is protected. Hence, since fetuses lack the requisite mental states, they will not have the right to life. However, all of these gerunds refer to what philosophers have sometimes called pro-attitudes. The reason the severely depressed are counterexamples to the Tooley-Singer theory is because they lack a pro-attitude toward their future existence, no matter whether that pro-attitude is described in terms of desiring to continue to exist, or preferring to continue to exist, or taking an interest in continuing to exist, or valuing their future existence or caring about their future existence. Accordingly this strategy for repairing the Tooley-Singer account does not successfully deal with the apparent counterexamples to it.

---

[8] An account in terms of interests can be found in Bonnie Steinbock, *Life Before Birth: The Moral and Legal Status of Embryos and Fetuses* (New York: Oxford University Press, 1992). An account in terms of caring can be found in Jeffrey Reiman, *Abortion and the Ways We Value Human Life* (Lanham: Rowman and Littlefield, 1999). An account in terms of valuing can be found in John Harris, "The Concept of the Person and the Value of Life," *Kennedy Institute of Ethics Journal* 9 (1999), pp. 293–308.

A third strategy for repairing the Tooley-Singer account is suggested by Singer's analysis of the moral permissibility of euthanasia. Singer holds that there are circumstances in which physicians may practice euthanasia, but only when based on "the free and rational decisions of their patients" (*Practical Ethics*, p. 143). We may infer that Singer would not permit killing the suicidal and depressed unless their decisions are free and rational. Because the apparent counterexamples to the Tooley-Singer view are precisely cases of individuals whose desires are not free and rational, Singer appears to have a clear way to deal with those counterexamples. On the one hand, there is nothing in Singer's account of the ethics of abortion and infanticide to suggest that his account should be understood in terms of free and rational preferences rather than actual preferences (which are sometimes clearly different). On the other hand, because the "free and rational preference" move seems to solve some problems for Singer, and because it is found elsewhere in his writings, the move is certainly worth examination.

It is not immediately clear how the "free and rational preference" move is supposed to work in the abortion and infanticide context. Although Singer holds that the euthanasia of typical adults is permissible only when the adult's desire for euthanasia is free and rational, he cannot similarly hold that a fetus may be killed only when her desire to die is free and rational. Because fetuses have no desires, this move does not underwrite abortion choice.

Perhaps this dismissal is too abrupt. Let us suppose that Singer's account of the wrongness of killing is worked out, not in terms of the desires that individuals actually do have, but in terms of the desires that individuals would have under certain idealized conditions. Let us suppose that Singer's account is understood in terms of the desires that an individual would have if she were fully rational and the desires an individual would have if one had full information concerning all of the courses of action open to one, and what one's desires would be if they were not skewed by propagandistic social influences. Presumably the best alteration to the Tooley-Singer account will incorporate all of these changes. Let us call this strategy for revising the Tooley-Singer account, following Boonin, an 'ideal desire' strategy.[9] Can this strategy succeed?

It cannot be faulted for purging the value-incorporating rationale from the Tooley-Singer account of the wrongness of killing, for it does not. Many philosophers have tried to offer an account of welfare in

---

[9] Singer has indicated (personal correspondence) that he now prefers such an account. See Boonin, *op. cit.*, pp. 70–85.

terms of such idealized desires.[10] An account of the wrongness of killing in terms of (a reduction of) the welfare of the victim is plausible. Furthermore the strategy cannot be faulted for failing to deal adequately with the apparent counterexamples to the original Tooley-Singer theory, for it plainly does.

The problem with this ideal desire strategy, at least from the point of view of Singer and Tooley, is different. On the one hand, an account of the wrongness of killing an individual in terms of the *actual* desires of that individual certainly will permit abortion and infanticide, for it is clear that neither fetuses nor infants possess the conceptual apparatus to desire to continue into the future. The trouble is that an account of the wrongness of killing an individual in terms of her actual desires is clearly unsatisfactory. On the other hand, an account of the wrongness of killing an individual in terms of the *ideal* desires of that individual does seem to be a far better account of the wrongness of killing. The trouble is that it is not nearly as evident that fetuses lack the relevant ideal desires as it is that they lack the relevant actual desires. The inference from 'A lacks the actual desire to X' to 'A lacks the ideal desire to X' is unsound. Hence, how can the ideal desire view justify abortion choice?

An individual's ideal desires are just the desires one would have if one were rational and fully informed. If a fetus were rational and fully informed, it would desire to live. It follows that fetuses have an ideal desire to live. It also follows this strategy does not underwrite abortion choice.

Could this conclusion be avoided? What is needed is some account of ideal desires which would not permit attributing ideal desires, or, at least, the ideal desire to continue to exist in the future, to fetuses. In fact, Boonin's ideal desire account is such an account. According to Boonin ideal desires are actual desires that have been revised to account for mistakes. Since fetuses cannot have actual desires they cannot have ideal desires either. However, nothing forces us to understand ideal desires in Boonin's way. We could instead understand them as desires that an individual would have under certain ideal conditions. We could understand the ideal desire of an individual who suffers from severe depression as the desire that individual *would* have (but plainly does not) if she did not suffer from the handicap of mental illness. We could understand the ideal desire of an individual fetus as the desire that individual *would*

---

[10] For one such account see Richard Brandt, "Goodness as the Satisfaction of Informed Desire," in George Sher, ed., *Moral Philosophy*, second edition (New York: Harcourt Brace, 1997), pp. 622–636.

have (but plainly does not) if she did not suffer from the handicap of underdevelopment. Thus, it is clear that Boonin's moral-status-of-the-fetus defense of abortion choice rests, in the final analysis, on Boonin's *decision* to *define* an ideal desire so that abortion choice is permitted. This won't do. If moral permissibility can rest in the final analysis on such a linguistic stipulation, then anything is permitted. I see no way of revising Singer's argument strategy to avoid these difficulties. An account of the wrongness of killing in terms of actual desires underwrites abortion choice. However, the account is unsound. An account of the wrongness of killing in terms of ideal desires may well be sound. However, it does not underwrite abortion choice unless it is restricted in an arbitrary way.

It seems fair to conclude that Singer's account of the wrongness of killing with its corollaries concerning abortion and infanticide is unsatisfactory. Singer has shown that the sanctity of human life theory is unsatisfactory. Many of those who are convinced that the Tooley-Singer theory fails will infer that the sanctity of human life theory must be somehow resuscitated to avoid moral disaster. Many of those who are convinced that the sanctity of human life theory is hopelessly unsound will search for the some variant of the Tooley-Singer theory that will work. Surely these philosophical moves are moves born of desperation. They will seem plausible only if one assumes that no other account of the wrongness of killing is a realistic possibility. Happily, there is an alternative.

The Future of Value Account of the Wrongness of Killing

Consider those adults and children whom, we all believe, it would be seriously wrong to kill. Why do we believe that killing them is wrong? Here is a simple answer: Killing them would harm them greatly. What is the nature of that harm? Killing them would deprive them of the goods of life that they would have experienced had they not been killed. If I am killed now, my entire life contains fewer goods than if I am not killed now and I don't die of something else in the meantime. Therefore, killing me will have harmed me. Killing deprives an individual of her future of value.[11] This account fits in well with other things that we believe. Suppose I discover that I have incurable cancer. I would regard

---

[11] I have defended this account in "Why Abortion Is Immoral," *Journal of Philosophy* 86 (April 1989), pp. 183–202.

this as a very great misfortune. What makes the incurable cancer a very great misfortune for me? It causes me to experience fewer of the goods of life than I presumably otherwise would. The cancer harms me. The future of value account of the wrongness of killing fits in nicely with the way we actually think of the misfortune of premature death and the harm caused by it.

The future of value account has implications very different from the Tooley-Singer theory. We were all fetuses once. The valuable futures of those fetuses are nothing more than those aspects of our past and future lives that are now, will be (or would be), and were valued by us. If it is wrong to kill us because we have futures of value and killing us would deprive us of our futures of value, then it would have been wrong to have aborted us, for the fetuses we once were had futures (very much!) like ours. Those futures consist of our own future and past lives. Therefore, abortion is wrong. Infanticide is wrong for the same reason.

This account of the wrongness of killing is based upon a plausible account of wrongness. Unlike sanctity of human life theories it is not based upon a merely biological characteristic. The value of the future of a standard human being consists in those aspects of her future life she will value when she lives them or she would value when she would live them. These aspects are such things as enjoying hiking or fishing, enjoying one's children or grandchildren, figuring out a problem, or luxuriating in the loveliness of a live performance of the Mendelssohn E-flat Major string quartet. The value of a future is constituted by those aspects of our future lives that make those future lives worth living. Therefore, unlike a sanctity of human life account, it does not imply an obligation to prolong the lives of anencephalic newborns or persons in persistent vegetative state. The valuable aspects of the lives of anencephalic newborns or persons in persistent vegetative state are forever closed to them. Our being biologically alive makes it possible for us to enjoy the good things of our lives. But our being biologically alive is not, on the future of value view, intrinsically valuable. Biological life is like a Rawlsian primary good. It almost always makes possible life's goods but it is not itself intrinsically good. Thus, the future of value view does not entail that it would be wrong to kill someone whose suffering cannot be relieved and who wants to die.

The future of value view is superior to the Tooley-Singer view because it accounts for the wrongness of killing those who do not desire to live. The suicidal have futures of value—at least, they will have valuable lives if they receive psychotherapy or psychotropic drugs. Although most people desire their continued existence, the *reason* most people desire their continued existence is because they anticipate that their future will be valuable to them. The reason the suicidal have an ideal desire to continue to exist is that they have futures of value. Our futures of value underlie our desires, or in the case of the depressed and fetuses, underlie their ideal desires. The future of value account explains why a desire account of the wrongness of killing appears to account for cases in which killing is wrong, to the extent that it does.

The future of value view does not suffer from speciesism. It is entirely possible that beings from other planets have futures very much like ours. If so, it will be wrong to kill them if we encounter them. Do other mammals have futures sufficiently like ours that it is wrong to kill them? Nothing in the future of value theory itself gives us a definitive answer to this question. Singer has argued that we can have reasons for thinking that the life of a human is more valuable than that of a mouse (*Practical Ethics*, pp. 89–90). This could be the basis for saying that the killing of human beings is, *ceteris paribus,* especially wrong.

Potentiality

The sanctity of human life theory and a desire theory of the wrongness of killing base the wrongness of killing some individual at some particular time on some actual property of that individual at that time. The future of value theory, by contrast, bases the wrongness of killing on some property an individual will have, or would have, not ultimately on a property she actually has now. Of course, you now have a future of value in virtue of now being an individual having a certain potentiality. That potentiality is grounded upon your present nature as a human being. Nevertheless, it is not that present potentiality itself that is intrinsically valuable to you. Your actual or potential future is the source of the value of your (future) life to you and therefore the basis for the wrongness of killing you. Accordingly, the future of value theory is a potentiality theory through and through. The wrongness of killing fetuses resides in their potentiality because the wrongness of killing YOU resides in your potentiality.

Singer has offered many objections to potentiality accounts of the wrongness of killing fetuses and infants. Do any of these objections undermine the future of value theory?

Singer has claimed that it is impossible to harm an individual in a morally significant way unless she is now actually sentient (*Embryo Experimentation*, p. 73). Since some fetuses are not yet sentient, but only potentially sentient, Singer's claim implies, in opposition to the

future of value theory, that it would not be wrong to end the life of a
fetus that lacks sentience. Singer's argument for his view is that (1) no
individual that lacks sentience has interests and (2) no individual that
lacks interests can be harmed (*Embryo Experimentation*, p. 73).
Consider some adult human who, because of an accident, is temporarily
unconscious but who, after a period in intensive care, will recover and
within a month will be functioning well. We believe that disconnecting
such a person from his life supports would harm him. Because such an
individual is not actually sentient, there is a problem with Singer's argument. What went wrong?

'Having an interest' is ambiguous. The human being who is unconscious in the ICU cannot *take* an interest in anything including his
future. If we want to count someone as having an interest in something
only if she takes an interest in that thing, then our temporarily unconscious human being lacks any interests, so (1) is true. If we understand
'interests' in this way, then (2) is false, for it is clearly possible to harm
this temporarily unconscious individual. However, we do not have to
understand 'interests' in this way. We want to say that it is in the best
interest of this temporarily unconscious person to remain on life supports. This notion of interest identifies interests with the welfare of this
being as a whole. If we understand 'interests' in this way, then (2) is true,
but (1) is false. Either way, Singer's argument is unsound.

Singer has considered the claim that it is wrong to kill a normal
human infant or fetus because it "has good prospects of a worthwhile,
happy, and fulfilling life, a life with many of the experiences which we
think of as making our own lives rewarding and satisfying" (*Should the
Baby Live?*, p. 132). The future of value theory entails exactly this claim.
Singer believes arguments exist for rejection of this claim. If Singer is
right, then Singer has an argument for rejecting the future of value
account. So is he right?

Singer believes that the moral irrelevance of the act-omission distinction is a basis for rejecting this claim. However, *merely* rejecting the
moral significance of the act-omission distinction will not undermine
the future of value view or, for that matter, a sanctity of human life view.
People who believe that infants have the right to life usually think that
deliberately omitting to feed an infant is as wrong as poisoning it.
Hence, the moral irrelevance of the act-omission distinction does not
undermine a potentiality view in the absence of additional analysis.

Singer believes that the moral irrelevance of the act-omission distinction when combined with a view in which potentiality is valuable
implies an absurdity. He says "if one holds that it is wrong to kill a new-

born infant (or foetus) because that infant (or foetus) will eventually become a person with a worthwhile life, then why is it not also wrong to omit to do an act which would have the consequence that a person with a worthwhile life comes into existence?" *(Should the Baby Live?*, p. 133). Thus, Singer seems to think that a potentiality theorist is committed to holding that abstaining from sex (when reproduction would have taken place) is wrong. However, even Singer notes that the argument is not quite convincing. "When we refrain from reproducing, there is no being whose life has already begun. Intuitively, this makes a difference" *(Should the Baby Live?*, p. 133). The difference is more than merely intuitive. In the first case an individual has been harmed. In the second case no individual has been harmed. Accordingly, even if one agrees with Singer that the act-omission distinction is morally irrelevant, the future of value theory does not seem to imply that it is wrong to refrain from reproducing.

Perhaps Singer would think that this point about harm is not important, for he does not think that *he* could have been harmed in infancy. He says: "When I think of myself as the person I now am, I realize that I did not come into existence until some time after my birth" *(Should the Baby Live?*, p. 133). This is an odd claim. It implies that Peter Singer was never a fetus nor was he born. Because the biological organism that the name 'Peter Singer' is ordinarily thought to denote certainly was born, it follows that Peter Singer is not a biological organism. This remarkable view surely requires defense. Singer offers none.

Finally, Singer has objected to potentiality accounts of the right to life on the grounds that "a potential X does not have all of the rights of an X" *(Practical Ethics*, p. 120). What Singer means is that the fact that an actual X has a right R does not entail that a potential X has R. Singer is correct. This is no objection to the future of value account. On the future of value account an actual person has the right to life in virtue of her potentiality. Since having this potentiality is a sufficient condition for having the right to life, potential persons who have this potentiality also have the right to life. There is no illicit inference here. Singer's objections to potentiality arguments are not sufficient to show that the future of value account is incorrect.

Human Embryos

Let 'human embryo' refer to the human product of fertilization until the time of implantation. Singer has defended the moral permissibility of embryo experimentation in which human embryos are destroyed. He has argued that sanctity of human life arguments do not show that embryos have the right to life (*Embryo Experimentation*, pp. 68–71). About that he is surely correct. He has argued that a human embryo's lack of sentience shows that it cannot be harmed (*Embryo Experimentation*, pp. 73–74). I have discussed that argument above and have given reasons why it is not successful. The Tooley-Singer desire account of the wrongness of killing implies that human embryos are not victimized by their deliberate destruction, whether located in another human being or not. However, this does not help much because of the difficulties that plague the Tooley-Singer desire view. Should we conclude that the future of value view shows that the destruction of human embryos is wrong and that Singer's view of this matter is incorrect?

There are special problems with this conclusion. A human individual has a future of value only if a later stage of that individual will have or would have a life that it then would value. It follows that a precursor of YOU had your future of value only if that precursor was an earlier stage of the same individual you are. Therefore, according to the future of value theory, the embryo that was my precursor had the right to life only if that embryo was an earlier stage of the same individual I am. Indeed, the unfertilized ovum (hereafter UFO) that was my precursor had the right to life only if it was the same individual as I. If the future of value theory implied that UFOs have the right to life, the future of value theory would have to be rejected. Therefore, consideration of these issues is important.

Jim Stone has offered an argument for the view that I am not the same individual as the UFO that was my precursor.[12] Suppose I were the same individual as the UFO that was my precursor. There is equal reason for supposing that the sperm that was my precursor is the same individual as I. (Surely sexism should be rejected as vigorously as speciesism in an essay on Peter Singer's views.) But if I am the same individual as the UFO that was my precursor and if I am the same individual as the sperm that was my precursor, then, since identity is transitive, the sperm and the UFO that were my precursors are identical. This is false. Therefore the supposition that I was either a sperm or a UFO is false. Therefore, I did not exist prior to fertilization.

Did human beings begin at fertilization? As Singer has pointed out, if the fertilized egg that is the precursor of the identical twins Bill and Harry is the same individual as both of them, then it follows that Bill and Harry are identical. But this is false. Therefore, the lives of Bill

---

[12] Stephen Buckle, "Arguing from Potential." In *Embryo Experimentation*, p. 100.

and Harry did not begin at conception (*Embryo Experimentation*, pp. 66–68). Notice that this result, like the result concerning the sperm and UFO, are just consequences of the general thesis that identity does not survive fission or fusion. The fact that the cells produced up to the sixteen cell stage are totipotent, and therefore can split into one or more individuals suggests a difficulty with the view that a human individual (a later stage of which is an adult) begin to exist at conception. Indeed, perhaps at the sixteen-cell stage there are sixteen human individuals (*Embryo Experimentation*, pp. 66–68).

There are other problems with the view that we begin to exist at conception. As Stephen Buckle has pointed out, much of the embryo becomes placenta. Therefore, perhaps the human embryo prior to implantation is some primordial stuff out of which a human individual arises rather than a human individual.[13]

Still another problem derives from the fact that many people believe that we are essentially human organisms. An organism is an entity in which life functions are carried on by means of parts that are separate in function, but mutually dependent.[14] The parts of the human individual that differentiates itself from the placenta begin to form during the third week after conception. Therefore, there is some reason for holding that the individual human organism that you are began during the third week after conception. All these considerations suggest that Singer's view that the destruction of human embryos is morally permissible may well be correct, even if the future of value theory of the immorality of abortion is true.

Conclusion

The purpose of this essay has been to evaluate Peter Singer's views on the ethics of abortion and infanticide. Singer has offered compelling arguments for rejecting the doctrine of the sanctity of human life. He has endorsed, in the final analysis, Tooley's 1972 account of the wrongness of killing. This account permits abortion and infanticide. However, the Tooley-Singer view is subject to counterexamples that show that it is unsound. Furthermore, if my analysis is correct, no revision of the Tooley-Singer view is both an adequate account of the wrongness of killing and also permits abortion and infanticide. I believe that the future

---

[13] Webster's New International Dictionary, second edition.
[14] Jim Stone "Why Potentiality Matters," *Canadian Journal of Philosophy* 17:4 (December 1987), pp. 815–830.

of value view is a superior alternative to the Tooley-Singer view or any revision of it. The future of value view explains why the Tooley-Singer view is correct when it is. It is untouched by Singer's arguments against potentiality theories of a fetal right to life. The future of value account does not permit abortion and infanticide. Therefore, we must conclude that Singer's defense of abortion and infanticide is inadequate. However, Singer's views on human embryo research emerge unscathed.

The argument of this essay could be extended in important respects. Because the future of value account is a secular account of the ethics of abortion that supports the conclusion that abortion is seriously wrong, it has been criticized extensively. Although I believe that none of those criticisms are sound, this essay contains none of the analysis that supports that. Furthermore, Tooley has updated his account of the wrongness of killing.[15] I have not discussed that updated account in this essay.[16]

---

[15] Michael Tooley, *Abortion and Infanticide* (Oxford: Clarendon, 1983).
[16] I thank Peter Singer for all of his help at a number of stages in the preparation of this essay.

Reply to Don Marquis

PETER SINGER

A Critique from Shared Premises

There are two distinct elements to Don Marquis's paper: his trenchant but fair critique of my position on abortion and infanticide, and his necessarily brief and limited defense of his own view. I shall begin by responding to the criticism of my view before offering my own critique of his account of what is wrong with abortion.

First, however, it is important to note how much common ground there is between Marquis and myself. We agree that the fact that a being is a member of the species *Homo sapiens* is not, in itself, sufficient to justify the claim that it is has a right to life. Hence the traditional doctrine of the sanctity of life view must be rejected. We also agree that giving parents of very low birth-weight newborns the right to decide whether their children should be kept alive by the use of modern medical technology is not, in principle, different from allowing infanticide. We must therefore either deny parents this option, or accept that permitting infanticide is sometimes justifiable.

Although in *Practical Ethics* I consider various possible ways of approaching the issue of killing, as Marquis notes, the account I have favored for many years is that the most serious reason against killing arises when the being has an awareness of his or her existence over time, and wishes to continue to live. Before discussing Marquis's objections to this view, I need to make two preliminary comments.

First, I am, for the purposes of this discussion, putting aside the effects that killing a being may have on others—those who love and will grieve for the victim, and those who, as a result of the killing, may be in fear of being killed themselves. These are, in some cases, extremely serious reasons against killing. The strongest ground for a general rule against killing infants is the wishes and feelings of the parents who love and cherish their child.

Second, since we commonly discuss the issue of killing by asking which beings have a *right* to life—and I have myself used that terminology as a convenient shorthand—I should preface what follows by saying that I do not regard rights as the foundation of any tenable view of the wrongness of killing, but rather as derivative from the goal of bringing about the greatest possible net satisfaction of the preferences of all those affected by an action. Rights are derived from this foundation in that we can justifiably say that X has a right to Y when it is desirable, to further this goal, that there be a generally accepted moral rule that recognizes and protects X's claim to Y.

Two Counterexamples

To the general theory that the wrongness of killing depends on the preferences of the person who is killed, Marquis offers two counterexamples: the depressed woman whose desire to die is linked to her depression, and the religious believer who wants to be sacrificed to the gods because he believes that he will be gloriously rewarded in a life to come. In each case Marquis thinks that the theory commits me to saying that it would be permissible to kill, but this judgment is unacceptable. Do these counterexamples refute the theory?

First regarding the depressed person who wants to kill herself. Marquis says flatly "it is not morally permissible to kill" this person. Is this so obvious? If a person suffers from long-term depression and wants to die, and all possible efforts to relieve her condition over a period of many years have been made, without success, then her request seems to be based on a reasonable view of her situation, and I would say it is morally permissible to act on her request for assistance in dying. So this situation is not a counter-example to my view.

Perhaps Marquis has in mind someone who may well recover from depression, but, because of her condition, is excessively pessimistic about her prospects of recovery. In that case, she is unable to judge her future accurately. Her situation therefore resembles that of the religious believer who desires to die because he believes—we assume falsely—that he will be rewarded in an afterlife. These cases raise the issue of how we should respond to people whose preferences are based on false beliefs or beliefs that are influenced by mental states like depression that interfere with a rational consideration of the situation.

Preferences and False Beliefs

Some cases seem straightforward. After playing tennis on a hot day, a man forms a preference to drink the contents of a bottle that he believes to contain only water. We know that the bottle contains poison. If I keep silent while watching him take the bottle and drink it, I could not defend my inaction by saying that "His preference was to drink the contents of the bottle." I knew this preference was based on a false belief, and he had no desire to drink poison. From this case we can draw the general conclusion that if a person's preference to die is based on a false belief, it does not justify providing assistance in satisfying the preference. If a teenager whose girlfriend has just spurned him tells us he can't live without her, we don't take this preference seriously, let alone assist him to act on it. We tell him to wait a few weeks until his emotions have stabilized. From this case we can conclude that for a preference to be one we should act upon, it should be based not only on accurate information, but also on a calm and rational assessment of the situation. This is an "idealized desire" view.

Marquis argues that the idealized desire view supports his position that abortion and infanticide are normally wrong. Against David Boonin, who also defends an idealized desire view, Marquis claims that it is arbitrary to require that desires be well-informed and rational in the case of people who are depressed or suffering from religious delusions, but not in the cases of fetuses and newborn infants; and he contends that the well-informed and rational fetus or newborn infant would desire to live.

> We could understand the ideal desire of an individual who suffers from severe depression as the desire that individual *would* have (but plainly does not) if she did not suffer from the handicap of mental illness. We could understand the ideal desire of an individual fetus as the desire that individual *would* have (but plainly does not) if she did not suffer from the handicap of underdevelopment.

This response seems plausible if we regard preference utilitarianism as recommending something like:

> We should satisfy the preferences a being would have if that being were fully informed and thinking clearly.

This formulation, taken literally, suggests imagining desires where there are none, and supposing a being might think clearly even if it has no capacity at all for thought of any kind. Adjusting a person's actual desires for errors is one thing; attributing a wholly new desire to a being that is not capable of having any desires at all, or any desires of the relevant kind is something else altogether, and something for which there is no obvious motivation. Preference utilitarianism should be formulated to cover only the former, as follows:[17]

> We should satisfy, to the greatest extent possible, the preferences a being has, except that we should not satisfy a preference that results from errors of reasoning or errors about matters of fact.

The depressed person has a preference for living without depression and prefers death only because of her erroneous belief that she will be depressed and miserable for the rest of her life. We should therefore satisfy her preference for living without depression, if that is possible, and not her preference for death. On the other hand, the fetus makes no errors of reasoning or fact—it simply has no preferences and so there is nothing we should satisfy.

Another way of distinguishing the situation of the fetus from that of the depressed person is to start by distinguishing intrinsic from instrumental preferences, as follows:

> An intrinsic preference is something that is desired for its own sake. An instrumental preference is a preference for something as a means to satisfying either another instrumental preference, or an intrinsic preference.

We could then formulate preference utilitarianism as follows:

> We should act so as to satisfy, to the greatest extent possible, the intrinsic preferences a being has.[18]

It follows that instrumental preferences should be satisfied only in so far as they can reasonably be expected to lead to the satisfaction of intrinsic preferences. In the case of the depressed person who may recover from her depression, but is too depressed to take her chances of recovery into account, the desire to die is an instrumental one. The more fundamental, or intrinsic, preference is not to suffer from her depression. She pre-

---

[17] I am grateful to a personal communication from Sebastian Knell for this formulation.
[18] I am grateful to Evan Williams, personal communication, for suggesting this approach.

sumably also has an intrinsic desire to live without depression. If we act so as to satisfy her intrinsic desires, we will not seek to satisfy her instrumental preference for death. Similar points apply to the case of the person who desires to be sacrificed to the gods because of his false belief that he will be rewarded in an afterlife. If we describe death, accurately in my view, as the end of all experiences, he has no desire to die. His intrinsic desire is to experience various forms of pleasure or ecstasy. That is the preference we should try to satisfy. The fetus, on the other hand, has no intrinsic preferences to satisfy.

Matthew Flannagan has pressed further Marquis's argument about the person who desires to be sacrificed to the gods. If I deal with this case by saying that we should not sacrifice him because his desire is based on a false belief, Flannagan asks, what do I say to a religious believer who knows that his future existence on this earth will be miserable, and refrains from committing suicide only because of his false belief that suicide is a sin for which he will be punished in the afterlife? Since he would wish to die if he did not have a false belief in an afterlife, am I committed to holding that he has no right to life, because he has no well-informed desire to go on living?[19]

At the level of ethical theory, as distinct from the world in which we live, Flannagan is right; but it scarcely needs saying how dangerous it could be for people to take it upon themselves to judge whether others—who have their own views about whether they want to go on living—would have the same views if their beliefs were accurate, and, on the basis of this judgment, to kill those who would not want to go on living if their beliefs were corrected. With John Stuart Mill, I think we should generally assume that, for competent adults at least, "each is the best judge and guardian of his own interests."[20] This will not always be literally true, but in the interests of providing everyone with the assurance of some basic liberties, we should normally treat it as if it were. Hence, at least in the real world, we should not deny the right to life of the miserable person to remain alive only because of the falsity of the belief on which this desire is based.

When Did I Begin?

There is an another way of responding to Marquis's suggestion that being a fetus is a "handicap" that an individual suffers in the way that

---

[19] Matthew Flanagan, personal communication
[20] John Stuart Mill, *On Liberty* (first published 1859).

severe depression may be a handicap to clear thinking about one's future. One could argue that the change from the fetus to an individual capable of having desires about his or her continued life is a change from one kind of being—a physical organism—to a quite different kind of being—an embodied mind. That is utterly different from the change that occurs in an adult when severe depression is successfully treated. I will shortly say a little more about this idea of a change in kind of being because it offers a distinct way of responding to Marquis's own account of what is wrong with abortion and infanticide—one that is not dependent on the desire-based view I have defended so far. But before I develop this argument, I want to return to the general problem I raised many years ago for all anti-abortion positions that rest on claims about the value of the future the fetus can be expected to have, if it is not aborted. My objection to this view was, as Marquis here notes, that it implies not only that abortion is normally wrong, but that abstaining from sex that will probably result in conception is normally wrong, because both the abortion and the abstention from sex will cause one fewer valuable life to be lived.

Marquis's response seems convincing: "In the first case an individual has been harmed. In the second case no individual has been harmed." But in fact, as Marquis later acknowledges, the question of when an individual exists is not as clear as it at first seems. He writes:

> The fact that the cells produced up to the sixteen-cell stage are totipotent, and therefore can split into one or more individuals suggests a difficulty with the view that a human individual (a later stage of which is an adult) begins to exist at conception. Indeed, perhaps at the sixteen cell stage there are sixteen human individuals.

The fact that our early cells are totipotent raises a problem for the "future of value" objection to abortion that is not solved by specifying that the human individual begins to exist only once the cells become more specialized. Take my own case. As far as I know, I have never had a twin. I put it in this cautious way, because it is possible that the early embryo from which I developed was one of a pair of identical twin embryos, one of which failed to implant in my mother's uterus, or fused with the embryo from which I developed. But let's assume that this did not happen. It is then at least arguable that I began to exist at conception. The arguments for this view are familiar—once the egg and sperm fused, the genetic basis of the organism was set, and many of my characteristics were determined. If we believe that we should protect the life of any individual with a future of value, it seems reasonable to hold that we should protect the life of the early embryo, and even of the zygote, from which I developed.

So far so good, for the future of value view. But what about those sixteen totipotent cells, which Marquis says perhaps are sixteen totipotent individuals?[21] We now have the technology to separate them, allow each to grow into an embryo, transfer that embryo to a woman's uterus, and thereby give each of them a future of value. Assume that we have sixteen women willing to receive an embryo into their uterus. Is that something we should do? On the future of value view, it would seem that we should. The resulting sixteen individuals will then be able to look back on those separated cells and say: "That is when I began to exist as an individual human organism." Failing to separate the cells is thus denying them a future of value, in the same way that aborting a fetus denies that human organism a future of value.[22]

If this seems a strange outcome for the future of value view, things are only going to get worse. Human cloning from an adult cell is likely to be achieved in the next decade or two. If it is, then we could consider every cell in our body as a (possible) new individual with a future of value. Since each new individual will itself generate more cells, the number of individuals with a future of value becomes infinite.

Marquis thinks that we are not required to provide the environment for totipotent cells to develop into individuals, because they are not yet individuals. Similarly, he would hold that if cloning from an adult human cell were possible, we would be under no obligation to do it. In both cases, the decision not to do what is necessary to enable the cell to develop further is, on his view, very different, morally, from preventing an individual from continuing to develop. What this shows, however, is how much weight Marquis has to place on a very fine distinction. Marquis believes that it is, other things being equal, seriously wrong to deprive an individual of a future of value, but not at all wrong to refrain from bringing into existence an individual with a future of value. Hence on his view determining when an individual begins to exist is absolutely

---

[21] I'm here accepting that, as Marquis says, each cell remains totipotent at the sixteen-cell stage. There is some evidence suggesting that totipotency declines after the eight-cell stage. If that is correct, the argument developed here can be restated with "eight" substituted for "sixteen" throughout.

[22] I am indebted to Agata Sagan for some very helpful discussion of the points made in this section. For a more detailed discussion, see Agata Sagan and Peter Singer, "The Moral Status of Stem Cells," *Metaphilosophy* 38:2–3 (April 2007), pp. 264–284.

vital. This is a problem because the human organism develops very gradually, rather than in sudden leaps. The problem is even less tractable if the idea that the human organism begins at conception is abandoned. (Although even those who hold that human life begins at conception need to reckon with the fact that after the sperm first begins to penetrate the egg, it takes about twenty-two hours before the genetic material from the egg and sperm unite. Midway through that process, do we have a human being? A senior figure in the Roman Catholic Church, Cardinal Carlo Maria Martini, has said that in the zygote stage, eighteen to twenty-four hours after fertilization, "There are still no signs of singularly definable human life."[23]) Marquis must pick one moment in the gradual process of development and say: "Before this moment, there is no individual, but after this moment, there is one."

What Am I?

All of this is premised, of course, on the idea that we are biological organisms. If he were to abandon this idea, Marquis could avoid these problems, and still preserve a "future of value" view. He refers to my assertion that "when I think of myself as the person I now am, I realize that I did not come into existence until some time after my birth" as "an odd claim" and the view that "Peter Singer is not a biological organism" as a "remarkable view" that requires defense. Perhaps it does need defense, but it doesn't strike me as remarkable. Other philosophers have defended the view that personal identity requires psychological continuity. In his book *The Ethics of Killing,* Jeff McMahan argues strongly that we are not human organisms.[24] One of his arguments is based on consideration of the following scenario, which requires us to imagine only an advance in transplant skills:

> I am brought into hospital after an accident. My brain is intact, but my body is mangled beyond repair. At the same time, a stranger is also brought into

---

[23] On the first twenty-two hours after conception, see Stephen Buckle, Karen Dawson, and Peter Singer, "The Syngamy Debate: When Precisely Does a Human Life Begin?" *Law, Medicine, and Health Care* 17:2 (Summer 1989), pp. 174–181. For Martini's comments, see Nicole Winfield, "Cardinal: Condoms 'Lesser Evil' than AIDS," *Associated Press,* April 21st, 2006; they originally appeared in the Italian newsweekly *L'Espresso,* in response to questions from Ignazio Marino, a scientist and bioethicist.
[24] Jeff McMahan, *The Ethics of Killing* (Oxford: Oxford University Press, 2002), pp. 24–39.

hospital after an accident. His body is fine, but his brain has been destroyed. So my brain is transplanted into his body. My memories and personality are intact, although I'm now much more handsome than I was before. The stranger's memories and personality have been lost.

Who has survived the accident? Despite the fact that most of the biological organism that was me has been destroyed, and most of the stranger's biological organism has survived, the majority of people considering this case conclude that it is I, rather than the stranger, who has survived. Nor is this only because the brain somehow regulates and controls the entire body. As McMahan points out, this would be our view even if it were just my cerebrum, rather than my entire brain, that had been transplanted. It is the memories and personality that determine who survives, not what regulates the organism's breathing and heartbeat.

McMahan offers another reason for thinking that we are embodied minds, rather than biological organisms. Abigail and Brittany Hensel are conjoined twins, born in 1990, now living in America's Midwest. They have separate heads and necks, but share two shoulders, two arms, one trunk, one pelvis, and two legs. Inside their body, they have two hearts, three lungs, two stomachs, one large intestine, one small intestine, one bladder, one uterus and one vagina. They are surely two persons—they have different tastes in food, clothing style, and so on. Brittany is better at writing than Abigail, but Abigail is better at math. When they reply to emails, they use the first person singular if they are in agreement, but the third person, using their names, if they do not agree. Nevertheless, they share a single biological organism. It's difficult to think of them in any other way. When they walk, swim, ride a bike, or hug their mother, there is only one organism doing these things. If the organism gets a fever, Abigail and Brittany both feel ill. If, tragically, their liver should develop an incurable cancer, both Abigail and Brittany will die, but the death will involve only one organism.[25]

For these reasons, it is plausible to think of ourselves as persons, rather than as organisms, and this supports my claim that "when I think of myself *as the person I now am*, I realize that I did not come into existence until some time after my birth." The claim only seems remarkable if we ignore the phrase I have now put in italics. Here is the ethical significance of this claim: we do not have to see coming into existence *as a biological organism* as crucial to the wrongness of killing. Depending

---

[25] For details see the Wikipedia entry, "Abigail and Brittany Hensel", http://en.wikipedia .org/wiki/Abigail_and_Brittany_Hensel.

on the exact criteria of psychological continuity we choose, I can identify myself either with the late fetus, when consciousness begins, or with the developing infant, when self-awareness develops, or perhaps even with the young child I can remember being. Since I have no psychological connection with the fetus I once was, and that fetus had no desires for the future, we are not compelled to say that it was in the interests of the fetus to live.[26]

But in any case, from my perspective, personal identity isn't such a big deal. I don't have to point to any precise moment when a person begins to exist. What matters, on my view, are the consequences of what we do. Before there is a being with future-directed desires, the consequences of destroying an individual organism, and refraining from bringing an individual into existence, are often virtually identical. Once there is a being conscious of its own future, with desires about that future, which we can satisfy or frustrate, the consequences of ending its life are different, but just as the development of such desires is gradual, so is the seriousness of thwarting them. A consequentialist moral theory can accept a gradual increase in the intrinsic seriousness of killing that parallels the development of self-awareness in the infant and child. Granted, society, and the law, may need some boundaries to indicate when killing will be treated as a crime and punished, but that is a pragmatic issue, not a matter of underlying moral theory.

---

[26] I am grateful to Brent Howard for helpful comments on this point.

4

Singer's Unsanctity of Human Life: A Critique

HARRY J. GENSLER

My goal here is to convince Peter Singer to give up his attack on the sanctity of human life, an attack that I argue is flawed and counterproductive, and to refocus his energy on an area where he could do much good, namely the eating-meat phase of animal liberation.

Moral Hero, But

A few years ago, I wrote a review on two of Singer's books, a review called "Peter Singer: Moral Hero or Nazi?"[1] I began by saying that Singer is very controversial: some think of him as a moral hero for promoting famine relief and the humane treatment of animals, while others see him as a neo-Nazi for his views on killing disabled infants. I ended by stating my own view, that Singer is a moral hero. I noted that Nazis do not regard everyone's good as equally important or give away a fifth of their income to help poor people who are mostly of other races. But I added that I saw being a moral hero as compatible with having wrong ideas about the sanctity of human life.

---

[1] I reviewed Dale Jamieson, ed., *Singer and His Critics* (Oxford: Blackwell, 1999), and *Ethics into Action: Henry Spira and the Animal Rights Movement*, by Peter Singer (Lanham: Rowman and Littlefield, 1998), in the *Times Higher Education Supplement* (8th October, 1999), p. 26. I remarked (and Singer in an e-mail agreed) that it was unfortunate that *Singer and His Critics* had no critics directly confronting Singer's controversial views about killing.

How can I praise Singer for what he says about famine and animals, but yet reject what he says about killing disabled infants? Don't all these views rest on utilitarianism?

When arguing about famine and animals, Singer mostly appeals, not to utilitarianism, but to weaker principles that can be accepted from various perspectives. His classic article on famine relief[2] appealed to the modest principle that we ought to prevent very bad things from happening, if we can do so without sacrificing anything of comparable moral importance; he wisely did not mention his extreme utilitarian views (for example that we would have a similar duty to help hungry animals, or that we are required to contribute so much that we would end up poor ourselves). Similarly, most of his suggestions about animals depend on the modest idea that it is wrong to inflict great pain on animals for the sake of trivial human interests; few of his suggestions depend on his more extreme utilitarian views (for instance that a mouse has the same right to life as your infant daughter, if both have the same mental level).

In my opinion, Singer is at his best when he acts as a prophet who denounces what can be seen as evil from various perspectives. He is at his worst when he theorizes about utilitarianism or uses it to advocate extreme views, like the killing of disabled infants. I see his view about infants as doubly unfortunate; besides being flawed (as I will try to show), it has destroyed his credibility for large groups of people—so Singer cannot now have the influence that he might have had on important areas like factory farming.

Animal Liberation and Infanticide

I see the animal liberation movement as having two phases. Phase 1 was about reducing cruel experimentation on animals. This phase had much success, largely through the work of Singer and his follower Henry Spira (1927–1998).[3] The activist Spira, who got interested in animal rights through an adult education course offered by Singer, started by organizing protests against senseless and painful animal experiments at the New York Museum of Natural History. After success here, Spira turned to Revlon, which used animals to test the safety of cosmetics; the cruel Draize test put toxic chemicals on the eyes of rabbits. Revlon at first

---

[2] "Famine, Affluence, and Morality" in *Unsanctifying Human Life* (Oxford: Blackwell, 2002), pp. 145–156. This article was first published in *Philosophy and Public Affairs* 1 (1972), pp. 229–43.

[3] See Singer's *Ethics into Action: Henry Spira and the Animal Rights Movement*.

ignored Spira; but a full-page ad in the *New York Times* on 15th April 1980 caught their attention and threatened to hurt sales. So Revlon yielded to Spira's modest demand, that they put some money aside to fund research into alternative tests not involving animals; these tests turned out to be more accurate and less expensive, besides avoiding pain to animals. Then Spira turned to other projects; he was successful in many of these, leading to better treatment of animals. While much remains to be done, there is far less cruelty in animal experimentation now than there was thirty years ago. When you see "Not tested on animals," think of Singer and Spira.

Singer's book on Spira has good advice for activists. It suggests that we focus on concrete, achievable projects; get the ball rolling instead of trying to do everything at once. Do not divide people into saints and sinners; instead, put yourself in the place of the people you want to change and explore how they can achieve their goals without, for example, being cruel to animals. Be patient, and change your strategy if needed. Above all, do your homework and get the facts straight.

Phase 2 of the animal liberation movement, which is about eating meat, has not had the same success. While there are more vegetarians and vegans than before, their numbers are small; the average consumption of meat has, if anything, increased in the last thirty years.[4] Yet arguments against our eating practices are strong. We eat so much meat that it (1) harms our health (clogging our arteries and making us obese); (2) aggravates world hunger (since many more resources are required to produce a gram of animal protein than a gram of vegetable protein); (3) harms the environment (especially since its heavy use of fossil fuels and forest-clearing promotes global warming); and (4) harms animals (especially those raised in inhumane factory-farming conditions[5]).

The American government's "food pyramid" emphasizes heath.[6] It advocates cutting down on meat (especially fatty meat) and eating more fruits and vegetables. We should eat about $5\frac{1}{2}$ ounces each day from the protein category;[7] and we should vary our protein more, eating less

---

[4] A 1998 study reported that per capita meat consumption in America was at an all-time high; see http://www.findarticles.com/p/articles/mi_m3765/is_3_21/ai_56013998/pg_1.

[5] See http://www.petatv.com/tvpopup/Prefs.asp?video=mym2002 for a graphic PETA video showing the cruelty to animals in current factory-farming practices. This video, narrated by the actor Alec Baldwin, is also at http://meetyourmeat.com.

[6] See http://www.mypyramid.gov. Few people follow these recommendations; obesity in America is at an all-time high.

[7] Many say we need less protein than that and typically get seven times the amount that is needed.

meat and poultry and more fish, beans, peas, nuts, and seeds (which also are in the protein category). These recommendations contrast sharply with American practice. From the Outback Steakhouse menu,[8] for example, it would be difficult to pick a single meal that doesn't by itself exceed the meat recommendation by several times. And I've seen several of my overweight friends eat "Aussie sized" helpings of meat leftovers, and almost nothing else, at lunch. We continue to eat unhealthy amounts of meat; so we get fat, clog our arteries, harm the environment, aggravate world hunger, hog the world's resources, and perpetuate cruelty to animals.

We need to adopt the achievable goal of radically reducing meat consumption.[9] The time is ripe for this; many people see problems with our current practice but are unclear about how to change things. What can we do? One helpful step might be to add two categories to the "Nutrition Facts" box found on most foods. First we might add a resources-environment category, about the food's resource and environmental costs. This would say, for example, that producing the one-pound steak required five pounds of grain, 2,500 gallons of water, and a gallon of gasoline,[10] and had such and such results that are thought to contribute to the greenhouse effect. People in drought areas of the Southwest should know how much their steak contributes to water shortages. We

---

My point is that, even on the conservative government figure, we get much more than we need.

[8] See http://www.outbacksteakhouse.com

[9] R.M. Hare's contribution to *Singer and His Critics* (pp. 233–246) defends the "demi-vegetarian" policy of eating little meat and selecting it carefully. He argues that this is at least as healthy as strict vegetarianism, better for world hunger (since some hilly or arid land is suitable for grazing but not farming), and in the interest of farm animals who are raised in a happy manner (since otherwise they would not exist). If meat is labeled as to its source, demi-veg buying habits can discourage cruel factory-farming practices and thus bring about much good for animals. With some qualification, Singer in that book (p. 325) accepted Hare's defense of demi-vegetarianism, which he saw, along with vegetarianism, as being a justifiable approach. While just *reducing* our consumption of meat may not be the final solution, it surely is a step in the right direction—and a step that many more people could be persuaded to take.

[10] These figures are from a study mentioned in Peter Singer's *Animal Liberation*, revised edition (New York: Avon, 1990), p. 166. Higher figures are common, for example that a pound of beef requires twenty or forty pounds of grain and 5,000 or 12,000 gallons of water. We need better numbers if we are to pick foods, in part, by their resource and environmental impact. We also need transportation data; after enjoying a delicious Fuji apple from New Zealand this morning, I wondered how much gasoline its 9,000-mile trip to Cleveland required.

could also add an animal-treatment category; this would say, for example, that the chicken grew up in a factory farm with half a square foot of space. The NRT (nutrition-resources-treatment) "Food Facts" box could be extended to restaurants and to supermarket meat and produce. Later there could be taxes or prohibitions on foods that are very harmful in terms of health, resources, or cruelty. These steps could be phased in, perhaps over a twenty-year period, to allow the food industry to adjust, much like how gas-mileage and emissions standards were gradually applied to the automotive industry. The important thing is to start simply, get the ball rolling, and make refinements later.

This goal, of radically reducing meat consumption, is achievable and could produce much good for health, resources, the environment, world hunger, and the humane treatment of animals. My suggestions may be misguided; I'm not an expert in this area. We need knowledgeable and creative people to construct a workable plan and put it into effect; they need to study what succeeded in phase 1 and why phase 2 is stalling.

The one to guide and inspire this is Peter Singer. His expertise and charisma, and that of his followers (especially Spira), were the driving force behind the successful animal-experimentation phase of animal liberation; and he is the ideal person to guide and inspire the meat-eating phase. As the holder of a prestigious bioethics chair at Princeton, he has many resources; since producing and eating food are biological phenomena, he could easily convince Princeton that food issues are an important part of bioethics.

The problem with this, of course, is that Singer's views on infanticide have discredited him in the eyes of many Americans. "Discredited" is an understatement; when Singer assumed his chair at Princeton in 1999, we read about protests by disabled people, threats to his life (and how he had an unlisted office and guards at his classroom), and alumni who vowed to stop contributions. Even today, the name "Peter Singer" is apt to bring reactions like "Oh, that intellectual kook who wants us to kill disabled infants." Singer's extreme views on human life have unfortunately lessened the practical influence that he might have on phase 2 of the animal liberation movement.

I am not suggesting that Singer change his mind on the sanctity of human life just to influence society more effectively and promote the social good; this utilitarian suggestion ignores the duty to be true to oneself and one's beliefs. But I do suggest that Singer's views on human life are hurting his effectiveness and that this would be a good time for him to reconsider these views—which, I will argue, are so full of problems that they are better abandoned.

Singer's Views about Killing Infants

The traditional sanctity-of-life ethic says it's seriously wrong, either always or with very few exceptions, to kill an innocent human being— even a young infant. Singer's originality lies, not in his arguing for more exceptions for the sick, but rather in the radical and innovative way he wants to repaint the whole moral landscape. I'll here focus on his views about killing infants and how this fits into his broader perspective.[11]

According to Singer, infants and fetuses have very little right to life. Let's imagine we have a newborn infant called Laurie. Killing little Laurie isn't seriously wrong in itself. Killing her is seriously wrong if it brings misery to older folks who *want* her—but not otherwise. Laurie will merit a strong right to life, on Singer's view, when she develops personhood (rationality and self-awareness).

Singer holds *preference utilitarianism*, that we ought to do whatever maximizes the satisfaction of preferences. It's not seriously wrong to kill a lower animal, as long as this is done painlessly.[12] But it is seriously wrong to kill an animal with self-awareness and strong desires (preferences) about its future. The difference depends on development, not species; killing an adult pig, which has some self-awareness and desires about its future, is in itself more serious than killing a human infant, which lacks these. Since preference utilitarianism recognizes that it's more serious to kill a *rational* animal, it seems preferable to *classical utilitarianism*, which says that we ought to do whatever maximizes the balance of pleasure over pain, even in cases of killing.

Singer sees utilitarianism as solidly based on reason. To think morally in a *rational* way is to be impartial in considering everyone's interests. Similar interests of every being are equally important—regardless of

---

[11] Some of these ideas are from a debate that Singer and I had on the sanctity of human life at John Carroll University on 4th December, 2000; the audio is on the Web at http://www.jcu.edu/pubaff/eyeonjcu/singer_gensler.htm. In that debate, I also questioned Singer's very dismissive attitude toward religion. While this relates to the sanctity of life (note that Singer uses the religious term "sanctity"), I don't have time here to explore Singer's views about religion; this would require another paper.

[12] On Singer's view, killing a lower animal (such as a fish or a human infant) could have some wrongness if it cuts off what would have been a pleasant life. This wrongness is cancelled if the animal is replaced by another who has a pleasant life not otherwise possible. Singer wants this "replacement" idea *not* to be applied to the killing of persons; I suspect this is due, not to the demands of preference utilitarianism, but rather to Singer's intuitions that a person's life has worth beyond being a container for valuable experiences. See his *Practical Ethics*, second edition (Cambridge: Cambridge University Press, 1993), pp. 121–34.

whether the being is black or white, male or female, next-door neighbor or far-off stranger, human or animal. To think morally is to favor whatever maximizes the sum-total of the interests of every sentient being.

Singer sees the point of birth as morally irrelevant in the development of a human. Since he believes it can be right to abort a defective fetus, he similarly believes it can be right to kill a disabled infant. His often quoted statement goes: "Killing a disabled infant is not morally equivalent to killing a person. Very often it is not wrong at all."[13]

Many object that, while it is wrong to kill a defective infant (for instance, by poisoning it), it is not necessarily wrong just to let it die (for example, by refusing to perform an extraordinary operation needed to save its life). Singer disagrees. He sees killing and letting-die as morally equivalent, since both have the same result.

Many object that we should follow our moral intuitions about such matters, not some theory like utilitarianism. Singer disagrees. He thinks following intuitions tends toward conformity, where we just follow what our culture taught us. Rational moral principles should sometimes lead us to change our moral intuitions and take unpopular stands.

Three Initial Problems

1. Singer's view is very vague on when it is right to kill our unwanted children. Recall that the newborn infant Laurie will merit a strong right to life when she develops personhood or rationality—more specifically, when she develops self-awareness and strong desires about her future. But she develops these gradually. Is Laurie's "sense of self" at age one developed enough to give her a strong right to life? Or must we wait until an age-three or age-five "sense of self"? Singer's view leaves it very unclear when, in Laurie's first few years of life, it becomes seriously wrong in itself to kill her.

I asked James Swindal, a philosophy colleague with several young children, when his children became Singerian persons. He thought they achieved this by age three; at this time, they can use personal pronouns (especially "I," "you," "he," and "she"), speak of their desires about the future, and contrast their desires with those of other people. Children at age two typically can't do such things. So perhaps the Singerian perspective should see the right to life emerging between ages two and three.

---

[13] *Practical Ethics*, p. 191.

But there are complications. Since personhood emerges gradually, maybe a three-year-old has some right to life, but not much. Maybe a stronger right to life emerges only later, when the child develops a stronger web of desires; or maybe the right to life of adults, too, depends on the strength and sophistication of their desires. Or maybe we should see the beginnings of personhood even earlier. At age two, a child can respond to a question like "Should we go outside and play?" by non-verbal behavior, like crying or laughing. Does this give it some right to life? And even young infants prefer to be held in certain ways. Singer once suggested that we be permitted to kill our disabled children until they are twenty-eight days old; he thought that personhood clearly was not achieved before this point (although he now realizes that twenty-eight days is too arbitrary). But it's hard to be sure even about this; it's conceivable that the baby in the womb has some sense of self and personal desires—even though these aren't manifested in clear behavioral ways.

From my perspective, this point of self-awareness is morally irrelevant. It's wrong to kill your children, regardless of whether they have reached some vague or arbitrary degree of self-awareness. If you think otherwise—you think it right for her parents to kill an unwanted little Laurie before she achieves self-awareness, but wrong afterwards—let me ask you a question. Would it have been right for your parents to have killed you before this point, but wrong afterwards? To be consistent, you must answer yes; but that's a difficult answer to give.

2. Studies show, despite Singer, that the disabled have roughly the same degree of happiness as the non-disabled. While measuring happiness is not an exact science, we can look at external signs like rates of suicide or drug addiction (which generally correlate with being very unhappy), and we can ask people to evaluate their lives. The disabled have lower rates of suicide and drug addiction than the rest of us; and they report about the same degree of life satisfaction as do other people. They are overwhelmingly glad that their lives were not ended and they oppose views like Singer's.[14]

---

[14] See http://www.notdeadyet.org/docs/disqual.html, whose first item (of many) says "86% of spinal cord injured high-level quadriplegics rated their quality of life as average or better than average; only 17% of their ER doctors, nurses, and technicians thought they would have an average or better quality of life" (from a study described in *Annals of Emergency Medicine* 23 (1994), pp. 807–812). Not Dead Yet (notdeadyet.org) is a civil-rights group for the disabled, started by Diane Coleman, J.D., M.B.A., who was disabled since birth and has used a wheelchair since age eleven; this group is a strong critic of Singer. One famous study compared major lottery winners with people paralyzed by accidents; the two groups a year later had relatively little difference in their perceived

Singer argues that disabilities must detract from the quality of one's life, and make it less worth living, since we would not desire our child to be disabled.[15] I admit that disabilities are negative; but so are many other things, like being born clumsy or into an uncaring family. If we kill off those with negatives, no one would survive. Life gives us a complex mix of positives and negatives, and from this we struggle to become the person that we will be. Overcoming negatives is an important part of "soul making" (to use a theological term from Irenaeus and John Hick); humans have a marvelous ability to overcome negatives or even turn them into positives.[16]

Suppose the facts were otherwise; suppose that the disabled as a group *were* significantly less happy. Even so, why single them out? There likely are other groups (perhaps racial, religious, or socio-economic groups) that turn out less happy; ought babies from these other groups to be killed too?

Instead of killing disabled infants, I suggest that we love and nurture them. Most with extreme disabilities will die off naturally; in the meantime we can help ease their pain. Those who survive will tend to live satisfying lives. Families with disabled children often develop a special love and concern for each other; and individuals who struggle with disabilities often develop special abilities that enrich the lives of others.

3. While Singer talks mostly about killing *disabled* infants, his principles apply also to killing *non-disabled* infants. On his principles, there's little moral objection to killing *any* unwanted infant, healthy or not, since such beings lack self-awareness and thus have no significant right to life.

People can be disabled in different degrees, from slight to severe; you might, for example, have a bad foot, or be confined to a wheelchair (like Franklin D. Roosevelt), or be almost completely paralyzed (like Stephen Hawking). I'm unclear, when Singer talks about killing disabled infants, how much of this spectrum he intends. Does he have in

---

general happiness. See Philip Brickman, Dan Coates, and Ronnie Janoff-Bulman, "Lottery Winners and Accident Victims: Is Happiness Relative?" *Journal of Personality and Social Psychology* 36 (1978), pp. 917–927; this article also refers to other research showing that the disabled are about as happy as the non-disabled. For further studies showing this, see Charlene DeLoach and Bobby G. Greer, *Adjustment to Severe Physical Disability* (New York: McGraw-Hill, 1981), pp. 122–26.

[15] *Practical Ethics*, pp. 53–54, 188.

[16] One of most the memorable events of my life was when I met Bill Irwin hiking in northern Virginia. Even though blind, he hiked the whole 2,000-mile Appalachian Trail, from Georgia to Maine; this is an almost impossible achievement.

mind only the most severe cases (like complete paralysis)? Or does he have in mind also cases like being confined to a wheelchair?[17]

Singer holds that the point of birth is morally irrelevant in human development; so infanticide and (late) abortion are morally on the same level. Many people who accept abortion see it as permissible regardless of whether the fetus is defective. With a defective fetus, on their view, there is greater reason for aborting; but, since the fetus has no right to life, killing an unwanted fetus is permissible in any case. Perhaps this is Singer's view about abortion. If so, then it should be his view also about infanticide. So then he should hold that, while there is little moral objection to killing any unwanted infant (since such beings lack self-awareness and thus have no significant right to life), there is a greater reason for killing an infant that is disabled over one that is not, and a still greater reason for killing an infant that is more severely disabled.

Singer seems much more guarded about infanticide than about abortion. Maybe he is anxious about shocking people. His principles commit him to a more radical view than what he sometimes expresses.

I agree with Singer that the point of birth is morally irrelevant. Birth is about where you are, not how developed you are; a late fetus may be more developed than a premature infant. So infanticide and a late abortion are in the same boat morally; both are permissible or both are wrong. Singer thinks both are permissible; I think both are wrong.[18]

Maximize Preferences or Pleasure?

Singer talks much about maximizing interests. As a preference utilitarian, he interprets interests in terms of preferences—we are to maximize the satisfaction of everyone's preferences—although he talks instead about pleasure and pain when discussing animals.

Satisfying preferences seems like an uncongenial basis for Singerian ethics. Doesn't satisfying preferences lead to a majority-rule conventionalism instead of a framework for criticizing popular views? People

---

[17] See *Practical Ethics*, p. 182 (where he talks about no infant having a right to life) and pp. 342–43 (where he seems to say just that the most severely disabled infants can be killed); these two passages (and others) give very different impressions of where Singer stands.

[18] I have argued that golden-rule consistency favors the belief that abortion is wrong in at least most cases. See my "A Kantian Argument against Abortion," *Philosophical Studies* 49 (1986), pp. 83–98. The last chapter of my *Ethics: A Contemporary Introduction* (London: Routledge, 1998) has a newer formulation of the same argument.

prefer to eat much meat. People prefer that infants not be killed. People prefer that Singer give up his outlandish views. Are these things thereby good? These conclusions go entirely against Singerian ethics. While there may be ways to deal with this obvious problem, I can only speculate on what they could be.

In *Practical Ethics*, Singer first suggests that "we count anything people desire as in their interests (unless it is incompatible with another desire)."[19] One problem with this is that misinformed people can desire what isn't in their interest; so Singer later tentatively suggests that we take "a person's interests to be what, on balance and after reflection on all the relevant facts, a person prefers."[20] This is better but unfortunately drops the element of consistency from the first definition. Perhaps it is better to interpret one's "interests" as "what one would desire if one were *rational* (informed, consistent, vividly aware of consequences, etc.)." Tweaking these definitions in various ways would lead to different forms of preference utilitarianism.

Many preference utilitarianisms are possible. Should we count *all* preferences? Or should we ignore ones that are misinformed, antisocial, or sadistic? Should we count only what people would desire if they were rational? Should we count preferences more if they are more intense (so my pleasure counts more than yours if both are identical except that I desire mine more)? If we kill you at time t, then do we ignore desires that you have for yourself at time $t + 1$ (since you then wouldn't be around to experience their frustration)? Should we count preferences that people have because they were brainwashed to have them? Should we count preferences that people would have had if they were not brainwashed? Should we count preferences that the infant Laurie would have later if we did not kill her now? This last question suggests that different forms of preference utilitarianism may have different implications about infanticide.

This all raises two special problems for Singer.

1. How is Singer to decide which form of preference utilitarianism to accept? The answer seems to be that he wants certain things to be right or wrong, and so he sets up his preference utilitarianism to match these. For example, he wants abortion and infanticide to be permissible, and so he doesn't count the preferences that the infant Laurie would have later

---

[19] *Practical Ethics*, p. 13. I am puzzled that this definition and the next apply only to people.

[20] *Practical Ethics*, p. 94.

if we do not kill her now (namely, her being glad that she was not killed).
So Singer follows his moral intuitions in deciding which form of preference utilitarianism to accept.

On Singer's view, basing moral theory on moral intuitions about particular cases is unacceptable. Singer criticizes Rawls for saying that
moral theory largely systematizes our moral intuitions; and he criticizes
those who interpret Sidgwick along similar lines.[21] Yet selecting which
form of preference utilitarianism to accept, from dozens of possibilities,
seems to require such an appeal to intuitions. Appealing to intuitions
weakens Singer's case about infanticide, since most people have contrary intuitions.

2. Any form of preference utilitarianism that fits Singer's intuitions
is apt to have a very doubtful application to animal rights. While it
makes perfect sense to speak of the chicken's pleasure-pain, it is more
questionable to speak of what the chicken would prefer if it reflected on
all the relevant facts.

A central plank of Singerian ethics is that the same moral principles
that apply to our treatment of human beings also apply to our treatment
of animals. Singer argues like this:[22] Let us assume that racism is clearly
wrong. Why is it clearly wrong? Is racism clearly wrong because it is
clear that all races have equal abilities (factual equality)? No, unfortunately this isn't clear. Instead, racism is clearly wrong because it is clear
that similar interests of *all* beings ought to be given equal consideration
(moral equality).[23] But this equal-consideration principle, which gives a

---

[21] See Singer's "Sidgwick and Reflective Equilibrium," in *Unsanctifying Human Life*,
pp. 27–50; this article was first published in *The Monist* 57 (1974),pp. 490–517.
Practical Ethics often appeals to intuitions; see especially pp. 101–05 about choosing
between the "total view" (that we ought to maximize the total pleasure) and "prior existence view" (that we ought to maximize the pleasure of those now existing). This latter
discussion is perplexing, since it suggests that Singer holds a pleasure-maximizing utilitarianism instead of a preference utilitarianism. Did Singer write this section, and others about animals, when he held the pleasure-maximizing view? Or is the ambivalence
about which is to be maximized a continuing feature of his utilitarianism?
[22] See *Practical Ethics*, pp. 55–62 and, more especially, Singer's *Animal Liberation*, pp.
1–23.
[23] Or perhaps racism is clearly wrong because it violates the golden rule, which applies
also to how we treat animals. See R.M. Hare's *Freedom and Reason* (Oxford: Clarendon,
1963) and Harry J. Gensler's *Formal Ethics* (London: Routledge, 1996) and *Ethics: A
Contemporary Introduction* (whose last chapter gives a golden-rule argument against
abortion and infanticide). Spira's *New York Times* ad implicitly appealed to the golden
rule (see *Ethics into Action: Henry Spira and the Animal Rights Movement*, pp. ix and
96): "Imagine someone placing your head in a stock. As you stare helplessly ahead,

strong reason for rejecting racism, can then be used to argue for animal rights too.

The argument fails if "X's interests" means "what X would prefer if X reflected on all the relevant facts"—since then it is unclear that animals have interests. Singer spends much time arguing that animals can feel pleasure and pain. This would be appropriate if he held that we ought to maximize the balance of pleasure over pain. Since he is a preference utilitarian, he must instead argue that animals have *preferences*; indeed he must argue that it makes sense to ask what animals (including the lowest animals) would desire if they reflected on all the relevant facts.

Apart from problems about how to take "interests," Singer's moral-equality principle ("Similar interests of all beings ought to be given equal consideration") seems clearly true, but only if "similar" is understood broadly enough that his principle is compatible with other judgments, like these, that seem just as clearly true:

1. We have a greater duty not to harm others than we have to help them.[24] It is not in general right to hurt A, by inflicting 20 units of harm, in order to help B, who thereby receives 21 units of good.

2. We have a greater duty toward some other people, because of our special relationships toward them, than we do to others. For example, parents can have a greater duty toward the interests of their children.

3. Other factors besides interests, like keeping your word, are important in determining our duty. Suppose you make a serious promise to your friend; but then you find that breaking it would promote your interests a little more than it would harm your friend's. Here, if other interests aren't affected, you ought to keep your promise, even though it maximizes interests to break it.

---

unable to defend yourself, your head is pulled back. Your lower eyelid is pulled away from your eyeball. Then chemicals are poured into the eye. There is pain. You scream and writhe hopelessly. There is no escape. This is the Draize Test."

[24] William K. Frankena, in *Ethics*, second edition (Englewood Cliffs: Prentice-Hall, 1973), p. 47, suggests that we have four basic duties about good and evil, in increasing order of stringency: to promote good, to remove harm (what is evil), to prevent harm, and not to inflict harm. (See also pp. 34–52, where he sketches other problems with utilitarianism's maximizing approach.)

Thus understood and qualified, Singer's moral-equality principle cannot be used to derive a maximizing-interests utilitarianism.

Another problem is that preferences are fairly soft. Studies show that we do not have well-defined preference orderings that we can just introspectively "read off" when asked. Instead, we construct a preference ordering on the spot; how we do this is greatly influenced by how questions are expressed and arranged. And we may well give a different ordering if we are asked again about our preferences later.[25]

Would you rather starve or eat a delicious meal? Which do you prefer? Well, that one is clear. Would you rather take a raft trip down the Grand Canyon or be promoted to full professor? Maybe that is not so clear. Your answer may depend on what you were asked just before that. Were you asked "How long have you wanted to be full professor?"? Or were you asked "How long have you wanted to raft down the Grand Canyon?"? The previous question is apt to influence your answer. So people seem not to have well-defined preference orderings about a lot of things. If so, then there is yet another reason for not basing ethics on maximizing the satisfaction of preferences.

Act or Rule Utilitarianism?

Act utilitarianism (AU) says that we ought to do the *individual act* with the best consequences. We can apply AU directly (by estimating the likely consequences of each option) or indirectly (by applying a "rule of thumb" about what kinds of action tend to have good or bad results).

Rule utilitarianism (RU), in perhaps its most plausible version, says that we ought to do what would be prescribed by the *rules* with the best consequences for people in society to accept. RU takes a two-step approach to determining our duty. First, we ask what rules (or policies) would have the best consequences for people (with their imperfections and limitations) to accept. Second, we apply these rules to our action.

Richard Brandt pointed out some of AU's bizarre implications (and there are dozens of similar examples that could be mentioned):

> Act utilitarianism has implications difficult to accept. It implies that if you have employed a boy to mow your lawn and he has finished the job and asks for his pay, you should pay him what you promised only if you cannot find

---

[25] See Alvin A. Goldman's survey article "Ethics and Cognitive Science," *Ethics* 103 (1993), pp. 337–360, especially pp. 345–350. Appraisals of one's personal happiness are similarly soft.

a better use for your money. When you bring home your monthly pay check, you should use it to support your family and yourself only if it cannot be used more effectively to supply the needs of others. If your father is ill and has no prospect of good in his life, and maintaining him is a drain on the enjoyments of others, then, if you can end his life without provoking public scandal or setting a bad example, it is your duty to bring his life to a close. Rule utilitarianism avoids some of these objectionable implications.[26]

In the lawn-mowing case, RU asks, "What rule about agreements would have the best consequences for society to accept?" This rule would likely require strict observance (especially since a loose rule would tend to destroy the practice of making agreements), with perhaps some carefully specified exceptions; then we would follow this rule instead of trying to maximize the good consequences of an individual act. RU brings guidelines that are stricter and harmonize better with common sense. A society that followed RU instead of AU would likely prosper better. With AU, it is too easy to talk ourselves into doing foolish things; compare AU's "Take heroine as a recreational drug in this case if you judge that this would have the best consequences" with RU's "Just say no."[27]

Is Singer an act or a rule utilitarian? Officially, he holds R.M. Hare's "two-levels" view,[28] which resembles RU. Hare thought humans in some ways are like *archangels* (with superhuman powers of thought and no human weaknesses) and in some ways are like *proles* (with many weaknesses and little ability to think things out). The "critical level" of moral thinking tries to think things out rationally, as would an archangel; it rests on critical thinking instead of moral intuitions, and it follows act utilitarianism. One task of critical thinking is to arrive at RU rules that would be built into the intuitions of proles and humans; these RU rules would likely resemble conventional morality. The "intuitive level" of moral thinking follows intuitions instead of thinking things out. So AU and RU each have their place: AU at the critical and RU at the intuitive level.

---

[26] Richard B. Brandt's "Rule Utilitarianism," in Harry J. Gensler, Earl W. Spurgin, and James C. Swindal, eds., *Ethics: Contemporary Readings* (London: Routledge, 2004), pp. 215–220. This was first published as "Toward a Credible Form of Utilitarianism," in *Morality and the Language of Conduct*, ed. Hector-Neri Castañeda and George Nakhnikian (Detroit: Wayne State University Press, 1965), pp. 107–143. While Brandt invented the term "rule utilitarianism," the idea goes back much earlier.

[27] I think that RU generally leads to the right judgments, although often for the wrong reasons. For example, while RU may lead to strong principles against breaking promises, it doesn't see anything inherently wrong in breaking your word.

[28] R.M. Hare, *Moral Thinking* (Oxford: Oxford University Press, 1981).

Whether correctly or not, I've always interpreted Singer as holding AU, instead of the less radical RU. So, in a debate with him a few years ago, I posed this question (here by "utilitarianism" I mean "act utilitarianism"—I'm sorry I wasn't clearer on this):

> My second objection is that Singer's underlying ethical principle, utilitarianism, leads to absurdities. . . . Here's an example that I call the lynching-is-fun case. Imagine a town where the racist lynch mob so enjoys hangings that it maximizes pleasure if they hang you, who are of a different race. Utilitarianism approves of this act, since it maximizes the pleasure total—since the racist mob gets so much pleasure from your lynching. If you were a consistent utilitarian, you'd have to desire that if you were in this situation then you be hanged. Since almost no one can desire this, almost no one can be a consistent utilitarian. . . . The problem with utilitarianism isn't that it permits killing in a few exceptional cases; the problem is rather that it leads to bizarre results—about killing and other things—in lots of cases—especially ones where you maximize good results at the expense of someone's basic rights.[29]

Singer responded as follows:

> The second objection was a general one to utilitarianism—interesting and important, but it has been fairly well covered. My view about the kind of lynching-is-fun case is that this is not the way to maximize the interests of all those affected, that if you allow this kind of practice where people get fun out of killing others or making them suffer, it's clearly going to spread and it's going to lead to a worse society in which there are some people who are in fear of their lives and terrorized, while others get some fun about it. It's much better to say, no you can't get fun that way, you've got to go to the football game instead, where you can still see people crunching each other, but not with such severe consequences, and they're all willing participants. That's also too brief an answer, I know, but for my purposes there's no time for more.[30]

This quick response, which might not represent Singer's considered opinion, seems to presume RU instead of AU. In my example, this particular instance of lynching is stipulated to maximize interests, which on

---

[29] See http://www.jcu.edu/pubaff/eyeonjcu/singer_gensler.htm. I went on to say that my objection addresses the critical level of moral thinking; it appeals to facts and consistency, not moral intuitions. While I expressed my case in terms of maximizing pleasure, I could have expressed it in terms of maximizing the satisfaction of preferences.

[30] See http://www.jcu.edu/pubaff/eyeonjcu/singer_gensler.htm.

AU would make it right.[31] But Singer focuses on the *practice* of lynching (instead of on the individual act): "If you allow this kind of practice where people get fun out of killing others or making them suffer, it's clearly going to spread and it's going to lead to a worse society in which there are some people who are in fear of their lives and terrorized, while others get some fun about it." Is Singer saying that this act of lynching is wrong, on his view, because it would be forbidden by the rule about lynching whose adoption by society would have the best consequences? If so, then Singer is a rule utilitarian and can avoid my objection. But is RU consistent with the great bulk of his writings on ethics?

I went through *Practical Ethics* again, looking for what it says about AU and RU. I was surprised that the index had no entries for "act utilitarianism" or "rule utilitarianism." I couldn't find any place in the book that uses these terms (although the ideas come up, as we will see). Also, I couldn't find any discussion of objections to act utilitarianism based on its bizarre implications (like Brandt's lawn-mowing case). Rule utilitarians usually present their view by first explaining the standard objections to AU and then showing how RU overcomes these objections. Singer doesn't mention these standard objections or explain how he deals with them (by moving to RU, biting the bullet, or whatever); this seems strange. Maybe he thinks utilitarianism is more plausible to people if they aren't aware of the standard objections to it. Or maybe he is so impatient with ethical theory that he doesn't want to spend time on this.

Singer introduces utilitarianism in this way:

> Now, imagine that I am trying to decide between two possible courses of action—perhaps whether to eat all the fruits I have collected myself, or to share them with others. . . . Suppose I then begin to think ethically. . . . I now have to take account of the interests of all those affected by my decision. This requires me to weigh up all those interests and adopt the course of action most likely to maximize the interests of those affected.[32]

---

[31] If it is objected that this individual act of lynching will not maximize pleasure (or preference satisfaction), because of such and such further factors, then we can specify the situation more carefully to sidestep these further factors. For example, maybe the people (like the ancient Romans) enjoy lynchings much more than football and maybe the effective time to change this is not now but later (when a new emperor comes into power). Hypothetical cases give the best way to evaluate AU, since they let us stipulate that a given action maximizes the total pleasure. With actual cases, AU rarely leads to clear results—since long-range consequences are so uncertain.

[32] *Practical Ethics*, p. 13; the example about X and Y on page 21 also seems to presume AU. Note how quickly the quoted passage slides from "taking account of the interests of

This seems like act utilitarianism: I am to do that individual action that maximizes the interests of everyone affected. But then he talks more like a rule utilitarian:

> There are utilitarian reasons for believing that we ought not to try to calculate these consequences for every ethical decision that we make in our daily lives, but only for very unusual circumstances, or perhaps when we are reflecting on our choice of general principles to guide us in future. . . . We must consider whether the effect of a general practice of sharing gathered fruits will benefit all those affected, by bringing about a more equal distribution, or whether it will reduce the food gathered, because some will cease to gather anything if they know that they will get sufficient from their share of what others gather.[33]

While this sounds more like RU, his position still isn't clear. The passage could be interpreted in an AU manner. Maybe it just points out that my act of sharing may promote the laziness of others; this would have to be taken into account as I calculate the pros and cons of this particular act. Or maybe it just points out the usefulness of having a "rule of thumb" about whether sharing tends to maximize interests; we can override such rules if we see that our particular action does or does not maximize interests. It is unfortunate that Singer doesn't resolve the issue, perhaps by saying something like this (picking either "shouldn't" or "should" at the end):

> Suppose that the most useful rule for society to accept about the practice of sharing forbids me to share—and yet sharing in this individual case has the best consequences. Then I shouldn't / should share.

Saying "I shouldn't share" would accept RU (which would let Singer avoid the standard objections to AU and my lynching-is-fun objection). Saying "I should share" would accept AU (and leave him having to bite the bullet about these strong objections).

Later Singer talks about Hare's two-level approach, which he endorses. But only at the end of this discussion does he make it clear where he stands on the AU-RU issue:

> Perhaps very occasionally we will find ourselves in circumstances in which it is absolutely plain that departing from the principles will produce a much

---

all" (which most moral philosophers would support) to "maximizing interests" (which only utilitarians would support). See my discussion of the equal-consideration principle in the previous section.

[33] *Practical Ethics*, pp. 13–14.

better result than we will obtain by sticking to them, and then we will be justified in making the departure.[34]

This seems to express AU's rules-of-thumb approach: moral rules tell us what kinds of action usually maximize interests and may be departed from if we see that they don't maximize interests in a particular case. So if it is clear (or probable) that lynching this person in this particular case maximizes interests (by satisfying the desires of the crowd), then this is what ought to be done.

In practice, Singer's reasoning about killing seems to be on the AU side, with occasional concerns about what the law should be (which bring in something like RU reasoning). This is especially clear in his discussion about the difference between killing and letting-die. Most non-consequentialists say that, while it is wrong to kill a defective infant (for example by poisoning it), it is not necessarily wrong to just let it die (for example by refusing to perform an extraordinary operation needed to save its life). Singer disagrees; he sees killing and letting-die as morally equivalent, since both have the same result:

> Which approach is right? I have argued for a consequentialist approach to ethics. The acts/omissions issue poses the choice between these two basic approaches in an unusually clear and direct way. What we need to do is imagine two parallel situations differing only in that in one a person performs an act resulting in the death of another human being, while in the other she omits to do something, with the same result.[35]

Singer's consequentialist approach says that the two acts, which have the same result, are morally equivalent.

This same example also poses the choice between AU and RU in an unusually clear way. AU weighs the consequences of individual acts; this is Singer's approach. RU, in contrast, looks at the usefulness of two policies or rules. Imagine two parallel societies that differ only in what rule they accept about killing and letting die:

A. While it is wrong to kill a defective infant (for example by poisoning it), it is not necessarily wrong to just let it die (for

---

[34] *Practical Ethics*, p. 94. Since no assessment of total consequences in real situations is "absolutely plain," there is still some unclarity in the view here. I take the statement to be saying that we should override a moral rule if it is *probable*, on the basis of our evidence, that doing so would have the best consequences. This is act utilitarianism aided with rules-of-thumb.

[35] *Practical Ethics*, p. 207.

example by refusing to perform an extraordinary operation needed to save its life).

B. It is not necessarily wrong either to kill a defective infant or to just let it die; both are morally equivalent.

It is arguable that a society that accepts A would produce better consequences than one that accepts B; this would give a rule-utilitarian justification of the moral importance of the killing versus letting-die distinction.[36] But this is not my point. My point is rather that Singer does not reason in this RU way but instead reasons in the AU manner (with all the problems that that brings).

Rule utilitarians would approach the issue of killing by looking for the rules whose acceptance by people (with their imperfections and limitations) would have the best consequences. Consider these two possible rules about killing humans:

A. Killing another human being is strictly wrong, with perhaps exceptions for a few carefully defined cases (like self-defense).

B. Killing another human being is right if it has the best consequences.

Rules against killing need to be firm and definite; otherwise, people will twist them for their own purposes. I'd be afraid to live in a society that followed the act-utilitarian rule B, where people could kill whenever they speculated that this would have better results; people would apply this in irresponsible ways, with disastrous effects. It would have better results if society followed a strict rule against killing, like A. So we see that RU brings guidelines about killing that are stricter and harmonize better with common sense.

Consider these two possible rules about killing your children:

A. Killing your child is strictly wrong.

B. Killing your unwanted child is permissible if the child has not yet attained self-awareness and rationality.

---

[36] Singer, even though he regards some meat-eating as justifiable in theory, in practice advocates the simple rule "Don't eat meat"—because of the usefulness of having a simple rule that reinforces important attitudes. Similarly, one might prefer a simple rule "Don't kill your children" over a complex and vague one that allows for exceptions— because it's useful for society to have simple rules against killing that reinforce respect for human life.

It's hard to take seriously the idea that accepting B would have better consequences for society than accepting A. Rule B is extremely vague; since children develop gradually in their rational powers, it's arbitrary to pick some "point of rationality" at which killing your children becomes wrong. Rules against killing need to be firm and definite. A vague rule like B may lead to a large amount of killing and erode respect for human life at all levels. It's frightening to imagine a society that lives by rule B.[37]

Singer mentions societies that allow infanticide but otherwise have a great respect for human life. He doesn't mention that much infanticide was done for very unenlightened reasons; for example, the first-born was sacrificed to bring the favor of the gods, female babies were killed out of a preference for males, and infanticide was used as a form of genocide (Exodus 1–2 tells how Moses barely survived the Pharaoh's order to kill all Hebrew boy babies). Ancient Rome is the textbook example of a society that practiced infanticide, and it was known also for its killing-is-fun Coliseum entertainment that featured the killing of gladiators and Christians.[38] Would allowing the killing of unwanted infants and toddlers move us somewhat in that direction, if not at first then perhaps after several generations? Singer thinks not, but that is only his guess. The best answer is that no one really knows what would happen. Allowing the killing of unwanted infants and toddlers is an extremely dangerous idea.

Singer is in a dilemma. If he is an *act utilitarian*, then his ethical framework is subject to strong objections. If he is a *rule utilitarian*, then he will have a more difficult time justifying his views about killing infants and toddlers from that perspective.

My view, which I base on the golden rule,[39] is that we should take into account the interests of animals and we should avoid inflicting needless pain on them. The interests of humans, however, are more

---

[37] B is less frightening if qualified to apply only to disabled children. But recall what was said earlier about the disabled being roughly as happy as the non-disabled.

[38] Recall the 2000 movie *Gladiator*, starring Russell Crowe, about ancient Rome. AU entails that the rightness of killing for entertainment depends on how the numbers work out; we have to weigh the pleasures of the crowd against displeasures caused to others. Note that several science-fiction movies portray a future age that has similarly lost respect for human life.

[39] See my *Ethics: A Contemporary Introduction*. In forming our moral beliefs, we need to be informed on the facts, be consistent, imagine ourselves in the place of the various parties involved, and treat others only as we are willing to be treated ourselves in the same situation. If we do this, I contend, most of us will be closer to the views sketched in this last paragraph than to Singer's views or to act utilitarianism.

important. Any member of a rational species[40] (including *Homo sapiens*) has a higher dignity than that of animals—even if the individual is very young, or is physically or mentally disabled. It is seriously wrong to kill an innocent human being. Every human life deserves such respect, because (a) all humans are members of a rational species; (b) it maximizes good results if, instead of arbitrarily drawing lines, we respect all human life; and (c) we are all made in God's image and likeness, have a special role in creation, and are destined to eternal life with God.

Conclusion

Peter Singer thinks out of the box. He has come up with some very good ideas and some very bad ones. I have argued that his ideas about the unsanctity of human life are deeply flawed and are hurting his credibility and his ability to carry through on the remaining work of the animal liberation movement—where he could do so much good for people, for animals, and for the environment.[41]

---

[40] Singer might object that it is inconsistent to hold, as I do, that species can be morally relevant while race is not. But this charge of inconsistency cannot be taken seriously until the additional premises needed to generate the alleged inconsistency are presented.

[41] I got useful ideas on how to refine this paper from members of my department (especially Jen McWeeny) during a colloquium on it.

Reply to Harry J. Gensler

PETER SINGER

Philosophy, Utilitarianism, and Reticence

I warmly welcome Harry Gensler's emphasis on the importance of alleviating global poverty and ending factory farming. Before I discuss the aspects on which we have deep philosophical differences, I have a few factual quibbles.

Gensler begins by saying that in my writings about famine I "wisely" did not mention my "extreme" view that "that we are required to contribute so much that we would end up poor ourselves." Perhaps I'm not as wise as he imagines, because, as other contributors to this volume are well aware, this is exactly what I did say.[42] Another example of my wisdom, according to Gensler, is my reticence about referring to our duty to feed hungry animals. If this is referring to wild, rather than domestic animals, however, I'm doubtful that we have such a duty, for the ecological consequences of feeding hungry wild animals might make things worse in the long run. With humans, we can encourage them to control their fertility in order to avoid ecological catastrophe. With wild animals, that is difficult to do.

Perhaps more interesting than either of these points is Gensler's claim that by advocating the killing of disabled infants, I have reduced the influence I might otherwise have had on more important issues like factory farming. If I had been able to see into the future, no doubt I

---

[42] "Famine, Affluence and Morality," *Philosophy and Public Affairs* 1 (1972), pp. 240–41; other contributors who note this implication of my position include Arneson, Cowen, Lichtenberg, Narveson, and Schmidtz. For fuller discussion of the distinction between what we should advocate in this area, and what we might privately believe we should do, see Peter Singer, *The Life You Can Save* (New York: Random House, 2009), Chapter 10.

would have considered the question Gensler's claim raises. But I did not foresee how controversial my views in this area would become. If today this seems difficult to believe, then consider that a full ten years elapsed between the time I first stated my views on infanticide for disabled infants (in the first edition of *Practical Ethics,* published in 1979) and the first public protests against my views, in 1989. (The autobiography in this volume gives further details.) In 1979, and even in 1985 when *Should the Baby Live?* appeared, I was not aware of any disability movement objecting to allowing babies with severe disabilities to die on the grounds that this is discrimination against those with disabilities. Opposition from the anti-abortion movement was more predictable, but that opposition was inevitable, given my views on abortion, and there was nothing unusual about defending legal abortion.

In any case, even if I had been able to foresee all the consequences of expressing my views on infanticide, I would not have acted differently. There are two distinct reasons for this. One is factual: I am not at all sure that my views on infanticide have reduced my influence on other issues. True, these views have led to protests, but that is a double-edged sword. The protests over my appointment at Princeton, for example, led to far more people becoming aware that I was taking up a chair in the United States than would otherwise have been the case. As a result, I had opportunities to express my views in the media that I would not otherwise have had. Among those opportunities was an invitation to contribute an article to the *The New York Times Sunday Magazine,* an opportunity I used to write "The Singer Solution to World Poverty" which, as I note in my autobiography, led to more than $600,000 being donated to Oxfam and UNICEF.

The other reason why I might not have acted differently is that as a philosopher I follow the argument where it leads. Should I, as a utilitarian, resist that urge, if the argument will lead me to say something counterproductive? That isn't so clear. Developing sound positions in ethics should, in the long run, have better consequences than doing bad philosophy, or refusing to discuss some issues for fear of losing influence on others.

Animal Liberation and Infanticide

Gensler says that the first phase of the animal liberation movement was to reduce the number of cruel experiments on animals, and in this the movement achieved significant success, while the second phase of the movement, to discourage people from eating meat, has not had the same success, despite the strength of the arguments against eating meat. He contends that I would be capable of inspiring a more successful campaign against meat-eating, were it not for the fact that I have been discredited by my views on infanticide.

What is wrong with this picture? For a start, Gensler is contrasting the reforms achieved in animal experimentation—which have not stopped experiments on animals—with the failure to abolish or substantially reduce meat consumption. A more balanced comparison would be between reforms that reduce cruelty in animal experimentation, and reforms that reduce cruelty in farming. If Gensler were to make that comparison, he would find that in Europe there has been at least as much success in reducing cruelty in farming as there has been in reducing cruelty in experiments on animals. Although the United States lags behind Europe in both areas, the American animal movement has recently achieved some notable successes for farm animals. The suffering of pigs will in future be reduced by the decisions of Smithfield Foods and Maple Leaf Foods—the largest pork producers in the United States and Canada, respectively—to phase out gestation crates, which are commonly used to confine pregnant sows in metal crates too small for them even to turn around or walk a few steps. Burger King has announced that it will start to buy some of its eggs from producers who do not keep their hens in cages, and many colleges no longer buy eggs from caged hens. Since 2002, Florida, Arizona, Oregon and Colorado have banned some forms of factory farm confinement, either as a result of referenda or through legislation at the state level. The biggest success of all came in the election of November 2008, when Californians voted overwhelmingly in support of an initiative that will, from 2013, allow all farm animals room to turn around and stretch their limbs freely, thus effectively banning sow crates, veal crates, and battery cages for laying hens.[43]

In any case, though I am flattered that Gensler should link the animal movement's failure to reduce meat consumption with the damage done to my reputation by my views on infanticide, any such connection is far-fetched. It is quite true that, as Gensler says, I can "easily convince Princeton that food issues are an important part of bioethics." In fact,

---

[43] For reports on Smithfield's decision, see Alexei Barrionuevo, "Pork Producer Says It Plans to Give Pigs More Room," *New York Times* (January 26th, 2007); on the Californian vote see "Californians Make History by Banning Veal Crates, Battery Cages, and Gestation Crates, Humane Society of the United States Media Release, November 4, 2008, http://www.hsus.org/farm/news/ournews/prop2_california_110408.html

that is exactly what I have done. In 2006 I organized a major conference at Princeton on "Food, Ethics and the Environment." It attracted so many people that we had to use the university's largest auditorium, one used in recent years for speeches by Bill Clinton or Condoleeza Rice, but very rarely for conferences. *The Ethics of What We Eat,* the book I wrote with Jim Mason, contains much of the information that Gensler says is need-ed, including a discussion of how much water it takes to produce meat and other foods. In promoting that book, I saw no evidence that people were taking it less seriously than they might have because of my views on infanticide.

The real problem is that it is notoriously difficult to change eating patterns. To persuade a significant number of people to stop eating meat takes a lot more than one person, no matter how prestigious a university chair he may hold. Whether from habit or because they like the taste of it, people continue to buy meat even when they have been exposed to all the arguments against doing so, including arguments based on their own health, which with many people are more powerful than ethical argu-ments that presuppose some concern for animals or the environment.

When Killing Is Wrong

Gensler finds three initial problems with my view about when it is most seriously wrong to kill. The first is vagueness. This is not so much a philosophical objection as a practical problem. It may be true that it is worse to kill a self-aware being who wants to go on living than it is to kill a being who lacks self-awareness, and yet, since self-awareness develops gradually, and is difficult to detect, it may also be the case that in practice we should ignore this distinction and simply hold that it is wrong to kill any human being after birth. (We could also, while main-taining the moment of birth as the crucial line of demarcation, allow some exceptions for extraordinary circumstances.)

Gensler thinks that the criterion of self-awareness is irrelevant to the wrongness of killing a child, and he defends this view by saying that those who support such a criterion must answer the question: "Would it have been right for your parents to have killed you before this point, but wrong afterwards?" (The formulation of this question doesn't entirely square with my views, since the rightness or wrongness of such an action may depend on more than self-awareness, including the desires of others to adopt or care for the child, but we can let that pass.) Gensler seems to think that an affirmative answer is difficult to give. To me it seems no more difficult than it is to give an affirmative answer to the question: "Would it have been right for your parents to have taken steps to avoid conception, around the time when you were conceived?" In both cases, I would not have lived the life that I have enjoyed living. In neither case would I have ever had any thoughts or plans about my future that would have been cut tragically short. Yet most people think it would not have been wrong for their parents to use contraception (or, for those opposed to conception, to have succeeded in avoiding conception by abstaining from sexual intercourse during times when your mother was likely to be fertile).

Gensler's second initial problem with my view on killing infants is that studies show "that the disabled have roughly the same degree of happiness as the non-disabled." Since the quality of life of people with disabilities is the central issue in Harriet Johnson's article in this volume, I shall postpone a full discussion until my response to her. Gensler's theologically flavored remark on the value of "overcoming negatives," however, proves too much. If suffering always has a silver lining, why does he think we should seek to alleviate poverty? Should we abandon all efforts to prevent suffering? If not, where is the line to be drawn? Would Gensler share the view expressed by the Christian philosopher Richard Swinburne: "Suppose that one less person had been burnt by the Hiroshima atomic bomb. Then there would have been less opportunity for courage and sympathy . . ."[44]

Gensler asks whether if there are other groups—racial, religious or socio-economic—that turn out to be less happy, babies from these groups ought to be killed too. That question implies that I think disabled babies ought to be killed because they are less happy. But that is a fundamental misunderstanding of my position. I don't think severely disabled babies ought to be killed. I think the parents of severely disabled babies who think it would be better if their babies died, ought to have the option of either allowing them to die, or killing them where that is the more humane course to take. Gensler himself seems to accept that parents should have the first of these choices, because he goes on to say: "Most with extreme disabilities will die off naturally, in the meantime we can help ease their pain." The implication is that we don't have to use all the medical technology at our disposal to prolong these lives. That in turn involves a judgment that some human lives are not worth prolonging. I agree, of course, but let's not slough off the responsibility for those

---

[44] Richard Swinburne, *The Existence of God* (Oxford: Oxford University Press, 2004), p. 264; quoted by Richard Dawkins, *The God Delusion* (London: Black Swan, 2007), p. 89n.

deaths with a casual reference to the deaths occurring "naturally." Neonatal intensive care units are replete with expensive and highly effective means of preventing deaths that would otherwise occur "naturally." If in specific cases we choose to withhold those means, we must take responsibility for doing so. The difference between Gensler's position and mine, in these cases, comes down to the fact that he would allow only the withholding or withdrawing of treatment to bring about death, whereas I see little difference between causing death by withdrawing a respirator, when one knows that the infant is unable to breathe unaided, and causing death by a lethal injection. (In practice, the difference between what Gensler recommends and what I recommend may be even less than this—among health care professionals, talk of "easing the pain" is often a euphemism for a life-shortening dose of morphine.[45])

In setting out his third problem with my views on infanticide, Gensler claims that I vacillate in whether I hold that there is no moral objection to killing any infant, or that it is only in the case of severely disabled infants that killing is permissible. But the first of the two references in *Practical Ethics* that Gensler cites makes my position clear: "The difference between killing disabled and normal infants lies not in any supposed right to life that the latter has and the former lacks but in other considerations about killing."[46] I then go on to discuss the importance of the wishes of the parents, and the relevance of the desires of other couples to adopt a child. These factors almost always provide ample reason to protect the lives of normal infants, at least for those of us living in industrialized societies where there is a shortage of babies for adoption. In addition, the already-mentioned desirability of basing laws on clear lines, rather than on differences that emerge gradually, is a reason for prohibiting the killing of normal infants.

Preference Utilitarianism or Hedonistic Utilitarianism?

I am a preference utilitarian, but the choice between preference and hedonistic utilitarianism has always seemed to me one about which reasonable people can disagree. There are advantages and disadvantages to

---

[45] See, for example, Patrick Devlin, *Easing the Passing: The Trial of Dr John Bodkin Adams* (London: Bodley Head, 1985).

[46] *Practical Ethics*, p. 182.

either choice. Gensler brings out some of the difficulties with preference utilitarianism. I was not, however, ambivalent about the issue when I wrote *Practical Ethics*. The passage to which Gensler refers in his footnote 21 was written in terms of "maximizing pleasure" only as a simplifying assumption, to make the discussion of a complex topic a little easier to follow. "More pleasure and less pain" is, after all, an important and widely shared preference.

I have already discussed, in my response to Don Marquis, the questions Gensler raises about whether I should include all preferences in my decisions about what to do, or only the preferences people would have if they were fully informed and thinking clearly. Similarly, in my reply to Michael Huemer, I consider and reject a claim very like the one Gensler makes, that my own views are based on moral intuitions, rather than on the most defensible form of preference utilitarianism. I need only add here that preference utilitarianism does not lead to "majority-rule conventionalism" because preferences are weighted in accordance with how much they matter to people. Majority rule, on the other hand, allows the majority to outvote the minority, even if the majority doesn't care much about an issue that is all-important to the minority.

In addition, in the specific case of people's desire to eat meat, Gensler overlooks the crucial fact—which he so eloquently stated earlier—that meat-eating involves cruelty to animals. The animals' preferences count too, and would decisively out-weigh the preferences of the meat-eaters. Gensler suggests that there is some problem about knowing what animals would prefer if they reflected on the relevant facts, but it seems obvious that they would prefer not to suffer merely so that humans can pay less to eat their flesh. As it happens, there is experimental work that demonstrates clearly the preferences—and even the "informed" preferences—of chickens. I have already mentioned, in my response to Frey, the work of Marion Stamp Dawkins, a professor in the department of zoology at the University of Oxford. Dawkins has tested how hard chickens will work to change their conditions—for example, by having to repeatedly peck at a button in order to move from a wire cage to a grass run. She "informed" the chickens about their choices, by familiarizing them with both sets of conditions. She found, not surprisingly, that they prefer the grass run. She also found that hens have a strong preference to lay their eggs in darkened, soft-floored nesting boxes, rather than in a bare wire cage.[47]

---

[47] See Marian Stamp Dawkins, "The Scientific Basis for Assessing Suffering in Animals," in Peter Singer, ed., *In Defense of Animals: The Second Wave* (Oxford:

Now we come to a genuine difficulty for preference utilitarianism: the way in which a question is framed can greatly influence the preferences people give in response.[48] It isn't clear how pervasive this problem is. We know that some of the preferences people express in response to questions will vary in accordance with the way the questions are framed, but as Gensler acknowledges, others will persist through a range of different ways in which we ask about them. Beyond that, the issue is one to which I need to give more thought. Is it merely a problem of how to get at the "real" preferences that underlie the different responses people may give to questions put to them in different ways, or does it show that there is no such thing as a "real" preference, apart from the fluctuating preferences that people may feel, and express, in different circumstances? If we are forced to conclude that the latter option is correct, this would be a significant reason for abandoning preference utilitarianism for hedonistic utilitarianism, or some other version of consequentialism.

Act- or Rule- Utilitarianism?

If I see the choice between preference and hedonistic utilitarianism as in some way open, I am more clearcut about the choice between act- and rule-utilitarianism. I have never been a rule-utilitarian. Act-utilitarianism can take over many of the features that make rule-utilitarianism attractive, without ceasing to be, properly speaking, act-utilitarianism. But this issue, too, is central to another essay in this volume, that by David Schmidtz, and my defense of this claim will be found in my response to him.

This leaves only one further point to make in response to what Gensler says about act- and rule-utilitarianism. His account of my views is generally fair and free from innuendo. But in this discussion he lets his standard slip. Saying that I fail to deal with the obvious objections to act-utilitarianism that rule-utilitarians usually present, he writes: "Singer doesn't mention these standard objections or explain how he deals with them (by moving to RU, biting the bullet, or whatever); this seems strange." He then suggests that I may be trying to hide the bizarre implications of utilitarianism from my readers in order to make it more plausible. This interpretation of my writings stands in stark contrast to other

---

Blackwell, 2005), pp. 26–39; Marian Stamp Dawkins, *Animal Suffering: The Science of Animal Welfare* (London: Chapman and Hall, 1980).

[48] The classic article on this topic is Amos Tversky and Daniel Kahnemann, "The Framing of Decisions and the Psychology of Choice," *Science* 211 (1981), pp. 453–58.

views expressed in this volume, for example, Beryl Benderly's assertion that I knowingly make statements that "will appall and scandalize many people." What is even stranger, however, is that Gensler himself has already attacked me for explicitly—and in his view, unwisely—stating my support for infanticide. Is that also part of my strategy to make utilitarianism seem plausible? And just a few pages further on he acknowledges that I *do* explain how I deal with the standard objections to act-utilitarianism. As he correctly notes, I do this by moving to the two-level view—he even quotes the passage in which I say that sometimes we have to depart from the usual moral rules. Later he adds: "My point is rather that Singer does not reason in this RU way but instead reasons in the AU manner (with all the problems that that brings)." In other words, his accusation that I am trying to hide these problems is a smear that he has himself shown to be baseless.

Gensler's Defense of the Sanctity of Human Life

As an alternative to my critique of the doctrine of the sanctity of human life, Gensler presents his own:

> Any member of a rational species (including *Homo sapiens*) has a higher dignity than that of animals even if the individual is very young, or is physically or mentally disabled. It is seriously wrong to kill an innocent human being. Every human life deserves such respect, because (a) all humans are members of a rational species; (b) it maximizes good results if, instead of arbitrarily drawing lines, we respect all human life; and (c) we are all made in God's image and likeness, have a special role in creation, and are destined to eternal life with God.

This idea of privileging all members of "a rational species" will not do, in part for reasons that I gave in responding to Williams. Strictly, no species is either rational or irrational—such capacities adhere to individuals, not species. What Gensler means is that if normal mature members of a species are rational, then *any* member of that species has a higher dignity than any member of another species, normal mature members of which are not rational. But why should belonging to such a species give an individual higher dignity, if the individual is not rational itself? Or if it is actually *less* rational than some members of other species, as some intellectually disabled human beings are less rational than normal mature chimpanzees? Isn't this the same fallacy that people make when they engage in racial or ethnic stereotyping—

judging individuals by some impression, accurate or not, of what most members of the group are like? In the absence of further argument, we should reject Gensler's reason (a). His (b) is a factual claim that, if true, would indeed show that it is seriously wrong to kill an innocent human being. But it hasn't been shown to be true, at least not in the absolute form in which it is stated. How do we know that the relief of suffering, and of burdens on families, that results from permitting euthanasia for severely disabled infants, is outweighed by respecting all human life? Gensler offers no evidence or further argument for his claim. Finally, in Gensler's (c), our alleged special relationship with God and life and death come into the picture. I can only wonder why a philosopher feels entitled to put forward such claims without making the slightest attempt to show that they are true.

5

Unspeakable Conversations, or, How I Spent One Day as a Token Cripple at Princeton University

HARRIET McBRYDE JOHNSON

He insists he doesn't want to kill me. He simply thinks it would have been better, all things considered, to have given my parents the option of killing the baby I once was, and to let other parents kill similar babies and thereby avoid the suffering that comes with lives like mine and satisfy the reasonable preferences of parents for a different kind of child. It has nothing to do with me. I should not feel threatened.

It is a chilly Monday in late March, 2002. I am at Princeton University. My host is Professor Peter Singer. He is the man who wants me dead. No, that's not fair. He wants to legalize the killing of certain babies who might come to be like me if allowed to live. He also says he believes that it should be lawful under some circumstances to kill, at any age, individuals with cognitive impairments so severe that he doesn't consider them "persons." What does it take to be a person? Awareness of your own existence in time. The capacity to harbor preferences as to the future, including the preference for continuing to live.

At this stage of my life, he says, I am a person. However, as an infant, I wasn't. I, like all humans, was born without self-awareness. And eventually, assuming my brain finally gets so fried that I fall into that wonderland where self and other and present and past and future blur into one formless all or nothing, then, he says, my family and doctors might put me out of my misery, or out of my bliss or oblivion, and no one count it murder.

In the morning, I talk to 150 undergraduates on selective infanticide. In the evening, it is a convivial discussion, over dinner, of assisted suicide. I am the token cripple with an opposing view.

I had several reasons for accepting Singer's invitation, some grounded in my involvement in the disability rights movement, others personal. Among the personal reasons: I was sure it would make a great story. By now I've told it to family and friends and colleagues and I keep getting interrupted by questions—like these:

Q: Was he totally grossed out by your physical appearance?
A: He gave no sign of it. None whatsoever.

Q: How did he handle having to interact with someone like you?
A: He behaved in every way appropriately, treated me as a respected professional acquaintance and was a gracious and accommodating host.

Q: Was it emotionally difficult for you to take part in a public discussion of whether your life should have happened?
A: It was very difficult. And horribly easy.

Q: Did he get that job at Princeton because they like his ideas on killing disabled babies?
A: It apparently didn't hurt, but he's most famous for animal rights. He's the author of *Animal Liberation*.

Q: How can he put so much value on animal life and so little value on human life?

That last question is the only one I avoid. I used to say I don't know; it doesn't make sense. But now I've read some of Singer's writing, and I admit it does make sense—within the conceptual world of Peter Singer. But I don't want to go there. Or at least not for long.

So I will start from those other questions. That first question, about my physical appearance, needs some explaining.

It's not that I'm ugly. It's more that the sight of me is routinely discombobulating. The power wheelchair is enough to inspire gawking, but much more impressive is the impact on my body of forty-five years of a muscle-wasting disease. At this stage of my life, I'm Karen Carpenter thin, a jumble of bones in a floppy bag of skin. Two or three times in my life—I recall particularly one largely crip, largely lesbian cookout in

Colorado—I have been looked at as a rare kind of beauty. But most often the reactions are decidedly negative. Strangers on the street are moved to comment: I admire you for being out; most people would give up. I'll pray for you. If I had to live like you, I think I'd kill myself.

I used to try to explain that it's a great sensual pleasure to zoom by power chair on these delicious muggy streets, that I have no more reason to kill myself than most people. But God didn't put me on this street to provide disability awareness training. In fact, no god put anyone anywhere for any reason, if you want to know. But they don't want to know. They think they know everything there is to know, just by looking at me. They don't know they're really expressing the discombobulation that comes in my wake.

So. What stands out when I recall first meeting Peter Singer in the spring of 2001 is his apparent lack of discombobulation, his immediate ability to deal with me as a person with a particular point of view.

Singer has been invited to the College of Charleston to lecture. I have been dispatched by Not Dead Yet, the national organization leading the disability-rights opposition to legalized assisted suicide and disability-based killing.

I arrive early and am confronted with the unnerving sight of two people I know sitting on a park bench with Singer. Sharon is a veteran activist for human rights. Herb is South Carolina's most famous atheist. Good people, I've always thought—now sharing veggie pitas with a proponent of genocide. I try to beat a retreat, but Herb and Sharon come over. I sit where I'm parked. Herb makes an introduction. Singer extends his hand.

I shouldn't shake hands with the Evil One. But he is Herb's guest, and hereabouts, the rule is that if you're not prepared to shoot on sight, you have to be prepared to shake hands. "Good afternoon, Mr. Singer. I'm here for Not Dead Yet." I want to think he flinches, but if he does, he instantly recovers. When he says he looks forward to an interesting exchange, he seems entirely sincere.

It is an interesting exchange. In the lecture hall, Singer lays it all out. The "illogic" of allowing abortion but not infanticide, of allowing withdrawal of life support but not active killing. He spins out his bone-chilling argument for letting parents kill disabled babies and replace them with non-disabled babies who have a greater chance at happiness.

I get the microphone and say I'd like to discuss selective infanticide. As a lawyer, I disagree with his jurisprudential assumptions. Logical inconsistency is not a sufficient reason to change the law. As an atheist, I object to his using religious terms ("the doctrine of the sanctity of human life") to characterize his critics. Singer jots down my points, and I proceed to the heart of my argument: that the presence or absence of a disability doesn't predict quality of life. I question his replacement-baby theory, with its assumption of "other things equal." I draw out a comparison of myself and my non-disabled brother Mac, each of us with gifts and flaws so peculiar that we can't be measured on the same scale.

He responds with clear and lucid counterarguments. We go back and forth for ten minutes. Even as I am horrified by what he says, and by the fact that I have been sucked into a civil discussion of whether I ought to exist, I can't help being dazzled by his verbal facility. He is so respectful, so focused on the argument, that by the time the show is over, I'm not exactly angry with him. Yes, I am enraged—but it's for the two hundred of my fellow Charlestonians who have listened with polite interest, when in decency they should have run him out of town.

My encounter with Singer merits a mention in my annual canned letter that December. I decide to send him a copy. In response, he sends me the nicest possible e-mail. Just back from Australia, agrees with my comments on the world situation, then some pointed questions to clarify my views on selective infanticide. I answer his questions, and pose some of my own. Answers and more questions come back.

Singer seems curious to learn how someone who is as good an atheist as he is could disagree with his views. At the same time, I am trying to plumb his theories. What has him so convinced it would be best to allow parents to kill babies with severe disabilities, and not other kinds of babies, if no infant is a "person" with a right to life? I learn it is partly that both biological and adoptive parents prefer healthy babies. But I have trouble with basing life-and-death decisions on market considerations when the market is structured by prejudice. I offer a hypothetical comparison: "What about mixed-race babies, especially when the combination is entirely non-white, who I believe are just about as unadoptable as babies with disabilities?" Wouldn't a law allowing the killing of these undervalued babies validate race prejudice?

Singer agrees there is a problem. "It would be horrible," he says, "to see mixed-race babies being killed because they can't be adopted, whereas white ones could be." What's the difference? Preferences based on race are unreasonable. Preferences based on ability are not. Why? To Singer, it's pretty simple: disability makes a person "worse off."

Are we "worse off"? I don't think so. For those of us with congenital conditions, disability shapes all we are. Those disabled later in life adapt. We take constraints no one would choose and build rich and satisfying lives within them. We enjoy pleasures other people enjoy, and pleasures peculiarly our own. We have something the world needs.

Back and forth we go over several weeks. Finally, I tell Singer we've exhausted our topic. He responds by inviting me to Princeton. I fire off an immediate maybe.

Of course I'm flattered. Mama will be impressed. But disabled lives should not be subject to debate. If I decline, Singer can say we refuse rational discussion. I inform a few movement colleagues, and advice starts rolling in. I decide to go with the advisers who counsel me to do the gig, lie low and get out of Dodge.

I ask Singer to refer me to the person who arranges travel at Princeton. He refers me to his assistant, but almost immediately jumps back in via e-mail. It seems the nearest hotel has only one wheelchair-accessible suite available with two rooms for $600 per night. What to do? I know I shouldn't be so accommodating, but I say I can make do with an inaccessible room if it has certain features. Other logistical issues come up. Do I really need a lift-equipped vehicle at the airport? Can't my assistant assist me into a conventional car? How wide is my wheelchair?

By the time we're done, Singer knows that I am twenty-eight inches wide. I have trouble controlling my wheelchair if my hand gets cold. I am accustomed to driving on rough, irregular surfaces, but get nervous turning on steep slopes. Even one step is too many. I can swallow purees, soft bread and grapes. I use a bedpan, not a toilet. None of this is a secret; none of it cause for angst. But I do wonder whether Singer is jotting down my specs as evidence of how "bad off" people like me really are.

After a grueling day of travel, I wake up tired. My personal assistant, Carmen, props me up to eat oatmeal and drink tea. Then there's the bedpan and then bathing and dressing, still in bed, and we ease into the day. Carmen lifts me into my chair and straps a rolled towel under my ribs. She switches on my motors to give me the power to move without anyone's help. I roll out.

I wait in the pit of a big lecture hall. Singer is loping down the stairs. So. On with the show.

My talk is pretty Southern. I pound them with heart, hammer them with narrative and say "y'all" and "folks." I talk about justice. Even beauty and love. I figure they haven't been getting much of that kind of talk from Singer.

Of course, I give them some argument too. I lead with the hypothetical about mixed-race, non-white babies and build the ending around the question of who should have the burden of proof as to the quality of disabled lives. And throughout I present myself as a representative of a minority group that has been rendered invisible by prejudice and oppression, a participant in a discussion that would not occur in a just world.

Singer's response is surprisingly soft. His reframing of the issues is abstract, entirely impersonal. There is a question about keeping alive the unconscious. In response, I tell about a family I knew as a child, which took loving care of a non-responsive teenage girl, acting out their unconditional commitment to each other. Later, when we're taking a walk around campus, I learn this doesn't satisfy Singer. "Let's assume we can prove, absolutely, that the individual is totally unconscious and that we can know, absolutely, that the individual will never regain consciousness. Assuming all that, don't you think continuing to take care of that individual would be a bit—weird?"

"No. Done right, it could be profoundly beautiful."

"But what about the caregiver, a woman typically, who is forced to provide all this service, unable to work, unable to have a life of her own?"

"That's not the way it should be. Not the way it has to be. As a society, we should pay workers to provide that care, in the home."

My Dinner with Peter

At the evening forum, I introduce the issue of assisted suicide as framed by academic articles recommended by Not Dead Yet. Andrew Batavia argues for assisted suicide based on autonomy. In general, he says, the movement fights for our right to control our own lives; when we need assistance to effect our choices, assistance should be available, even if the choice is to end our lives. But Carol Gill says that it is disability discrimination to try to prevent most suicides while facilitating the suicides of ill and disabled people. The case for assisted suicide rests on stereotypes that our lives are inherently so bad that it is entirely rational if we want to die.

I side with Gill. In the discussion that follows, I argue that choice is illusory in a context of pervasive inequality. We shouldn't offer assistance with suicide until we all have the assistance we need to get out of bed in the morning and live a good life. Common causes of suicidality—dependence, institutional confinement, being a burden—are entirely curable.

Singer, seated on my right, participates in the discussion but doesn't dominate it. During the meal, I occasionally ask him to put things within my reach, and he competently complies. At one point, my right elbow slips out from under me. This is awkward. I gesture to Singer. He leans over, and I whisper, "Grasp this wrist and pull forward one inch, without lifting." He follows my instructions to the letter. And he may now understand what I was saying a minute ago, that most of the assistance disabled people need does not demand medical training.

Sympathy for the Monster

When I get home, people are clamoring for the blow-by-blow. Within the disability rights community, people worry that my civility may have given Singer legitimacy. I hear from Laura, a beloved movement sister. She is appalled that I let Singer provide even minor physical assistance. How could I put let Singer appear so human, even kind? I struggle to explain. I didn't feel disempowered; it seemed good to make him do some useful work. And then, the hard part: I've come to believe that Singer actually is human, even kind in his way. I'm not good at sustaining righteous anger; my view tends more toward tragedy.

Like the protagonist in classical tragedy, Singer is a man of unusual gifts, reaching for the heights. He writes that he is trying to create a system of ethics derived from fact and reason, that largely throws off the perspectives of religion, place, family, tribe, community and maybe even species—to "take the point of view of the universe."

But he has his flaw. It is his unexamined assumption that disabled people are inherently "worse off," that we "suffer," that we have lesser "prospects of a happy life." Because of this all-too-common prejudice, and his rare courage in taking it to its logical conclusion, catastrophe looms. I can't look at him without fellowfeeling.

I am regularly confronted by people who tell me I should make Singer an object of implacable wrath, to be destroyed absolutely. And I find myself lacking a logical argument to the contrary.

I am talking to my sister on the phone. "You kind of like the monster, don't you?" she says.

I am unable to evade, unwilling to lie. "Yeah, in a way. And he's not exactly a monster."

"You know, Harriet, they say the SS guards went home and played on the floor with their children every night."

Her harshness comes as a surprise. She changes the topic. I put the phone down with my argumentative nature frustrated. In my mind, I replay the conversation, but defend my position.

"He's not exactly a monster."

"He's advocating genocide."

"That's the thing. In his mind, he isn't. He's only giving parents a choice. He thinks the humans he is talking about aren't 'persons'."

"But that's the way it always works, isn't it? They're always objects, not persons. He's repackaging old ideas. Making them acceptable."

"His ideas are new, in a way. It's not hate. It's a misinformed, warped kind of beneficence. His motive is to do good."

"What do you care about motives?" she asks. "Doesn't this beneficent killing make your disabled brothers and sisters just as dead?"

"But," I say, "it's just talk. It won't matter in the end. Ultimately we'll make a world that's fit for all its flawed creatures."

"What if you're wrong? What if he convinces people that a baby is just like a fetus, infanticide no worse than abortion? What's between that and genocide?"

"Singer wouldn't allow the killing of anyone who prefers to live."

"Oh yes, that overarching respect for individual preferences. Isn't it a bit naïve?"

"I'd call it a fiction, a quasi-religious belief. Once you kill someone, all preferences are moot."

"So what if you wind up in a world where the disabled person's 'irrational' preference to live must yield to society's 'rational' interest in reducing the incidence of disability? When does horror kick in? As you watch the door close behind you in the gas chamber?"

"That's not going to happen."

"Do you have evidence? An argument?" she asks.

"Of course not. And I know it's happened before, in what was considered the most progressive medical community in the world. But it won't happen. I have to believe that."

Belief. Is that what it comes down to? Or am I clinging to foolish hope that the tragic protagonist, this one time, will shift course before it's too late?

I don't think so. It's more about a need for ideas I can live with. I must live in a world that by and large thinks it would be better if people like me did not exist, among people who share Singer's prejudices. I'm unwilling to make monsters of them all. As a disability pariah, I must struggle for a place, for kinship, for community, for connection. My goal isn't to shed the perspective that comes from my particular experience, but to give voice to it. I want to be engaged in the tribal fury that rages when opposing perspectives are let loose.

As a shield from the terrible purity of Singer's vision, I'll look to the corruption that comes from interconnectedness. To justify my hopes that

Singer's theoretical world—and its entirely logical extensions—won't become real, I'll invoke the muck and mess and undeniable reality of disabled lives well lived. That's the best I can do.

Afterword

When asked to contribute to this book, I was disinclined. I felt I had said what I had to say about Singer and his ideas in "Unspeakable Conversations," the long essay from which the above was adapted. That essay did not seem right for this book because it didn't make an argument but told a story. However, within the story, there is some argument. I decided to pull the argument out here and offer it for what it's worth.

Focusing on argument, I have removed most of what seems to have had the greatest impact on many readers: the incidental details, the twists and turns of events, the surprises of human interaction. These made some see for the first time that even a severely disabled person can be fully engaged in the world and maybe it's not such a bad thing that we disabled people exist. Maybe it would be bad to have special dispensations to kill us in various circumstances. Maybe it would be good to give us what we need to contribute to society, even to care for us even when there's no realistic hope of a practical reward. By conveying that disabled lives can be rich and interesting, my pointless details seemed to make some points after all. The fact that they hit so many as a revelation surprised me and made me more than a little sad. Part of me hates revisiting the discussion, but clearly it will go on with or without me.

One thing I learned rather late in my day at Princeton is that I am not a "philosophical" but a "tactical" thinker. Singer and I speak in different terms and work in different spheres.

Singer seems to be trying to figure out what's right and wrong in some ultimate sense. He imagines a universally applicable ethical system logically derived from a few simple principles. His arguments tend to be deductive. For him, key touchstones of validity are clarity and internal consistency.

I do law and politics. I don't look for social consensus—let alone ultimate resolution—of basic questions of right and wrong. I expect that different people will have different notions of right and wrong, depending on their experiences, influences, and needs. In politics and law, we come together and figure out what we'll do without necessarily agreeing why. We bring our own notions into the arena, and if we want to be effective we'll be alert to the notions of our opposition and potential allies. Because societies make laws in response to social, political, and economic realities that are both complex and conflicted, simplicity and consistency are not the law's natural state. As Singer seems to distrust the messiness of experience, I distrust abstract simplifications, whether derived from the Ten Commandments or from Singer's apparently neutral, apparently incontrovertible propositions.

I don't claim to be free of notions. My experience, influences, and needs have led me to put a very high value on justice. Tactically I don't think we can get justice without equality: all participants in the polity need a reasonably equal chance to get out there and mix it up and push their agenda or it won't work. Beyond that, I have been unable to imagine a society sustaining egalitarian political structures without legal structures that put a high value on human life.

Throughout history, certain categories of people have been excluded from the polity, often based on ideologies that define some human lives as worthless or not worth living, unduly burdensome or burdened, or otherwise problematic. Laws that address problems by killing problematic individuals subvert the social commitment to justice—giving each member what he or she needs, striving to hear all voices. As a matter of policy, I favor an irrebutable legal presumption that every human life is inherently and uniquely valuable. I think this presumption is so useful toward building a just society that I just don't worry about whether it can be validated or is ultimately "true."[1]

I might be tempted to just let Singer and his crowd argue philosophically among themselves while I work with others on the real stuff, and in general that's what I do. However, Singer insists that his philosophy should be "practical," that it should guide both individual actions and social policy. And there we get into trouble. Singer is infected by common social prejudices about disability. He would validate those prejudices with the life-and-death power of the law. At a minimum, validating those prejudices undercuts the disability rights movement's struggle for a significant social investment in people commonly considered to lack potential usefulness. At the worst, it puts genocide on the table for "rational" discussion.

Singer says clearly that he would not legalize the killing of anyone who prefers to live, disabled or not, but I've never quite understood his basis—within his intellectual framework—for this particular thou-shalt-not. If we have a society in which most people prefer not to deal with

---

[1] I take no position on whether this presumption should extend (for different reasons, presumably) to nonhuman animals. I try to avoid making public pronouncements on subjects I know very little about.

disabilities like mine, why let my individual preference to live trump all those other people's preferences, especially since my preference will vanish the moment I'm killed, while those others will continue to enjoy theirs? If we go by logic and preference utilitarianism, I really don't see anything substantial between selective infanticide, selective euthanasia, and selective assisted suicide on the one hand and selective genocide on the other. So long as the categories are drawn in a way that leaves most people secure in their own lives and the lives they value, where's the objection? These concerns are often dismissed as "slippery slope" arguments, but I think they are in fact logical extensions of Singer's thinking; in the practical world of law and policy, you have to be prepared to cope with the logical extensions.

Yikes. I'd really rather not think in those terms. Not just because I don't like where the argument is headed, but because playing within Singer's rules demands that we assume away so much that gives real life its richness. Part of life is learning that you don't always get what you want—and confronting the surprises that wait on the other side of disappointment. No child's life can be predicted at birth; a disabled child's path is equally mysterious. Parenthood is in its essence a leap into the unknowable. When you eliminate a life of supposed suffering, you also eliminate the possibility of transcendence for that individual and for the people around him or her. Calling such killing right is profoundly disrespectful to the lives many of us lead and the joys we know. It gives an easy out, an cheap escape from the difficult struggle to make each life good.

Beyond that, it rests on false dichotomies between pain and pleasure, suffering and happiness, limits and possibilities. When we live with a commitment to see one another through—whether as parents and children, til-death spouses or lovers, or members of a political community in pursuit of justice—we may live to know that what is most painful, most difficult, most dreaded may prove to most precious.

It doesn't make sense, but here we are.

Reply to Harriet McBryde Johnson

PETER SINGER

Disability and the Quality of Life

We are all fortunate that Harriet Johnson overcame her reluctance to allow her essay to be included in this volume, for she has provided what is surely the most engaging piece of writing to be found between its covers. Her eloquent, entertaining, and yet deeply unsettling account of our interactions is accurate and generous. She is an astute observer. "Singer seems curious to learn how someone who is as good an atheist as he is could disagree with his views" is right on target. So what did I learn? Why do we disagree?

For a start, we probably disagree on what Johnson describes as "the heart of [her] argument": "that the presence or absence of a disability doesn't predict quality of life." I say "probably" because this claim can be read in two ways. If we understand it as saying "from the fact that a person has a disability, we cannot reliably predict that he or she will have a poor quality of life" then there is no disagreement. Or at least, there is no disagreement unless we consider extreme states of disability, involving either severe intellectual disability or a high level of pain. I shall return to these rare situations shortly. For less devastating conditions, Johnson shows by example that it is possible to be very seriously physically disabled, and to have a rich and full life.

If, however, we read Johnson's claim as "the presence or absence of a disability gives us *no* indication of whether that person's life is likely to be better or worse than the life of an otherwise similarly situated person without a disability," then we do disagree. Most people take it for granted that having a disability has some tendency to make a person worse off. If having a disability has *no* tendency to reduce quality of life, there seems no reason for pregnant women to give up smoking and drinking alcohol, nor for taking folic acid to reduce the risk of having a child with spina bifida. Immunizing girls against rubella would be a waste of time, since the only serious effect the illness has is to produce a disabled child. We could even rescind the ban on thalidomide—why should pregnant women not take advantage of this drug, so helpful in reducing morning sickness, if the fact that your child is likely to be born without arms or legs has no tendency to reduce his or her quality of life? If this sounds grotesque, that is because the view that implies it is so difficult to take seriously.

Admittedly, the fact that majority opinion is on my side does not show that I am right. As I have argued in other areas, the majority view may be based on prejudice—and that is what Johnson believes. She sees people with disabilities as "a minority group that has been rendered invisible by prejudice and oppression." But even within the community of people with disabilities, there are many who actively support research to prevent or cure disabilities—as Christopher Reeve lobbied for stem cell research in the hope that it might one day lead to a cure for paralysis. It is not impossible that people who themselves have disabilities are also prejudiced against people with disabilities, but it begins to seem more probable that there is another explanation—namely, the obvious one, that quality of life often is significantly reduced by having a disability.

In his critique of my views of the sanctity of life, Harry Gensler refers to studies that show, he says, that "the disabled have roughly the same degree of happiness as the non-disabled." It isn't so clear, however, that the studies do show this. Three different reasons make Gensler's conclusion more doubtful than he acknowledges. First, even if we take the data at face value, some studies show significant differences between people with disabilities and people without disabilities, and the differences point to people without disabilities being happier.[2] Admittedly, these differences are smaller than I would have expected, and that is certainly relevant to any discussion of the treatment of disabled infants. But should the data be taken at face value? The second reason for doubt is that, as Tyler Cowen points out in his essay in this volume, what these studies measure is not the degree of happiness that people have, but the degree of happiness that they report themselves as having. This is, of course, because we do not know how to measure happiness directly. Since we are dealing only with reported happiness levels, however, it is possible that, as

---

[2] See Ruut Veenhoven, "Is Happiness Relative?" in J.P. Fargas and J.M. Innes, eds., *Recent Advances in Social Psychology: An International Perspective* (Amsterdam: Elsevier Science, 1989), pp. 235–247, available at http://www2.eur.nl/fsw/research/veenhoven/Pub1980s/89f-full.pdf. See especially p. 13.

Cowen suggests, people with severe disabilities "adjust their expectations" or "lower their aspirations in life." They may then be reporting how well their life meets their expectations, and this could make it misleading to use their reports to compare their degree of happines to that of people with normal expectations. The third reason for doubting that the studies show what Gensler claims they show is that the method they use—obtaining people's own reports of how happy they are—skews the sample of people with disabilities, since it omits those who have intellectual disabilities severe enough to prevent them understanding the question they are being asked. People with severe intellectual disabilities may be much less happy than the rest of us. If they are, the studies to which Gensler refers would not detect it.

Caring for the Irreversibly Unconscious

Johnson describes an exchange we had about the case of a totally unconscious person who we can be sure will never recover consciousness. With the development of techniques for obtaining images of soft tissue in the brain, such cases do exist. If we can see that the cortex has been destroyed, consciousness can never be restored, even if brain-stem functions continue. Johnson says that continuing to take care of such an individual could be beautiful. Perhaps it could. Since a totally unconscious person cannot suffer, I don't really object to it, if that is what people want to do, and if they use their own resources to do it. But when I suggested to Johnson that keeping such people alive imposes a burden on the care-giver, usually a woman who is then unable to have a life of her own, her reply was that society should pay workers to provide that care in the home. I would give priority to meeting the needs of conscious beings—like the billion people currently living in extreme poverty—before spending our limited resources on those who cannot experience any benefit at all from the care they receive.

Similarly, Johnson explains her opposition to assisted suicide by saying that choices to end one's life are illusory until "we all have the assistance we need to get out of bed in the morning and live a good life." She suggests that "common causes of suicidality—dependence, institutional confinement, being a burden—are entirely curable." Perhaps they are, in theory, but I can only wonder when she thinks that utopia is going to arrive, and indeed whether she thinks it *should* arrive in, say, the United States, while, as discussed elsewhere in this book, thousands of children are dying *every day* from poverty-related causes, and the cost of providing a good level of care to one severely disabled person in the United

States could save the lives of many of those children. Meanwhile, is it really promoting free choice to say that people who now want to end their lives—and cannot do so without assistance—should not be permitted to receive that assistance, because one day—but who knows when?—they *might* receive such good care that they *might* change their minds about whether they wish to continue to live?

The Philosopher and the Activist

In her "Afterword," Johnson suggests that I am, as a philosopher, looking for clarity and internal consistency in our ethical beliefs, whereas she is, as a lawyer and an activist, more interested in moving an agenda forward. That's another perceptive observation. I'm aware of the difference of perspectives, because, as I describe in my autobiography in this volume, I am both a philosopher and an activist in some areas, especially for animals. In regard to the issues about which Johnson and I disagree, I am no doubt, thinking primarily as a philosopher. But the division between the philosopher and the activist should not be too sharp. People with agendas need to stop and think about whether their agendas really are worth achieving. As it happens, I think that most of the things that Johnson tries to achieve for people with disabilities—stopping discrimination against them in employment or education, for example, or getting them out of sub-standard institutions—are very much worth achieving. But when the agenda includes opposition to physician-assisted euthanasia, or trying to prevent disability being taken into account when life-and-death decisions are made for infants, I think that one can't escape the philosophical questions about whether these are worthwhile goals.

It is possible, of course, that from a tactical point of view, the simple rallying-cry "No discrimination against people with disabilities" is more effective than any more nuanced stance could be. Admitting that different cases require different judgments can divide a movement that remains united only as long as its agenda does not get into the messy details. As I've indicated in my response to Frey, I've seen this in the animal movement, where many animal advocates campaign under the slogan "no experimentation on animals" since that makes it unnecessary to discuss which experiments might be defensible and which are not. Political movements tend to think in simplistic slogans. But it may not be, in the long run, the best way of achieving their goals, because it mean that the activists lose touch with the mainstream they are trying to convince. I wonder if that is happening in the militant disability movement as well.

Disability Rights and Speciesism

In my response to Bernard Williams's defense of "the human prejudice" I argued that there is no justification for giving special value to human beings, simply because they are members of our species. Although Johnson herself says that she takes "no position" on extending the irrebutable legal presumption of inherent and unique value to nonhuman animals, let's try it out for her. Rewritten to include all sentient beings, her argument would read as follows:

> I have been unable to imagine a society sustaining egalitarian political structures without legal structures that put a high value on sentient life. Throughout history, certain categories of sentient being have been excluded from the polity, often based on ideologies that define some sentient lives as worthless or not worth living, unduly burdensome or burdened, or otherwise problematic. Laws that address problems by killing problematic individuals subvert the social commitment to justice—giving each member what he or she needs, striving to hear all voices. As a matter of policy, I favor an irrebutable legal presumption that every sentient life is inherently and uniquely valuable. I think this presumption is so useful toward building a just society that I just don't worry about whether it can be validated or is ultimately "true."

Is this position less coherent than the original? It might be objected that Johnson is talking about building a just society, and animals can't be members of a human society. But why not? Johnson cannot give the obvious response—that nonhuman animals lack the rational capacities needed to participate in the community—because that would also rule out human beings with profound intellectual disabilities. For the same reason she cannot say that all humans have "voices" that need to be heard, whereas animals do not. But since she acknowledges that she doesn't worry about what position can be validated or is "true," she presumably would brush aside these suggestions and instead argue that it is good policy to include all human beings, because we can imagine a society that is fully egalitarian with respect to humans but it is far-fetched to imagine one that would include all sentient beings. She might add that whether the boundary of species is in itself morally significant or not, it is at least clearcut. It is easy to tell which beings are human and which are not. So we should protect all human life, not because it is "truly" of greater value than nonhuman animal life, but to avoid starting down a dangerous slippery slope that will lead to injustices against some humans that we would all deplore.[3]

This argument is in some ways similar to an argument that, as I indicated in my response to Gensler, might justify using birth as a clearcut line that the law can take as marking the point at which it is wrong to take an innocent human life. But even taken purely on the level of public policy, "an irrebutable legal presumption that every human life is inherently and uniquely valuable" will cause problems. Gensler is far from being an advocate of euthanasia, but he accepts that it is right to allow infants with "extreme disabilities" to "die off naturally" while merely easing their pain, not prolonging their life. That is difficult to defend if their lives have the same unique inherent value as the life of every other human being. Those who support abortion rights will also need to explain why the irrebutable legal presumption does not come into effect at conception. And even the removal of organs from people we declare to be "brain dead" could come into question, as I explain in my response to Stephen Drake.

A Final Challenge

Johnson puts the following question, drawing out what she believes to be an implication of my position: "If we have a society in which most people prefer not to deal with disabilities like mine, why let my individual preference to live trump all those other people's preferences, especially since my preference will vanish the moment I'm killed, while those others will continue to enjoy theirs?" But the fact that a preference vanishes the moment someone is killed does not mean that it does not have weight. That is one of the differences between hedonistic utilitarianism and preference utilitarianism. Preference utilitarians are not concerned only about the conscious experience of having one's preferences frustrated. When they talk of the "satisfaction" of preferences, they are not thinking of the sense of satisfaction that a thirsty person may have when she is at last able to drink. Instead, it is the sense of satisfaction that we use when we say "Freud's desire to have a statue erected in his honor in Vienna has been satisfied" even though the statue was only erected after Freud died. This raises the puzzle of whether preference

---

[3] See A.V. Townsend, "Radical Vegetarians," *Australasian Journal of Philosophy* 57 (1976), pp. 85–93.

utilitarians should take into account the past preferences of those who are now dead. Preference utilitarians may divide on that question, but they all agree that preferences in existence at the time the act is carried out must count, even if the act extinguishes the preference by killing the being whose preference it was.[4]

Even if the preferences of the person killed count, however, why couldn't they be trumped by the preferences of others, as Johnson suggests? In theory, they could be. But, for a start, if someone wants to go on living, that preference is normally going to be much stronger and more significant than the preferences of even a very large number of prejudiced people who prefer not to encounter people with disabilities. More significantly, perhaps, in the interests of a better future, we should encourage people to overcome such prejudices. This is, after all, what happened with racial integration in the American South. White Southerners who, in the 1950s, were repulsed by the idea of sitting next to an African American on a bus or at a lunch counter found, once they were compelled to do it, that it really wasn't bad at all. If we had not acted against the prejudices they had, we might still have a situation in which the preferences of white southerners to maintain racial segregation prevent African Americans from satisfying their—much stronger and more significant—preferences for equality. Only by refusing to yield to such prejudiced preferences were we able, in the long run, to satisfy the preferences of everyone. And lastly, if we do not protect the right to life of everyone capable of wanting to go on living, the result will be a level of fear and insecurity that will greatly reduce the quality of life of all those who fear that they might be killed.

Postscript

Harriet Johnson's sudden death, while this volume was in preparation, has robbed me of a critic who was often sharp, but always fair. My reply was written before her death, and refers to her in the present tense. I have decided to leave it like that, not because I imagine her watching me from above—one thing on which we were one hundred percent in agreement is that there is neither god nor afterlife—but because her presence is still so fresh and vivid in my mind. I was looking forward to seeing her opinion of my response, and I deeply regret the end of our dialogue.

---

[4] On counting the preferences of the dead, see *Pushing Time Away* (New York: Ecco, 2003), Chapter 36.

6

Not Dead Yet!

STEPHEN DRAKE

I am going to make some claims that may seem outrageous or even shocking about the work of someone who was hired at Princeton, whose work is widely respected, and whose texts are standard fare in college classrooms all over the world. The standard "defense" of Peter Singer and his works, is that no matter how offensive you may find them, they meet a high standard of intellectual integrity and rigor. This was the standard "Princeton defense" of the appointment of Peter Singer in a tenured position.

That, in a nutshell, is what I challenge. Peter Singer's work, as it pertains to euthanasia, infanticide, and personhood—the idea that some human beings are persons and others are not—is riddled with sloppiness and even dishonesty. To be fair, those traits aren't Singer's unique domain in the field of bioethics. Bioethics is a field that doesn't seem to demand intellectual integrity or honesty from professionals within its fold.

Before I move onto that, I'd like to demonstrate that academia and people who like to think of themselves as progressives have wholeheartedly embraced social agendas dressed up with a veneer of reason, rationality, and science in the past. Specifically, let's spend a minute considering the eugenics movement in this country.

In the first part of the twentieth century, the now-discredited eugenics movement was immensely powerful. Leaders of the movement wanted to "prove" that society's ills were caused by those who had bad genes. This gave the rich and powerful the added benefit of being able to view

213

their own status as a natural consequence of their own good breeding. Major universities taught classes on the subject. Texts that we now find laughable in their logic were respected for their rigor and fearless application of science to social problems.

One of the main goals of the movement was mandatory sterilization for those deemed "unfit." Another was the forced segregation of the so-called feebleminded, alleged to be the source of most of the crime, prostitution, and alcohol abuse in the country. There were even some in the eugenics movement who advanced the agenda further, advocating extermination of those who were severely disabled, including a Chicago physician, Harry Haiselden, who became famous briefly in the early twentieth century for publicly stating he killed infants with disabilities.

There were other activists in Chicago as well. In 1922, a major eugenics book was published by the Psychopathic Laboratory of the Municipal Court of Chicago. I quote now from the introduction to that book, written by Harry Olson, Chief Justice of the Municipal Court:

> Segregation is necessary, even though sterilization were invoked. Sterilization protects future generations, while segregation safeguards the present as well.

In spite of the best efforts of Olson and others, Illinois was one of the minority of states that failed to pass mandatory sterilization laws. They were very successful with the goal of segregation, though. A simple look at the structure of our school systems and the number of people housed in institutions in this state shows that very bad ideas can have very long lives.

I am not saying that Peter Singer is a new eugenicist. What I hope to have established—briefly—is that there is a precedent for bad ideas to gain wide respect. The reason eugenicists were successful and respected was that their claims reinforced the prejudices of other white, privileged professionals. As a result, the shaky foundations of their claims and policy recommendations went unchallenged by many we might think should have known better.

And some try to resurrect those old bad ideas, wrapped up in new rhetoric and new forms. In the US, the book *The Bell Curve* topped the best-seller list by resurrecting claims of genetic determinism and racial differences in intelligence. The book was soundly condemned by researchers from many disciplines—for making unfounded assertions and reporting incomplete and biased examples of research related to intelligence, race, and genetics. No matter how shaky the work, the real message to be learned was the latent audience receptive to this newest piece of ideology masquerading as science and rationality.

The respect Peter Singer receives is built on the same foundations. Singer's works are carefully constructed. He relies heavily on stories and also on the wisdom of selected "authorities." The world is filled with stories. When using stories, the questions should always come up: Why was this story chosen? Are there things being left out? Are there other stories that might even undermine the conclusions or policy agenda being advocated and what might they be?

In the only face-to-face encounter Professor Singer and I have had, he made some revealing comments. The occasion was an exchange at a private school in Chicago that belatedly invited Not Dead Yet to provide a counterpoint to Singer, whom they had brought in as an invited speaker. During Singer's address to the students, he described bioethics as a field that relied heavily on "stories," even describing "brain death" as a story that bioethicists "sold" to the public.

Even though that should be self-evident from anyone who has read Singer's work or any one of a great many bioethics texts, it's helpful to have this admission out in the open. Many of the stories used—and misused—in bioethics involve people with disabilities.

The career of Jack Kevorkian is one that is told in many different ways. Professor Singer has written about Kevorkian in admiring terms. In one of the instances that can probably be attributed to "sloppiness," Professor Singer has described the people who died at Kevorkian's hands as "terminally ill." For those who don't know, there is ample documentation that only a minority of the people who make up Kevorkian's body count were "terminal" in any commonly understood sense of the word. When confronted with this on a radio show, Professor Singer expressed what I believe was honest surprise—it didn't stop him from asserting that "all" the people were given careful consideration by Kevorkian. I pointed out it was outrageous to make that claim when he didn't know enough about the people who went to Kevorkian to know anything at all accurate about their medical status. In fact, it's well documented that Kevorkian did not even follow his own criteria in selecting people to assist in suicide.

Many readers of this book should be familiar with the following passage by Peter Singer, originally published in *Rethinking Life and Death* in 1994.

We cannot expect a child with Down syndrome to play the guitar, to develop an appreciation of science fiction, to learn a foreign language, to chat

with us about the latest Woody Allen movie, to be a respectable athlete, bas-
ketballer or tennis player.

Criticisms of the accuracy and the bias of that passage have come from
countless individuals and organizations—almost from the date of publication. Certainly, enough people had weighed in by 2000 that one would
think it was a point Singer would be willing to concede. But judging
from the republication of the essay and the lack of a disclaimer regarding factual accuracy, evidently Singer finds old bigotries and stereotypes
hard things to let go of. Or maybe it's just that, in the end, factual accuracy and rigor aren't high on his agenda when it comes to talking and
writing about people with disabilities.

Let's go back to stories. In *Rethinking Life and Death*, Singer relies
heavily on the stories—as he tells them—of the Indiana Baby Doe and
John Pearson. Both were infants with Down's syndrome. In both cases
the parents are claimed to have initiated and stood by the request for
death of their respective infants. Baby Doe, who needed fairly standard
corrective surgery, was starved and dehydrated to death. John Pearson
was killed through excessive doses of narcotic.

It's no accident these stories were chosen. There are actually pretty
slim pickings when looking for stories about parents initiating a request
for killing a newborn with a disability. Usually the doctor raises the idea.
It's telling that Singer did not choose to tell the story of Baby Jane Doe
in New Jersey, which happened the year after the Indiana Baby Doe was
killed. Both the Indiana and New Jersey Baby Doe cases are described
in detail in a book that Singer cites as a source in his "acknowledgments" in *Rethinking Life and Death*. The book, titled *Classic Cases in
Medical Ethics*, by Gregory Pence, is one of the few bioethics text I can
recommend for a complex discussion of infanticide and related issues.

Baby Jane Doe was born with spina bifida. From the start there was
conflict. The surgeon recommended immediate treatment of the baby
while the pediatric neurologist told the parents their choices were to
have the baby die soon through nontreatment or live a longer life filled
with suffering if she was treated. The surgeon withdrew from the case
and the parents, based on the way the physician framed their choices,
decided on nontreatment.

The story became public. A lawyer active in the right to life movement filed suit in state court to force treatment on the baby's behalf. As
a result of the suit, a guardian ad litem was appointed to represent the
baby in court. The guardian ad litem found that the written medical
notes of the pediatric neurosurgeon were at odds with the testimony of

the doctor in the hearing—in at least two crucial medical details. In other words, the doctor lied on the stand and apparently, to the parents. Eventually, through several hearings, decision-making was given back to the parents. While all this was happening, though, the parents had changed their minds. They requested surgery and treatment for the baby. A follow-up story five years later revealed that Kerri-Lynn was a happy child—very different from the suffering, noncommunicative child the pediatric neurologist had told them to expect.

Gregory Pence, the source for this story and who Singer also used in *Rethinking Life and Death*, spends some time discussing the media coverage of the Baby Jane Doe case. According to Pence, who is not really a friend to the disability perspective, the media coverage was inaccurate and biased—all in the direction of supporting the death of Baby Jane Doe. The pronouncements of the pediatric neurologist who favored death were treated as fact and the guardian ad litem who favored life, according to Pence, was dismissed as a fanatic. Pence points out the irony and absurdity that the lead reporter on the case—the source of so much bias—won a Pulitzer for her coverage.

Is there any real surprise that Singer didn't select this story as one to present?

The fact is, Peter Singer's so-called practical ethics have little relation to the real world. The real world is filled with physicians with prejudices they are willing to act on, who will lie for self-protection, and have little in the way of oversight over their profession and practice.

Here's some bits from the real world, and unlikely to be discussed in anything Peter Singer writes or in any other major bioethics texts in the near future:

- In 2001, a formal inquiry found that the Royal Brompton Hospital in London discriminated against children with Down's syndrome because doctors believed operating on them was not worthwhile;

- In 1998, family members of David Glass, a young boy with multiple disabilities, was in the hospital with pneumonia. Hospital staff told the family that he was dying, withdrew treatment, and supplied diamorphine, which further depressed his breathing. Several family members literally fought staff to re-initiate care. They were arrested, but David was given treatment and still lives with his family. The family members charged with assault all served almost a year in jail. No penalties were leveled against the medical staff.

- In the disability community, the so-called "Oklahoma Study" is infamous. The Oklahoma "study" was conducted in the late 1970s. Twenty-four sets of parents were given inaccurate information about their children and recommendations of nontreatment. Two sets of parents who changed their minds about nontreatment sued the hospital after they learned that they had been given inaccurate information and manipulated by the hospital staff. They lost every count in the courts, all the way up to the Supreme Court. This study is remarkably conspicuous in its absence in virtually every major bioethics text, including anything written by Singer. Can you wonder why?

None of this is surprising to disability advocates, activists and scholars. There is a consistent body of research that shows medical professionals have more negative attitudes about disability than the general population, not to mention people with disabilities themselves. These professionals believe their prejudices are "objective," which is a fiction supported and promoted by Singer and his colleagues.

Our belief, in part, is that an unspoken goal of most bioethicists is to protect the reputations, authority and status of the medically-related professions. Stories that call these into question are not discussed, let alone analyzed.

There is one more aspect of story construction that deserves discussion here. I suspect that even opening this topic up will generate more criticism than anything else I write in this chapter. It's the story constructed about Singer's mother.

Early on in the press coverage leading to Singer's arrival at Princeton, the press caught wind of the situation of Singer's mother, who was in an advanced stage of dementia. Arguably, Singer's mother no longer had the qualities relating to the status of "personhood" and Singer was asked about the apparent contradiction.

Here, for example, is what he told Michael Specter, in a *New Yorker* article:

> Singer would never kill his mother, even if he thought it was what she wanted. He told me that he believes in Jack Kevorkian's attempts to help people die, but he also said that such a system works only when a patient is still able to express her wishes.

Singer repeated variations on this theme with various reporters during this time period. It resulted in op-eds and essays that either accused him of hypocrisy or offered his failure to end his mother's life as proof that his ethical views were too harsh for even him to live by.

The second theme served as a vehicle that softened and humanized him at a time when attacks from both the disability community in the U.S. and from the pro-life community were gaining public attention.

It turns out that this wasn't the *whole* story, at least according to what Singer told journalist Ronald Bailey in an interview for *Reason* magazine. *Reason* magazine has a limited readership and one that is inclined to be more agreeable with Singer's worldview than the general public. Here is what he said for this specialized audience, as reported by Bailey, after that initial wave of press coverage:

> Rigorous adherence to a single principle has a way of hoisting one by one's own petard. Singer's mother suffers from severe Alzheimer's disease, and so she no longer qualifies as a person by his own standards, yet he spends considerable sums on her care. This apparent contradiction of his principles has not gone unnoticed by the media. When I asked him about it during our interview at his Manhattan apartment in late July, he sighed and explained that he is not the only person who is involved in making decisions about his mother (he has a sister). He did say that if he were solely responsible, his mother might not be alive today.

It's quite possible that both of Singer's stories are true. Family life is complicated. But it's interesting that this second story was not told during his introduction to the American public. At the very least, it would have generated very different—and less sympathetic—commentaries from many quarters. For those who resist the idea this might have been a deliberate choice, it would be good to remember that Professor Singer has familiarity with the "street theater" of animal-rights activism as well as the polemics that characterize his bioethics work.

When Professor Singer complains of being silenced, he uses the word "silenced" in a curious manner. Most curious for someone who prides himself on rational, nonemotional discourse. To him, getting a speaking engagement cancelled equals being silenced.

We in the disability community know what "silencing" is. The voice of Rus Cooper-Dowda was very nearly silenced by her doctors and husband, ignoring her desperate attempts to communicate and discussing when and how to end her life. Dr. James Hall was nearly silenced, as his friends fought time and the open derision of medical staff, to establish communication with him to prevent cessation of life support. There have been people with disabilities that medical professionals were wrongly sure were unconscious.

There are other kinds of silencing too. Over the past year, there were countless bioethics conferences and symposia around the anniversary of the death of Terri Schiavo. In spite of the fact that over twenty national disability rights groups opposed her death by court-ordered dehydration, there was no inclusion of disability representatives in any of these events across the US.

We will continue to do what we've done. Struggle with limited resources against an array of prejudices backed by money, power, and prestige. We know that in many cases we will be ignored and marginalized. Nevertheless we will continue to fight with what we have—experience, passion, and knowledge. It may not be enough—we know it wasn't enough for sixty to seventy thousand people in this country who were victims of involuntary sterilization. But the alternative is to be passive participants in an increasingly organized assault on the integrity, dignity, and worth of our lives. That alternative is unacceptable. We will not be silent. Thank you.

The use of the phrase "the most dangerous man in the world" has been widely and incorrectly attributed to Not Dead Yet president Diane Coleman. The metaphor most often used by Not Dead Yet to describe Peter Singer is "the ugly tip of the iceberg." Singer is more visible and blatant than many of his mainstream colleagues, but there is plenty of agreement and movement in that larger arena of bioethics, at least in the United States.

And if bioethics is an iceberg, let's hope we can get our societal ship to steer clear. Because right now bioethicists are getting to decide who gets to have a place on the lifeboats and who doesn't. That doesn't bode well for people with disabilities, especially those with cognitive disabilities.

Reply to Stephen Drake

PETER SINGER

Charges Without Substance

Stephen Drake's fanfare about how he is going to question my intellectual integrity must be intended to make up for the lack of substance in his charges.

His first charge seems to be based on a misunderstanding that I can only assume—since I am not as ready as Drake is to accuse someone of dishonesty—is due to an incomplete grasp of my work. Drake says that when we had a debate in Chicago, I made a "revealing comment," describing "bioethics as a field that relied heavily on 'stories', even describing 'brain death' as a 'story' that bioethicists 'sold' to the public. The implication is that I am one of these bioethicists who 'sold' the idea of 'brain death' to the public, and here I let slip the truth about what my colleagues and I are doing, which shows that our field has no intellectual integrity. But as anyone who reads all of *Rethinking Life and Death* will soon discover, I am a critic of the idea of 'brain death'. I think it is a fiction.[1] By redefining human beings whose brains have irreversibly ceased to function as dead, we can cut out their still-beating hearts and give them to other people while fooling ourselves into thinking that we have not violated our belief in the sanctity of human life.[2]

In case this sounds as if I am opposed to doing heart transplants from human beings whose brains have irreversibly ceased to function, I should make it clear that I am not. Once your brain has irreversibly ceased to function, you can get no further benefit from continued life. So—unless you have previously objected to this—there is no reason why you should not be killed, and if removing your heart enables someone

---

[1] See, for example, *Rethinking Life and Death* (New York: St Martin's Press, 1994), p. 4.
[2] See *Rethinking Life and Death*, Chapter 2.

who would otherwise die to have a good quality of life for many years, it is a good thing to do. In other words, I accept heart transplantation from patients whose brains have irreversibly ceased to function, because I do not think there is any value in continuing the life of someone who will never again be conscious.

Not Dead Yet Fails to Defend Those Who Are Not Dead Yet

It would be interesting to know what position Drake takes on brain death. "The admission that 'brain death' is an artificial construction," he writes, "is a useful one." This suggests that he agrees that brain death is an artificial construction, and that those whose brains have irreversibly ceased to function are well described by the name of the organization he works for, "Not Dead Yet." But once you have seen through the fiction of describing human organisms as 'dead' when their brains have irreversibly ceased to function, you must either accept that quality of life is important, and not all human lives are equally worthy of prolongation, or you must regard cutting a beating heart out of the chest of a warm human body as murder. I haven't noticed either Drake or Not Dead Yet out there campaigning against heart transplants. Why not, I wonder? Should the organization rename itself Not Even Close to Dead?

Drake's other main piece of evidence of my alleged lack of intellectual integrity is that I reprinted a passage from *Rethinking Life and Death* about Down syndrome in a later collection of my work, even though many people had previously criticized the passage. But the critics had read the passage carelessly, as Drake seems to have done. They saw it as suggesting that no child with Down syndrome could learn to play the guitar, appreciate science fiction, learn a foreign language, chat with us about a Woody Allen movie, and so on, and they wrote to tell me about people with Down syndrome they knew who could do at least one of those things. But the passage doesn't say that no child with Down syndrome can do any of these things, it says—and Drake does at least quote it accurately—"we cannot expect" a child to have such abilities. I know very well that people with Down syndrome vary greatly. In particular, those with "mosaic Down syndrome" who have the extra chromosome that is the cause of the syndrome in only some of their cells, have IQ scores that are ten to thirty points higher than those who have the extra chromosome in every cell.[3] I noted, in *Rethinking Life and Death,* that people at the upper end of the range can live independently with very little supervision.[4] But that doesn't mean that parents who have just been informed that their fetus or newborn infant has Down's syndrome can expect their child to be at the upper end of the range. My reading of the literature indicates that most children with Down syndrome cannot do the things I listed. If Drake has evidence that this is wrong, it was his responsibility to cite that evidence, for example, a survey of people with Down syndrome that indicates their abilities and achievements. People who make accusations of dishonesty have a responsibility to show that the statement they are criticizing is false, and could reasonably be known to be false by the person making it. Drake does not even bother to show that the statement he complains about is false.

Defending a Mother's Decision

Drake refers to the case of David Glass, saying that I was "called in to comment on this case in media coverage." What really happened is that the producer of a documentary about me drew my attention to what had happened to David Glass, and asked me if I would be willing to travel to Portsmouth, England, to meet him on film. I did so, because the case disturbed me. As Harriet Johnson notes, but contrary to the view prevalent among those who have read only snippets of my work I am not an advocate of killing the disabled: I am an advocate of giving parents a greater say on whether their severely disabled child lives or dies. This includes supporting parents who want their child to live, even if the doctors take a different view, as long as the child's life is not inevitably going to be one of suffering, no matter how much love and care the parents can provide. The transcript of the documentary includes the following passage:

> **PETER SINGER:** [*speaking to David*] Hi. Hello David! All right, well he's certainly making eye contact. I can see he's looking at me. . . . David is clearly a very severely disabled boy, but he's not suffering. He's not in misery. Perhaps his enjoyment of life is limited, but he seems like he can enjoy life. And what I thought was really wrong about the doctors' refusal to support David, when he needed life support, was that they

---

[3] International Mosaic Down Syndrome Association website, "What Is Mosaic Down Syndrome?" http://www.mosaicdownsyndrome.com/faqs.htm.
[4] *Rethinking Life and Death,* p. 106.

were putting themselves above David's mother in being the judges of whether his life was worth continuing.[5]

David's mother, Carol, was among those who had accepted the image of my views often propagated in the circles of disability activists. In the film she says: "When I read about you on the internet, I thought that you were a monster, and that you'd never agree with David being allowed to have any sort of independent life."

It is true that I have not written about David Glass, but then, apart from responding to critics, over the past decade I haven't written much at all about life and death decisions for people with disabilities. But the documentary, entitled *Singer: A Dangerous Mind* has been shown on television in more than a dozen countries, so I can hardly be accused of keeping quiet about cases in which doctors get things wrong.

Bioethics and the Medical Profession

Drake broadens his attack from me to bioethicists as a whole, saying that the "unspoken goal" of most bioethicists is "to protect the reputations, authority, and status of the medically-related professions." Applied to me personally, this statement is difficult to reconcile both with my efforts to give parents, not doctors, greater say in whether their disabled children live or die, and with my long-standing critique of research on animals, which the "medically-related professions" generally support. Applied to bioethics as a whole, Drake's statement is one that could only be made by someone who knows little of the field and its history. Bioethicists have played a leading role in combating the power of the medical profession, especially in opposing medical paternalism and insisting on the right of patients to give free and informed consent to medical procedures. The strict controls that exist today on experimentation on human subjects is at least in part the result of the work of people in bioethics. Although those battles have largely been won in the United States, they are still raging in many other nations, including some Mediterranean nations and several countries in Asia. Most bioethicists in these countries continue to stand on the side of greater patient autonomy.

---

[5] From *Singer: A Dangerous Mind*, directed by Terry Carlyon and produced by Margie Bryant for Serendipity Productions, 2003. A transcript by Steven Barney is available at http://www.utilitarian.net/singer/interviews-debates/2003———.htm.

Who Represents People with Severe Intellectual Disabilities?

Drake sees the fact that disability representatives were not included in bioethics conferences that discussed the death of Terri Schiavo as an attempt to keep the views of the disabled out of bioethics. I'm tempted to respond that the quality of Drake's essay suggests a less sinister explanation, but that would be unfair to others in the disability movement. The more serious issue raised by his comment is: Who should represent people in a persistent vegetative state, or, for that matter, people with severe intellectual disabilities? Those with purely physical disabilities can, of course speak for themselves. Sometimes those with mild-to-moderate intellectual disabilities can too, depending on the nature of the issue they are addressing. But what gives a person of normal or above-average intelligence a particular claim to speak on behalf of people in a persistent vegetative state, or people with severe intellectual disabilities? I fail to see how the fact that someone is in a wheelchair makes her or him better qualified to represent the interests of people with intellectual disabilities than someone who can walk.

III

GLOBAL ETHICS

7

Famine, Affluence, and Psychology

JUDITH LICHTENBERG

> An ethic for human beings must take them as they are, or as they have some chance of becoming.[1]

I am not sure I can live up to the task assigned to me to put Peter Singer or his work "under fire." Doing so risks displaying a lack of appreciation for Singer's unparalleled contributions to moral and political philosophy over the last three decades in areas as diverse as poverty and global justice; abortion, euthanasia, and medical ethics; and the moral status and treatment of animals. Singer is more responsible than any philosopher in recent memory (or perhaps ever) for putting questions of global poverty and justice—my topic in this paper—on the moral philosopher's agenda, and in a way that is without jargon and entirely accessible to the general public. That by itself is an achievement for which he deserves our gratitude. I doubt that any essay has been assigned more often in introductory ethics courses over the last thirty years than Singer's "Famine, Affluence, and Morality,"[2] with the possi-

---

[1] Peter Singer, *The Expanding Circle: Ethics and Sociobiology* (New York: Farrar, Straus and Giroux, 1981), p. 157.

[2] "Famine, Affluence, and Morality," *Philosophy & Public Affairs* 1 (1972), reprinted in Charles R. Beitz et al., eds., *International Ethics* (Princeton: Princeton University Press, 1985). References to the paper are to the reprinted edition; page numbers are given in parentheses. I have no hard evidence for this claim, which is based on observation and experience over thirty years of teaching.

ble exception of Judith Jarvis Thomson's "A Defense of Abortion."[3] Singer's essay and subsequent works on the subject have spawned a large and important philosophical literature. Perhaps someone else would eventually have come along and put the issue of absolute poverty and famine relief front and center to philosophers and generations of students, but in fact it was Singer who did it.

So whatever the flaws in Singer's work, I am certain they are far outweighed by its benefits (to put matters in the utilitarian terms dear to Singer's heart). There's also a danger of blaming Singer for faults that may belong more to his critics and disciples than to him. Philosophy no less than economics and technology is "path-dependent," so influential philosophical ideas can move subsequent thought in directions that may exaggerate flaws at the origin. It may be overly harsh in such cases to fault the source.

Having excused myself, I turn to the task at hand. This essay proceeds as follows. In Part I, I briefly recount Singer's view about the moral obligations of affluent people to relieve global poverty. Part II describes what I believe are the two main lines of criticism against his view. Some recent critics have challenged what they take to be Singer's account of global poverty and its solutions. I explain why I think these are not valid criticisms of Singer. The traditional set of criticisms, more familiar to moral philosophers, denies that our obligations are as demanding as Singer says they are. I argue that this debate about how much we owe, morally speaking, is no longer fruitful. In Part III I consider some puzzles about the meaning of moral obligation arising from this controversy. Having explained why it is not useful to argue about the extent of our obligations—while fully acknowledging the significance of the problem Singer tackles—in the remainder of the paper I ask what we know already, and what we should try to learn, about the circumstances under which people give to others and might be influenced to give more.[4] Part IV describes some relevant findings of social psychol-

---

[3] "A Defense of Abortion," *Philosophy & Public Affairs* 1 (1971). It's notable that both essays appeared in the first volume of *Philosophy & Public Affairs*.

[4] The language we employ in these matters is fraught with controversial connotations. "Giving" seems to imply charity, and charity is often contrasted with justice. Exactly where justice ends and charity begins is a question I cannot address here, but it is difficult even to find neutral language in which to state the problems at hand. The distinction between justice and charity closely tracks, although it is not identical with, the distinction between negative duties not to harm and positive duties to aid. For a good discussion see, for example, Allen Buchanan, "Charity, Justice, and the Idea of Moral Progress," in J.B. Schneewind, ed., *Giving: Western Ideas of Philanthropy* (Bloomington: Indiana

ogy and their implications; Part V considers the comparative aspects of well-being. Parts VI and VII concludes with some further observations on what we might learn from the social sciences and history (and anywhere else we can) about producing widespread changes in moral beliefs and behavior.

I

As almost everyone likely to be reading these words now knows, Singer's initial and most forceful statement of his view about the duties of rich people to the global poor relies on an example meant as an analogy. You are walking by a pond and see a drowning child, whom you can rescue with little cost and no risk to yourself. Singer concludes that you "ought to wade in and pull the child out" (p. 249). Who, one might ask, would disagree? Well, depending on what one means by "ought," some *would* disagree. If by "You ought to do it" one means "It would be a good thing for you to do it," or even "It would be a bad thing if you didn't do it," or, more strongly still, "You would be a defective human being if you didn't do it," few people would dissent. But if "You ought to do it" means "You have a moral obligation to do it," some people hesitate.

Why? An important part of the explanation is this. For some, particularly modern secular moral philosophers, talk of moral obligation is simply a way of expressing very strong moral imperatives. But others see in such language the specter of coercion; they think (or at least their resistance to such talk suggests that they think) that to say one is morally obligated to do something implies that one may be coerced—by the state, for example—to do that thing. Political libertarians are among those who tend to connect obligation with coercion and thus resist the conclusion that one is morally obligated to rescue the child.[5]

University Press, 1996). In "Famine, Affluence, and Morality," Singer strongly suggests that the issue is one of charity and positive duties rather than justice and negative duties, although the utilitarian view to which he subscribes largely conflates these distinctions.
[5] See, for instance, Judith Jarvis Thomson, "A Defense of Abortion," pp. 48–49, and Robert Nozick, *Anarchy, State, and Utopia* (New York: Basic Books, 1974), passim. Nozick's view that the state may not coerce a person to aid another and Thomson's view that the unborn fetus has no right to life seem to rely on the assumption that there is no obligation to aid on a par with the obligation not to harm. In her classic essay, "Modern Moral Philosophy" (*Philosophy* 33, 1958), Elizabeth Anscombe argues that the concept of moral obligation makes no sense outside a theistic moral system in which God backs moral commands with the full force of His authority and power, and it may be the remnant or analogue of this belief that is at the root of the libertarian view. But resistance to

Still, almost everyone agrees that in some sense of "ought" the bystander ought to rescue the drowning child. Ordinary people might stop there, seeing no need to explain. What could be more obvious? But in seeking to uncover the assumptions underlying this conclusion, Singer takes us far beyond the obvious. He articulates two premises. First is the uncontroversial one that "suffering and death from lack of food, shelter, and medical care are bad." No serious person I know of has challenged this assumption and I don't mean to start now. Second is the principle that "if it is in our power to prevent something bad from happening, without thereby sacrificing anything *of comparable moral importance*, we ought, morally, to do it" (p. 249; emphasis added). This is a very strong principle whose "uncontroversial appearance . . . is deceptive" (p. 249), as Singer is the first to admit and as many others have emphasized. It drives the far-reaching conclusions Singer draws. If we acted on it "our lives, our society, and our world would be fundamentally changed" (p. 249). We would have to give up all luxuries and even some things we don't view as luxuries. For the faint of heart, he offers a weaker alternative principle: "if it is in our power to prevent something very bad from happening, without thereby sacrificing anything *morally significant*, we ought, morally, to do it" (p. 249; emphasis added). Given the extent of desperate poverty and suffering in the world, endorsing even this weaker premise would force a radical reduction in our standard of living.

I shall not linger over the phrases "comparable moral importance" and "morally significant," which could preoccupy (and have preoccupied) anyone concerned with Singer's argument. I assume instead that however we understand these phrases, it's clear they yield very demanding conclusions. On the strong principle, according to Singer, "we ought to give until we reach the level of marginal utility—that is, the level at which, by giving more, I would cause as much suffering to myself or my dependents as I would relieve by my gift" (p. 259). Even on the weaker principle, "we would have to give away enough to ensure that the consumer society, dependent as it is on people spending on trivia rather than giving to famine relief, would slow down and perhaps disappear entirely" (p. 259).

Recently Singer has muted his message. Thus, for example, in *One World: The Ethics of Globalization*, he proposes that "anyone who has

---

obligation-talk is not limited to libertarians or academic philosophers; over the years I have found many students who object as well, even though they are willing to admit that one who doesn't save a drowning child when he can without cost is an awful human being.

enough money to spend on the luxuries and frivolities so common in affluent societies should give at least one cent in every dollar of their income" to those lacking basic necessities.[6] Singer makes clear that the more modest proposal is rooted not in a change in his ethical position but in pragmatism.[7] Conceding that it is unrealistic to expect people to give aid in anything remotely approaching the amounts he endorses in "Famine, Affluence, and Morality," he articulates a conclusion that is more likely to be accepted. Still, Singer believes that rich people's obligations are much stronger than most think they are.

II

Since the publication of "Famine, Affluence, and Morality," a thriving philosophical literature has centered on Singer's claim that we (that is, relatively rich people in rich countries) have powerful moral duties to alleviate the dire circumstances of poor people, especially those in less developed countries. Singer has been joined by philosophers such as Peter Unger and Shelly Kagan in defending the demanding view.[8] Critics (in the form of professional philosophers as well as students who have encountered Singer's views in their introductory philosophy courses) have found this view counterintuitive and impossibly demanding, and have worked hard to vindicate what they conveniently think of as common sense. Broadly speaking, Singer's critics have argued that we cannot be required by a plausible morality to make such large sacrifices. Certainly, they would say, we can't be required to reduce our standard of living to or near the level of subsistence, and even much smaller sacrifices are beyond the call of duty. Consider, for example, a family of four with an annual income of $150,000, rich by any global standard and far above the median U.S. income. The family pays about $36,000 in federal income tax (at the twenty-eight percent rate). Add in state and local taxes and any deductions, and let's estimate that about $100,000 a year remains. Such a family could give away $35,000 a year and still be well above the median income for U.S. families of four.[9] But few people

---

[6] See, for example, *One World: The Ethics of Globalization*, second edition (New Haven: Yale University Press, 2002), Chapter 5, p. 194.

[7] *One World*, pp. 191–92; for further discussion see below, section III.

[8] Peter Unger, *Living High and Letting Die: Our Illusion of Innocence* (New York: Oxford, 1996); Shelly Kagan, *The Limits of Morality* (Oxford: Clarendon, 1989).

[9] According to U.S. Census figures, the median income for a four-person family in 2003 was about $65,000 before taxes. See http://www.census.gov/hhes/income/4person.html (accessed January 30th, 2006).

believe that giving at this level is morally obligatory; a family that gave away a third of its post-tax income would normally be considered heroic or saintly.

Philosophers have argued that such a demanding morality impermissibly infringes people's autonomy and their ability to live their lives as they see fit. They have tried to show that much of what makes life worth living would disappear if we acted in accordance with Singer's conclusion.[10] The effort to discredit the demanding view is sometimes part of a larger attack on utilitarianism, which is often taken to imply that a person ought to maximize the good. But one need not be a utilitarian to accept Singer's conclusion, and it is not obvious that a utilitarian must.[11]

It is not hard to see why many people—philosophers and others—have wanted to resist Singer's conclusion. That conclusion conflicts with what most people believe and how we live our lives. To embrace it would involve large personal sacrifices, if a person acted on it, or feelings of guilt, if one didn't. Although the arguments against the demanding view lack the simplicity and clarity of Singer's, and often involve intricate arguments accessible only to the philosophically trained, their conclusions more closely track ordinary thinking—as well as the interests of those most likely to be listening.

I shall return to this debate shortly. But questions about whether we have the demanding moral obligations Singer believes we do are not the only ones relevant to his conclusion. Other challenges to his view have recently become prominent. The question for some is not whether we *ought* to aid the poor but whether we *can*. Singer and others have often emphasized fulfilling the demanding duties through donations to organizations such as UNICEF, Oxfam, and (in "Famine, Affluence, and Morality," written against the backdrop of the 1971 crisis in East Bengal) the Bengal Relief Fund. But in recent years critics—many of them former insiders in the aid business—have mounted an attack on the efficacy of humanitarian assistance. The titles of their books speak for themselves: *The Road to Hell: The Ravaging Effects of Foreign Aid and International Charity*; *Lords of Poverty: The Power, Prestige, and*

---

[10] Among the many attempts to stem the Singerian tide are Samuel Scheffler, *The Rejection of Consequentialism* (Oxford: Clarendon, 1982); Liam Murphy, "The Demands of Beneficence," *Philosophy and Public Affairs* 22 (1993); Jean Hampton, "Selflessness and the Loss of Self," *Social Philosophy and Policy* (1993); Garrett Cullity, *The Moral Demands of Affluence* (Oxford: Clarendon Press, 2004).

[11] On the latter point see Judith Lichtenberg, "The Right, the All Right, and the Good," *Yale Law Journal* 92 (1983).

Corruption of the International Aid Business; *Famine Crimes: Politics and the Disaster Relief Industry in Africa*; *Condemned to Repeat?: The Paradox of Humanitarian Action*; *Aid as Obstacle: Twenty Questions About Our Foreign Aid and the Hungry*; *The Dark Sides of Virtue: Reassessing International Humanitarianism.*[12]

Aid in the form of disaster relief must be distinguished from long-term efforts to improve the circumstances of the world's poorest people. But many critics have attacked both forms of assistance as at best ineffective and at worst harmful. The central charge, as Garrett Cullity explains, is that large-scale aid programs "damage the local economy and pauperize the 'target population'. . . . The effect is to create aid-dependent economies in which the task of developing economic self-sufficiency has been made much harder than it was before."[13] Aid programs, it is charged, disrupt traditional institutions, undermine incentives to work, erode recipients' self-respect, and encourage corruption by local governments. According to some these problems may plague not only institutions like the World Bank and the International Monetary Fund, but also NGOs like Oxfam and Save the Children. Michael Maren, one of aid's harshest critics, claims that such organizations (he focuses on Save the Children) prey on the pity of donors and spend an inordinate amount of time and money jockeying with competing organizations for position and media attention, while their young and privileged employees live high on the hog amid the poverty they are supposedly there to fix.[14]

Building on these criticisms and on other evidence, some philosophers have recently argued that the picture Singer paints of global poverty and its solutions—emphasizing, as it does, traditional humanitarian and development assistance—is acontextual and ahistorical. As Andrew Kuper puts it: "Given the structure of the world as it is, the most serious problem for Singer is that we may do better for South Africans by

---

[12] Michael Maren, *The Road to Hell* (New York: Free Press, 1997); Graham Hancock, *Lords of Poverty* (London: Mandarin, 1991); Alex de Waal, *Famine Crimes* (London: Africa Rights and the International African Institute, 1997); Fiona Terry, *Condemned to Repeat?* (Ithaca: Cornell University Press, 2002); Frances Moore Lappé and David Kinley: *Aid as Obstacle* (San Francisco: Institute for Food and Development Policy, 1980); David Kennedy, *The Dark Sides of Virtue* (Princeton: Princeton University Press, 2005).

[13] Cullity, *The Moral Demands of Affluence*, p. 39. Chapter 3 of Cullity's book provides an excellent discussion of the issues.

[14] See Maren, *The Road to Hell*; and Cullity, *The Moral Demands of Affluence*, pp. 41–42.

buying furniture and clothes from ethical manufacturers and manufacturers in developing countries than by donation."[15] Dale Jamieson argues
that "rather than advocating ambitious agendas to remake the world," we
should first "do no harm" and focus "primarily on challenging those
structures that bring and maintain global poverty."[16] Mathias Risse
(who, unlike the other two, does not address Singer's view directly)
believes that a country's prosperity is primarily a function of the strength
of its institutions, and that what is required for the rich to discharge their
duties to the poor is support in institution-building. But this is a role in
which, he argues, outsiders are constrained in both what they can and
what they ought to do.[17]

Risse acknowledges that duties to assist "in institution-building may
be extremely taxing,"[18] and Jamieson's advice to challenge structures
that produce poverty could also, if taken seriously, require great effort.
In fact, only Kuper suggests that rich people might best help the global
poor without discomfiting themselves. On his view, although Singer "is
right that rich individuals can survive without [luxuries]," he is "wrong
that poor people can," because they depend on the market in luxury
goods.[19] Kuper's proposal may nevertheless prove demanding, if it
means that consumers must learn which products come from socially
responsible sources and which purchases will actually benefit poor people. Still, the message many well-off people will take away from these
accounts is "Whew! I don't have to make huge sacrifices after all. And
wow, the best way for me to be a good global citizen is to shop till I
drop." They are more likely to hear Jamieson's message to "do no harm,"
with its implication that the safest route is to do nothing at all, than the
part about challenging poverty-producing structures. And they may latch
onto Risse's warnings about the constraints on what outsiders can do
rather than his assertion that helping to building institutions may be
"taxing."

There are several important points to take away from these critiques
of the efficacy of humanitarian aid. First, as Kuper and Singer agree, in

---

[15] Andrew Kuper, "More Than Charity: Cosmopolitan Alternatives to the 'Singer
Solution'," *Ethics and International Affairs* 16 (2002), p. 111.
[16] Dale Jamieson, "Duties to the Distant: Aid, Assistance, and Intervention in the
Developing World," *Journal of Ethics* 9 (2005), pp. 167–68.
[17] Mathias Risse, "What We Owe to the Global Poor," *Journal of Ethics* 9 (2005), pp.
116. Risse suggest several reasons why they are constrained, having to do with the evils
of paternalism and the idea that "what is needed cannot be imported" (pp. 90–92).
[18] Ibid., p. 117.
[19] Kuper, "More Than Charity," p. 112.

deciding how to act on a moral principle such as Singer's, much "will depend on the story you believe"—that is, on how you think the world actually works and on which explanations of economic, political, and social phenomena you accept.[20] If the critics of aid are right, then what it takes to alleviate dire poverty may be very different from what "experts" previously thought. For practical purposes—how to alleviate deprivation and dire suffering in the world—the *how* is the heart of the issue; nothing is more important.

But questions about the *how* do not touch the moral argument for a powerful duty to render assistance. Unless every kind of expenditure is counterproductive, the critics of aid haven't laid a hand on Singer's con- clusion that "people in rich nations ought to be using a substantial amount of our income in the way that will most effectively help the world's poorest people."[21] If traditional aid doesn't work, then we shouldn't give traditional aid. We should do something *else*. But that in no way defeats Singer's conclusions. To do that we would need strong evidence that nothing we could do could alleviate the problem of dire poverty and suffering.

Finally, as Singer notes, "most people are only too happy to find an excuse for not giving money away,"[22] so those who agree with Singer that rich people ought to do more than they are doing for the global poor should be careful in how they frame their views. It is easy to mislead people who may take disagreement about *how* to alleviate suffering for disagreement about whether we ought to, and how much we are required to do.

It looks, then, as if we are back to the original question about whether rich people have the powerful moral obligations Singer says

---

[20] Kuper uses the phrase in quotes but it's not clear whether it originates with him or Singer. Ibid., p. 117.

[21] Singer, "Poverty, Facts, and Political Philosophies: Response to 'More Than Charity'," *Ethics and International Affairs* 16 (2002), p. 123. For a good defense of this view, see Cullity, *The Moral Demands of Affluence*, Chapter 3. Singer puts his point in terms of expenditures of money and income, but the argument would also seem to require expenditures of time and effort—even more precious commodities, perhaps—if their use tended to produce the benefits in question. The moral consumer might be obli- gated to devote a lot of time researching the products she buys and the companies she patronizes, or getting involved somehow in institution-building. Some of these activities could probably be turned into monetary commodities; instead of doing the work herself the moral consumer could contribute to organizations committed to institution-building or to monitoring the practices of corporations.

[22] Singer, "Poverty, Facts, and Political Philosophies," p. 124.

they do. And this is where I want to change the subject. After thirty years of debate, I don't believe anyone on either side is likely to convince anyone on the other side, and the strengths and weaknesses of each position seem clear.

On the one hand, no sensible person can deny that dire poverty and deprivation are terrible, and the scope of suffering is by any standard staggering. According to the United Nations Human Development Report 2005, more than forty percent of the world's population constitute "a global underclass, faced daily with the reality or the threat of extreme poverty." "More than 850 million people, including one in three preschool children, are still trapped in a vicious cycle of malnutrition and its effects."[23] In the context of extreme inequality both within and between countries, and alongside the levels of consumption and excess prevalent among the rich and even the not-so-rich, the facts are even more disturbing.

On the other hand, very few people are moved to anything like the lengths Singer and his defenders say they should be. It is a weakness of a normative view that its conclusions leave us uninclined to act on them. Even Singer falls short; according to a 1999 *New Yorker* profile, he gives away twenty percent of his income—far more than most people, an admirable amount according to any "standard" view, but far less than the demanding requirement set out in "Famine, Affluence, and Morality."[24] The ad hominem attack (here, the attack of inconsistency) is often thought to be irrelevant to evaluating the philosophical merits of a view. But it's hard to dismiss it in this case, because a fundamental question that Singer's view poses is precisely whether human beings are built to believe and act on his conclusions.[25] If he himself cannot, what can we expect of lesser mortals? Must we rethink his conclusions if his demands will fall largely on deaf ears?

---

[23] United Nations Human Development Report 2005, p. 24, at http://hdr.undp.org/reports/global/2005/pdf/HDR05_chapter_1.pdf (accessed December 14th, 2005).

[24] Michael Specter, "The Dangerous Philosopher," *The New Yorker* (September 6th, 1999), at http://www.michaelspecter.com/ny/1999/1999_09_06_philosopher.html (accessed December 14th, 2005). I leave aside the criticism that if everyone did what Singer suggested in "Famine, Affluence, and Morality," the economy would come to a screeching halt, the poor would not benefit, and the not-poor would become so. Singer would presumably revise his prescriptions to avoid this possibility.

[25] As Alan Ryan puts it, "human beings just aren't put together the way that he wishes they were." Quoted in Specter, "The Dangerous Philosopher." Specter continues: "In Ryan's view, no moral philosophy that departs so fundamentally from such common sentiments could possibly make sense."

The views of Singer's opponents have the advantage of matching more closely to common sense. But because common sense tells us what we want to hear, we need to regard these conclusions with a touch of suspicion. (This is not to impugn the motives of Singer's critics, nor is it to deny that we have learned something from them.)

Of course, the fact that the sides are no closer and that the strengths and weaknesses of the positions are clear has never stopped philosophers before from continuing to defend their positions and attack their adversaries. Those who find this activity worthwhile don't need my blessing to continue. I think we can learn more of interest, however, by asking what influences people to give or not to give, to help or not to help. I think this for two reasons. Most important is that these issues originally aroused the interest of philosophers—myself and, I assume, Singer among them—because we were disturbed by the worldly facts of desperate poverty and inequality, and so we should find out what is known, and what might be learned, about the influences on people's propensities to behave more or less generously. Moreover, I believe that people's moral obligations in these matters are partially indeterminate, and so it makes no clear sense to ask, in these contexts, what an individual's moral obligation is. In the next section I explain why I think this is so.

III

Even if we accept my diagnosis that the debate about Singer's demanding view has reached an impasse and is no longer fruitful, it would seem that there are two possible ways of describing the moral landscape. One is that we (rich individuals) ought to do much more than we are doing, even though it is unlikely that we will. The other is that Singer demands more than can reasonably be demanded of ordinary human beings, even if it would be a good thing if they gave much more. In the first case he is right about our obligations, in the second case he is wrong.

Does it matter which we say? One would think the answer is yes. That answer stems from the assumption that our moral obligations are determinate, and Singer is either roughly right or roughly wrong about what they are. The truth will be approximate, of course; ethics is not an exact science. But in fact the matter is even less determinate than we might suppose from the imprecision of ethics. Singer has at least a measure of rightness on his side because there is little doubt that it would be better if we did more, and this betterness is not a matter of bringing the world from a state of adequacy to ideality, but of bringing it from badness to adequacy. But the widespread intransigence and skepticism found in the face of his arguments cast doubt on their validity. The question arises whether it is useful to insist—and even whether it is true—that people ought to do so much more than most ever will.

The view that if people believe that something is not wrong then it's not wrong is crude relativism, a view not worth taking seriously (I shall assume). If killing suddenly became widespread, so that many or most people engaged in killing other human beings, we would not say that killing was morally permissible, even if we found the killers immune to argument on the subject. That many people engage in a certain kind of behavior (such as not giving away a large part of their income) does not make it acceptable, nor does the fact that many people believe that kind of behavior is acceptable. (Because of the demonstrated psychological need to reduce cognitive dissonance, the two—acting in a certain way and believing that acting in that way is morally acceptable—tend to go together.[26]) Nevertheless, the more widespread a practice within a society, the more problematic it becomes to condemn those engaged in it. We judge that slavery is wrong, but how do we judge those who owned slaves or sold slaves? Well, we say that what they did was wrong. But that is just another way of saying that slavery is wrong. Is there necessarily an implicit moral judgment of the individuals themselves? That they should have known better? That they should be blamed? Should have been punished? To answer these questions we need to know more about the situations of particular individuals.[27] We often hesitate to blame those involved in practices that are wrong, not only because blaming them might not be productive but also because we think that the cultural entrenchment of the practices in which they were engaged, conjoined with facts about human psychology, make it unreasonable to expect average people to resist the mores of their times. (We may, of course, blame some people—the Jeffersons and the Washingtons and others whom we think could have and should have known better.) Largely for these reasons, would-be critics may feel reluctant to pass judgment, wondering what they would have done in the same situation.

---

[26] The classical experiments on cognitive dissonance were done by Leon Festinger. See *A Theory of Cognitive Dissonance* (Stanford: Stanford University Press, 1957). See also below, discussion at the end of section VII and experiments cited in note 71.

[27] I have made a similar argument about the responsibilities of soldiers fighting on the wrong side of a war in "How to Judge Soldiers Whose Cause Is Unjust," in David Rodin and Henry Shue, eds., *Just and Unjust Warriors* (Oxford: Oxford University Press, 2008).

Of course, we think nevertheless that slavery was wrong. Yet statements like "Slave-holders violated their moral obligations" or "Slave-holders ought not to have had slaves" sound peculiar. They are obvious in one sense and pointless in another: obvious insofar as they mean only "Slavery was wrong," pointless insofar as they ignore the culture and context that exerts influence on, and often excuses, those engaged in such practices.

From the fact that most people in our society don't give away a lot of their income, and don't believe they or others have a duty to, we cannot infer that they don't have such a duty. But the customs, mores, and beliefs widespread in our society give us reason to be skeptical that it is appropriate to frame these moral aspirations in terms of individual duty.

What would be the point of asserting that people ought to give away a lot of their income?[28] Singer has recently acknowledged that there might not be a point, and that in fact doing so could be counterproductive. Responding to the objection that "it is poor policy to advocate a morality that most people will not follow" because doing so could threaten "to bring the whole of morality into disrepute," he invokes Henry Sidgwick's distinction between "what it may be right to do, and privately recommend," and "what would not be right to advocate openly."[29] If a widespread reaction to Singer's original conclusion is "This is too demanding, and I won't do it; so I might as well ignore other moral injunctions that conflict with my interests too," Singer agrees that the moralist should temper the message: "The question then becomes: What policy will produce the best consequences."[30]

This response is problematic for several reasons. First, for a utilitarian like Singer there is no difference between what a person ought to do and what policy will produce the best consequences. This is true not only for rule-utilitarians but for all utilitarians insofar as they hope to

---

[28] One might argue that "You ought to give away a large proportion of your income" means something different from "You have a moral obligation to give away a large proportion of your income," and that some of the ambiguity I have been exploring rests on those different meanings. "A is morally obligated to do x" means "A is morally required to do x," but "A ought to do x" suggests something less stringent—although more stringent than simply "It would be a good thing if A did x." What that meaning might be is a question worth pursuing. But I do not think anything significant here rests on the possible ambiguity.

[29] Singer, *One World*, pp. 191–92, quoting Sidgwick, *The Methods of Ethics*, seventh edition (London: Macmillan, 1907), pp. 489–490.

[30] Singer, *One World*, p. 192.

shape policy or public opinion.[31] When speaking publicly rather than to particular individuals, they must frame their statements in general terms. Since utilitarianism is defined in terms of what will produce the best consequences, there is no independent criterion of what people ought to do.

A second, related point is that ethics is often said to be "action-guiding." If general statements of duty are ineffective or even counterproductive, that seems to undermine their validity.

Third, if publicity is a requirement of an adequate moral theory, as some have argued,[32] then "the moral law" must be capable of public declaration; morality cannot be esoteric. But then invoking Sidgwick's distinction is not an adequate response to the charge that an overly demanding morality is self-defeating.

The first of these reasons applies only to utilitarianism. But the second and third apply more broadly to other ethical approaches. Together, they give us reason to doubt the validity of a judgment such as "People in our society who are reasonably well-off are morally obligated to give away a large portion of their income," even if we think the action it recommends is an enormously important one.

IV

Nevertheless, as I indicated earlier, my purpose here is to change the subject. For those who wish to influence human behavior, and thereby improve the situation of the world's poorest people, the debate about how demanding the obligations of rich people are is beside the point, because most people in our society, constituted as it is now and with the incentives presently in force, will not give a great deal more than they are giving. The important thing is rather to understand the springs of action (as the eighteenth century philosophers would have put it) in order to see how people might come to act differently. In one sense I don't think this is very controversial. Looking at the world objectively— imagine that we could take a snapshot of it, or that we approach the earth

---

[31] For a similar idea see Robert Goodin, *Utilitarianism as a Public Philosophy* (Cambridge: Cambridge University Press, 1995).

[32] See for example Immanuel Kant, *Perpetual Peace*, Appendix II; John Rawls, *A Theory of Justice* (Cambridge: Harvard University Press, 1971), pp. 177–182, 582; and David Luban, "The Publicity Principle," in Robert Goodin, ed., *The Theory of Institutional Design* (Cambridge: Cambridge University Press, 1996). Singer does not appear to accept the publicity principle, however.

from some distant place—it's hard to deny that the state of affairs in which more than two billion people face extreme poverty while a few hundred million live in luxury is unacceptable, if not outrageous and obscene. Even the beneficiaries of this state of affairs will be hard pressed to disagree.

To understand how people might come to act differently—without supposing utopian transformations or demanding more than can reasonably be expected of ordinary human beings—requires knowledge of history and the human sciences. We are in possession of some of this knowledge and should aim to learn more.

I think it's fair to say that the popular view is that "human nature" poses severe limits on how much we can expect people to give or to sacrifice, in the normal course of things, for the well-being of strangers.[33] But this view seriously oversimplifies the matter. Hundreds of experiments performed over the last fifty years show that the particulars of the situations in which people find themselves exert enormous influence on human behavior. Small differences in circumstances can radically affect people's propensity to volunteer their services, to do someone a favor, to help—or even to hurt—other people. Psychologists have identified a number of situational factors that significantly affect outcomes—for example, being put in a good mood by a trivial benefit, being in a hurry, having been previously persuaded to make a small commitment to perform an action, having received something from someone who wants something from you. One of the most notable, for our purposes, is the extent to which a person's behavior is strongly influenced by what he believes others are doing.[34]

Situationism is the psychological theory according to which behavioral differences among people are due much more to differences in their situation and much less to variations in personality and character than is usually thought. Explaining human behavior primarily in terms of personality or character, as we typically do, commits what situationists call the "fundamental attribution error": "[p]eople's inflated belief in the importance of personality traits and dispositions, together with their failure to recognize the importance of situational factors in affecting

---

[33] Sacrifices by individuals for those they love—such as their children, spouses, and dear friends—and sacrifices by soldiers for their cause or country are obvious exceptions.

[34] For some of the classic experiments see Lee Ross and Richard E. Nisbett, *The Person and the Situation: Perspectives of Social Psychology* (Philadelphia: Temple University Press, 1991), especially pp. 27–46, and Robert Cialdini, *Influence: Science and Practice*, fourth edition (Boston: Allyn and Bacon, 2001).

behavior . . ."[35] The term is contentious, and may unnecessarily raise hackles, as I'll argue in the next section. Nevertheless, situationists cite a wealth of experiments confirming their view.

In 1964, Kitty Genovese was murdered outside her apartment building in Queens while thirty-eight people watched from their windows; not a single person so much as called the police. (The crime took place over thirty minutes, leaving plenty of time for action.) Much public handwringing about human selfishness and apathy followed. Social psychologists (whose field was in a fertile period at this time) became interested in the circumstances under which people would or would not engage in "helping behavior." Here I describe a few of the best-known experiments on the question.

1. In one experiment, the subject, who has just emerged from a phone booth, comes across a woman (a confederate of the experimenter) who has dropped a sheaf of papers on the ground. Will the subject stop to help her pick up the papers? The determinative factor turns out to be whether the subject has found a dime in the coin return of the public phone: of those who found a dime, fourteen people helped and two didn't; of those who didn't find a dime, one helped and twenty-four didn't.[36] The results of this experiment are so counterintuitive that it is tempting to dismiss them as some kind of fluke. How could something as trivial

---

[35] Ibid., p. 4. Situational factors act on creatures who are not *tabulae rasae*. If human beings didn't have certain propensities, they wouldn't necessarily respond as they do. So, for example, in his popular and informative book *Influence*, Cialdini considers six modes of influence (reciprocation, commitment, social proof, liking, authority, scarcity). Reciprocation is the rule "that we should try to repay, in kind, what another person has provided us" (p. 20). He argues that the desire to reciprocate is an "adaptive mechanism" that helps maintain societies by allowing for the division of labor, contractual agreements, and the like. According to Cialdini, people have a powerful desire to repay debts. For this reason it's easier to get people to do what you want if you do something for them—even something they don't want—first. Experiments confirm this conclusion: giving people something, even something they don't want and much less significant than what you want from them—will sharply increase the chances that they will give you what you want. (Cialdini gives the example of the Hare Krishna, a religious sect whose members would approach wary travelers in airports, giving them a flower before requesting a donation. According to Cialdini, the tactic was highly successful. See *Influence*, pp. 23–25.) But such effects still capitalize on a human disposition. The situationists' point is that these dispositions do not vary as much as we have thought; it's the situational factors that produce variations in behavior.

[36] A.M. Isen and P.F. Levin, "Effect of Feeling Good on Helping: Cookies and Kindness," *Journal of Personality and Social Psychology* 21 (1972), pp. 384–88. For discussion of this and other experiments see John Doris, *Lack of Character: Personality and Moral Behavior* (Cambridge: Cambridge University Press, 2002), pp. 30–39.

as finding a dime influence whether people helped a stranger on the street? The result was explained in terms of its effect on mood; finding a dime (not much even in 1972) apparently elevated a person's mood and so increased the chances she would help others. Other experiments have confirmed that seemingly inconsequential situational factors can produce large effects on mood and, through mood, on behavior.[37]

2. In one of the most striking (and, in its way, amusing) experiments, John Darley and Daniel Batson recruited divinity students at Princeton Theological Seminary to prepare a brief talk on the parable of the Good Samaritan.[38] Some subjects were told that they were a few minutes late, others that they were a few minutes early. On the way to the building where they were to speak, subjects encountered a man slumped in a doorway, motionless and with his eyes closed. As they went by he coughed and groaned. Only ten percent of the late seminarians offered assistance, while sixty-three percent of those who were early did.[39]

How could so many who had chosen a vocation of offering succor to others—and focused precisely on that subject at the moment of the experiment—fail so miserably to do so? According to Ross and Nisbett, "When we find an apparently small situational circumstance producing a big behavioral effect, we are justified in suspecting we have identified a channel factor, that is, a stimulus or response pathway that serves to elicit or sustain behavioral intentions with particular intensity or stability."[40] Being in a hurry, or not; having one's mood elevated; committing oneself to taking some small, apparently insignificant steps along the way toward a goal of more significant actions—are examples of channel factors.[41] As Ross and Nisbett warn, however, "contextual details, sometimes very subtle details, matter a great deal," so those who hope to

---

[37] For references see Doris, *Lack of Character*, p. 30.

[38] John Darley and Daniel Batson, "From Jerusalem to Jericho: A Study of Situational and Dispositional Variables in Helping Behavior," *Journal of Personality and Social Psychology* 27 (1973).

[39] More interesting still would have been two pairs of experiments, testing the hurry/no hurry variable among seminarians delivering the Good Samaritan sermon and another sermon on a more neutral topic. Darley and Batson argue that "Thinking about the Good Samaritan did not increase helping behavior, but being in a hurry decreased it" (p. 107). But it's possible that seminarians preparing a sermon on an unrelated topic would have been even less likely to help.

[40] *The Person and the Situation*, p. 46.

[41] The "getting one's foot in the door" strategy—asking for a small commitment, as a way of raising the probability of getting a larger one later—has been demonstrated in a variety of experiments. See *The Person and the Situation*, pp. 50–52, and Cialdini, *Influence*, Chapter 3, for descriptions and references.

influence behavior should not draw hasty inferences from particular cases or experiments.[42]

3. In the late 1960s John Darley and Bibb Latané conducted a series of experiments on helping behavior. Their book *The Unresponsive Bystander: Why Doesn't He Help?*[43] describes these experiments, highlighting in particular one factor relevant to determining whether a person gives assistance or not.

In one experiment, male Columbia University undergraduates were recruited to participate in what they thought was a market research survey. When a subject arrived he met an attractive and lively young woman who described herself as the "market research representative." She brought him to the testing room, and set him up with some questionnaires to fill out. The room was separated from another office by a collapsible curtain. The young woman left the room, saying she would go next door to do a few things and return in ten or fifteen minutes. While subjects worked on the questionnaire, they heard the woman moving around next door; those who were listening carefully heard her climb up on a chair to retrieve something from a high shelf. After a few minutes, subjects "heard a loud crash and a woman's scream as the chair fell over. 'Oh, my God, my foot . . .' cried the representative. 'I . . . I . . . can't move . . . it. Oh, my ankle. I . . . can't . . . can't . . . get . . . this thing off . . . me.' She moaned and cried for about a minute longer, getting gradually more subdued and controlled . . ."[44] The sounds were prerecorded, but only six percent of subjects expressed any suspicion later that they were not live and real.

Some subjects were alone in the waiting room when they heard the noise next door, others were in the presence of a confederate of the experimenter or of another subject. Among those who were by themselves, seventy percent offered the victim help; when a passive confederate was present, only seven percent intervened. Even in pairs of two naïve subjects, another person's presence strongly inhibited people from helping—a result confirmed by other experiments as well.[45]

---

[42] *The Person and the Situation*, p. 51.

[43] New York: Appleton-Century-Crofts, 1970. The experiments, previously published in psychology journals, include Latané and Darley, "Group Inhibition of Bystander Intervention," *Journal of Personality and Social Psychology* 10 (1968); Darley and Latané, "Bystander Intervention in Emergencies: Diffusion of Responsibility," *Journal of Personality and Social Psychology* 8 (1968); Latané and J. Rodin, "A Lady in Distress: Inhibiting Effects of Friends and Strangers on Bystander Intervention," *Journal of Experimental Social Psychology* 8 (1969).

[44] *The Unresponsive Bystander*, p. 58, and generally Chapter 7.

[45] Ibid., pp. 60–61. Altogether there were four experimental groups, run as two pairs. In

At least three explanations, not mutually exclusive, can be offered for the inhibiting effect of other people. One is diffusion of responsibility: in a group, each person may expect or hope that others will intervene; that belief relieves the burden on any given individual to act. The second explanation is conceptual rather than moral. We interpret situations partly in light of others' interpretations. When others in our presence act as if all is well, we are inclined to believe that all is well. Although some who depart from the standard interpretations of events turn out to be heroes and sages, more commonly we deem them crazy or at least "unreasonable," to use the law's term. The third reason concerns embarrassment and self-image. Even if we feel confident that something is amiss, if everyone else is acting as if nothing is wrong, we may hesitate to act because of fears of looking foolish.[46]

Many other experiments, as well as events in real life, support the situationists' claim that seemingly small features of the situations in which people find themselves play a crucial role in influencing behavior.[47] Put this way, of course, the claim is hardly controversial. What gives the situationists' thesis its bite is its corresponding demotion of the role of personality traits in determining behavior. The "fundamental attribution error" seems to say that character is a myth, and situationists may encourage that interpretation. Psychologists who study personality don't take kindly to this view, nor does the ordinary person in the street. It's hard for most of us to believe that differences in people's behavior do not arise from differences in personality and character.

Fortunately for my purposes here, we need not resolve this dispute. I myself am skeptical of the radical understanding of situationism that grants little explanatory power to differences in personality and character. But what the situationists have established indisputably is that small differences in circumstances—including the behavior of others—can produce large differences in how people act. To acknowledge this finding is to invite further inquiry into the conditions under which people might give more than they now do. And it limits (even if it does not

---

the first pair, subjects were alone in the room during the emergency, or together with a confederate of the experimenter who remained passive throughout. In the second pair, two naïve subjects were in the room; in half they were strangers and in the other half friends who had been recruited together. See also the smoke experiment in *The Unresponsive Bystander*, Chapter 6.

[46] These factors are discussed at various places in the articles and book by Latané and Darley and in Ross and Nisbett, *The Person and the Situation*.

[47] For many examples see Ross and Nisbett, *The Person and the Situation* and Cialdini, *Influence*.

eliminate) the role of such traits as selfishness, indifference to others, and sadism in explanations of human action. If the circumstances had been slightly different—if, for example, only one witness had been present—a bystander to Kitty Genovese's murder might well have intervened; apathy and lack of altruistic feeling do not account for inaction. Similarly for our understanding of the infamous Milgram experiments, in which two out of three subjects were willing to shock another person beyond the "danger: severe shock" level, all the way to the lethal level, simply because they were instructed to do so by an apparent authority.[48] When Milgram altered the experimental conditions, the results varied sharply. Thus, "when subjects were free to choose the shock levels to administer to the victim, only three percent delivered the maximum shock."[49] Moreover, although, in the standard variant, subjects complied with the experimenter's order, they did so not indifferently but in anguish.[50]

Not surprisingly, the results of the Milgram experiments have produced in some people profound pessimism, because they show the horrible things that people are capable of doing (in case we hadn't known already). But the subtlety of the influences on subjects' behavior demonstrate that it is not simply "human nature" that caused them do these horrible things. In some environments, people may refuse to do horrible things or may be more likely to perform generous actions. If we have reason to be pessimistic, it's because altering circumstances in the relevant ways is often difficult and not because human dispositions are fixed.

To explain why people act differently in the same circumstances it's difficult to avoid explanations in terms of differences in personality and character. After all, even in the original Milgram experiments a third of

---

[48] Stanley Milgram, *Obedience to Authority* (New York: Harper and Row, 1974). The findings were originally published in Milgram, "Behavioral Study of Obedience," *Journal of Abnormal and Social Psychology* 67 (1963). For situationist interpretations of the Milgram experiments see Ross and Nisbett, *The Person and the Situation*, pp. 52–58, and Doris, *Lack of Character*, pp. 39–51.

[49] Doris, *Lack of Character*, p. 46, citing Milgram, *Obedience to Authority*, p. 61, and A.G. Miller, *The Obedience Experiments: A Case Study of Controversy in Social Science* (New York: Praeger, 1986), p. 210.

[50] A social scientist watching through a one-way mirror reported: "I observed a mature and initially poised businessman enter the laboratory smiling and confident. Within twenty minutes he was reduced to a twitching, stuttering wreck, who was rapidly approaching a point of nervous collapse" (Milgram, "Behavioral Study of Obedience," p. 377, quoted in Ross and Nisbett, p. 55).

the subjects refused to comply.[51] So acknowledging the force of situationism does not imply that parents, teachers, and others should abandon traditional efforts to engage in moral education and character development. Nevertheless, if we hope to make changes in individual behavior that have significant consequences for social life, we should pay close attention to the findings that situationist psychology has uncovered, and look for further developments.

VI

In addition to the findings of psychologists, there are also other reasons to think that people's giving habits could be altered without effecting a transformation of their natures or a newly-awakened appreciation of their duties. These have to do with what can be called the relativity of well-being. Resistance to Singer's demanding view of our obligations derives largely from the belief that it requires large—unreasonably large—sacrifices on the part of ordinary people, and, certainly in his earlier writings, Singer has done little to assuage that fear. But what if the sacrifices did not have to be as large as they appear, while still producing the same results? To the degree that a person's well-being depends on the well-being of others, costs to donors can shrink without reducing benefits.

Although all human beings have certain basic needs—for a minimum number of calories, protection from the elements, and basic health, for example—above the minimum what people need depends a great deal on what others around them have, for several reasons.[52] One has to do with the infrastructure of the culture in which a person lives, and with what economists call networking effects. In a city without good public transportation, you need a car to get around; a family may need two. In a wired society, students and citizens require computers and Internet

---

[51] See David Luban, "Integrity: Its Causes and Cures," *Fordham Law Review* 72 (2003), p. 295. Radical situationists are inclined to explain these differences in behavior in terms of differences in how individuals construe the situation they find themselves in rather than in terms of personality or character differences. So what are externally the "same" circumstances are not the same, from the point of view of the subjects. See Ross and Nisbett, *The Person and the Situation*, pp. 11–13 and Chapter 3.

[52] The discussion here briefly summarizes a longer paper; see Judith Lichtenberg, "Consuming Because Others Consume," *Social Theory and Practice* 22 (1996); reprinted in David A. Crocker and Toby Linden, eds., *Ethics of Consumption: The Good Life, Justice, and Global Stewardship* (Lanham: Rowman and Littlefield, 1998).

access, without which they are severely disadvantaged. These needs are not absolute in the way the need for 1,500 calories a day is; your need for a car or a computer depends partly on the role these goods play in the economic infrastructure and thus in the lives of other people. But they are no less real for being relative.

A second way in which well-being is relative has to do with salience or availability, in the sense that psychologists use these terms. We want things partly because we see them, and we see them because others around us have them. I'm crazy about those boots Jennifer wore to the office yesterday! (And the boots are just a few clicks away, at Zappos.com!) He loves that hundred-dollar wine opener he saw at Doug's the other night! Whether our well-being is actually enhanced by having these items is a question I shall not pursue here. But it's clear that our desire for them, and thus whatever dis-ease we feel at not having them, depends partly on their availability and their possession by others around us.

The idea that a person's well-being is relative to the well-being of others is likely to evoke, first and foremost, thoughts about the status functions of goods, and this is the third and probably the most complex aspect of relativity. In every society certain things function as markers of respect and self-respect, or the lack of them; they denote a person's status relations with others. These "things" need not be material objects; they can be educational degrees or even accents and speech patterns. In eighteenth-century England it was linen shirts and leather shoes, "the want of which," according to Adam Smith, "would be supposed to denote that disgraceful degree of poverty, which, it is presumed, no body can well fall into without extreme bad conduct."[53] Smith deemed such goods "necessaries."

These status functions are closely connected with what the economist Fred Hirsch calls "positional goods."[54] The value of a positional good depends on its place in a system—on how it compares to what other people in the system have. It's misleading to talk about positional *goods*, because goods are likely to have both positional and nonpositional aspects; instead we should talk about the positional *aspects* of goods. One might prefer a Jaguar for its intrinsic properties and also for

---

[53] Adam Smith, *An Inquiry into the Nature and Causes of the Wealth of Nations* (New York: Modern Library, [1776]), Book V, Chapter 2, pp. 821–22.

[54] Fred Hirsch, *Social Limits to Growth* (Cambridge: Cambridge University Press, 1976), Chapter 3; see also Robert Frank, *Choosing the Right Pond: Human Behavior and the Quest for Status* (New York: Oxford University Press, 1985).

what it says about the status of its owner; similarly for an Ivy League education. The relevant point here is that to the extent that the value of a good is positional, the absolute amount of the good is irrelevant; what matters is what one possesses compared to others.

How do positionality and relativity—which together we can think of as comprising the comparative aspect of well-being—bear on the psychology of giving? To the extent that our consumption of goods is rooted in comparative reasons, we could consume less, and give away more, without reducing our well-being. We could live in smaller houses, drive smaller cars, buy fewer gadgets, and be just as well off. (I leave aside other reasons for thinking that material consumption doesn't increase our well-being.) These sorts of reductions would not require changes in the degree to which people are altruistic or self-sacrificing.

This conclusion could hold for donations of time as well as material things. Suppose that some of what is needed to help the poor cannot be transformed into monetary terms. Suppose, that is, that for aid to be effective people would have to donate more time than they now do to volunteer organizations or other nonremunerative work. For many, time is an even more precious commodity than material goods, so sacrifices of time may seem especially onerous. But time's preciousness is in some cases also partly positional. Spending three hours a week volunteering in a soup kitchen or researching the practices of clothing manufacturers in developing countries might cut into a person's work life and put him at a disadvantage compared with his colleagues, who are busy working overtime while he doles soup or surfs the Web for information about employment practices. But if all the colleagues cut their work time to engage in non-employment-related activity, the sacrifice to each would be reduced.

We should note several qualifications. First and most obviously, we consume goods also for noncomparative reasons. Second, there are, as we saw earlier, complex questions about how consumption by rich people helps or harms the poor, and thus how much helping poor people need involve material sacrifices by the rich.[55] Finally, a fuller understanding of these matters requires that we look more closely at those individuals and groups whose well-being we are assessing. People compare themselves

---

[55] See the earlier questions raised by Andrew Kuper, who suggests that consumption of luxury goods might be beneficial to the poor in developing countries. Of course, the details matter. The arguments of this section are relevant also to other issues, such as environmental degradation, where it is clear that lowered consumption is necessary to slow the rate of climate change and reverse other environmental harms.

not with everyone, not even, usually, with everyone in their society, but with certain others, deemed in the sociological literature the *reference group*.[56] How to factor in the comparative aspects of well-being will vary from case to case according to the appropriate reference group.

Still, the relativity of well-being gives us reason (in addition to any other reasons we may have) to think that the relationship between the well-being of the rich and the poor is not a zero-sum game.

VI

The conclusions of the last two sections can be seen as dynamic and static aspects of the problem confronting anyone who wishes to effect a change in people's giving behavior. In the last section I argued that well-being is in many respects comparative, from which it follows that people could have less and be no worse-off as long as others in their reference group also had less. Viewed statically, the well-being of group A with material goods n might be equal to the well-being of group B with material goods $n+m$, and the distribution of well-being within each group might be the same. Thus whatever inequalities and status differences exist in group A might exist in group B. But this fact doesn't explain how to get from B to A: how to get people to act differently so that the goods they relinquish get to others who need them. The findings discussed in the previous section provide some insight into what moves people to act, and in particular to act with the aim of helping others. We should be encouraged by the realization that small differences in situations can produce large differences in behavior, and more specifically that individuals' behavior is highly sensitive to the behavior of others around them.

A caveat is in order. A central finding of situationism is that the factors influencing people to act are subtle, so we cannot straightforwardly extrapolate from one set of circumstances to another, particularly not from experimental situations to the real world. Moreover, the situations psychologists have explored often differ in another obvious but crucially important respect from the circumstances confronting anyone interested in the redistribution of global wealth. In the latter case we are dealing

---

[56] See for example Robert K. Merton and Alice Rossi, "Contributions to the Theory of Reference Group Behavior," in Robert K. Merton, *Social Theory and Social Structure*, enlarged edition (New York: Free Press, 1968). A person's reference group will vary from context to context; for different aspects of consumption it could be one's neighbors, one's co-workers, or the parents of one's children schoolmates.

The influence of the "we" on the "I" bears also on another prominent philosophical debate about alleviating global poverty. I began by considering a question that has lately preoccupied moral philosophers: what responsibilities do rich people have for alleviating dire poverty? My focus was on the duties of individuals. But some philosophers have emphasized that the obligations to relieve poverty are collective ones possessed by societies (or other groups) rather than individuals. Such duties could be rooted in charity alone, but are often thought to rest also on the fact that it is societies or nations as a whole that have been "supporters of, and beneficiaries from, a global institutional order that substantially contributes" to the destitution of poor people around the world.[64] In addition to any conceptual and moral reasons we have for thinking the locus of responsibility is the collective entity rather than the individual person, the evidence and arguments I have been adducing provide additional psychological and material reasons for that focus. The psychic and economic burdens of acting diminish when we act in concert with others.

Lest we imagine an elaborately choreographed ritual involving the synchronized movements of millions, consider instead government. A society as a whole takes action when it uses tax revenues for some public purpose. Significantly increasing the federal budget for international assistance, and directing that assistance intelligently, is an obvious way of achieving such results.

VII

I have focused in this essay on actions rather than beliefs, asking how we might bring it about that people act more generously. To the extent that people act on their beliefs, and stand committed to their actions, the two go hand in hand. In any case, lurking in these topics are difficult questions about how widespread changes come about in people's beliefs about right and wrong, the acceptable and the unacceptable, rights and responsibilities. Consider Adam Hochschild's description, in *Bury the Chains: Prophets and Rebels in the Fight to Free an Empire's Slaves*, of the British antislavery movement:

> When the twelve-man abolition committee first gathered in May 1787, the handful of people in Britain who openly called for an end to slavery or the

---

[64] Thomas Pogge, *World Poverty and Human Rights* (Cambridge: Polity Press, 2002), p. 117; see also pp. 168–177.

with the actions of very large numbers of people, most of them personally unknown to each other—as opposed to would-be Good Samaritans physically present or at least proximate to others, as in the experiments described in section IV.

Despite these differences, however, I believe there is reason for optimism and much room for investigation, for several reasons. First, some of the factors increasing the probability of more generous action seem to operate independently of size and scale issues. Psychologists have demonstrated "the effectiveness of commitment tactics like written pledges and foot-in-the-door procedures in increasing such energy conservation behaviors as recycling, electricity usage, and bus ridership,"[57] and there is no reason to believe such approaches couldn't work to reduce poverty as well. The Internet appears to be a "channel factor" that can make it easy to give, as we learned after the tsunami and Hurricane Katrina, when many online businesses made it possible, with a click of the mouse, to donate small amounts of money (or large amounts) while shopping.[58] These are small changes, and are unlikely to produce the kind of transformations hoped for by those concerned about global poverty. Still, when carried out by thousands or millions of people, they could be more than negligible. And, at least as important, the principles they demonstrate may very well work—we should try and find out—at more ambitious levels.

One thing seems clear: pervasive changes in giving behavior will not come about in the absence of beliefs that others (in whatever reference group is appropriate for the purpose) are giving more. In addition to the situationist evidence and the argument for the relativity of well-being, both of which I have explored in this essay, this conclusion finds support elsewhere as well—in work by psychologists and economists on "cascades," and in a vast array of historical and sociological evidence on the power of trends and broadbased changes in belief and behavior. Before closing with some very brief remarks about these, I will describe one further study that illustrates how beliefs about what other people are

---

[57] Cialdini, *Influence*, p. 90, citing studies by Richard Katzev and colleagues: R. Katzev and T. Johnson, "Comparing the Effects of Monetary Incentives and Foot-in-the-Door Strategies in Promoting Residential Electricity Conservation," *Journal of Applied Psychology* 14 (1984), pp. 12–27; R. Katzev and A. Pardini, "The Comparative Effectiveness of Token Reinforcers and Personal Commitment in Promoting Recycling," *Journal of Environmental Systems* 17 (1988), pp. 93–113.

[58] See above, p. 245, for discussion of channel factors. Similarly, for a time Whole Foods put small bags of groceries at the checkout; the shopper paid six dollars, and the store supplied the groceries to poor people in the vicinity.

doing—even people unknown to the subject and not physically present—can affect a person's behavior.

Noah Goldstein, Robert Cialdini, and Vladas Griskevicius studied the efficacy of conservation efforts in a hotel.[59] Guests found one of several different signs in their rooms, each attempting to persuade the guest to reuse his towels. Each of the five signs had a headline in bold capital letters: "Help the Hotel Save Energy," "Help Save the Environment," "Partner with Us to Help Save the Environment," "Help Save Resources for Future Generations," "Join Your Fellow Citizens in Helping to Save the Environment." Each sign provided further text elaborating on the message. The last message—"Join Your Fellow Citizens in Helping to Save the Environment"—was followed by this sentence: "Almost seventy-five percent of guests who are asked to participate in our new resource savings program do help by using their towels more than once . . ."

Participation rates for those receiving the last message were 41.3 percent; for the other four combined, 29.2 percent.[60] In other words, the belief that others were recycling their towels was more effective in producing participation than the appeal to environmental values, the worth of future generations, and the like.

In section IV I discussed three possible reasons (not mutually exclusive) why the *in*action of others increases the probability of inaction on the part of a person: diffusion of responsibility, the influence of others on our interpretation of events, and possible embarrassment and self-consciousness effects. For the most part, explaining why one is more likely to *act* when others act can be understood analogously. Begin with the third reason: obviously, we will not be embarrassed or self-conscious to act in the way that others are acting. Now the second: since we are generally influenced by others' interpretations of events, when others see the situation as one that makes giving appropriate, we are

---

[59] "A Room With a Viewpoint: The Role of Norm Specificity in Motivating Conservation Behaviors," unpublished paper. The authors are at Arizona State University.

[60] The authors argue also that the results underestimate the true rate of participation. A second experiment demonstrated the effectiveness of appeals to reciprocation. In that experiment, one of the five signs, reading "We're Doing Our Part for the Environment. Can We Count on You?," claimed that the hotel had already made a financial contribution to an environmental organization, and appealed to the guest to "do her part." Guests seeing that sign were almost as likely as those seeing the "Join Your Fellow Citizens" sign to participate—46.7 percent and 47.9 percent respectively. These two signs were significantly more successful in producing participation than the others.

---

likely to as well. The first reason—diffusion of responsibility—requires some revision in the case of action rather than inaction. With inaction, the hypothesis says that we feel less responsibility in the presence of others who could act. But why do we? Is it because we think others also have the *responsibility* to act, or because we think they are more *likely* to act? Each belief may play a part. Similarly, two responsibility-related reasons could explain why others' action might impel us to act. One is a Kantian thought of universalizability: "They're doing their part; I'm no different, so I should help too." The second is the imagining of the joint effects of many people's action, which might spur us on in a way that thinking only of my own little contribution might not: "Look, if we all pitch in we can really solve this problem and do more than put drops in the bucket."[61]

These explanations of the ways people are influenced by the behavior of others are buttressed by a line of research among psychologists and economists on "cascades"—bandwagon or snowball effects. "Informational cascades" occur when people "start attaching credibility to a proposition P . . . merely because other people seem to accept P."[62] Informational cascades correspond to the idea that we look to others to interpret events. If no one is helping Kitty Genovese, then perhaps, appearances to the contrary notwithstanding, she doesn't need help after all. "Reputational cascades" come about when people conform not because they are committed to a belief or an action but in order to look good among their peers. In the bystander situations we have examined, the point may be to avoid looking foolish rather than to gain positive approval. But the desire to be thought upright or generous—or in any case at least as good as the next guy—could play a part in motivating people to give more, if facts about giving were publicly known. Informational and reputational cascades together are part of what Timur Kuran and Cass Sunstein call "availability cascades," in which the availability or prominence of a view in public discourse triggers like responses among individuals.[63] As more people act in a certain way, the belief at issue is more "available" and its effects on others more powerful.

---

[61] I have discussed this point in "Absence and the Unfond Heart: Why People are Less Giving Than They Might Be," in Deen Chatterjee, ed., *The Ethics of Assistance and the Distant Needy* (Cambridge: Cambridge University Press, 2004), p.

[62] Timur Kuran and Cass R. Sunstein, "Availability Cascades and Risk," *Stanford Law Review* 51 (1998), p. 721.

[63] For a discussion (directed to a different subject, risk perception and risk) and further references, see Kuran and Sunstein, "Availability Cascades and Risk."

slave trade were regarded as oddballs, or at best as hopelessly idealistic. Yet in less than a year something unprecedented burst into being. Britons were challenging slavery in London debating societies, in provincial pubs, and across dinner tables throughout the country. Antislavery arguments filled bookshop shelves and newspaper columns. By a few years later, Equiano's autobiography [Equiano was a slave who earned his freedom] had become a surprise bestseller, at least 300,000 people [out of a total population of around eight million] were refusing to eat slave-grown sugar, and Parliament was deluged with the most petitions it had ever received on any subject.[65]

Slavery was outlawed almost everywhere by the end of the nineteenth century.[66]

How did such a sea-change take place? Hochschild's book explores some of the reasons for the spread of anti-slavery sentiment in Britain, among which were factors of geography, the rise of mass media, high literacy rates, the Quaker presence, the influence of some extraordinary individuals, Caribbean slave revolts, war with France, and the American Revolution. Some details are telling. A diagram of a slave ship, with measurements in feet and inches and showing 482 slaves "closely lined up in rows, lying flat, bodies touching one another or the ship's hull," began appearing in "newspapers, magazines, books, and pamphlets" around 1788, long before the public was used to graphic pictures.[67] According to Thomas Clarkson, one of the central figures in the anti-slavery movement, it made "an instantaneous impression of horror upon all who saw it"—and many saw it.[68] Hochschild argues that "the campaign in England was something never seen before: it was the first time a large number of people became outraged, and stayed outraged for many years, over someone else's rights. And most startling of all, the rights of people of another color, on another continent."[69] And this despite the economic benefits of slavery to the British. Yet activists thought it important also to emphasize the mortal effects of the slave trade on English sailors: about twenty percent of each crew had perished by the time ships returned to Britain from the triangular voyage to Africa and the New World.[70]

---

[65] Boston: Houghton Mifflin, 2005, p. 213.

[66] Ibid., p. 3.

[67] Ibid., p. 155.

[68] Ibid., pp. 156, quoting Clarkson.

[69] Ibid., p. 5.

[70] Ibid., pp. 94–95.

Common sense has it that people act mainly out of self-interest, or at least the interests of those near and dear to them. If so, appeals to improve the lot of distant strangers will have to be grounded, at least in part, in "self-interest rightly understood," in Tocqueville's phrase. Yet the abolition movement does not bear out the supremacy of self-interest as a motive. And some experimental findings hint at the complexity of the question.[71]

Hochschild observes that "There is always something mysterious about human empathy," about "when we feel it and when we don't."[72] We are in no danger of dispelling the mystery entirely. But we can learn more about these matters from history and the human sciences. I believe this is a more fruitful direction for inquiry than intricate analyses of the limits of our moral obligations.

---

[71] For example, in a study of young boys told not to play with an attractive toy, boys in one group were warned they would be punished if they played with it; boys in the other group were not threatened. When the experimenter left the room, almost all the boys in both groups refrained from playing with the toy. Six weeks later, boys in both groups were given the opportunity to play with the toy, but were not reminded of the earlier episode. Most of the boys in the group that had been threatened played with the forbidden toy, but most of the boys in the unthreatened group did not. J.L. Freedman, "Long-term Behavioral Effects of Cognitive Dissonance," *Journal of Experimental Social Psychology* 1 (1965), pp. 145–155 (discussed in Cialdini, *Influence*, pp. 82–84). In another experiment, student subjects were paid to tell fellow students that a very boring task they had performed was actually interesting. Subjects who were paid $1 were more likely to decide the task really was interesting—to internalize the message they had communicated—than those who were paid $20. The results are explained by cognitive dissonance theory: subjects who received very little external reward experienced dissonance about lying to their peers, while those who were paid a lot felt they had a justification for the deception. L. Festinger and J.M. Carlsmith, "Cognitive Consequences of Forced Compliance," *Journal of Abnormal and Social Psychology* 58 (1959), pp. 203–210, discussed in Ross and Nisbett, *The Person ad the Situation*, pp. 66–67. Obviously these results would have to be examined very carefully for broader implications.

[72] Hochschild, *Bury the Chains*, p. 5.

Reply to Judith Lichtenberg

PETER SINGER

Obligation and Charity

Judith Lichtenberg has made a thoughtful and constructive contribution to the problem of how we should respond to the co-existence of extreme poverty with affluence. Believing that the ethical debate over my demanding view of our obligations to the poor has reached an impasse, she turns to some relevant work in psychology in order to understand how people might be persuaded or induced to respond more adequately to a situation that is, she says, "unacceptable, if not outrageous and obscene."

Before commenting on the psychological questions Lichtenberg raises, however, I need to respond to some of the comments she makes, early in her essay, about the view of morality that lies behind my argument. She notes that one of the reasons why my view arouses a strong negative response in some people is that I write of our moral obligations to the poor, and some of my opponents take this to mean that if people do not meet this obligation, they may be coerced, perhaps by the state, to do so. But my use of the term "obligation" is not intended to imply that coercion would be justified if the obligation is not met. I've never thought that the state ought to tax people a hundred percent of their income above what they need to meet their basic needs, and then give the money thus raised through foreign aid programs.

I originally used the term "moral obligation" in order to break away from the idea that giving to assist the poor is "charity," that is, something that is good to do, but not wrong not to do. I wanted to suggest that failing to make a significant effort to assist the desperately poor is a failure to meet some minimal standard of moral decency. I am therefore one of those "modern secular moral philosophers" Lichtenberg mentions for whom "talk of moral obligation is simply a way of expressing very strong moral imperatives."

Admittedly, my claim that failing to make a significant effort to assist the poor makes one a less than morally decent person needs to address the point that Lichtenberg makes in regard to slaveowners in the American South before the Civil War. When people who, though morally decent or even admirable in many respects, nevertheless do something seriously wrong, should we excuse that wrong if they were living in a setting in which almost everyone was acting wrongly in that particular way? Here Lichtenberg is absolutely correct when she writes: "To answer these questions we need to know more about the situations of particular individuals." But there is a difference between a past wrong and an ongoing one. As Lichtenberg points out, today it sounds odd to say "Slave-holders violated their moral obligations," because in one sense that statement is obvious, and in another sense it is pointless. On the other hand, there is nothing odd about saying "People violate their moral obligations if they can easily afford to help the desperately poor, but fail to do so." That statement is neither obvious nor pointless, because it challenges widely accepted views about what we ought to do.

Lichtenberg says that I have recently acknowledged that "there might not be a point" in asserting that people ought to give away a lot of their income, and that this might in fact be counterproductive. Though this acknowledgement is not recent—it goes back as far as 1979, when I first suggested tithing[73]—it is true that I have speculated that it might be possible to raise a larger sum, in total, by advocating a lower target that people will be ready to meet, rather than a higher target so far beyond what most people would even consider that they will ignore it. Whether this speculation is correct depends on the facts. How do people respond to plausibly argued, but highly demanding moral judgments? At present, we don't have much data on this question, although I will shortly discuss some relevant research. If the speculation is correct then my view is that we should advocate the target that will lead to raising the largest possible sum—assuming also that the critics of aid that Lichtenberg mentions are wrong, and we can find effective ways to use this sum for the relief of global poverty.

Doing Good, Privately

In this context, Lichtenberg suggests that it is problematic for me to invoke Sidgwick's distinction between what it is right to do privately,

---

[73] *Practical Ethics*, first edition (Cambridge University Press, 1979), pp. 180–81; cf. second edition (Cambridge University Press, 1993), pp. 245–46.

and what it is right to advocate publicly. But Lichtenberg goes astray when she says "for a utilitarian like Singer there is no difference between what a person ought to do and what policy will produce the best consequences." The insertion of the word "policy" here is crucial. Without it the statement would be a tautology; with it, it is false. Consider the recent debate over whether torture is ever justifiable. Those who defend an affirmative answer often challenge their opponents with a situation in which a captured terrorist has information that would enable us to thwart a plot to detonate a nuclear bomb in the midst of a major city. If torture is the only way to get the information out of the terrorist in time, wouldn't we be justified in torturing him? As a utilitarian, I cannot deny that, if this situation really were to arise, torture would be justified. On the other hand, as a utilitarian I may also believe that, given the repeated well-documented instances of people who work in security and intelligence services abusing their captives, and the difficulty of enforcing a nuanced policy in the conditions of extremely restricted access in which interrogations take place, acceptance of a policy that permits torture, no matter how narrowly specified, will lead to the torture of many people who have no knowledge of plots involving nuclear bombs, or any bombs at all, and some of whom are completely innocent of any wrongdoing. If these are indeed the facts, then utilitarians who find themselves able to thwart a plot to use nuclear bombs only by using torture on a captured terrorist will use it, secretly, while at the same time publicly defending a policy that rules out torture in all circumstances. And they will be right both in their use of torture, and in their public rejection of a policy that permits what they were right to do.

This is a dramatic and rare case in which one may have far better consequences by doing something in secret that it is better not to advocate publicly. But there are many much more trivial, but common, instances. When asked by their spouse what they think of a new outfit that he or she has just bought, some people privately consider themselves justified in being less than entirely truthful, but they do not publicly advocate lying in such circumstances, for to do so would undermine the effect they are seeking to achieve by their lie. Another example might be privately accepting a very demanding morality with regard to how much we should give to relieve global poverty, while publicly advocating the more modest level that, if the facts are as I have suggested they could be, would maximize the total amount given by everyone in our society, and would not lead to cynicism about morality as a whole.

Lichtenberg offers two further reasons, applicable not only to utilitarians, against distinguishing between what we rightly do privately, and what we publicly advocate. One is that morality is action-guiding, and if general statements of duty are ineffective or counterproductive, that seems to undermine their validity. But as the examples I have given show, the general statements *are* action-guiding, and are not counter-productive. So are the private judgments about what it is right to do in secret. Thus there is no problem regarding the action-guiding nature of these statements. Lichtenberg's other reason is that "if publicity is a requirement of an adequate moral theory" it follows that whatever is morally right "must be capable of public declaration; morality cannot be esoteric." But the claim that publicity is a requirement of an adequate moral theory is exactly what is here being denied. Why should a utilitarian—other than, perhaps, a rule-utilitarian—accept such a claim, when doing something in secret is obviously very different, in terms of its consequences, from publicly advocating that it be done?[74]

If there is a problem here, it lies in the paradox of actually saying, in a book or journal article, that it may be right to do things in secret that one cannot publicly advocate. For the book or journal is available for anyone to read and saying that it is right to do something in certain situations—for example, what I have just said about torture—is therefore a form of public advocacy. In *The Methods of Ethics* Sidgwick wrote:

> Thus the Utilitarian conclusion, carefully stated, would seem to be this; that the opinion that secrecy may render an action right which would not otherwise be so should itself be kept comparatively secret; and similarly it seems expedient that the doctrine that esoteric morality is expedient should itself be kept esoteric. Or if this concealment be difficult to maintain, it may be desirable that Common Sense should repudiate the doctrines which it is expedient to confine to an enlightened few. And thus a Utilitarian may reasonably desire, on Utilitarian principles, that some of his conclusions should be rejected by mankind generally; or even that the vulgar should keep aloof from his system as a whole, in so far as the inevitable indefiniteness and complexity of its calculations render it likely to lead to bad results in their hands.[75]

---

[74] For further discussion, see Katarzyna de Lazari-Radek and Peter Singer, "Secrecy in Consequentialism", forthcoming in *Ratio*. See also Ben Eggleston, *Self-Defeat, Publicity, and Incoherence: Three Critieria for Consequentialst Theories,* Ph.D. thesis, University of Pittsburgh, 2002, Chapter 4; available at http://etd.library.pit.edu/ ETD/available/etd-04292002-131105.

[75] Henry Sidgwick, *The Methods of Ethics*, seventh edition (London: Macmillan, 1907), p. 490.

Expressing this view on the 490th page of an academic treatise on ethics is not exactly keeping it secret, but it is very different from promoting it in the popular media. The distinction may be harder to draw today, however, when philosophy professors appear on radio and television talk shows. Normally, they are protected from awkward questions by the fact that their host is unlikely to have read their work. But a few interviewers do read, or are briefed by researchers who read, and then the philosophers who defend the idea of a distinction between what it is right to do privately and what it is right to advocate publicly may find themselves forced to acknowledge this fact in a very public forum.

If Sidgwick is right, utilitarianism is a morality that is, in Derek Parfit's terms, partly esoteric, and partly self-effacing.[76] Some people find the idea of an esoteric morality deeply objectionable. Sidgwick's reference to "the vulgar" doesn't help, for it disturbs today's more egalitarian attitudes—or at least, our more egalitarian rhetoric. Bernard Williams called Sidgwick's view "government house utilitarianism," suggesting that it shows the mentality of colonial governors who accept one morality for themselves, while propagating another among "the natives."[77] But the problem with imperial governors in Britain's colonial heyday was not that they followed Sidgwick's utilitarianism, which would have required them to govern for the benefit of all, but that they very often governed to promote the interests of Britain, or their own interests, above the interests of those they governed. Sometimes, of course, they managed to deceive themselves into thinking that what was in Britain's interests was also in the interests of their colonial subjects. So using the evils of colonialism as a ground for rejecting the view that there is a difference between what we do in private and what we advocate in public is suggesting guilt by association.

Critics of the distinction between private morality and public policy need to address the fact that private acts and public advocacy have different consequences. For a utilitarian, there is no getting around this difference between the two. One could, of course, decide never to do anything that one would not publicly advocate, but that would mean that on some occasions one would have to forego doing something that would have better consequences than anything else one could do. This could be the right decision for a utilitarian to make—there may be a parallel here

---

[76] Derek Parfit, *Reasons and Persons* (Oxford: Clarendon, 1984), pp. 40–43.

[77] Bernard Williams, "The Point of View of the Universe: Sidgwick and the Ambitions of Ethics" in Bernard Williams, *The Sense of the Past: Essays in the History of Philosophy* (Princeton University Press, 2006), Chapter 19.

with the commitment to long-term relationships that Richard Arneson discusses in his contribution to this volume—but it isn't obvious that this is the case, and one would need to have good reason to believe that sticking to such a rule would, in the long-term, have better consequences than departing from it on some occasions.

From Philosophy to Psychology

I turn now to the most original and significant part of Lichtenberg's essay, on what we can learn from recent experimental work in psychology about the circumstances under which ordinary people are likely to give to strangers, and the possibilities of increasing both the likelihood that they will give, and the amount they donate.

Lichtenberg asserts that if our interest is in influencing human behavior, it is "beside the point" to discuss how demanding the obligations of rich people are, because "most people in our society, constituted as it is now and with the incentives presently in force, will not give a great deal more than they are giving." Even if "most people" will not be influenced by this argument to give a great deal more than they are now giving, however, discussing how demanding the obligations of rich people are is not pointless if it leads even a very small number of rich people to give a great deal more than they would otherwise give. There is some evidence that it can have this effect. A year or two after "Famine, Affluence, and Morality" was published, in 1972, a wealthy New York philosopher told me that the article had persuaded him to give thousands of dollars each year to Oxfam America. To the best of my knowledge he is still doing so. And as mentioned in my autobiography in this volume, an article I wrote for the *New York Times Sunday Magazine*—in which I argued for a very demanding standard—led to at least $600,000 being donated to Oxfam America and UNICEF.

Nevertheless, the fact that a small number of people are moved by such arguments to give significant sums does not answer the "fundamental question" that Lichtenberg sees my views as posing, namely "whether human beings are built to believe and act" on my conclusions. In that connection she quotes and appears to endorse Alan Ryan's comment that "human beings just aren't put together the way that he wishes they were." The psychological research that Lichtenberg goes on to describe, however, is in some respects at odds with that conclusion. I do not want to suggest that the research supports the opposite conclusion, that human beings are altruists with a natural tendency to share their resources with those in need. Rather, as Lichtenberg herself points out, it suggests that circumstances play a significant role in determining how generous we are.

Here lies the great practical merit of Lichtenberg's essay: it points a way forward. Among the more significant points she draws from the research is that our behavior is strongly influenced by what we believe others are doing, and that small differences in circumstances can lead to big differences in what people do. Her example of the anti-slavery movement also supports this view. The movement to abolish slavery seemed "hopelessly idealistic" when it began in 1787, but a century later it had triumphed almost everywhere. That gives us grounds for cautious optimism about the possibilities of far-reaching change. There may be a "tipping point" at which so many people are giving a significant amount to reduce global poverty that doing so becomes normal.[78]

A useful addition to the material Lichtenberg assembles is some recent work on the impact of defaults. Consider organ donation. In Germany, only twelve percent of the population are potential organ donors. In Austria, the comparable figure is 99.98 percent. Germans and Austrians are not so different in their cultural backgrounds, so this striking difference is puzzling—until we learn that in Germany, you become a potential organ donor by registering your consent with a central register, whereas in Austria you are a potential organ donor unless you register your objection with a central register. This pattern applies across Europe. In four countries with "opt in" systems, the highest percentage of potential donors is 27.5, in the Netherlands. In seven countries with "opt out" systems, the lowest percentage of potential donors is 85.9, in Sweden.[79] Defaults have also been shown to have a major impact on such things as savings and insurance rates. If we could set a modest level of contribution to fighting global poverty, a default position that required people to opt out, rather than one that requires people to opt in, could result in a significant increase in the level of donations. The percentage contributing would be boosted still further if it were widely known that most people did not opt out. Opting out would then be seen as abnormal behavior.

I am not suggesting that merely switching the default would lead to people giving as much as they ought to give. At some significant level,

---

[78] See Malcolm Gladwell, *The Tipping Point: How Little Things Can Make a Big Difference* (New York: Little Brown, 2000).

[79] Eric Johnson and Daniel Goldstein, "Do Defaults Save Lives?" *Science* 302 (21st November, 2003), pp. 1338–39. I owe this reference to Eldar Shafir, whose comments on this topic were very helpful.

most people would decide it was worth the trouble of opting out, and then that would become normal behavior. There could, however, be a significant rise in overall donations before that level is reached. Because that significant rise would be widespread, it might be enough to reduce very sharply the demandingness of my ethical view for individuals. In *The End of Poverty,* Jeffrey Sachs estimates that the shortfall in the annual income of the world's poorest people that would bring them up to a level at which they could meet their basic needs is only $124 billion per annum.[80] This is, admittedly, not a very meaningful figure, because no one thinks that simply handing out money to the poor would end global poverty. But it does suggest that the problem of widespread global poverty could be virtually ended for two or three times that sum. Even if it took eight times that sum, this would still be less than five percent of the $20 trillion annual income of the twenty-two industrialized nations that are members of the OECD's Development Assistance Committee. So if most people were to give, none of them would have to make huge sacrifices.

For these reasons, Lichtenberg is absolutely right when she suggests that the solution to the problem of the demandingness of our obligations to the global poor is to change social structures in ways that are informed by our growing psychological understanding of what it is that will lead us to do more to end global poverty. To adapt Marx, the philosophers have only debated our moral obligations in the world as they find it; the point is, to change it.[81]

---

[80] Jeffrey Sachs, *The End of Poverty*, Chapter 15.

[81] Cf. Karl Marx, *Theses on Feuerbach,* Thesis 11, reprinted in Lloyd Easton and Kurt Guddat, *Writings of the Young Marx on Philosophy and Society* (New York: Doubleday, 1967), p. 402.

8

What Do We Owe to Distant Needy Strangers?

RICHARD J. ARNESON

As an affluent person in a world of needy poor, I should probably do more to aid badly off persons around the globe. Many people subscribe to this thought, which prompts guilt and chagrin. However, the thought readily becomes an extremely demanding vise.

If I am contemplating using a few dollars of mine to go to a restaurant and a movie, I might reflect that the money would do more good, yield more moral value, if I refrained from the personal expense and gave the money to a relief agency serving the global poor. Transferred to the relief agency, the money would save a life or prevent a severe deterioration in the quality of someone's life. The vise tightens when I reflect further that if I give the few dollars to a relief agency, essentially the same decision problem recurs. I could contribute another similar increment of resources to a worthy cause and further reduce my expenditures to enhance my own quality of life. And another, and another, and so on.

Peter Singer has observed that virtually all of us would agree that if we chance upon a child drowning in a pond we ought to save the child's life even if the life-saving activity imposes a considerable sacrifice on us. We live in a world in which, in effect, children drowning in ponds, or the moral equivalent, are ubiquitous, and thanks to the existence of networks of institutional aid already in place, we are always in the position of being well placed to act to save some of the many people whose lives are at risk. Singer thinks that the reason we believe that we ought to save the drowning child, thought through, generalizes and becomes a principle of beneficence that has been called the Principle of Sacrifice:

"If it is in our power to prevent something bad from happening, without thereby sacrificing anything of comparable moral importance, we ought, morally, to do it."[1]

This formulation leaves it open that moral constraints of a deontological sort might limit the moral demands of beneficence. Maybe we should not tell a lie or steal or commit physical aggression against an innocent person in order to help prevent some significant bad from occurring, because the violation of the deontological constraint would be sacrificing something of comparable moral importance. As I understand Singer's stance in this essay, he wants to set the issue of constraints to the side. Let us confine our attention to situations in which whatever moral constraints there are have no bearing on our situation, and the issue is how we should use resources that we legitimately own and could use to benefit ourselves, those near and dear to us, or distant strangers. In that setting, the Principle of Sacrifice dictates that we are morally required to use our resources in whatever way would bring about the best outcome, do the most good. The Principle of Sacrifice so construed is act consequentialism except that the issue of deontological side constraints on what we permissibly may do to bring about the best outcome is bracketed. Like act consequentialism, the Principle of Sacrifice denies options. One is morally required (when constraints are not in play) to do whatever would bring about the best outcome and is not morally allowed to choose any course of action that would induce a less than best outcome.

Singer proposes that the best explanation of the truth that we ought to undertake rescue efforts to save a drowning child that we encounter in the circumstances he describes is that the Principle of Sacrifice is true and it implies that we ought to save the child from death in the specified circumstances. But now the vise is pinching hard. Given stable conditions in the modern world, the Principle of Sacrifice implies that we ought to keep giving to the relief of global destitution until another increment of aid would do more good spent on ourselves than transferred to any distant needy strangers. Roughly speaking, the implication is that we affluent persons should reduce our consumption levels to the point that leaves us just barely better off than the poorest of the global poor.

The "roughly speaking" qualifier of this last conclusion is needed because nothing stated so far warrants the identification of the goods

---

[1] Peter Singer, "Famine, Affluence, and Morality," *Philosophy and Public Affairs* 1 (Spring, 1972), pp. 229–243. Further thoughts are in Peter Singer, "Outsiders: Our Obligations to Those Beyond Our Borders," in *The Ethics of Assistance: Morality and the Distant Needy* (Cambridge: Cambridge University Press, 2004), pp. 11–32. See also Peter Unger, *Living High and Letting Die* (New York: Oxford University Press, 1996).

that constitute moral value and with aggregate human well-being. Perhaps it is intrinsically morally more valuable to achieve a well-being gain for a saint than an identical well-being gain for a sinner. Perhaps bringing about a well-being gain for a person is more morally valuable, the lower her lifetime well-being would otherwise be. Perhaps it is intrinsically morally more valuable that friends help friends rather than strangers and that parents help their own children rather than other people's children. Perhaps human well-being largely consists in excellent achievements and not pleasure or desire satisfaction. There are many issues here, but they are not relevant to settling the moral issue that Singer has pressed on our attention. No matter how we decide these and other issues concerning the nature of moral value, it will remain uncontroversially true, on any noncrazy conception of moral value, that affluent people reducing their consumption and massively transferring resources to the global poor would result in massive increase in aggregate well-being and in moral value. According to Singer, this is what each affluent person is morally required to do.

This Singeresque extreme demand is extremely counterintuitive. Hardly anybody feels obligated to such an extent, or holds others to this standard. Yet the argument that begins with the idea that we ought to save any drowning child near at hand and ends with the conclusion that we ought to contribute resources to Good Samaritan rescue operations to the point at which a further increment of expenditure would reduce the contributor's well-being more than it would enhance the potential aid recipients' well-being is hard to fault. This dialectical situation suggests a puzzle to be solved: find the flaw in the reasoning that issues in the extreme demand.

Proposed solutions to this puzzle abound.[2] Many are obviously unsatisfactory.[3] In the first three sections of this essay I examine two

---

[2] Jean Hampton, "Selflessness and the Loss of Self," *Social Philosophy and Policy* (1993), pp. 135–165; also Liam Murphy, "The Demands of Beneficence," *Philosophy and Public Affairs* 22 (1993), pp. 267–292; also Richard W. Miller, "Beneficence, Duty, and Distance," *Philosophy and Public Affairs* 32 (2004), pp. 357–383; also Samuel Scheffler, *"The Rejection of Consequentialism* (Oxford: Oxford University Press, 1994 [1982]). For elaboration of a view on the obligations of beneficence from a virtue ethics perspective, see Michael Slote, "The Justice of Caring," *Social Philosophy and Policy* 15:1 (Winter, 1998), pp. 171–195; also Slote, *From Morality to Virtue* (Oxford: Oxford University Press, 1995). For a response to Singer from a deontological standpoint, see Frances M. Kamm, "Famine Ethics: The Problem of Distance in Morality and Singer's Ethical Theory," in Dale Jamieson, ed., *Singer and His Critics* (Oxford: Basil Blackwell, 1999), pp. 162–208.

[3] For criticism of Murphy, Hampton, and Scheffler, see Richard Arneson, "Moral Limits

seemingly plausible closely related lines of argument that purport to show that the obligations of beneficence we ought to accept are not nearly as demanding as the Singeresque extreme demand. In the end, both of these lines of argument peter out inconclusively. Our initial puzzlement remains standing. The final sections of this essay attempt to hold on to the Singeresque extreme demand while reducing its counterintuitive air of paradox. Here I venture gentle criticism of Singer. Further progress on this front requires that we move beyond the enterprise of paradox mongering to the enterprise of paradox defusing.

In broad terms, Singer's argument to the conclusion that well-off people in contemporary wealthy societies morally ought to contribute to the relief of the misery of distant needy strangers around the globe and keep contributing until the point at which they are only marginally better off than those they could help relies on a moral premise, the Principle of Sacrifice. It also relies on empirical premises, such as the existence of global poverty and frequent natural and man-made disasters and the existence of mechanisms through which giving aid can provide genuine relief to people.[4] One might challenge Singer's argument by attacking either its moral premise or the empirical premises or both. In this essay I shall focus exclusively on what might be said for and against the crucial moral premise. The factual issues are important and tricky but I set them to the side in order to frame a manageable issue for discussion.

Demanding Too Much?

Garrett Cullity advances a promising criticism of Singer's position.[5] He holds that Singer goes wrong in taking an iterative rather than an aggregative approach to the demands of beneficence. The iterative approach is relentlessly forward-looking: whether one should contribute a further increment of aid or not depends only on the moral costs and

---

on the Demands of Beneficence," in *The Ethics of Assistance: Morality and the Distant Needy*, ed. Deen K. Chatterjee (Cambridge: Cambridge University Press, 2004), pp. 33–58.

[4] On these issues, see Mathias Risse, "What We Owe to the Global Poor," *Journal of Ethics* 9 (2003), pp. 81–117; also Leif Weinar, "What We Owe to Distant Others," *Philosophy, Politics, and Economics* 2 (2003), pp. 283–304.

[5] Garrett Cullity, "Asking Too Much," *The Monist* 86 (2003), pp. 402–418. A more extended discussion appears in Cullity, *The Moral Demands of Affluence* (Oxford: Oxford University Press, 2004). In the more extended discussion, Cullitty renames the principle he opposes. "The Severe Demand" in the essay becomes "the Extreme Demand" in the book. My discussion focuses on the essay version of the argument.

benefits of using that resource in one or another way. (Of course what has happened in the past may affect the costs and benefits that alternative current courses of action would achieve.) The aggregative approach allows backward-looking considerations partially to shape the right answer to such decision problems: an agent may sometimes be justified in declining to contribute a further increment of aid on the ground that his past contributions have on the whole imposed a sacrifice on him that entitles him to resist further demands to give even when the cost of giving to benefit to potential beneficiary is very favorable.

Cullity supports the aggregative approach by arguing that the iterative approach assumed by Singer leads to contradiction. In a nutshell, his proposal is that we must reject the iterative approach in order to preserve options. Among the good reasons to supply easy rescue is that those we save from death or devastation will then be able to achieve the various goods contained in ordinary human lives, lives that do not conform to what he calls the Severe Demand. But if we ought to conform to the Severe Demand, then people's interests in gaining the goods of ordinary human lives, oriented to advancing their own interests and the interests of those near and dear to them, are interests that it is wrong for them to pursue and fulfill. But interests that it is wrong for people to fulfill, we ought not to help them to attain. In Cullity's words, "If a gangster's gun jams, I ought not to help him fix it." But then it turns out that people's interests in achieving the goods of ordinary human lives, lives that do not conform to the Severe Demand, are not after all interests that generate good reasons for us to supply easy rescue of them if they are in peril. On the other hand, if these interests do generate perfectly good reasons to help people by providing easy rescue, as seems intuitively obvious, then the Severe Demand must be rejected.

The Severe Demand as formulated by Cullity is roughly this: Faced with a series of easy rescue opportunities, one should either (1) continue to contribute what is required for easy rescues until no further opportunities for easy rescues present themselves, or (2) stop contributing at the point at which "contributing another increment would itself harm me enough to excuse my failing to save any single life directly at that cost."[6] I shall broaden the idea of an easy rescue, so that it applies when one could at small cost to oneself bring it about that a person is saved, not from imminent death, but from some serious devastation such as chronic malnutrition or lack of decent shelter. I shall also stipulate that when

---

[6] Cullity, "Asking Too Much," p. 403.

an opportunity for easy rescue occurs, efficient rescuing action will result in a net increase in moral value (the cost to the rescuer and others is outweighed by gains to rescuee and others).

Cullity claims acceptance of the Severe Demand leads to a dilemma, which is best avoided by rejecting the Severe Demand and accepting instead some less demanding norm of beneficence. The reasoning to this conclusion proceeds as follows:

1. Everyone ought to conform to the Severe Demand.

2. In order to satisfy 1, everyone ought to aim to satisfy the Severe Demand.

3. A person who aims to satisfy the Severe Demand must lead an altruistically-focused life. Cullity writes: "I have an altruistically-focused life if a guiding aim of mine is to constrict my pursuit of my own fulfillment as much as I bearably can, for the purpose of benefiting others," up to the point at which any further restriction would involve a sacrifice on my part that would not be required by the Severe Demand because the excuse specified in condition 2 of its definition above is triggered by that level of sacrifice.

4. A person ought to aim to satisfy the Severe Demand and contribute to easy rescues in order to satisfy the potential rescuees' interests in leading lives rich in life-enhancing goods.

5. Potential rescuees' interests in the fulfillments contained in non-altruistically-focused lives provide good reason to satisfy the Severe Demand.

6. But potential rescuees' interests in the fulfillments contained in non-altruistically-focused lives are interests in gaining what it is wrong for them to have.

7. People's interests in gaining what it is wrong for them to have are not interests we ought to help them fulfill.

8. People's interests in gaining the fulfillments contained in non-altruistically-focused lives are not interests we ought to help them fulfill (from 6 and 7).

9. People's interests in gaining the fulfillments contained in non-altruistically-focused lives are interests we ought to help them fulfill (from 4 and 5).

8 contradicts 9. To avoid the contradiction, we must renounce the Severe Demand.

So urges Cullity.

In response, I claim we should accept 9, so we should reject 7 and 8. Rejecting these claims eliminates the pressure to reject the Severe Demand.

Below I present an example in which a beneficent agent has good reason to assist another person by helping that person fulfill interests it is morally wrong for her to have. If the example is convincing, we have reason to reject 7 and 8.

Suppose a well-off person, Wealthy, has only two choices: she can either pursue her own projects, which would yield one unit of moral value, or she can contribute some resources to a needy stranger, Needy, who predictably will use the resources to further her personal projects, which would yield two units of moral value. Needy could instead donate the given resources to a still needier stranger, Grim, located where Wealthy cannot assist her but Needy can. Grim would in turn devote the extra resources to her own personal projects. This turn of events would yield three units of moral value. All else is equal here, so the only morally relevant differences between these choices and outcomes as regarded by moral principle are the net gains of one, two, or three units of moral value.

In the situation as described, Needy's interest in using the resources given to her by Wealthy to further her own personal projects is an interest it is wrong for her to have, because according to the Severe Demand, Needy ought to pass the resources along to Grim. In this example I submit that even if Wealthy knows that Needy will not pass along the resources but will use them for herself, Wealthy ought to give the resources in question to Needy. This decision is vindicated when Needy spends the resources on herself and brings about an extra unit of moral value, compared to what would have happened had Wealthy kept the resources for herself. In this scenario Needy's interests in gaining the fulfillments contained in an non-altruistically-focused life are interests that Wealthy ought to assist Needy to fulfill.

This example hinges on a fact about the nature of moral requirements that will prove important later in this essay. Actions are not merely morally right (permissible) or morally wrong. The wrong acts vary in degree of wrongness. The same goes for interests. Some interests, though wrong, are less wrong to have and pursue than others. The interest that a very well off person has in hoarding resources and using them for herself when she should transfer them to other people is more or less wrong depending on the degree of shortfall in moral value between pursuing her interests and pursuing the fulfillments of other needier people. Hence in our example Wealthy's interest in using resources for herself is "wronger" than the comparable interest that Needy has in using those resources for herself (if they are given to her) rather than transferring them to a still needier person. I submit that Needy's interest in using the resources in question to gain the fulfillments of a non-altruistically-focused life is less wrong than the interest Wealthy has in using these resources for herself and that accordingly Needy's interest in gaining these fulfillments provides good reason for Wealthy to transfer these resources to her.

The conclusion we should draw is that Cullity's argument against the Severe Demand (and with it, the iterative approach) fails, so this defense of options collapses.

Allowing Personal Projects

Although Cullity's argument is unsuccessful, merely pointing this out does not dispose of the main considerations to which he appeals in the course of building his case.

One such consideration is the problematic status of immensely valuable components of human life such as friendship and family ties and other personal commitments according to the Principle of Sacrifice applied to the conditions of the modern world.[7] These personal projects are thought to share a special feature. Participation in these projects does a lot of good, but for the most part this good accrues only on the condition that the individuals involved are devoted to them. One is devoted to a project only if one is disposed to channel resources to it beyond the level that would be justified by neutral values as mediated by Singer's Principle of Sacrifice or act consequentialism or the like. It might seem that the advocate of Singer's position must endorse devotion to personal projects (it produces good) and condemn it (it leads us to do bad).

There is no paradox lurking in this train of thought. All that follows is that if we are Singerites we should engage with these personal projects in ways that achieve an optimal trade-off of goods and bads. Consider this argument articulated by Bernard Williams.[8]

---

[7] Richard Arneson, "Consequentialism vs. Special-Ties Partiality," *The Monist* 86 (2003), pp. 382–401.

[8] Bernard Williams, "A Critique of Utilitarianism," in J.J.C. Smart and Bernard Williams, *Utilitarianism: For and Against* (Cambridge: Cambridge University Press, 1973), pp. 75–150.

1. If utility is maximized, people are devoted to personal projects.

2. If people are devoted to personal projects, they are disposed to pursue their projects sometimes even when pursuing a different course of action would produce more utility.

3. If people are disposed to pursue their personal projects sometimes even when pursuing a different course of action would produce more utility, they are not disposed to act in conformity with act utilitarianism.

4. If utility is maximized, people are not disposed to act in conformity with act utilitarianism.

The conclusion 4 is an empirical claim that may well be true, and that is true if the empirical premises 1 through 3 are true. If true, it is an interesting fact of moral psychology. Notice that it does not bear on the normative question, whether act utilitarianism is a correct moral principle that states the correct criterion of morally right and wrong action. Act utilitarianism is one specification of the more generic act consequentialist doctrine, which says that one morally ought always to do an act that would bring about an outcome no worse than the outcome that would be brought about by any other act one could instead choose.

Consider friendship. It may well be the case that forming and sustaining a friendship do a lot of good but also lead one to sometimes act in ways that show loyalty to one's friends when that act does not lead to the best outcome and is morally wrong according to the act consequentialist standard. That being so, if the amount of good that friendship generates is sufficiently large, sometimes the acts of forming and sustaining friendship are what one morally ought to do according to act consequentialism even though these acts predictably lead one to do some further acts that according to act consequentialist assessment are wrong. What holds for friendship may hold for many other personal projects, including devotion to family, kin, communal goals, job and career, accomplishments of many types, and so on.[9]

With these points in mind, return to Cullity's Severe Demand and his claim that to fulfill it, one must lead an altruistically focused life. Recall that an *altruistically-focused life* is defined as one in which "a guiding aim of mine is to constrict my pursuit of my own fulfillment as much as

---

[9] Peter Railton, "Alienation, Consequentialism, and the Demands of Morality," *Philosophy and Public Affairs* 13 (1984), pp. 134–171.

I bearably can, for the purpose of benefiting others." Cullity adds that having that aim "would mean adopting an attitude of vigilant self-constraint toward your friendships" and other personal projects. But wait a minute. A penny-pinching attitude toward friendship (and other personal projects) that seeks to make one's choice of friends and engagement with them as cheap as possible in resources that might be used to help distant needy strangers is itself a force that greatly reduces the good that friendship generates. This does not mean that one is never morally required to pinch pennies to comply with the demands of beneficence. It does mean that one should balance the good and bad that vigilant self-constraint generates and optimize, presumably by adopting an attitude that mixes vigilance and money-is-no-object caring.

Recall also the point that one might be morally required by act consequentialism sometimes to act in ways that will increase the chances of acting against the moral requirements of act consequentialism on other, less consequential occasions. Consequentialism morally requires me to devote myself to some personal projects in ways that will lead me to act from this devotion in ways that consequentialism forbids me to do. Singer's Principle of Sacrifice, a close cousin to act consequentialism, bids me to do the same.

One needs to distinguish what one is morally bound to do over one's life as a whole and what one is morally bound to do, situation by situation, as each occasion of choice arises. Situation by situation, one morally ought to conform to the Severe Demand and strive to lead an altruistically-focused life (taking on board the optimizing qualification). Over one's life as a whole, one can be morally required sometimes to act in ways that ensure that over one's life as a whole, one will not conform to the Severe Demand and will not lead an altruistically focused life.

Following Common Sense?

Perhaps the simplest response to the Singer argument is just to assert baldly the common-sense view about the limited demandingness of the moral requirements of beneficence that Singer has challenged. The common-sense view is vague, in that it allows that we are required morally to some extent to help distant needy strangers but does not include any quantification of the extent. The common-sense view insists that ordinary persons living their own lives without doing anything that harms others in ways that might be thought to violate their rights have considerable moral freedom to live as they choose in any of a wide variety of innocent ways pursuing any of a wide variety of innocent pursuits. This claim too is vague, but maybe this is not a problem. The project would then be to elaborate a consistent and coherent approach to the problem of what we owe distant needy strangers that above all does not wander off the tracks and end up in denial of the common sense starting point. Success in executing this project is achieved when we are able to exhibit a stable mutually supportive set of views that cohere with common sense and do not latently or inchoately give any support to the claim that morality properly understood is extremely demanding.

Richard Miller follows the strategy of response to Singer just described.[10] He supposes that common sense endorses the judgment, on which Singer relies, that if one encounters a drowning toddler close at hand and can bring about a rescue at reasonable cost one morally is required to do so. Part of his task then is to find a way of endorsing Singer's judgment about the drowning toddler case without eliminating options across the board. If scrutiny reveals that Miller's project runs into serious difficulties, that provides some support for the suspicion that the plain common-sense beliefs that oppose Singer's view of obligations of beneficence are in tension and do not form a coherent and plausible set.

Miller explicitly rejects Singer's Principle of Sacrifice and proposes that we should instead accept this Principle of Sympathy: "One's underlying disposition to respond to neediness as such ought to be sufficiently demanding that giving which would express greater underlying concern would impose a significant risk of worsening one's life, if one fulfilled all further moral responsibilities; and it need not be more demanding than this."[11]

An initial response is that the Principle of Sympathy imposes nil or next to nil requirements of responding to need. In a world such as ours in which strangers often will be afflicted with serious unmet needs unless they receive help, any nontrivial disposition to help will require one to give up personal resources that could otherwise have been spent to improve one's own life. Any disposition to help will worsen one's life, unless one restricts the disposition so that it is triggered only when giving aid is costless. This proposal sounds more like a principle of stinginess than one of sympathy. However, Miller is of the opinion that being deprived of some resources that would have enabled one to satisfy a few extra desires does not per se worsen one's life. Worsening only occurs if

---

[10] Miller, "Beneficence, Duty, and Distance." See also Richard Miller, "Moral Closeness and World Community," in *The Ethics of Assistance*, pp. 101–122.

[11] Miller, "Beneficence, Duty, and Distance," p. 359.

one passes some threshold of lessened satisfaction. So we might read his Principle of Sympathy as setting this upper bound on the required disposition to give: having a stronger disposition to give would impose a significant risk of significantly worsening one's life. (A disposition to respond to neediness could be stronger by involving a tendency to respond to a lesser level of need or to respond to a given level of need with greater aid or to be less prone to fatigue in responses to repeated episodes of neediness or some mix of these.)

Even with this clarification, Sympathy looks remarkably undemanding. Why is it written in the stars that the requirements of beneficence must be so undemanding that fulfilling them never significantly worsens one's expected well-being? We impose no such constraint on any other moral duty.

Sympathy is also counterintuitively unbending in a certain respect. Even if the fans of common-sense moral opinion reject Singerism, they surely want to allow that the requirements of beneficence can vary in their demands depending on circumstances and in particular can impose greater sacrifice on those placed in the giving role as the ratio of the cost of giving to the giver to the gains that giving would yield for its beneficiaries becomes more favorable. Even if one need not give a thousand dollars to save a single life, one might be required to give a thousand dollars when that would save several lives. On its face, Sympathy lacks this feature. If giving a thousand dollars imposes on oneself a significant risk of worsening one's life, the disposition that requires such giving cannot be morally required, according to Sympathy. A qualification is needed here, but with the qualification in place, the criticism against Sympathy stands. The qualification is that according to Sympathy it is having the disposition that cannot impose risk of worsening one's life; the disposition that Sympathy licenses might be to give to the point where further giving would involve a ratcheting upward of the disposition past the no-significant-worsening line, but within that limit, to give wherever and whenever giving will do the most good to alleviate neediness as such.[12] However, it remains the case that the location of the threshold line beyond which Sympathy judges a sympathetic disposition to be excessively demanding does not itself vary depending on the ratio of the cost to the giver to the gains

---

[12] To clarify: It would be consistent with the Principle of Sympathy to hold that one ought to be moderately disposed to charitable giving and within the limit of moderation, to deploy one's charity wherever it will do the most good. Miller rejects this view in embracing the Principle of Nearby Sacrifice.

to potential beneficiaries that would be associated with boosting the threshold line upwards.

Miller elucidates the no-worsening constraint on sympathetic disposition as follows. The constraint becomes binding when making an individual's disposition to respond to neediness more expansive would worsen the individual's life "by depriving him of adequate resources to pursue, enjoyably and well, a worthwhile goal with which he is intelligently identified and from which he could not readily detach." On this interpretation of the constraint, its bite for each person is relative to the goals that particular individual happens to have embraced, provided the goal is worthwhile and relinquishing the embrace would take some doing. The more ambitious and expensive the pursuit of the goals one has embraced, the less demanding the requirements of beneficence that Sympathy imposes on one. If a person grows up in an affluent community and forms the life aim of owning all of the world's best thoroughbred racing horses or any comparably stupendously expensive but worthy life aim, the requirements of beneficence according to Sympathy for that person shrink to insignificance. If on the other hand one grows up in destitute surroundings and forms very modest life aims, the no-worsening constraint on the demands of beneficence binds much less tightly. Miller explicitly avows this implication of his doctrine, so I hesitate to press it as an objection, beyond noting that he makes no effort to demonstrate that enlightened common sense really shares these particular opinions that are shaping his account.

Miller places his Principle of Sympathy in a contractualist framework and asserts that this placement justifies Sympathy. He distinguishes the moral attitude of equal concern for all people and equal respect for all people. Having equal concern for all, I would count a utility or well-being gain for any person as having exactly as much weight as a same-sized gain that might be obtained for any other person instead, in the calculation of gains and losses from actions one might perform that determines which action one morally ought to do. Except for saints and fanatics, nobody has the attitude of equal concern for all, and this does not seem to be any sort of moral failing. Lacking equal concern for all is fully compatible with having equal respect for all, and it is the latter that Miller finds the attitude that the moral point of view prescribes for each of us.

What then is having equal respect for all? I found this idea as deployed by Miller to be oddly elusive. He often says that *this* is compatible with equal respect and *this other thing* is not, but I could never see what was supposed to be determining these judgments. He ties the equal respect norm to a general contractualist framework for determining what is morally required, permissible, and forbidden.[13] According to contractualism, acts are wrong just in case they are forbidden by moral principles that no one could reasonably reject as a basis for living together with others motivated in this very same way—to live together with others on a mutually acceptable basis. As Miller puts it, "a choice is wrong if and only if it could not be made in the circumstances by someone displaying equal respect for all persons; equivalently, a choice is wrong if and only if it is incompatible with the ascription of equal worth to everyone's life." As I see it, the cash value of these phrases about "equal respect" and "equal worth" is just this: one shows equal respect for everybody (every rational agent) by always behaving in ways that every fully rational agent will endorse. In short, one should always behave according to correct moral principle. Even shorter: One should morally always do what one should morally always do. Miller's formulations under scrutiny reveal themselves as lacking in content. One does not disagree, because there is nothing substantive here to agree or disagree with.

When Miller asserts that not giving aid to distant needy strangers because one is favoring oneself or those to whom one is closely connected does not fail to show equal respect for all or is compatible with moral principles that nobody who respects all could reasonably reject, he is saying he believes not giving aid to distant needy strangers in deference to this sort of moral partiality is morally permitted. He is asserting his conviction that the demands of beneficence are limited and moderate, not extreme as Singer would have them. Despite the appearance of the rhetoric he employs, in using the language of equal respect and equal worth he is reasserting his opinion that beneficence requirements are limited not providing any sort of argument for that opinion.

A slight retraction might seem to be called for at this point: Maybe talk of equal respect and equal worth does have miniscule content. Equal respect may rule out certain kinds of partiality that are bad such as racism and sexism and tribalism. Some kinds of partiality are morally okay and some sorts are morally bad and the norm of equal respect rules out the bad sorts as impermissible. Of course, if one asks, which kinds of partiality are okay and which kinds are not, the norm of equal respect and equal worth is silent. Once again it is functioning as a slogan not as a substantive argument.

---

[13] On contractualism, see T.M. Scanlon, *What We Owe to Each Other* (Cambridge: Harvard University Press, 1998).

Although Miller might be right to insist that the moral demands of beneficence are moderate, not extreme, his norms of equal respect and equal worth and the contractualism to which they allude provide no argument to support this insistence, so should not stampede anyone not initially inclined to agree with Miller against Singer to reject Singerism. I turn now to a genuine argument offered by Miller in support of the position he affirms.

Miller says that the main argument offered by Singer to support his extreme interpretation of the moral demands of beneficence is that it provides the only, or perhaps the best, explanation of why if one happens to encounter a drowning toddler and can rescue the endangered child without incurring undue risk or cost one is morally required to do so. Miller then argues that he can provide an alternative explanation of why we must save the drowning toddler, an explanation that coheres with his moderate doctrine of the demands of beneficence and doers not lend support to Singer's rival view of this matter. If this explanation succeeds, he will have removed the main support of Singer's doctrine and undermined his position.

Miller's alternative explanation of why we should save the drowning toddler invokes what he calls the "Principle of Nearby Rescue: One has a duty to rescue someone encountered close by who is in imminent peril of severe harm and whom one can help to rescue with the means at hand, if the sacrifice of rescue does not itself involve a grave risk of harm of similar seriousness or of serious physical harm, and does not involve wrongdoing."[14]

Straightaway one might object that the Principle of Sympathy is flatly incompatible with the Principle of Nearby Rescue. If one happens to find oneself in the rescuer role in a Nearby Rescue scenario, one's life may be worsened. However, Sympathy is constrained by no-worsening.

As it stands, this objection fails. Sympathy requires that one's disposition to respond to neediness be such that if the disposition were stronger, it would then impose a significant risk of significantly worsening one's life. Miller asserts that from a suitable *ex ante* perspective, acceptance of Nearby Rescue when others accept the same principle as well is advantageous. The possible costs of finding oneself in the rescuer role are more than offset by the benefits of finding oneself in need of nearby rescue. Having a disposition that conforms to the requirements of Sympathy and that is fine-tuned to include a disposition to Nearby

---

[14] Miller, "Beneficence, Duty, and Distance," p. 378.

Rescue would not require one to incur a significant risk of significantly worsening one's life.

However, the reference here to a suitable ex ante perspective should set off alarm bells. What is "suitable"? Notice that if one is choosing principles of beneficence from behind a thick veil of ignorance that blocks knowledge of one's particular circumstances including one's talents, inherited traits that will render one more or less likely to suffer accident or illness, one's personal wealth, how wealthy one's society is and how comparatively well off one's society is compared to others, and so on, then Singer's Principle of Sympathy will be *ex ante* advantageous and I submit more advantageous than weaker requirements of beneficence including Miller's Sympathy. Miller's Sympathy or something close to it might be expected to emerge as a social contract agreed to by people who know their expected wealth and vulnerability. In this setting the wealthy would have a reason of self-interest to object to schemes of beneficence that require significant transfers of wealth to the poor. But Miller himself rejects egoistic contractarianism.[15] At this point I have no idea how one is supposed to choose a veil of ignorance of any particular degree of thickness and with it a suitable *ex ante* perspective that sets the requirements of beneficence. Since this choice is so unconstrained by reasons of principle, nothing blocks Miller from choosing an *ex ante* perspective that delivers a Principle of Nearby Rescue tailored to his antecedent moderate convictions about the limits of beneficence.

One thought that appears to influence Miller's choice of formulations is that if it were morally permissible to decline to give aid to someone immediately endangered on the ground that giving aid would expose one to any risk, however tiny, of suffering significant harm oneself, morality would endorse refusal to respond in cases in which the ratio of expected costs to the giver to expected gains for beneficiaries is immensely favorable. The requirement that only significant risk of significant harm to self gets one off the hook of moral obligation to aid sets some limit to the permissibility of declining to give aid on the basis of possible cost to oneself.

Nonetheless, Miller does not succeed in justifying a set of beneficence requirements that accounts for the judgment that one must help the drowning toddler without doing so in a way that opens the door to

---

[15] On egoistic contractarianism, see David Gauthier, *Morals by Agreement* (Oxford: Oxford University Press, 1986).

wider beneficence requirements. First, if Nearby Rescue is to be clearly justifiable without conflicting with Sympathy, the requirement will be to be disposed to offer Nearby Rescue provided other people are similarly disposed. But the moral judgment in the drowning toddler case is not that rescue must be supplied if there is a social norm to that effect generally accepted in one's society. The judgment is that rescue must be supplied, period.

Second, Nearby Rescue makes distance relevant to obligation, but this is counterintuitive. Nearby Rescue also makes obligation vary with vagaries of personal encounter, but this also is a counterintuitive feature of the view. Suppose that one could save one person nearby with whom one has made eye contact. This person is sitting on a rock soon to be covered by the tide. Alternatively one could save many persons who are not nearby and in fact are out of eyesight. They too are sitting on a rock that is about to be covered over by the rising tide. One cannot save both the one and the many. Nearby Rescue applied to this setting gives the clearly wrong verdict that one ought to save the nearby person with whom one has established personal contact, since that person's plight triggers the special requirements of that rescue principle. Since the many are located just beyond the jurisdiction of Nearby Rescue, no special requirement to save applies to them.

Another feature of the Nearby Rescue Principle renders its implications counterintuitive when the principle is applied to a broad range of cases. Nearby Rescue as formulated by Miller limits the duty to rescue those in imminent peril whom one encounters nearby *whom one can save with the means at hand*. But why does it matter whether the tool one needs to save a life is at hand or available at a distance? Surely what matters in rescue scenarios is how much good one can do, in a setting in which the good one leaves undone will likely be done by no one else, at what cost to self.

Miller proposes reasons that in his view support Nearby Rescue. The one that strikes me as having most heft is his assertion that this norm efficiently coordinates rescue efforts that we feel morally should be undertaken. However, the two rock case described two paragraphs back shows that Nearby Rescue does not efficiently coordinate rescue efforts. It tells people to channel their beneficence to those close at hand in imminent peril rather then wherever beneficent aid would do the most good in one's circumstances. This objection shows that Miller fails in his task of showing the latent coherence and good sense of common moral opinion in this area.

Further Anti-Singer Strategies

Although I have raised objections against Miller's defense of a moderate view of the demands of beneficence, his strategy might yet be broadly defensible even though his execution of it is flawed.

In broad terms, the issue is whether or not each individual is morally permitted to give extra weight to her own interests and personal concerns in deciding what to do when deontological constraints are not in play. Coherent moderate doctrines can be constructed along this line. Singer himself in his 1972 essay suggests one. Alongside his favored Principle of Sacrifice he sketches a principle that I would render in these words: if one can prevent something bad from happening, without thereby violating anyone's rights or whatever other moral side constraints there may be, and without incurring a significant cost as assessed from the perspective of one's reasonable personal concerns, one ought morally to do the act that prevents the bad from materializing.

This version of moderation is problematic in that it is unbending: In any case in which helping others would cause one to suffer some significant cost in terms of one's personal concerns, the obligation to extend help ceases, no matter what amount of help to no matter how many people is at stake. This feature is eliminable. A more plausible replacement is the idea that the greater the absolute amount of good that one can bring about by beneficent action, and the more favorable the ratio of the cost to one's personal concerns if aid is provided to the net gain that would accrue to beneficiaries and others indirectly affected if the aid is provided, the stronger the reason to do the beneficent action. The principle of moderate beneficence then becomes: If one can prevent something bad from happening, without thereby violating anyone's rights or whatever other moral side constraints there may be, and without incurring excessive cost as assessed from the perspective of one's reasonable personal concerns, one morally ought to do so. A personal cost is excessive just in case the net moral value of the gain to beneficiaries and others indirectly affected if one does the beneficent act is smaller than the moral disvalue of the net loss to one's personal concerns multiplied by a positive number M, where the value of M is constant in all such decision problems and registers the extent of the morally appropriate extra consideration that one is entitled to give one's own personal concerns when deciding on an innocent course of action.[16]

---

[16] This version of moderation rehearses an idea first proposed by Samuel Scheffler in *The Rejection of Consequentialism*.

Notice that the version of moderation just sketched gives up the thought that fundamental moral norms should distinguish nearby rescues and other opportunities to extend aid. Spatial distance and personal encounter are neither morally significant in themselves nor reliably correlate with anything that is per se morally significant. Spatial closeness and personal encounter are psychologically powerful triggers to dispositions to respond to neediness, but these factors do not per se have normative significance. In this important respect this version of moderation renounces Richard Miller's project.

The version of moderation currently under review also dispenses with the attempt to defend an aggregative rather than an iterative approach to the issue of the moral limits of beneficence requirements. In this important respect this version of moderation renounces Garrett Cullity's project.

I suggest that an adequate assessment of the plausibility of moderation, the idea that the demands of beneficence are not so strong as to eliminate options, must take seriously the idea that options and constraints are not independent and separable features of fundamental moral principles but are to be considered together. Options and constraints are a package deal requiring holistic assessment. Although investigation of the logical space of theoretical alternatives here might always turn up surprising new candidate moral theories possessing unexpected virtues, my own hunch is that the most plausible representative of the moderate family of beneficence doctrines will be some version of Lockean natural rights theory.[17] The rough idea of the Lockean tradition is that each and every person has basic moral rights not to be harmed in certain ways such as theft and fraud and physical aggression and that along with these rights is a complementary right to live as one chooses, doing whatever one wants, so long as one does not thereby violate anyone's basic moral rights. A slightly less rough version of this doctrine allows that people's basic rights include moderate rights to be given aid but that the correlative duty to aid the needy is subordinate to the negative duty not to harm in specified ways. On this version of the doctrine of side constraints,

---

[17] See John Locke, *Second Treatise of Government*, ed. C.B. Macpherson (Indianapolis: Hackett, 1980 [1690]). On side constraints, see Robert Nozick, *Anarchy, State, and Utopia* (New York: Basic Books, 1974), Chapter 3. An excellent recent interpretation of Locke's doctrine is in A. John Simmons, *The Lockean Theory of Rights* (Princeton: Princeton University Press, 1992). For the idea that options and constraints form a package deal, see Eric Mack, "Prerogatives, Restrictions, and Rights," *Social Philosophy and Policy* 22 (2005).

these constraints pose limited demands, and within those limits, one is at liberty to do whatever one chooses. The world being as it is, generally respect for people's rights leaves one at liberty to choose among a wide array of morally acceptable options.

The Lockean tradition is associated with a conception of moral rights as absolute exceptionless constraints, and no one has articulated a plausible list of such exceptionless constraints. But in the apt phrase of Judith Thomson, rights might take the form of spongy side constraints, that give way and may acceptably be infringed if the consequences of not infringing them are excessively bad.[18]

The consequentialist will wonder why certain traditional negative moral rights should have pride of place in a moral theory. Her hunch is that the imperative to respect rights is most appealing when we suppose that respecting rights is an efficient and generally reliable strategy for bringing about good outcomes, and lacks appeal otherwise. But the issue of consequentialism versus broad Lockeanism is unresolved in the present state of ethical theory.[19] Insofar as the issue of moderation versus extremism on the issue of the moral demands of beneficence aligns itself with that monumental stand-off, there will I predict be no quick resolution of it.

Swallowing Singer's Stone

So far this essay has defended Singer's arguments against two critics. The flaws in the critics' positions point the way toward a more plausible moderate doctrine of beneficence, but even as lightly sketched, this doctrine looks complex, hedged, and qualified, and not obviously superior to Singer's simple powerful reasoning. Despite the cogency of the principle that powers Singer's reasoning, there remains a huge stone to swallow. The conclusion of his argument is extremely counterintuitive.

Singer sometimes incautiously expresses the thought that we should not be troubled by this fact, because our moral intuitions about cases have no particular epistemic authority anyway.[20] They likely just reflect

---

[18] Judith Jarvis Thomson, *The Realm of Rights* (Cambridge: Harvard University Press, 1990). Thomson believes that rights, though spongy to a degree, have an iron core.

[19] Richard Arneson, "The Shape of Lockean Rights: Pareto, Fairness, and Consent," *Social Philosophy and Policy* 22 (2005), pp. 255–285.

[20] Peter Singer, "Sidgwick and Reflective Equilibrium," *The Monist* 58 (1974), pp. 490–517.

the fact that we are socialized in a bad society that grossly underestimates the true moral demands of beneficence. But the trouble is that reliance on moral intuitions (judgments concerning what is morally so) cannot be avoided.

Suppose someone proposes a clever argument to a clearly incredible conclusion, for example, "No human person has ever suffered pain." If the argument consists in a derivation of the conclusion, the deductive reasoning may be valid or invalid, suppose it is clearly valid. If the conclusion of the argument is sufficiently incredible, it can never be rational to accept the argument and its conclusion—a more sensible response is to reject one or more of the premises from which the crazy conclusion follows. If the premises in question all look pretty good, we may not be sure which one or more to reject, but we may provisionally decide that some of them must be defective even if we are not sure which these are, if the only alternative is believing something that after reflection and thought we simply cannot believe.

The same goes if someone proposes a clever argument to a clearly incredible moral conclusion, for example, "Hitler's plan to exterminate the German Jews was just and fair."

Of course, there is no specifying in advance any limits on the novel conclusions to which we might eventually be led by novel moral reasoning that reveals undetected prejudice and presses unnoticed similarities on our attention and proposes hitherto unformulated moral principles that after scrutiny and reflection command our allegiance. Practical reason goes where it goes. But the fact that what seems incredible to us at one time may not seem so at a later time after absorbing the force of novel reasons does not mean that it is rational at any time to accept as true what all things considered strikes us as incredible and so false.

The difficulty that Singer's train of thought imposes on us can be simply stated:

1. We are morally required to rescue a child drowning at our feet in a shallow pond when the gain from rescue outweighs the moral cost.

2. The same reasoning that justifies claim (1) also justifies a parallel claim that we are morally required to aid distant needy strangers when the gain from aid outweighs the moral cost.

3. It is not the case that morality requires us to help distant needy strangers up to the point at which the moral gain that could be secured by providing any further aid would be outweighed by the moral cost of providing such aid.

1, 2, and 3 conflict. I agree that the best response is to reject 3. The challenge then is to reduce the counterintuitive sting of this response. So far in this essay my criticisms of two critics of Singer suggest that any available stance on this terrain will be counterintuitive to some extent, and that defenders of plain common sense will have their own problems once they try to articulate an explicit and detailed consistent position. I have also urged that act consequentialism by its own lights is committed to accommodating goods that are generated by devotion to personal projects when they are really conducive to aggregate human well-being. Moreover, act consequentialism can accommodate personal devotion without becoming trapped in inconsistency. So far, so good. What else can be done to mollify grouchy anticonsequentialist "common sense"?

The next two sections of this essay answer this question. I pursue two lines of response. One involves (a) distinguishing between acts that are wrong according to fundamental moral principle and acts that fail to comply with the moral code that either actually is or ideally should be established in the agent's society and (b) tying blameworthiness to moral code noncompliance. The idea would be to allow the Singerite to deny that people are blameworthy generally for failure to live up to the very demanding requirements of Singerite beneficence requirements. This gambit is only partially successful, it turns out. A second line holds that the act consequentialist should downplay the distinction between acts that are right and wrong. Her more important task is to grade acts as "righter" and "wronger" depending on the extent of the shortfall between the act being evaluated and the best that could have been done in the circumstances. Once this task is taken seriously, one sees that although the act consequentialist must deny options as understood by the deontologist, she will accept options of a sort.

Distinguishing Moral Principles, Moral Codes, and Blameworthiness

In his 1972 essay Singer had raised the worry that acceptance of his strong view of the moral requirements of beneficence might be counterproductive. That is to say, perhaps if a society were to attempt to train people to accept the Principle of Sacrifice as part of its moral code, people might become alienated from such a demanding moral code, and become less disposed generally to conform to the code's requirements. In this way the consequences of instituting a less demanding moral code might be better than the consequences of promulgating a more severe code.

Singer countenances the possibility that in practice ratcheting up the requirements of morality beyond some threshold point in a code to be socially enforced might be counterproductive. He then adds, "it should be emphasized that these considerations are relevant only to the issue of what we should require from others, and not to what we ourselves ought to do." This comment sounds to me both correct and incorrect, but obviously we then need to sort out the mixture of insight and error it expresses.

Correct: Whatever moral code has been established in the society I inhabit, that code does not by itself settle the issue, what I myself should do here and now. Suppose for good reasons a lax code has been established, which as applied to my situation says I am not obligated to give more to distant needy strangers. For all that, the moral reasons for me giving more now may be stronger than any opposed reasons. Then surely what I morally ought to do here and now is whatever the balance of moral reasons that bear on my particular circumstances singles out as the thing to do.

Incorrect: But if a moral code is instituted in society, and internalized by its members including myself, then that code guides my sense of what is morally acceptable and unacceptable for me to do. How can the code be irrelevant to the assessment of my choice of conduct as right or wrong and of me as culpable or praiseworthy for doing it?

The key here is to see that the issue is not what we demand of ourselves versus what we demand of others. We should rather distinguish fundamental moral principle and derived public code, both principle and code being applicable both to self and others. The distinction I have in mind is essentially R.M. Hare's distinction between the critical and intuitive levels of moral thinking. At the critical level, one seeks to discover fundamental moral principles that constitute the theoretical criterion of morally right and wrong action—what is morally required, permitted, and forbidden. At the intuitive level, one responds to moral decision problems on the basis of moral rules that people in a society are trained to accept as the guide to their conscience. From the standpoint of an act consequentialist critical morality, the social code that ought to be maintained in a given society and time is the one that would function best as assessed by the consequences of its operation. Since humans have cognitive, affective, and volitional disabilities, and also lack access to information relevant to choice of conduct, the moral rules to be established even in perfect compliance with critical morality standards will be coarse-grained and designed to produce good results when imperfect people are guided by them. The moral code of one's society, even if the moral code is as good as it could be, may tell one that the acts one might do have a moral permissibility status different from the status they have from the critical morality standpoint.

The question then arises, is blameworthiness and praiseworthiness determined from the critical morality standpoint or from the moral code standpoint? Suppose we try the latter option: then fitness for blame to be administered by self or others would be triggered only by acts that violate the code of moral rules that is, in the down to earth sense, actually established in the agent's society, and in an ideal sense, would be established if the code were selected by whatever standards ought to govern this choice. An act consequentialist will suppose that the ideal code to be established in society is the one, the selection and institution of which here and now would be productive of best consequences.

One might hope that this line of thought will reduce the counterintuitiveness of Singer's stringent morality of beneficence. Given that human beings are by nature prone to selfishness and to favoring those near and dear, the best moral code will not make war against human nature but will compromise with it. The best moral code will then not be act consequentialism, nor will it be a set of rules equivalent in practice to act consequentialism. The code will be less demanding than act consequentialism (or Singer's Principle of Sacrifice) in its beneficence requirements. This will all be compatible with holding that act consequentialism is the correct theory that at the critical level determines what one morally really ought to do. But blameworthiness is generated not by failure to conform to critical level morality but rather by the unexcused failure of a competent agent to conform to the moral code that is actually established in practice at least if that moral code is best according to critical theory standards.

An alternative stance on blameworthiness would also have the effect of mitigating the conflict between Singerism and common-sense morality. The alternative stance holds that an act is blameworthy only if some act of punishing it is warranted, and adds in a consequentialist spirit that punishing is warranted only if it would produce better consequences than any alternative course of action. Since in many cases not even the smallest reproach directed against someone who fails to aid distant needy strangers in a society with a social code that regards aiding as morally optional would produce any good consequences, once again the Singer position's opposition to common-sense opinion is muted. His position will imply that the person who fails to give aid according to the Principle of Sacrifice is standardly morally wrong but probably not morally blameworthy.

However, the line of thought just sketched is incorrect. It blurs the distinction between holding someone responsible and someone's being responsible. We hold people responsible for the quality of their actions in various ways by praising and rewarding in response to good quality and reproaching and punishing in response to bad. These holdings are (I claim) acts to be judged by their consequences. Supposing it to be wrong in some case to blame me for my action, this still leaves open the possibility that I am blameworthy. Whether or not I am blameworthy in doing an act surely depends only on the assessment of features of *my moral performance in the process that caused the act* and not at all on the consequences of acts of punishment that other persons might or might not perform.

The line of thought that tries to tie the praiseworthiness and blameworthiness of an agent's conduct to whether or not it conforms to the established moral code is also going crookedly astray. When an agent does what is morally wrong but permissible according to the established moral code of her society, the presumption is that the wrong act is not seriously culpable. But the relevant standard of blameworthiness is whether the agent had a reasonable opportunity to behave rightly. To the degree that in her circumstances it would have been difficult or painful or both for the agent to have done the right thing, to that degree culpability is lessened, and at some threshold vanishes altogether. Since the established moral code exerts a massive gravitational pull on individual judgment and choice, when doing the morally right act requires the agent to act against the code, often we should judge that the agent lacked a reasonable opportunity to do the right thing. Often, not always: there still may be cases in which the agent who does the right thing against the grain of the established moral code is hardly praiseworthy for doing so, because in her circumstances doing the right thing was as easy as falling off a log and as pleasant as eating ice cream, and likewise cases in which the agent who conforms to the established moral code and does what is morally wrong is seriously blameworthy for doing so, because doing the right thing in her circumstances would have been easy and pleasant.

The consequentialist need not conflate an act's being blameworthy and its being the case that any act of blaming the agent for having done the first act would be morally right according to act consequentialist standards. Nor should we identify the blameworthy act as one that is of a type the blaming of which would generally be productive of the best outcome. These standards would render culpability (and the same goes for praiseworthiness) independent of the quality of the agent's moral performance itself. Whether what I do is blameworthy depends on the character and quality of what I do and not on the further question whether blaming me or administering sanctions would produce good consequences. My act is blameworthy if a blaming attitude to it is appropriate on the merits of the case, which could be so even if no act of forming such a blaming attitude in oneself or another would be desirable by consequentialist standards.

Reintroducing Options of a Sort

Considerations about the necessary conditions for reasonably holding people blameworthy for doing morally wrong actions interact with another feature of an act consequentialist morality that Singer's position should adopt. The upshot is to modify the denial of options that Singer affirms.

Ordinary common-sense morality insists that so long as one does not violate what are in most circumstances fairly undemanding rights of other people not to be harmed in certain limited ways, one is morally free to live as one chooses. Any act that does not violate anyone's moral rights is a legitimate option eligible for choice, according to common sense. Singerism denies options and insists that one must do whatever (without violating constraints) would bring about the best outcome. Leaving aside the possibility of acts tied for best in their consequences, this position denies options altogether. In any situation there is one act one morally must do.

However, this denial of options is relaxed once one notes that act consequentialism properly construed holds that acts are righter or wronger depending on the amount of the shortfall in value between the outcome of what one actually does and the outcome of the act that would in one's circumstances have led to the very best outcome. A wrong act can be trivially wrong, a whisker away from the best one could have done, or it can be a horrendously wrong act that, for example, prevents millions of people from enjoying decent lives without giving rise to significant offsetting benefits. We can think of the acts an agent could do on some occasion as ordered in an array of groups of acts that have consequences that range from very close to the consequences of the best act to very close to the very worst one could have done. With this picture in view, we can see that options of a sort have an important role in moral life and moral assessment. Far more important that determining whether one's act on an occasion was right or wrong would be fixing the degree of wrongness if it is not the very best one could have done. For any given extent of shortfall from the very best act, there will be a set of acts that are eligible for choice in the sense that none is morally worse than the act whose consequences lie just at the edge of this boundary. In virtually any circumstances in which an agent is placed, there will be sets of actions she might perform, whose consequences though not the same are sufficiently similar that there is very little that is morally at stake if the agent chooses any option within the set. Call these vague equivalence classes "consequentialist options." Act consequentialism can be formulated as a righter/wronger test: an act that an agent does is righter or wronger, depending on the amount of shortfall, if any, between the value of the total inclusive consequences of doing that act and the value that would accrue if the act that would produce the best outcome attainable were done instead.

The righter/wronger formulation enables the act consequentialist to avoid being required to hold that it is morally a big deal if I am in a restaurant and order the fish tacos rather than the chicken tacos if ordering the chicken tacos would have led to the best available outcome (slightly more pleasure for me) and hence qualifies as the uniquely morally right act, the act that one morally ought to be done.

However, one should note that the righter/wronger formulation may enhance, rather than lessen, our sense that the ordinary consumer of luxury goods and a wasteful lifestyle in an affluent society is doing something that is seriously morally wrong, given that he could have used the same resources to make a big dent in the misery suffered by some distant needy strangers. The idea that morality should make room for some notion of options, and leave individuals moral freedom to pursue a variety of life courses without thereby doing anything seriously wrong, is an idea that the act consequentialist can readily embrace, as has been shown. But this still leaves intact the harsh assessment of modern capitalist consumerism that any reasonable version of act consequentialist morality must imply.

Conclusion

The upshot of this lengthy discussion is that the vise that Singer has clamped on us still binds tightly. The common sense moral opinions that have made it seem to some philosophers as though morality could not be as demanding as he supposes have turned out under examination to be either not relevant to the key issue or lacking in force.

Reply to Richard Arneson

PETER SINGER

Utilitarians and Close Personal Relationships

In the first two-thirds of his fine essay, Richard Arneson rebuts some leading alternatives to my position on our obligation to aid the poor, a position that he calls the "Principle of Sacrifice." Arneson's arguments are sound and provide welcome support for my views, so I have little to add to them.

I especially welcome Arneson's careful response to the objection that consequentialism is in conflict with immensely valuable aspects of human life like close family relationships and friendship, because the implications of this objection are often not understood. As Arneson notes, if the facts of human psychology are that these relationships are of great utility, but being in such relationships precludes, on at least some occasions, acting as a utilitarian, then utilitarians will espouse such relationships, and as a result, sometimes will not do what would produce the best consequences. These utilitarians have chosen lives that lead to higher utility than any other life open to them. They are like Odysseus blocking his sailors' ears with beeswax and then having himself bound to the mast so that he can hear the sirens, but will not be lured to destruction by them.[21] A rational egoist would approve of this procedure, for Odysseus thereby maximized his overall preference satisfaction, even though he knew that he would, when tied up, be unable to satisfy his preference to get closer to the sirens. Similarly, rational utilitarians maximize overall utility by committing themselves to relationships that, taking a long-term view, produce greater utility for themselves and others than they could produce if they were not committed to such relationships. There is nothing in this procedure that conflicts with the util-

---

[21] Homer, *The Odyssey,* XII, line 39.

itarian claim that the right act is the one that produces the best consequences. Simply stated, an initial choice precludes certain later choices,
but since the initial choice maximized utility, it was the right choice to
make.

Moral Intuitions and the Principle of Sacrifice

In the final third of his paper, Arneson seeks ways to make the Principle
of Sacrifice less counterintuitive. Before assessing the merits of
Arneson's suggestions, I have three general comments to make about
this project.

Early in his article, after explaining my view of our obligations to aid
the poor, Arneson asserts: "This Singeresque extreme demand is
extremely counterintuitive. Hardly anybody feels obligated to such an
extent, or holds others to this standard." I don't find the extreme demand
so counterintuitive. As I mention in the autobiography that appears in
this volume, it has always struck me as obvious that there is something
wrong with spending money on luxuries when that money can make
such a huge difference to the lives of other people who are desperately
poor. Nor am I the only one to think this. James Otteson, a forceful critic of my views on our obligation to give to the poor, describes it as "a
simple and powerful statement of an ethical position that many find
intuitively attractive, if hard to adopt."[22]

Why then does Arneson find it "extremely counterintuitive? Later in
his essay he writes: "Ordinary common-sense morality insists that so
long as one does not violate what are in most circumstances fairly undemanding rights of other people not to be harmed in certain limited ways,
one is morally free to live as one chooses." This may be accurate as a
description of the ordinary common-sense morality of some
Americans—those who have been significantly influenced by Lockean
ideas of individual rights—but I very much doubt that it applies more
broadly to the ordinary common-sense morality of Europeans, or
Australians, or many other cultures, which recognize an obligation to
provide assistance to those in need, at least when that assistance can be
provided at little cost to oneself, and will make a big difference to the
recipient. Arneson's account of the freedom that he believes "ordinary
common-sense morality" insists on is strikingly similar to the freedom
that John Stuart Mill famously insisted the state should permit us—that

---

[22] James Otteson, *Actual Ethics* (Cambridge: Cambridge University Press, 2006), p. 130.

is, freedom to live as we choose, as long as we do not harm others.[23] But setting limits to the power of the state over the individual is one thing, and setting limits to what morality can oblige us to do is something quite different. (On this, see also my response to Judith Lichtenberg in this volume.)

It is true that the claim that it is our moral obligation to give away *everything* beyond what we need to meet our basic needs is contrary to the ordinary common-sense morality even of Europeans and Australians, but perhaps all this shows is that we don't reflect on the implications of moral judgments that we do accept. That failure to think through the implications of our moral judgments may say more about our selfishness, and our desire to conform to social standards, than it does about our moral intuitions. In any case, while I would not wish to claim that we intuitively accept a principle as demanding as the one I defend, I don't think the mismatch between our intuitions and that principle is as sharp as Arneson suggests.

My second general comment relates to my oft-stated position that in deciding what is right, we should not take our moral intuitions as authoritative. To this Arneson objects that we cannot avoid relying on moral intuitions. This raises a fundamental issue about method in ethics, one that is central to Michael Huemer's contribution to this volume, so I shall have more to say about it in responding to him. Here I shall limit myself to a minor criticism of one particular claim Arneson makes. After accepting—as an argument against taking our intuitions as authoritative—that it is not possible to specify in advance where novel moral reasoning might lead us, for example in revealing previously undetected prejudices or proposing new moral principles, Arneson attempts to blunt the force of this concession by saying: "the fact that what seems incredible to us at one time may not seem so at a later time after absorbing the force of novel reasons does not mean that it is rational at any time to accept as true what all things considered strikes us as incredible and so false." This statement seems to envisage a two-step process that can lead to change in our moral intuitions:

1. At time T_1, novel reasons are presented to us for accepting as true a moral conclusion that strikes us as incredible and so false.

2. At time T_2, we have absorbed the force of these reasons, and the conclusion no longer seems to us incredible, and so no longer seems to us false.

---

[23] John Stuart Mill, *On Liberty,* first published 1859.

Arneson appears to assert that it would not be rational for us to accept the moral conclusion as true at T_1. But how can that be right? We have been given adequate reasons for accepting the conclusion. No additional reasons are offered between T_1 and T_2. So how could it be irrational to make up our mind about the moral conclusion on the basis of the reasons we have been given? On the contrary, it is the delay in accepting the conclusion—our tendency to irrationally cling to moral intuitions in the face of sufficient reasons for abandoning them—that is irrational.

The Role of a Moral Code

Notwithstanding the two previous comments, it is no doubt true that many people reject my views about our obligations to relieve poverty because these views are at odds with the way they ordinarily think about what we need to do to lead morally good or even morally decent lives. Since widespread acceptance of my views on this topic can be expected to have good consequences, my final general comment on this topic is that I support efforts to reduce the contrast between my views and ordinary moral attitudes. Indeed, that is something that I have been trying to do in all my work. As Arneson notes, the idea can already be found in "Famine, Affluence, and Morality" and, as mentioned in my response to Judith Lichtenberg in this volume, it is also in *Practical Ethics*, where I suggest that we publicly advocate only that tithing, or giving ten percent of one's income, is obligatory. Giving above that level would be seen as good but optional. More recently, in *One World*, I went even further and suggested that as little as one percent might be enough as a minimal, though not optimal, level—if it were really possible to make that a widely accepted norm.[24] (Why so little? Partly because of new evidence about how modest a sum it may take to bring most of the world's poor up to a minimum at which they could satisfy their basic needs, and partly because as the years pass and little changes in terms of how much people give, I have become increasingly anxious to get *some* kind of norm accepted, even a minimal one.) In *One World* I wrote: "Those who do not meet this standard should be seen as failing to meet their fair share of a global responsibility, and therefore as doing something that is seriously morally wrong. This is the minimum, not the optimal, donation." As these remarks suggest, I favor Arneson's idea of a moral code that allows for options, and I also agree that we should recognize degrees of "righter

---

[24] *One World* (New Haven: Yale University Press, 2002), pp. 193–94.

and wronger"—or more seriously and less seriously wrong—actions, rather than just the black and white distinction of right and wrong.[25]

Arneson is critical of my comment, in "Famine, Affluence, and Morality," that the reasons why we might encourage the existence of a moral code that sets a low standard (but will nevertheless, because it will gain wide acceptance, yield the greatest possible amount) "are relevant only to the issue of what we should require from others, and not to what we ourselves ought to do." He thinks that this comment is correct in that whatever code has been established in my society does not settle the amount I ought to give, for this amount is determined by "the balance of moral reasons that bear on my particular circumstances." Nevertheless, he thinks it is incorrect in that "if a moral code is instituted in society, and internalized by its members including myself, then that code guides my sense of what is morally acceptable and unacceptable for me to do." This is true, because to say that I have internalized a moral code just is to say that it guides my sense of what is morally acceptable and unacceptable for me to do. In making the comment Arneson quotes, however, I had in mind someone who thinks for herself about moral issues. She will be aware of the code, but she has not internalized it to the extent of allowing it to determine her sense of what she ought to do. That is the situation in which the issue is, contrary to what Arneson says, "what we demand of ourselves versus what we demand of others."

As Arneson says, a moral code, if well entrenched in a society, can exert a "massive gravitational pull" that is relevant to assessing the actions of members of that society. If we have a well-entrenched moral code that requires the giving of a significant amount—but not so much as to eliminate all optional spending—a failure to give more would sometimes still be blameworthy, but it would only be in very unusual circumstances that blaming an agent who gave as much as the code required would have good consequences. Nevertheless, reflecting on our own conduct, we might think that we should have done more, even though, because we have given as much or more than the code required, no one else is in a position to blame us, or at least not publicly, for that would not have good consequences.

Arneson's concluding discussion of the ways in which a consequentialist can still allow for some options is useful, and his suggested way of thinking about this issue is one we would do well to adopt, although

---

[25] In my most recent work on this issue, I acknowledge Arneson's point here, and incorporate it into my own views. See *The Life You Can Save* (New York: Random House, 2009), Chapter 10.

the actual language "righter/wronger"is jarring. We do already, of course, distinguish between more and less serious wrongs, and greater emphasis on this may be a good thing. Arneson's account of the difference between an act being blameworthy, and it being right, on consequentialist grounds, to blame the agent for the act, is another helpful contribution to making my view less counterintuitive without weakening it to any significant degree.

9

Should Peter Singer Favor Massive Redistribution or Economic Growth?

TYLER COWEN

I. Introduction

Peter Singer is well-known for advocating very high levels of wealth redistribution. He argues with force that we should give most of our incomes to charity. After all, how could your consumption of ice cream cones be more important than somebody's life in East Africa? Perhaps you should also give up your second car, your desire for fancy clothing, and your yearly vacation at Club Med. Singer himself gives twenty percent of his income to charitable causes, mostly to fight poverty.

Singer also has suggested that government should take a lead role in directing such redistribution. This would involve much higher levels of taxation and government spending in both the United States and Western Europe. Nonetheless, if the gainer's gain exceeds the loser's loss, such policies will pass the utilitarian test. If you will not give to the poor voluntarily, the money can be taken from you and redistributed in any case. Preventing suffering and death is, under a utilitarian perspective, more important than protecting you from coercive taxation.

Singer (1999, p. 8) writes of "[being] on the side of the weak, not the powerful; of the oppressed, not the oppressor; of the ridden, not the rider. And he [Singer is referring to Henry Spira] talks of the vast quantity of pain and suffering that exists in our universe, and of his desire to do something to reduce it. That, I think, is what the left is all about."

Not surprisingly, utilitarianism is seen as a very demanding morality. It appears that the claims of the suffering are so enormous that few able or wealthy individuals would be able to carry out individual life projects. We can imagine, for instance, that every individual is obliged to work for charity, or to send most of his or her income to the poor in India. Western doctors should spend most of their careers in African villages. Many more of us would have to become doctors or nurses. A mother might have to abandon or sell her baby to send food to the babies of others, and so on. But can this be true?

I wish to examine Singer's policy conclusions, specifically his embrace of widespread redistribution. I will argue that his faith in both government and redistribution is misplaced. Instead Singer should consider a stronger attachment to growth-affirming institutions, often of a capitalist nature. In lieu of the focus on more redistribution, arguably governments should be doing more to encourage savings, investment, and production. If we hold a long enough time horizon, as I argue we should, these policies will likely do more for the very poor. Dare we think of Singer's utilitarianism as implying some form of (properly sophisticated) supply-side economics?

I will not seek to pin down this case in every detail. Instead I will show that Singer's own moral theory plausibly suggests such a conclusion. Under some assumptions about parameter values, redistribution may be welfare-dominated by a market economy with strong incentives for savings and investment. Furthermore most professional economists—not just free-market extremists—believe such parameter values to be true. Singer's case for redistribution is then driven by his out-of-fashion "immiseration thesis," and not by his moral theory *per se*. Utilitarianism, taken alone, should in most circumstances direct our attention toward incentives for growth and production.

The essay will proceed as follows. Section II will briefly outline the case for a zero rate of discount. Since Singer (consistently) appears to accept a zero discount rate, or some approximation thereof, I will not consider every nuance of these debates. Section III will consider the implications of a zero discount rate in more detail. In particular, a truly long time horizon suggests a greater importance for maximizing the rate of sustainable economic growth. Section IV will consider whether greater wealth in fact brings more happiness. Section V offers some concluding remarks.

Throughout the essay I shall take Singer's "cardinal utilitarianism" as given. It will be assumed that utilities are measurable and comparable, at least in principle or in very rough terms. Furthermore it will be assumed that a very poor person (usually) values a dollar more than does a very rich person. Finally, it will be assumed, in line with Singer, that cardinal utility is the only relevant moral value. My own moral theory is more pluralist in nature, but it is nonetheless interesting to see where pure utilitarianism will lead. Even a pluralist typically holds utility to be one very important value. So while these conclusions could be overturned by the consideration of non-utility values, they should be of interest to pluralists as one part of a broader policy calculus.

II. Zero Discount Rates

Singer's writings focus on cardinal utility, so we should ask how to compare cardinal utility today to cardinal utility tomorrow. Using the terminology of economics, we must choose a suitable rate of utility discount.

Most cardinal utilitarians see a strong case for a zero or otherwise very low rate of utility discount. That is, pleasures and pains which come in the future should not be worth less, simply because they are removed in time. When those pleasures and pains come, they will be no less real.

The alternative implications of a strongly positive rate of discount are intuitively repelling. For instance imagine a decision-maker weighting present and future interests. The table represents some tradeoffs, assuming that we use various positive rates of intergenerational discount:

If we discount the future by five percent, a death, five hundred years from now, is worth more than 39 billion times less than a comparable death would be worth today. Alternatively, at that same discount rate, one death two hundred years from now is equal in value to 131.5 deaths, of comparable lives, three hundred years from now. Few cardinal utilitarians would endorse these conclusions.

Parfit and Cowen (1992, p. 145) wrote:

TABLE 9.1

Estimated Number of Future Benefits Equal to One Present Benefit Based on Different Discount Rates

Years in The Future	1%	3%	5%	10%
30	1.3	2.4	4.3	17.4
50	1.6	4.3	11.4	117.3
100	2.7	19.2	131.5	13,780.6
500	144.7	2,621,877.2	39,323,261,827	4.96×10^{20}

Why should costs and benefits receive less weight, simply because they are
further in the future? When the future comes, these benefits and costs will
be no less real. Imagine finding out that you, having just reached your twenty-
first birthday, must soon die of cancer because one evening Cleopatra wanted
an extra helping of dessert. How could this be justified?

Consider similar comparisons prospectively. Under any positive discount rate, no matter how low, one life today can be worth more than one
million lives in the future, or worth the entire subsequent survival of the
human race, if we use a long enough time horizon for the comparison.

Time preference does not justify the positive discounting of well-
being across long time horizons, especially when those horizons cross
the generations. Time preference means that an individual prefers to
have a benefit sooner rather than later. Perhaps I am impatient to enjoy
my dinner, or I wish to put off a boring departmental meeting. Even if
such preferences are rational, they do not justify pure time preference
across the generations. Our unborn great-great-grandchildren will not
receive benefits for some time, but in the meantime they are not waiting
impatiently. Similarly, medieval peasants did not receive a utilitarian
benefit from the mere fact of having been borne before us.[1]

It can be argued that we should not endorse a zero rate of utility discount for all problems in all settings. Perhaps different utilities are het-
erogeneous, intra-personal discount rates should differ from interpersonal rates, and the exact discount rate should vary with the length of the
time horizon, to cite just a few complications. Surely a single number—
zero—cannot contain all of the information required to express such
complex intertemporal trade-offs. This point is well-taken. For this reason, a zero rate of discount is best thought of as a rough approximation
of how we approach discounting and the value of the distant future.
More complex mathematical tools allow us to express a strong concern

---

[1] Some individuals object that a zero rate of discount encounters problems with infini-
ties. This will be true if there is some expectation that the world will last forever. But
the resulting difficulties with infinity are not unique to issues of intertemporal value.
Many plausible cosmologies allow for infinite expected value throughout the universe,
with or without a zero discount rate (Bostrom 2004). These cosmologies may not be
true, but they need only have some positive chance of being true for the infinity to surface in our expected value calculations. Pascal's Wager and the St. Petersburg Paradox
bring related issues to the fore, again without relying on a zero discount rate. So we face
the infinity problem in any case, regardless of our attitude toward the very distant future.
Whatever the force of the infinity issue, it does not particularly discriminate against a
zero discount rate on utility.

for the distant future, yet without requiring that we boil all trade-offs down to a single, unalterable, final discount rate number. The general principle is that we should not count future cardinal utilities for close to nothing, simply because those utilities come much later in time. Provided that we accept that intuition, the remaining arguments of this paper will follow, whether or not we commit to the exact number of zero for all comparisons and purposes.[2]

Note also that economists (for example, Broome 1994) have developed good arguments for why small increments of *wealth* should be subject to positive discounting. For instance I should prefer a dollar today to a dollar tomorrow. In the meantime I can invest the dollar today at a positive rate of return. These arguments, however, do not offer a comparable justification for discounting cardinal utility. Unlike dollars or physical resources, utilities cannot be invested at positive rates of return. We therefore can accept this standard article of economic reasoning, while continuing to maintain zero discounting of cardinal utility or some more generalized version thereof.

III. Economic Growth

A look at the longer run suggests that wealth should be invested rather than redistributed. Just as Table 1 shows the dangers of positive discounting of utility, it also shows the immense potential for compound returns. For instance if we invest a million dollars for fifty years at five percent return, we will have $11.4 million. That same dollar, at a ten percent return for one hundred years, will produce over $13 billion of value. That will produce benefits for the world's poor, and of course for the wealthy and middle classes as well.

It is true that sending a large chunk of American GDP to Africa would raise African welfare in the short run. But if current total income were divided equally around the world, global per capita income would be about $3,500.[3] This average would then fall rapidly, due to incentive effects. Civilization as we know it could not survive and the world's poor would fall into a deeper state of misery than they currently experience.

---

[2] For instance, in a work in progress, I argue for "The Overtaking Criterion" as one means of comparing present and future utility streams; other approaches also generalize some of the basic intuitions behind a zero discount rate for utility, while retaining scope for flexibility. I will not enter into the details here, but for most practical problems they yield broadly similar results.

[3] See www.geocities.com/combusem/WORLDGDP.HTM.

So rather than redistributing most wealth, we would reap greater utilitarian benefits by investing it in high-return activities. While the benefits of growth often lie in the future, we already have seen that future benefits should not be subject to significant temporal discount.[4]

A sufficiently long time horizon will favor growth over redistribution even if we are counting *only* the interests of the very poor in the social welfare function. The benefits of radical redistribution are one-time in nature. We can try to equalize all wealth today, but we would not be able to draw on comparable resources for the next generation. Such a widespread collective redistribution would lead rapidly to negative economic growth. Furthermore redistribution often corrects problems for only a short period of time. Most of the world's poor suffer under many burdens, including poor access to health care, poor infrastructure, low literacy, lack of access to markets, and most of all weak institutions and poor governance. These conditions cannot be cured overnight or even within a few years' time. Immediate redistribution may alleviate some of these problems for a while, but after the transferred money has been used, often the problems will reemerge to considerable degree. We are not investing in a permanent cure for poverty.

In contrast the benefits of economic growth will compound over time. It is common to scorn the phrase "trickle down economics," but in fact a steady and ongoing flow of benefits is exactly what we are looking to achieve. A flood is better than a trickle, but a lasting trickle is better than eating our cake today and cashing in our chips.

To be sure, we wish to maintain higher growth over time, and not just for a single year. Maximizing the sustainable rate of economic growth does *not* imply pursuing immediate growth at the expense of all other values. Policies that seek growth at breakneck speed are frequently unstable. The Shah of Iran tried to bring his country into the modern world very rapidly. Growth rates were high for a while but in the longer run could not be maintained. Since the revolution Iran has done poorly. The Shah's forced modernization did not in fact maximize economic growth, and a more cautious set of policies likely would have been better. Environmental factors also may constrain how much growth is possible in the longer run.[5]

---

[4] On utilitarian obligations, Scarre (1996, Chapter 8) offers a good survey. In addition to Williams 1973, see Rand 1967, Scheffler 1982, Wolf 1982, Railton 1984, and Nagel 1986 for other critiques of extreme utilitarian obligations.

[5] For a formal look at the concept of sustainability, see Heal 1998, Chapter 1. Singer 1995, pp. 48–54, correctly notes that environmental constraints may limit how high a rate of growth we can achieve.

Furthermore pursuing economic growth ought to refer to gross domestic product as properly understood, and not as currently measured by governments. "True GDP," if I may use that term, accounts for leisure time, household production, and environmental amenities. Current GDP statistics have a bias towards what can be measured, rather than what contributes to human welfare. For this reason, "maximizing the rate of growth" does not mean that everyone should work the maximum number of hours in a day. An eighteen-hour workday might maximize measured GDP but would not maximize true GDP over time, once we take the value of leisure into account, not to mention the possibility of labor burnout.

The Benefits of Growth

Singer sometimes sees economic growth as the enemy rather than friend of the poor. He (1999, p. 45) writes: "I doubt that greater wealth for the middle and upper classes could make up for the increase in human misery this [market competition] has brought to the poor."

At other times Singer (2004, pp. 88–90) cites evidence that globalization has helped rather than hurt of the lot of the poor. He appears to have mixed feelings. On one hand, he claims that globalization increases inequality (this is not true, once Chinese economic growth is considered; see Firebaugh 2003). On the other hand, he does not argue that globalization makes people poorer. Singer (2004, pp. 89–90) ends on an agnostic note: "With so many different ways of assessing inequality, and so many different findings, what is the ordinary citizen to think? No evidence that I have found enables me to form a clear view about the overall impact of economic globalization on the poor. Most likely, it has helped some to escape poverty and thrown others deeper into it; but whether it has helped more people than it has harmed and whether it has caused more good to those it has helped than it has brought misery to those it has harmed is something that, without better data, we just cannot know."

Many complex issues are on the table, not the least of which is how globalization, market competition, and capitalism fit together as concepts. Nonetheless, reading Singer's body of work as a whole, I interpret him as expressing skepticism of this entire bundle of ideas. He is not willing to endorse a capitalist market economy—based on global trade relations—as our best available means of poverty alleviation.

In reality, few economists dispute the positive links between capitalism, trade, globalization, and growth. If we look over the last fifty years, the spectacular growth in East Asia has been accompanied by, and indeed been driven by, capitalism and globalization. The Chinese miracle has required foreign investment, as well as the growth of private enterprise and urban migration. Outsourcing, while still modest in absolute terms, is bringing higher living standards to India. The opening of that economy, combined with partial privatization, is bringing current growth rates of eight percent. These empirics are not accidents, but rather stem from a fundamental understanding of property rights, incentives, and the benefits of voluntary exchange.[6]

Singer (2004, p. 85) admits that "poverty has fallen more in the past fifty years than in the previous 500." He then strikes a note of caution, largely because African nations have become poorer. Nonetheless Africa has seen by far the smallest degree of economic globalization and the African nations have in general been the least successful in building capitalist institutions. Pointing to Africa seems to *support* the view that economic growth is important. Furthermore Africa would benefit more from the wealthy countries if the latter would open up their agricultural markets. This would more mean more capitalism and globalization, not less.[7]

Putting aside these factual debates, Singer's analysis does not take a long enough time perspective. No matter how we view current world trends on a year-to-year basis, economic growth over a longer time horizon alleviates human misery and lengthens human lives. Wealthier societies have better living standards, better medicines, and offer greater autonomy, greater fulfillment, and more sources of fun.

In the United States in 1995, forty-one percent of "poor" households owned their own homes. The average poor home had three bedrooms, one-and-a-half baths, a garage, and a porch or patio. Seventy percent of poor households own a car; twenty-seven percent own two or more cars. Ninety-seven percent of the poor have a color television, and almost half of the poor have two or more color televisions. Sixty-four percent own microwave ovens, half have a stereo system, and over a quarter have an automatic dishwasher. Two-thirds of "poor" households classified as poor have air conditioning. (For purposes of comparison, only thirty-six percent of the entire U.S. population had air conditioning as recently as the early 1970s.) Most have access to antibiotics and many own cell phones and personal computers. Today's American poor are more likely

---

[6] For surveys of such evidence, see Mandle 2002, Wolf 2004, and LeGrain 2004.

[7] Singer 2004, p. 87, does note a conflict between two perspectives. On the one hand, more people than ever before are living below the world poverty line. At the same time, more people than ever before are above—often well above—the poverty line.

to be overweight than are middle-class persons. Most poor children today grow up to be, on average, one inch taller and ten pounds heavier than WWII American GIs. In quantitative terms, the evidence suggests that the bottom quintile of an economy shares proportionally in growth (Dollar and Kraay 2000).[8]

Just as the present appears remarkable from the vantage point of the past, our future may offer comparable advances. Continued robust growth might bring greater life expectancies, cures for debilitating diseases, and cognitive enhancements. Millions or billions of people will have much better and longer lives. The future "poor" will have benefits we do not dream of, just as today's poor in many ways live better than did Napoleon.

The economic growth of the wealthier countries also benefits the very poor. For instance a richer economy will have a greater capacity to absorb immigrants. Poor people who migrate to rich countries earn much higher incomes, and their children become much richer yet. A typical migrant from rural Mexico to the United States will move from earning about two dollars a day to about ten dollars an hour. Of course, the richer the host country, the more new immigrants tend to benefit.

Immigrants also send remittances back home. Total remittances around the world are now about eighty billion dollars a year, about twice the amount of the formal category of foreign aid. Remittances, however, bypass governments and do not encounter comparable problems with waste or corruption. To cite one example, Mexicans working in the United States send back home twenty billion dollars every year, circa 2003. This sum is twice the value of Mexico's agricultural exports, and over a third more than tourist revenue. Many Mexicans have used received remittances to start new businesses or revitalize their communities through infrastructure investments.[9]

Many migrants return to their home countries, bringing skills and liberal democratic ideas. Software repatriates have helped build India's competitiveness in high-tech industries. Thousands of Asian students have obtained science or engineering degrees from American universities, thereafter returning home to start new businesses. If a country is willing to offer some scope for entrepreneurship, it need not fear a "brain drain." Instead foreign contacts, training, and periods of residency will help promote domestic development.

---

[8] The U.S. Census provides the data, I am indebted to the summary by Rector (1998).

[9] All the figures are from the November–December 2004 issue of *Foreign Policy*.

The global poor also benefit from new medicines, new global technologies, and research and development efforts. E. Helpman (2004, p. 84) summarizes: "the main finding—that R&D capital stocks of trade partners have a noticeable impact on a country's total factor productivity—appears to be robust . . . [consider] a coordinated permanent expansion of R&D investment by one-half of GDP in each of twenty-one industrial countries. The U.S. output grows by fifteen percent, while Canada's and Italy's output expands by more than twenty-five percent. On average the output of all the industrial countries rises by 17.5 percent. And importantly, the output of all the less-developed countries rises by 10.6 percent on average. That is, the less-developed countries experience substantial gains from R&D expansion in the industrial countries . . ."

Taking yet a longer view, look back at how human beings climbed out of the poverty of the year 1000 A.D. or 5000 B.C. Welfare states have done considerable good, but it was not redistribution that accounted for the significant growth in wealth. If we are sufficiently forward-looking, sustainable economic growth will be our priority.

What Role for Redistribution?

We do see circumstances under which a utilitarian *should* favor large-scale redistribution toward the very poor. Perhaps, for whatever reason, the world would end in the near future. Redistribution then would stand a greater chance of being favored in utilitarian terms. The scope for compounding investment value over time would be correspondingly limited and the immediate returns to charity would weigh more heavily in the decision calculus. Alternatively, the real return on investment might be permanently negative or zero. In this case compounding would not operate and we again would see greater reason to redistribute wealth. So utilitarianism *might* yield the prescription of extreme redistribution, but there is no general presumption in this direction.

We still can find good arguments for some degree of redistribution, simply not for extreme redistribution. For instance redistribution plausibly enhances the rate of sustainable economic growth. To cite some pluses from redistribution, a welfare state can give the poor greater access to education and nutrition. These individuals not only enjoy a higher quality of life, but they produce goods and services, they contribute to tax revenues, and they are less likely to end up as a destructive social force. Other growth-enhancing benefits of redistribution are political in nature. Welfare payments sometimes "buy" the loyalties of special interest groups, thereby inducing them to support public order. Some of the poor will be less desperate and will feel less desperate as well. Those groups receive a financial stake in the system and a socially-sanctioned legitimacy for their claims.[10]

These factors may mean more redistribution than we currently undertake, or perhaps redistribution of a different kind, namely growth-enhancing redistribution. (It is debatable how much today's government programs in fact redistribute to the poor at all.) It will not, however, suggest that a utilitarian is obliged to redistribute most of national income to the very poor, whether at home or abroad.

Beyond some point a sufficiently generous welfare state limits the rate of growth. It withdraws some individuals from the labor force, weakens productive incentives, necessitates higher tax rates, and is usually combined with static, insider-oriented labor market regulations. Furthermore if everyone approaches government looking for a handout, basic mechanisms of governance can break down, leading to rent-seeking, corruption and fiscal bloat. Alternatively, welfare may create urban cultures of dependency and crime, which endanger social order. The empirical literature suggests that non-infrastructure government spending is correlated positively with lower growth rates.[11]

More subtly, high levels of welfare make it harder for wealthy countries to afford large numbers of poor immigrants from around the world. Many immigrants increase government revenue in the short run, but many, especially the poorer ones, do not. They require resettlement assistance, emergency medical care, extra police and public works expenditures, or they otherwise tax the resources of the state. The more we spend on domestic welfare, the less we can spend on absorbing immigrants. Furthermore a larger welfare state may make society less willing to take in many immigrants. Many voters resent it when their tax dollars go to support foreigners.

In some cases utilitarian prescriptions will have morally counterintuitive implications, but running counter to the usual fears of enslaved American doctors serving Africa. Namely utilitarianism may support the

---

[10] See for instance Alesina and Rodrik 1994 and Persson and Tabellini 1994. For a survey of the growing literature on how income distribution can affect growth, see Greiner, Semmler, and Gong 2005, pp. 132–33.

[11] See, for instance, Barro 1991. Goodin, Headey, Muffels, and Dirven 1999 argue that a democratic social welfare state does not lower the rate of economic growth, but they use only two data points, the Netherlands and the United States. See also Lindert 2004. He argues that higher welfare spending tends to be packaged with other growth-enhancing policies, such as low taxation on capital income. He does not show that higher spending at Western European levels is itself good for economic growth.

transfer of resources *from the poor to the rich*. A talented entrepreneur, for instance, can probably earn a higher rate of return on invested resources than can a disabled great-grandmother. So we will have some reason, when thinking about the future, to redistribute *additional* resources to the more productive members of society. The implications will be anti-egalitarian at first, but over a sufficiently long time horizon the poor will benefit increasingly from the high rate of economic growth. The results need not be anti-egalitarian if we take the appropriate broader stretch of time, but they still will appear anti-egalitarian by the usual metrics.

Being a pluralist, I would not favor redistribution toward the super-rich for reasons related to human rights. Nonetheless such an example shows just how far the burden of argument can be shifted to the other side. Direct, short-term redistribution to today's poor is no longer the default option for an impersonal moral theory that emphasizes individual well-being.

III. Does Wealth Bring Greater Well-being?

Singer (1995, p. 50) asks whether economic growth has made people much happier. He cites some evidence:

> The problem is that our conception of the good life depends on constantly rising levels of consumption . . . Despite this dramatic increase in material goods, people felt neither more affluent nor happier . . . The proportion [of Americans] describing themselves as 'very happy' has hovered around one-third since the 1950s. Why has it not risen with material levels of affluence? Essentially, because though the society was still becoming more affluent, the rate at which it was doing so had slowed . . .

Singer (p. 52) also cites relative status effects: even if I am wealthier, my neighbors are too and so I do not feel much better off if at all.

Singer (pp. 53–54) then calls for a decrease in the rate of economic growth:

> If we retain our narrow view of our own self-interest . . . we will see the reduction in material affluence as nothing but a setback. Even if we recognize that the reduction is inevitable and that the present economy cannot be sustained, we will consider it a regrettable necessity, desirable in the interests of the world as a whole, but bad in its impact on our own lives. But if we have a broader view of self-interest we will welcome the change, not just for the good of the global environment, but also for our-

selves . . . a nation's Gross National Product is no guide to the level of welfare of the population.

Apparently consistent with Singer's claims, a large literature suggests that additional riches do not make citizens in wealthy countries any happier, at least not above a certain level of wealth. Using information taken from questionnaires, once a country has a per capita income of roughly $10,000 a year or more, the aggregate income-happiness link appears weak. Helliwell (2002, p. 28) argues that the curve flattens out at about half of current American per capita income, or roughly the standard of living in contemporary Greece. These results lead us to wonder whether economic growth is very important for human well-being.[12]

Despite this evidence, I see wealth and happiness as closely linked, especially in the long run. At most the "happiness literature" shows that many small changes are irrelevant for human well-being, compared to what we had previously thought. Buying a new sailboat, for instance, might not make you happier at all. But this result would not eliminate the major benefits of economic growth, as experienced over longer periods of time. I am much better off than my medieval counterparts, and if growth continues most people in the more distant future will be much better off than I am.

The observed flat-lining of the happiness-wealth relationship may in part reflect changes in verbal framing. The literature usually focuses on aspiration or treadmill effects, whereby you get more but you start expecting more as well. The greater wealth translates into less happiness than might have been expected. But this is not the only adjustment occasioned by growing wealth. The wealthy also recalibrate how they should respond to questions about their happiness; they call themselves "happy" only at increasingly high levels of true satisfaction. If happiness itself is subject to framing effects, most likely *talk* about happiness is subject to framing effects as well. The wealthy develop higher standards for reporting when they are "happy" or "very happy." If you are a millionaire living next door to a billionaire, you might be less likely to report that you are ecstatically well-off. This does not mean that you

---

[12] See Argyle 1999; Oswald 1997; and Myers 2000. Wealthy countries, when they become wealthier over time, do not become happier in the aggregate. In some cases (such as the U.S., 1946–1991) greater wealth is correlated with *lower* levels of self-reported happiness; see Dieter 1984; Blanchflower and Oswald 2000; Diener and Oishi 2000; Myers 2000; Lane 1998; Frey and Stutzer 2000; and Easterlin 1995. On the United States, see Frey and Stutzer 2002a, pp. 76–77.

spend your entire time envying the billionaire or that you suffer under your lower relative status. Part of the "downgrading" of your condition is a more modest standard of verbal reporting rather than reflecting an underlying flatness of welfare.

So assume that both framing effects—concerning happiness *and* talk about happiness—operate at the same time. This will imply that even a constant measured level of reported happiness implies *growing* real happiness over time. Life improvements do usually make us happier, while *both* our expectations *and* our reporting standards adjust upwards. This is the most plausible interpretation of the aggregate data. Furthermore it is supported by an observation of revealed preferences. Most individuals strive to earn higher incomes even after they have experienced the strength of "aspiration" and "treadmill" effects.

Consider another example. If I buy a Mercedes, my polled neighbor may express greater dissatisfaction with his Volkswagen. That same neighbor, if he had a Lada in Moscow, circa 1978, might express a very high level of satisfaction on a questionnaire. After all, most of his peers would not have any car at all. Nonetheless in absolute terms he still is probably happier having the Volkswagen in contemporary America. So my neighbor may envy my new car, but when I buy a Mercedes, the gainer's gain still likely exceeds the loser's loss. Buying expensive baubles—even when done for status—is often a positive-sum game.

The happiness literature also tends to confuse the flatness of the income-happiness curve with whether that curve can be shifted upward over time. Yes, the observed happiness-wealth correlation flattens out at some level of income. But economic growth still can shift the curve as a whole. The standard of living found in contemporary Greece—even if comparable in happiness to the current U.S.—would not match up to what people will likely enjoy in a wealthier society of the future. So there is no strong case for remaining at the wealth level of Greece; we should instead seek to make people even wealthier, so as to push up the (possibly) flat part of the curve.

We can see the same point—the long-run irrelevance of the observed flattening—by going back to the past. The happiness-wealth curve may have had a flat range in the Stone Age, but the entire range of that curve—even the top—would not make for a very happy existence by modern standards. This is not just a zero-sum comparative effect, but rather reflects the greater ease and variety of modern life. So a flat range of the curve, at any point in time, does not break the long run link between happiness and wealth. Economic growth still shifts the curve up over time, even if the far end of that curve remains flat in the short run.

The happiness literature also takes a limited view of well-being. The contemporary empirical literature on happiness starts with the operational definition of whether an honest, self-aware person would report himself or herself as being happy, if so asked. Even if this accurately captures one notion of happiness, it is not the only relevant variable concerning well-being.

For instance a wealthier economy probably gives us more "fleeting" happiness experiences, or at least greater chances to trade-off long and short-term sources of happiness. Recent research (Kahneman, et.al. 2004) looks at the allocation of time during the day and classifies events according to how much (temporary) happiness they produce. It turns out that intimate relations, time spent with friends, and television, all appear to make people happier in this sense. Working and commuting make people less happy. A wealthier economy will offer greater options for structuring these choices, again recognizing trade-offs between long- and short-term happiness. Wealthier economies, on average, are associated with higher levels of leisure time, although they accommodate workaholics as well.

Often context effects matter for temporary happiness. An individual will admit to being happier if he has recently found a dime, or if his soccer team won rather than lost (Schwarz and Strack 1999). These sources of happiness will likely be systematically more potent in a wealthier society. A diverse commercial economy offers more sources of temporary stimulations and more short-term turns of good fortune. This means more new gadgets, more fun videos, and more serendipitous encounters with new people. Although a new gadget may make you happy for only a short while, if the stream of new gadgets is steady, your boost in happiness can be quite real.

Another form of well-being simply involves the avoidance of great tragedies. For most people life catastrophes create significant misery. Very sick individuals have less autonomy, experience more pain, and face high stress. The death of a child or close family member has a strongly detrimental affect on happiness for most individuals, often persisting for many years. Torture, extreme stress, rape and severe physical pain also produce depression, trauma, and persisting unhappiness. Individuals who have been through wars, revolutions, and collapses of civil order typically experience recurring flashbacks, nightmares, irritability, depression, alcoholism, troubled relationships, and an inability to concentrate. Well-functioning and wealthy societies tend to minimize these problems, or to offer higher levels of care once they occur.[13]

It is sometimes questioned whether even extreme catastrophes make people less happy. Individuals who experience severe disabilities or physical handicaps do to some extent adjust their expectations. Often these victims compare themselves to individuals who are even worse off than they are, or they lower their aspirations in life. The loss in happiness is not as great as a naïve perspective might expect. Nonetheless victims of catastrophe still report lower levels of happiness than do comparable healthy individuals. The happiness difference is most distinct, the greater the extent of the disability. At the very least, a significant percentage of victims experience an ongoing "core of distress" for many years.[14]

People cope least successfully when the catastrophe or malady is ongoing and involves an ongoing deterioration of condition. Most of the counterintuitive results come when the bad event has a "once and for all" nature, such as a one-time physical handicap. In these cases many people recover their initial level of self-reported happiness. But individuals remain subjectively badly off when they suffer from progressive or degenerative problems.[15] So to the extent that a poorer society brings an ongoing worsening of conditions for many individuals, the associated human suffering will again be greater.

Finally, even if we accept the "flat-line" empirical result as valid, the happiness surveys are given to individuals in normal life circumstances. The answers will not pick up the ability of wealthier economies to postpone or mitigate extreme tragedies, whether in the wealthier or poorer parts of our world. For instance the happiness surveys do not pick up the benefits of greater life expectancy. The dead and incapacitated cannot complain about their situation, at least not in questionnaire form. If an immigrant, or a child of immigrants, fills out the form, there is no comparison with a pre-immigration state of affairs. By its very nature, happiness research draws upon a fixed pool of people in relatively normal

---

[13] On the link between catastrophes and unhappiness, see Dyregrov 1990; Lehman et. al. 1987; Sanders 1980; Weiss 1987; Frederick and Loewenstein 1999; Lehman, Wortman, and Williams 1987; Archer 2001; and Wortman et. al. 1992.

[14] On coping, see Brickman, Coates, and Janoff-Bulman 1978; Bulman and Wortman 1977; Kessler, Price, and Wortman 1985; Meyer and Taylor 1987; and Wortman and Silver 1987. On the "core of distress" idea see Frey and Stutzer 2002a, p. 56; Wirtz and Harrell 1987; and Stroebe et. al. 2001.

[15] See Frederick and Loewenstein 1999.

circumstances. This will limit its ability to measure some of the largest welfare changes brought by economic growth.

IV. Concluding Remarks

A welfare state can be justified using a variety of arguments. And at the individual level, we probably are obliged to help the poor more than most of us have been doing. But we do not run the risk of personal enslavement or massive redistribution of the wealth of the Western world. In the long run, growth is a better means of helping the poor than is redistribution. We should therefore invest our energies in working hard, being creative, building good institutions, and encouraging the rest of the world to do the same. These recommendations also suggest that utilitarianism does not lie so far from common-sense morality.

Peter Singer (1999, p. 5) has suggested: "The left needs a new paradigm." Dare I suggest that we find such a paradigm in the idea of economic growth?

REFERENCES

Archer, John. 2001. Grief from an Evolutionary Perspective. In *Handbook of Bereavement Research: Consequences, Coping, and Care*, edited by Margaret S. Stroebe, Robert O. Hansson, Wolfgang Stroebe, and Henk Schut (Washington, D.C.: American Psychological Association), pp. 263–283.

Barro, Robert J. 1991. Economic Growth in a Cross Section of Countries. *Quarterly Journal of Economics* 106: 2 (May), pp. 407–443.

Brickman, Philip, Dan Coates, and Ronnie Janoff-Bulman. 1978. Lottery Winners and Accident Victims: Is Happiness Relative? *Journal of Personality and Social Psychology* 36: 8, pp. 917–927.

Broome, John. 1994. Discounting and Welfare. *Philosophy and Public Affairs* 23: 2 (Spring), pp. 128–156.

Broome, John, and Ulph, David. 1992. *Counting the Cost of Global Warming.* Cambridge: White Horse Press.

Bulman, Ronnie Janoff, and Wortman, Camille B. 1977. Attributions of Blame and Coping in the "Real World": Severe Accident Victims React to Their Lot. *Journal of Personality and Social Psychology* 35: 5, pp. 351–363.

Clark, Andrew E., and Andrew J. Oswald. 1996. Satisfaction and Comparison Income. *Journal of Public Economics* 61, pp. 359–381.

Cowen, Tyler. 1992. Consequentialism Implies a Zero Rate of Discount. In Peter Laslett and James Fishkin, eds., *Philosophy, Politics, and Society*, sixth series (New Haven: Yale University Press), pp. 162–68.

————. 1997. Discounting and Restitution. *Philosophy and Public Affairs* 26: 2 (Spring), pp. 168–185.

————. 2003. Policy Implications of Zero Discounting. *Social Philosophy and Policy.*

Cowen, Tyler, and Derek Parfit. 1992. Against the Social Discount Rate. In Peter Laslett and James Fishkin, eds., *Philosophy, Politics, and Society,* sixth series (New Haven: Yale University Press), pp. 144–161.

Diener, Ed. 1984. Subjective Well-Being. *Psychological Bulletin* 95, pp. 542–575.

Diener, Ed, and Eunkook Mark Suh. 1999. National Differences in Subjective Well-Being. In Daniel Kahneman, Ed Diener, and Norbert Schwarz, eds., *Well-Being: The Foundations of Hedonic Psychology* (New York: Russell Sage Foundation), pp. 434–450.

Dyregrov, A. 1990. Parental Reactions to the Loss of an Infant Child: A Review. *Scandinavian Journal of Psychology* 31, pp. 266–280.

Easterly, William. 2002. *The Elusive Quest for Growth: Economists' Adventures and Misadventures in the Tropics.* Cambridge: MIT Press, 2002.

Firebaugh, Glenn. 2003. *The New Geography of Global Income Inequality.* Cambridge: Harvard University Press.

Frank, Robert H. 1997. The Frame of Reference as a Public Good. *The Economic Journal* 107 (November), pp. 1832–1847.

Frederick, Shane, and Loewenstein, George. 1999. Hedonic Adaptation. In Daniel Kahneman, Ed Diener, and Norbert Schwarz, eds., *Well-Being: The Foundations of Hedonic Psychology* (New York: Russell Sage Foundation), pp. 302–329.

Frey, Bruno S., and Alois Stutzer. 2000. Happiness, Economy, and Institutions. *Economic Journal* 110 (October), pp. 918–938.

————. *Happiness and Economics: How the Economy and Institutions Affect Well-Being* Princeton: Princeton University Press.

Greiner, Alfred, Willi Semmler, and Gang Gong. 2005. *The Forces of Economic Growth: A Time Series Perspective.* Princeton: Princeton University Press.

Grier, Kevin B., and Gordon Tullock. 1989. An Empirical Analysis of Cross National Economic Growth. *Journal of Monetary Economics* 22 (September), pp. 259–276.

Helliwell, John F. 2002. How's Life? Combining Individual and National Variables to Explain Subjective Well-Being. NBER Working Paper 9065.

Kagan, Shelly. 1991. *The Limits of Morality.* Oxford: Oxford University Press.

LeGrain, Philippe. 2004. *Open World: The Truth about Globalization.* Chicago: Dee.

Lehman, Darrin R., Camille B. Wortman, and Allan F. Williams. 1987. Long Term Effects of Losing a Spouse or Child in a Motor Vehicle Crash. *Journal of Personality and Social Psychology* 52: 1, pp. 218–231.

Mandle, Jay R. *Globalization and the Poor.* Cambridge: Cambridge University Press, 2002.

Oswald, Andrew J. 1997. Happiness and Economic Performance. *Economic Journal* 107 (November), pp. 1815–1831.

Parfit, Derek. 1987. *Reasons and Persons*. Revised edition. Oxford: Clarendon.

Rector, Robert E. 1998. The Myth of Widespread American Poverty. Washington, D.C.: Heritage Foundation, Executive Summary #1221 (September 18th).

Schelling, Thomas C. 1995. Intergenerational Discounting. *Energy Policy* 23: 4–5, pp. 395–401.

Schwarz, Norbert and Strack, Fritz. 1999. Reports of Subjective Well-Being: Judgmental Processes and Their Methodological Implications. In Daniel Kahneman, Ed Diener, and Norbert Schwarz, eds., *Well-Being: The Foundations of Hedonic Psychology* (New York: Russell Sage Foundation), pp. 61–84.

Silver, Roxane L., and Camille G. Wortman. 1980. Coping with Undesirable Life Events. In Judy Garber and Martin E.P. Seligman, eds., *Human Helplessness: Theory and Applications* (New York: Academic Press), pp. 279–340.

Singer, Peter. 1993. *Practical Ethics*. Cambridge: Cambridge University Press.

———. 1995. *How Are We to Live? Ethics in an Age of Self-Interest*. Amherst: Prometheus.

———. 1999. *A Darwinian Left: Politics, Evolution, and Cooperation*. New Haven: Yale University Press.

———. 2004. *One World: The Ethics of Globalization*. Second edition. New Haven: Yale University Press.

Solow, Robert. 1974. The Economics of Resources or the Resources of Economics. *American Economic Review* 64, pp. 1–14.

Stroebe, Margaret S., Robert O. Hansson, Wolfgang Stroebe, and Henk Schut, eds. 2001. *Handbook of Bereavement Research: Consequences, Coping, and Care*. Washington, D.C.: American Psychological Association.

Williams, Bernard, and J.J.C. Smart. 1973. *Utilitarianism: For and Against*. Cambridge: Cambridge University Press.

Wolf, Martin. 2004. *Why Globalization Works*. New Haven: Yale University Press.

Wortman, Camille B., and Roxane Cohen Silver. 1987. Coping with Irrevocable Loss. In Gary R. Vanderbos and Brenda K. Bryant, eds., *Cataclysms, Crises, Catastrophes: Psychology in Action*. Master Lecture Series, Volume 6 (Washington, D.C.: American Psychological Association), pp. 185–235.

Reply to Tyler Cowen

PETER SINGER

What Do I Really Advocate?

Tyler Cowen spends much of his time arguing against positions I have never held. His misunderstandings begin with the reference to "massive redistribution" in his title. They continue in his second paragraph when, after correctly stating that I favor high levels of giving to fight poverty, he says: "Singer also has suggested that government should take a lead role in directing such redistribution. This would involve much higher levels of taxation and government spending in both the United States and Western Europe." A couple of paragraphs later he writes: "I will argue that his faith in both government and redistribution is misplaced." Later in his essay he appears to attribute to me the view that "most of national income" should be redistributed to the poor.

All of these claims about my views are false. I do not have great faith in government—at least, not much more than Cowen, who acknowledges the advantages of a welfare state in providing the poor with access to education and nutrition. (I would add health care.) As far as poverty in the developing world is concerned, however, my emphasis has always been on voluntary giving to non-government organizations. I do not favor much higher levels of taxation in order to fight global poverty, nor "most of national income" being redistributed to the poor. On the contrary, I have consistently argued that non-government organizations like Oxfam tend to be more effective than government aid. In my 1999 *New York Times Sunday Magazine* article, "The Singer Solution to World Poverty," I gave telephone numbers for readers to donate to Oxfam America and Unicef. I did not list the phone number of the Internal Revenue Service, nor tell people to call their congressional representatives to demand much higher levels of taxation.

le and thousands are dying every day of poverty-related causes? The
cond is: how much should the billion or so affluent people in the
orld, taken as a whole, be giving to poverty relief?

Since at present neither governments nor the majority of affluent
eople are giving even one percent of their income to poverty relief, it
emains possible that, as Cowen puts it, the money you spend on an ice
cream could save the life of someone in Africa (although that too is not
a claim I would make—it surely takes a lot more than that[18]). Acting on
our own, none of us, not even Bill Gates, can give so much that there
would be no more people whose lives, or whose children's lives, could
be saved for the price of things that many of us buy without much
thought. Hence the answer to the first question is that you should give
a great deal, because it is unjustifiable to spend money on satisfying
trivial or frivolous desires when that money could save a child's life. On
the other hand, if we ask how much the world's affluent people—taken
as a whole—should give, the answer that follows from my argument is:
as much as, but no more than, is needed to end extreme poverty and the
preventable poverty-related deaths that it causes. We could probably
achieve that goal by giving quite a modest amount of our income,
almost certainly less than ten percent, and very probably less than five
percent, as long as most affluent people give. Hence if the desirable
increase in foreign aid were to be funded through taxation, with the
governments of the rich nations agreeing to introduce an additional tax
for that purpose, the tax itself could be at that modest level. Scarcely a
"massive redistribution."

Sometimes Cowen's barrage is even wider of its presumed target:

if current total income were divided equally around the world, global per
capita income would be about $3,500. This average would then fall rapidly,
due to incentive effects. Civilization as we know it could not survive and the
world's poor would fall into a deeper state of misery than they currently
experience.

Since I have never advocated such an equal divi
quences are irrelevant to a critique of my views
advocated just handing money to the poor, so the f
is equally irrelevant:

_____
[18] For some estimates, see Peter Singer, *The Life You C*
House, 2009), Chapter 6.

In a democracy, no government can afford to g   lit
views of the voters in the amount they give to fc   se
however, inform their citizens accurately about hov   w
ing. In surveys in the United States, when people we
of the government's budget is spent on foreign aid, t.   p
in four different surveys ranged from fifteen to twenty
rect answer is less than one percent. But when people
much of the government's budget should go for foreign
answer ranged from five to ten percent![16] Government
view, increase foreign aid beyond the UN target of 0.7 p
domestic product. Arguably, they should increase it to two
that figure, as long as it is targeted at the poorest of the po
most U.S. aid currently is, to countries that serve U.S. geopc
(At the time of writing, by far the biggest recipient of U.S. c
aid is Iraq, followed by Afghanistan and Egypt. Only about
all U.S. development aid goes to the least developed coun
other low-income countries.[17]) But given that foreign aid is
countries, less than one percent of government spending, do
tripling it would not require a substantial increase in taxation.

Cowen's most fundamental misconception appears to be abc
much I think needs to be given overall. Perhaps he thinks that I an
ing for some kind of radical egalitarianism, rather than just for an
the extreme poverty that is responsible for the loss of millions of
each year. This misconception is suggested by the frequent recurrenc
the word "redistribution" in Cowen's essay, usually preceded by an adj
tive such as "massive," "widespread," "large" "collective" or "extrem
There is good reason to believe that the problem of widespread extren
poverty is soluble, and that the kind of expenditure required to solve i
would not be very large. As I mention in my response to Judith
Lichtenberg, even allowing for a substantial margin of error, it is likely to
take no more than five percent of the annual income of the twenty-two
industrialized nations that are members of the OECD's Development
Assistance Committee—and it could be much less than that.

How did Cowen get me so wrong? One possible explanation is that
has confused two very distinct questions. The first is: how much
ld I give to poverty relief, given that other people are giving very

International Policy Attitudes, *Americans on Foreign Aid and World*
of U.S. Public Attitudes (February 2nd, 2001), www.pipa.org
statistics for 2005, the most recent available at the time of writing.
rg/dataoecd/42/30/1860571.gif

Immediate redistribution may alleviate some of these problems for a while, but after the transferred money has been used, often the problems will reemerge to considerable degree.

Discounting the Future, Markets, and Economic Growth

Once we get beyond Cowen's misconceptions about what my views are, it is possible to find significant agreement between us. We agree that the welfare of future generations should count equally with our own. Discounting future cardinal utilities, just because they are in the future, is wrong. We can, however, discount for uncertainty. There is some uncertainty about whether there will actually be any future generations at a given future date, because a global catastrophe like nuclear war or collision with an asteroid is always possible.[19] We also cannot be certain about the effect of decisions we make now on future generations, if there are any. Cowen assumes that economic growth will benefit future generations. Let's put aside a possible caveat about the link between income and happiness—to be discussed shortly—and agree that, if all goes well, it will do so. But many things may go wrong. If there had been less economic growth, and therefore less use of fossil fuels, we would not now be facing the threat of irreversible climate change, with a host of possible adverse consequences. Damage to the ozone layer is also the result of economic growth, for if we had no refrigeration or air conditioners, we would not have put chlorofluorocarbons into the atmosphere. The risk of nuclear war and of nuclear weapons falling into the hands of terrorists is something else we owe to economic growth, for nuclear science and nuclear technology requires resources that no society had before the twentieth century. Further economic growth may bring other, as yet unforeseen, threats. To forestall additional misunderstandings, I should make it clear that I am not putting forward these considerations as an argument against economic growth. It is impossible to avoid risk, and it may be that the benefits of economic growth outweigh the risks. Increasing foreign aid could also carry its share of risks. Perhaps helping millions of people to survive and prosper will further increase greenhouse gas emissions, pushing us beyond some threshold at which climatic systems will spiral towards disaster. The point I want to make now

---

[19] See Richard Posner, *Catastrophe: Risk and Response* (Oxford University Press, 2005).

is only that even if we agree that future cardinal utilities are to be given the same weight as present ones, there are significant uncertainties that provide good practical grounds for discounting the future. This discount limits our obligation to postpone giving aid now in order to invest in economic growth for the future.

Another point on which Cowen and I agree is that many African nations would benefit from an end to the agricultural subsidies that both the United States and the European Union pay to their farmers. American subsidies on cotton, for instance, make it impossible for peasant cotton growers in West Africa to sell their cotton on global markets, even though their costs of production are much lower than those of American cotton producers, before subsidies. As this example indicates, I am in favor of global trade as a means of reducing global poverty, as long as developing nations are given fair opportunities to benefit. Cowen claims that I am "not willing to endorse a capitalist market economy—based on global trade relations—as our best available means of poverty alleviation." It would have been more accurate for him to say that I am not willing to endorse a capitalist market economy as a *sufficient* means of poverty alleviation.

In making his case that I am hostile to markets, Cowen takes a sentence from *A Darwinian Left* out of context when he quotes me as writing: "I doubt that greater wealth for the middle and upper classes could make up for the increase in human misery this [market competition] has brought to the poor." In the preceding paragraph, I made it clear that I was discussing the balance between cooperation and competition that is struck in different societies. I gave America and Japan as examples, and said that "I am talking about societies that differ in degree, rather than in kind . . ." Both Japan and America are, of course, market economies. Against this background, and presuming that recent cutbacks in the welfare system in developed countries were fresh in the minds of my audience, I referred to the fact that "the gap between rich and poor has widened, and support for the poor has been cut back." It was in regard to these measures to increase competition by cutting support for the poor, not in respect of market competition in general, that I questioned whether the benefits for the middle and upper classes outweighed the costs for the poor.[20]

I could, of course, be wrong about this. For various reasons, including the difficulty of measuring interpersonal utilities and of running

---

[20] *A Darwinian Left* (Yale University Press, 1999), p. 45.

properly controlled economic experiments, no one can really be sure
what economic arrangements lead to the greatest overall utility. I accept
that a capitalist market economy can be a powerful means of poverty
alleviation, and in the right circumstances, perhaps even the best
means. But as tools for relieving poverty internationally, trade and aid
should be complementary, not mutually exclusive. Often the poorest
people need aid in order to be able to benefit from new trade opportunities. Cowen's proposal that we should "invest our energies in working
hard, being creative, building good institutions, and encouraging the
rest of the world to do the same" is all very well, but in some parts of
the world, working hard and being creative will not, on its own, bring
prosperity. Warren Buffett, one of America's shrewdest investors, and
the world's second richest person—although he may not hold that title
for long, as he is in the process of giving almost all of his money
away—has aptly said: "If you stick me down in the middle of
Bangladesh or Peru, you would find out how much this talent is going
to produce in the wrong kind of soil."[21]

Another reason I am less sanguine than Cowen about the beneficial
effect of unrestrained market capitalism is that in some circumstances,
trade can make developing countries worse off. As Thomas Pogge has
pointed out, international corporations are willing to make deals to buy
natural resources from any government, no matter how it comes to
power. This provides a huge financial incentive for any armed gang to
attempt to overthrow the existing government. Successful rebels are then
rewarded for their violent and illegal insurrection by being recognized
as the country's legitimate government, with the ability to sell off its oil,
minerals, or timber. This gives them access to riches beyond the dreams
of ordinary people in developing countries. They can divert some of the
proceeds of their sales into their personal accounts and use the remainder for rewarding their supporters and strengthening their armed
forces.[22] This legal situation is beneficial for the industrial nations,
because it enables us to obtain the raw materials we need to maintain our
economic growth, but it is a disaster for resource-rich developing countries, turning the wealth that should benefit them into a curse that leads
to a cycle of coups, civil wars, and corruption. Research indicates that

---

[21] Janet Lowe, *Warren Buffett Speaks: Wit and Wisdom from the World's Greatest Investor*
(New York: Wiley, 1997), pp. 164–66.
[22] Thomas Pogge, "'Assisting' the Global Poor" in Deen K. Chatterjee, ed., *The Ethics
of Assistance: Morality and the Distant Needy* (Cambridge: Cambridge University Press,
2004), pp. 260–288.

the more a developing country's economy depends on natural resources the less likely it is to be a stable democracy.[23]

In other areas, too, Cowen's account of the benefits of economic growth overlooks its costs. In writing about the benefits that accrue to poor countries that provide immigrants to the rich nations, he mentions remittances that are sent home, and the immigrants who return to their country of origin, bringing back their newly learned skills and entrepreneurial spirit, but he omits any mention of the problem of the loss of educated professionals, including health-care professionals, and the nation's brightest young people, many of whom will never return.[24] Cowen also says very little about the well-known environmental costs of economic growth, some of which, like climate change, I have already mentioned. It is true that, with still more economic growth, we may have the ability to solve some of the environmental problems created by an earlier stage of economic growth. We can all hope that this will prove to be the case. But we cannot know that it will.

Cowen's discussion of the link between income and well-being is only indirectly related to the aid issue, since there is no dispute that increasing the income of the poor will improve their well-being. Nor can it be denied that, given diminishing marginal utility, adding $100 to the income of someone living on $500 a year will confer a greater benefit than adding $100 to the income of someone earning $50,000 a year. On the other hand, to strengthen his case for economic growth as generally good, Cowen needs to address the objection that, once we have achieved a reasonable level of income, further increases leave us no happier than we were before. The discussion raises important issues about how we assess someone's welfare—issues that are also raised in a different context in the essays in this volume related to my views on the treatment of severely disabled newborn infants.[25]

---

[23] See Leif Wenar, "Property Rights and the Resource Curse," *Philosophy and Public Affairs* 36:1 (2008), pp. 2–32. See also Nathan Jensen and Leonard Wantchekon, "Resource Wealth and Political Regimes in Africa," *Comparative Political Studies* 37 (2004), pp. 816–841.

[24] See, for example, T. Pang , M.A. Lansang, and A. Haines, "Brain Drain and Health Professionals: A Global Problem Needs Global Solutions," *British Medical Journal* 324 (2004), pp. 499–500.

[25] See especially my response to Harriet Johnson, although the issue is also raised by Harry Gensler and Stephen Drake.

Does Economic Growth Make Us Happier?

The field of research that I drew on in *How Are We to Live?*[26] has grown since 1993, when that work was first published. Cowen refers to recent studies as continuing to support the earlier results, suggesting that once average per capita income exceeds the approximate level of contemporary Greece, or about half current United States levels, further increases in average per capita income do not increase happiness. Nevertheless, Cowen questions these finding, at least when applied to large changes over long periods of time. Granted, the fact that the existing literature is based on subjective reports given by people when they are asked how happy they are makes it possible that, as Cowen suggests, an increase in real happiness linked to rising income is not revealed by the answers people give to surveys, because their expectations and reporting standards have risen along with their income and happiness. To that extent, Cowen has a point. But he is on more dubious ground when he argues that revealed preferences indicate that most individuals strive to earn higher incomes. This is, of course, easily explained by the fact that they are striving to retain or improve their status in a competitive society in which status is closely linked to income. No one disputes that there is a link between perceived status and happiness. The problem is that since improving status is a zero-sum game—if my status rises, someone else's must fall—if everyone works equally hard to improve their status, no one benefits, or at least not directly from improved status. There may be incidental benefits from the increased productivity that this encourages, but there will also be costs from the excessive investment in work. Cowen himself cites Daniel Kahnemann's findings that "intimate relations, time spent with friends, and television, all appear to make people happier in this sense. Working and commuting make people less happy." So the revealed preference for more work (and the longer commutes that the desire for a highly-paid position may require, especially in dual-career couples) seems likely to lead to more income, but less happiness.

To make the link between higher income and greater happiness seem plausible, Cowen argues "I am much better off than my medieval counterparts, and if growth continues most people in the more distant future will be much better off than I am." The claim that we are better off than our medieval counterparts is, of course, consistent with the research mentioned above, since the average per capita income in medieval times was far below the point at which the research indicates that the curve of

---

[26] Melbourne: Text, 1993; Amherst: Prometheus, 1995.

increasing happiness begins to flatten out. It is, however, not clear what basis Cowen has for asserting that people in the distant future will be much better off—much happier, that is—than we are. On the other hand some additional research that has become available since Cowen completed his essay, and indeed after I had completed my response to him, has cast serious doubt on the view that I, and most others, previously held about the link between happiness and income. Using the most reent Gallup World Poll data, my Princeton University colleague Angus Deaton argues that increasing income even beyond the threshold of contemporary Greece does increase wellbeing, although it takes quite a large increase in income to make a significant difference to happiness.[27] The debate is by no means over, but the evidence for Cowen turning out to be right about this point is stronger now than it was when he wrote his essay.

Conclusion: Staying Open to the Evidence

In conclusion, I should emphasize that I'm not committed to any particular view about the role of markets, regulated or unregulated, in overcoming global poverty. I'm open to listening to the arguments, assessing the evidence, and supporting whatever means of reducing global poverty has the highest expected utility. Free markets and global trade will no doubt have an important role to play in overcoming poverty, but I doubt that they can do it alone. In particular, on the available evidence so far, globalization has not helped the poorest of the poor.[28] To reach them and bring them into a position where they are able to participate in global trade, aid has a vital role to play.

---

[27] Angus Deaton, "Income, Aging, Health, and Wellbeing around the World: Evidence from the Gallup World Poll," *Journal of Economic Perspectives* 22:2 (2008), pp. 53–72. Also arguing in the same direction is Betsey Stevenson and Justin Wolfers, "Economic Growth and Subjective Well-Being: Reassessing the Easterlin Paradox," National Bureau of Economic Research Working Papers 14282 (2008), available at http://ideas.repec.org/p/ces/ceswps/_2394.html.

[28] See Branko Milanovic, *Worlds Apart: Measuring International and Global Inequality* (Princeton: Princeton University Press, 2005); Branko Milanovic, "Why Did the Poorest Countries Fail to Catch Up?" Carnegie Endowment for International Peace, Carnegie Paper No. 62 (October 2005), available at http://www.carnegieendowment.org/publications/index.cfm?fa=view&id=17557&prog=zgp&proj=zted.

10

The Ethics of Assistance: What's the Good of It?

DAVID FAGELSON

What Is to Be Done?

In a stark and powerful observation about the ethical implications of the choices we make, Peter Singer observed in 1971 that Great Britain, that year, valued the opportunity to shave two hours off a flight from London to New York thirty times more than the lives of nine million starving Bengalis. Australians, on the other hand, preferred to build a new opera house twelve times more than saving those same nine million lives.[1] Before feeling too smug, we should recall that these were two of the more generous nations per capita. Singer's varied and wide ranging inquiries into the rights of animals, the disabled, the poverty stricken, and indeed, even the member of common room, have a constant theme running through them: what do we owe each other? Looking though the body of his work, one can see a carefully constructed fabric detailing the ethical relationship of each of us, and by us he means all sentient beings, to each other.

Singer's answer is clear, and deceptively simple, do whatever produces the most good and the least harm. In its strong version, this requires us to give to others until we reach the point of marginal utility, or the point at which doing so would sacrifice something of equal moral significance. This answer only seems simple, because unlike many util-

---

[1] Peter Singer, "Famine Affluence And Morality," *Philosophy And Public Affairs* 1:3 (Spring 1972), p. 230.

itarians, Singer gets down to the dirty work of defining who counts in this ethical aggregation of pain and happiness. The devil is always in the details and Singer never shies away from wrestling with them. Unfortunately, clarifying the reach of this ethical theory has only served to highlight some of its weaknesses.

In this essay I want to re-examine Singer's argument for aiding the poor. I refer here to the issue of famine, affluence and our obligations to the poverty stricken people of what we might call the burdened states of the world. I use the term burdened states advisedly because I am not referring to Rawls's sense of our obligations in a reasonable utopia. Rather, I mean to focus on the obligations we have here and now in the imperfect sovereignty-laden world we now inhabit. In his recent book, *One World*,[2] Singer makes a compelling case against the partiality of our obligations. The idea that we only owe obligations to our countrymen is at root no more acceptable than the idea that we would only owe obligations to our race, our co-religionists or, indeed, members of our political party. This case is somewhat muddied by the arguments in favor of partiality to kin and community he makes elsewhere.[3] Singer doesn't rest on these issues long enough to reconcile the different positions they represent but one gets the impression that he is advocating someone with a liberal identity who identified his or her good as more tightly bound up in the community. Yet even if we stipulate that this obligation exists, it still remains to discover who owes what to whom. Singer points to a personal obligation from each of us, to everyone in need. That our governments may prefer to build monuments to themselves instead of caring for the needy, or indeed, even if our governments give, albeit insufficiently, we are still personally obligated to help to the extent that we can do so without causing more harm than the relief we produce. But this does not dictate the terms of our help. If we could help others better through our governments than individually, our efforts and money would be better spent in that endeavor.

My essay will focus on two issues. The first, rather narrow and concrete, is what actually works and whether Singer's practical proposals for an ethical life actually make the world better off in the way that he (and I) would hope to see it. In particular, I speak of his proposals for

---

[2] New Haven: Yale University Press, 2002.

[3] *How Are We to Live?* (Amherst: Prometheus, 1995). In Chapter 6, for example, he gives a positive description of Japanese society and its people's deep identification with the community. He compares this identification favorably as against the self-interested behavior of Americans.

helping others outside one's own country, whether it be feeding the hungry in Somalia or reducing greenhouse gases. That is to say, would it actually maximize the good consequences that could be achieved without any extra effort expended or harm caused? I argue that it would not. Does this matter? If we help are we acting more ethically by helping more efficiently?

Answering this question leads to the second issue which concerns the meaning and substance of ethics that Singer uses to justify this obligation in the first place. This will be more tricky to evaluate than usual because although much of Singer's work places him squarely within the utilitarian ethic, he often espouses ideas from other conceptions of justice that are incompatible with utilitarianism. So for example, when considering the destruction of the rainforests and other natural resources, he asks why we haven't reconsidered our commitment to Smith's idea of human nature and adopted Rousseau's (*How Are We to Live?*, p. 38). This is a perfectly good question which we perhaps ought to reconsider. But if we do, we will have to give up much if not all of the rest of Singer's position. The different ideas of the good in Rousseau and Smith go down to the very idea of human identity and what sort of animals we are. The conflicts they represent go deeper than any idea of justice. They are rooted in different epistemological questions of what is really out there in the world. While Singer's eclectic invocation of different positions is always interesting, he never explains how they would all fit together in one coherent idea of the good apart from an ultimate reliance on the distinctive universal capacity of humans to reason.

My conclusions are that his policy proposals do not produce the best outcomes and that part of the reason for this can be found in the idea of ethics he relies on. In an essay of this size it is impossible to cover these questions comprehensively. I hope here to raise questions about certain of his conclusions which, taken together, could support a call for more rather than less self interest and partiality so long as that partiality is based on liberal tolerance and an equal concern and respect for the agency of each person. You might call it the partiality of universal respect for individual agency, although I propose this ethic because I think it is right even if it produces less good consequences than another theory of ethics would achieve. I cannot defend this position based on the idea that it will produce the greatest good, because my preference is itself based on the belief that the greatest good consists in carrying out these ethical principles.

I will begin with this argument by asking what we can do in practice to fulfill Singer's mandate to do that which produces the best consequences. Singer suggests giving to some worthy international charity such as Oxfam or getting governments to commit more money to relieve poverty. But I would argue here that this does not fulfill the obligation that Singer himself has so convincingly detailed. For if we are obligated to help the poor, then as he himself points out, we are clearly obligated to help them in the most effective way that we know how to do, subject to causing the least possible pain. The problem is that in fulfilling this obligation, we may be obligated to intervene in their societies in ways we once thought intolerable, and which the recipients of our aid, or their governments, almost certainly still do. Singer addressed this question in the postscript to "Famine, Affluence, and Morality," when he raised the problem of population control.[4] Accepting a causal link between population growth and famine, Singer argued that no policy to alleviate world hunger could succeed without also addressing overpopulation. Rejecting the charge of coercion or illegitimate derogation of national sovereignty, Singer noted, quite rightly, that any obligation to help relieve famine, can only be an obligation to do what one knows to the best of one's knowledge will be effective. Since no nation is forced to accept our aid, conditioning such assistance upon the agreement of recipient countries to impose population reform entails no coercion.[5]

The issue, however, is more complicated because the sort of intervention I speak of is highly partial to a given sort of cultural, historical, political and economic practices. While there may be no intrinsic moral or epistemological foundation to consider our political and legal institutions superior, if it produces the most good then there is compelling ethical reasons for partiality. Indeed, if it would produces this greatest good, there is a compelling reason to get the governments of these impoverished states to adopt our partial view of what is good, and to build institutions to achieve those ends. An additional twist to this problem arises if the most effective way to produce the most good is for individuals to be more rather than less self-interested and perhaps more partial to one's cultural political and legal practices. Of course, our calculation of the greatest good will hinge on our partial ideas of what is good and this might bias our sense of how well we are achieving the best consequences. For a liberal, the best consequence might be one in which everyone's ability to pursue his or her own conception of the good is maximized, while for Jerry Falwell, the best consequences would be

---

[4] *Philosophy and Public Affairs* 1:3 (1972), p. 229.
[5] http://www.utilitarian.net/singer/by/1972——.htm

those in which all of us recognize Jesus Christ as our savior. Is the truly best set of consequences that which constitutes the greatest aggregate set of preferences or is there some truly best set of consequences that is independent of what the most people want?

This is a terribly difficult issue made all the more complicated by the fact that Singer never really defines a general theory of the greatest good so that we could specify those consequences that lead to it. Each policy aims at a specific moral end but we do not know whether that end is itself the best consequence or whether that end is only instrumentally valuable because it leads to some more abstract set of consequences that are the goal of those ends. We know that we should treat animals with respect, refrain from despoiling the planet or extracting excessive resources and direct our resources where they are most needed. Yet many ethical frameworks from libertarianism to social democracy to a Christian theocracy could conceivably adopt these goals. So we must know what the comprehensive good is that requires us to manifest ethical concern in his way. Without it each task of helping the poor, preserving the environment or clothing the naked is something that has to be defended *ad hoc*. Singer cannot simply say that helping the poor is its own best consequence because then we are saying that there is something inherently, not consequentially important about helping them.

I suspect that if we compared notes, Singer and I would agree on those things he identifies as part of the greatest good. But I cannot see why they are good in any universal ethical sense that goes beyond my own partial ideas of justice and value. Moreover, the sophisticated argument for the unity of self-interest and ethical behavior that Singer makes in *How Are We to Live?* seems to contradict his plea for less selfishness. Most Americans appear to pursue their self-interest quite enthusiastically and America as a nation appears similarly motivated. This doesn't appear, however, to result in the sort of international cooperation that would address the pressing issues of our time.

Why has our pursuit of the greatest good resulted in such bad results? Are we misaggregating the actual beliefs of what people believe is their greatest good or does this good exist apart from what the aggregate believes it to be? Most modern theories of utilitarianism, including Singer's, reject the hedonistic premise that the good consists in this simple aggregation.[6] As we shall see, this is problematic because it simply

---

[6] *How Are We to Live? Ethics in an Age of Self-Interest* (New York: Oxford University Press, 1997), p. 231.

makes the idea of what is really good not a consequence of people's preferences but rather the preferences we want people to have in order to pursue the correct policies. This conflict, inherent in utilitarianism could be avoided by viewing the failure of people to act ethically for the greater good as a collective action problem. If people had more information, they would rationally cooperate in the sort of Tit for Tat (*How Are We to Live?*, pp. 132–142), which while not ideal, at least produces cooperation and concern for others. But this result would be achieved purely out of hedonistic self-interest, and not some idea of aiming at the greatest good for all.

How could we achieve Singer's ends? Fashions change and for now at least, development theorists and practitioners believe that the nature of a country's political and legal institutions affect development more significantly than resources or population growth. This view, however, puts even more pressure on the benefactor to intervene in the internal mechanisms of state power and community identity. Deciding whether or not to have an independent judiciary or democratic legislature goes right to the heart of state sovereignty and more importantly from Singer's point of view, it affects the core ethical ideas that either do or do not justify the force of the state. So demanding reform of these policies and institutions as a condition of assistance must be recognized as partiality by overriding the community's values and sense of what makes life important. Singer's position on this sort of partiality is a little ambiguous. On the one hand, in evaluating George Bush's Millennium Challenge Account Singer appears to accept the idea of aid conditioned on political reform, if not Bush's ultimate implementation of this concept.[7] In Chapter 4 of *One World*, Singer confronts the question directly and puts Westphalian Sovereignty in its rightful, subordinate role. What benefit is their in respecting the "right" of a sovereign to cleanse, "re-educate" or otherwise persecute its own people? Because we think very little, we have breached the barrier of sovereignty in Kosovo and in East Timor, and wish we had done so in Rwanda. So the question is not whether intervention in state sovereignty can be justified, but when and under what circumstances. Here, Singer becomes more circumspect. In a short section on cultural imperialism, he warns that the link between democracy and legitimate sovereignty is not proven because the only arguments we could give in favor of it are necessarily culturally partial

---

[7] Peter Singer, *The President of Good and Evil: The Ethics of George W. Bush* (New York: Dutton, 2004), p. 126.

ones that in the end, would be no different than asserting that our religion was the one true avenue to eternal salvation (pp. 142–44).

This cannot be true unless one believes that Aung San Suu Kyi's belief in the connection of democracy and legitimacy can only be the product of partial "Western" values rather than some indigenous Burmese belief. That view would be its own sort of cultural partiality. The problem in arguing for the universal connection of democracy and legitimacy, however, is not one of cultural partiality but ethical partiality. Yet one could say the same thing about his, or indeed, any theory of ethics that claims universal application. The truth of utilitarianism as an ethical theory stands on no firmer or weaker ground, than the truth of democracy as a precondition of legitimate political authority. As Bernard Williams put it, the first question for philosophy, is not whether one agrees with utilitarianism's answers but rather, does one accept it is even asking the right questions?[8] Any theory of ethics must start with the view that it is asking the right questions and in that sense no ethical theory can be neutral about itself.

Singer is a strong advocate for democratic sovereignty but not because of its intrinsic qualities. Rather, he supports it, and interventions to promote it, when the consequences of doing so would be better than not intervening to support it. Nobody could dispute that standard but the rub is in defining what the best consequences would consist in. While Singer may reasonably take into account issues like the viciousness of a non-democratic government and the effect of an intervention to promote democracy, others else might just as reasonably ignore his set of consequences if they feel them subordinate to their own idea of the good.

Moreover, it would seem that democracy is a necessary tool to put the ethical theory of utilitarianism into political practice. Since Singer is not willing to excuse lapses in utilitarian obligations across boarders to stop genocide, or to void the duty to help the poor, why should obligations to implement the political institutions of utilitarian principles be optional or conditional in some way on other benefits or costs? We need not resolve that question here because it is part of my argument that Singer's own criterion that such action do more good than harm would, by its own lights, require us to intervene in burdened non democratic states to help ensure the political and legal rights of people to pursue their own happiness. But this intervention is entirely partial and risks

---

[8] J.J.C. Smart and Bernard Williams, *Utilitarianism: For and Against* (Cambridge: Cambridge University Press, 1973), p. 78.

being correct only for partial reasons. If determining the greatest good depends upon each person's expression of that good, then it is actually an ethical requirement of Singer's utilitarianism that we be partial and self interested.

I began this paper with the assumption that wealthier states have an obligation to assist poorer states.[9] The obligation to help poorer states derives from a requirement to help people whether or not they live within a well-ordered society. It cannot be correct that those who have the misfortune of being born in an impoverished hierarchical society have less call on our assistance than someone born in a completely dysfunctional society at the same level of impoverishment. For this obligation to exist, it must be possible to accomplish. As Isaiah Berlin pointed out, we cannot be unfree to do something we are not able to do in the first place. Similarly, we cannot be morally obliged to accomplish the impossible. Foreign assistance, when sincerely given, is premised upon the notion that it is possible to help impoverished societies improve their lot in life. In order to understand the contours of our obligation to assist we must understand practically how to accomplish it. Surely, our obligation to assist must be an obligation to assist in the best way we understand this assistance to work. Gestures might make us feel good, but there is no moral obligation to provide them. The relief of suffering might be the most we can accomplish, but if real development is possible, then anything less would be inconsistent with our obligation.

Pace Singer, I do not believe that the ethical obligation of the donor requires each of us to keep giving until the benefit we derive from the resource is no greater than the benefit derived by the beneficiary. One problem with this obligation is that few people, including most utilitarians, appear willing to act ethically in the way he says is required. That's serious, because by Singer's own lights, it strips his proposals of their ethical foundation. Any system of ethics, in his view, must be suited to the "rough and tumble of everyday life . . . ethics is practical or it is not really ethics" (*How Are We to Live?*, p. 179). The overwhelming numbers of wealthy people who have failed to share their ample wealth to help the poor stands as a testament to the failure of Singer's ethics to pass his own test. This might be because people are selfish or that our self-interest does not in fact jibe with the greatest good. Or it might just be that as, Singer notes about Kant's duty-based idea of ethics, people

---

[9] I use the term states rather than well-ordered and burdened peoples to emphasize that this obligation exits now, prior to the realization of any realistic utopia.

don't think the results of sharing would be particularly good (*How Are We to Live?*, pp. 182–87). They might be correct because the donations to charitable organizations he suggests, to the extent they would be effective at all, would be primarily palliative with regard to the overall problem of global poverty.

While providing medical care to the impoverished is critically important, unless a society is able to get to the point that it can provide this care on its own, we are not producing the greatest good that we could accomplish with the least harm and effort. This is true whether one thinks the corresponding rights claim derives from each individual or his or her society. Indeed, two of the most prolific fundraisers for development assistance, the record producer Bob Geldorf and the U2 rock singer Bono, have accepted that they are obligated to help the poor as Singer suggests. Yet they have turned away from expending their efforts on individual fundraising for food deliveries or medical care in favor of lobbying government officials to implement policy reforms both in the donor and beneficiary countries.

The sort of obligation that I am referring to in this paper entails helping a society get to the stage where it can provide, on its own, the basic necessities of life to its entire people. This improvement is commonly referred to as sustainable development. We must define explicitly what these necessities are because that will define what sort of improvement we are obligated to help others achieve. In truth, however, naming these necessities is part of what theories of justice do, so there cannot be any universal obligation without a universal belief about what people absolutely need. Hence, we must decide whether we are obligated to give what a society believes most necessary to its own survival or what we believe is most necessary for it to receive. This will necessarily be a partial decision that cannot be divorced from partial ideas of what the greatest good consists in. Should we choose ours or the beneficiaries?

We can imagine donors as missionaries converting unwilling peoples on the belief that their salvation is the most necessary feature of life itself. Indeed, for them it was more important than a native people's "transient" temporal needs for food and other comforts. Conversely, we can imagine a beneficiary that is a fundamentalist theocracy. This group believes the aid it most needs is to shore up its religious foundations by preventing women from leaving the home to get an education or health care. If these two sorts of views matched, I suppose donors and beneficiaries might work out a way to achieve the best of all possible consequences. More likely their dealings would be tense and unconstructive. Even if they worked out a modus vivendi, we should note that the best of all possible consequences they will achieve eschews basic human needs for survival as their primary concern. Most of us find this odious yet at some level we admire those who can *freely* merge their interest and indeed their identity with the community and aim for some transcendent purpose. Indeed, this is what Singer urges us to do (*How Are We to Live?*, pp. 206–218). The problem is that in many cases we are skeptical about the freedom of their commitment to the group, particularly when some members are in clearly subordinate and undesirable positions. Authoritarian hierarchical communities appear to bother Singer less if, in his view, it is producing better consequences according to the idea of self-interest the community fosters (*How Are We to Live?*, p. 108). Singer is no relativist, but his adoption of Rousseau's and in some respects Japan's communitarianism leads one to wonder how we will find some universal definition of good that we could use to measure ethical behavior across all the different communities of our one world. Any liberal committed to autonomy would argue that no outcome is good that rests on the subordination of others. That answer, like any, will represent ethical if not cultural partiality. Yet is there any other way? If so, Singer has not explained it as much as one would hope. The only objective way to measure the best consequences of any given act or rule entails aggregating the self-interest of each person. Singer, correctly in my view, rejects this but we still need some abstract principle that bridges this gap if we will be able to act ethically.

What Has Been Done

In order to support my claim about the efficacy and ethics of development assistance, it is necessary to discuss some of the history and policies of the post–Bretton Woods development efforts. Most of my comments are based on the actions of The World Bank and the United States Agency for International Development (USAID). Although most bi-lateral aid programs give much more per capita than the United States, America nonetheless plays a central role, along with the World Bank, in defining the goals and practice of development assistance.

When looking back at the modern era of aid, it is necessary to distinguish between the pre- and post-Communist donor practice and purpose. If one looks solely at the mis-steps of the World Bank and USAID during the Cold War, one might infer that development was never the goal of the development process. That inference would be correct because for most of its modern life, foreign aid was simply an extension of larger foreign policy goals. Realists like Morgenthau or Kennan hardly felt any moral obligation to help poorer states and for many policy makers, foreign aid was simply another weapon in the Western Cold War arsenal.[10] Indeed, even now, policy makers at the heart of the foreign aid process regard foreign aid as a subset of geo-strategic policy rather than an end in itself.[11] This motive might explain the spectacular failure of donor initiatives during that period. Otherwise, why would the World Bank permit perhaps as much as one third of its loans to be siphoned off by corrupt borrowers (government officials)?[12] Many donors felt this was merely part of price of gaining allies. If so, it was also part of the price for the recipient nations since they would be paying off the World Bank debt long after the money had been siphoned into private bank accounts. Whether this was misfeasance or malfeasance, it permitted self interested people to get rich at the expense of the poor.[13]

The international financial donor agencies are somewhat schizophrenic about their identities.[14] Sometimes they are a bank and other times, a development institution. While the stated purpose is "sustainable development," promotions, pay raises, and program evaluations are centered, as with any bank, on how much lending is going on. But the idea of being developed is rather amorphous and does not seem susceptible to either absolute or objective meanings. If we define development in terms of GDP, for example, the United States would come towards the top of the list. Yet if we measured social equality, leisure time, infant mortality, or even literacy, it moves down the list. The idea of development has gone through fashion cycles and, until fairly recently, it was understood almost strictly in terms of wealth creation. Yet it has proven

---

[10] GAO Report, *World Bank: US Interests Supported but Oversight Needed to Ensure Improved Performance*, Report No. GAO/NSIAD-96-212 (Washington, DC: General Accounting Office, 1996), Chapter 2.

[11] For a particularly frank account of this reasoning by a former Deputy Administrator of AID, see Carol Lancaster, *Transforming Foreign Aid* (Washington, DC: Institute for International Economics, 2000), Chapter 2. This view leads her to recommend that efforts at development be reduced in favor of efforts to protect the United States against the "externalities" of pollution, disease, and political volatility (pp. 72–76).

[12] Jeffrey Winters, "Criminal Debt," in J. Pincus and J. Winters, eds., *Reinventing the World Bank,* (Ithaca: Cornell University Press, 2002), p. 101.

[13] For a particularly skeptical account of the World Bank's function and purpose see, S. George and F. Sabelli, *Faith and Credit: The World Bank's Secular Empire* (Boulder: Westview, 1994).

[14] Article 1§(i) of the World Bank's Articles of Agreement, states that its purpose is, "[t]o assist in the reconstruction and development of territories of members by facilitating the investment of capital for productive purposes, and the encouragement of the development of productive facilities and resources in less developed countries."

remarkably difficult to figure out how to become wealthy. During the early years of the World Bank's existence, economists viewed access to resources as the main criteria for growth. The solution to this problem appeared to be in developing infrastructure. No country could grow without good transportation links and sources of energy production. During this phase, much effort was devoted towards the construction of roads and hydroelectric dams. When this failed to produce significant results, the focus shifted to macro-economic policy as an obstacle to growth. Much effort was expended to change taxing and spending patterns in recipient nations but again there was little impact on growth. Then the emphasis shifted towards micro-economic policies such the privatization of industry and soon after that directed its focus on the development of sound financial and management techniques.

The problem with these approaches is that they assumed institutional foundations that were absent. The theory of the firm suggests that rational actors freely trading for their own benefit can create efficiencies that ultimately benefit everyone. But these trades require the protection of contract rights to guarantee the integrity of the trade and property rights to guarantee the resources that are traded. The actual enforcement of these rights requires a legal structure that goes to the heart of a state's constitutional organization and a community's identity. One cannot assume that property rights exist simply because they are recognized at law or because state owned property has been privatized.

Property rights require judicial independence which in turn, requires an executive willing to clip his own wings and forgo his ability to expropriate resources. Few leaders since Cincinnatus and Washington have voluntarily given up power and the poor nations were no exception. The privatization boom that was the hallmark of development assistance in the 1980s and early 1990s served primarily to enrich the government officials who could afford to buy them. It had little effect on the productivity of those resources that were denationalized.

So while the idea of free-market capitalism *à la* Smith might be true, none of the legal infrastructure existed to support it. No rational actor would invest in these companies because there was no way to ensure that the stock one purchased bore any relationship to its assets or current revenue. Few domestic let alone foreign creditors of these newly privatized entities would lend capital unless they could be sure that the collateral the debtor pledged for the loan actually belonged to the debtor and hadn't already been pledged to five other creditors for ten times its actual value. That requires a registry system which most dictators usually destroy in order to ensure that no one shows up to assert a claim over land he has expropriated. The lack of these legal rights made it irrational for people to do the sort of trading which the development agencies thought would unleash the efficiencies of the marketplace.

While this has led to a focus on legal reform assistance over the past decade, very few countries have developed rule-governed institutions as a result of these efforts. The problem is partly due to the way donor institutions approach the legal reform process and partly due to deep ambivalence, if not hostility, among recipient governments to creating the sort of legal institutions that would enforce the rights necessary for growth.

Until fairly recently, the World Bank charter prohibition against political activities was read very strictly by its general counsel to preclude any utterance that might affect the political or legal structure of any of its member states. This didn't concern most Bank economists because in their view, the type of government or its legal system had little impact on growth. Their only concern with the state was that it be as inactive as possible. As they later learned, the government activity that impeded growth was related to its accountability and willingness to enforce the law even against itself.

While admitting the checkered past of development efforts, Singer bases his call for increased aid funding partly on the increased capacity of development institutions to actually deliver on their *aims (One World*, p. 109). The World Bank's claim of new-found abilities is dubious because often its measure are based on the claims used to justify the projects rather than the actual results of those projects. Even when they are based on the latter it is very difficult to show the causal link between an aid project and development. Oftentimes an improvement in aid "efficiency" is due to the Bank's unwillingness to lose a customer even after that country has long since graduated to the point of sustainable rapid economic growth. Lending a little money to a country with a strongly growing economy will show wonderful results on paper although the improvement may not be causally related to the aid given.

The shortcomings of the Bank's evaluation of its abilities and accomplishments can be seen most clearly in the area of its new found expertise: law reform. It is difficult to know how to create the rule of law in another country and perhaps even more difficult to measure the impact of such assistance. But it is easy to see that the programs and measures of Bank legal reforms accomplishments do not measure anything pertinent to the rule of law. While these programs have been rebottled with contemporary jargon, most of the post cold war legal reform projects of the past decade are similar to the one's pursued by USAID in Latin America during the 1960s. These programs focus primarily on infrastructure and management because that is what the aid agencies know how to do. An independent judiciary is ostensibly achieved by building shiny new courthouses and outfitting them with new phones and computers. Another measure of an independent judiciary used by many World Bank projects includes the ability of the courts to clear their dockets efficiently. While justice delayed might be justice denied, a quick decision from one of Papa Doc's courts is perhaps worse than a slow one.

Could the Bank really nurture independent judiciaries if it rose above its *deus ex machina* approach? It is difficult to know given that the only successful transfers of judicial systems come from military conquest as with the Roman Empire and the occupation of Japan and Germany after World War II. This is unlikely to be an attractive model for these institutions let alone for Singer. Yet greater strides could be made if the World Bank stopped treating legal reform as an ethically neutral piece of technical assistance. The lack of an independent judiciary in most of these countries has less to do with technical ignorance than the unwillingness of local powers to subordinate themselves to the law. Perhaps no country was more devoid of legal capacity then Cambodia in the 1990s. Almost every single judge and lawyer had either fled or been liquidated by the Khmer Rouge. Yet after the UN arrived in the early 1990s, it took only six months to train a cadre of judges competent in local law. The inability of these judges to adjudicate independently did not stem from their technical ignorance but rather from the unwillingness of Hun Sen or the army to submit to the law.

None of this means that the legal reform is unimportant to development or that international institutions like the World Bank cannot play a role in bringing about that end. But in order to do so, it must first abandon its mantle of impartial technical advisor. There are many ways to deal with conflict and social cooperation. Using law to achieve these goals implies decidedly partial attitudes about the correct way that people ought to govern themselves. Democratic accountability, while no magic bullet, also provides a check on power that is necessary to limit the sort of rent seeking that contributes to the impoverishment of many borrowing nations.

If the Bank really has the new-found abilities that Singer contends, and which that institution believes rests in the area of legal and political reform, then there is very little need for new money. These legal reform projects are not capital intensive and the labor is relatively cheap compared to the major construction projects it used to carry out. Indeed, while it may be true that Singer's one-percent solution would dwarf the money now allocated towards the millennium development goals, it is also true that the amount of capital that could be secured with the implementation of real measures to protect property and contract rights would raise still more. At a conference on secured transactions in Moscow in the early 1990s, the senior vice president of Citicorp joked that the most impressive sight he saw on his approach to the city was not the Kremlin or Cathedral Square but rather all the unsecured capital the city represented. If Russians had been able to mortgage their land a decade ago, it would have provided much more capital for investment and employment and more tax revenues for social services than their one-percent share of Singer's global donation proposal. The same would be true for poorer countries when one took account of the multiplier effects of employment and tax revenues resulting from capital investment rather than simple food or medicine transfers. This is true even if we assume that the aid stuffs are not corruptly diverted to private entities who sell this aid in the marketplace.

The second greatest factor inhibiting the growth and well being of people in the poorest countries relates to the social, educational, and legal opportunities of women. Several Bank sponsored and independent studies have shown that one of the biggest returns for development expenditures would derive from extending equal property and contract rights to woman and opening up equal opportunities to get an education, start business and work outside the home.[15] None of these policies are especially expensive but achieving them will entail concerted action because these woman are not illiterate or subordinate through some benign oversight. The state of affairs that put women in this situation is very much part of the culture of many of these beneficiary countries who regard women as subordinate to men. This is a cultural issue that goes back several millennia and there is no way around the fact that Western attitudes about sexual equality are a product of a radically different cultural perspective. What are we ethically required to do in the circumstance when a beneficiary nation pleads, accurately, that their cultural practices are central to their communal identities and that they do not wish to abandon them? What will produce the greatest good in this situation? Are we obligated to leave the country alone—as they request but cut off aid, continue aid but abandon efforts to enforce women's equality—or are we to use all the economic and other non military tools we have to push for sexual equality while continuing aid?

---

[15] Amartya K. Sen, *Development As Freedom* (New York: Knopf, 1999), pp. 189–204.

Democracy, another cultural artifact of western partiality, appears also to contribute directly to human well being. Amartya Sen has studied the relationship between democracy and famine and the results appear to suggest that accountable government is more closely correlated with the ability of a state to avoid famine than it is with aid or natural resources (pp. 146–160).

So Singer's call for more money is misplaced because it will not take more money to bring about the sort of institutional reform that is required. Indeed, bringing about the greatest good to those in most need might require the transfer of resources in the opposite direction. In order to see why, one needs to consider the role of agricultural trade barriers and farm subsidies in the impoverishment of developing countries. But for these policies, many farmers could sell their products to American consumers. The benefits to these poor farmers cannot be overstated and are generally agreed to be far in excess of even the most generous aid program. The odd thing about this policy proposal is why it hasn't already happened given that it would be in the overwhelming interest of most Americans to eliminate agricultural trade barriers and farm support. After all, only two percent of the US population lives on the farm while one hundred percent of us are consumers of food. It is not only Egyptian cotton farmers or Vietnamese rice farmers who suffer when the Army Corps of Engineers redirects major rivers hundreds of miles away to permit California farmers to grow rice on arid land. American consumers could probably get more value for their tax dollars by buying the California rice farmers an annuity, forgoing the diversion of major waterways and purchasing rice from countries that can produce it far more cheaply and more benignly.

Why do so many Americans act contrary to their own interests and the interests of those in the global community? Part of the answer lies in the logic of collective action. The money milk producers get from price supports is vitally important to them while the cost to the remaining ninety eight percent of Americans is minor when compared to the costs of organizing a remedy. So the milk producers lobby hard while most of us don't even realize what is going on. What would it take for Americans to realize how distorted and harmful their trade and farm policies were? For a start it would take education and more prosaic propaganda to explain the situation sufficiently so that each individual understood where his or her true interests lay. Americans are unlikely to appropriate money to educate themselves about a problem they aren't aware exists. So this means that others who do understand must spend their money to educate Americans about what is truly in their self-interest. The same general rule holds true for the excessive use of fossil fuels. In many cases the full cost of production is not borne by the producers but rather is subsidized by taxpayers. This distorts the market and encourages increased consumption to points that are harmful to the Earth and ourselves. Most Americans are oblivious to the subsidies they pay and even if they learned of them, the logic of collective action would obviate a very strong response. The war in Iraq may serve to focus attention on this matter with regard to energy policy and to show that the costs are indeed, quite high.

Given the logic of collective action, it seems that the problem of American overconsumption and protectionism derives not from selfishness but ignorance where Americans' self-interest really lies. If they understood the destructive impact of farm supports to themselves, as well as to African farmers, they would see the benefit of organizing to change the policy. If the costs and benefits of farm supports and trade protectionism really do dwarf the benefits of aid programs, then it seems that the only ethical course would be to transfer money from other countries to engage in a massive education and propaganda campaign to educate Americans (and the Japanese and Europeans) about their policies. From the standpoint of increasing the general welfare, this money would be better spent than if it had been sent to developing countries.

Defining the Greatest Good

Singer is nothing if not practical and would not cling dogmatically to ineffective policies. So presumably he would support my approach if I could prove that it would produce a better outcome. But this presumes that the greatest good consists in economic growth and the attendant social benefits of food, housing, education, and medical care that accrue from it. These are certainly good things but they are not the only good consequences one could aim at. If we insist on these material necessities we risk falling into the same trap as the economist Robert Barro, who believes growth to be the greatest good even if a people want something else, like democratic accountability or equality.[16] Some communities pull back when faced with the option of changing basic cultural practices that go to the heart of their identity. Evidently, their idea of the greater good exceeds their fear of famine or premature death. This is a reasonable position from a communitarian perspective of justice but it's

---

[16] Robert Barro, *Getting It Right: Markets and Choices in a Free Society* (Cambridge: MIT Press, 1996).

not clear whether it is better, on the whole to preserve these central aspects of identity or to increase life expectancy and literacy rates.

How then could we tell what the best outcome overall would be? This is important because without this basic information, we could not know the consequences we need to pursue in order to act ethically. One of the original virtues of utilitarianism was its ability to provide an objective, empirically verifiable answer to the question of what justice consists in. That is because the only preference one needed to account for were one's own purely egoistic ideas of the best consequences. So the best outcome could be calculated simply by aggregating all the individual conceptions of what would produce the greatest pleasure. This approach is problematic because it ends up declaring all sorts of horrifically evil acts as morally correct. After all, the aggregation of these preferences in the Third Reich or the antebellum American South would have yielded sizeable majorities in favor of slavery and the liquidation of the Jews.

While most utilitarians, including Singer, reject this hedonistic conception of determining the best consequences, doing so abandons the virtue of objective ethical certainty. Once we switch from merely reporting what each person believes is best to determining what turns out really to be best we open up the possibility of error. People can be mistaken about which act or rule will actually produce the best consequence. Yet then, what is really the best consequence in the ethical sense? If there is some objective measure then why bother asking people in the first place? Wouldn't we get better consequences by having experts decide these matters? Another cause for uncertainty about ethics in non self interested utilitarianism derives from what each person must now consider. Rather than assessing just one's own preferences, which one knows better than anyone, each person is required to have an idea of the best consequences that includes what other people, also taking everyone's idea of the good life into account, would also think is the best consequence. But this doesn't fit the way we employ ethics. When I vote against free trade, and lose, I don't then recognize free trade as the correct policy or the best consequence. Rather I become determined to convince others back over to my position because I still believe my policies will produce the best consequences for everyone overall. Indeed, there is some question whether or not one is actually acting morally, if all one is doing is attempting to channel everyone else's idea of the best consequences. To act morally implies the use of reason and judgment to decide what to do. That one would cede this decision to an aggregation of what people think others would think is the best result is to cede judgment about the central question about the morality of any given action.

Singer argues that trying to aim for what is best for the group turns out to produce the best consequences for people individually within the group. But this goal is too abstract to be useful as a guide to practical action because what anyone believes is best for the group will depend on things that are prior to what the actual consequences are of any given choice. The Klansman who fights miscegenation of the races believes that he is taking everyone's idea of what is best for them into account because prior to any consequences; he believes that the value of preventing inter breeding is what all reasonable people would pursue. If they wouldn't pursue it, then in the Klansman's view, it is only because the are misinformed about what is good for them, and they would prefer his view if they knew better.

This is more than simple bias. There is an epistemological barrier to determining the best consequences not merely for oneself but for everyone overall. It is impossible both from the perspective of Adam Smith, who, being a liberal, believed that each person was sovereign over his or her own idea of the good life. So no one else could begin to determine this for anyone else, even if well intentioned. It is also impossible from Rousseau's perspective which Singer apparently endorses (*How Are We to Live?*, p. 41). For Rousseau, personal identity was itself the product of inter-subjective meanings and constitutive understanding about many important social phenomena. Anyone outside of these hermeneutic circles of shared meaning could not comprehend let alone agree or disagree about the content of ethical behavior.

Unlike the Adam Smith route that Singer laments, Communitarians thought there were actual moral truths about the way people ought to live that were encompassed in the General Will. These ethical precepts were as true as any social phenomena could be because they were incorporated into our language and hence our idea of reality itself. Yet notwithstanding his admiration for Rousseau he inexplicably goes on to embrace the logical positivist rejection of theology and absolute truth in ethics (*How Are We to Live?*, p. 188). But Ayer wasn't just rejecting the notion of any absolute truth in ethics. He was arguing that the very idea of ethics and truth in the same sentence was meaningless. For Ayer, ethics were not absolutely or even relatively untrue. They were irrational emotional expressions that could no more be associated with truth than the idea of a best-flavored ice cream. To Ayer, ethics were purely an expression of taste. One cannot get much more subjective than taste and yet Singer urges us to reject the egoistic subjective idea of ethics. Indeed, for him, the moral of the epic, *Gilgamesh*, King of Uruk, is that we ought not to pursue "hedonistic" pleasures like being with our children or wife (or husband), but rather find the meaning of life through help-ing others (*How Are We to Live?*, p. 189). Yet if what produces the best consequences is ultimately an aggregate of our personal preferences for a particular state of affairs, then this is necessarily an egoistic-based morality.

Singer tries to steer a middle path between some idea of ethics as empirically true and the logical positivist view of morality as nonsense. But ultimately, his notion of the ethically correct consequence, that of relieving the suffering of others, depends not only on our ability to iden-tify with the suffering of others, but deciding that for whatever reason, it is in our self-interest to help them. This is a notoriously weak founda-tion for ethics. While many majorities might take that path, it would have to follow, according to this view that if most people decided it was not in their interest to relieve the suffering of others, than it is evidently not ethically necessary to do so. Singer may reject that characterization of his theory, but when you get down to the last turtle all the good con-sequences are good, only if we decide that it is in our subjective self interest that they happen.

This cannot be where Singer leaves us given that his whole profes-sional corpus has promoted the incorporation of ethical thinking into our lives. Yet to embrace the positivist view of ethics as expressions of taste leaves no basis to make judgments about the correct way to live one's life. After having endorsed an epistemological view that puts ethics outside the world of reason, Singer concludes that the only way we will be able to reach those best consequences that are ethically cor-rect will be by using our distinctively human capacity to reason out our place in the world and understand the benefits that concern for others and cooperation will bring (*How Are We to Live?*, pp. 225–235).

The turn to reason, while sensible, seems oddly out of place in Singer's ethics. In addition to the epistemological issues, it seems to con-tradict other aspects of his work. Indeed, in the same book where he embraces reason as a basis of ethics, he attacks Kant's ethical framework for its reliance on duty rather than consequences. Yet the essential fea-ture of Kant's ethics is our capacity to reason ourselves to the ethically correct outcome. Reason is at the root of our ability to act ethically in Kant's world, and indeed, Singer partially rehabilitates Kant for this rea-son. But if reason won't work to create duties, why should it work to make better consequences? Singer disposes of Kant, by noting that Adolf Eichmann justified his war crimes on the basis of his supposedly Kantian derived duties. The idea that Eichmann's actions would have passed Kant's universality requirement is laughable. But if Singer really thinks Kant is sunk on this basis then his ethical notion of reason is just as vulnerable. One could just as easily imagine Eichmann testifying that he was morally bound to carry out the Final Solution because it would produce the *best consequences*. While I think this idea is mistaken, there is nothing inherent in Singer's utilitarian ethics that precludes this conclusion. Reason after all, just enables us to identify with another's suffering and perhaps conclude that it is in our self-interest to help. But ultimately it is self-interest that moves things along and our reasoned self interest might lead us to believe that we ought not to care about the suffering of others.

Singer's turn to reason is even more out of place when we consider the corpus of his work related to animal rights. Notwithstanding his rejection of subjective self-interest as a basis for the good consequences that produce ethical obligations, his defense of animal rights depends just on that notion. In his defense of animals he rejects reason as an ethically pertinent characteristic to distinguish humans from other animals. In his landmark essay, "All Animals Are Equal," Singer argues that the ability to suffer, not reason, is the cornerstone of an animal's ethical standing to be counted as one and no more than one, equally with all other creatures, human and otherwise.[17] Quite apart from the merits of this argument, it is important to note that this is precisely the sort of hedonistic self-interested foundation that Singer rejects in his idea of how we ought to live (*How Are We to Live?*, pp. 142–45).

Suffering, after all, is the ultimate subjective experience that no one else can appreciate exactly as we do. Indeed, we experience suffering in the same way we experience taste, through our senses. Like taste, people are the experts in what causes them the most pain or pleasure. That is why Bentham thought that our interests in pursuing happiness and avoiding pain are non-comparable. While we might identify with another being's pain or suffering, as with matters of taste, only that animal can experience the actual suffering and decide just how bad it is. The pleasure I get from eating a ripe avocado or mango, on this view, cannot be compared with the happiness you get from feeding a starving family or the joy they feel in alleviating their hunger pain. Moreover, these tastes are by definition, irrational. There is no reason one could give to explain his preference for mangos over oranges because it would simply boil down to 'This is what I like'. Were we to rank all these different pains

---

[17] Tom Regan and Peter Singer, *Animal Rights and Human Obligations*, second edition (Englewood Cliffs: Prentice Hall, 1989), pp. 149–152.

and pleasures for people, we would be overriding their taste. Apart from being paternalistic, this would not treat each living thing as one and no more than one. So if Singer is going to protect animals on the basis of their hedonistic interest in not suffering, than he cannot disclaim this as the foundation of his ethical theory. While aggregating the self-interest of rational maximizers might end up protecting animals, it would not provide a very firm ground for many of the other consequences that Singer wanted to pursue. More importantly, it subordinates reason in favor of our sense of pain and pleasure.

I believe that the ethical goals that Singer outlines are both inspiring and correct. Yet I come to this view based on a liberal outlook that focuses not on the consequences of actions but the autonomy of each person. I think this autonomy comes from the same unique reasoning capacity that Singer tries to draw on as his basis for ethical behavior. But I believe this means that we must protect that autonomy even if doing so does not on the whole produce the best consequences. In the end, while I embrace the substantive positions and attitudes Singer proposes for living an ethical life, I do not see how his theory of justice or human nature leads him to those beliefs—other than that, like me, he thinks they are inherently, not consequentially, the right thing to do.

Reply to David Fagelson

PETER SINGER

Two Senses of Partiality

At the core of David Fagelson's critique of my views about foreign aid and globalization is a confusion about what it is to be partial. Fagelson correctly states that in *One World* I argue against "the partiality of our obligations" and that I reject "the idea that we only owe obligations to our countrymen." But a page or two later he refers to some forms of intervention in other nations as "highly partial to a given sort of cultural, historical, political and economic practices." These are distinct senses of the term "partial."

A true cosmopolitan might say: "I consider myself a citizen of the world. I owe loyalty to no state, and I have similar obligations to every human being, or perhaps to every sentient being." This is a fully impartialist position. Next consider a citizen of Ruritania who says: "Every citizen of every nation has a primary loyalty to his or her country. Hence I have obligations first and foremost to my fellow-Ruritanians." In one sense, he is clearly being partial—if he has to choose between saving the life of a Ruritanian or an Urbanian, he will save the Ruritanian and leave the Urbanian to die. On the other hand his principle implies that an Urbanian, faced with a similar choice, ought to save the life of the Urbanian and leave the Ruritanian to die. This is an impartial argument for partiality. I don't accept it, or at least not in such an extreme form, but I have argued in *One World* and in *How Are We to Live?* that an impartial case can be made for a limited degree of partiality towards one's children, and perhaps to other kin and to members of one's community. If the structure of the argument is clear—that is, that the partiality is justified within the framework of an impartial ethic—I don't believe that it "muddies" the case for impartiality, as Fagelson seems to think, although it does moderate the practical applications of impartiality.

351

In contrast, imagine that we meet a Molvanian[18] who says: "Since I am a Molvanian, I have obligations only to other Molvanians. But everyone else should put Molvanians first, too, because we are more important than anyone else." Suppose also that when we question this Molvanian about why he thinks his compatriots are more important than anyone else, he just says "Because they are *my* compatriots." We point out that since we are Urbanians, we could say the same about Urbanians, but he responds "Yes, but I care more about Molvanians, and so you should care more about them too." Further attempts to draw out reasons for this judgment produce only repetition. We might then say that the Molvanian is partial all the way down. His partiality has no impartial foundation.

This distinction should give us a clear sense of what it is to be partial, in the first sense of the term mentioned above. The Cosmopolitan is impartial in every sense. The Ruritanian is partial, but defends his partiality in impartial terms. He is an impartialist, as far as the ethical foundations of his position are concerned. If it turns out that his impartialist defense of partiality is incorrect, he would presumably switch his view about his obligations. The Molvanian is partial at all levels of justification.

Now consider the work of Rational Aid, an international aid organization that has as its mission statement: "Give equal weight to the interests of all the world's people." Rational Aid collects money to assist people in some of the world's poorest nations. Before going ahead with an aid program, it conducts a cost-utility analysis—that is, a study to ensure that there are no other possible programs that, for the same cost, are likely to bring about a greater increase in the welfare of extremely poor people. Among the poor countries in which Rational Aid works is Faithland, where AIDS has become widespread, and the rate of people newly infected with HIV, the virus that causes AIDS, is rising. Most of the citizens of Faithland have strong religious beliefs and little education, and the only thing their government tells them about AIDS is that it is God's curse on those who disobey his laws. This is consistent with their culture, religion, and values.

Before the AIDS epidemic, Rational Aid ran effective village-level programs in Faithland providing improved seeds and agricultural methods, so that families were better nourished. Three years ago, it became clear that these programs were imperiled by the high death rate from

---

[18] For information about this little-known country, see Santo Cilauro, Tom Gleisner, and Rob Sitch, *Molvania: A Jetlag Travel Guide* (New York: Overlook Press, 2004).

AIDS, particularly among young adults who normally work the land. Therefore after the usual cost-utility scrutiny, the Rational Aid leadership decided to switch the focus of its Faithland programs to directly combating AIDS. To that end, it set up health clinics staffed by paramedics who have taken Harvard-designed online courses in health care. These paramedics offer basic health care and give out information that says AIDS is most commonly transmitted by unprotected sexual intercourse, and advises people on how to avoid being infected by it. Rates of new infections in the villages served by these clinics have fallen. Nevertheless, the Faithland government has threatened to shut down the clinics, saying that they are undermining the religious faith of the people. Pressure from foreign governments that provide official aid to Faithland has, so far, prevented these threats from becoming reality.

Is Rational Aid acting impartially? In the sense outlined—the sense in which the cosmopolitan is impartial—it is. But it seems that Fagelson might disagree. He might say that the actions of Rational Aid are, to quote from his essay, "highly partial to a given sort of cultural, historical, political and economic practices." In this case, the cultural and historical practices would be those of the biomedical science, and the economic practice would be that of cost-utility analysis.

If Fagelson were to claim that the practices of Rational Aid are partial, that would obviously be a sense of the term that is distinct from the sense in which cosmopolitans are impartial. In my view it would be a misuse of the term. Rational Aid is simply trying to do the most good it can with its limited resources. On scientific questions like the cause of AIDS, it follows the best evidence available to it at the time, while always remaining ready to change its views if new and conflicting evidence should emerge. There is nothing partial about preferring evidence-based practices to religious faith.

Fagelson appears to have confused impartiality with belief in cultural relativity. Impartiality does not require equal respect for every culture. I can be impartial and still think that my society's culture, institutions, practices, and values are superior to those of another society. Of course, I should be aware of the likelihood that my comparison is biased, and that I may have difficulty in seeing the merits of a culture that is foreign to me. In *One World* I urged sensitivity to other cultures, and a recognition that we in the West may have much to learn from them. But the likelihood of bias in favor of our own culture is not a reason for denying that some cultures are better than others. One ground for this judgment may be that some cultures do more than other cultures to satisfy the needs and desires of those who live in accordance with that culture. This is, of course, a complex question, and it will be especially difficult to resolve if the cultures differ in their conception of human nature and the needs and desires that are part of that nature. Accounts of human nature are often molded by religious thinking, so that the account describes not what human nature really is, but what religious teachings say it should be. (The account of human nature accepted by Roman Catholic proponents of natural law is one example.) But what our nature is, and what it takes to make us happy and fulfilled is, at least in principle, an empirical question and one about which scientific inquiry is making progress.[19]

This point is related to another of Fagelson's critical comments. He suggests that I "espouse ideas from other conceptions of justice that are incompatible with utilitarianism." His example is my reference to Rousseau's thinking about nature in *How Are We to Live?* But this claim reads too much into a few brief comments. To provide a counterpoint to the views of Adam Smith, who applauded the way in which humans "have turned the rude forests of nature into agreeable and fertile plains," I mentioned Rousseau's advocacy of greater harmony with forests and with nature generally. I did not adopt Rousseau's conception of human nature.[20]

Beneath this erroneous attribution to me of Rousseau's conception of human nature, however, a more significant philosophical error is lurking. Fagelson says that the conflicts between Smith and Rousseau "go deeper than any idea of justice. They are rooted in different epistemological questions of what is really out there in the world." I doubt that the differences between Smith and Rousseau are epistemological—at least, I'm not aware of differences between them over whether knowledge is possible, or how we can gain knowledge. They do differ over the empirical question of what human nature is like. But in any case, neither epistemological nor empirical questions are deeper than normative questions, they are simply different. As I say in *A Darwinian Left*—a book that should have dispelled any illusion about my Rousseauian tendencies—we should not allow our values to dictate our view of human nature, as the left has often done in preferring Marx to Darwin. Instead, we should accept the theory of human nature best supported by the evidence, and then use that theory in order to work out how to achieve the society that best accords with our values. Even if I had accepted

---

[19] For a recent summary of what scientific inquiry has to say on this topic, see Jonathan Haidt, *The Happiness Hypothesis* (New York: Basic Books, 2005).
[20] *How Are We to Live?*, pp. 40–41.

Rousseau's conception of human nature, there would have been no conflict with my utilitarianism.

Some further errors need correction. The utilitarian criterion does not always require us to intervene in burdened nondemocratic states, although it may do so in some circumstances. Intervention in a burdened, nondemocratic state is, after all, the policy followed by the United States in Iraq, and that may well have done more harm than good. We must always closely consider the costs of our actions for others and military intervention risks particularly high costs.

Fagelson's comment on my views, in *One World,* of the link between democracy and sovereignty, is even more misleading. He claims:

> In a short section on cultural imperialism, [Singer] warns that the link between democracy and legitimate sovereignty is not proven because the only arguments we could give in favor of it are necessarily culturally partial ones that in the end would be no different than asserting that our religion was the one true avenue to eternal salvation.

Fagelson's reference is to the following passage:

> How can we give reasons, independent of our culture, for the view that legitimacy requires popular support, rather than resting on, say, religious law? Attempts to argue for the separation of church and state will not work, since that begs the question against the defenders of the religion that rejects such a separation. In the end, the challenge cannot be met without confronting the basis for belief in the religion. But one cannot argue that the religious faith of people of a different culture is false, while upholding a religious faith of one's own that rests on no firmer ground. That really would be cultural imperialism. In the end, at least as far as we are concerned with practices based on propositions about the existence of a god or gods and the authenticity of what are claimed to be divinely inspired scriptures, it is our capacity to reason that is the universal solvent. But this is not a question into which we can go further here.

Even a casual reader of my work would know that I am not a religious believer. So in this passage, far from suggesting that to argue in favor of a link between democracy and legitimacy is necessarily culturally partial, I am arguing for the opposite view: there *is* a culturally impartial way of arguing for such a link. It requires an appeal to reason against the religious faith that is invoked by undemocratic rulers to justify their rule. The catch is that such an appeal works equally effectively against all religions that believe in a god or gods, or divinely inspired scriptures. But for me, that's no catch at all.

Fagelson writes: "If determining the greatest good depends upon each person's expression of that good, then it is actually an ethical requirement of Singer's utilitarianism that we be partial and self interested." Since Fagelson elsewhere refers to collective action problems, he should know that this is false. If we all act in a manner that is partial and self-interested, the result will often be worse for all of us.[21] A second reason why Fagelson's claim is false is that I may achieve my greatest satisfaction and fulfilment from living in a world in which others are not suffering unnecessarily. To take such a view is hardly to be "partial and self-interested" in the usual sense of those terms.

When I wrote that any system of ethics must be suited to the "rough and tumble of everyday life. . . . ethics is practical or it is not really ethics," I did not mean that ethics could not demand things that most people will not do. I meant only that *if* people act, in increasing numbers, as the ethic advocates, it should bring about consequences that we can accept. "Turning the other cheek," for example, is not practical because if people started doing it, the number who commit assault and robbery would increase, and no one would want that.

I can't see the relevance to my views of Fagelson's discussion of the activities of the World Bank. As with the reference to Rousseau, and with the later suggestion that I am a logical positivist, Fagelson is here grabbing at a sentence or two from one of my books and reading much more into them than is really there. Although I hope that the World Bank is serious about reforming itself and focusing on the reduction of global poverty, I have never imagined that a reformed World Bank would be sufficient to solve the problem of global poverty.

Finally, Fagelson's suggestion that the poor nations need institutional reform, and therefore there is no need to give money, seems to me disingenuous for two reasons. First, the poor need various kinds of assistance, and institutional reform is just one of them. Given the wealth of the affluent world, the children of the poor shouldn't have to die from avoidable poverty-related causes while they wait for their national institutions to reform. Second, if we do want to promote institutional reform, there are organizations like Transparency International[13] already doing so, and they will be able to do so more strongly and effectively if we give them some of our money.

---

[21] See my discussion of the Prisoner's Dilemma in *How Are We to Live?*, pp. 132–34, and of climate change as a collective action problem in *One World*.

IV

ETHICAL THEORY

11

Singer's Unstable Meta-Ethics

MICHAEL HUEMER

1. Singer's Meta-Ethics

Peter Singer's stated view about the nature of ethics is both non-cognitivist and Humean. This meta-ethical view, however, clashes with the rest of his philosophy on three levels. First, it clashes with his view of what we are ethically required to do; second, it leaves him with no plausible account of why we should be moral given his conception of what morality demands; and third, it clashes with his methodology in ethics. Instead, Singer should embrace his latent sympathies for a rationalist intuitionism. In what follows, I explain and defend these points. In this first section, I set the scene by explaining Singer's meta-ethical views and contrasting them with an alternative, intuitionist view.

A *meta-ethical* theory is a theory about the general nature of values and value judgments. There are two noteworthy elements of Singer's meta-ethical view:

i) Non-Cognitivism: This view holds that evaluative statements, such as "Enjoyment is good" and "Eating chickens is wrong," do not describe any objective facts and cannot be either true or false. Instead, such statements function to express the speaker's feelings, desires, or other attitudes, or to issue a kind of imperative.[1] Thus, "It is wrong to eat chickens" is compa-

---

[1] This is a traditional characterization of non-cognitivism, of the sort found in Ayer's *Language, Truth, and Logic*, Chapter 6. More recently, non-cognitivists have preferred to define the view in terms of the thesis that evaluative statements do not express beliefs, rather than in terms of the thesis that evaluative statements are neither true nor false.

rable to "Eating chickens—boo!" or "Don't eat chickens!"—neither of these sentences can be true or false because they simply are not factual claims at all. Criticizing the idea of objective values, Singer writes:

> If the universe has not been constructed in accordance with any plan it has no meaning to be discovered. There is no value inherent in it, independently of the existence of sentient beings who prefer some states of affairs to others. Ethics is no part of the structure of the cosmos, in the way that atoms are.[2]

ii) The Humean Conception of Reasons: This is the view that the only reason a person can ever have for doing anything is that it will enable him to satisfy some desire of his, or at least increase the chances of his satisfying some desire of his.[3] Thus, Hume and his followers would say that the fact that an action is morally right can give you a rational reason to do it, only if you *want* to do what is right, or you want something else that you think doing the right thing will help you accomplish. Furthermore, Humeans deny that there is anything that all rational beings must desire. Thus, what reasons for action we have depend on contingent facts about our emotional/conative makeup. If someone simply does not care about ethical concerns at a fundamental level, there need be nothing irrational about him; though we may call such a person "immoral," we will be unable to give him any reason why he should be moral.[4]

Because Singer embraces this Humean view, he faces the task of explaining how ethical behavior contributes to satisfying one's own desires. Though he need not and does not maintain that it is *always* rational to act ethically, his view of ethics would be implausible unless he could at least argue that we *normally* have good reason to be ethical. Singer meets this challenge by suggesting, in essence, that consciously leading an ethical life can give one a sense of meaning and purpose that more self-centered ways of living do not provide. Without a sense of

---

Singer defends non-cognitivism, albeit with reservations (admitting some sympathy with Sidgwick's intuitionism) in *Singer and His Critics*, pp. 269–273, and *Practical Ethics*, p. 7. Singer's sympathy with intuitionism was clearer in his "Sidgwick and Reflective Equilibrium."

[2] Singer, *How Are We to Live?*, p. 188; the context makes clear that Singer believes the universe in fact has not been created in accordance with any plan. Compare p. 231 ("Ethical truths are not written into the fabric of the universe") and *Practical Ethics*, p. 8 (discussing "the non-existence of a mysterious realm of objective ethical facts").

[3] Hume, *Treatise of Human Nature*, pp. 413–18; Singer, *Practical Ethics*, pp. 320–22.

[4] *Practical Ethics*, pp. 334–35.

meaning, we are unlikely to find our lives fulfilling, and such a sense of meaning can be achieved only through devotion to something we see as larger than ourselves. Thus, adopting the moral perspective may indirectly help us to satisfy the desire for happiness, a desire that nearly all people share.[5]

In the following sections, I argue that Singer ought to give up his Humean non-cognitivism in favor of a *rationalist intuitionism*, embodying the following three theses:[6]

i) Objectivism about Value: This is the view that some evaluative statements are true independently of the attitudes of observers towards the objects they are about. For example, the wrongness of murder is objective if "murder is wrong" is true regardless of what attitudes anyone takes towards murder.

The question of objective values is not to be confused with a question as to *what* is valuable. The question is not, for example, whether *the good things* are things that depend on sentient beings, but rather whether a thing's *being good* is a matter of the attitudes that observers take towards it. Thus, Singer's view that the sole intrinsic value is preference-satisfaction is neither subjectivist nor objectivist *per se*; though it implies that the good things are dependent on sentient beings, it says nothing about whether preference-satisfaction is good in virtue of our attitude toward it, or whether it is good objectively. Analogously, facts about (human) medicine are dependent on human beings in an obvious sense, but this does not impugn the objectivity of medicine.

ii) A Rationalist Conception of Reasons: This is the view that we sometimes have reason to do something solely in virtue of being in some cognitive state. For instance, my believing (or knowing) that meat-eating is wrong—where this is a cognitive state, as opposed, say, to an emotion or desire—might give me a good reason not to eat meat. According to the rationalist, it is not necessary to specify in addition that I desire not to act wrongly. This is not to say that I necessarily will in fact refrain from eating meat (I might suffer from weakness of will); it is only to say that I have a *good reason* to refrain from eating meat, given that I believe meat-eating to be wrong.

---

[5] *Practical Ethics*, pp. 331–35.

[6] I defend this view at length in my *Ethical Intuitionism*. The following is a simplified version of the view. See *Ethical Intuitionism*, Chapter 5 for elaboration on the notion of ethical intuition, and Chapter 7 for elaboration on the rationalist conception of reasons. Note that what follows in the text characterizes my version of intuitionism; not all intuitionists would characterize their views in this way.

iii) *An Intuitionist Conception of Moral Knowledge:* This is the view that all of our knowledge of value derives ultimately from our ethical intuitions. Ethical intuitions are cognitive, intellectual states in which we seem to directly see certain things to be good, bad, right, or wrong. For example, most people know that it is bad to inflict suffering on others for no reason; this seems immediately obvious when we think about it. This state of its "seeming obvious" amounts to an ethical intuition, and according to intuitionists, it gives us good reason to believe that infliction of gratuitous suffering is in fact bad, absent any specific grounds for doubting this.

In brief, Singer holds that there are no objective values, that ethical claims reflect nothing other than our subjective preferences, and that our only possible reason for behaving ethically is to satisfy our own desires. As we shall see presently, these views fit poorly with his conception of the content and methods of ethics; instead, he should adopt the view that ethical claims are claims about objective facts that provide us with reasons for action independent of our desires, and that we have an intuitive, intellectual awareness of some of these facts.

2. The Content of Ethics

Singer adopts a *preference-utilitarian* ethic, according to which the right action in any situation is determined by what will best satisfy the preferences of all sentient beings affected, with each being's preferences weighed according to their strength.[7] This leads to what are perhaps Singer's two most discussed ethical positions: First, that each of us who are relatively well-off has a strong moral obligation to donate large portions of our wealth to international famine-relief efforts, since the suffering we could alleviate by doing so is much greater than the pleasures we would obtain by spending that money on ourselves. I, for example, probably ought to donate at least eighty percent of my current income, to save the lives of individuals in the Third World. My failure to do so, Singer would say, is morally comparable to murder.[8] Second, Singer believes that our current treatment of non-human animals is seriously wrong, and in particular that we ought to refrain from eating meat, since

---

[7] Singer, *The Expanding Circle*, pp. 100–111.

[8] *Practical Ethics*, Chapter 8. The comparison to murder is discussed on pp. 222–29. It is worth noting that Singer makes a case for his views, both about famine relief and about animals, that does not depend on utilitarianism. The case is, however, particularly clear for a utilitarian.

the suffering (and presumable preference-frustration) of farm animals greatly outweighs the amount of pleasure that we obtain by eating them.[9]

Are these *ethical* views coherent with Singer's *meta-ethical* views? On a non-cognitivist construal, when Singer says it is seriously wrong to eat meat, what he is saying is roughly, "Eating meat—ugh! Don't do it!!" He is not claiming to report any objective fact; he is simply expressing his aversion to people's eating meat. In itself, there is nothing incongruous in this. A non-cognitivist philosopher can be expected to have just as many moral emotions and preferences as anyone else; his theory of how moral discourse functions will not prevent him from having those non-cognitive states, nor will it make it any the less appropriate for him to express them by moral language.

But Singer does not hold just any ethical views. His ethical views are highly *revisionary* ones. It is important to see this point clearly because it is central to my objection in this section. Let us therefore review some of the positions that Singer has taken or that his utilitarianism commits him to:

1. Failure to donate to famine relief is morally comparable to murder.

2. Animals deserve equal moral consideration to human beings—it is just as wrong to frustrate the desires of an animal as it is to frustrate equally strong desires of a human.

3. Bestiality is acceptable (where it does not harm the animal).[10]

4. Infanticide is permissible when one has a good reason for killing the infant, such as that the infant is severely disabled, because newborn infants have no right to life.[11]

5. It is morally right to sacrifice one individual to produce a greater benefit for others; thus, in the example discussed below, the doctor should kill the healthy patient.

Item 5 refers to the following well-worn scenario:

Organ Harvesting: A doctor in a hospital has five patients who need organ transplants; otherwise, they will die. They all need different organs. He also has one healthy patient, in for a routine checkup, who happens to be

---

[9] *Practical Ethics*, Chapter 3; Singer and Posner, "Animal Rights."

[10] Singer, "Heavy Petting."

[11] *Practical Ethics*, pp. 188–191.

compatible with the five. Should the doctor kill the healthy patient and distribute his organs to the other five?[12]

Given certain predictable stipulations about the case,[13] the doctor would produce a greater good by harvesting the organs, since only one life would be taken while five would be saved. If so, a utilitarian must say that this would be the morally correct course of action. Indeed, the *refusal* to harvest the organs would be an extremely serious wrong, morally comparable to committing four murders.[14]

I do not introduce these examples for the purpose of discrediting Singer's ethical views. On the contrary, I think Singer may well be right in all or most of these points, and in any event, I view conventional morality as very badly misguided. What these examples illustrate, again, is that Singer adheres to a revisionary ethics—his views clash with the moral sensibility of the vast majority of people in our society. If Singer were an objectivist, his view would be that most of us are seriously mistaken, that our moral attitudes fail to correspond to moral reality. As a non-cognitivist, he thinks there is no such reality for us to get wrong; instead, he is simply expressing non-cognitive attitudes that clash with those of most people.

What sort of attitudes might Singer be expressing in his moral discourse? I shall assume that Singer would claim to be expressing a kind of preference or desire.[15] Presumably, moral language does not function to express just *any* kind of preference—we should not expect a non-cognitivist, for example, to declare Mozart's music immoral, simply because he (the non-cognitivist) does not like it. But presumably the non-cognitivist will say there is a *kind* of preference, which we might

---

[12] James Rachels originally introduced this example in informal conversations in the 1960s; it has since become a standard alleged counter-example to utilitarianism.

[13] Assume, for example, that the healthy patient's murder will not be discovered; the doctor can make it look like a death from natural causes and can also produce a forged document giving him permission to take the organs. This blocks most of the negative consequences that would otherwise result from harvesting the organs. If you think there are negative consequences that would still occur, use your imagination to come up with the sort of stipulations one would make about the case to ensure that they would not occur.

[14] Utilitarians, Singer included, deny that there is a significant distinction between killing someone and letting someone die, or between acts and omissions generally (*Practical Ethics*, pp. 205–213).

[15] Singer (*The Expanding Circle*, pp. 105, 108, 110) treats the view that moral claims express subjective preferences as the salient alternative to objectivism.

call a "moral preference," that one aptly expresses by making moral statements. Thus, in taking the moral stands mentioned above, Singer is expressing the following sort of attitudes:

- Singer wants people to donate to famine relief about as strongly as he wants them to avoid murder.

- Singer has equally strong preferences for the welfare of animals as for that of human beings.

- Singer does not mind bestiality.

And so on. Now, there are a few things that are odd about this.

First, it is very odd that Singer should have such a set of preferences—so odd, in fact, that we must question whether he really does. I believe, for example, that a harm to an animal may well be equally bad, objectively speaking, as an equally serious harm to a human. But certainly my *desires* pertaining to the two kinds of harm are not equally strong; I just don't care as much about animals as I do about other people. By the same token, while I have no difficulty believing that Singer *believes* that animal-suffering is equally bad (other things being equal) as human-suffering, I would find it very odd if he had equally strong preferences with regard to both. I find it even more difficult to believe that Singer's desires for his own happiness and that of his friends and family are no stronger than his desires for the happiness of strangers; yet this seems to be the mental state that, according to non-cognitivism, he would be expressing in saying that his own happiness and that of his family and friends does not matter more, morally, than that of strangers.[16]

How might a non-cognitivist explain what is going on here? Perhaps we need to attend here to the distinction, drawn above, between preferences in general and *moral* preferences. Perhaps while Singer's overall desire for his own happiness is stronger than his overall desire for the happiness of a stranger in India, his *moral* preference for his own happiness is of equal strength to his moral preference for the happiness of the stranger in India. But this suggestion is phenomenologically bizarre. It seems to imply that Singer has two distinct desires for his

---

[16] This is a familiar theme in Singer's work. See for example, *The Expanding Circle*, p. 106: "[O]ne's own interests are one among many sets of interests, no more important than the similar interests of others." And he would clearly say the same of the interests of one's family and friends (see *How Are We to Live?*, pp. 229–230).

own happiness, one much stronger than the other. As far as I can tell, I only have one desire for my own happiness and one desire for the happiness of strangers in India, and the former is much stronger than the latter. I would be very surprised if things were different for Peter Singer.

So it seems that, if moral language functions to express desires or preferences, then Singer's moral positions are largely *insincere*—in adopting the moral positions he does, he purports to express desires he does not in fact have. Perhaps we should say, instead, that moral language functions to express some other sort of non-cognitive mental state, such as moral emotions. But the same sort of problem will likely arise for any such state one chooses. I would find it very odd if, for example, Singer's moral *emotions* followed his ethical theory, so that he felt the same degree of disapproval towards failures to donate to famine relief that he felt towards murder.

Perhaps the non-cognitivist should abandon the idea that moral statements express any sort of mental state at all. Perhaps Singer should say that, in taking the ethical positions he does, he is simply telling people to behave in certain ways. But, if the above points stand, this is scarcely less strange. It would be quite odd for Singer to be telling us to behave in certain ways if he had no corresponding mental state, such as a desire that we should so behave. Even if on some level, or to some degree, he wants us to behave in the ways he describes as ethical, it would be odd for him to issue these imperatives if they did not reflect what he most wanted overall.

Be that as it may, there is a second oddity in all of this. Even if Singer has the preferences that his moral statements supposedly express, it would be strange that the rest of us should be expected to take an interest in Peter Singer's preferences, or in the commands that Singer wishes to issue to us. This would be more understandable if the preferences Singer expresses were ones that most of us share. But of course that is not the case—if Singer has the sort of preferences we have been discussing, he must be among a very few people in the world who do.

Perhaps instead Singer would say that the preferences he expresses are ones that the rest of us *should* adopt. But what is the force of that "should"? Does it function merely to express another subjective preference of Singer's? If so, this does not seem to get us any further. Or is the claim perhaps that reason dictates that we adopt these preferences? But this would be to abandon Singer's non-cognitivist, Humean view, according to which reason alone cannot dictate any preferences. Or perhaps the claim is that, given the *rest* of our preferences, it would be most consistent for us also to adopt Singer's preferences. But this claim is very implausible. It is implausible that the set of moral views that best coheres overall with typical people's preferences (or moral preferences, or moral emotions) is one that permits bestiality and infanticide, demands organ-harvesting, treats animals and humans as equals, and treats failure to donate to charity as on a par with murder. Surely it is possible to construct a consistent set of values that comes closer to most people's preferences (moral and other preferences) than *that*.

How does Singer arrive at his utilitarianism? He tries to show that a utilitarian ethic results uniquely from the idea of ethics as a system of *impartial* rules of conduct, rules in terms of which actions could be justified to all members of society.[17] (An example of a *partial* ethic would be the rule: everyone must do what promotes *my* interests. This rule does not provide a basis on which conduct could be justified from anyone's point of view other than my own.) Now on the surface, it seems that there are many other ethical systems that are as impartial as utilitarianism. Conventional morality, including the aspects of it that Singer rejects, is impartial. Singer, however, wonders on what basis one could recommend the rules of conventional morality:

> One possibility is that whoever says that we ought to obey certain moral rules is merely expressing his or her subjective preference for obedience to these rules. *But then this preference should not, from an impartial point of view, count for any more than any other preferences of similar strength.* This desire for obedience to the rules must therefore be weighed against conflicting desires which are frustrated by obedience.[18]

At which point, Singer seems to suggest, we are thrown back to preference utilitarianism. He goes on to consider and reject the view that the rules of conventional morality are objective moral truths. Treating these as the only two ways in which one might put forward moral rules—either as subjective preferences or as putative objective truths—Singer concludes that we must embrace preference utilitarianism.

One objection to this reasoning is that the italicized sentence in the quotation above begs the question against non-utilitarian ethical theories; it simply assumes preference utilitarianism as the default way of adjudicating among conflicting preferences. Of more immediate interest for our purposes, however, is that Singer's reasoning in the quoted passage does not follow a non-cognitivist approach. On the non-cognitivist

---

[17] *The Expanding Circle*, pp. 100–111.
[18] *The Expanding Circle*, pp. 108–09, emphasis added.

picture, what one is doing in taking a moral stance is expressing *one's own* preferences (of a certain kind) as to how people should behave. The idea of weighing those preferences against the preferences of other people or animals does not come into it at all.[19] (Even if one had a preference for satisfying others' preferences, this would already be taken account of in one's expression of one's own preferences, so that one still would not have to weigh others' preferences *against one's own*.) Now while Singer himself might prefer that people should generally act so as to maximize preference-satisfaction of sentient beings (though as we have seen, even this is doubtful), it is obscure how his remarks could be expected to induce others to express a similar preference. On a non-cognitivist view, if I do not in fact experience a desire for utility-maximization, then, regardless of what others prefer, I cannot sincerely say that utility-maximization is right.

I do not think Singer's ethical claims are insincere. I think that they express his moral *beliefs*, rather than his desires or emotions. And so I think that non-cognitivism is false. Ethical non-cognitivism is ill-equipped to account for individuals, such as Peter Singer, who hold ethical positions that diverge, not only from the dictates of conventional morality, but also from their own personal feelings and desires.

3. Why Be Moral?

Singer's account of why one should be moral is, in essence, that adopting an ethical way of life can give one a sense of meaning in life, thereby leading to greater happiness. We are now in a position to see why this account is inadequate, given Singer's view of the content of ethics.

On Singer's view, ethics is incredibly demanding. Ethics demands that I give up the consumption of meat and the use of nearly all animal products; that I donate almost all of my money to charity; and in general that I sacrifice my interests and the interests of those I care about whenever I stand to produce a greater good for someone else by doing so. This leaves me with two alternatives. Either I behave ethically, or I do not. It seems clear that if I behave ethically according to Singer's standards, my life will be miserable; at any rate, it would be absurd to

---

[19] According to Hare, with whom Singer expresses much sympathy (see "R. M. Hare's Achievements in Moral Philosophy"), the preferences one expresses using moral language cannot be just any personal preferences; they must be universalizable. This does not affect the present point, however; it remains the case that they must be preferences *that one has*, if one is not simply being insincere.

suggest that this would be the way to maximize the satisfaction of my preferences. And indeed, probably no human being has ever come close to living ethically according to Singer's standards.

My other option, if I accept Singer's ethical perspective, is hypocrisy: I can fulfill my ostensible obligations only partially, or not at all. Recall that on Singer's view, when I fail in my obligation to give to famine relief, my behavior is comparable to that of a murderer. So on this alternative, I should regard myself as horribly immoral, on a par with how most people would see Ted Bundy.[20] It seems unlikely that this, either, is the route to maximizing my own happiness and desire-satisfaction in general. And it is unclear that fulfilling my ostensible obligations *partially* gives me much of an advantage here—perhaps it would enable me to be comparable to a murderer of fifty people a year, rather than one hundred. It is unclear how much of a sense of fulfillment one can derive from leading a partially ethical life, given Singer's views as to what this amounts to.

Recall that on Singer's Humean conception of reasons, the only reason one can have for doing anything is that it would satisfy some preference one has. It seems that we must conclude that, for Singer, it is extremely irrational to adopt the ethical perspective. Nearly everyone— perhaps absolutely everyone—has much more reason to continue in our usual, relatively self-centered way of thinking and acting. This is not an *inconsistency* on Singer's part—he can consistently maintain that adopting the ethical perspective is morally required but irrational. But this makes his writings about ethics seem irrelevant, and it makes his conception of ethics implausible—a plausible conception of ethics, again, should imply that it is at least usually rational to be moral.

Let us return to the idea of giving oneself a sense of meaning or fulfillment in life. For the reasons just discussed, adopting the ethical perspective as Singer characterizes the latter does not seem an effective way of doing this. It seems that there are many alternatives that would be much better from the standpoint of satisfying our preferences. Many people find fulfillment in religious faith. Or devotion to their family. Or the study of philosophy. Or even stamp-collecting. None of these alternatives requires one to give up one's favorite foods, give away more than eighty percent of one's income, or sacrifice loved ones for the good of strangers.

---

[20] On Singer's view, of course, Ted Bundy is worse than me, because he killed many people *in addition* to failing to give to charity.

Singer does consider alternative ways of finding fulfillment, but he feels that a commitment to an ethical life "is the commitment with the firmest foundation," because "no amount of reflection will show a commitment to an ethical life to be trivial or pointless," as can happen with some other commitments.[21] Relatedly, he describes such ethical commitment as a matter of "identifying ourselves with the most objective point of view possible," and with taking "the point of view of the universe."[22]

This certainly sounds like something that might give meaning to one's life, even more so than the alternatives I have mentioned. The problem is that, on Singer's meta-ethical view, the most objective point of view possible, the point of view of the universe, is in fact entirely *non-ethical*—for as Singer also tells us, "Ethical truths are not written into the fabric of the universe";[23] they are merely a matter of subjective preferences. Singer's characterization of the ethical perspective as "the point of view of the universe" adverts to his view that, from the point of view of the universe, or from an objective point of view, no individual's interests are more important than any other individual's interests. Since ethics, on his view, takes account of all sentient beings' interests equally, it may fairly be said to embrace the point of view of the universe—or so it would seem. But suppose we add—as any good anti-objectivist about value should—that from the point of view of the universe, no individual's interests matter more than those of any other individual, *because nothing matters whatsoever*. To be sure, there is nothing in the objective facts that determines that my happiness, say, is more valuable than anyone else's; but then, there is allegedly nothing in the objective facts that determines that happiness is valuable at all. If I am truly to adopt the point of view of the universe, I should be a nihilist.

I, of course, do not believe that we have no reason to be moral. I think, with the rationalists, that moral beliefs already constitute reasons for action, so that no further reason for being moral is required. To explain this view to a Humean, we may compare it to what a Humean might say in response to the question, "Why should I act so as to satisfy my desires?" "That an action would satisfy a desire of yours," the Humean might say, "already inherently constitutes a reason for performing that action; hence, no *further* reason for satisfying desires is required." Just so, I maintain that the fact that some result is objectively good already

[21] *How Are We to Live?*, p. 218.
[22] *Practical Ethics*, p. 334.
[23] *How Are We to Live?*, p. 231.

inherently constitutes a reason for pursuing it, so no further reason for being moral is required. There is of course much more to be said about this than can be said here.[24] But if we adopt such an account, we have a straightforward explanation of why it is rational to behave morally even when doing so is not in our own interests. Furthermore, as an added reason for being moral, we can now embrace Singer's conception of the ethical perspective as "the point of view of the universe," together with his account of how adopting this perspective gives meaning to our lives. This does not resolve the problem of the demandingness of morality, but it does remove the threat of nihilism.

4. The Methods of Ethics

We turn at last to Singer's moral methodology. There are four salient aspects of Singer's approach to moral reasoning. First, Singer disapproves of the practice of testing moral theories against our intuitions about concrete situations, because he thinks that those intuitions are highly unreliable: "Even though it has always seemed to me so evidently erroneous, the view that we must test our normative theories against our intuitions has continued to have many adherents."[25]

His reason for thus rejecting particular case intuitions reveals a second important aspect of his methodology: Singer embraces intuitions about *moral relevance*, that is, intuitions about what sorts of factors may make a difference to the moral properties a thing has. In his approving discussion of Unger's *Living High and Letting Die*, Singer remarks thus on Unger's attempts to explain why typical people have the intuitions about concrete cases that they do:

> [Unger's] explanations are devastating for the view that we should take our intuitive responses to particular cases as the test of a sound theory, because the explanations show that our intuitive judgments are based on things that are obviously of no moral significance at all.[26]

For example, Unger had argued that our intuitions about whether and how strongly we are obligated to give aid to others are strongly influ-

---

[24] See my *Ethical Intuitionism*, Chapter 7.

[25] *Singer and His Critics*, p. 316; see also Singer's review of *Living High and Letting Die*. I take it that, as the rest of the context makes fairly clear, by "intuitions" here Singer has in mind specifically moral intuitions about concrete cases, such as the intuition that one should not kill the healthy patient in the Organ Harvesting example.

[26] *Singer and His Critics*, p. 316.

enced by the *conspicuousness* of the others' needs—that is, how well the needs attract and hold our attention.[27] Singer himself has argued that our intuitions about whether and how much we are obligated to assist others are biased by the physical proximity of those others, so that we think we have much stronger obligations to people who are in front of us than we do to people who are thousands of miles away.[28] He has also suggested that our intuitions about the wrongness of infanticide are biased by the cuteness of infants.[29] In all of these cases, Singer regards the factors allegedly influencing our intuitions as "obviously of no moral significance." "These factors just *cannot* be morally signficant," he says.[30] Singer does not see a need to, and does not *argue* that these factors are not morally significant; it just is obvious that they aren't. It is this that leads me to construe Singer as appealing to intuitions about moral significance.

Third, Singer also embraces one very general ethical intuition, the intuition that any being's interests are equally important, objectively, as any other being's (equally strong) interests (he calls this the principle of equal consideration of interests). Thus:

> [I]t would be best to forget all about our particular moral judgments, and start again from as near as we can get to self-evident moral axioms.[31]

> I cannot deny the plausibility of Henry Sidgwick's claim that it is a self-evident truth that from 'the point of view of the universe', the good of one individual is of no greater significance than the good of any other. . . . I have tried to argue that this, or something like it, is a common element in many developed ethical traditions, and that it is something that we come to understand through our capacity to reason.[32]

The talk of "the point of view of the universe" suggests that Singer is discussing an *objective* ethical principle, and the talk about self-evident truths, or axioms, suggests that Singer is discussing an ethical intuition.

---

[27] Singer, review of *Living High and Letting Die*, p. 184.

[28] *Practical Ethics*, p. 232.

[29] *Practical Ethics*, p. 170.

[30] *Singer and His Critics*, p. 317 (emphasis Singer's), referring to a list produced by Unger of factors allegedly influencing our intuitions. I have little doubt that Singer would say the same about such factors as conspicuousness, physical proximity, and cuteness.

[31] "Sidgwick and Reflective Equilibrium," p. 516.

[32] *Singer and His Critics*, p. 270. Compare *The Expanding Circle*, pp. 105–06; *How Are We to Live?*, p. 229; and *Practical Ethics*, p. 334.

Henry Sidgwick is among the most prominent figures in the history of ethical intuitionism, and in the above passages, Singer sounds strikingly like an intuitionist, as he is no doubt aware. I think, therefore, that there is a deep ambivalence in Singer's thought between his official non-cognitivist meta-ethics, and a lingering sympathy with an objectivist intuitionism in the tradition of Sidgwick.

Fourth and finally, despite what we have said above, there are some cases in which Singer seems perfectly happy to appeal to ethical intuitions about particular cases. The most notable is that of the Shallow Pond example. Singer appeals to the intuition that, when one sees a child drowning in a shallow pond, one is obligated to wade in and pull the child out, despite inconvenience to oneself. He does not *argue* that one ought to save the child; this is simply taken as obvious ("Would anyone deny that I ought to wade in and pull the child out?")[33] This intuition is then parlayed into an argument for an obligation to donate to famine relief—in fact, possibly the most celebrated and most forceful argument in all of Singer's work. Nor is this an isolated case. In discussion of the abortion issue, Singer makes important use of the intuition that it is not wrong to refrain from fertilizing an ovum.[34] In discussion of the moral status of animals, he invokes the intuition that it would be wrong to use retarded humans for painful experiments or for food.[35] In discussion of the law of double effect, he appeals to the intuition that it would be wrong to dump pollution into the nearest river, where harm to wildlife and other humans is a foreseen but not intended side effect of this.[36]

From this summary, some of the tensions in Singer's philosophy are no doubt apparent. Most obviously, his general stricture against appealing to intuitions about particular cases stands in conflict with his own use of such intuitions on many occasions. One might want to make something of the fact that he says we should not use such intuitions *to test an ethical theory*, rather than that we should not use such intuitions for any purpose at all. But in fact, Singer uses intuitions about cases to test ethical theories—in the examples listed above, he criticizes the law of double effect, the idea that potential persons have rights, and the thesis that only intelligent beings have rights by appeal to intuitions about cases. Moreover, the *reason* Singer gives for why one should not appeal to intuitions about particular cases is that our

---

[33] *Practical Ethics*, p. 229.
[34] *Practical Ethics*, p. 162.
[35] *Practical Ethics*, pp. 74–75.
[36] *Practical Ethics*, p. 210.

intuitions are systematically unreliable and biased by irrelevant factors; it is difficult to see how this can be reconciled with his own reliance on such intuitions in any of the cases in which he relies on them. In my view, Singer's use of particular intuitions has been extremely effective; his ethical views would be far less compelling if he were to argue for them by appealing solely to the abstract principle of equal consideration of interests, or to other similarly general principles. A deduction of the obligation to donate to famine relief solely from utilitarianism, without drawing the Shallow Pond analogy, would understandably have had very little impact on moral philosophers or others concerned with living an ethical life. So I think that what Singer should give up here is his disparagement of particular intuitions.

A second tension is between the rejection of particular intuitions and the acceptance of more abstract intuitions, such as intuitions about moral relevance and about the principle of equal consideration of interests. Granted, this is not inconsistent, but it is unclear why one sort of intuition should be thought more reasonable to rely on than another. Why should general intuitions be more reliable than particular intuitions? Perhaps Singer would say that he believes this because many particular intuitions have been refuted, or shown to be influenced by irrelevant factors, whereas this is not true of general intuitions. But that argument *assumes* that abstract intuitions, particularly those about moral relevance, are reliable. If one assumed our intuitions about cases to be reliable, one could as well argue that our intuitions about what is morally relevant must be systematically unreliable.

But the problems are most acute when we take into account Singer's anti-objectivist non-cognitivism. On that theory, again, moral judgments are solely a matter of feelings or preferences. On this view, I suggest, it is *incoherent* to claim that our intuitions about cases are either "biased" or "unreliable"; instead, we shall be forced to conclude that it is Singer's judgments about moral relevance that are wrong.

First, consider the notions of bias and reliability, as they apply to beliefs in general. Biases are influences on our belief-formation that detract from reliability, that tend to lead us astray. A reliable belief-forming method is one that tends to lead us to the truth. Thus, for example, we would say a scale is reliable if, when the object on the scale *in fact* weighs fifty pounds, the scale reads "fifty pounds"; when the object in fact weighs seventy-five pounds, it reads "seventy-five pounds"; and so on. If this is even roughly correct, then these notions cannot be applied to ethical intuitions, on a non-cognitivist view. A non-cognitivist cannot say, "A reliable way of forming moral beliefs is one such that, when an action is *in fact* wrong, the method will lead us to the belief that it is wrong." Nor can a non-cognitivist complain of our ethical intuitions being biased—he cannot say, "Our ethical intuitions are often affected by factors that *lead us away from the truth*." Again, for the non-cognitivist, the moral attitudes are all there is; there is nothing for them to correspond to, so there is no question of their leading us astray or being unreliable.

Thus, for example, suppose that Singer is correct that our intuitions about when we should help others are influenced by how far away those others are. This would simply be one influence among others on our emotions and preferences. In what sense would the preference for helping nearby people rather than far away people be any less "correct" than a preference for vanilla rather than chocolate? Or suppose Singer is right that our intuitions about the wrongness of infanticide are caused by evolutionary or cultural programming.[37] Again, what would be "wrong" about this? Indeed, it can be assumed that most if not all of our feelings and desires are caused by genes and culture—what else could they be caused by? So how is this supposed to undermine the corresponding ethical judgments or give us reason not to act on those desires? It almost seems as though Singer were assuming that ethical judgments should be based on reason, rather than subjective preferences!

What of the notion of "moral relevance"? For an *objectivist*, a "morally relevant" property is a property whose presence or absence makes a difference to the moral properties that a thing has—for instance, the property of "causing suffering" is morally relevant, because when an action causes suffering, this tends to make the action wrong. Now, what becomes of the notion of moral relevance if we remove the moral properties, leaving only *moral attitudes*? The best I can make of it is that for a non-cognitivist, a morally relevant property is a property that affects our moral attitudes.

If this is right, Singer's critique of concrete moral intuitions is incoherent. He complains that our moral attitudes are influenced by morally irrelevant features of situations—but the fact that a feature of a situation influences our moral attitudes *ipso facto* makes it morally relevant, if non-cognitivism is correct.

Perhaps Singer would say that by a "morally significant feature," he means a feature that influences *his*, Peter Singer's, moral attitudes. But then it would be unclear why others should be impressed with his cri-

---

[37] *Practical Ethics*, pp. 170–74.

tique of intuition—"We should not rely on ethical intuitions about particular cases, because most people's intuitions are influenced by factors that obviously do not influence *my* attitudes."

Or perhaps in calling a feature "morally irrelevant," Singer is simply expressing his disapproval of our being influenced in our moral attitudes by that feature. But again, it is unclear why others should take an interest in Singer's expression of disapproval. So suppose instead that Singer claims that most people's moral intuitions are influenced by factors that they themselves would disapprove of their being influenced by. But what would be the ethical upshot of this? If I approve of *A* because *A* has feature *F*, but I disapprove of my being thus influenced by *F*, what should I say about *A*—that *A* is good, or that it is bad? If I am a non-cognitivist, I should still say "*A* is good," because that is the sentence that expresses my actual attitude. Furthermore, it is quite dubious that most people would disapprove of their being influenced in the ways that they are. For example, Singer seems to regard our disproportionate concern for members of our own species as a bias—"speciesism," he calls it—yet it seems unlikely that most people would disapprove of their own speciesism.

I therefore see no way of sustaining anything like Singer's critique of particular ethical intuitions without introducing the assumption of a truth that is independent of our attitudes—in short, objective values.

5. A Revisionary Intuitionism?

Singer's normative ethical views, considered in themselves, are perfectly coherent. Many find them implausible, but, in my view, Singer has defended them with skill and plausibility. He should not give up any of his arguments in normative ethics because of the problems discussed above. Instead, he should embrace his latent intuitionist sympathies and renounce non-cognitivism.

Can an intuitionist really embrace the sort of ethical views that Singer has? Can an intuitionist, for example, coherently embrace utilitarianism? At least one intuitionist has—Henry Sidgwick—but there is reason to doubt that he was fully coherent in doing so. And I suspect that this may explain Singer's reluctance to accept the way of intuition. The line of thinking would be something like this:

"Ethical intuitionists believe that our intuitions are a source of at least *prima facie* justification for ethical claims. For example, our having the intuition that bestiality is wrong makes us justified in believing that bestiality is in fact wrong, unless and until specific grounds for doubting this appear. To be sure, such grounds for doubt may well be forthcoming, but they must themselves derive from other ethical intuitions, because intuitionists believe that intuition is the *sole* ultimate source of justification for ethical claims. As a result, it seems that when we reason in a manner consistent with intuitionism, we must seek an ethical system that coheres best, overall, with our ethical intuitions. While this may require occasional adjustments to our ethical views here and there, it seems unlikely, perhaps impossible, that we should arrive at a truly revisionary ethical view. Intuitionism represents a fundamentally conservative approach to ethics."

I disagree with this reasoning. For the reasons discussed in the previous section, I think it is the anti-objectivist views that demand a conservative ethics. I believe that intuitionism, in contrast, very likely leads to a *revisionary* ethics. To see how this is possible, notice two points. First, although intuitionism as I understand it takes intuition to be the sole ultimate source of justification for ethical claims, an intuitionist should *not* claim that only intuitions can function as *defeaters* for ethical claims. The fact that ethical belief E is a product purely of my cultural programming can rationally undermine E for me, given that I accept the notion of objective evaluative facts. This is because I know that beliefs produced purely by cultural programming are in general unreliable, I know that there are many other cultures with different beliefs, and I have no reason to think my culture would be more likely to get the ethical facts right than another culture. Similarly, "Many people have the intuition that ~E" can defeat my justification for believing that E, given that I have no reason to expect other people's intuition to be less reliable than my own. An intuitionist should therefore seek to build his ethics on intuitions that are neither culturally specific nor controversial. This can result in jettisoning a great many ethical intuitions.

Second, we may on reflection find ourselves more confident of some intuitions than others, and it might well turn out that many of our intuitions about specific moral issues conflict with other intuitions of which we are more confident. For instance, we may well find it more intuitively obvious that the physical proximity of a suffering person is morally irrelevant to whether we should help them, than that we are not obligated to give money to famine relief organizations.

All of these reflections are consistent with how Singer in fact reasons about ethics—in short, Singer argues about ethical issues in exactly the way an intuitionist should. This fact is sometimes obscured by his disagreements with other purveyors of intuition. In his debate with Singer,

Richard Posner appealed repeatedly to the unreflective "intuition" that human beings matter more than animals:

> I do not feel obliged to defend this reaction; it is a moral intuition deeper than any reason that could be given for it and impervious to any reason that you or anyone could give against it. Membership in the human species is not a "morally irrelevant fact," as the race and sex of human beings has come to seem. If the moral irrelevance of humanity is what philosophy teaches, and so we have to choose between philosophy and the intuition that says that membership in the human species is morally relevant, then it is philosophy that will have to go. [38]

This makes it seem that intuition stands in conflict with philosophical reflection, and that Singer must take the side of the latter against intuition. But Posner is a poor advocate for intuition. In fact the conflict between Posner's and Singer's methods is not one between intuition and philosophy. It is a conflict between an inflexible and parochial reliance on intuition, and a more reflective, more inclusive use of intuitions. It goes without saying that any intuitionist should prefer the latter.

Here is an analogy. Many scientists and philosophers of science agree that science is based entirely on observation. Let us suppose this is true (if it is not, at least science is *mostly* based on observation). It does not follow from this that science will tell us the world is pretty much the way it appears, to casual observation, to be. On the contrary, science teaches us such things as that the sun is 1.3 million times larger than the Earth, that invisible force fields fill all of space, and that ordinary material objects are composed of tiny, colorless particles in rapid motion, with great spaces between them. None of these things are apparent to *casual* observation, yet all of these conclusions are adequately supported, indirectly, by observation. Imagine a philosopher insisting that the sun is obviously much smaller than the Earth, because he can just see this with his eyes, and "if we have to choose between observation and science, then it is science that will have to go." This philosopher would not be a good empiricist; he would merely be a dogmatist.

For the ethical intuitionist, intuition is to ethics what observation is to science. There is no general requirement that ethics should vindicate what appears, to casual consideration, to be correct. This is not to say that an ethicist may simply disregard intuitions that conflict with his theory. Just as scientists can explain why the sun falsely appears much

---

[38] From Posner's letter of June 12th in Singer and Posner, "Animal Rights."

smaller than it is and can support their theory with other observations, an ethicist should be able (perhaps with the help of psychologists) to explain why people have mistaken ethical intuitions and to support his theory with other intuitions.

None of this is to say that Singer is in fact correct in his normative ethical views. But there is no simple methodological consideration that precludes his justifying those views within an ethical intuitionist framework. Indeed, I believe it is only an intuitionist framework that enables us to appreciate Singer's unique contributions to normative ethics.

REFERENCES

Ayer, A.J. 1952. *Language, Truth, and Logic*. New York: Dover.

Huemer, Michael. 2005. *Ethical Intuitionism*. New York: Palgrave Macmillan.

Hume, David. 1992 [1739]. *A Treatise of Human Nature*. Buffalo: Prometheus.

Singer, Peter. 1974. Sidgwick and Reflective Equilibrium. *The Monist* 58, pp. 490–517.

———. 1981. *The Expanding Circle: Ethics and Sociobiology*. New York: Farrar, Straus, and Giroux.

———. 1993. *Practical Ethics*. Second edition. Cambridge: Cambridge University Press.

———. 1995. *How Are We to Live? Ethics in an Age of Self-Interest*. Amherst: Prometheus.

———. 1999a. A Response. In Dale Jamieson, ed., *Singer and His Critics* (Malden: Blackwell), pp. 269–335.

———. 1999b. Review of *Living High and Letting Die* by Peter Unger. *Philosophy and Phenomenological Research* 59, pp. 183–87.

———. 2001. Heavy Petting. *Nerve*, at nerve.com/Opinions/Singer/ heavyPetting/main.asp. Accessed August 1st, 2005.

———. 2002. R.M. Hare's Achievements in Moral Philosophy. *Utilitas* 14, pp. 309–317.

Singer, Peter, and Richard Posner. 2001. Animal Rights. *Slate* (June 2001), at: slate.msn.com/id/110101/entry/110109. Accessed August 1st, 2005.

Unger, Peter. 1996. *Living High and Letting Die: Our Illusion of Innocence*. New York: Oxford University Press.

Reply to Michael Huemer

PETER SINGER

My Ambivalence

Michael Huemer asserts that I am "officially" a non-cognitivist but that I sometimes argue more like an intuitionist. He thinks I should resolve this tension by dropping my non-cognitivism and becoming an intuitionist.

Am I a non-cognitivist? As evidence that I am, Huemer quotes me as saying that the universe has not been constructed in accordance with any plan, has no value inherent in it, independently of the existence of sentient beings, and that ethics is not part of its structure. The first two claims do not imply non-cognitivism. The first excludes only forms of objectivism that link ethics to the plans or commands of some divine creator. The second is compatible with those forms of objectivism that see value as related to the preferences, desires, attitudes or states of consciousness of sentient beings, not in the sense that our judgments of right and wrong are subjective preferences, but in the sense that what is objectively good is the satisfaction of preferences, or the existence of positive states of consciousness, and what is objectively bad is the opposite of one, or both, of these (Huemer acknowledges, in his section "Objectivism about Value," that the latter position is compatible with objectivism.) The third claim, that ethics is not part of the fabric of the universe, does take us closer to non-cognitivism, but for reasons that will become clear in the course of this response, I now would accept only a more nuanced statement of it. I am, in other words, ambivalent about non-cognitivism.[39] Hence I welcome the opportunity to consider Huemer's arguments that I

---

[39] As I have previously indicated when Frank Jackson asserted that I am a non-cognitivist. See my "A Response" in Dale Jamieson, ed., *Singer and His Critics* (Oxford: Blackwell, 1999), p. 269.

should be an objectivist rationalist intuitionist. His essay raises important philosophical issues and merits a full response.

The Content of My Ethics

Huemer begins with a very crude notion of non-cognitivism: "On a non-cognitivist construal, when Singer says it is seriously wrong to eat meat, what he is saying is roughly, 'Eating meat—ugh! Don't do it!!'"

This is the position advocated by the early non-cognitivists, A.J. Ayer and C.L. Stevenson, but many more sophisticated versions have been developed since. I am inclined to agree with R.M. Hare's view, according to which a moral judgment is a special form of prescription. As I have argued in several places—for example, in the first chapter of *Practical Ethics*—there is plenty of scope for argument about moral judgments. First, our judgments must be coherent and consistent. We can't, for example, simultaneously hold that all human life is of equal value, that human life begins at conception, and that it is acceptable to kill a fetus for reasons that do not justify killing an adult. If we find that we hold all of these views, then we have a problem that can only be overcome by giving up at least one of the trio. Just as an officer who gives inconsistent commands will leave his troops in a quandary, not knowing what to do, so inconsistent prescriptions are of no use in deciding how to act.

In addition to being coherent and consistent, moral judgments must be universalizable, and indeed universalizable in a special sense that means that we must be prepared to hold them after putting ourselves in the position of—and taking on the preferences of—all those affected by our actions. Huemer eventually gets to something like this answer, quoting a passage from *The Expanding Circle* that suggests it. He then accuses me of begging the question against non-utilitarians by treating their support for obedience to moral rules as just another preference, rather than some objective moral truth. That accusation overlooks the fact that the sentences Huemer quote begin with a phrase indicating that here I am discussing "one possibility." In the paragraph that immediately follows the quoted sentences, I go on to consider the other possibility, that the rules are valid independently of any preferences. I reject that possibility because "it unnecessarily imports the puzzling idea of an objective moral reality into an area of human life which, as we have seen, can be explained in a more natural and less mysterious way."[40]

---

[40] *The Expanding Circle,* Farrar, Straus, and Giroux, p. 109.

Huemer then argues that the requirement to take on the preferences of others is incompatible with non-cognitivsm. Again, he seems to be operating with a crude definition of non-cognitivism. Here I would direct the reader to Huemer's footnote 19, which notes that for Hare, "the preferences one expresses using moral language cannot be just any personal preferences; they must be universalizable." Actually for Hare moral judgments don't express preferences. As already noted, they are prescriptions, and have only an indirect relationship to my preferences. The misunderstanding of Hare's position becomes more serious when Huemer goes on to say: "This does not affect the present point, however; it remains the case that they must be preferences *that one has*, if one is not simply being insincere." But the fact that moral judgments must be universalizable means that they must be prescriptions we are willing to make *for all possible circumstances*. Since "possible" here includes hypothetical cases, to be able to make a moral judgment one has to put oneself in the position of all those affected by the prescription. The prescription one can accept about, say, the obligation to aid the poor, is naturally very different if one makes it only from the position of a comfortably-off person in an industrialized nation, or if one also considers whether one would make it if one were living in poverty in Mozambique. So it is not surprising that one's universalizable prescriptions may bear little resemblance to one's non-universalized preferences.

The most interesting response Huemer could make to this would be to assert that so strong a notion of universalizability cannot be defended by an appeal to moral language, and therefore goes beyond non-cognitivism. It must, instead, be grounded in some claim about the requirements of reason, and it presupposes a view of reason that goes beyond Hume's instrumentalist view of reason as the slave of the passions. Had Huemer said this, I would have been in sympathy with him—it is, in fact what I attempt to argue in the pages of *The Expanding Circle* that follow the sentences Huemer has quoted. These pages reflect "Singer the objectivist" rather than "Singer the non-cognitivist." I made a similar argument, but with more explicit reference to Hare's non-cognitivism, in "Reasoning towards Utilitarianism," my contribution to *Hare and Critics*.[41] Still, Huemer has not excluded the possibility of a form of non-cognitivism that recognizes morality as an area of discourse with constraints on the kind of attitudes that count as moral attitudes. The issue then is what the basis of that constraint might be.

---

[41] "Reasoning towards Utilitarianism," in D. Seanor and N. Fotion, eds., *Hare and Critics* (Oxford: Clarendon, 1988), pp. 147–159.

Why Be Moral?

Before I discuss the fundamental issues Huemer raises in this section, I should correct his repeated statements that, on my view "when I fail in my obligation to give to famine relief, my behavior is comparable to that of a murderer." The reference Huemer cites the first time he says this is to *Practical Ethics*, pp. 222–29. But the section of Chapter 8 that begins on p. 222 is headed "The Moral Equivalent of Murder?"—and the question mark is not a typo. Over the next seven pages I examine five differences between killing and allowing to die, in the context of absolute poverty and overseas aid, and conclude that among these are differences that "show that not aiding the poor is not to be condemned as murdering them; it could, however, be on a par with killing someone as a result of reckless driving, which is serious enough."[42] So Huemer should have said that on my view, "when I fail in my obligation to give to famine relief, my behavior is comparable to that of someone who kills someone as a result of reckless driving." But then he couldn't have made his dramatic claim that when I fail to give almost all I earn to famine relief, I have to regard myself as most people regard a serial killer like Ted Bundy.

It also isn't correct that the only alternative to doing everything that my highly demanding ethic requires is hypocrisy. If I were to say that we ought not to spend anything on luxuries when others are starving, while I spend money on luxuries *and* pretend that I do nothing wrong, that would be hypocritical. But I have often acknowledged that I do not do everything I believe I ought to be doing. That is certainly a moral failing, but hypocrisy doesn't seem the right term for it.

Huemer goes on to argue that without objectivism, taking the point of view of the universe doesn't get you anywhere except nihilism. We can't say, he thinks, that happiness is valuable. But if I value my own happiness, and recognize that when I make a moral judgment, universalizability requires me to give the same ultimate weight to the happiness of a stranger that I give to my own happiness, then I will treat the happiness of strangers as valuable, even if its value is not somehow written into the structure of the universe beyond the processes that have led me to the judgment I make.

Huemer concludes this section by presenting his alternative to the Humean view. According to Huemer, the fact that some result is

---

[42] *Practical Ethics,* p. 228.

objectively good "already inherently constitutes a reason for pursuing it, so no further reason for being moral is required." Aware, perhaps, of the likely demand from followers of David Hume for some further explanation of how this can be, given that not everyone desires to do what is objectively good, Huemer attempts to pre-empt such a response by suggesting that one can equally well ask the Humean: "Why should I act so as to satisfy my desires?" He imagines the Humean responding that the fact that an action would satisfy a desire "already inherently constitutes a reason for performing that action" and no further reason is required. If the Humean can say that, Huemer seems to be arguing, why can't he say the same about the fact that an action is objectively good? But this response fails to grasp exactly what Hume's position is, and why it is so difficult to refute. Hume headed the section of his *A Treatise of Human Nature* in which he discusses the role of reason in conduct "Of the Influencing Motives of the Will." As that heading suggests, his concern is about what kinds of things can influence our will, and thereby, our actions. Only desires—or as he calls them, passions—can do that. So it is not as if we recognize that we have a desire to, say, help a stranger, and then say to ourselves "Now I have a reason to help a stranger, so I will do so." On the contrary, Hume says, "reason alone can never produce any action, or give rise to volition." So the question isn't what we have reason to do, the question is what can possibly move us to action. Desires can, and beliefs alone cannot. That's a plausible view, for while it is possible to regard the fact that an action is objectively good as a reason for doing it, we then still need an explanation of how this reason actually connects with anyone's will.

Here's an illustration of the problem. Let's accept Huemer's view that some things are objectively good—for example, let's suppose that the relief of great suffering at a small cost to oneself is objectively good. We then inform a friend of ours, let's call him David, of this fact. He replies:

> I know I can relieve the suffering of this stranger at a very small cost to myself, and I know that this would be an objectively good thing to do, indeed it would be the objectively morally right thing to do. But I don't care about the stranger, nor about doing what is morally right. I just want to live as interesting, satisfying and fulfilling a life as I can. So why should I do what is objectively right?

The response "Just because it is objectively right" fails to engage with what David is telling us. It won't motivate him to act. Suppose, on the other hand, we reply:

You may think that you don't care about this stranger, but you do care about living a satisfying life. If you start by helping this stranger and then do more to relieve suffering generally, and live in a way that can be defended from an impartial point of view, your life will become more meaningful and satisfying for you and you will face each day with new purpose. As you get older, you will be able to look back on your life and feel that you have not wasted it.

True or false, this at least engages with what David has said. If we can convince David that it is true, he will be motivated to help the stranger. So there is a difference between an appeal to someone's desires, and an appeal to objective goodness, or to the objective reasons for action to which such goodness is supposed to give rise.

Many people are not motivated to act by objective reasons. Are they simply irrational? With standard cases of irrationality, we can show people where their error lies. If they are sane and of at least average intelligence, they will be able to recognize and acknowledge that they have made a mistake. But if someone is selfish and doesn't care about objective goodness or objective reasons for action, what mistake in reasoning can we point out to them that they would be able to recognize and acknowledge as a mistake?

Even if some people are "irrational" in the sense of not being motivated by objective reasons for action, it would still be important to find considerations that will persuade them to relieve the suffering of strangers. For example, we could try to make such people more emotionally attuned to the suffering of others, or to show them that it is in their interests to be concerned about anyone's suffering. Without something of this sort, establishing claims about what is objectively good will make no difference to how they act.

Now that we have seen the difficulty for the kind of rationalism that Huemer advocates, I have to admit that a Humean view of the limited role of reason, when combined with a demanding ethical view like mine, also faces a problem. Hume, like Shaftesbury, Butler, and Hutcheson, his predecessors in the moral sense school of ethics, stressed the benevolent and virtuous side of our nature, and the idea that we would be more likely to find happiness by living a virtuous life. In that way the conflict between our preferences and what morality requires of us was ameliorated, if not eliminated. But Hume also took a more conservative view of morality than I do. The following passage shows nicely how he harmonized our natural preferences and our duties:

A man naturally loves his children better than his nephews, his nephews better than his cousins, his cousins better than strangers, where every thing else is equal. Hence arise our common measures of duty, in preferring the one to the other. Our sense of duty always follows the common and natural course of our passions.[43]

Hume also held that "there is no such passion in human minds as the love of mankind, merely as such, independent of personal qualities, of services, or of relation to ourself."[44] Hume's pre-Darwinian observations can now be seen to accord remarkably well with what evolutionary theory would lead us to expect, especially in regard to the strength of preference for one's kin varying in accordance with the degree of genetic relationship. If he is right, then it is reasonable to ask, as Huemer does, how I can base a much more demanding ethic on his theory of the role of reason in action.

Let's be clear, however, about the implications of accepting Hume's position and my demanding ethic. It does *not* follow, as Huemer maintains, that "it is extremely irrational to adopt the ethical perspective." Although Hume famously wrote: "'Tis not contrary to reason to prefer the destruction of the whole world to the scratching of my finger," he made it clear that he was not saying that self-interest is more rational than altruism when he continued: "'Tis not contrary to reason to choose my total ruin, to prevent the least uneasiness of an Indian or person wholly unknown to me." On Hume's view, having these preferences, or any other preferences, is not a matter of reason at all, unless some faulty reasoning is involved: "a passion must be accompany'd with some false judgement, in order to its being unreasonable." So if some people prefer to follow my arguments and give almost all their money to aiding those in great need, there is nothing at all irrational about this. Equally, giving away money to those in great need is not rationally required.

Still, it may be said, if the demanding morality I espouse conflicts with what most people would prefer to do, and if I cannot argue that it is irrational for them to do what they would prefer to do, what is the significance of arguing that morality is so demanding?

I grant that there is a problem here, but it seems to me no greater than the problem involved in telling people that they are rationally required

---

[43] David Hume, *A Treatise of Human Nature*, ed. L.A. Selby-Bigge (Oxford: Clarendon, 1978), Bk. III, Pt. 2, Sec. i.
[44] *A Treatise of Human Nature*, Bk. III, Pt. 2, Sec. i.

to do what is objectively good, when this concept of practical reason has no necessary connection with what they want to do, or with anything at all that they care about. Aren't the rationalists and non-cognitivists really all in the same boat here? Or if not in exactly the same boat, at least in boats that are equally unable to get to their destination. To stretch the metaphor, we could say that in the rationalist boat the person at the helm is steering the wheel in the right direction, but the link between the steering wheel and the rudder is broken, so the movement of the boat is unrelated to the direction in which the steering wheel is turned. In the noncognitivist boat the steering is working properly, but the person at the helm is unpredictable and may steer in one of several directions. Some of these directions are better than others, but she is unlikely to steer exactly in the right direction. In both boats, therefore, getting to the right destination will require some aid from circumstances beyond the control of the person at the helm.

We are now facing one of the deepest problems in moral philosophy. To solve it, various strategies have been tried. Here are some of the main ones:

Linking Morality and Motivation

1. An Objectively Rational Morality

This is the position Huemer holds. On this view, it is rational to do the act that is objectively right, or that results in the most objective goodness. As we have just seen, this doesn't solve the problem because the problem is one of motivation, and objective reaons will not be motivating for everyone.

2. Ethical Egoism

We could accept that most people are self-interested, and argue that since we cannot recommend a morality that is not linked to the actual motivations people have, the only possible morality is one that holds that it is ethical for a person to do whatever is in his or her own interest. The content of such a morality will vary according to whether or not we see self-interest as linked with, or opposed to, such things as concern for others. (Although I am not an ethical egoist, in *How Are We to Live?* I sought to answer the egoist's challenge, invoking both ancient and modern arguments for linking self-interest, broadly conceived, with commitment to concern for others. Some readers have thought this attempt persuasive. Others, like Huemer, have not.)

3. Humean Morality

We could soften our moral demands to the point at which they coincide with what most people want to do anyway, or at least would want to do, given some social encouragement and sanctions for noncompliance. This is, very roughly, Hume's solution, and perhaps Narveson has some sympathy with it too, although in some passages of his essay in this volume he seems closer to ethical egoism. Judith Lichtenberg's contribution to this volume works within the broad framework of natural and social virtues, enhancing the social side of it by focusing on the need to arrange social institutions so as to encourage actions that lead to better results.

4. Humean Ideally Rational Choice

Richard Brandt held that the rational thing to do is the action that would most satisfy our desires, provided that we were choosing under ideal conditions of rational choice.[45] These include full information, and in Brandt's view, that means we must also understand the nature and origin of our desires—in other words, we should undergo a form of cognitive psychotherapy before we make the choice. We should also be fully aware of the consequences of our choice for everyone affected, by imaginatively putting ourselves in their position. Under these conditions, Brandt argues that most of us would give much more weight to the serious interests of others than we do in our everyday lives.

5. An Impartial Morality, Not Rationally Required

This position understands morality in terms of judgments that we can universalize or accept from an impartial perspective. To this can be added other requirements of rationality, for instance consistency and the avoidance of arbitrary distinctions. This is the view I have defended. It provides scope for reason and argument within ethics, but it leaves open the question of why one should be interested in, or committed to, acting only on those judgments that we are prepared to accept from an impartial perspective.

Does the fact that the impartial perspective can be rejected without opening oneself to the charge of irrationality make ethics irrelevant, as Huemer charges? That will depend on whether a significant number of

---

[45] R.B. Brandt, *A Theory of the Good and the Right* (Oxford: Oxford University Press, 1979). See also Michael Smith, *The Moral Problem* (Oxford: Blackwell, 1994).

people are interested in acting in ways that they can prescribe univerally, or justify impartially. If, as Hare and others have argued, putting yourself in the position of others is a defining characteristic of moral discourse, then the prevalence of such discourse is itself evidence that many people are interested in acting in ways that can be justified from this perspective.[46] For those who question whether to take this perspective, we can appeal to the arguments that are also available to the ethical egoist to link self-interest with concern for others. The difference is that for the egoist, what it is ethical for a person to do will depend on the success of such arguments, whereas for my position, the success or failure of that argument does not change what it is ethical to do, but rather what it is rational for a self-interested person to do. Accepting or rejecting the ethical perspective is not an all-or-nothing thing. It is possible to have a strong, but not overriding, desire to act ethically. I know many people like this. Here is one, whom I'll call Helen. Helen accepts that, given the needs of the poor, she is morally justified in keeping for herself only what she requires to meet her basic needs. She also thinks it is important to do what is right, but she really wants to go hiking amidst spectacular mountain scenery, which involves spending money on travel, accommodation, and hiking equipment. She doesn't think that her desire to go hiking provides a moral justification for spending this money, but she also doesn't think that it is irrational for her to spend it. She has some other similarly strong desires that she also goes to some expense to satisfy, without considering this defensible from an impartial perspective. The upshot is that she gives a substantial part of her income to agencies working to overcome poverty, but she spends substantially more on herself than she can defend morally. In these circumstances, Helen's ethical views are clearly relevant to her actions.

Huemer suggests that, on my view, partially fulfilling my ethical obligations "would enable me to be comparable to a murderer of fifty people a year, rather than one hundred." He wryly comments that it "is unclear how much of a sense of fulfillment one can derive" from such a perspective. I've already pointed out that this misrepresents my view, and that a better comparison with not giving to poverty relief would be killing people by reckless driving. Suppose, then, that I live in a society in which most people drive so recklessly that they kill one hundred

---

[46] On this, see my response to Marcus Düwell in this volume. See also Mane Hajdin, *The Boundaries of Moral Discourse* (Chicago: Loyola University Press, 1994), Chapter 2. Hajdin uses the term "the shoehorn maneuver" for putting yourself in the position of others, and offers a more precise formulation of it.

people a year. This is considered normal, and few people suggest that there is anything wrong with this level of recklessness, or that those who drive in this manner are not decent people. By hard work and great effort—making a real sacrifice, in comparison to the blithely indifferent recklessness of most of my fellow-citizens—I manage to drive more carefully and kill only fifty people per year. Perhaps I can then take some satisfaction in knowing that there are fifty people alive who, without my efforts, would be dead.

Helen's way of living is not so different, in terms of what she gives and what she spends on herself, from Garrett Cullity's proposal, in *The Moral Demands of Affluence*, that we are obliged to give until we reach the point at which, if we gave more, we would be depriving ourselves of "intrinsically life-enhancing goods."[47] This would mean, presumably, that Helen is not violating her obligations if she continues to spend money on hiking trips in the mountains, because hiking in the mountains is definitely life-enhancing for her. I doubt, however, that this expenditure can be defended from an impartial perspective, for the money Helen spends on a single hiking trip could probably save the life of at least one person dying from a preventable, poverty-related disease—and that has to be more important than her hiking trip. On the other hand, Cullity thinks that what is morally required is also rationally required. He and I could agree, therefore, that no one is rationally required to sacrifice intrinsically life-enhancing goods in order to save a stranger, while disagreeing on whether this is morally required.[48]

The Methods of Ethics

Huemer accurately describes the first aspect of my moral methodology, my rejection of the idea that we can test moral theories by seeing if they clash with our intuitions about what we ought to do in concrete situations. The existence of such a clash is, at best, an *ad hominem* argument. If I am a utilitarian with the intuition that lying is always wrong, I have a problem, but that doesn't mean I have to reject utilitarianism. I could also reject the intuition.

The second aspect of my moral methodology to which Huemer refers, my appeal to intuitions about whether something is morally relevant, is an instance of such an *ad hominem* argument. If Peter Unger's

---

[47] Garrett Cullity, *The Moral Demands of Affluence* (Oxford: Clarendon, 2004).
[48] For further discussion, see my review of Cullity's book in *Philosophy and Phenomenological Research* 75 (September 2007).

account of the factors that generate our intuitive responses to the cases he discusses in *Living High and Letting Die* is right, few people will want to defend the *moral* relevance of these factors. Similarly, I believe, few people will want to defend the moral relevance of physical proximity in determining our obligations to assist someone who is in danger (as long as we are careful to isolate physical proximity from factors like the probability of success). If people are prepared to defend the moral relevance of the factors that I say "are obviously of no moral significance at all," then different arguments will need to be produced, on both sides.

The third aspect of my moral methodology, Huemer claims, is my acceptance of "one very general ethical intuition," the principle of equal consideration of interests. Here Huemer touches upon another central unresolved issue in my metaethics. On what basis do I hold the principle of equal consideration of interests? One possibility is, following R.M. Hare, to derive it, at least as a provisional or default position, from the requirement that moral language be universalizable.[49] The other is to follow Sidgwick and see it as a self-evident truth.[50] In the passage that Huemer quotes I take the latter course. On the other hand in the opening chapter of *Practical Ethics* I take a line that is closer to Hare, suggesting that the idea of putting yourself in the place of others is a feature of a particular kind of discourse, in which we seek to justify our conduct to others, and in order to do so, have to take a point of view that they can share.[51]

If, with Hare, we take the view that universalizability is a requirement of moral discourse, but nothing more, then we have to admit that the logic of amoralists who reject moral language entirely and refuse to universalize, cannot be faulted. (Although we can, of course, fault them on moral, and perhaps also prudential, grounds.) Given this, we may find the Sidgwickian alternative more attractive, for if the principle of rational benevolence is a requirement of reason, that would seem to ˙able us to show why amoralists are irrational. But in fact Sidgwick ˙ not claim that much. He acknowledges that:

˙goist strictly confines himself to stating his conviction that he ought
˙ own happiness or pleasure as his ultimate end, there seems no

ˮom and Reason* (Oxford: Oxford University Press, 1963), and
ˮrendon, 1981); and see also Mane Hadjin, *The Boundaries
ˮgain, see my response to Marcus Düwell in this volume.
of Ethics, p. 382.

opening for any line of reasoning to lead him to Universalistic Hedonism as a first principle; it cannot be proved that the difference between his own happiness and another's happiness is not for him all-important.[52]

All that can be done in this case, Sidgwick says, is to try to find reasons that will appeal to the egoist's own interests. It is only when "the Egoist puts forward, implicitly or explicitly, the proposition that his happiness or pleasure is Good, not only for him but from the point of view of the Universe" that the argument for the principle of rational benevolence will succeed. In the concluding chapter of *The Methods of Ethics,* Sidgwick returns to this problem, but is unable to make further progress towards reconciling egoism and utilitarianism, because

> It would be contrary to Common Sense to deny that the distinction between any one individual and any other is real and fundamental, and that consequently "I" am concerned with the quality of my existence as an individual in a sense, fundamentally important, in which I am not concerned with the quality of the existence of other individuals: and this being so, I do not see how it can be proved that this distinction is not to be taken as fundamental in determining the ultimate end of rational action for an individual.[53]

Thus although Sidgwick writes of rational axioms and Hare about the meaning of the moral terms, they agree that consistent amoralists or egoists cannot be convicted of irrationality. That agreement may explain why I have been unable to make up my mind between Sidgwick's intuitionism and Hare's non-cognitivism. For although the metaphysical implications of their positions diverge profoundly, if there are no practical differences between them, the choice is less momentous than it may at first appear.

Finally, the fourth and last aspect of my moral methodology that Huemer mentions is my appeal to intuitions in particular cases, for instance the intuition that we should save the child drowning in the shallow pond. But here I am again making only an *ad hominem* argument, an appeal to those who do hold this view and are not ready to give it up. If someone does say "I don't think we would do anything wrong if we decide not to save the child because we don't want to ruin our shoes" then this particular argument doesn't work. The same is true for the other appeals to intuitions in particular cases that Huemer mentions.

---

[52] *The Methods of Ethics,* p. 420.
[53] *The Methods of Ethics,* p. 498.

How Revisionary an Intuitionism?

When Huemer turns, in the final section of his essay, to the need for a revisionary intuitionism, he comes close to views I have put forward in my most recent published work on this topic, which presumably appeared too late for Huemer to take into account in his own essay.[54] In some ways that work lends support to his claim that I am an intuitionist of sorts, for in it I again express tentative support for Sidgwickian rational axioms of a highly general kind. But at the same time my arguments go beyond Huemer's in the extent of the intuitions that I consider unreliable, and so threaten to undermine even an intuitionism as revisionary as the one he holds.

Huemer writes: "The fact that ethical belief E is a product purely of my cultural programming can rationally undermine E for me, given that I accept the notion of objective evaluative facts. This is because I know that beliefs produced purely by cultural programming are in general unreliable." From this he concludes: "An intuitionist should therefore seek to build his ethics on intuitions that are neither culturally specific nor controversial." Cultural programming, however, is not the only source of unreliable intuitions. Recent research in psychology and neuroscience has suggested that some intuitions may be part of our evolutionary inheritance.[55] They may then be universal, rather than culturally specific, but that doesn't make them any more reliable as a guide to any kind of moral truth. There is no reason to believe that moral attitudes that enhanced the reproductive fitness of our ancestors, and are therefore now something we are all born with, are a source of objective knowledge of moral truth. In contrast to the case of evolved senses like sight or hearing, it is difficult to think that the best explanation of our evolved intuitions would need to refer to objective moral truths. Moreover these intuitions may be disastrous in our present, greatly altered circumstances. Even if the intuitions are still fitness-enhancing, however, since evolution has no moral direction, that says nothing about whether we ought to follow them.

---

[54] "Ethics and Intuitions," *Journal of Ethics* 9:3–4 (October 2005), pp. 331–352.

[55] See Jonathan Haidt, "The Emotional Dog and Its Rational Tail: A Social Intuitionist Approach to Moral Judgment," *Psychological Review* 108 (2001), pp. 814–834; Joshua D. Greene, R. Brian Sommerville, Leigh E. Nystrom, John M. Darley, and Jonathan D. Cohen, "An fMRI Investigation of Emotional Engagement in Moral Judgment," *Science* 293 (2001), pp. 2105–08; and Joshua Greene and Jonathan Haidt, "How (and Where) Does Moral Judgment Work?" *Trends in Cognitive Sciences* 6 (2002), pp. 517–523. More recent work can be found on the websites of each of these researchers.

I shall conclude by quoting the final paragraph of my paper on "Ethics and Intuitions," since this states my current views on the fundamental meta-ethical issues Huemer has raised:

> In the light of the best scientific understanding of ethics, we face a choice. We can take the view that our moral intuitions and judgments are and always will be emotionally based intuitive responses, and reason can do no more than build the best possible case for a decision already made on non-rational grounds. That approach leads to a form of moral skepticism, although one still compatible with advocating our emotionally-based moral values and encouraging clear thinking about them. Alternatively, we might attempt the ambitious task of separating those moral judgments that we owe to our evolutionary and cultural history from those that have a rational basis. This is a large and difficult task. Even to specify in what sense a moral judgment can have a rational basis is not easy. Nevertheless, it seems to me worth attempting, for it is the only way to avoid moral skepticism.

I cannot here carry out the ambitious program outlined in the second part of this paragraph, but I hope it is sufficiently clear what kind of distinctions I would draw. For instance, the fact that we intuitively regard incest as wrong is not in itself a reason to reject incest and regard it as immoral. Incest will be wrong when it leads to reproduction, because of the higher risk of abnormalities in the children, and that, no doubt, is why we intuitively reject it. We may also be able to find other reasons for considering incest to be wrong, for instance, where it involves the exploitation of a child by a parent. But what of sex between adult siblings who use reliable forms of contraception?[56] The intuition that incest is *always* wrong may be one we owe to our evolutionary history, rather than to rational reflection on what sex between adult siblings involves. On the other hand, acting altruistically to strangers we are unlikely to come into contact with again is something that evolutionary psychology struggles to explain. If, after putting ourselves in the position of all those affected by our actions, we conclude that it is our obligation to act altruistically to strangers, this judgment looks very much like a judgment that has a rational basis, rather than one that is the result of our evolutionary history.

---

[56] The example is suggested by Jonathan Haidt, Fredrik Björklund, and Scott Murphy, "Moral Dumbfounding: When Intuition Finds No Reason," unpublished manuscript, Department of Pschology, University of Virginia, 2000.

12

Philosophical Presuppositions of *Practical Ethics*

MARCUS DÜWELL

0. Introduction[1]

In my contribution to this volume I primarily want to discuss some philosophical presuppositions of Peter Singer's approach. But before doing so I want (1) to briefly describe Singer's impact on the bioethical debate and (2) to give a short comment on the debate about Singer in the German-speaking countries. Then I want (3) to give an outline of his philosophical position in *Practical Ethics*, (4) to discuss the Principle of equal consideration of interests, (5) to consider the 'Sanctity of life' Doctrine and the criticism of speciesism, (6) to look at the role of the state and international justice, and (7) to make some final remarks.

1. Singer and the Bioethical Debate

Utilitarianism plays a prominent role in contemporary bioethical debates. Its significance in bioethics is even stronger than in the more fundamental discussions in meta-ethics and moral philosophy. In the 1960s and 1970s differences between several versions of utilitarianism were discussed. In the more recent debate, we more often find attempts to combine basic themes of utilitarianism with elements of other traditions in

---

[1] I want to thank Klaus Steigleder for suggestions on an earlier version of this article and Frederike Kaldwaij who translated parts of this paper from a German text.

moral philosophy, so we see approaches that combine a utilitarian framework with elements of rights-theories, liberalism, rational choice approaches, or virtue theory.[2] That is one of the reasons why it's often not easy to classify different approaches as utilitarian approaches.

In classical utilitarianism, when moral principles were derived from the utility of all, this was usually understood in terms of common welfare. Sometimes 'utility' has been interpreted in a hedonistic sense. Moreover, some utilitarian theorists were prepared to demand sacrifices of and harms to the few for the sake of the happiness of the many. Many extreme positions have negatively affected the image of utilitarianism. In the more recent debates the 'utility' that is to be promoted is usually not understood in a purely hedonistic way. Many utilitarians attempt to integrate the concern for the common good into more comprehensive theories of justice, in which the rights of individuals also play a central role.[3] The greatest-happiness principle is rarely proposed as a moral principle without further specification.

That utilitarian theorists play a prominent role in bioethics can partly be explained by the fact that the exploration of concrete moral problems has always been emphasized in the utilitarian tradition. Utilitarianism has a strong tradition of dealing with very concrete moral and political debates, while in practical continental philosophy or in analytic meta-ethics there often have been a cautious attitude towards 'applied' issues. A lot of scholars of meta-ethics considered that we should only analyze moral language and discuss the possibility of moral knowledge; topics of applied ethics were merely employed as examples for illustrative purposes. Other approaches in practical philosophy wanted to restrict themselves to topics like the concepts of the political and historical subjects. In all these discussions there was great reticence concerning concrete moral or political issues. Only academic colleagues in the theology departments had a strong tradition of dealing with the casuistry of controversial moral cases.[4] When the bioethical debates started in the 1970s, utilitarians and theologians were better prepared to discuss these new challenges than other philosophers.

When utilitarianism entered the bioethical debate, it was not in the first place classical utilitarian concerns for the common welfare that were of central importance in their investigations. The debate about the

---

[2] Several important texts are collected in Scheffler 1988.
[3] See for instance Brandt 1983.
[4] See for example the influence of bioethicists with a theological background, like Albert Johnson, Paul Ramsey, and Warren T. Reich.

moral status of, especially, embryos and animals—the question of what kind of features are morally significant in determining moral status—and the criticism of the so-called *sanctity of life doctrine* were much more central. In consequence of the bioethical issues that arose in the context of new medical technologies, utilitarians have become—in their own view[5] as well as that of their opponents—the public spokespersons of a challenge to traditional conceptions of morality. The utilitarian emphasis on the no-harm principle implied, firstly, that the pain of animal should be of moral importance, secondly, that the life of human beings only deserves moral protection if these human beings are capable of feeling pain, and finally, that it should be morally permitted to end a human life when it is completely dominated by pain.

Many saw in Peter Singer the spokesperson of utilitarianism, which, with regard to the more fundamental philosophical debates about utilitarianism, is questionable. But for us it's not so important to discuss here to what extent Singer has to be seen as a representative of utilitarianism. Singer argues that the interests of all beings who are capable of having interests deserve equal moral consideration, and that we only owe moral consideration towards those beings. This moral principle conflicts with the doctrine that *human* life is sacred and inviolable. In fact the doctrine combines—from Singer's point of view—two elements: the prejudice that member of the human species should morally be treated differently than member of other species and that the life of members of this species should be inviolable. Singer claims that this view lies at the heart of our traditional ethics. In the context of increased technical possibilities for prolonging life and of our increased scope for intervening in human life in its early forms (contraception, abortion, prenatal diagnosis, embryo experimentation), Singer can offer lot of examples that seem to demonstrate, that the so-called 'sanctity of life' doctrine leads to absurd consequences in medical practice.

The dualist opposition between preference utilitarianism and traditional ethics has played an important role in the public perception of bioethics, in Central Europe as well as in other parts of the world. The impression was formed that the primary task of bioethics should be discussion of the 'sanctity of life'. This has resulted in hostile confrontations between utilitarian bioethicists on the one hand and representatives of the churches and the handicapped on the other. In such quarrels, the range of relevant bioethical positions is reduced to the alternatives:

---

[5] As an example, the subtitle of Singer 1994 is *The Collapse of Our Traditional Ethics*.

either one accepts the doctrine of 'sanctity of life' and then one is indiscriminately against abortion, reproductive medicine, active and passive euthanasia, cloning, and embryo research, or one opposes this doctrine and has no objections worth mentioning to all these developments. Especially in traditionally Catholic countries, like Italy, this dualistic view is very dominant; taking my cue from a famous mid-twentieth-century Italian film about the battle between a Catholic priest and the Communist mayor of his village, I would like to call it the 'Don-Camillo and Pepone' principle of bioethics. This dualistic perspective has it roots in a specific perception of the basic theoretical difference in bioethics, that Joseph Ratzinger, George W. Bush, and Peter Singer seem to share: It's the conviction that the bioethical positions are in the first place divided by their view of the sanctity of life doctrine. It all depends on whether you are in favor or against it, *tertium non datur*. These two alternatives have been set against each other in the academic and public debate to the point where they dominate the entire field of discussion, as much by conservative moral philosophers and theologians as by theorists who have made the challenge to the sanctity of life doctrine their motto. The public debate concerning Singer's claims should be regarded in this context.

2. Singer in Germany: Some Remarks

Being of German origin—though living and teaching in the Netherlands for the last few years—I want to make some short remarks about Singer's experiences in Germany, before I discuss his meta-ethical presumptions in more detail. The history of the appearances of Peter Singer and Helga Kuhse in Germany and Austria in the early 1990s is widely known. Several groups, especially from disabled organizations, made it impossible for Singer and Kuhse to speak before an audience. On several occasions, workshops and university courses on bioethics couldn't go ahead. During the 1990s other bioethicists, like Norbert Hoerster, had similar experiences. But at this time nobody was perceived as *the* personification of bioethics in the way that Peter Singer was.

In my view there is no doubt that these activities were unjustified restriction of some of Singer's basic rights. But perhaps one should in the first place try to reconstruct the context that leads to such forms of public protest. And it's clear that in this case it was related to a specific historical moment. When I had a discussion with Singer on a public forum in Heidelberg in 2004, only a very small group of peacefully protesting citizens made their presence felt. It seems, then, that the episode of intense opposition to Singer had passed into history. I don't want to review the whole debate in detail, but I want to mention some aspects to explain why it happened in Germany at that time; aspects that are normally not sufficiently understood in the wider international debate.

Perhaps it's worth mentioning that until the 1970s in Germany ethics were more or less nonexistent as a philosophical discipline. Germany had a tradition in ethics (especially with Kant) but the criticisms of this tradition by Hegel and Nietzsche were so omnipresent in German philosophy that more or less the whole tradition of moral philosophy has been under pressure. In the twentieth century, both left-wing critical theory (deriving from Marx and Lukacs) and the conservative theory (deriving from Heidegger, Gadamer, or Joachim Ritter) shared a fundamental skepticism of philosophical ethics, generally accepting the validity of Hegel's criticism of Kant's idea of a morality of reason. In the 1970s there was a significant group of German conservative philosophers[6] who held Kant's ethics, seen as unhistorical and as an abstract and radical form of rational moral criticism, responsible for all wrong developments on the left, sometimes even for the terrorist attacks of the 'Rote Armee Fraktion'. In their perspective Hegel has shown that the *Rechtsstaat* is the best realization of moral standards while all other kinds of philosophical ethics are in danger of radicalism and abstract critical attitudes. Until the end of the 1970s, ethical debates in the analytic tradition were barely noticed. So for the German philosophical tradition of Husserl, Heidegger, Adorno, Horkheimer, Gadamer, and so forth, philosophical ethics was not a serious topic—at least, ethics was not of systematic importance; to write essays about ethical topics was another story.

Very slowly philosophers in the 1970s tried a 'rehabilitation of practical philosophy', to mention the title of a very important book.[7] Still, dealing with applied ethics in general, and bioethics in particular, was totally unknown until the end of the 1980s or beginning of the 1990s. When I got a job in 1991 at the Inter-Departemental Center for Ethics in the Sciences and Humanities in Tübingen (in the 1990s the biggest institute for Applied Ethics in Europe), most philosophers reacted with total lack of understanding towards all colleagues who decided to pursue such a weak topic as bioethics. And to the wider public, the whole term

---

[6] Like Joachim Ritter, Günter Rohrmoser, or Hermann Lübbe.
[7] Riedel 1972.

'Bioethik' was totally unknown. A lot of Germans probably heard the term 'Bioethik' for the first time in the context of the Singer controversy. At the same time the Council of Europe prepared a convention on the regulation of the life sciences in Europe, a document that was called the "Bioethics Convention." Chiefly as a reaction to this convention, small centers of resistance against bioethics were established in several German cities, mainly related to disability groups, but well connected to religious and political groups.[8]

At that time the German public had no clear picture of what the label 'bioethics' could mean. And indeed the way ethical sub-disciplines are classified is very confusing for people because some labels refer to areas of discussion, like meta-ethics, environmental ethics, animal ethics, while others are names for specific approaches in ethics, like Kantian ethics, utilitarian ethics, and the like. In the beginning of the bioethical debate the term 'bioethics' was understood as the name for a specific approach, and in general people supposed that it referred to Peter Singer's approach. In the perspective of the international debate, that doesn't make any sense. If there is internationally a dominant approach, one could refer to the *principlism* of Beauchamp and Childress,[9] which in fact is much more widely accepted than Singer's approach.

At the same time the debate on the ethics of the life sciences was overshadowed in Germany by some aspects that perhaps are typical for the German situation at that time: the memory of the activities of physicians in the concentration camps of the Nazis and as a result: the high importance of the notion of human dignity in the German constitution. The last point is worth mentioning since the interpretation of the extension of dignity very much dominated the German debate, and it's a notion that is not directly familiar to the utilitarian tradition Peter Singer is committed to.

But two other factors have to be mentioned: In Germany the status of the medical profession has been traditionally very dominant. It's a combination of the authority of a physician with the authority of a German professor. To mention only one indicator: the establishment of a separate profession of nurses started very late in Germany. Therefore the debate about questions of medical ethics or bioethics started in a situation,

---

[8] It's worth mentioning that those critical groups are not affiliated to one political party but nearly across the whole political spectrum, from the religious members of the Christian Democrats, to feminist segments of the Green Party and a significant number of Social Democrats.
[9] Beauchamp and Childress 2001.

where the whole area of medicine was on the one hand dominated by power-relationships, on the other hand still under the impression of a lack of trust in the memory of Mengele and his colleagues. The disability movement was not very well organized, so for example disability studies became established much later in Germany than in the United Kingdom or the United States. There was a disability movement (the so-called "Krüppel Tribunal") that dealt, for instance, with the memory of the history of the disabled in Nazi Germany, but this movement was only beginning to get established, and it had few academically trained speakers. Consequently, when some representative of the disability movement undertook their actions against Singer, they did so with the feeling that they lacked access to meaningful freedom of speech. And in the historical circumstances, this perception was not entirely wrong.

This situation has now changed considerably: There are several places in Germany where disability studies is established, the disability movement has itself organized Internet discussions as an important platform for internal debate,[10] and they have founded a research institute in Berlin.[11] For the disability movement it was important to have their own academically trained spokespersons and some visibility in the public discussion. The traditional dominance of the physicians was not helpful. The debate on bioethics and the life sciences was in the first place a debate between representatives of medicine and law and theologians.

All these aspects have influenced the debate about Peter Singer. Additionally, some organizers of the meetings where Singer wasn't permitted to speak didn't try to create the room for a critical confrontation of Singer with other perspectives, especially from the disability movements. With the appearance of Singer people felt confronted with a debate from the English-speaking world, a discourse that introduced a new 'label' in the debate, in a situation where the academic debate wasn't prepared for that and where the societal status of medicine wasn't favorable to an open discussion. That Singer's position was to some extent a provocation is of course another important factor.

All that isn't a justification for the reactions, but perhaps it explains some of the relevant motives behind the discussion. In that situation, it would have been necessary to discuss Singer's position in very different settings and formats and to organize it in such a way that eloquent critics could be part of the meetings. Interpretations of this history that see nothing more than aggressive disabled people obstructing Singer's

---

[10] www.1000fragen.de
[11] www.imew.de

freedom of speech are totally ignoring the context. Once again: my comment is not an attempt to justify the attacks against Singer, but for an adequate understanding of the whole discussion it's necessary to understand this context that in general isn't known internationally.

3. Peter Singer's *Practical Ethics*: A First Outline

Since the beginning of the 1970s Peter Singer has taken positions on issues in applied ethics. Many of his views should be seen in the context of the American civil rights movement as well as the developing animal liberation movement, which found an important spokesperson in Singer.[12]

In 1979 his book *Practical Ethics* was published (with an expanded and revised new edition in 1993). In this book Singer explains his bioethical positions in the context of some general meta-ethical considerations. First he explains his view of the theoretical foundation of ethics and clarifies the *principle of equal consideration of interests*, according to which "we [should] give equal weight in our moral deliberations to the like interests of all those affected by our actions."[13] Singer's position has been classified as preference utilitarianism, because the interests or preferences of all those affected by an action are weighed against each other. *All* preferences count and all preferences count *equally*. Singer does not attempt to morally evaluate those preferences themselves, they are taken as they are. Their moral importance is merely that these preferences or interests are to be given equal consideration in our moral deliberation.

Practical Ethics can be understood as a presentation and elaboration of this principle of equal consideration and as the criticism that many of our traditional conceptions of morality fail to take this principle seriously. As a direct consequence of this principle we have to accept that the pure fact that some entity belongs to a specific biological species cannot be a decisive factor in the moral consideration of interests. Singer claims, however, that our traditional ethics is dominated by the bias that the interests of fellow members of the species *Homo sapiens* should be accorded more weight than those of other species. He calls this bias 'speciesism' and regards this as an analogy of the unjust discrimination that occurs when in sexism or racism the members of a certain sex or

---

[12] For an overview see Jamieson's contribution (1999) in a collection of articles on Peter Singer (edited by Jamieson himself).

[13] Singer 1993, p. 21.

race are favored. The principle of equal consideration demands that the similar interests of animals are also equally considered. Differences in the treatment of animals and human beings can only be justified when there is a difference in the interests that they have. For instance, animals as well as human beings have an interest in the avoidance of pain. But self-conscious beings (persons) do have interest other than not self-conscious beings that—as far as we can tell—are not equally capable of anticipating the future. The human capacity—or more precisely, the capacity of persons—to anticipate their future causes a different perception of death. Because persons can make plans for the future, they have a different understanding of the significance of death: they can regard death as something that would thwart these plans. Therefore, the proscription against killing turns out to apply differently to persons than to (not conscious) animals. Because those animals cannot have preferences regarding their future, their interests are not thwarted in the same way by death as in the case of persons. The principle of equal consideration does not require that all beings are treated equally. It only requires that all interests are considered equally. If those interests differ however, this should be taken into consideration in the process of moral deliberation.

For the above-mentioned specification of interests the introduction of the concept of "person" is decisive. Singer proposes "rationality and self-consciousness"[14] as the defining characteristics of persons. Insofar as rationality and self-consciousness are necessary conditions for the capacity to have preferences regarding one's own future existence, the proscription against killing in the strict sense only applies to persons. If there is a moral reason, normally, to treat human beings differently from animals, then this is only because members of this species normally have the relevant capacities of personhood. The principle of equal consideration demands that the no-harm principle be extended to all beings that are capable of having preferences, and demands the prohibition of killing persons.

But the principle of equal consideration has the implication that only those beings who are capable of having interests are morally considerable. This moral consideration too has been obscured in our traditional conceptions of morality by the speciesist bias. There are beings who belong to our biological species, but who do not (yet or not any more) have interests, such as embryos, fetuses, and coma-patients. There are severely handicapped people who—as far as we can judge—will never

---

[14] Singer 1993, p. 87.

be able to have interests. Singer discusses our moral obligations to fetuses and embryos at length and explains why an abortion is not a case of morally impermissible killing, insofar as no interests are thwarted by this procedure. As embryos and fetuses are not yet persons, the proscription against killing does not apply to them.

Singer also discusses the case of people whose lives are completely dominated by pain. In such a situation, the principle of equal consideration actually demands an acknowledgement of the individual's desire to die. It is precisely in this context that—according to Singer—the conflict between the principle of equal consideration and the sanctity of life doctrine is particularly evident. When severely handicapped newborns are being kept alive with all possible technical means,[15] and when people who suffer severe and unrelievable pain are denied the possibility of ending their lives, their interests are ignored in order to be able to maintain the inviolability of human life.

The issues that have been discussed above concern those aspects of *Practical Ethics* that have particularly given rise to dispute in the bioethical debates. Other parts of the book are concerned with economical and political inequality between the poor and the rich, with moral obligations towards refugees, and with environmental ethics. I will not pursue these matters here. At the end I will discuss our moral obligations to the distant poor since Singer's position on that topic has stimulated some discussions.

4. The Principle of Equal Consideration of Interests

As was explained above, the principle of equal consideration is the fundamental principle of *Practical Ethics*, and its implications are explored for various practical issues. The justification of this principle is already advanced in the first chapter. Singer rejects a number of views of ethics, especially relativist and emotivist theories, in which moral beliefs are solely regarded as beliefs that vary across cultures or as expressions of moral feelings. Singer argues against these views that all moral judgments share a universal aspect. He wonders: "How do moral judgments differ from other practical judgments?"[16] When we refer to a way of life as "moral" or when we characterize an action as "moral" or "immoral," then we do not merely appeal to convention or self-interest. We assume rather that moral judgments should be backed up by universally valid

---

[15] See Kuhse and Singer 1985 for an elaborate description of such cases.
[16] Singer 1993, p. 9.

principles. This view can also be found in the ideas of many moralists and philosophers throughout the history of ethics. From the Golden Rule to the categorical imperative and utilitarian views, the different thinkers "agree that an ethical principle cannot be justified in relation to any partial or sectional group. . . . ethics requires us to go beyond 'I' and 'you' to the universal law, the universal judgment, the standpoint of the impartial spectator or ideal observer, or whatever we choose to call it".[17] The idea of an impartial consideration of interests is, then, already included in the concept of morality itself. My interests or the interests of a particular group do not count for more or less than the interests of all others. When I make moral judgments, I accept the position that all interests are to be considered impartially. Singer points out that this is merely one view of ethics, but that it is a plausible view.[18] But it is not only one concept of ethics next to others, it is the concept of morality as such. The moral point of view is the point of view of the impartial weighing of interests and whoever argues morally, commits himself or herself to this very idea of impartiality. Therefore—according to Singer—it is necessary to examine whether our various moral judgments and convictions really do follow from the principle of equal consideration. As was explained above, he comes to the conclusion that this is often not the case. In many cases we do not consider interests impartially, but rather favor the interests of the members of our biological species.

The derivation of this principle appears to have the advantage that it does not require many complicated theoretical assumptions or disputable presuppositions. The explanation of this moral view appears to be quite plausible. It is not tied to any particular world view and does not require elaborate moral-philosophical argumentation. The equality-principle follows from a simple explanation of what it means to make a moral judgment, and appears to be included within the concept of morality itself. If this is correct, then we can expect for everybody to respect the validity of this principle, and everyone has to make sure his moral convictions accord with this principle. With very thin philosophical assumptions, a principle with wide-ranging implications appears to have been found, which, when it is explored, turns out to unhinge the entirety of traditional ethics.

The way this principle is derived has evoked criticism. There is one objection that I would like to discuss. Anne Maclean has presented an extensive critique of various bioethical theories, including for instance

---

[17] Singer 1993, pp. 11–12.
[18] Ibid., p. 8.

the approaches of John Harris and Peter Singer.[19] Her sharp, partly polemical criticism of various utilitarian approaches is tied to the expectation of eliminating bioethics altogether, because: "bioethicists are utilitarians".[20] Even paging through the book's table of contents, however, it becomes apparent that the various approaches to bioethics are quite diverse. Maclean's distinction of "pure utilitarianism" and "impure utilitarianism" will also cause more confusion than clarification to the classification of various ethical theories.[21] Now, I would assume that her statement "bioethicists are utilitarians" in the first place shows her severe lack of knowledge in the field of bioethics; one cannot take that seriously. However, even if the entire enterprise of bioethics does not stand or fall on Maclean's criticism of the utilitarian approaches to bioethics, it is possible that her criticism is persuasive for the specific approaches she is discussing, especially the approach of Singer.

Maclean accuses Singer of a fundamental ambiguity in the notion of impartiality as he uses it when introducing the principle of equality. Maclean reconstructs Singer's argumentation in the following way: Singer claims that a moral system consists of judgments about what we ought or ought not to do, which are based on a certain standard or justification. These standards have to be impartial. We cannot justify moral judgments by appealing to our self-interest, nor does it suffice that we express our subjective convictions or feelings. After establishing this impartial character of the moral standards that we draw on to justify our judgments, Singer goes one step further: impartiality requires equality, that is, the equal consideration of all those affected by our actions. Maclean now points out that the way that impartiality is understood changes very fundamentally by introducing the notion of equality. When impartiality and universalizability are taken to be characteristics of the concept of morality itself, this merely means that the standards which underlie moral judgments, are generalizable. This, however, does not yet imply equality in the sense of a substantial moral criterion. Singer has attempted to derive the equality-principle from the concept of morality. However, when we consider impartiality as a characteristic of all conceivable moral systems, this only means that the moral standards that we refer to in order to justify judgments have to be generalizable. So, if I claim that we have the moral obligations to persons not to kill them, than I say that all persons shouldn't be killed. If I claim that we are morally

---

[19] See Maclean 1993, pp. 52–77, for her discussion of Singer's views.
[20] Ibid., p. 37.
[21] Ibid.

obliged to treat elderly philosophers with special respect, then this obligation is valid for behavior towards all elderly philosophers.

This demand, though, is compatible with various moral standards. We could say that parents have special obligations to their children. It is possible to generalize this maxim of action in the sense that we suppose that all parents have such obligations to their children.[22] It is not irrational to suggest moral obligations that are group-specific and non-egalitarian, even if one accepts that the concept of morality implies generalizability and impartiality. When we hold that all moral systems are made up of standards, principles, rules, or maxims that are universalizable, this only means that we have to bring these standards to bear not only in one particular case, but also in other similar cases. The content of these standards is still undetermined.

We could then say that every person has moral obligations to take care of his children and to care for his own children in a special way. He may also care for other people's children, but is not morally obligated to do so. When there is a conflict, for instance when he has to decide to save either his child or his neighbor from a burning house, then he is obligated to save his child. Such a moral view is a possible moral view. It still remains to be seen whether this moral rule or this moral standard is properly justified, whether it is a good moral view and everybody is obligated to accept it. But it is *a* moral view. In his exploration of the concept of morality Singer asked the question of what separates moral judgments from other judgments. Moral standpoints "cannot be justified in relation to any particular or sectional group" but must be "in some sense universal".[23] When one regards universalizability and impartiality as general characteristics of the concept of morality, then one has to agree with Maclean that very inegalitarian conceptions of morality can also be universalized.[24]

---

[22] Ibid., p. 55.

[23] Ibid., p. 11.

[24] That doesn't mean that no concept of universalizability with stronger implications can be defended. Kant for example tried to ground his highest principle of morality in a concept of universalizability that holds the position that there are maxims that a reasonable person cannot think or rationally want. This is a much stronger conceptual claim. Accordingly Kant defends the specific moral position of persons not with a specific structure of their interests but with regard to the fact that persons are autonomous beings, meaning that they are capable of practical and moral considerations, basic requirements for morality. Therefore the specific relevance of personhood in Kant's conception varies significantly from the function in Singer's approach. According to Kant persons have to be treated as ends-in-themselves; only if we see rational beings as

Maclean does not conclude from her deliberations that Singer's position is irrational or wrong. However, she points out that Singer's equality principle is only based on *a* view of morality. In referring to Maclean it is not at all my intention to adopt her own conception of morality (though she has some suggestive examples). However, in her central criticism of Singer, in my opinion, she has a point. When we make moral judgments, we assume that the rules and principles that underlie these judgments do not only apply to us, but to all moral agents. Yet it does not at all follow from this characteristic of the concept of morality that the interests of all who are affected by our actions should be weighed equally.

Klaus Steigleder has elaborated this criticism in a similar way (with less suggestive examples).[25] Steigleder holds the opinion that we have to distinguish between criteria that determine the scope of moral actions, judgments, obligations, convictions, and so forth, from criteria that determine *right or valid* moral actions, judgments, obligations, convictions, and so forth. Criteria of the first kind would only show us how moral actions or judgments are different from other judgments or actions. They are criteria that show that moral judgments differ from esthetic judgments or judgments of taste. But this class of moral judgments can have totally different content. One can for example hold the opinion that we are morally obliged to treat all humans with respect, that all women have to serve the male, or that we are morally obliged to do everything possible to promote the well-being of Bavaria. One can hold the position that the whole world is morally obliged to serve the interests of the United States in oil resources or to promote the worldwide spread of Christianity. One can even hold the position of an egoistic ethics that everybody is obliged to do everything possible to promote the interest of himself or herself. One can be of the opinion that those moral positions are not very agreeable or even strange and dangerous, but that is another question than the question whether or not they are moral positions in the first place. And I see no reasons why they shouldn't be seen as moral positions. It's even *necessary*, in order to discuss whether or not

---

beings with worth can the will of such a rational being ground a commitment for us. And the claim of universalization of our maxims is grounded in the fact that it is the maxim a pure rational being would choose. The key argument in that context is however the intrinsic relation between the idea of universalizability with the will of a rational being and the specific value we have to give to a rational being. So Kant's attempt to give substantive content to his moral principle in the idea of the dignity of a person does not find an analogy in Singer's attempt to combine the demand of universalizability with the substantive concept of equality.

[25] Steigleder 1991 and Steigleder 1999, pp. 20f.

those moral positions are valid moral positions, to accept that they are moral positions. Concerning criteria for determining the scope of morality, universality only means that it's a characteristic of moral claims that they have a universal scope of application: If you think that women are morally obliged to serve men, than you hold the moral position that every woman is obliged to do it. One could therefore say: we can recognize a moral judgment or conviction in contrast to other judgments or convictions by the universal pretension of that claim.[26] A criterion for valid moral judgments, as Steigleder states, can be distinguished from the criteria of the first kind. If I accept that a racist maxim is a moral maxim I do not need to accept that it is a valid moral maxim. I can, however, strongly oppose it and I can strongly hold the opinion that this moral maxim is totally indefensible.

I think that this distinction of Steigleder is valid and it's even necessary for the possibility of moral discourse that we make this distinction. Concerning Singer's principle of equal consideration we can say: Singer is wrong to believe that it is the criterion for determining the scope of morality. It may however be possible that he could defend the principle of equal consideration as a criterion for valid moral convictions. In doing so one especially would have to show why the fact that some beings can suffer, can feel pain and can have preferences is a sufficient reason to assume that they have rights and others have corresponding obligations. Singer does not argue for that, but he should if he wants to convince us that we have the obligations he assumes we have. Singer tries to avoid this justification of his moral principle by showing that it follows from the very idea of morality as such. The criticisms of McLean and Steigleder, however, indicate that the principle of equal consideration does not follow from the concept of morality itself; non-egalitarian principles are candidates for moral principles. Since Singer derives his principle of equal consideration from the concept of morality alone, it follows that the principle of equal consideration has not been justified in *Practical Ethics*.

5. Speciesism and Sanctity of Life

"Traditional ethics," the moral view against which Singer directs his critique, is discussed under the concepts of *speciesism* and *sanctity of life*.

---

[26] We can always presuppose that these universality aspects include considerations that all other things are equal, context-specific aspects, and the like. Normally universal claims are only referring to principles, rules or maxims, not to single actions.

Many attempts have been made to defend this view of traditional ethics against Singer. Various ethicists appear to identify with the view of ethics that Singer campaigns against. In fact all the ideas that Singer criticizes are represented in the debate. In the bioethical debate, however, a lot of nuances in the valuation of the human species and our obligation to human life have been introduced partly in reaction to Singer's claims, so Singer has certainly made important contributions to this discussion. He is correct in pointing out that belonging to a specific biological species can, as such, not be a valid justification for morally special treatment. In ethical argumentation it simply does not suffice if, to explain why human beings deserve special moral attention, one were to appeal to the fact that these are our conspecifics. A biological fact does not justify a moral 'ought'. It is also clear that developments in medicine have forced us to formulate clearer definitions of traditional concepts. Human embryos and fetuses have only in the last couple of decades become visually accessible to us. We have detailed knowledge of the various stages in the development of the fertilized egg. When Kant and Hume were talking about humans they didn't differentiate between the different stages of embryological development because they didn't have precise knowledge about it. So, if one uses terms like "person" or "human dignity" one has to specify and justify the use of these terms with regard to early stages and to other phases in the life of humans.

The question presents itself, however, whether Singer is right that the demand to include human beings who are not yet persons, or who have severe disabilities, into the sphere of beings who deserve moral protection, can only be explained by species bias. It may also be asked whether the criticism against the 'sanctity of life'-doctrine has as many consequences as Singer presupposes. In Singer's view, his criticism of this doctrine is significant insofar as the fundamental objections against euthanasia, assisted suicide, and abortion are necessarily dependent on the assumption that human life is sacred and inviolable.[27] So, if this doctrine is not valid, then—according to Singer—the objections to those practices are not valid. As the assumption of the sanctity of human life can only be justified by appealing to religious views, this doctrine is unsuitable as a morality for a secular society. This latter idea, in my opinion, is correct. A secular society cannot derive moral obligations

---

[27] We are only talking here about fundamental objections to those practices. Singer accepts that there can be arguments against euthanasia and abortion, if those actions are not freely chosen or happen under specific, morally relevant circumstances.

from religious assumptions. And I agree that the 'sanctity of human life' cannot be defended as a valid moral principle.[28] The question is, however, whether the sanctity of life doctrine really does offer the only possible justification of the objections mentioned above, and I want to briefly discuss that.

Traditional moral convictions have changed substantially in the last few decades. However, the concepts of *human dignity* and *human rights* lie at the normative heart of an ethical view that justifies the special status of human beings. The history of ideas contains various threads that lead to these concepts. It does stand out that various traditions refer to the idea that human beings were made in God's image. The justification of the special status of human persons is, however, related to their specific moral capacities: their freedom, their capacity for reason, communication, action, or morality.[29] In the history of moral philosophy it is usually not human life—as the life of members of one biological species—that is declared to be sacred and inviolable. On the contrary, there is no lack of examples of human beings actually being morally required to sacrifice their lives for the sake of freedom or other goods. In Kant's moral philosophy—the most important and influential theory of human dignity—human beings, as rational beings, are viewed as ends in themselves. The question may be asked whether the inclusion of human beings who are not yet or may never be persons into the moral sphere can be justified by the such theories or whether here—as if through the back door—the doctrine of the sanctity of human life is necessarily showing up again. In the actual attempts to justify such moral-

---

[28] If we hold a human dignity position we can only defend a moral claim like that: If persons are morally ends in themselves, and if the species *Homo sapiens* is the species where normally personhood appears, than we can, however, ask for specific justification for the treatment of all human life. That would be an argumentation without religious pretensions. So, there could be reasons to defend something like the 'sanctity of life' doctrine as a rule for the 'burden of proof' or to translate it in a kind of precautionary principle. But there are clear limits to this in terms of an ethics of human dignity. Especially if the protection of non-personal human life (such as embryos) is in conflict with a right of a person, those limitations cannot be defended anymore. To defend the protection of an embryo against the rights of a woman to her body seems to be clearly an immoral act for an ethics of human dignity.

[29] In the religious tradition also, it's not the membership of a biological species that is the reason for the specific moral duties to humans, but their participation in the rational capacities of God, their capability of communicating with God, and so on. Especially if we want to look to the tradition of human dignity that assumed great importance in philosophy after the Renaissance, we can perceive the high value that is given to the rational capacities of human beings. Cf. Trinkaus 1970.

philosophical approaches, this is usually not the case. To justify the special status of embryos and fetuses, the relationship of continuity, potentiality, or identity between embryos and persons is usually appealed to.[30] It is argued that embryos and fetuses are entities that are on their way to become persons, and that they have the potentiality for freedom and personhood, and these are morally relevant features. It is pointed out that there are no clear places to draw lines in the development from fetus to person. One can discuss whether those arguments are valid. But the argument that an embryo deserves specific moral protection as a potential person cannot be criticized as a speciesistic argument. It cannot be claimed that occidental ethics stands or falls with the doctrine of the 'sanctity of human life'. The question arises whether there are good reasons to accord the dignity of persons to all members of the human species. Some ethicists, for example, hold a gradualist position. However, in the discussion to what extent the moral respect to a person should be extended to different phases of the life of human persons, the 'sanctity of life'-doctrine is not of decisive importance.

In order to emphasize my point more clearly I want to add another remark concerning Singers' criticism of speciesism. There are at least two different reasons for referring in ethical debates to the species that a certain entity belongs to. One can either desire to give a *justificatory reason for moral consideration* or to indicate the *scope of moral protection*. The first way of referring to species-membership would be the following argument: due to the fact that x is a member of the species *Homo sapiens* we have a moral reason why we should grant moral protection to x. The second way of referring to species membership could be, for example, the following: we should grant moral protection to persons (since they are the subjects of morality), the characteristics of personhood can only be found at members of the human species, therefore we should treat members of the human species (with regard to potentiality, precaution and other reasons) as special.

The former way of referring to species-membership is—as has been pointed out before—not a cogent ethical argument: that an entity is a member of a specific species does not provide us as such with a justificatory reason why we are morally obliged to tread this entity in a specific way. In addition—as has also been indicated above—the biological species that human beings belong to is not advanced in the ethical discussion as the justifying reason for their special status.

---

[30] See Damschen/Schönecker 2003; Düwell 2006.

But not all ways of referring to species-membership are of this kind. It can be an outcome of an ethical discussion that we have moral obligations to all human beings (although it may be seriously doubted whether such a demand can be justified indiscriminately). This is a point for discussion. In any case it is not yet an error in ethical reasoning and an expression of thoughtless bias, if one tries to extend the scope of moral protection to cover all members of the species. All references to a protection of human embryos due to their potential to become persons, and so forth, presuppose the justificatory reasons why we grant moral protection to persons and that we have reasons to extent this protection of personhood to potential persons. One can criticize this view, but not as a speciesistic one, since personhood is the justificatory reason and not species-membership.

When an allegation of speciesism is made, it is not entirely clear what the accusation is. It is an evocative battle cry. When one is of the opinion that it is ethically unjustified to extend moral protection to all members of the species, this is a point for debate. Someone who argues for or against this view does not yet commit an argumentative error, or a speciesist fallacy. It would be a speciesist fallacy if one referred solely to the species membership as a justification for an entity's being entitled to moral protection, and this—it seems to me—lies well beyond the scope of the moral-philosophical discussion.

To conclude this section, I have an observation in response to Singer's criticism of the potentiality argument with reference to the Prince Charles argument. If the King of England has specific powers, it doesn't mean that the crown prince, as the potential king, also has the same powers. This argument seems to go only so far. That the status of the crown prince is different from the status of an actual king doesn't mean that he has the same status as—let's say—a London taxi-driver. He can merit some kind of special status due to his future powers. This seems actually to be the situation in nearly all ways of protecting the human embryo (except in some very Catholic countries). Most countries give some protection to embryos either by substantial regulations (that say what you may or may not do with them) or by procedural regulations (as in the UK, defining in the first place a procedure that regulates their treatment). Both approaches to regulation presuppose that we have some reasons to treat human embryos differently from other things (a presupposition that Singer finds not legitimate). But most regulations presuppose at the same time that embryos do not have the same status as actual persons (since they allow the possibility of abortion under specific circumstances, for example).

I don't want to go into detail here. But it seems to me that the recognition of a specific status for a potential person, granting some kind of moral status without granting the full moral status possessed by actual persons, is a much more plausible reconstruction of the reasons for those regulation then the assumption that species membership is seen as a justificatory reason.

6. International Justice and the Role of the State

I want to give some brief comments on Singer's proposals concerning the discussion on international justice, especially our obligations to the distant poor. This topic has growing importance in the international debate.[31] Singer employs his principle of equal consideration to argue for a substantial change in our attitude towards the distant poor.[32] We are using our financial and other resources to fulfill desires and needs beyond the scope of basic needs while a growing amount of people in the world are lacking basic goods. The bias is growing over the years and is now accompanied by the development of globalization that—due to the pressure of international economic concurrence—reduces the possibilities of intervention in this process even more. This situation comes to be under pressure even more since the ecological crises would grow significantly if the underdeveloped countries would start to use the same amount of natural resources as the developed countries are using. In this situation a substantial limitation of fulfillment of preferences in the rich countries seems morally to be urgently demanded, both with regard to moral obligations to the distant poor and in relation to intergenerational responsibilities.

Singer is criticized as being over-demanding in his moral demands towards the people in the first world. Singer seems, however, to have a strong point in this discussion, and one can wonder why a situation where a growing number of people are lacking basic opportunities of living is not seen as morally scandalous. It seems to be a moral scandal not only for a utilitarian approach, but as well for a lot of other ethical frameworks.

This debate however raises some questions of political philosophy that haven't been of central importance in Singer's writing and that seem to reflect problems he shares with other utilitarian approaches. I'm talk-

---

[31] Pogge 2001; 2002; Cullity 2004; Chatterjee 2004.
[32] Especially in Singer 2002.

ing about the role and the task of states in his philosophical framework. In this debate about international justice Singer's opponents are not religious thinkers with whom he is disputing about bioethical issues. Quite the contrary: very similar ideas to those Singer defends can be found in the writings of religious authors. Singer's opponents are liberal thinkers, holding the opinion that the liberal state should limit its power to the protection of the negative freedom of its members. The radical *libertarians* could argue for this limitation of the state in a contractarian tradition that legitimizes the role of the state with reference to well considered judgments of its members. Singer's opponents could be the defenders of a *political liberalism* that requires us to explain our ideas of justice as an overlapping consensus between different comprehensive doctrines and not in terms of an ethical theory as Singer proposes it. Singer's opponents could also be the *communitarian* thinkers who defend a commitment of the state to promote the wellbeing and the common good of the members of a specific community.

But in any case Singer wants to rule out their objections by referring to a universal moral principle of equal consideration of the interests of all beings capable of developing preferences. In that perspective Singer is criticizing the limitations of the liberal idea of protection of negative freedom as well as a limitation to special weight that could be given to the members of the own community. I think that Singer has good reasons to give emphasis to the universal perspective, but up to now, a clear focus on the role of states and political authority is missing.

That is even more problematic as Singer's own normative framework lacks sound justification. The contractualist perspective has its strong point in referring to the idea of a political contract as the basis of common activities relying only on the presuppositions that are internally related to the idea of politics and common activities. The contractualist in the Hobbesian tradition avoids all kind of moral justification of his claims. But also the Kantian tradition, that provides a moral justification, gives specific weight to the role of the state in the realization of a rationally required political and social order.

So, even if one thinks that the tasks of the state should be morally justified (and I strongly think they should), it seems necessary to reflect on differences between specific moral obligations of states and citizen. That seems even more necessary in a situation of globalization where we are in danger of losing the opportunity of political regulations due to uncontrollable concurrence between international economic powers. If one is justifying moral demands one should give special attention to the subjects towards whom those demands can be addressed. I'm strongly sympathetic to the emphasis Singer give to the question of international justice, but with respect to the role of political institutions his theory is clearly underdeveloped.

7. Concluding Remarks

It has not been possible here to analyze Singer's treatment of various issues in applied ethics. I have only been able to make some remarks regarding some basic assumptions of Singer's views. In view of the many misconceptions and ambiguities in the debate on Singer's views, it seemed more important to give an introduction to his basic approach and to critically assess his approach in terms of moral philosophy. One can agree or disagree with single ideas of Singer from the perspective of various ethical approaches. In my opinion, however, this is not as important as subjecting the ethical justification of his position to serious discussion. It seems to me that it would have been better if this latter approach had been taken in the debates in Germany. Peter Singer was right in working out a range of criticisms of common ethical convictions. He does not stand alone in this. The special popularity of his position also seems to be connected to the fact that Singer, in writing his books, has always had the larger audience in mind, and has always sought a connection with political movements. In my opinion, his criticisms of speciesism and the sanctity of life doctrine have been overrated. At the same time, some of his critics, carelessly defending the sanctity of life doctrine, have inadvertently ended up merely defending traditional ideas in ethics. It would be better to pay careful attention to Singer's own arguments than to go on haplessly committing the mistakes he has criticized.

The justification of the principle of equal consideration of interests turns out to be quite weak. The question why the fact animals can feel pain is morally relevant also remains unanswered. Basically, Singer confronts us in his writings with an articulation of his moral convictions. One can wonder why Singer doesn't take more effort to justify these convictions. He very easily starts to criticize concurrent positions by a simplification and unclear polarization of the debates. Singer's use of the polemic label 'speciesism' and his insufficiently specified criticisms of the sanctity of life doctrine are symptoms of the fact that Singer tends to get rid of alternative positions without nuanced discussion. Bioethical debates could be more serious if we would avoid such an attitude. With respect to the justification of Singer's own position, a lot of work needs to be done.

REFERENCES

Beauchamp, Tom L., and James F. Childress. 2001. *Principles of Biomedical Ethics*. Fifth Edition. New York: Oxford University Press.

Brandt, Richard B. 1983. The Concept of a Moral Right and its Function. In *Journal of Philosophy* 80, pp. 29–45.

Chatterjee, Deen, ed. 2004. *The Ethics of Assistance: Morality and the Distant Needy*. Cambridge: Cambridge University Press.

Cullity, Garrett. 2004. *The Moral Demands of Affluence*. New York: Oxford University Press.

Damschen, Gregor, and Dieter Schönecker, eds. 2003. *Der moralische Status menschlicher Embryonen. Pro und contra Spezies-, Kontinuums-, Identitäts- und Potentialitätsargument*. Berlin.

Düwell, Marcus. 2006. Moralischer Status. In Marcus Düwell, Christoph Hübenthal, and Micha H. Werner, eds., *Handbuch Ethik* (Stuttgart), pp. 434–39.

Jamieson, Dale, ed. 1999a. *Singer and His Critics*. Oxford: Blackwell.

————. 1999b. Singer and the Practical Ethics Movement. In Jamieson 1999a, pp. 1–17.

Kuhse, Helga, and Peter Singer. 1985. *Should the Baby Live? The Problem of Handicapped Infants*. Oxford: Oxford University Press.

————, eds. 1999. *Bioethics: An Anthology*. Oxford: Blackwell.

Maclean, Anne. 1993. *The Elimination of Morality: Reflections on Utilitarianism and Bioethics*. London: Routledge.

Oderberg, David S. 2000. *Moral Theory: A Non-Consequentialist Approach*. Oxford: Blackwell.

Pogge, Thomas. 2002. *World Poverty and Human Rights*. Cambridge: Polity.

————, ed. 2001. *Global Justice*. Oxford: Blackwell.

Riedel, Manfred, ed. 1972. *Rehabilitierung der praktischen Philosophie*. Freiburg i. Br.

Scheffler, Samuel, ed. 1988. *Consequentialism and Its Critics*. Oxford: Oxford University Press.

Singer, Peter. 1979. *Practical Ethics*. Cambridge: Cambridge University Press.

————. 1993a. *How Are We to Live?* Melborne: Text.

————. 1993b. *Practical Ethics*. Second edition. Cambridge: Cambridge University Press.

————. 1994a. *Rethinking Life and Death: The Collapse of Our Traditional Ethics*. Melbourne: Text.

————. 1994b. Wie man in Deutschland mundtot gemacht wird. In *Anhang der deutschen Übersetzung von Singer, Peter, Praktische Ethik, Praktische Ethik*, übs. v. Oskar Bischoff, Jean-Claude Wolf u. Dietrich Klose (Stuttgart), pp. 425–451.

————. 2001. *Unsanctifiying Human Life: Essays on Ethics*. Oxford: Blackwell.

————. 2002. *One World: The Ethics of Globalization*. New Haven: Yale University Press.

Steigleder, Klaus. 1991. Die Abenteuer der Bioethik: Ein kritischer Vergleich der Ethikkonzeptionen H. Tristram Engelhardts und Peter Singers. In *Ethik ohne Chance? Erkundungen im technologischen Zeitalter*, hg. v. Jean-Pierre Wils u. Dietmar Mieth (Tübingen 2. erw. Aufl), pp. 225–246.

————. 1999. *Grundlegung der normativen Ethik*. Der Ansatz von Gewirth, Freiburg/München.

Trinkaus, Charles. 1970. *In Our Image and Likeness: Humanity and Divinity in Italian Humanist Thought*. Two volumes. Chicago: University of Chicago Press.

Reply to Marcus Düwell

PETER SINGER

Germany Revisited

Before I discuss the important philosophical issues Marcus Düwell raises, I have to differ with his account of the controversy over my work in Germany, which I have described in the autobiographical chapter of this volume. Though he does not seek to justify the attempts to stop me speaking, Düwell wants to make the actions of my opponents understandable to those who, outside the German-speaking world, find it hard to believe that such outright opposition to free speech on serious philosophical issues could still exist in a modern liberal democracy. But he tilts too far when he seeks to explain the actions of the protestors on the grounds that the organizers of meetings at which I was not permitted to speak were not planning to engage me in debate with people from the disability movement. The first protests against my speaking in Germany were directed against a congress organized by Lebenshilfe, the largest German organization of parents of people with disabilities. As a result of the protests, initially my invitation was withdrawn, and later the entire congress—called by the protesters a "euthanasia congress" because it was to discuss that issue—had to be cancelled. But had it gone ahead, almost all of those present and speaking would have been associated with the disability movement and with areas of research and academia related to disability. As Lebenshilfe's letter withdrawing my invitation stated, their plan was that I should discuss my views "with critical scientists who want to convince you that your attitude infringes human rights." The second of my lectures to be cancelled was at the invitation of Christoph Anstötz, Professor of Special Education—in other words, education for people with disabilities—at the University of Dortmund. Although Anstötz was an academic rather than a member of the disability movement, his area of expertise and the students he taught gave him extensive contacts with people in the disability movement, and they would have been involved in the discussion had threats of physical obstruction not forced its cancellation. The sharpest disproof of the suggestion that the protests were related to the organizers' exclusion of the voices of people with disabilities, however, occurred at the lecture I was invited to give on animal rights, not on issues to do with disability at all, at the University of Zurich. In front of me when I got up to speak, using the flat floor space where they could be accommodated, was a row of people in wheelchairs. While they listened calmly to my opening words a group of black-clad "Autonomen" (Literally, "autonomous ones," a self-styled anarchist organization) began to chant "Singer *raus!*" to drown out my words. After my glasses had been smashed and my host cancelled the lecture, those in wheelchairs spoke up, saying they had not wanted this to happen, but instead had been looking forward to having the chance to challenge my views in open discussion. Here it was not the organizers of the event, but the protesters who prevented people with disabilities from having a critical confrontation with me.

Düwell is right to say that the problem was not just "aggressive disabled people obstructing Singer's freedom of speech," but he ignores the extent to which it was aggressive able people who obstructed my freedom of speech. Certainly one or two leaders of militant disability groups opposed any airing of my views, but had the opposition come only from the disability movement, it would have been much less aggressive, and few, if any, of my lectures would have had to be cancelled. Right-wing Christians also played a role, but they too would most likely not have physically stopped me speaking (although on one occasion they did demand, in vain, that I should not be permitted to enter Germany). The most forceful protests came from the militant left, people who managed to delude themselves that by stopping me speaking, they were saving Germany from a resurgence of fascism.

As Düwell says, these protests occurred at a specific historic moment in the development of bioethics in Germany, and that moment appears to be over. Since 2004 I have spoken in Germany on several occasions without any disruption. Nor have my talks been disrupted in other countries. In 2007 I had an invitation to speak at the seventh Gniezno Convention, in Poland withdrawn after people protested to the conference organizers, but the real surprise here is that I was invited in the first place, since the conference was organized by the Roman Catholic Church. I later spoke on two other occasions in Poland without any protests.

Equal Consideration of Interests and the Nature of Ethics

Düwell asserts that my derivation of the principle of equal consideration of interests rests on an equivocation. "Singer has attempted to derive the equality-principle from the concept of morality." (This sentence occurs in Düwell's paraphrase of Anne Maclean's argument against me, but Düwell later endorses that argument.) The objection to this attempt is that while the concept of morality involves a notion of impartiality, it is impartial only in the sense that "the moral standards that we refer to in order to justify judgments have to be generalizable" and therefore the concept of morality is compatible with moral obligations, like those of parents to their children, that are "group-specific and non-egalitarian."

Put more simply, I am accused of philosophical conjuring: into the hat goes a minimalist criterion of what it is to be a moral principle; out of the hat I pull a substantive moral principle that excludes many possible moral views. This would indeed be a philosophical conjuring trick. But I'm well aware of the impossibility of pulling that rabbit out of that hat. Although Düwell attributes the objection to Anne Mclean's 1993 book, *The Elimination of Morality*, it goes back at least as far as J.L. Mackie's 1977 critique of Hare's use of universalizability in *Ethics: Inventing Right and Wrong*. In fact, I set out the Mackie-Mclean-Düwell problem myself in the first chapter of *Practical Ethics:*

> The problem is that if we describe the universal aspect of ethics in bare, formal terms, a wide range of ethical theories, including quite irreconcilable ones, are compatible with this notion of universality; if, on the other hand, we build up our description of the universal aspect of ethics so that it leads us ineluctably to one particular ethical theory, we shall be accused of smuggling our own ethical beliefs into our definition of the ethical—and this definition was supposed to be broad enough, and neutral enough, to encompass all serious candidates for the status of "ethical theory".[33]

Accordingly, when I introduced the idea of universalizability in *Practical Ethics*, I was careful to make it clear that I was *not* using it to exclude non-utilitarian moral principles:

> What does this show? It does not show that utilitarianism can be deduced from the universal aspect of ethics. There are other ethical ideals—like

---

[33] *Practical Ethics,* p. 12.

individual rights, the sanctity of life, justice, purity and so on—that are universal in the required sense, and are, at least in some versions, incompatible with utilitarianism.[34]

I then went on to say what I thought the universal aspect of ethics does show:

> The utilitarian position is a minimal one, a first base that we reach by universalizing self-interested decision making. We cannot, if we are to think ethically, refuse to take this step. If we are to be persuaded that we should go beyond utilitarianism and accept non-utilitarian moral rules or ideals, we need to be provided with good reasons for taking this further step. Until such reasons are produced, we have some grounds for remaining utilitarians.

Now Düwell might well think that this attempt to put the onus of proof on those who defend a non-utilitarian principle fails. But it would have been better if he had addressed the actual argument I put forward, rather than one that I expressly disavowed.

Let's take a closer look at my argument. I start with the claim that if I am thinking or acting ethically, I cannot give my own interests greater weight, simply because they are my own, than I give to the interests of anyone else. If we imagine people with a normal concern for their own interests accepting universalizability, then they will give the same weight to the interests of others that they give to their own interests. This is, of course, compatible with giving zero weight to everyone's interests, including one's own, and it is also compatible with allowing some quite distinct ethical principle to override one's own interests and everyone else's. But who would do such a thing, without a good reason for doing so? That is all I am saying in the passage quoted above, and it is consistent with the way I proceed in the remainder of *Practical Ethics*. I do not simply assume that the principle of equal consideration of interests is correct, and deduce my conclusions from that. I take it as no more than a starting point, and throughout the book I examine alternative ethical views—for example, the doctrine of the sanctity of human life—and argue that they are unsound.

Equal consideration of interests is therefore no more than a default position, one that emerges from applying universalizability to the most obvious motive for human action, self-interest. To override the default, all that is neceessary is to show that there are sound moral principles that

---

[34] *Practical Ethics*, second edition, p. 14.

are incompatible with it. Düwell suggests this is the case with principles that are "group-specific and non-egalitarian." Again, let's look more closely at this suggestion.

Düwell refers to the obligations parents have to their children. Suppose the principle he has in mind is: "Parents have an obligation to take care of their children, showing them love and affection and giving greater weight to their interests than they give to the interests of others." This looks like a principle that violates equal consideration of interests, but as I have argued elsewhere, it is possible to give an impartial defense of this principle by arguing that children are, in general, better off if brought up in loving homes.[35] (Problems with attempts to rear children collectively in communities like the Israeli kibbutzim provide evidence for this claim.) Since the very idea of parental love implies the legitimacy of giving greater weight to the interests of one's children, however, we have to accept this, in order to obtain the benefits of having children brought up in loving homes. If the facts are as suggested, then allowing parents to give greater weight to the interests of their children does not violate the principle of equal consideration, even though parents acting in accordance with it do not act directly on that principle. (This defense of the principle is similar to Richard Arneson's argument, in this volume, that people acting in accordance with consequentialism may develop relationships that preclude them doing what will have the best consequences on every occasion.)

There are, of course, other group-specific principles for which no such defense is available. For example, a principle that told parents to give absolute priority to the interests of their own children over the interests of other children is unlikely to be compatible with the principle of equal consideration of interests. But I can also see no good reason to accept such a principle. Other group-specific principles need their own justification, and again, the most plausible candidates are those that are compatible with the principle of equal consideration of interests. Compare the principles "I should help my fellow-citizens before I help anyone else" and "I should help people of my race before I help anyone else." Neither of these principles is self-evident, and therefore neither should be accepted without further argument. But whereas there appear to be no good arguments for racial priority, some arguments for recognizing a special obligation to one's fellow-citizens—for example, that

---

[35] *How Are We to Live?*, pp. 95–96 and *One World*, pp. 160–67.

we are part of a "community of reciprocity"—are worth serious consideration.[36] My view is that only those principles that appeal to equal consideration of interests are at all persuasive. But this isn't an *a priori* claim derived from any view about the nature of morality. It is the outcome of an examination of the merits of each argument.

In addition to arguments for alternatives to, or constraints on, the principle of equal consideration of interests, many of these alternatives are simply put forward on the basis of our intuitive judgments. In my response to Huemer, I discuss my reasons for doubting the reliability of these intuitions.[37]

There is one more thing to add on this issue. I have, in the preceding paragraphs, restated the route I took in *Practical Ethics* to the principle of equal consideration of interests. I have focused on that line of argument because Düwell took it as his target. As I make clear in my response to Huemer, there is another possible way of arguing for equal consideration of interests, and indeed for consequentialism. This is the line of argument I attempted in *The Expanding Circle*. On this view, the principle of equal consideration of interests is not derived from the concept of morality, but rather from a substantive conception of reason similar to the one that Sidgwick appeals to in setting out the axioms that are the foundation of his utilitarianism.[38] I remain doubtful about whether a successful defense of this view is possible, but I do not entirely reject the possibility.

"Human Dignity" and the Special Value of Human Life

Düwell accepts my rejection of speciesism and of religious grounds for defending the doctrine of the sanctity of human life, but he believes that something akin to the traditional doctrine can nevertheless be defended. He mentions, in this context, the desirability of drawing clear lines in the gradual development from fetus—he could have said zygote—to person. I have already commented on this in my response to Gensler, and acknowledged that there is something to be said for taking birth as the cut-off line, at least in terms of the criminal law.

---

[36] *One World*, pp. 168–180.

[37] See also my "Ethics and Intuitions," *Journal of Ethics* 9:3–4 (October 2005), pp. 331–352.

[38] Henry Sidgwick, *The Methods of Ethics*, p. 382.

In regard to speciesism and our attitudes to human life, perhaps part of the difference between Düwell and me concerns our intended audience. He writes:

> It would be a speciesist fallacy if one referred solely to the species-membership as a justification for an entity's being entitled to moral protection, and this—it seems to me—lies well beyond the scope of the moral-philosophical discussion.

I hope it is true that the moral-philosophical discussion has moved beyond the simple fallacy of speciesism, although Bernard Williams's essay in this volume gives grounds for doubting that claim. But in any case, I am interested not only in the moral-philosophical discussion, but also to change our practice with regard to speciesism, and here it is glaringly obvious that speciesism plays a crucial role. Species-membership determines whether a sentient being is a person protected by the law, or an item of property that can be bought and sold. Neither the absence of any capacity to reason, nor even the absence of any potential to develop such a capacity, makes a difference. (Consider, for example, the refusal of courts to permit the removal of organs from anencephalic babies, even when the parents request it and when the organs could be be used to save the life of another baby, and compare that with the routine way in which nonhuman animals may be killed for meat or in research.[39]) Perhaps the academic debate in moral philosophy has moved beyond simple speciesism, but the law and popular consciousness certainly has not.

In defending something akin to the traditional ethic, Düwell suggests that the argument from potential is a non-speciesist way of defending opposition to abortion. Perhaps, he suggests, human embryos and fetuses should have special status because they have the potential to become persons, with rational capacities that exceed those of any nonhuman animals. This claim is not speciesist, but is it defensible? We could question, for example, whether there is any reason to protect an entity with the potential to become a person, if we do not favor a policy of encouraging people to produce more such beings—in other words, if we think that, for environmental reasons, there are already enough persons in the world. But perhaps the greatest challenge for the argument from potential comes from our advances in reproductive technology. When we have an early embryo *in vitro,* consisting of, say, two cells, each of these cells

---

[39] See *Rethinking Life and Death*, pp. 53–54, 163–65.

has the potential to become a person. We could divide them and culture them separately. Then when each of these cells itself splits and becomes two, we could divide them again. The process cannot be continued indefinitely, but if there are women willing to take the resulting embryos into their wombs, we could allow many more potential persons to develop. In the near future, we may be able to do the same with the nuclei of many of our cells, using somatic cell nuclear transfer to clone ourselves. (This has already been done with many species of mammals, including primates, so there is little reason to doubt that it could be done with humans.) Will the availability of this technology confer a special moral status on all the cells that will then have the potential to develop into persons?[40]

Finally, as far as the discussion of the sanctity of human life is concerned, it is worth pointing out that Düwell has focused on only two aspects of my discussion of this topic, mainly on the objection that the doctrine is speciesist, and on my grounds for rejecting the argument from potential. There is more to my critique of the doctrine that he does not discuss, in particular my objection to the absolutist nature of the doctrine—that is, the claim that it is *always* wrong intentionally to take the life of an innocent human being. This aspect of the doctrine is used, for example, as an objection to voluntary euthanasia. Another aspect of the doctrine that I criticize extensively is the idea that all human life has *equal* value or worth—something that seems to suggest that the life of an anencephalic baby is as valuable or worthy of protection as the life of any other human being. Hence even if Düwell thinks that something like the traditional view can survive my objections to speciesism and to the argument from potential, this does not show that the traditional view, or anything like it, is defensible against these other objections.

International Justice

I welcome Düwell's support for the view that those of us living in the affluent world have demanding obligations to do more for those who cannot satisfy their basic needs. As for his criticism that I have no developed theory of political institutions in the international arena, I can only acknowledge that this is true. I make some suggestions about this in *One*

---

[40] For discussion, see Agata Sagan and Peter Singer, "The Moral Status of Stem Cells," *Metaphilosophy* 38:2–3 (April 2007), pp. 264–284 and also in Lori Gruen, Laura Grabel, and Peter Singer, eds., *Stem Cell Research* (Oxford: Blackwell, 2007).

World, especially in regard to the need for global institutions to deal with problems like climate change and humanitarian intervention, but this is more of a sketch than a developed theory. The argument I make about our obligations to those in extreme poverty is not affected by this deficiency, because I argue that these obligations are specifically those of individuals, not governments. Nevertheless I agree that a more comprehensive account of international justice would need to pay more attention to political institutions.

13

Separateness, Suffering, and Moral Theory

DAVID SCHMIDTZ

What I call the Singer Principle has an awkward consequence. Section I explains the principle. Section II explains the problem. Later sections discuss implications for morality and moral theorizing.

I. The Singer Principle

In "Famine, Affluence, and Morality," after describing the famine in East Bengal circa 1971, Peter Singer says:

> I shall argue that the way people in relatively affluent countries react to a situation like that in Bengal cannot be justified; indeed, the whole way we look at moral issues—our moral conceptual scheme—needs to be altered, and with it, the way of life that has come to be taken for granted in our society.
>
> In arguing for this conclusion I will not, of course, claim to be morally neutral. I shall, however, try to argue for the moral position that I take, so that anyone who accepts certain assumptions, to be made explicit, will, I hope, accept my conclusion.
>
> I begin with the assumption that suffering and death from lack of food, shelter, and medical care are bad. . . . Those who disagree need read no further.
>
> My next point is this: if it is in our power to prevent something bad from happening, without thereby sacrificing anything of comparable moral importance, we ought, morally, to do it. By "without sacrificing anything of comparable moral importance" I mean without causing anything else comparably bad to happen, or doing something that is wrong in itself, or failing

to promote some moral good, comparable in significance to the bad thing that we can prevent. This principle seems almost as uncontroversial as the last one. It requires us only to prevent what is bad, and not to promote what is good, and it requires this of us only when we can do it without sacrificing anything that is, from the moral point of view, comparably important.[1]

Here, then, is what I call the Singer Principle:

SP: If it is in our power to prevent something bad from happening, without thereby sacrificing anything of comparable moral importance, we ought, morally, to do it.

SP has weaker and stronger forms. SP's weaker form lets us rewrite "anything of comparable importance" as "anything significant." SP's stronger form requires us to interpret the original phrase literally. Singer acknowledges that SP's uncontroversial (!) appearance is deceptive. If SP were acted upon, even in its *weaker* form, our lives would be very different. SP's *strong* version, though, requires "reducing ourselves to the level of marginal disutility," by which Singer means "the level at which, by giving more, I would cause as much suffering to myself or my dependents as I would relieve by my gift. This would mean, of course, that one would reduce oneself to very near the material circumstances of a Bengali refugee." Singer adds, "I should also say that the strong version seems to me to be the correct one."[2]

SP has an implication that a moral principle should not have.

II. SP Cannot Be Right
The Symmetry Problem

Here is what I have in mind. If we interpret SP from a straightforwardly utilitarian perspective, it would seem to be calling on us to ship food and money to wherever people need it more than we do.[3] Is that a problem? Not from a utilitarian perspective. It will conflict with some of our intuitions about the limits of our obligations to others, but utilitarians are accustomed to biting that bullet.

---

[1] Peter Singer, "Famine, Affluence, and Morality," *Philosophy and Public Affairs* 1 (1972), pp. 229–243, at pp. 230–31.

[2] Ibid., p. 241.

[3] If we do not presume to flesh out the principle in utilitarian terms, then what it calls for becomes wide open.

What about toxic waste? Might shipping toxic waste to wherever it will do the least harm fall into the category of preventing something bad without causing anything comparably bad? Yes, of course. It may even be the rule rather than the exception that our own back yards will not be the best possible place to store toxic waste.

Both exporting goods and exporting bads could prevent something bad without sacrificing anything of comparable importance. If this leaves us realizing that SP, as seen through a utilitarian lens, is not the whole story of morality when it comes to exporting bads, we may suspect it is not the whole story for exporting goods either. What we build into our theories to disrupt the symmetry of bads and goods—acknowledging the separateness of persons, say—is likely to limit the obligation (and perhaps the right) to export goods at the same time as it limits the right (and perhaps the obligation) to export bads.

Before pursuing this, I want to mention a further awkward consequence SP has when combined with Singer's position on animal equality.[4]

Species Equality

Not every utilitarian shares Singer's concern about animals. It is a separate decision where to locate the boundaries of moral concern, and the location of boundaries normally is not dictated by the principle one adopts for guiding decisions within those boundaries.

SP requires us to prevent bad whenever we can do so without sacrificing anything comparably important. SP's strong form, interpreted in a sufficiently narrow way (that is, ignoring the suffering of animals), requires us to reduce ourselves to the circumstances of a Bengali refugee if Bengali refugees are the worst off people we can help. However, if human and animal suffering are comparably important, then what SP actually requires has little to do with Bengali refugees. Animals everywhere are dying from easily preventable thirst or hunger, and from easily preventable diseases. If we let nature take its course, the best that many animals can hope for is that their throats will be torn out by predators before they starve: not exactly merciful, but at least quicker. However, we could prevent that too. There are animals by the millions, perhaps billions, whose circumstances are worse than those of Bengali refugees. SP (conjoined to species equality) entails no obligation to Bengali refugees. On the contrary, SP's strong form, conjoined to

---

[4] Peter Singer, *Animal Liberation*, second edition (New York: Random House, 1990), pp. 1–23.

species equality, requires us to "reduce ourselves to a level of marginal disutility" defined by the material circumstances not of Bengali refugees but of the worst off animals we can help. (If we humans were "utility monsters" compared to other animals, utilitarianism would require us to favor humans in our investment decisions, but Singer does not believe we are.)

III. But How Can SP Be Wrong?

Yet, SP is a plausible idea about how we ought to respond to suffering (including animal suffering). I want to say SP can't be wrong as a *reason for action*. On my view, SP is telling us to do the best we can, which is uncontroversial, as Singer says. There is always reason to do the best we can. Having identified any given course of action X as the best we can do, our reason for doing X is that we believe X is, after all, the best we can do. To have picked out X as the best we can do is by that very fact to have seen some reason to do X.

I am not claiming that SP is a *comprehensive* account of our reasons for action. Why not? Briefly (the next section elaborates), many of our reasons for action in this world stem from the fact that this world is not a parametric world. Ours is a strategic world: other agents respond to what we have done and also to what they anticipate from us. To give one of the simplest and most amply confirmed examples, players respond in one way to a strategy of unconditional cooperation, and respond quite differently to a strategy of tit-for-tat. SP must be, if not abandoned, at least interpreted in light of this fact. When suitably interpreted, that is, when interpreted as a strategy whose consequences will be a result of what happens when it is implemented in a strategic world, SP will not have the implications Singer says it has regarding how much we should contribute, when, or even why.[5]

A second concern, related but in any case the sort of concern we might express *qua* moral philosophers rather than *qua* game theorists, is that sometimes the best response to value is to respect it rather than to promote it. There comes a time for doing the best we can, which is to say there comes a time for SP or something like it. When? John Stuart Mill seemed to think SP, or something like it, would be required in but one

---

[5] Singer circa 1998 is alive to such complications. See his thoughtful "Darwin for the Left," reprinted in Peter Singer, *Writings on an Ethical Life* (New York: HarperCollins, 2000).

case in a thousand.[6] However, it is hard to see any resources in Mill's utilitarianism to so limit the scope of SP's application. Many readers in the aftermath of twentieth-century utilitarianism dismiss Mill's claims as pandering to common opinion, an unconvincing disavowal of his theory's patently radical nature. But Mill was neither a stupid man nor a man overly concerned to ally himself with the prejudices of his day. So, perhaps he saw something that got lost in the shuffle of twentieth-century utilitarianism's development as a simple-minded decision procedure.

IV. Respecting versus Promoting[7]
Elaborating the Game Theoretic Point

TRAGIC COMMONS: A baby is drowning in the pool beside you. You can save the baby by a process that involves giving the baby's family a hundred dollars. If you do not save the baby, the baby will die. You save the baby. A crowd begins to gather. Seeing what you have done, two onlookers throw their babies into the pool. The babies will drown unless you give each of their families a hundred dollars. More onlookers begin to gather, waiting to see what you do.

I am not saying our world is like TRAGIC COMMONS. I would say, though, that TRAGIC COMMONS is not a world we have any good reason to want to live in. And one way to make our world more like TRAGIC COMMONS is to embrace SP. Moreover, people do react to opportunities, including opportunities presented by the predictable actions or commitments of other people. Which is to say, our world is a strategic world. (Substitute "dictator" for "onlooker" in TRAGIC COMMONS. May we *assume* our world is nothing like that? Anyone committed to getting actual good results will assume no such thing but will instead investigate, one case at a time, how dictators and the rest of us actually react to incentives.)

TRAGIC COMMONS illustrates one kind of type-token issue.[8] In TRAGIC COMMONS, the token-benefit is a saved life, but this token-benefit is wildly misleading as a characterization of your action's real

---

[6] John Stuart Mill, *Utilitarianism* (Indianapolis: Hackett, 1979/1861).

[7] This section revises parts of David Schmidtz, "Islands in a Sea of Obligation: An Essay on the Duty to Rescue," *Law and Philosophy* 19 (2000), pp. 683–705.

[8] As analytic philosophers use these terms, a *type* is a general category, whereas a *token* is a particular instance of the more general category. For example, there are many blue shirts in the world. The one I am wearing is a token of the general type.

consequences. The token-result of your action is a saved life, but the type-result is an escalating catastrophe. Knowing that foreign aid has a history of driving such wedges between token-benefits and type-disasters, I now get a letter asking me to participate in what may or may not be another commons tragedy in the making. I have to make a decision. Does morality require me to accept a theorist's or professional fund-raiser's all-too-predictable assurance that if we turn on the spigots in response to problems and turn them off in response to solutions, we'll eventually have fewer problems and more solutions?[9]

To whatever extent we take responsibility for other people as well as ourselves, our actions are encouraging people to depend on us rather than on themselves. Act-utilitarianism usually would not permit people opportunistically to arrange circumstances so that our act-utilitarian commitments require us to support them, but unless they too are committed act-utilitarians, that will not stop them from doing it. Theories often have implications other than ones they formally acknowledge. A theory can stipulate an action guide and an intended result. But a theory cannot stipulate that following its action guide will have its intended result, for that is an empirical matter. So it is with maximizing utility. One can say that trying to maximize utility actually tends to maximize utility, but saying it does not make it so. A simple maximizing strategy may tend to lead to the best possible outcome for beings like us in situations like ours. Then again, it may not. It has no history of doing so.

Elaborating the Moral Theoretic Point

SP is a suggestion about how to go about *promoting* value. However, promoting value is not the only concern if either (a) value itself is not the only concern, or (b) being moral sometimes is a matter of *respecting* rather than promoting value. Under what conditions might respecting value conflict with promoting it? Here are two notorious philosophical thought experiments.

> TROLLEY: A trolley is rolling down a track on its way to killing five people. If you switch to another track on which there is only one person, you will save five and kill one.

Most people say you ought to switch tracks and kill one to save five.

---

[9] One need not be an ideologue to be a skeptic about foreign aid. Foreign aid's actual history appalls Brian Barry as much as it does me. See Barry, *Why Social Justice Matters* (Cambridge: Polity, 2005), Chapter 3.

Compare this to:

> HOSPITAL: Five patients are dying for lack of suitable organ donors. A UPS delivery person walks into the hospital. You know she is a suitable donor for all five patients. If you kidnap her and harvest her organs, you save five and kill one.[10]

People have a different intuition here. Among students (and U.S. Congressional staffers, at whose workshops I sometimes lecture) that I informally poll, almost everyone responds to HOSPITAL by saying you cannot kidnap and murder people, period. Not even to save lives. On a trip to Kazakhstan, I presented the cases to an audience of twenty-one professors from nine post-Soviet republics. They said the same. Why? Are the cases really so different? How?

TROLLEY tells us numbers matter. Although HOSPITAL seems to have TROLLEY's logical structure, it leads us to a different conclusion. Why? The literature discusses several differences, but one difference I have not heard mentioned is this: HOSPITAL tells us that sometimes what matters is being able to trust others to respect us as separate persons. Hospitals cannot exist, and more generally we cannot live well together, unless we can trust each other to acknowledge that we all have lives of our own. HOSPITAL shows we sometimes get the best result—a community of people living well together—not by aiming at a result so much as by being trustworthy, so people can plan to deal with us in mutually beneficial ways.

To a cartoon utilitarian thinking about TROLLEY, all that matters is numbers. But in a more realistic institutional context like HOSPITAL, we intuitively grasp a more fundamental point. Namely, if we don't take seriously rights and separate personhood, we won't get justice; in fact, *we won't even get good numbers*. This is why I said morality sometimes is about *respecting* value, not because value does not matter, but precisely because it does.

---

[10] It generally is understood that the trolley conductor is not using the lone victim as a mere means of saving five. TROLLEY's victim simply is in the wrong place at the wrong time, unlike the victim in HOSPITAL who in effect is being hunted down for use as a mere resource. The seminal article on this point probably is Philippa Foot, "The Problem of Abortion and the Doctrine of Double Effect," *Oxford Review* 5 (1967) pp. 5–15. Foot argues persuasively against attaching too much weight to the idea of double effect, but see the discussion of acts and omissions in Horacio Spector, *Autonomy and Rights* (Oxford: Oxford University Press, 1992). For a classic discussion of HOSPITAL-type cases, see Judith Jarvis Thomson, "Killing, Letting Die, and the Trolley Problem," *Monist* 59 (1976), pp. 204–217.

Acts versus Practices

A consequentialist theory needs to treat some topics as beyond the reach of utilitarian calculation. Rights can trump (not merely outweigh) utilitarian calculation even from a broadly consequentialist perspective. Why? Because, from a consequentialist perspective, results matter, and because, as an empirical matter, there is enormous utility in being able to treat certain parameters as settled, as not even permitting case by case utilitarian reasoning.

Unconstrained maximizers, by definition, optimally use any resources to which they have access, including their neighbors' organs. To get good results in the real world, though, we need to be surrounded not by unconstrained maximizers but by people who respect rights, thereby enabling us to have a system of expectations and trust, which allows us together to transform our world into a world with greater *potential* (a world where delivery companies are willing to serve the hospital). When we cannot count on others to treat us as rights-bearers with separate lives, we are living in a world of lesser potential.

John Stuart Mill famously observed that it is better to be a dissatisfied Socrates than to be a satisfied pig.[11] Of course, it is better to hit an optimum than not, other things equal. On the other hand, Mill's insight is that other things are not equal. If our choice is between making the best of a low-potential situation versus falling short of making the best of a high-potential situation, we may prefer to fall short, and be a dissatisfied Socrates. Mill, wanting his society to operate as high as possible in utility space, considered it more important to live in a world with a higher ceiling than to make sure every action hits the ceiling. Mill was right.

All optimizing is done with respect to a set of constraints and opportunities. Some of our constraints may be brute facts about the external world, but most will be to some extent self-imposed; some will reflect our beliefs about what morality requires. (We have limited time to spend looking for an apartment, limited money to spend on dinner, and there are things we will not do for money.)[12] We may be constrained not to murder—constrained both by choice and by external factors such as the presence of Joe's bodyguard. If other people can count on us not to murder

---

[11] *Utilitarianism*, Chapter 2.

[12] See Schmidtz "Rationality Within Reason," *Journal of Philosophy* 89 (1992), pp. 445–466, or Schmidtz, *Rational Choice and Moral Agency* (Princeton: Princeton University Press, 1995).

them, new possibilities open up—opportunities people would not otherwise have. In contrast, if people *cannot* rely on us not to murder them, then our murderous act may be as good as possible under the circumstances—it may hit the utility ceiling, but the ceiling itself will be lower than it would have been had murder been ruled out. (Someone who says a true utilitarian will take all that into account is saying a true utilitarian cares not so much about consequences of acts as about consequences of practices that permit some acts and not others, thereby enabling citizens to make some kinds of plans rather than others. I agree. My point is only that a true utilitarian in that sense is not an act-utilitarian.)

When doctors embrace a prohibition against harvesting organs of healthy patients without consent, doctors give up opportunities to optimize—to hit the ceiling—but *patients* gain opportunities to visit doctors safely. They gain a world with a higher ceiling. Such utility comes from doctors refusing even to ask whether murdering a patient would be optimal.

But what if your doctor really could save five patients by murdering one? Would not a rule letting your doctor do it, just this once, be the rule with the best consequences? Compare this to a question asked by Rawls: in baseball, batters get three strikes, but what if there were a case where, just this once, it would be better if a batter had four?[13] Rawls's crucial and neglected insight is that this question presumes to treat "three strikes" as a rule of thumb, to be assessed case by case. Rules of thumb are "rules made to be broken." But in baseball, "three strikes" is a rule of practice, not a rule of thumb. If an umpire were to allow a fourth strike in an exceptional circumstance, baseball would not be able to go on as before.

"Rule of thumb" utilitarians may say, and even believe, they respect the rule against murder, yet they treat whether to obey as a question to decide case by case. By contrast, "rule of practice" utilitarians decline even to *ask* about the utility of particular actions in particular cases. Facing a case where violating a rule would have more utility, rule of practice utilitarians say, "Our theory sorts out alternative practices, like three strikes versus four, by asking which has more utility as the kind of practice that even *umpires* have no right to evaluate case by case. Our theory *forbids* us to consider consequences in a more case-specific way. We need not say why—the theory says what it says and letting that be

---

13 See "Two Concepts of Rules," reprinted in John Rawls, *Collected Papers* (Cambridge, Massachusetts: Harvard University Press, 1999).

the end of it would be fine—but if we wanted to defend the theory rather than merely specify it, we would say our being forbidden to consider case-specific consequences has better consequences. For one thing, it gives other people the option of rationally trusting us."

What do we think about a HOSPITAL-like case where we are certain no one will ever know what we've done, therefore certain that our action will not undermine trust? Perhaps it does not matter, since I am not speaking of a world where we can be certain it will never occur to UPS Inc. to wonder what is happening to all the delivery personnel they keep sending to our hospital. Suffice it to say, real world morality has the shape it does in part because real world uncertainty is what it is.

Some utilitarians find it a mystery why morality would incorporate any constraints beyond a requirement to do whatever maximizes the good.[14] But from an institutional perspective, there is no mystery. Moral institutions constrain the good's pursuit because the good is pursued by individuals. If the good is to be realized, then institutions—legal, political, economic, and cultural institutions—must get the constraints right, so as to put individuals in a position to pursue the good in a manner conducive to the good's production in general.

There are parallels between rational agents and moral institutions in terms of how they operate in the face of real-world complexity. For example, individuals adopt satisficing strategies in pursuit of particular goals. They impose constraints on local goals so as to bring their various goals into better harmony with each other, thereby making life as a whole go as well as possible.[15] Likewise, moral institutions get the best result not so much by aiming at the best result as by imposing constraints on individual pursuits so as to bring individual pursuits into better harmony with each other. Institutions (hospitals, for example) serve the common good by leaving well enough alone—creating opportunities for mutual benefit, then trusting individuals to take advantage of them. That is how (even from a utilitarian perspective) institutions have a moral mandate to serve the common good that does not collapse into a mandate for ordinary moral agents to maximize utility.

In effect, there are two ways in which institutional utility is based on trust. First, people have to be able to trust their society to treat them as

---

[14] See Shelly Kagan, *The Limits of Morality* (New York: Oxford University Press, 1989), pp. 121–27. Samuel Scheffler, *The Rejection of Consequentialism* (New York: Oxford University Press, 1982), p. 129, expresses similar skepticism, despite departing from utilitarianism in other respects.

[15] See Schmidtz "Rationality Within Reason," supra note #10.

rights-bearers. Second, society must in turn trust people to use the opportunities they have as rights-bearers within society.

A reflective consequentialist morality is not about one versus five, nor even about costs versus benefits. It is about how we need to live in order to be glad we are neighbors. It's about getting on with our lives in a way that complements rather than hinders our neighbors' efforts to get on with theirs. It accepts constraints on optimizing in order to have a higher ceiling.

Acts aren't the important thing in the long run. They are not the main variable on which long-run utility depends. The ceiling itself is the main variable. An optimizer on the ground in Bangladesh can do only so much. What Bengalis need is not to optimize or be surrounded by optimizers so much as to live in a society with a western-style ceiling: a society where people (men *and* women, people of all religions, all castes, and so on) have the opportunity and the responsibility to do what meets needs: that is, to produce. If we care about people meeting needs on a global scale, our task is to throw ourselves not into meeting needs but into encouraging processes by which people meet needs. Such encouragement, I surmise, would never involve or even be compatible with reducing ourselves to the material circumstances of a Bengali refugee.

Postscript on Trolley Problems

Experimental psychologists have demonstrated repeatedly that their subjects' intuitions regarding such things as probability and logical implication become more unreliable as the experimental context becomes more abstract or unworldly. In the face of such findings, why would moral philosophers continue to treat intuitive moral reactions to bizarre thought experiments as if such intuitions were reliable? I doubt there is any good reason; their teachers did it, so they do it. I am glad Singer seldom partakes of this tradition. (I wonder how he feels about SHALLOW POND; authors today are still writing on it, without even knowing it began life in an article of Singer's.) I seldom do as much thought-experimenting as I am doing here. I am glad I did it in Kazakhstan, though. Here's why.

Wherever I go, whether my audience consists of local students, congressional staffers, or post-Soviet professors, when I present the TROLLEY case and ask them whether they would switch tracks, about ninety percent will say, "there has to be another way!" A philosophy professor's first reaction is to say, "Please, stay on topic. I'm trying to illustrate a point here! To see the point, you need to decide what to do when there is no other way." When I said this to my class of post-Soviet professors, though, they spoke briefly among themselves in Russian, then two of them quietly said (as others nodded, every one of them looking me straight in the eye), "Yes, we understand. We have heard this before. All our lives we were told the few must be sacrificed for the sake of many. We were told there is no other way. What we were told was a lie. There was always another way."

I was speechless, but they were right. The real world does not stipulate that there is no other way. (Have you, or anyone you know, ever been in a situation like TROLLEY, literally needing to kill one to save five? Why not? Have you been unusually lucky?) In any case, I now see more wisdom in the untutored insight that there has to be another way than in what TROLLEY originally was meant to illustrate. As Rawls and Nozick (in different ways) say, justice is about respecting the separateness of persons. We are not to sacrifice one person for the sake of another.[16] If we find ourselves seemingly called upon to sacrifice the few for the sake of the many, justice is about finding another way.[17]

V. Ethical Theory in an Ethical Life

Is it *important* to reject the argument that SP can require us to export bads? An all-the-way-down utilitarian should yawn, saying, "So what? Utilities may or may not add up that way in the real world. If they do, so be it. It's not as if recommending that we move bads to wherever they do the least harm is an embarrassment for the theory. What's the problem?"

Would we feel uncomfortable in reacting to the symmetry problem by saying "So what?" I would (and I *am* uncomfortable insofar as we do in fact export bads). What is the source of my discomfort? Something like this: people have lives of their own. Exporting bads (when we do so without recipients' consent—the *real* recipients, not just their governments) would treat recipients as mere means rather than as separate agents with lives of their own.

---

[16] I insert the word 'actively' here to distinguish Rawls and Nozick from utilitarians who say not rescuing people amounts to sacrificing them, so that at any given moment, we are sacrificing everyone who would not have died if individually or collectively we had acted differently.

[17] Jean Hampton argues that the moral argument against sacrificing one person for the sake of another applies to self-sacrifice as well. See "Selflessness and the Loss of Self," *Social Philosophy and Policy* 10 (1993), pp. 135–165.

Singer is smart, skilled philosopher. He may say, "So what?" He may say something more clever. No doubt Singer could respond in an interesting way to the species equality problem too. Among analytic philosophers, the bare fact that Singer can give a good account of himself in philosophical debate is too predictable to be interesting. (Any suspense will concern whether Singer manages to extract utility from these responses.)

My main reason for raising the Symmetry and Species Equality problems (especially the latter) is not to prove I can "spot the fallacy" but simply to reflect on how to take human nature into account when doing moral philosophy. I do not mean to be pointing out a mistake when I observe that what fires Singer's imagination changes from time to time. Sometimes, what fires Singer's imagination is information that there are laboratories where animal experiments are being conducted that have little point and where, even if the research were important, the animals are suffering unnecessarily. Sometimes Singer is gripped by reports of human famine. Sometimes what grips Singer is how animals are treated on factory farms. Singer is normal. He does one thing for a while, then moves on. Moving on is human. It is not a mistake. It is not immoral. Singer is not obliged to commensurate his projects—to show that a moral imperative to spend his days exactly as he does is derivable from SP. He does not need to show that his positions on species equality and on SP fit nicely together. Animal liberation and famine relief are different projects, as are euthanasia, abortion, and so on. Moreover, not everything that matters to Singer is a *project*. Henry Spira was a friend, not a project. *Friend* is something to be rather than something to do.

Selective Focus[18]

FAST PAIN RELIEF: There is a button you could push. If you push it, all sentient life will painlessly vanish from existence. You will, of course, minimize suffering in the process.

FAST PAIN RELIEF shows that minimizing suffering is not the only thing that matters. Neither is it always what matters most.

What FAST PAIN RELIEF leaves open is whether minimizing suffering matters a lot, or relatively little, in the cosmic scheme of things. We need not settle this, because suffering could matter quite a lot without it being

---

[18] The last two parts of this section revise parts of David Schmidtz, "Islands In a Sea of Obligation: An Essay on the Duty to Rescue," *Law and Philosophy* 19 (2000), pp. 683–705.

true that we ought to spend quite a lot of our lives working to put an end to it. Let me approach the point obliquely, beginning with a story. Environmental activist Paul Watson, founder of the Sea Shepherd Society, confronted a Japanese fishing fleet in 1982 and negotiated a halt to a netting process that was killing dolphins. During the discussion, a fisherman asked Watson which is of more value, the life of a dolphin or a life of a human?

> I answered that, in my opinion, the life of a dolphin was equal in value to the life of a human. The fisherman then asked, "If a Japanese fisherman and a dolphin were both caught in a net and you could save the life of one, which would you save?"
>
> All the fishermen in the room smirked. They had me pegged for a liberal and felt confident that I would say I would save the fisherman, thus making a mockery of my declaration that humans and dolphins are equal. I looked about the room and smiled. "I did not come to Japan to save fishermen; I am here to save dolphins."[19]

There is power in Watson's response. It is no mere philosophical inconsistency. We can learn from it. It is a pivotal feature of our moral psychology that when we focus on something, it takes on added moral significance to us. We can call it *selective focus*.[20] A lot of people are consumed by one burning issue or another, and sometimes make the mistake of thinking everyone ought to be consumed by the same issue. In fact, we freely choose to be consumed by one issue rather than another. Singer may think what he has chosen to focus on is the thing on

---

[19] Paul Watson, "Tora! Tora! Tora!" *Earth Ethics*, edited by James Sterba (Englewood Cliffs: Prentice Hall, 1995), pp. 341–46, here p. 341.

[20] Human beings including Peter Singer are what Elijah Millgram (in personal correspondence, June 2005) has called serial hyperspecializers. What Millgram has in mind is that humans adapt to ecological niches by adapting software, not hardware, and the flexibility of human software permits equisitely refined adaptation: to niches for such organisms as Antarctic nature photographer, corporate merger lawyer, or animal rights activist. Moreover, that flexibility persists to some extent, such that humans retain the capacity to colonize new niches. Individual humans do not pursue only one project, although they may be gripped by one main project at any given time. One of the problems with a project such as that suggested by SP—the project of making sure that no one in the world is worse off than oneself—is that the project cannot be brought to a state of satisfactory completion. There never comes a time to move on to the next project, and so serial hyperspecilizers (including Singer) cannot possibly take SP as seriously as Singer says they should, and their lives would be grossly unlivable if they were seriously to try. See note # 21.

which we are all obliged to focus, but it only looks that way to someone already focusing on the same thing. Paul Watson was telling the fishermen that although he may be committed to seeing humans and dolphins as equals, he is not obliged to be preoccupied by that particular commitment. He is committed to *respecting* humans and dolphins alike, but not to giving them equal time when deciding how to plan his life.

Paul Watson believes in fighting injustice. Does that commit him to fighting injustice wherever he finds it? Not at all. There is injustice everywhere. Is Watson committed to fighting whichever injustice currently is firing the imagination of Peter Singer? Not at all. That's not what Watson is here for. Like Singer, Watson decides for himself where to make his stand, as do we all.[21]

Western Civilization: What Makes It Work

Distant problems are types of which there are innumerable tokens. Local emergencies are simply tokens. If one falls in your lap today, you can be fairly sure there won't be another in your lap tomorrow. You help and that's the end of it. Life goes on.

When professional fund-raisers exhort us to help relieve famine, they talk about token-cost (without using that name), going into some detail explaining how a hundred dollar donation can change a recipient's life. Yet, it is no particular token of the type "starving person" they have in mind. It is the type itself, and famine relief's type-cost is not small. If we embrace the duty to relieve famine in the way Singer says we should, life does not just go on.

Singer himself rightly stresses that pious talk is not enough. "What is the point of relating philosophy to public (and personal) affairs if we do not take our conclusions seriously? In this instance, taking our conclusion seriously means acting upon it."[22] Can Singer's conclusion be taken seriously in this sense?[23]

---

[21] I have argued that we can and do deliberate about our ends, even our final ends, and that having to grapple with the potentials and perils of human psychology can make a choice of final ends straightforwardly rational. See David Schmidtz, "Choosing Ends," *Ethics* 104 (1994), pp. 226–251. I put these arguments in context in *Rational Choice and Moral Agency*.

[22] "Famine, Affluence, and Morality," p. 242.

[23] Zell Kravinsky takes SP seriously. He gave away nearly everything he owned, including a kidney, and feels unquenchable guilt over not yet having given away the other one. See Ian Parker, "The Gift," *The New Yorker* (August 2nd, 2004), pp. 54–63.

Singer gives the impression he is not keen on western civilization. Having endorsed SP in its strong form, Singer adds, "Even if we accepted the principle only in its moderate form, however, it should be clear that we would have to give away enough to ensure that the consumer society, dependent as it is on people spending on trivia rather than giving to famine relief, would slow down and perhaps disappear entirely. There are several reasons why this would be desirable in itself."[24]

Desirable. Desirable *in itself.* We might have expected that Singer would classify the collapse of western society as a cost, albeit an acceptable one. Evidently not. Singer calls it desirable in itself, and seems to find it so obviously desirable that the "several reasons why" need not be mentioned. And if this is the moderate principle's predictable result, what happens if we follow the strong principle Singer favors? What else disappears along with consumer society? Books? Art? By the lights of SP, spending *time* on "trivia" is no more allowable than spending money on it.

How much should we give? Singer's theory gives a simple answer: more. To get something we can take seriously in Singer's sense, we must do better than that. Theorists need to realize that moral theorizing isn't a game you win by having the most demanding theory.

Peter Unger imagines a world in which "whenever well-off folks learn of people in great need, they promptly move to meet the need, almost no matter what the financial cost. So, at this later date, the basic needs of almost all the world's people will be met almost all the time. . . . What's more, should any of these descendants find herself facing such preventable suffering as now actually obtains, she'd devote almost all her energy and resources toward lessening the suffering."[25]

I doubt that Unger's vision is even coherent. It has the following logic. The productive output of the western world is put up for grabs. A world-wide competition ensues. And the way for a country's leaders to win the competition for that output is to have a population that needs (or seems to need) it more than anyone else. But if we devote almost all our energy and resources to meeting such need, *then how do we get to be so well off?* Where does Unger think prosperity comes from in the first place?

Imagine what our community would be like if a lot of us did as Unger asks. There were about five thousand people in Humboldt, the

[24] Ibid., p. 241.
[25] Peter Unger, *Living High and Letting Die: Our Illusion of Innocence* (New York: Oxford University Press, 1996), p. 20.

nearest town when I was growing up on a farm in Saskatchewan. Suppose we farmers gave up that part of our crop that we would have cashed in to buy movie tickets. If we do that, the Towne Theater goes out of business. No big deal, perhaps. The handful of employees seek work elsewhere. Maybe they find work at the Princess or Lucky Cafes. Fine, but we also stop exchanging grain for burgers at the café, instead sending that part of our crop abroad. The cafes close, over a dozen people are out of work, and we exceed Humboldt's ability to find work for them.

Unger says we would not have nice cars and homes.[26] We sacrifice that part of our crop that would have bought new cars. Fine. Car dealers and their employees are out of work. *They* no longer send money to Bangladesh; neither do they buy trivia from local shops, so furniture and clothing shops close, defaulting on their business loans. Their employees stop making mortgage payments, and of course, they stop sending money to Bangladesh. Banks start foreclosing on houses, relieving occupants of the obligation to liquidate their houses in service of famine relief. There is no one to buy the houses, though, so the banks close too.

Those able to leave Humboldt do so, becoming refugees themselves, searching for a community that has not yet succumbed to Unger's call to prevent suffering. So, Singer was right that obeying SP would result in our reducing ourselves to the circumstances of a Bengali refugee. It would do little for Bangladesh in the long run, but would have the result for western civilization that Singer calls desirable in itself.

Singer would allow that we have to keep doing our part to maintain our incomes so that we remain able to send money overseas. But in the above thought experiment, the problem isn't that we aren't working but that we aren't *consuming*, which is to say, we aren't sustaining other people's work. We aren't *doing* business, so we aren't *sustaining* business. It is the lack of business—our declining to spend money on trivia—that shuts down the theater and the coffee shop. Moreover, the experiment is not merely a thought experiment. Historically, with few exceptions, this is how thoroughly communal societies crash, unless they switch to some other way of doing business first.[27]

Singer says we need a "Darwinism of the left."[28] I agree. No doubt we would disagree on what such a view would imply. We might agree,

---

[26] Ibid., p. 145.
[27] See David Schmidtz, "The Institution of Property," *Social Philosophy and Policy* 11 (1994), pp. 42–62 for some exceptions to this historical rule and also for some explanation of why it is the rule.
[28] See note #4.

though, with an observation recently made by David Miller. Miller reflects that if someone in France were getting far better health care than Miller was getting in England, Miller's first instinct would be to suspect that France has a better system and England ought to consider adopting it, not that resources ought to be transferred from France to England so as to reduce inequality.[29] Why? Because the aim of Miller's egalitarianism is to improve life prospects, not to equalize them. Miller's credentials as a spokesperson for the left are beyond question, and the point he makes here is more or less Darwinian. That is, the thing to do with failed social systems is not to *subsidize* them but to *replace* them with something having a history of working.

We must of course remain (or become) humbly aware that revolutions imposed by alien cultures and philosophies have no history of working. Nothing we do will have only the effects we intend. The only course with a history of helping people long term is whatever enables them to take responsibility for their own futures (and even that is not a guarantee).

VI. The Nature of Moral Theory

Perhaps we need not reject SP. It may suffice to understand what SP is: it is a piece of a theory, nothing more. Theories are maps, not attempts to specify necessary and sufficient conditions.[30] We begin with a terrain (a subject matter), and with questions about that terrain. Our questions spur us to build theories—maps of the terrain—that articulate and systematize our answers. To know how to reach Detroit, we need one kind of map. To know how to be a good person, we need another map. Note: *maps* do not tell us where we want to go. (This is equally true of scientific theorizing. For example, to those who want to understand nature in secular terms, Darwinism is a serviceable map. It does not explain everything, but it explains a lot. Darwinism is rejected by Creationists, though. Why? Not because it *fails* to help them understand the origin of species in secular terms, but precisely because it succeeds. They have a different destination; understanding themselves in secular terms is not

---

[29] David Miller, "Justice and Global Inequality," in Hurrell and Woods, *Inequality, Globalization, and World Politics* (Oxford: Oxford University Press, 1999), pp. 187–210.

[30] I thank Jenann Ismael and quite a few other people over the years for helpful and enjoyable conversations about theories as maps. This section revises portions of Part 1 of David Schmidtz, *Elements of Justice* (New York: Cambridge University Press, 2006).

what they want.) Our questions predate our theorizing, and constitute our reasons to theorize in the first place. In different words, moral theorizing primarily is for those who aim to be moral. It is when we aim to be moral that we make moral theory the kind of map we have reason to consult.

Theories Are Abstractions

A map of Detroit is an artifact, an invention. So is a map of morality. In neither case does the terrain being mapped *really look like that*. A map of Detroit is stylized, abstract, simplified. It otherwise would fail as a map. Yet a map can be accurate in the sense that it does not mislead. A given map will for some purposes have ample detail; for other purposes it will be oversimplified.

A map is not itself reality. It is at best a serviceable representation. A theory likewise is a more or less serviceable representation of a terrain. A theory cannot be more than that.

Fine Detail Is a Means to an End

When we construct a map, we leave out details that would merely confuse users. Fine detail is not an end in itself. We do not try to show current locations of every stalled car on the side of the road, and we do not call a map false when it omits such details. The question is whether users honestly wanting to follow directions would be led astray.

Road maps would be better in the sense of allowing more detail if we printed them on ten square meter sheets rather than the roughly one meter sheets we use today. What does that tell us? It tells us that road maps are functional artifacts. We design and create them for a purpose. Their purpose limits how accurate they can be, limits how detailed they can be, limits how much information they can represent. Moral theories are the same. We could "blow them up" in an effort to make them correspond exactly to the moral terrain that they are supposed to represent. At some point, though, loading in more detail causes users to lose sight of the forest for the trees. There also is a limit to how much detail a finite mapmaker can possibly anticipate needing to represent. Giving someone directions to your house is not an exact science. It is an art. We get better at it with practice, but still it takes wisdom and judgment. It makes sense to say one thing for daylight hours and something else to a person who will be navigating at night. We have no reason to expect any set of instructions to be apt for all contexts. It does not help to tell someone to look for Starbucks if that person has never been outside rural China before and has no idea what a Starbucks is. Likewise, in 1990, it may help to tell a driver to turn left at Starbucks, yet the same instruction becomes useless in 2005 when there is a Starbucks every second block.

Comprehensive Scope Is a Means to an End

Existing theories tend to be like maps of the globe: a striving for comprehensive scope—for a principle or set of principles that covers everything. Real moral questions, though, often are more like questions about getting to campus from the airport. When we want to get to campus, a map of the globe does not help. It is not even relevant.

Local maps do not say how to reach all destinations. Yet, though noncomprehensive, they almost always are what we want when we want a map. Why? Because they provide the detail we need for solving problems we actually have. The distant perspective from which we view the whole globe of morality is a perspective from which the surface looks smooth. Principles we stretch to cover the globe fail to make contact with the valleys of moral life. They do not help people on the ground to make moral decisions.

Theories Have Counterexamples

Typically, a counterexample's point is to show that a theory is not algorithmic: we could follow the letter of a theory and still arrive at the wrong destination. But we can consider it a folk theorem of analytic philosophy: *any* theory simple enough to be useful, including SP, has counterexamples. (This is a simple theory. Therefore, if correct, it has counterexamples.)

Counterexamples are warnings, telling us theories should not be trusted blindly, any more than a map should be trusted blindly in the face of signs warning that the bridge ahead is washed out. Even simple travel instructions require interpretation, judgment, and experience. (Carbury said the turn was "about a mile." Have we gone too far? Is that the gas station he told us to watch for?) There is virtually no such thing as simply following instructions.

Theories Say What to Do in Context C, Not that
We Are in Context C

Like it or not, we apply theories, not merely follow them. Put it this way: when we formulate *rules*, we try to formulate instructions that agents can follow, but when we formulate *principles* rather than rules, we are not even trying to formulate instructions that agents can simply follow.

(The idea of following is comforting, seeming to relieve us of responsibility, whereas *applying* a theory requires good faith, wisdom, and experience, and leaves little room for doubt about who is choosing and who is responsible for the consequences.) Those who want principles of justice to be "idiot-proof" have the wrong idea about what a theory can do.

If your destination is the campus, a city map may tell you to turn left at 1st and Broadway, but by itself an ordinary map cannot tell you what to do right now unless you already know from experience and observation that you are at the corner of 1st and Broadway. An ordinary road map does not come with a red X saying, "You are here." Ordinary maps depend on a user to know where he or she is, and where he or she wants to go.

Theories are like ordinary maps in that respect. Even if a theory says unequivocally that principle P applies in context C, we still need to decide whether our current situation is enough like C to make P applicable. Unequivocal though principle P may be, we still need wisdom and experience to judge that the time for principle P has come.

Different Destinations Call for Different Maps

Our purposes change. We seek answers to new questions, calling for a new map. A map of the city is for one purpose; a map of the solar system is for another. Likewise, a theory that maps a public official's duties may be quite different from a theory that maps a parent's duties. Note: If we have more than one purpose, we may need more than one map *even if* there is only one ultimate reality. (My theory that theories are like maps is a theory: a way of systematizing and articulating how I see the activity of theorizing. The activity of theorizing is the reality; my "map theory" is my attempt to describe that reality. If my "map theory" is correct, it will have the limitations that maps tend to have.)

When Maps Overlap, They Can Disagree. So What?

Suppose I have two maps, and they disagree. I infer from one that I should take the freeway; the other says the freeway is closed. If I discard one, I make disagreement vanish, but that doesn't solve the problem. Disagreement is informative, telling me I need to pay attention. I cannot trust any map blindly. So, when maps are imperfect, there are worse things than having more than one. If I notice that they disagree, I check whether one is out of date, or consult a local resident. If I see grains of truth in incompatible theories, must I discard one for the sake of consistency? No, not if theories are maps.

Theories Are Compromises

When we theorize, we seek to render what we know simple enough to be understood, stated, and applied. If we try to describe verbally every nuance of morality's complexity, we get something so unwieldy that it may not appear to be a theory at all. If instead we try to simplify, homing in on justice's essence, we get incompleteness or inaccuracy. The task is like trying to represent three-dimensional terrain in two dimensions. Mapmakers projecting from three dimensions onto two can accurately represent size or shape, but not both. Mercator projections depict lines of longitude as parallel, representing shapes more or less accurately at a cost of distorting relative size. Greenland looks as big as Africa but in fact is one fourteenth as large. Goode's Homolosine is better at representing individual continents, at a cost of depicting the world as a globe whose surface has been peeled like an orange.

Like other theories, utilitarianism is rather like a Mercator projection. It has an equator around which its implications seem intuitively accurate, and it has poles around which its exclusive emphasis on consequences seems wildly distorted.

In short, mapmaking, like theorizing, is a messy activity. Mapmakers choose how to represent worlds, and there is no perfect way of representing three-dimensional truth in two dimensions. Moral theorists choose how to represent complex thoughts in simple words, and there is no perfect way of representing in words everything we believe.

Yet, this is not a skeptical view! There remains an objective truth that the map can represent (or fail to represent) in a helpful way. Regardless of whether partisans of Mercator and Peters projections ever settle which representation best serves a particular user's purposes, there will remain a three-dimensional truth of the matter.

It need not be a skeptical view in the arena of moral theorizing either. We might think we see a huge disanalogy between geography and moral theory: We evaluate a geographical map's accuracy simply by checking the terrain, whereas in moral theory, there is no terrain out there to simply check. An alternative view: think of road maps as prescriptions rather than as descriptions. We choose to believe one moral theory rather than another, and there is no obvious way to prove that those who choose differently are wrong. However, the same is true of road maps. A road map cannot point us in the right direction until we choose a destination. We do not get our destination *from* the map. We bring it *to* the map. There are reasons for choosing one destination (for wanting to be one kind of person, say, or live in one kind of society) rather than another, but we do have to choose. Do we wish moral theories were *less* like road maps in this sense? Do we instead want a theory to be a *treasure* map, identifying X as the spot at which every agent *must* aim on pain of being irrational? Why?[31]

Articulating the Code

When hiking in the Tucson mountains, I can tell the difference between a pincushion cactus and a hedgehog cactus. I *see* the difference even while doubting I can *state* the difference. If I try to state the difference, my statement will be incomplete, or will have counterexamples. Our ability to track ethical norms similarly exceeds and precedes our ability to articulate the norms being tracked. Indeed, if being able to track X presupposed verbal skills we develop only in graduate school, then X could not function in society as moral norms must.

Any code we can articulate is no more than a rough summary of wisdom gleaned from experience, that is, wisdom about where we have been. Our articulated wisdom will be useful going forward, since the future will be somewhat like the past. Yet, the future will be novel, too. No code is guaranteed to anticipate every contingency, which is to say, no formula (so far) unerringly prescribes choices for all situations. (The theorists I know do not expect their theories to tell them what grade to assign, how to vote when the hiring committee meets, or whether to cancel class.)

Knowing which principle to apply requires judgment. Judgment is codifiable in a way, yet exercising judgment is not like following a code. Consider a simpler issue: can a code tell investors when to buy and sell stocks? Market analysts look at histories of price fluctuations and see patterns. Patterns suggest formulas. Occasionally someone markets a formula, offering proof that the formula would have predicted every major price movement of the last fifty years. Investors buy the formula, which promptly fails to predict the next major move. My point: many phenomena are codifiable—exhibiting a pattern that, after the fact, can be expressed as a formula—but that does not mean the formula will help us make the next decision.

---

[31] I thank Chris Freiman, Kevin Vallier, Jason Brennan, and Jenann Ismael for helpful discussion. I do want to portray being moral as inspiring, as the best life for normal human beings, and I do so in Schmidtz 1995. We want to be understood. We want to be esteemed, and we want our real selves, not merely our false facades, to be objects of esteem. To me, this reason for being honest is compelling, but I see no point in trying to convict of irrationality those who are unmoved.

So, when business majors in ethics courses ask for "the code" the following of which is guaranteed to render all their future business decisions beyond reproach, we may have little to say, even if we think such a code is, in principle, out there awaiting discovery. Business majors tend to understand stock markets well enough to know they can expect only so much from a stock-picking code. Responsibility for exercising judgment ultimately lies with them, not with any code. Some of them have not done enough moral philosophy to know they likewise can expect only so much from a moral code. But we can tell them the truth: philosophers are in the business of articulating principles, not rules and not codes. Moral wisdom is less like knowing answers to test questions and more like simply being aware that the test has begun (and that every day is a new test).

Moral theorizing doesn't necessarily have a global focus. Morality is about what should guide us given that our focus (yours, mine, Paul Watson's, Peter Singer's, everyone's) inevitably is a *focus*—something that does not cover everything. A humanly rational morality is one that can help people live well together, given that neither we nor the people around us are going to consider everything. A conception of morality that induces us to internalize negative externalities is both psychologically realistic and empirically effective: Conformity to such a morality is something we can and do reasonably expect from anyone with some real degree of moral motivation. Conforming to such a morality also enables people to live well together, to prosper individually, and to develop a significant capacity to make their society a better place (indeed a cornucopia of positive externalities) for other people as well as for themselves. This is the kind of morality that we find predominating in prosperous societies, and this is no fluke. I also think the ethos of prosperous societies is more a cause than an effect of prosperity. Not everyone believes morality makes a difference, but I do, and so does Singer.

VII. Conclusion

I argued that SP lends as much weight to exporting bads as it does to exporting goods, to the point of marginal disutility. If SP is not the only consideration relevant to the question of whether to export bads, it probably is not the only consideration relevant to the exporting of goods either. (Singer could concede here that foisting negative externalities on innocent people without their consent falls into the category of "wrong in itself" which he accepted from the start as a sort of catch-all category for counterexamples to SP. Fair enough. I will not try to develop the idea that there is an analogous problem with exporting goods. I think TRAGIC COMMONS is the form of a huge problem for SP in our world. Whether it is analogous to the symmetry problem, or whether we call it "wrong in itself" is immaterial.)

I argued that the SP conjoined to species equality does not direct us to relieve famine in Bangladesh, so long as there are rescuable animals in worse shape than the people of Bangladesh. I do not believe in species equality, but my point is not to fault Singer for either part of the conjunction that has this implication. Rather, my point is that Singer has more than one project, and is not obliged to fit them all together. Neither logic nor any conception of the good life requires that all our values and commitments fit together to make sense as a single project. Singer is not wrong to care about things other than famine relief, and to spend most of his life on other things. Neither are we. (At the risk of belaboring the obvious, let me stress that this is not an *ad hominem* argument. To say of a theory that its inventor should be able to live by it is to criticize the theory, not the inventor.)

I said SP can't be right, then asked, "but how can it be wrong?" SP is not quite right, but rejecting it does not seem quite right either. I suggest that the apparent dilemma is an artifact of a mistaken assumption about the nature of moral theorizing. The mistaken assumption is that the point of moral theorizing is to identify necessary or sufficient conditions for being moral, when in fact the point of moral theorizing is the same as the point of any other kind of theorizing, namely to draw a map. SP is a suggestion about how we might find our way around the terrain of morality.

Singer's theory is simple, and that is not a problem. It has counterexamples, and that is not a problem. The only problem comes when we treat SP as something more than a way of articulating an understanding about one facet of morality. SP is a piece of a map. It cannot be more than that. No principle can be more than that.

Singer has made a more tangible difference than any philosopher in living memory (at least outside the academy; the analogous distinction within the academy would go to John Rawls). It is no exaggeration to say Singer is among the inventors of what we today call applied ethics. It was Singer (along with some of the more thoughtful game theorists, virtue theorists, anti-theorists, and feminists, among others) who dragged moral philosophy back to the real world. I think we are a generation or so away from figuring out how to do applied ethics well, but applied ethics already is one of the most important things philosophers do, and its importance is growing. By that standard, Singer is a singularly great philosopher.

It is human nature to grope toward consensus, for better or worse. We try to convince and be convinced by each other, and we are taught as philosophers to treat consensus as a holy grail. I think the urge to find common ground is a recipe for philosophy that is (at best) boring. Singer is interesting, and his agreeing with me would not make him more so. So, I see no reason to search for common ground. Singer might agree that there is a big difference between what people can agree on and what is in fact true. (If he agreed, would that make what I just said more likely?) Thus, when I say Singer is entitled to his opinion, I mean it. (It was only during my early years in graduate school that winning philosophical arguments seemed even vaguely important. I still would rather win than lose—I'm only human—but no one including me will ever lose a minute's sleep wondering whether I won.) I offer this essay as food for thought, not as refutation. Perhaps despite myself, I value Singer's opinion, but what matters is whether we walk away from this exchange with better ideas than we had coming in.

I would say we need a better idea than twentieth-century utilitarianism. I think nineteenth-century utilitarianism was a better idea, and I think the "proto-utilitarianisms" of Locke, Hume, and Adam Smith were better yet. Maybe the most important idea in Adam Smith, and one of the most important ideas in any theorizing about morality: There is *some* tendency for self-interested behavior to be good for other people as well as for oneself. That tendency is *highly* variable, and highly sensitive to the details of culture and institutional structure. I also find in Smith a deeper idea that true self-interest is interest not only in what we can get, but in what we can be. That deeper self-interest too—our vision of the life worth living—is shaped by culture, upbringing, and for quite a few of us, by our acquaintance with Peter Singer.[32]

---

[32] This essay first appeared in David Schmidtz, *Persons, Polis, Planet* (New York: Oxford University Press, 2008), and is printed here by permission of Oxford University Press.

Reply to David Schmidtz

PETER SINGER

A Dangerous Principle?

The principle of utility, (I have heard it said) is a dangerous principle: it is dangerous on certain occasions to consult it. This is as much as to say, what? that it is not consonant to utility, to consult utility: in short, that it is *not* consulting it, to consult it.[33]

David Schmidtz seems to grasp Bentham's point. He gives his own version of it:

A consequentialist theory needs to treat some topics as beyond the reach of utilitarian calculation. Rights can trump (not merely outweigh) utilitarian calculation even from a broadly consequentialist perspective. Why? Because, from a consequentialist perspective, results matter, and because, as an empirical matter, there is enormous utility in being able to treat certain parameters as settled, as not even permitting case by case utilitarian reasoning.

But Schmidtz also seems to think that this is an objection to my views:

Someone who says a true utilitarian will take all that into account is saying a true utilitarian cares not so much about consequences of acts as about consequences of practices that permit some acts and not others, thereby enabling citizens to make some kinds of plans rather than others. I agree. My point is only that a true utilitarian in that sense is not an act-utilitarian.

This is a common mistake, one shared by Harry Gensler in his contribution to this volume, so before I say why it is a mistake, I need to say a little about the form of utilitarianism I hold.

---

[33] Jeremy Bentham, *An Introduction to the Principles of Morals and Legislation*, Chapter 1, n9.

R.M. Hare distinguished two levels of moral thinking, the intuitive level and the critical level.[34] This is not because, as Gensler puts it, Hare thought we "in some ways are like *archangels* (with superhuman powers of thought and no human weaknesses)"—Hare never held such a naive view of human nature. Rather, he thought that we are liable to go astray if we try to calculate the consequences of every action. In everyday life, it is best to act from an intuitive sense of right and wrong. What is important is to have the right intuitions—that is, the intuitions that will generally bring about the best consequences, if most people act on them. We can think of these intuitions as telling us to follow certain moral rules—not to lie, cheat, steal, murder, and to be a good, trustworthy and loyal parent, friend, spouse, lover, colleague, team-mate or citizen. Occasionally, however, we will find ourselves in situations in which we are able to think clearly, calmly, and in a manner sufficiently free from bias, and in which, thinking in this mode, we can see that following the usual moral rules will not have the best consequences. Then we should act at the critical level, doing what will have the best consequences even though this means choosing against our intuitions and departing from the usual rules.

Unlike rule-utilitarianism, this two-level model never tells us to follow a rule when we can be sure that breaking the rule will have better consequences. It thus avoids the charge of what J.J.C. Smart called "rule-worship"—that is, of putting you in a situation in which your only reason for doing one thing rather than another is because you are obeying a rule that says you must do it, although disobeying the rule would have better consequences.[35] Hence this is a form of act-utilitarianism, not rule-utilitarianism.

As an advocate of two-level utilitarianism, I respond to the case Schmidtz calls HOSPITAL in much the same way as I responded to Gensler's "lynching-is-fun" case in the debate he describes in his essay in this volume. The response looked at the long-term consequences, and not only the immediate ones, of yielding to the lynch mob. Though that response was, as I said at the time, too brief to be a full answer, Gensler is wrong to claim that because it refers to the practice of lynching, rather than the single occasion in front of us, it presupposes rule-utilitarianism. There's nothing in act-utilitarianism that says act-

---

[34] See R.M. Hare, *Moral Thinking: Its Method, Levels, and Point* (Oxford: Clarendon, 1982).

[35] See J.J.C. Smart and B. Williams, eds., *Utilitarianism: For and Against* (Cambridge University Press, 1973).

utilitarians have to focus only on the particular situations in front of them, and cannot take account of the fact that these situations are part of a general practice, the consequences of which are bad. If we want to stop a bad practice, we have to start somewhere, and stopping a particular instance of a bad practice may have good consequences, overall, precisely because it will contribute to stopping the practice as a whole.

What Gensler himself says later in regard to killing is exactly what an advocate of a two-level approach would say, if the facts are indeed as Gensler suggests they are:

> I'd be afraid to live in a society that followed the act-utilitarian rule B, where people could kill whenever they speculated that this would have better results; people would apply this in irresponsible ways, with disastrous effects. It would have better results if society followed a strict rule against killing, like A.

This is very similar to what Schmidtz says:

> When doctors embrace a prohibition against harvesting organs of healthy patients without consent, doctors give up opportunities to optimize—to hit the ceiling—but *patients* gain opportunities to visit doctors safely. They gain a world with a higher ceiling. Such utility comes from doctors refusing even to ask whether murdering a patient would be optimal.

The two-level view does not permit anyone to kill people whenever he or she speculates that doing so would have better results. That is certain to have bad consequences. So we should promote and respect a rule that we do not kill.

Hypothetical Cases

We can still ask, of course, as Schmidtz asks: "What do we think about a HOSPITAL-like case where we are certain no one will ever know what we've done, therefore certain that our action will not undermine trust?" This is the parallel to Gensler's footnote to the lynching-is-fun example, when he goes into hypothetical situations in which the best way to stop the practice of lynching is not to stop this particular instance, but to wait until a new emperor comes to power.

Schmidtz responds to his own question in just the way an act-utilitarian should respond:

Perhaps it does not matter, since I am not speaking of a world where we can be certain it will never occur to UPS Inc. to wonder what is happening to all the delivery personnel they keep sending to our hospital. Suffice it to say, real world morality has the shape it does in part because real world uncertainty is what it is.

Still, if pressed further to imagine some improbable but conceivable real-world circumstances in which we can know—not "speculate"—that killing will have the best consequences, even taking into account the possibility that it will reduce general respect for the rule, an act-utilitarian must accept—as I do—that we would be justified in killing. So, in Gensler's case, if we really have a better chance of stopping the practice of lynching if we appease the lynch mob this time, and wait until the new enlightened Emperor comes to power before we take our stand against lynching, then we do have to sacrifice the unfortunate person being lynched in front of us.

To say this is, of course, to take an agent's perspective, not an institutional perspective. Schmidtz is correct to say that there is no mystery about why an institution would include constraints on maximizing the good. The difference between the perspective of an agent and of an instituion is illustrated in the example I used in my response to Judith Lichtenberg, of the debate over whether torture is ever justifiable. As I argued there, if the "ticking bomb" scenario really were to happen, and torture were the *only* chance we had of stopping an unmitigated catastrophe, torture would be justified. On the other hand, given that this is a purely hypothetical scenario that is never likely to happen, and that acceptance of a policy that permits torture is likely to lead to the infliction of extreme pain on innocent people, it is best to have policies prohibiting torture. In other words, it is possible for an act to be justified, and for an institution that rejects that act to be justified as well.

Part of a complete response to Schmidtz on this issue would also draw on arguments like those put forward by Richard Arneson in his contribution to this volume, when he rebuts the objection that consequentialists cannot commit themselves to close personal relationships. What is true of commitment to a personal relationship can also be true of committing oneself to not violating one's professional ethics as a physician, for instance, or, in one's role as an intelligence agent and interrogator, to not even considering the use of torture As I wrote in my response to Arneson, if the facts are such that one will, over a lifetime, achieve greater utility by making such a commitment and not even giving any consideration to situations in which it might be better to violate it, then there is nothing in such commitments that conflicts with the utilitarian claim that the right act is the one that produces the best consequences.

My conclusion, then, is that act-utilitarianism is defensible, although often we should not consult it. This does not mean that utilitarianism is self-defeating; rather, it means that it is partially self-effacing: it will sometimes be better, for act-utilitarian reasons, to promote respect for rules rather than to promote direct utility-maximization.[36]

Western Civilizaton Is More than the Consumer Society

In saying that I give the impression that I am not keen on Western civilization, Schmidtz seems to equate Western civilization with our modern consumer society. That's an amusing example of an Americo-centric view, or even more narrowly, a view centered on America since about 1950. Fortunately, that is not the entirety of Western civilization, and hence it is false to suggest that rejecting the idea that the focus of our lives should be on earning more money, living in bigger houses, and consuming more goodies, is equivalent to rejecting Western civilization.

Moral Theory and the Role of Reason

Schmidtz has some interesting things to say about the role of a moral theory. He compares a moral theory to a map, and notes that a map does not tell you where to go, but only how to get somewhere, if you want to go there. "It is when we aim to be moral," he says, "that we make moral theory the kind of map we have reason to consult." This is a broadly Humean stance: reasons for action must start from something wanted. A Kantian, or an intuitionist, would dispute the analogy, contending that a moral theory tells us not only what to do *if* we aim to be moral, but why we must aim to be moral, if we are to be rational. But as my response to Michael Huemer makes clear, on this issue I am sympathetic to Hume, and hence also to Schmidtz. For moral theories to get a grip on us, we must, at least, aim to act impartially, and it isn't clear to me that this can be shown to be rationally required.

---

[36] For more on self-effacing morality, see my response to Judith Lichtenberg in this volume, and Derek Parfit, *Reasons and Persons* (Oxford: Clarendon, 1984), pp. 40–43.

Schmidtz's Appeal to Our Intuitions Against the "Singer Principle"

My response to Huemer also indicates that I am entirely in agreement with Schmidtz's doubts about the reliability of our intuitive responses to bizarre thought experiments. That skepticism must, however, also count against Schmidtz's own examples, including the two counter-intuitive implications that lead Schmidtz to say that the "Singer Principle" cannot be right. What can he mean by this, except that they don't match his intuitions, and those of many other people?

I was tempted not to respond at all to Schmidtz's two examples of what he takes to be unacceptable implications of my views, because Schmidtz disarms any response by saying that even the fact that I can give a good response will be "too predictable to be interesting." Why then does he even bother to make the objections? Can an objection be interesting, if the fact that there is a good response to it is not? But some readers may be curious as to how I would reply so here is my predictably good response.

First, on ethics and animals. Schmidtz writes: "Not every utilitarian shares Singer's concern about animals. It is a separate decision where to locate the boundaries of moral concern, and the location of boundaries normally is not dictated by the principle one adopts for guiding decisions within those boundaries." All three of the great nineteenth century utilitarians—Bentham, Mill and Sidgwick—would have disagreed with that comment. They were all aware that their theory extended to animals, and none of them regarded this as a separate decision. Their reasoning was, in effect: "Hedonistic utilitarianism says we should produce the greatest possible surplus of pleasure over pain. Animals are capable of experiencing pleasure and pain. Therefore the boundaries of moral concern include animals."[37] And for a preference utilitarian, concerned about conscious preferences, a parallel line of reasoning follows. So I'm not sure what form of utilitarianism—or what prominent utilitarian—Schmidtz has in mind when he says that the inclusion of animals is a separate decision.

---

[37] See Jeremy Bentham, *Introduction to the Principles of Morals and Legislation* (New York: Hafner, 1948), Chapter XVII, Section 1, par. iv, p. 311; John Stuart Mill, "Whewell on Moral Philosophy," reprinted in T. Regan and P. Singer, eds., *Animal Rights and Human Obligations* (Englewood Cliffs: Prentice-Hall, 1976), pp. 131–32; Henry Sidgwick, *The Methods of Ethics* (London: Macmillan, seventh edition, 1907), Book IV, Chapter 1, p. 414.

Schmidtz also claims: "If we humans were "utility monsters" compared to other animals, utilitarianism would require us to favor humans in our investment decisions, but Singer does not believe we are." My position is not as simple as that. It is true that I don't believe that mere membership of the species *Homo sapiens* is enough to give a being a greater capacity for utility than any being who is not a member of our species—how could it?—but I do think that the possession of certain cognitive capacities can produce a greater capacity for utility in some respects. With regard to pain or physical suffering, other mammals, birds, and perhaps all vertebrates, appear to have capacities that are broadly similar to our own—or at least, we cannot assert with any confidence that they are generally less sensitive to pain than we are.[38] For that reason, as I have argued in *Animal Liberation* and elsewhere, many of our current practices with regard to animals are indefensible. In regard to other preferences, however, the differences in cognitive capacities between normal humans and nonhuman animals do make a difference. As I have argued in many places—and in this volume, in my responses to Marquis and Gensler—normal humans, once they are beyond infancy, are aware of their existence over time in a manner that nonhuman animals are not. Therefore they can have preferences for what they will do next week, next summer, or over the course of their lives, that nonhuman animals cannot have. This means that, from a preference utilitarian perspective, they have more at stake when their lives are put in jeopardy.

That is one reason why coupling the "Singer Principle" with the rejection of speciesism may not require us to drop our concern for humans living in extreme poverty and instead give priority to helping animals. Where the lives of both humans and animals are at risk, we may do more good by helping the humans. But other factual considerations are also relevant, especially the ecological consequences of feeding starving animals, or of preventing predators from attacking their prey. I would not, in principle, rule out the idea that we should intervene in nature to reduce the suffering of animals, but our record of interfering in ecological systems is not good. Unless we have reason to think that we can reduce animal suffering not only in the immediate instance in front of us, but over the long term, we should not be doing it.

Second, on Schmidtz's idea that the Singer Principle requires us to "export bads" to wherever they do the least harm, I again have no

---

[38] For further discussion of such comparisons, see my response to Frey in this volume.

objection, in principle, to the implication. In our calculation of whether our toxic wastes really will do less harm if we export them, however, we have to take into account the utility lost by the people who live in the country to which we will export them. If we do this without first obtaining their consent, it is easy to imagine that they will feel outraged or humiliated at our use of their country as a dumping ground for our wastes. They may fight back. The result could therefore very easily be that our export of toxic wastes causes much more harm than would have resulted from disposing of them in our own country.

A similar requirement to calculate properly all the consequences of providing aid indicates why the "Singer Principle" would not require us to do anything that might lead to a situation like that in Schmidtz's TRAGIC COMMONS case, nor in general, to act in ways that have a damaging effect on markets and on people's motivations to become productive and self-sufficient. I have already discussed some of these issues in my response to Cowen. The obligation that the "Singer Principle" puts on us is to prevent something bad—and that should be read not merely as preventing something bad happening now, even if preventing it leads to something worse happening later, but as reducing the bad things things that happen, overall. Hence it does not mean, as Schmidtz suggests, that we should "ship food and money to wherever people need it more than we do." It might mean that, rather than ship food or money, we should provide better varieties of grain to farmers, or give people bednets so that they do not get malaria, or fund microcredit schemes so that they can borrow small amounts of money to set up new businesses, or set up family planning clinics that will help them to control their fertility. There is no obligation to give aid that is not effective, and we need to learn from past experiences and discover how to make aid more effective. A fuller discussion of these and other issues can be found in my book, *The Life You Can Save,* which appeared only after Schmidtz wrote his essay.

14

Singer on Moral Theory

JAN NARVESON

Peter Singer famously criticizes most of us for several things—notably, our evident disregard of animals, as also for our attitudes and actions regarding the poverty-stricken masses in various parts of the world. His criticisms are philosophical. He isn't just standing in a pulpit and sounding off—he claims, instead, to have a solid basis for these complaints. That's important, for although many who respond to his work do so out of antecedent attachment to those very goals—preaching to the converted is a familiar fact of life—still, he isn't going to convert others who do not share those attachments without arguments. Among those are some who will be impressed if indeed he can come up with solid reasons of a specifically philosophical sort, and it is those especially, I think, whom Singer hopes to appeal to. That philosophical basis is my particular concern here.

The basis of his critique is a leading principle, to the effect that *equal interests should get equal consideration, no matter whose interests they are.* We are to "weigh up interests, considered simply as interests and not as my interests, or the interests of Australians, or of people of European descent . . ." This he calls the "principle of equal considerations of interests."[1] He argues that this is the best understanding of a

---

[1] Peter Singer, *Practical Ethics*, second edition (Cambridge: Cambridge University Press, 1993), p. 21. All further references are to that source unless otherwise indicated.

basic idea of moral equality and universality, both of which he takes to be very fundamental to ethics.

> Ethics takes a universal point of view . . . in making an ethical judgments we go beyond our own likes and dislikes . . . Ethics requires us to go beyond 'I' and 'you' to the universal law, the universalizable judgment, the standpoint of the impartial spectator or ideal observer, or whatever we choose to call it."[2]

'Equal consideration' is a catchy phrase, and like most such phrases it is ambiguous. Strictly speaking, we could *consider* anything and then *reject* it. In fact, we could accept some, and reject others, even at random, and still have given them all "equal consideration" if *consideration* were literally all that is in question. But Ssinger means a lot more than that. What he apparently means is that each is to be given *equal weight*. The idea is that if any moral agent, A, judges that some other individual, B—among a set of organisms which in Singer's view is much wider than the human race—has an interest, I, of degree (or size, or intensity) n, such that A would be able, by doing x, to promote I as effectively as he could promote an interest of lesser degree m, held by himself or someone else whom A cares about, by instead doing something else, say y, then if x and y are alternatives available to A, and y would promote the lesser interest m, then what A morally ought to do is x. That is a very hefty principle—and, I shall argue, not only not self-evident, obvious, or plausible, but simply incredible.

But the plot thickens. For Singer later explained that he doesn't hold morality to be overriding. Thus,

> I could recognize that if I were totally committed to doing what I ought to do, I would give away my wealth up to the point indicated in my article [the point in question is the one at which you yourself would end up suffering as much as the person you give it to[3]], but at the same time I may, without any irrationality, choose to be less than totally committed to doing what I ought to do. My own interests, or those of my family, may counteract the demands of morality to some degree . . .[4]

---

[2] Singer, *Practical Ethics*, pp. 12–13; see also p. 47.

[3] The article to which Singer refers here is the widely-reprinted "Famine, Affluence, and Morality," originally in *Philosophy and Public Affairs* 1 (Spring 1972), pp. 229–243.

[4] Dale Jamieson, ed., *Singer and His Critics* (Oxford: Blackwell, 1999), "A Response", p. 309.

It is, I think, extremely and importantly unclear what this does to his overall thesis. Thus most of us, I think, would hold that morality at least *allows*, and some even that it *requires* that we give special regard to the interests of family, or friends, and so on.

There are, by my count, four crucial points to discuss about Singer's position.

First, there is the question of what constitutes "equality of interest." Sometimes Singer talks about the "morally comparable interests" of, especially, animals. But it is not altogether clear whether a *morally comparable* interest is simply an interest of similar "size" or intensity, or something else etc., or whether perhaps morals compares interests in further ways than in respect of intensity and duration. I shall argue that the latter option is correct, and that Singer is altogether wrong in the former contention—which is the central point in his ethical theory. Without it, he can't get the rather astonishing conclusions that his work so famously advocates.

Second, there is the question of the status of what he claims to be specifically moral 'ought' judgments. As we saw above, he does not think that morality is overriding. But it is unclear just what that is supposed to mean. The ancient Socratic question is whether a person *could*, at all, do what he himself judged to be wrong or even to be less good than some other option—to be what he (thinks he?) ought not to do. Everyone from Aristotle on has accepted that a person indeed *could* do so, but some have held that this would be in some way irrational or at least a sign of some kind of defect, for instancee.g. to exemplify action from weakness of will. Singer, however, doesn't accept that view. He holds, evidently, that it could be perfectly rational to act thus. Some philosophers seem to find this perfectly clear and in order; others, such as this writer, may find it puzzling. And its effect on his theses is, I shall argue, imponderable.

Third, and perhaps most fundamentally, Singer's writings on these matters raise questions about the rationality *of morality*. Singer says that the question, "Why act morally?" has *no rational answer*.[5] Is this just the preceding point, restated? Or is it something stronger: namely, an admission that morality itself might be quite nonrational? Or *is* that, as I claim, really 'stronger'?

Finally, and of course most fundamentally, there is the general question of the *foundations of morality*: why should we accept any moral obligations a t all, and therefore this one in particular?

---

[5] Singer, *Practical Ethics*, p. 355.

I shall try to make progress on all of these points here.

On the first point: I shall first sketch what we may call the "strongest" reading of Singer, a reading according to which, or so he claims, we should all feel obliged to become vegetarians, and most of us in the "wealthy" countries to donate a great deal of our incomes to the cause of famine relief—*and* in which it would be proper to use compulsion to bring about those alterations in our conduct. As noted, it is by no means clear that Singer holds the latter, and on the whole I am inclined to think that he does not, at least in practical terms. (He deplores, for example, the violence used by some animal rights enthusiasts in breaking up laboratories, and so forth.etc.) Still, the position would seem to lend itself to that conclusion.

I shall then state weaker versions of his position, ones that there is no reasonable doubt that we may ascribe to him. But I will argue that he is wrong in both. It is not true that we may be compelled to refrain from eating animal flesh or to give money to starving people—though the latter is enormously more important than the former. It is also not true that morality tells us that we *ought* to do the former, though it may in some few cases imply that we ought to do the latter—but it is not true across the board, and in any case runs into the problem that his proposed response to the fact of world poverty is really counterproductive, and people with a real interest in improving that situation should be acting very differently from what he recommends.

More generally, I will argue that we not only have a perfect moral right to pursue our wealthy and semi-sybaritic lives as we do, but that we characteristically act in a wholly nonblameworthy manner when we do so.

In the course of this discussion, I will argue that Singer's appeal to *impartiality* is misplaced. His leading principle, that all interests of equal "size" should get *equal moral weight*, will be shown to be ambiguous in such a way that either it has nothing at all like the implications he draws from it, or it should be rejected, and rejected precisely on the score of its failing of impartiality.

On the second point, there is a serious question how a serious moral claim could be thought not to be "overriding." There is, of course, the question just what it overrides, but to deny that they are overriding at all would seem to call in question their very meaningfulness.

On the third, I will suggest that we cannot say what Singer appears to say about the rational status of morality. Its being rational is crucial to its acceptability, and implies criticism of a kind that we indeed cannot rationally ignore. We should not think that morality is something we are rationally free to take or leave in the manner suggested.

And finally, I will sketch, very briefly, what I think must be recognized to be the right way to do moral theory. That way denies much of Singer's starting point and replaces it with a far more intuitively plausible one. Some, apparently including Singer, appear not to think we need—usually because they don't think we can have—a respectable answer to the question of the foundations of morals. If that were meant seriously, I shall suggest, then his book simply would not be worth reading. When we take it as seriously as it should be, we will, I shall also argue, find his view completely unacceptable.

1. The "Equal Consideration" Principle

According to Henry Sidgwick, it is axiomatic to morals that:

> the good of any one individual is of no more importance, from the point of view (if I may say so) of the Universe, than the good of any other; unless, that is, there are special grounds for believing that more good is likely to be realized in the one case than in the other. And *it is evident to me that as a rational being I am bound to aim at good generally*, so far as it is attainable by my efforts, not merely at a particular part of it.[6]

Singer, I think, has been enormously influenced by this idea, which he is tempted to give the same sort of axiomatic status that Sidgwick credits it with.[7] But he differs from Sidgwick on the important second point: that it is *as a rational being* that one is "bound" to aim at good generally—for Singer, as noted, is ready to admit that his position is not rational in the sense that every rational individual will, necessarily, go along with it, This leaves us with an interesting question: just *why* should we "aim at good generally" in the Sidgwickian sense? Why should we accept Singer's principle that we should give equal weight to the promotion of *any interest no matter whose*, given that it is of equal "size"? We will return to this aspect in points three and four.

In fact, we must back up one step: what is this idea about the "point of view of the universe"? It is fascinating that Singer, among many others, has been attracted to this metaphor and to the idea associated with it. But after all, it is of course strictly a metaphor, since there is no reason to think that the *universe* has a "point of view" at all, and Singer,

---

[6] Henry Sidgwick, *The Methods of Ethics*, XIII.3 (London: Macmillan, 1962), p. 382.
[7] Singer, p. 334: "The point of view of the universe is a lofty standpoint." See also Dale Jamieson, ed., *Singer and His Critics* (Oxford: Blackwell, 1999), p. 270.

who objects to those environmentalists who think that plants have some sort of desires, will surely agree with that.[8] Moreover, it is likewise clear that there is *no* "point of view" that it makes sense for *us* to try to identify and which has the singular features Sidgwick and Singer want to endow it with. For utility is *subjective*: to talk of utility is to talk of *someone's* utility; there is no "everyone's utility" left over once every individual's utility is reckoned. But even to talk of "reckoning" is misleading, for we must next recognize that utility *motivates*—but it *intrinsically* motivates *only* the individual *whose utility it is*. There is simply no sense to the idea of my acting on, that is, being motivated as such by, *your* utility. Thus the moralist who would be a utilitarian is evidently choosing to identify with everyone, by estimating what he supposes other people's utilities to be, and then *installing into his own utility function* some kind of representation of those "quantities" and, himself, for reasons of his own, deciding to attempt to promote them. Sidgwick and Singer apparently think that those are not just "reasons of his own"—but it is unclear what that could mean here, unless that somehow everyone *has* reasons so to identify. Whether they do will be discussed under point (4) below. Here I shall merely point out that this is so far from obvious that it would be much more plausible to say that the reverse is what is obvious.

How are we to understand this? Each of us, one hopes, identifies some, usually some *few*, people as the objects of our love, admiration, approval, and so on. In the case of the first of these emotions, it is sometimes true, I presume, that the lover would describe his or her attitude as *valuing* the other person as highly as, or quite possibly more highly than, himself or herself. People are often prepared to make great sacrifices for some one or perhaps some very few such persons.

There are obvious limits to this, of course. You have only one self, and if you devote all your energies to one other such person, then you won't have any left for the rest of the human race—contrary to Sidgwick's and Singer's axiom. Singer manages, we understand, to contribute perhaps twenty percent of his very substantial income to charitable causes generally; but this puts the rest of the world in sum rather lesser on the scale than, for example, his own wife and children. Is this something he classifies as some sort of moral failing? I for one hope not. But the point is clear enough: that is, that the Sidgwickian formula is hopeless as a supposed description of objects of affection even on the part of the most charitable people we encounter.

---

[8] Singer, *Unsanctifying Human Life* (Oxford: Blackwell, 2002), pp. 320–21.

Of course income matters here. It must be rather painful to people of Singerian tendencies to note that Bill Gates, who famously has a sixty-million-dollar house, manages also to contribute literally billions every year to large-scale charitable activities in Africa and elsewhere, and in doing so, he does more of the kind of good Singer approves of, objectively speaking, than all of the philosophers who have ever lived put together. We'll leave that as food for thought—except to point out that other billionaires, multimillionaires, and persons of much more modest means such as myself, tend to have different tastes. (And to point to the "widow's mite" if we move to the question of what measures virtue in this area.) We can understand Gates's behavior on the basis of his own distinctive set of sympathies (and those of his wife's, I understand). But, again, not only do others differ, but we misstate the situation by supposing that Gates succeeds, much better than Singer or I or any number of others, at *identifying with the universe*! What he does is to sympathize with the plight of a lot of people, and to do a good deal about it, which his wealth enables him to do. Others might instead promote the opera, or modern art, or architecture, or any number of other causes, which they find more important. On Singer's view, presumably, these other people are *acting in error*. On any more reasonable view, they are acting on their interests, interests shared by a good many others, indeed, but ones to which, as with all other interests whatever, the "universe" is sublimely indifferent, although we mere people are not at all so. We *care*, and the universe can just stay out of it.

What could make theorists imagine that the Singer-Sidgwick formula makes sense? A shot at it might go like this. We interact with a few people quite closely, with many more less closely, and with almost everyone in increasing degrees of indirectness. All these people react to each other in various ways, as their various interests dictate. In dealing with them, especially quite close to us, we must, if we are to do so at all effectively, be able, as Ken Binmore has pointed out, to *empathize* with them, that is, to be able to imagine ourselves in their situations, with their tastes, and so on.[9] If we can't do this, we will have a much harder time making sense of their patterns of activity, and if we can't do that, we can hardly respond to and engage them intelligently, if at all. Empathy, however, is not the same as *sympathy*. To be sure, there is in almost all of us a certain amount of the latter as well as the former: that is, we not only understand, more or less, how they feel and what they want, but we may also

---

[9] Ken Binmore, *Game Theory and the Social Contract* (Cambridge, Massachusetts: MIT Press, 1994), Volume 1, p. 56.

be moved to help them fulfill their desires in various respects. But *sympathy* is not peculiarly "rational"; and indeed, it is not fundamentally rational at all, other than that you will be hard put to sympathize with someone if you don't understand him or her at all. And especially, rationality does not impel us to sympathize with *everybody whatever* and try to devote all our energies to achieving their ends as if we actually *were* those people. Trying to do that is, normally, irrational—self-destructive in the extreme—, and of course also completely frustrating. Those endowed with an extreme level of sympathy for others will do best to try to suppress much of that emotion, for if they do not, it will disenable them from helping even some few.

The utilitarian is especially susceptible to the malady so beautifully illustrated by Dickens's portrait of Mrs. Jellyby, a woman of immense sympathies who spends much of her time and energy promoting missionary projects in Africa—and meanwhile her children go about in rags and suffer illnesses and, of course, especially suffer a decided lack of emotional support from their mother.[10] Whatever our sympathies, if we are to do anything effective about their objects, we will have to focus and suppress and channel so that our efforts do actually get something done rather than dissipating into fruitless blind alleys and byways. We also need to have an eye out for those near and dear which our grand programs might cause us to neglect.

Worse, however—much worse, potentially—is that in our efforts to do some good, we also do some harm, unintended or even perhaps intended or just ignored. Now, the utilitarian's maxim is such as to induce him to regard the harm he may do to some as simply a cost to be reckoned up in relation to the benefits he's trying to supply. Nozick invokes the language of "side constraint" here,[11] a rather effective metaphor for the purpose, in that the idea is that we channel our efforts, confining them to ones that have no significant evil consequences for others—we don't just look "ahead,", at the goals we are trying to accomplish, but we also look "to the side" and make sure that we don't cross borders into the domains of bystanders and incidentals.) We may not pursue good ends at the expense of people not in the circle of favored recipients of our beneficence—and we may *not* treat these "expenses" to them as *nothing but that*—nothing but costs *to me* which I can simply weigh against the positive values, as I suppose it to be, that I am pro-

---

[10] Mrs. Jellyby is encountered in Chapter 4 of *Bleak House*.

[11] Robert Nozick, *Anarchy, State, and Utopia* (New York: Basic Books, 1974), pp. 28–35.

moting. The moral fact of the matter is that we owe it to these uninvolved others that we do essentially *no* damage to them. No *net* damage, that is; we might accidentally do damage, and compensate for it; on many occasions we can enlist the help of others even though they don't have great interest in our project, but are ready to help to some minor degree just out of good nature. And in the case of many others still, we can enlist this kind of help from them by buying it, so that what would otherwise be damages to them are converted to positive benefits to them as well as us. I actively enlist the somewhat painful services of my dentist, confident than the improvement in functionality of my teeth makes it worthwhile, even including the financial pain involved; I also pay the dentist for his services, making his rendering of them beneficial to both of us. But the case is wholly different with other people—innocent bystanders. I cannot presume to inflict pain on them in order to benefit still others, or myself; and if I inflict it on them acceptably, what makes it acceptable is their consent—in which case they usually aren't just "bystanders" any more—and *not* a calculation by me that they will be better off on the whole as a result. In short, undercutting the practical reasoning of others is not acceptable. The Sidgwickian axiom, however, seems strongly conducive to this kind of undercutting.

Killing/Letting Die; Harming/Not-Helping

Along with many others, Singer thinks that any distinction between killing and letting-die in moral theory would be either just arbitrary, or else a function of incidental factors. In this I think he is wholly and greatly wrong, but there is indeed a question of just what is "essential" and what is "incidental" in the distinction in question. Many philosophers, including Mill, have allowed that the "negative" part of morals comes first: we must refrain from killing, and more generally from harming, defrauding, and so on; by comparison, the matter of caring for the sick and needy, even of saving people's lives, is less demanding, though it might (views vary) be still quite demanding. The specific application to killings versuss. lettings-die is but one of an indefinite number of such contrasts we can make. For example, it is (normally) wrong of us to lie, as such, but not obviously so wrong and perhaps not wrong at all to fail to correct someone else's misconception. I must not lie myself, but must I go to trouble to undo the mischief made by someone else's lies? (Not usually.) And how about just leaving things unsaid? It is obvious that I do not have the duty, in general, to tell people truths, even truths in which they are quite interested, whereas I do have a duty to refrain from lying to them. And so on. In general, even where x is a harmful type of action, and y a beneficial type of action, either of which we might be able to do, that we have a strong obligbation to avoid doing x, but either no duty, or at least a much attenuated duty, to do y.

Singer does discuss this subject at length. But he seems to think that the distinction of acts and omission *stems from* an "ethic consisting of specific duties, prescribed by moral rules that everyone can be expected to obey."[12] He seems not to consider the possibility that it's the other way around: that the rules are the way they are because, we, and life in our experience, is such that rules of that kind are what are called for. In typical cases, there is not just a trivial but a whopping difference between doing nothing and rendering aid. Putting the immediate responsibility of each of us on *not harming,* and by comparison putting rendering help, especially in distant and onerous cases, quite far down the list or, indeed, not on the same list at all, but a rather different one, makes sense. But I'll return to that in section (4). Meanwhile, Singer wants to apply this to the case of helping the world's poor and suffering. What's the situation there?

I certainly think that we do not have an *enforceable* duty to help with that, and am doubtful that we have any duty at all, though it is, of course, admirable, *prima facie*, to do such things, if done effectively. But a more salient test area might well concern liberation and defense. When people in country C are being butchered and tortured and oppressed by C's government, should we be thought to have a duty to go forth, if we can, and help liberate the hapless Cs by making war against C's government or taking other steps to relieve them? Singer has recently written a book excoriating the American President Bush for doing just that in Iraq. Given his principles, that seems astonishing. If we, and nations too, should be spending vast sums to relieve starvation, why not to relieve tyranny? But meanwhile, one would hope, a nation proposing to make war on some quite peaceable and decently governed but very poor country, in order somehow to promote prosperity therein would indeed be wrong. If Singer is prepared to condemn the latter, that's good news— but his principles don't make it obvious that they should. Much less do they make it obvious that he should be condemning the former. On the contrary, they seem seriously conducive to running afoul of all these strictures.

---

[12] Singer, *Practical Ethics*, pp. 206–213, 222–29; more generally, the whole chapter "Rich and Poor," pp. 218–246.

To be sure, war and espionage and so forth are indeed much more onerous than refraining from day-to-day murder on the street. This raises one general and one more specific question. The more general question is this: is it essential to the notion of x-ing that not-$x$ing is *easier*, requires *less* of some demanding human quality? Refraining from murder is easy, intervening to prevent a murder much more difficult (and typically dangerous). But is *that* fact alone the *basis* for distinguishing as sharply as we in general do between x-ing and letting-x?

Refutations of the view that there is a serious moral difference between doing a bad thing and not-intervening to prevent the bad thing from happening have mostly taken the form of constructing examples in which the difference really would be very small. For example, Rachels offers the case of the child in the bathtub. In case (1), his evil uncle A pushes him beneath the water; in case (2) the child slips beneath the water, and evil uncle A refrains from pulling him up, though he easily could. We in general can find cases where the distinction is indeed small: the ease with which we could avoid letting-h is nearly equal to that with which we can avoid h-ing. It is not, and we should not suppose it to be, actually identical. It is easier to refrain from pushing the child beneath the surface than to rescue him from drowning even if that requires only a small well-placed lifting action. The question is whether that is the difference that *makes* the difference. On Singer's hypothesis, it is the *only thing there is*. I disagree.

Even in these marginal cases, we may well ask whether there is not in fact a difference, morally, and whether that difference is somehow "proportional" to the level of difficulty to effect the action or inaction. Inaction usually costs nothing; we aren't even aware of it. At this very moment I am refraining from murdering some six billion people, yet so easy is this that it would never even occur to me, except when writing philosophical papers such as this, that that is what I am "doing." By contrast, rescuing someone from great danger or death normally consumes time and, energy, incurs emotional stress, and so on. Yet if A actually does watch a child drown and can establish that that's what she did, rather than that she in fact *killed* her, then she might be tried for criminal negligence but certainly not for *murder*. Even when assistance is quite easy to provide, we are not generally threatened with incarceration for failing to provide it; but we are definitely threatened with such when what we do is to commit the crime ourselves—even if the difference in energy requirements between committing it and not doing so was positively diaphanous, and the amount involved in saving that life rather inconsequential. Singer has pooh-poohed this, and he might indeed appeal to the disutility of enshrining into law requirements to aid as opposed to prohibitions on evil action. But as with so many such assessments in utilitarian terms, it is seems clear that the estimated disutility is a function of our pre-existing moral attitude, not vice versa. This does not show that those attitudes are irrational, either. What is irrational is to ignore the reasons why we should have these tendencies rather than the ones Singer commends to us.

But those reasons exist, and I suggest that they are very good indeed. They issue from a matter of principle: that we are individually acting agents, with our own agendas, our own set of interests and values. For such beings, *freedom matters*. If the actions of others affect us, as they so often do, we shall be concerned about those from *our* point of view—not from the point of view of the *others*. *If* our point of view happens to be conspicuously altruistic, we shall *then* no doubt take those others' points of view into our own with alacrity, and alter our own actions in ways that we judge will promote those other people's interests. But if we don't, then what? At this point, Singerians, evidently, have nothing to do but nag. They won't be able to argue that it is *rational* to take the others' interests into account as if they were our own, for it is, simply, a fact that they are not. Thus an argument would be needed to persuade the reluctant agent in question to take them on after all. But what argument could be available? What *argument*, that is—as opposed to *more preaching*? Arguments that we are all siblings under the skin, for example, are familiar, and their rather low rates of success a matter of record, starting with Cain—even though we are told that he *was* a sibling. . . .

A much better, and genuine, argument appeals to broad facts about human interaction. If we pay some attention to each other, extending help when it's greatly needed and the cost of supplying it is low, then the chances are that we will benefit from this. Such an argument is indeed persuasive—to most of us.[13] But it is very far from giving us what Singer wants. As applied to animals, it has virtually nothing to offer in the general case, though it does in the case of treating one's own pets. The "community of lions" isn't going to turn around and become highly and positively sensitive to our own utility functions just because we extract an occasional thorn from this or that lion's paw. And that's perhaps true of the community of mankind in general, were it not that they are capable of communicating at a much higher and more extensive level

---

[13] I discuss the matter in "We Don't Owe Them a Thing!" *Monist* (2003), pp. 419–433.

than the lion community. They are also capable of reasoning things out, tolerably well. It does not take much to see that we all stand to benefit from living among helpful people rather than narrow-minded, selfish recluses. The reason for being helpful oneself falls out very straightforwardly from this. But it doesn't get us to the point of abolishing the distinction between harming and not-helping. The fact remains that other people are *other*, and that leaving each other "alone" in the sense of refraining from intervening in their situations without their consent is wise general policy for all. It is so wise that it can plausibly be put forward as perhaps *the* basic *principle* of human association. Non-harm is the rule; help is nice, when it's wanted, but *requiring* it is going over the edge. Who, Everyman may well ask, are *you* to be telling *me* what to do? The only credible answer is that we are nothing more than fellow humans beings. Telling each other to keep off when not wanted makes sense; telling each other to treat us as if we were a part of someone else, or at very least their spouses, does not.

The "point of view of the universe," in short, is a philosophical fraud. That metaphor may serve to remind us that we are not alone in this world, that what we do to each other matters, and that we have much to lose at the hands of our fellows if we treat them badly, and much to gain if we treat them well,. But the expression loses all impact when it is taken to designate a genuine fact about how the world is put together, such as that there is really only *one* person in the world and all these apparently distinct entities we call "people" are really just so many interconnected computer work-stations. We have *no* reason to think this, and every reason to deny it.

I am not attributing this incredible doctrine to Singer. Rather, I am pointing out that in the absence of any such thing, the road to acceptance of his doctrine as stated goes almost vertically up hill. We must then ask, which world is morality concerned with? The answer is that there is no alternative to admitting that it's *this* one. Philosophers have no business trying to move us elsewhere, and in any case, we won't go. And in this one, the Singerian view is, in a word, incredible.

2. Overridingness

This brings us to the second point. How are we to understand the claim that morality is not overriding? Doesn't it override *anything*? Wouldn't a so-called "morality" that had *no* weight in comparison with *anything* be an empty set of words—nattering rather than serious talk? Surely he can't mean it that way.

One possibility is that discussion of Singer's idea here requires us to recall an important distinction within morals: namely, between (1) those things which it is our duty to do in a sense implying that others may *compel* us to do those things, and (2) those things with regard to which we are not properly to be compelled, though we may and should put moral pressure on ourselves (and others) to do them. For example, the duty to refrain from those killings of other persons which we reasonably classify as *murder* is one that we may indeed compel people to fulfil, and to punish severely when they do not. By contrast, there are "weaker" morals statements which propose various actions as ones it would be a *good thing* to do, that they would in a reasonably interesting sense be *morally right*, but still, *not* proper subjects of compulsion. It is fairly typical to classify charity as among those things. For that matter, we can frame a third class, of things that it is morally admirable to do but which normal people are not only not required to do but are scarcely expected to do. Morality, we think, does not *require* us to do heroic or saintly actions, though we all agree that heroic and saintly actions deserve high praise from us—and even though heroes and sdaints often do think that what they do is morally required of them. Of crucial interest regarding Singer is what he thinks about our duties, as he often says they are, regarding animals or the very poor. Many talk as though the latter, in particular, may properly be responded to by imposing taxes on people, which have the effect of compelling them to help contribute toward the relief of poverty. Is Singer one of those? In the revised version of his famous article on world poverty, he says "At the government level, no government has given the sort of massive aid that would enable the refugees to survive for more than a few days."[14] In context, this sounds like a complaint. He goes on to point out that Britain's contribution to this cause was about one-thirtieth of its contribution to the development of the supersonic Concorde airliner, and that Australia's contribution was about one-twelfth of the cost of the then-new Sydney Opera House. Indeed, he says,

> I shall argue that the way people in relatively affluent countries react to a situation like that in Bengal cannot be justified; indeed, the whole way we look at moral issues—our moral conceptual scheme—needs to be altered, and with it, the way of life that has come to be taken for granted in our society.[15]

---

[14] http://www.petersingerlinks.com/famine.htm, first page.
[15] *Loc. cit.,* note 14. In *Practical Ethics*, figures along the same general lines are supplied on p. 222.

Those are very strong words. It would be natural for one making such claims to endorse government action to bring about the alterations in question. But to my knowledge (which is admittedly imperfect) Singer doesn't do that.

Singer *may* agree with the many, like myself, who hold that we in the affluent countries have a perfect *right* to attend operatic performances and buy expensive wines, automobiles, houses, and so on, even though we have no right at all to murder, cheat, lie, or steal in the course of making it possible for ourselves to engage in these expensive but pleasant activities. He tends not to talk in terms of rights, and this makes it difficult to be clear about his position. I (and, I think, we) certainly do not agree that our way of life in the affluent countries "cannot be justified," and that it "needs to be altered." In fact, what we would all like is that the currently poor should by and by come to be in the same enviable position that we are—able to buy expensive automobiles and back-yard swimming pools, and able to regard questions of help to the distant needy as merely an interesting further issue, to which no one may *compel* us to respond. There are, certainly, many problems about what we do and the ways we do them, but these problems are nothing like the ones that Singer has in mind in the above. In the case of the poor, and so on, the situation is that by and large, those people have no *right* to our help; we have no compulsory duty to help them, and whatever we do in the way of help, and however much to our credit it may be to do it, it simply cannot be put in the same category as our duties to *refrain from harming* our neighbors, near or far. (I say this by way of general summary; detailed discussion of the question of what to do about the world's poor is not in place here, though I have certainly addressed it elsewhere.[16])

In saying this, of course, I implicitly reject another claim often made, that there is "no difference" between harming and not-helping. The rejection can be made explicit here: there is an obvious, and in most cases enormous such difference. When we merely don't-harm, we mind our own business, we leave others to live their lives as they please, whereas when we harm, we cross the boundaries between us and them, we invade them, we leave them worse off than if we had never existed or simply stayed home. If Singer thinks this is no difference, one wonders

---

[16] See especially, *Journal of Ethics* 8:4 (2004), Jan Narveson, "Welfare and Wealth, Poverty and Justice in Today's World," pp. 305–348, and "Is World Poverty a Moral Problem for the Wealthy?", 397–408. The articles by my co-discussant Larry Temkin in the same issue should be seen as well.

whether he feels as affronted with those of us who don't give him another million dollars and those who go and steal the million he (I'm told) already has! The argument that there is no difference, in short, is too absurd in its implications to be taken seriously.

Why do I think this? Because we must reject Singer's supposed axiom. Not only are not "all animals equal" but neither are all people, from the point of view of other people—the very "other people" (namely, all of us) to whom moral directives are addressed. But we will discuss this fundamental matter in my fourth point, below. For the present, my point is that the duty to refrain from engaging in violence to our fellows *overrides* any supposed duties we may have to help the poor, or animals, or whatever. We *may* compel people so to refrain, and for that very reason we may *not* compel them to refrain from eating animals, wearing fur coats, and so on.

How could anyone think otherwise? The man who proclaims that peace is our duty and then in his backroom prepares bombs and at night attacks his neighbors is a hypocrite. His claim that he "believes" that to be his duty is preposterous. We expect people's pronouncements about such things to be sincere, which means that their behavior can be expected to be appropriate. Absent such conformity between word and deed, we have a further beef with them, in addition to our beef concerning the evil of the deeds they actually do. The point of morality is to guide—hence to *direct*—behavior. The person whose behavior is immediately under the control of the person doing the speaking is, of course, the speaker, and so while others, being independent decision-makers, may not conform, yet if he doesn't either, then he misuses language, he deceives us, and we should treat him with contempt and likely, in any important cases, with suspicion. When Singer himself proclaims a duty to give much more than normal to the poor, we are impressed because he in fact does this. But what if he didn't? Would we still be impressed? I don't think so! (Thus philosopher Peter Unger, who candidly confesses that he does little along this line though claiming that there is an enormous duty to do so, is by comparison not taken seriously. Or better, he's taken to illustrate the fatuousness of the claim.)

Because the point of morals is to guide and direct behavior, it of course *must* override *something*, namely the behavior that is inconsistent with the directive in question, whatever it may be. Now in the case where one proclaims a strong duty to refrain from x, the behavior to be overridden is x-ing. But where one claims merely the *desirability* of doing y, that is quite another matter. One who says this is not committed to doing y, just like that. In the case of the strong duty claim, he would need a serious, moral-type justification for nonperformance, or a very good excuse. The normally pacific person who shoots an armed robber who refuses to surrender when called on has not acted inconsistently with his duty. But the normally pacific person who shoots someone in order to take his wallet, the victim being quite innocent in wrongdoing in the course of earning the contents, has acted inconsistently with his duty. Let's agree that it is not always easy to say precisely what justifies which apparent deviations from duty. But while it is not always easy, it very often is, and when it is, those who act otherwise are acting inconsistently with their professions, and those professions are failing to do what they are supposed to do—namely to guide his behavior accordingly. And when it is not, we will listen to reasons given; but if there are none, then again the charge of insincerity looks plausible, and is important.

But when we say that x is admirable or commendable or virtuous, we are not committed to doing x, just like that—routinely, normally. We may admire great basketball players without having any interest at all in playing ourselves; I approve strongly those who give large sums of money to the symphony, though I give only modest sums myself, and others who approve give little or none. And the person who gives large sums to cause X even though he also approves giving such sums to cause Y, though he does not himself, is again not necessarily, or even likely, acting inconsistently either. The way in which such assertions "guide" our behavior is understood to be much "looser" (as Kant puts it) than the way in which professions of right, or justice, or requirement do so. At the margin where other things are truly equal, approval of x implies that we'll support x, but that is- a condition very hard to realize for most of us, and we rarely bother to inquire.

These looser assertions, however, guide us in another way: if we think behavior z admirable, then we ought to applaud those who do z, including those we otherwise don't like very much. One who failed to give credit where his own assertions imply that it is due would indeed be acting inconsistently, prima facie, though the actions in this case are largely verbal.

So this gets us back to the issue between us and Singer in regard to his puzzling claims, that we have a duty to, say, treat "all animals equally," but also that morality is not overriding. Just what is he claiming? He cannot, of course, point to us carnivores and claim that *we* are acting inconsistently when *his* claims do not override *our* behavior. Obviously we differ from him, and our behavior, consistently, differs accordingly. What he needs to show is that somehow we are making a mistake about the nature of morality. And if he can, then indeed we really shall have to change our ways. We won't be able genuinely to agree with him but keep right on eating (unless we have some other sort of argument or a different set of utility calculations—buot of which, in this case, are all too likely!) On the other hand, he needn't change *his* ways if *we* are right, for no one, on our view, has the *duty* to eat meat. Our view is that people may eat what they like (not including the flesh of the very individuals they have a strong duty not to kill, namely their fellow humans.) If Singer shared our view, then, what he would then believe wouldn't override his habit of not eating meat, for it wouldn't *claim* to override that. It would, however, override his habit of claiming that we are doing something wrong.

All of which reinforces the point here: *of course* morality overrides behavior, overrides individual nonmoral values that may conflict with whatever the moral claim in question may be, and to say otherwise is to run a serious danger of trivializing the subject.

3. Is Morality *Rational*?

The claims that moralityit is rational, and likewise the claim that it is not, are in much need of clarification. At one end of the spectrum, as it were, we have the question of whether moral language actually *means anything*, whether it has any implications, whether it is logically possible for moral claims to be either consistent or inconsistent with other claims. My preceding discussion supports the thesis that it does mean something and has some implications. Indeed, my discussion there is very much in accord with the views of Singer's late mentor R. M. Hare, who held that morals claims were essentially a sort of imperatives. I do not in fact accept the claim that they are "essentially" that in the way that most would take it, but I certainly do accept the thesis that moral claims have implications for the behavior of those who make them. Moreover, these implications are not personal and private but public: all who hear are entitled to expect certain kinds of behavior from those who make such claims.

Nevertheless, the question whether morals is rational goes well beyond the preceding rather narrow point about the semantics, as it were, of moral language. Our question now is: is there any *reason to* be moral, or for that matter to have a morality at all? And of what nature might such reasons be? On this matter, I again side, so far as I can see, against Singer, or at least against several of his assertions which appear to imply the contrary. About those reasons, my positive case will be made under the umbrella of my fourth question. Here I mean only to indicate what seems to me to be involved in seriously denying the rationality of morals.

For this we urgently need to make distinctions. Whenever anyone says anything, no matter what, we might ask, "Why did you say that?" Sometimes when we ask this, the emphasis will be on why she *said* it, which may have quite a different answer from the question, "Why do you *think* that?" And it is essentially the latter kind of question, I take it, that we are asking when we ask whether morality is "rational."

Still, we need to make distinctions. Most importantly, we need to be clearer about what is meant by 'morality' here. For there are, so far as I can see, at least two[17] quite different, though certainly not unrelated, subjects that might be referred to by this term.

On the one hand, moralities have often been taken to be what we may call personal guides to life. I lean toward attempting to relegate the term 'ethics' for *this* subject, but accept that English usage does not provide a clear and reliable pattern here. At any rate, consider the subject of Aristotle's famous *Nichomachean Ethics*. This seems to me *par excellence* an example of a treatise on this very general, and of course exceedingly important, subject. Here, says Aristotle, is how all men ought to behave, given the Nature of Man. Here are various virtues, practice of which will enable us to live better lives, be "better people."

But only *some* of Aristotle's treatise is directly concerned with the other subject we need to distinguish here: morals, as a general set of principles or rules meant to apply specifically to people living in contact with each other, in "society"—that is, principles that claim *interpersonal authority*. Aristotle discusses justice, for example, and some of his examples of moral virtues are also generally of this type. But others are not. The man who eats too much is not doing himself a favor, we may think, but what he does isn't normally *immoral*, though if he were to eat too much by helping himself to other people's supplies without their permission, his vice would then have also impelled him into immoral behavior in this narrower sense that I am concerned with here.

And I take it that Singer is likewise making claims of this kind: claims that *we*, and not just people who *happen to feel this way* about it, *ought* to be doing a lot more for the poor, and refraining from eating meat, and so on. It is the mark of morals in this sense to deny that the

---

[17] A third would be the term 'ethics' as it applies to the codes of behavior of, say, corporations or specialized organizations such as professional bodies of lawyers or doctors. I take it that we are not concerned with such uses here.

matters in question are matters of personal taste or idiosyncrasy. People do differ in their tastes and fashions and "lifestyles," to be sure, and that is an extremely important point about them. Some moralists are ready to criticize most or all of those whose lifestyle differs from their own or ours, while others are more "liberal," say. Now, are some of these moralists right, and others wrong? And should we expect to be able to "prove" or at least give strong and good reasons against some and in favor of other views on this subject? Those of us who say that morality is (the sort of thing that can and should be) *rational*, are answering in the affirmative. We hold that there is a *rationale* for these rules on the basis of which we presume to criticize some behavior, and to applaud other behaviors, in the context of social life.

Well, what about these "reasons" then? Should we not be impressed by Hume's claim that "reason is and must ever be a slave of the passions," for example?

Well, obviously the subject here is *practical* reason, not pure mathematics, and so the kind of reasons we are talking about have to be of that kind. We do not base morality on the axioms of Euclid, say. That hardly means that morality is non-rational. But it does suggest that some who query the rationality of morals are barking up the wrong tree. Broadly speaking, we of course must agree with Hume—and, perhaps more surprisingly to some readers, with Aristotle. Both writers remind us that actions proceed from *desires, interests,* and indeed from *passions.* So far, so good. But to say this is not to say that there is no such thing as practical reason. It is, rather, to tell us where it lies, what it's about. Reason, says Aristotle, is a matter of *controlling* the passions. In so saying, he may have thought that "reason" is a sort of black box in the soul, telling us what we ought to like and dislike. If so, however, he is greatly mistaken, to the point of incoherence. It is, as he himself observed, just nonsense to think that we can have practical direction with no desire, no interest, no *wants*.

But remember: we are talking about *interpersonal* direction, not just any old direction. The man who has a passion for collecting stamps has reason for attending to the sale over across town, but I do not. That man will make many calculations, shrewd or ill-advised purchases, etc., but persons like myself, the philatelically challenged, will not have any of *those* problems and need do neither well nor badly at them. Perhaps the stamp-lover will get us to think that life would be much more interesting if we too got into stamp collecting, but if we judge otherwise, that's the end of the matter: we act perfectly reasonably in staying home and ignoring the sale.

If, however, we presume to issue judgments about the behavior of *just anyone*—which is the province of morals, roughly—then we will have to get into practical reasoning of a kind that can reach out across the variety of particular interests and involvements that give various people special reasons for doing or avoiding this or that, and—as, again, Hume noted—find principles such that we are *all* "in symphony and accord"and thus can be expected to have interests to which these principles suitably respond. We shall say that the murderer is evil, no matter who his victim may be, and no matter what particular gains he expects to make by assailing that person, because the thesis that murder is wrong is one based on aspects of human nature that we all share—including the murderer himself.

Can there be reasonable principles of that kind? Yes. Do we know *exactly* what they are? No, though the subject is rife with suggestions and more research. Do we have a decent idea what they are, broadly? Yes. And is it rational, reasonable, to think so? Indeed it is.

The question arises, then, what Singer is intending to say when he denies that morality is "rational." And unfortunately, there is a clear sense that can be given to such a claim that would make it plausible—but also irrelevant, or rather, would render his own distinctive principles of little interest, rather than of the level of great importance he obvious thinks they have. This clear sense is that the principles in question *are*, after all, just a matter of feeling, a matter of how *he* and *some* others feel about certain matters. I myself have an enormous aversion to broccoli, despite its well-confirmed nutritional virtues. This aversion might be said to be "irrational," no doubt: but what could this mean other than that it's a nuisance, and wouldn't it be nice if instead I just loved the stuff, considering how much good it could do me? Well, I concede all that, though I'm not about to go gulping it down, despite my aversion, in hopes of changing my tastes. (I would expect massive failure in any such experiment, but, who knows? Perhaps some food psychologist will show me how to make it succeed. . . .) Meanwhile, however, will someone claim that the taste *itself* is in some relevant sense "irrational"? But what they will mean, surely, is that it is *non*-rational: one does not acquire one's tastes by abstractly deciding which would be good to have and which not. At this level, it just is a fact about particular people that they do or do not *like* certain flavors. To each, as we say, his own. We say this for a good reason, too: we imply, in saying that, that the appropriate social rule, the appropriate, the rational *moral* attitude, is to *let* people act on their *own* tastes, insofar as this is practically compatible with others doing likewise.

Now, this latter is a pronouncement of reason. Tastes are not rational, but what to do about the fact of divergence of tastes can be a subject for quite rational deliberation—and with an easy answer. Rigid, narrow-minded, dogmatic types who insist on pronouncing in moral vein on the habits and tastes of others, are *mistaken*: their moral views are being wrongly based. That we regard such "rigidity" as a moral vice is not itself just a further matter of taste, but reflects a rational accommodation to an important fact of life. Indeed, as Singer himself says and we noted at the outset, " . . . Ethics takes a universal point of view . . . in making an ethical judgment we go beyond our own likes and dislikes. . . ." Very well. So in declaring morals to be not rational, then, is Singer claiming that the claimed duty to give a great deal of our incomes to the faraway poor, and to refrain from eating steak, are, after all, on a par with my aversion to broccoli? If so, fine—so be it! But equally obviously, it is small wonder that he should be modest about the prospects for these aversions of his to be *overriding*—specifically, that they should have the status of overriding the tastes and proclivities of the rest of us. For that purpose, they run up against a stone wall: people *differ*. If he couldn't do better than that, he should, as we say, dry up.

And, can he do better? That is our final question here.

4. Universalizability and Foundations of Morals

I quoted Singer at the outset thus:

> Ethics takes a universal point of view . . . Ethics requires us to go beyond 'I' and 'you' to the universal law, the universalizable judgment, the standpoint of the impartial spectator or ideal observer, or whatever we choose to call it.

But "But what we choose to call it really does matter, in fact. Those are not just names for the same thing.

First: *universal* judgments are easy to make: "everybody ought to do *x*" is universal. But easy as it may be to *make* such claims, many such judgments are by no means suitable for morals.

Second, the "impartial spectator" may not be the right person to ask. We, after all, are not just spectators, but agents, participants. The spectator *qua* spectator may enjoy the show, or not, but it is less than clear that he is necessarily the authority on what we should all do.

Third, the "ideal observer" may be still worse. Like the spectator, he's only an observer; and if he's "ideal" the question is, what makes him so and whether *ideal* observers are really in much of a position to tell us ordinary mortals what's what. More fundamentally: unless that observer is interested in *morals* in particular, his various observations may be of no interest. But that's why we can't define the moral point of view in terms of "ideal observers" except at pain of circularity.

The fundamental point is that there's me, and there's you, and so on; there's any given person, a moral agent, equipped with interests, desires, ideals, wants, values, and who guides his or her action in light of those; and then there's all the rest. Since his own interests and values are all he's got, we had better not go claiming that to be guided by those is somehow inadequate or irrational. We had better, instead, try to work from each person's practical reasons, plus the fact of life, and especially of human *interaction*, and see whether anything useful emerges.

What won't and can't work is to base our prescriptions for all on something peculiar to ourselves. That's where impartiality looms large as an imperative of morals. If we expect Jones to cooperate in refraining from actions of type y, we'd better not have a theory that says that people like Jones don't cut it, don't stack up. We had better, instead, find some basis such that each of us can see that he or she, in view of how everyone else is, would do well to avoid *y* and confine themselves to doing other things instead.

Singer and Singerians (including Hare) seem to think that the point of view of morality is, as we might put it, Martian—that when we do moral theory, we are allowed to ignore what we are, pound on the table and insist on ways of acting that will strike most of us as bizarre. As, for instance, when we are called on to make no distinction between our own children and anyone else's, or insisting that creatures we can't even talk to nevertheless deserve our most lavish attention. Or again, like insisting that what we have worked for and carefully attended to all this time should be given to others *simply because* they have a lot less than we do.

Hume held that in every breast there was a bit of universal sympathy, along with the elements of the wolf and the serpent. He was at least pretty close to right, and that is a fortunate thing for humanity. But a bit is a bit—it's not a flood, and it's no way equal to our concern for people near and dear to us, usually including our*selves*. Telling us that we must count all the others "equally" is plain foolishness. On the other hand, telling us that we must accommodate to others, get along with them, deal fairly with them, is the very reverse of foolish, but of the last importance for people wanting to make a go of it with their fellows.

The universal point of view of morals is the point of view of Everyman, who finds himself—or, of course, herself—among many others, similarly diverse and similarly capable of making life better or worse for her. The obvious strategy is the one recommended by Glaucon and then later by Epicurus: agree to refrain from the ones that make life worse for others, provided that they do likewise. Agreeing to do good to others provided they reciprocate is the other side of the coin, but those agreements will be specific and particular, whereas the general negative agreement, as we may call it, tells us all to refrain across the board from what is evil for others, so long as they do likewise. This general idea is, as the boys say, a "slam dunk." It appeals to all, and it is small wonder that the "golden rule" is the hands-down favorite general moral maxim in virtually all cultures. It requires the least from us that is compatible with expecting the desired reciprocation by all. No other moral view, as they say, can make that statement. And especially not one that refuses to take note of our being the sort of organisms we are, proposing instead to impose pointless or impossible duties on us for the sake of goodness-knows-what.

Actually, we are fairly sure we do know what happened: the "universality" that Hare and Singer think to appeal to is tunnel-vision universality. They look only at the side of us that receives, not the side that creates and gives. Pleasure, or anyway experienced value, is the good for all, they suppose, and pain, experienced evil, the bad for all, and universality consists in focussing on that, they say—forgetting that what *produces* these pleasures or pains are individual people with their own interests and aspirations—the very interests and aspirations, in fact, that motivate them to produce so much. To reason in the Sidgwick-Singer-Hare manner is to commit a kind of socialist fallacy, analogous to that committed by the followers of Marx in political matters. And just as the Marxian idea is a recipe for disaster in economics and politics, so the Harean idea is a recipe for disaster in morals. For the universality of morals isn't like that. It's rules, requirements, for all, to be imposed on these people who act and plan, and do so for the sake of persons they care about (including themselves), not for the sake of some kind of amalgamated "good" irrespective of who gets it or why. Once we appreciate this, we can see the irrelevance and impossibility of the kind of "impartiality" proposed by Hare. We shall then pay attention to real people, as they are, and make rules that make sense to them in their interactions. The attitude that it doesn't really matter who benefits from my efforts, that I should regard one potential recipient as on all fours (often literally!) with any others, is simply unreal. It in no way can serve as the starting point of a credible morality. By contrast, calling upon all to refrain from damaging others, and to be generally helpful in cases of near-to-hand need, looks to be a plausible formula for a good life in society. Looking at things this way will lead us not to regard the presence of billions of poor people in the world as some kind of moral failing on our part, nor as on a part with the sort of disasters that are due to the odd hurricane, flood, or volcano, but rather as a field of opportunity for the entrepreneur—and as an occasion for checking out the political apparatus in the places they live, which is likely preventing them from getting on in life. And as for animals, who of course play no part as moral agents in our lives, we can look on them in many ways—as objects for interesting study, as aesthetically interesting, as pets, and as sources of food, clothing, and very helpful sources of medically important information—but not as organisms whose pains and pleasures are of necessary moral significance to us simply as such.

Singer, along with his mentors Sidgwick and Hare, are by no means alone in this philosophical irrelevance. But my concern here is with Singer, and we'll leave the others for other days.

Reply to Narveson

PETER SINGER

Jan Narveson says that he will question four of the foundations of my ethical position: the principle of equal consideration of interests, whether morality is overriding, the rationality of morality, and why we should accept moral obligations at all. These are important questions, and some serious criticism of my views would provide a useful opportunity for further reflection and reconsideration. Unfortunately, however, Narveson uses the broad headings of these four points to take potshots at me on a variety of other issues, and it isn't always clear what principle, other than free association, has led him to group his points under the four main headings. Even when he does address the major questions, it isn't always easy to know exactly what point he is making. Nevertheless, I shall use Narveson's headings, and respond as far as possible to his criticisms in the order that they are made.

The "Equal Consideration" Principle

Narveson quotes Sidgwick's celebrated passage about taking "the point of view of the Universe" and correctly states that it has been highly influential on me. But he is less clearly correct when he adds that I differ from Sidgwick because I am "ready to admit that his position is not rational in the sense that every rational individual will, necessarily, go along with it." For Sidgwick's assertion, in the passage Narveson quotes, that "it is evident to me that as a rational being I am bound to aim at good generally, so far as it is attainable by my efforts, not merely at a particular part of it," is not his last word on the topic. On the contrary, Sidgwick was famously troubled by what he called "the dualism of practical reason" and in the concluding chapter of *The Methods of Ethics,* he acknowledged:

> It would be contrary to Common Sense to deny that the distinction between any one individual and any other is real and fundamental, and that consequently "I" am concerned with the quality of my existence as an individual in a sense, fundamentally important, in which I am not concerned with the quality of the existence of other individuals: and this being so, I do not see how it can be proved that this distinction is not to be taken as fundamental in determining the ultimate end of rational action for an individual.[18]

Because of this, Sidgwick held, we can only avoid "a fundamental contradiction in one chief department of our thought" if duty and self-interest can be reconciled, for example by belief in reward and punishment in a life after death. But Sidgwick, it seems, did not find the evidence for such a hypothesis compelling.

I agree, of course, as I have said in response to Bernard Williams, that the idea of "the point of view of the universe" is a metaphor. But Narveson's further claim that "there is *no* 'point of view' that it makes sense for *us* to try to identify and which has the singular features Sidgwick and Singer want to endow it with," seems unfounded, and certainly doesn't follow from his observation that after we have reckoned all the individual utilities, there is no "'everyone's utility' left over." It's not "left over," it just *is* the total of all the individual utilities. What's so difficult to grasp about that?

Narveson's further claim, that utility "intrinsically motivates" only the person whose utility it is, is just not relevant to whether we can usefully add up utilities. It is odd that Narveson should claim that "There is simply no sense to the idea of my acting on, that is, being motivated as such by, *your* utility." There is, of course, a perfectly ordinary sense in which most parents are motivated by the utility of their children, most spouses or lovers are motivated by the utility of their partners, most friends are motivated by the utility of their friends, and most people are at least sometimes motivated by the utility of strangers. Narveson can, of course, make it true by definition that these people are not being motivated "as such" by the utility of others, but are including the utility of the others in their own utility function. This definitional move is just a way of telling us how he wants to understand the concept of "intrinsic motivation" or "motivation as such." It doesn't tell us anything about what really motivates people. Since we virtually all are motivated, whether "intrinsically" or not, by the utility of our families, friends and

---

[18] Henry Sidgwick, *The Methods of Ethics,* seventh edition (London: Macmillan, 1907), p. 498.

of strangers, we will need to calculate, in some way, what is in the over-all utility of all those about whom we care. (I note, too, that Narveson himself seems to have difficulty in taking seriously his own view that when we are motivated by the interests of another, we have installed some representation of that person's utility into our own utility function. For if he did take that view seriously, why would he then say, in the very next paragraph, that "People are often prepared to make great sacrifices for some one or perhaps some very few such persons"? Since the person's own utility now includes—that is, has had "installed" in it—a representation of the utility of the other, why would it be a *sacrifice* for the person to maximize his or her own utility?)

Next Narveson points out that I do not give as much to good causes as I believe I ought to give. That's something I've frequently acknowledged. The sense in which this is a moral failing is something that Judith Lichtenberg and Richard Arneson usefully explore in their contributions to this volume, and I have commented on that in my responses to them. I shall say more about it when I come to what Narveson says about morality and rationality. Narveson then adds that this shows that "the Sidgwickian formula is hopeless as a supposed description of objects of affection even on the part of the most charitable people we encounter." Okay, but who ever said that the "Sidgwickian formula" was a description of objects of affection? It's a normative claim, and not a description of anything. (Sidgwick does describe comon sense morality, with regard to benevolence, in a different part of *The Methods of Ethics,* but he does not endorse it.[19])

From here Narveson goes on to imagine that it must be "rather painful" for people like me to note that Bill Gates gives away far more than all the philosophers put together. It's not painful at all, it's merely an application of a rule known to all fundraisers, that if you want to raise large sums, you should go to people who are very rich. Gates gives more than all the philosophers put together because he has much more than all the philosophers put together. If Gates causes pain to holders of any philosophical position, I would have thought it would be to defenders of egoism if they go to the website of the Bill and Melinda Gates Foundation—a foundation set up by the man who is arguably the most successful exponent of capitalism of our era, and now additionally endowed by the majority of the fortune of one of his close rivals for that title, Warren Buffett—and see, under the heading "Our Values," the

---

[19] See *The Methods of Ethics,* Book III, Chapter 4.

proclamation that "All lives—no matter where they are being led—have equal value."

I have no quarrel with accumulating wealth, if the purpose of the accumulation is to acquire the largest possible sum to give away. The key question is always how one can do the most good in the long run.

From here Narveson goes into an excursion about the harm that misguided utilitarians can do, citing the amusing example of Dickens's Mrs Jellyby. But as Bentham pointed out long ago, the claim that utilitarianism has bad consequences can't be an objection to utilitarianism, for that claim is itself an appeal to utility. All it can be is an objection to the misapplication of utilitarianism. Should it turn out to be true that utilitarianism is particularly prone to being misapplied and that the misapplications cause greater harms than the gains achieved by people acting correctly as utilitarians, then—as I have argued in my responses to Lichtenberg and Schmidtz—utilitarians will, in order to bring about the best consequences, cease to advocate utilitarianism as a guide to behavior, although it will still remain the ultimate criterion by which we judge good and bad outcomes.

That leads Narveson to assert that it is "not acceptable" to inflict pain on a bystander, without that bystander's consent, in order to benefit others. No argument is given for this claim—perhaps to Narveson it just seems obvious. But it isn't obvious to me, and—although I don't think we should test our theories by the extent to which they match common moral intuitions—it isn't obvious to most people, for in several different studies, more than eighty percent of people, from a variety of cultures, ethnicities, age, sex, and nationalities, said that you should throw a switch to divert a runaway trolley that otherwise will kill five people, even if by diverting the trolley you will kill an innocent bystander.[20] So Narveson's claim needs to be argued for—but argument is lacking.

When Narveson moves on to the distinction between killing and letting die, he still doesn't give any arguments, except the claim that we have the rules we have because, given the kind of beings we are, and what life is like, such rules are "called for." I can only think of two things that this might mean. The first is that there is some overarching purpose to the universe that calls for such rules. I doubt that Narveson wants to say this. The other is that having such rules will enable all of us to live better. That may be what Narveson means, but if so, he is putting

---

[20] See J.D. Greene, R.B Sommerville, L.E. Nystrom, J.M. Darley, and J.D. Cohen, "An Investigation of Emotional Engagement in Moral Judgment," *Science* 293 (2001), pp. 2105–08; Marc Hauser, *Moral Minds* (New York: HarperCollins, 2006).

forward a utilitarian argument for accepting rules, and if the facts are indeed as he claims, I would of course agree.

Narveson writes that in *The President of Good and Evil* I excoriate President George W. Bush for going to the aid of the oppressed people of Iraq. He cites no page reference, presumably because there is no passage in which I say anything of the kind. In that book I do excoriate Bush for many things, including his refusal to allow the UN inspectors to finish their work of ascertaining whether Saddam Hussein had weapons of mass destruction, and for accepting a military strategy that involved bombing targets of minor military significance in civilian areas where it could be foreseen that dropping bombs would be likely to kill many civilians. Anyone who listened to Bush or others in his administration in the buildup to the Iraq war would know that the overriding reason put forward for attacking Iraq was to stop Saddam building weapons of mass destruction and passing them on to terrorists. As any reader of *One World* would know, I support genuine humanitarian intervention when it foreseeably will prevent great suffering at much less cost. War should, however, be a last resort, because it so often brings enormous suffering. In Iraq, tragically but—since humanitarian intervention was never the primary motive for the invasion—not surprisingly, more people have died violent deaths in the five years since the American attack than in the previous five years under Saddam's repressive rule.

Other than an appeal to intuitions, the only reason Narveson gives for the distinction between acts and omissions is that we are individual agents, with our own agendas, for whom freedom matters. But no implications about the acts and omissions distinction can be drawn from that. Suppose that today, if I do nothing, I will be able to act on my own agenda and this matters to me; but ten other individual agents will be arbitrarily arrested by a tyrant. They will suffer a permanent loss of freedom, and never again be able to act on their own agendas, and this matters as much to each one of them as acting on my own agenda matters to me. As I am lying on the beach, enjoying the warmth of the sun on my back, I receive a text message telling me that I can save all ten from this fate, but to do so I will have to abandon my own agenda for the remainder of the morning. (My agenda was to continue to lie on the beach sunbathing.) How does the fact that freedom matters—to other agents as it matters to me—entail that in these circumstances I would be justified in continuing to follow my own agenda?

Narveson suggests that a better argument for extending help to others when we can do so at little cost to ourselves is that "the chances are that we will benefit from this." But in a world of more than six billion people, this is wishful thinking. It is extremely unlikely that any of the people who have been helped by my donations to Oxfam will ever be in a position to help me. Okay, Narveson may say, so don't give to Oxfam. What about offering my seat on a crowded bus to an elderly person, or, while driving in heavy, slowly-moving traffic, giving way to a driver trying to enter the road from a driveway? Narveson says: "It does not take much to see that we all stand to benefit from living among helpful people rather than narrow-minded, selfish recluses. The reason for being helpful oneself falls out very straightforwardly from this." Narveson is fooling himself here too. Unless we live in a very small town, the chances that we will benefit from these actions (other than from feeling pleased that we helped) are negligible. Of course, if we *all* helped in these ways, the community would become a better place, but the "what if everyone did it?" argument is a moral argument, so Narveson cannot invoke it without abandoning his self-interested stance. The cold reality is that if there are millions of us living in the same city, my actions are not going to make any noticeable difference to the community as a whole, let alone to me personally.

Narveson delights in pointing out that animals can't reciprocate whatever good we may do to them. He neglects to mention that future generations, born only after we die, are equally incapable of benefiting us. If I enjoy driving my large gas-guzzling sports utility vehicle, why should I care about the fact that I am contributing to climate change that, in a few decades, may cause millions of people to starve when the rains fail or rising sea levels flood their farmlands? But perhaps Narveson thinks we have no obligation to be concerned about future generations.

Overridingness

Whether morality is overriding, and if so, in what sense, is an important topic. Disappointingly, Narveson fails to pursue it systematically, instead diving rapidly into quite separate issues, such as whether my views imply that aid should come from governments or from individuals. I have discussed that issue in my response to Cowen. He also suggests that to say something is our duty means that we may be compelled to do it, whereas there are other things that it would be good to do, but which we are not justified in compelling people to do. For a utilitarian, any such distinction would be, at most, a set of secondary rules that would generally bring about better consequences. In any case, what I said about my use of the term "obligation" in my response to Lichtenberg applies equally to the term "duty."

Narveson evidently thinks that morality is overriding, in some sense, but he doesn't say much about what this means, beyond the statement that "*of course* morality overrides behavior, overrides individual nonmoral values that may conflict with whatever the moral claim in question may be, and to say otherwise is to run a serious danger of trivializing the subject." This sentence is frustratingly loose in its wording. I don't understand what it means to say that morality "overrides behavior" because that seems to confuse two different categories. Perhaps Narveson means that morality *should* govern our behavior. I'll come back to that claim in a moment. What about the statement that morality "overrides individual nonmoral values that may conflict with whatever the moral claim in question may be"? On its face, this statement asserts that morality in fact overrides whatever conflicting nonmoral values an individual may hold. Is this supposed to be a logical truth, perhaps true in virtue of the meanings of the terms involved, or is it supposed to be something we can observe? In the ordinary sense of the terms, it is not true by definition that morality overrides nonmoral values—we often say of someone that he let his ambition, say, override his moral principles. If morality were by definition overriding, this would be self-contradictory, and we would instead say "His morality is to satisfy his ambition." Hence if Narveson thinks that it is true by definition that morality is overriding we would need arguments in favor of a special, reforming definition of "morality" such that for a person to hold a moral principle, he must hold it in a way that overrides his nonmoral values. D.H. Monro put forward such a view in the 1960s, and I discussed it in one of my earliest articles, but generally the position has had few followers.[21] In any case, Narveson offers no arguments at all for this claim.

If, on the other hand, we read Narveson's claim that morality overrides conflicting nonmoral values as a factual claim, it is obviously false. Regrettably, people do, all too often, allow their ambition, self-interest, love for a friend, or many other nonmoral values to override their morality. Sometimes they themselves admit this, and apologize for having done what they knew to be wrong.

Narveson's claim that morality "overrides individual nonmoral values that may conflict with whatever the moral claim in question may be" is, then, neither true by definition, nor true as a matter of fact, so it is, as it stands, false. But since Narveson thinks that it is an obvious

---

[21] See D.H. Monro, *Empiricism and Ethics* (Cambridge: Cambridge University Press, 1967) and Peter Singer, "The Triviality of the Debate over 'Is-Ought' and the Definition of 'Moral'," *American Philosophical Quarterly* 10 (January 1973), pp. 51–56.

claim—remember the *"of course"*—he must have meant to say something that his words fail to express. Perhaps his thought was the one that I mentioned earlier and put aside: that morality *should* govern our behavior and override nonmoral values. But what could this mean? If the "should" is a moral "should" then it is a tautology. From a moral perspective, of course, morality should override all conflicting nonmoral values. But one might just as well say that from the point of view of etiquette, etiquette should override moral values.[22] (Doing the right thing can still be bad manners.) Is there some kind of neutral "should" that can adjudicate between morality and other conflicting perspectives? The best candidate is the one Narveson discusses in the next section—that is, that the "should" is one based on what it is rational to do. So, digressions apart, the section on whether morality is overriding hasn't got us anywhere yet.

Is Morality Rational?

It isn't easy to work out what question Narveson thinks he is addressing in this section. He writes: "Our question now is: is there any *reason to* be moral, or for that matter to have a morality at all?" That suggests that he is interested in the question "Why should I act morally?" and looking at whether we can give an individual reasons for acting morally. But later in the same section he writes: "We hold that there is a *rationale* for these rules on the basis of which we presume to criticize some behavior, and to applaud other behaviors, in the context of social life." That comment, like much else in this section, does nothing to answer the individual who supports the idea that there should be moral rules, yet can see no reason for obeying them herself, if she can break them without being sanctioned in any way. Other passages in this section discuss whether morality is subjective, or a matter of taste, or whether we can give rational arguments for reaching some conclusions rather than others. This issue is more carefully discussed by Michael Huemer, and my views on it can be found in my response to him.

Universalizability and Foundations of Morals

As I have already indicated in my responses to Huemer, Düwell, and Schmidtz, I follow Hare in holding that universalizability is a defining

---

[22] See Philippa Foot, "Morality as a System of Hypothetical Imperatives," *Philosophical Review* 81 (1972), pp. 305–316.

feature of a moral judgment. Universalizability requires me to put myself in the position of all those affected by my actions. Given this, there is no need to appeal to an impartial spectator or ideal observer, for the effect is the same. Nevertheless, Narveson is wrong to say that the ideal observer needs to make moral judgments, and therefore that the concept risks circularity. All the ideal observer needs to do is put herself in the position of all those affected by the action under scrutiny, and decide what choice she would then prefer.

"Why should I act morally?" arises as a question in need of an answer because, while I can decide to act only on those judgments I would be prepared to universalize, I can also act on judgments that I am not prepared to universalize—judgments that, for instance, give special weight to *my* interests when I would not be prepared to accept that others should give special weight to *their* interests if, in an otherwise similar situation, our roles were reversed. In these circumstances, I cannot claim that my action is morally justified. Does that make it irrational? Narveson appears to want to give an affirmative answer to this question, but he doesn't ever say why. He quotes Glaucon with approval, but seems to forget that when, in Plato's *Republic,* Glaucon puts forward his prototype of a social contract view of morality, he also adds that if one could get away with breaching this agreement—for example, by possessing the legendary ring of Gyges, which makes one invisible—everyone would act as Gyges did, seducing the queen and killing the king. Narveson doesn't tell us whether he thinks the answer that Socrates gives to this question is sound, or if not, how else Glaucon's challenge might be met. Moreover Narveson's agreement with Hume that "reason is and must ever be a slave of the passions" makes it difficult to see how he could argue that it is always rational to be moral. If reason is the slave of the passions, and a person's strongest passion is not for doing as morality dictates—not, that is, for acting only on judgments he can universalize—how could it be irrational for him to follow his strongest passion?[23]

Instead of fulfilling his initial promissory note to address this fundamental issue, Narveson returns to sniping at my ethical position on the treatment of animals, saying that it will strike most of us as "bizarre" to insist that "creatures we can't even talk to nevertheless deserve our most

---

[23] Michael Huemer makes the same point in his contribution to this volume: "Thus, Hume and his followers would say that the fact that an action is morally right can give you a rational reason to do it, only if you *want* to do what is right, or you want something else that you think doing the right thing will help you accomplish."

lavish attention." But we can't talk to infants, and insisting that they deserve our most lavish attention doesn't strike many people as bizarre. Even insisting that intellectually disabled people who can't use language deserve our most lavish attention is not bizarre. So if Narveson wants to exclude nonhuman animals from the social contract because we can't talk to them, or because they can't cooperate with us, he will have to exclude infants, people with severe intellectual disabilities, and, as already mentioned, future generations.

As the intellectual autobiography in this volume indicates, I have been grappling with the question "Why should I act morally?" since I began work on my master's thesis. I came back to it in the last chapter of *Practical Ethics,* and also in *How Are We to Live?* I am not fully satisfied with the answers I have given. Had Narveson systematically set out and defended a different answer, he would have done us all a valuable service. Alas, he has not done that.

---

[24] See J.D. Greene, R.B Sommerville, L.E. Nystrom, J.M. Darley, and J.D. Cohen, "An Investigation of Emotional Engagement in Moral Judgment," *Science,* 293 (2001), pp. 2105–08; Marc Hauser, *Moral Minds* (New York: HarperCollins, New York, 2006).

15

Animal Liberationist Bites Dog

BERYL LIEFF BENDERLY

"When a dog bites a man, that is not news, because it happens so often," said John B. Bogart, city editor of the nineteenth-century New York *Sun*. "But if a man bites a dog, that is news."

So what do you call it when a distinguished professor of ethics advocates the acceptability of killing (not just of allowing to die, but of actively putting to death) brain-damaged infants and harmless but terminally demented old people, including, perhaps, his own mother? Such pronouncements may well fit Bogart's stated criterion, because they probably occur, in the United States at least, not much more frequently than an adult human sinks his canines into a canine.

Bogart's definition goes further, though, and taps into an emotional element beyond mere rarity. An event can be unusual and still have little intrinsic interest, but a man biting a dog rivets the attention in part because its severely violates the ordinary experience and expectations of daily life, along with the assumptions that underlie those expectations.

The spectacle of an ethics professor endorsing views that many in the philosophically unsophisticated general public regard as repugnant and depraved has quite a similar effect. Ordinary people, were they ever to give the academic study of ethics any thought at all, would probably assume that professors of the subject spend their days exploring ways to do right and virtuous actions rather than thinking up justifications for acts that appear, at least to many without graduate philosophy degrees, to be monstrous. Many such people would probably agree that the professor's assertions exemplify a category of ideas defined by another journalist, George Orwell: those so preposterous that only an intellectual could believe them.

Aphorisms attributed to journalists may seem an odd way to approach the ideas of so consequential an intellectual as Peter Singer. Coming at those ideas from this direction comes naturally to me, however. First, I'm a journalist myself and unqualified to comment from a philosophical standpoint on the work of a thinker whom publications such as the *New Yorker* and the *New York Times* have called the most influential, famous, dangerous, and controversial philosopher alive. Second, the picture of Singer that these and other popular media have constructed, with his active collusion, has become an important part of his philosophic message, at least to the general run of people who are not ethics professionals. He has attained the status of a designated *bête noire* among conservative political commentators and in the right-wing blogosphere, as well as of a certified thorn in the side of bleeding hearts of all political persuasions. I may not know much about philosophy, but working in journalism does give some insight into news value, publicity, and fame. And to me, those decidedly unintellectual, even counter-intellectual, phenomena have something to say about Singer's ideas and their place in society at large.

Singer's status as an influential intellectual rests most securely on his views about the relationship of human beings to animals and the evils that he has perceived in what he calls speciesism, or the belief that humans are in some essential way different from and superior to other creatures. His iconic 1975 book *Animal Liberation* galvanized the eponymous movement that has, through the actions of a violent, fanatical fringe, attracted considerable popular attention and in its more serious manifestations has improved the treatment of animals used as research subjects.

Singer's standing as a danger to society or to common decency derives predominantly from his pronouncements on euthanasia, especially as applied to infants and the disabled. These have appalled those who disagree with his premises and disturbed some who do agree with either his premises or his conclusions but believe that his manner of stating them sets back the cause of changing public attitudes and policies.

Singer's status as an irritant to many who consider themselves generous, high-minded, and moral was earned by his argument for a radical reduction in personal consumption among even the moderately well-off, with the money saved going to aid the people who possess the least. His general celebrity, finally, comes from his being probably the only living philosopher that most people who know of him from the popular media—including some journalists who have rolodexes of contact information for assorted experts to call on short notice—have ever heard of.

So, his ideas have become news even though many of them may not actually be all that new. The utilitarianism on which he bases his reasoning, as any veteran of Philosophy 101 can attest, goes back, if in somewhat different form, to Bentham. The Hindu religious tradition has rejected a firm line between humans and other creatures and favored vegetarianism for uncounted millennia. Ascetic communities in the Christian and other traditions have long urged limiting consumption to survival or the most basic level of comfort. And even doing away with some hopelessly damaged individuals has been, if not openly advocated, then at least privately practiced for many years.

Not all that long ago, in this and many other countries, well-meaning midwives and kindly family doctors would quietly see to it that newborns with certain kinds of obvious abnormalities somehow never drew their first breath. In our own day, families routinely decide that the hopelessly ill should not get the most aggressive possible treatment for pneumonia or that they should be quietly detached from the machines that sustain their bodily functions. In recent years, physicians have gained increased freedom to prescribe painkillers in doses large enough to end intractable pain even if they may have the secondary effect of also ending processes that sustain life.

So Singer's status as a focus of controversy therefore probably arises not so much from what he says as how he says it. He has made statements that a person of his intelligence must know will appall and scandalize many people and has done so without apparent regard for the sources of critics' outrage. In fact, he generally appears to give the feelings at the base of many ordinary people's ethical views very little standing. (I have, however, read an interview in which he acknowledged that his experience caring for a mother with Alzheimer's showed him that end-of-life questions are more complicated in practice than he had previously thought). In short, he has bitten a dog with blithe and apparent disregard for the effect he has on observers.

I'm not sure, however, that I find that disregard entirely convincing. Why would someone of Singer's awesome intellect ignore something as obvious as a "decent respect for the opinions of mankind"? Thomas Jefferson, author of that immortal phrase, was of course not a journalist, but could be called one of history's greatest popularizers of ideas, having put the Enlightenment philosophers' tenets into language that continues to win them adherents around the globe 230 years later. Several possible explanations for Singer's approach come to mind. First, even an intellect as fine as Singer's does not necessarily preclude utter social cluelessness. Many individuals with autism-spectrum disorders that prevent even the simplest understanding of how to deal inoffensively with other people, for example, score high on tests of pure intellectual processing, especially within closed systems of reasoning.

But maybe this isn't really pathological cluelessness, but only the milder version that many academics display. These scholars believe that one can write whatever one wants and it will find a publisher and people will read it and be persuaded by it regardless of whether they find it arcane, ridiculous, or even repulsive. As far as publication goes, the professors may be right, given the plethora of academic journals needing material. But, as every journalist knows—and Jefferson knew, too—writers best entice readers to consider their work, and to read it, and to remember it, and possibly even to alter their thinking and actions because of it, by starting with what the reader knows and thinks and building from there. The first rule of journalism is that everybody on earth has a million things they could do rather than reading your article. You therefore have to give them reasons for doing so.

But this explanation doesn't seem to exactly fit Singer either, because his disregard for feelings actually appears to be a basis of his philosophical system, not just a style of presentation. Bentham allowed for happiness to figure in his calculation, I believe, and that of course is nothing but a feeling. Singer, however, appears to admit only "interests," which he seems to conceptualize as objective, and susceptible to being toted up by persons other than those who possess them. That is the basis for disabled people's objections: how can Singer possibly know what it feels like to have a condition that he has never experienced, so how can he judge what a person who does have it would want or feel? To tell the truth, no one has ever told us what it feels like to have advanced Alzheimer's. We don't even know how much people in the disease's latter phases can feel or perceive; we only know that, should it be anything at all, they are unable express it to the rest of us.

But anyway, unlike Singer, ordinary people generally don't base their ethical or moral thinking on abstract reasoning from a handful of intellectual premises. Rather, some combination of abstraction and gut reaction guides their responses to challenging situations. Basic premises do, of course, underlie those reactions, but, unlike Singer's, they generally have a large emotional component. The premises may include the notion that people one cares about have a greater call on one's attention and resources than those who don't, or that one should treat others as one would wish to be treated oneself, or that each person is entitled to life, liberty and the pursuit of happiness. In every one of these, the basic criteria depend on emotion.

But though Singer seems to disregard the public's sensibilities, he does seem to want at least some of them to adopt his view. He does a lot of writing, some of it in quite attention-getting popular publications, and also gives extensive interviews to reporters. At least in the case of animal liberation, he has succeeded in persuading a number of people. Interestingly though, this is the area in which his ideas comport most closely with what a substantial number of people seem already to have believed, and also to his own behavior. He has been a consistent vegetarian for many years. But he has not put his mother to death, instead spending considerable sums of money providing for her care, although he purports to place her in the philosophical category of a nonperson. Nor does he give away all of his income above his own subsistence needs, instead maintaining reportedly comfortable residences in both Princeton, New Jersey, and Manhattan. Clearly, as Orwell might well observe, even he doesn't believe some of his own pronouncements. But as Bogart doubtless knew from newspapering, a public figure failing to live up to his own ethical pronouncements is even less newsworthy than a dog biting a man.

So what is accomplished by putting forward an ethical system that derives from premises that the great majority of people don't agree with and that reaches conclusions that revolt them? Probably not persuading the public to adopt those views. Perhaps the idea is to draw attention to the questions under discussion. Or perhaps the idea is to draw attention to the intellectual personage doing the discussing. Biting the dog does seem to have been reasonably effective in winning people to the cause of animal liberation. And it has been succeeded extremely well at making Singer a public figure. But for actually bringing people around to accepting—or even listening to—his ideas on many other subjects, a Jeffersonian approach would be a lot more effective.

Reply to Beryl Lieff Benderly

PETER SINGER

Thanks for the Advice, But . . .

Beryl Lieff Benderly is intent on telling me how to write so that more people will read my work: "The first rule of journalism is that everybody on earth has a million things they could do rather than reading your article. You therefore have to give them reasons for doing so." Given that she has noticed that my writing appears in "quite attention-getting popular publications," I wonder why she thinks I need this advice. But wait, there's more. Once I have learned how to get the attention of my readers, I need to change my style of arguing if I am to succeed in persuading them to accept, or even listen to, my views. Once again it has not escaped Benderly's attention that, at least in my writings about animal liberation, I have succeeded in persuading "a number of people." But that can easily be explained, she thinks, because this is the area in which my ideas "comport most closely with what a substantial number of people seem already to have believed." I hadn't noticed, when I began writing on this topic in 1973, the existence of a substantial number of vegetarians, at least not outside India, and especially not people who were vegetarian because of their concern for animals. In fact, I recall, when *Animal Liberation* first appeared, a certain amount of incredulity and even derision regarding the idea that we should give equal consideration to the interests of animals, and that this might lead us to stop eating them. I must have missed all those heads nodding in agreement.

In areas other than the treatment of animals, Benderly apparently thinks I have failed to persuade people even to listen to my views, let alone accept them. I heartily wish I had persuaded more people to accept my views. But have I done so badly? I don't really know—I can only form a loose and totally unscientific impression based on book sales, speaking invitations, media interviews, requests to reprint my articles,

504

emails, letters and personal comments I receive. On that basis, the number of people listening seems quite high, and even the number persuaded doesn't seem entirely negligible. But Benderly seems to know better. Perhaps she has her own sources of information about how many people have, as a result of reading my work, changed their thinking on what it is to live an ethical life, on our obligations to the poor and on life and death issues in medicine. If so, it is a pity she hasn't shared her source with us.

Benderly thinks I would be more persuasive if I were to adopt a "more Jeffersonian approach" which involves "starting with what the reader knows and thinks and building from there." The curious thing about this final piece of advice is that I have been doing just that for thirty-five years. In "Famine, Affluence, and Morality" I started with the reader's moral sense that it would be wrong to walk past a child drowning in a shallow pond. In *Animal Liberation* I started with the reader's opposition to racism and sexism, and drew an analogy between these forms of discrimination, and speciesism. And in *Rethinking Life and Death*, I began with our acceptance of the idea of brain death, and of withholding or withdrawing life-saving medical treatment from severely disabled infants. I then argued that such decisions already involve a judgment that not all human life is of equal value, and that sometimes it is best that a severely disabled infant or a person who has irreversibly lost consciousness should die.

Benderly's claim that I must have known that my views would appall and scandalize my readers is an example of the benefit of hindsight. As I pointed out in my response to Gensler, for the first ten years after these views appeared in *Practical Ethics,* they didn't really cause any fuss at all. Her comments also reflect a distinctively American perspective, and perhaps more specifically an American perspective influenced by the resurgence of religious conservatism in the post-Reagan era. In Australia and New Zealand, in Britain, in the Netherlands and the Scandanavian countries, in Italy, France and Spain, in Japan and Korea, in Canada and generally among countries that are less religious than the United States, my views often meet with disagreement, but not with the level of emotional repugnance that Benderly's language suggests.

So, thanks for the advice, but I don't intend to take it. I hope this won't come across as complacent, but the audience I've reached and the contribution my writings have made to contemporary ethical discussions suggest that there is enough value in the approach I've taken to make it worth continuing in the same mode.

PETER SINGER
Bibliography

1968

Hitler, Mussolini, and Elizabeth Wiskemann. *Australian Outlook* 22 (April), 96–101.

1970

A Note on an Objection to Determinism. [Notes] *Philosophy* 45 (April), 156–57.

1971

Neil Cooper's Concepts of Morality. [Notes] *Mind* 80 (July), 421–23.

1972

Is Act-Utilitarianism Self-Defeating? *Philosophical Review* 81 (January), 94–104.
Moral Experts. *Analysis* 32 (March), 115–17.
Famine, Affluence, and Morality. *Philosophy and Public Affairs* 1 (Spring), 229–243.
Review of *The Foundations of Political Analysis*, by E.J. Meehan. *Times Higher Education Supplement* (29th December).
Review of *The Writings of the Young Marx*. *The Human Context* IV, no. 1.
Review of *Illich's Deschooling Society*. *The Human Context* IV, no. 3.

1973

The Triviality of the Debate over 'Is-Ought' and the Definition of 'Moral'. *American Philosophical Quarterly* 10 (January), 51–56.

Review of *Democratic Theory: Essays in Retrieval*, by C.B. MacPherson. *Times Higher Education Supplement* (2nd February).

Review of *Political Obligation*, by R. Flathman. *Times Higher Education Supplement* (2nd March).

Animal Liberation. *New York Review of Books* (5th April).

Animal Liberation. *New York Review of Books* (5th April, 1973), reprinted in: *The National Observer* (28th April).

Altruism and Commerce: A Reply to Arrow. *Philosophy and Public Affairs* 2 (Spring), 312–320.

Review of *Direct Action and Liberal Democracy*, by April Carter. *Times Higher Education Supplement* (31st August).

Review of *Locke*, by J.D. Mabbott. *Times Higher Education Supplement* (26th October).

Animal Liberation. *New York Review of Books* (5th April, 1973), reprinted in: [Italian translation] *Communita* no. 170, Milan (October).

Review of *Rousseau*, by J. Hall. *Times Higher Education Supplement* (23rd November).

Democracy and Disobedience. Oxford: Clarendon.

Review of *The Gift Relationship*, by Richard Titmuss. *The Human Context* 5, no. 3.

1974

Animal Liberation. *New York Review of Books* (5th April, 1973), reprinted in: *The Match* (January).

Discovering Karl Popper. *New York Review of Books* (2nd May).

Review of *Utilitarianism, For and Against*, by J.J.C. Smart and B. Williams. *Philosophical Books* 15 (May).

Should We Let Them Starve? *New Humanist* (June).

Philosophers Are Back on the Job. *New York Times Sunday Magazine* (7th July).

Looking Backwards. *New York Review of Books* (18th July).

Sidgwick and Reflective Equilibrium. *The Monist* 58 (July), 490–517.

All Animals are Equal. *Philosophical Exchange* 1 (Summer), 103–116.

Democracy and Disobedience. New York: Oxford University Press.

1975

Discovering Karl Popper, reprinted in: [Spanish translation] *Revista de Occidente*, Madris (January).

The Right to Be Rich or Poor. *New York Review of Books* (6th March).

Making Monkeys Neurotic, Dogs Shriek, Etc. Etc. *New York Times* (27th December).

Animal Liberation: A New Ethics for Our Treatment of Animals. New York Review/Random House.

Pp. 86–92 of *Democracy and Disobedience* reprinted in: *Moral Problems,* ed. J. Rachels, 2nd edition (Harper and Row).

Philosophers Are Back on the Job, reprinted under the title: [Abridged] The New Relevance of Philosophy. *Dialogue* 8, no. 2 (Washington, DC).

Animal Liberation. *New York Review of Books* (5th April, 1973), reprinted in: *Moral Problems,* ed. J. Rachels, 2nd edition (Harper and Row).

Animal Liberation. *New York Review of Books* (5th April, 1973), reprinted in: *Ethics in Perspective,* eds. P. and K. Struhl (Random House).

1976

The Case for Animal Liberation. *The Age,* Melbourne (13th March).

Review of *The Politics of Extinction,* by L. Regenstein. *National Review* (2nd–8th April).

Review of *The Existentialists and Jean-Paul Sartre,* by Max Charlesworth. *Meanjin* 35, no. 2 (June), 205–07.

Bio-Ethics and the Case of the Fetus. *New York Review of Books* (15th August).

Freedoms and Utilities in Health Care, reprinted in: *Ethics and Health Policy,* eds. R. Veatch and R. Branson. Ballinger.

Freedoms and Utilities in Health Care, reprinted in: *Working Papers for a New Society* 4, no. 2 (Summer).

Review of *Reason and Violence,* by S. Stanage. *Mind* 85, no. 340 (October).

Animal Liberation: A New Ethics for Our Treatment of Animals. London: Cape.

With Thomas Regan. *Animal Rights and Human Obligations: An Anthology.* Prentice-Hall.

Why Nozick Is Not So Easy to Refute. [Notes] *Western Political Quarterly* XXIX, 191–92.

A Utilitarian Population Policy. In *Ethics and Population,* ed. M. Bayles (Schenkman).

Animal Liberation. *New York Review of Books* (5th April, 1973), reprinted as a foreword in: [Swedish translation] *Djur,* eds. S. and R. Godlovitch and John Harris, Manniskor, Moral (Stockholm: Aldus).

Famine, Affluence, and Morality, reprinted in: *Understanding Moral Philosophy,* ed. J. Rachels (Dickenson).

Famine, Affluence, and Morality, reprinted in: *Philosophy Now,* eds. P. and Struhl, 2nd edition (Random House).

Altruism and Commerce: A Reply to Arrow, reprinted in: *Moral Problems in Medicine,* ed. S. Gorovitz (Prentice-Hall).

All Animals Are Equal, reprinted in: *Understanding Moral Philosophy,* ed. J. Rachels (Dickenson).

All Animals Are Equal, reprinted in: *Animal Rights and Human Obligations: An Anthology,* eds. T. Regan and Singer (Prentice-Hall).

All Animals are Equal, reprinted in: [Swedish translation] *Djurfront,* no. 2.

Chapter 3 of *Animal Liberation*, reprinted in: [Abridged] *Animal Rights and Human Obligations, An Anthology*, eds. T. Regan and Singer (Prentice Hall).

Chapter 5 of *Animal Liberation*, reprinted in: [Swedish translation] *Djurfront*, no. 4.

1977

Utility and the Survival Lottery. [Notes] *Philosophy* 52 (April), 218–222.

Philosophy. *The New York Times* (8th May).

Philosophical Vegetarianism: A Reply. *The Humanist* XXXVII, no. 4 (July–August).

Can Ethics Be Taught in a Hospital? [Notes] *Pediatrics* 60 (August), 253–55.

Animal Liberation: A New Ethics for our Treatment of Animals. New York: Avon.

Animal Liberation: A New Ethics for our Treatment of Animals. London: Paladin.

Animal Liberation: A New Ethics for our Treatment of Animals. [Dutch translation] *Pro Mens, Pro Dier*, Baarn: Anthos.

Freedoms and Utilities in Health Care. In *Markets and Morals*, eds. G. Dworkin, G. Bermant, P. Brown (New York: Halstead).

Reconsidering the Famine Relief Argument. In *Food Policy: U.S. Responsibility in the Life and Death Choices*, eds. P. Brown and H. Shue (The Free Press).

Animal Liberation. *New York Review of Books* (5th April, 1973), reprinted in: *The Little, Brown Reader*, eds. M. Stubbs and S. Barnet (Little, Brown).

Famine, Affluence, and Morality, reprinted in: *Social Ethics*, eds. T. Mappes and J. Zembaty (McGraw-Hill).

Famine, Affluence, and Morality, reprinted in: *World Hunger and Moral Obligations*, eds. W. Aiken and H.A. La Follette (Prentice-Hall).

Chapter 5 of *Animal Liberation*, reprinted in: [Swedish translation] *Djurfront*, nos. 1 and 2.

1978

The Fable of the Fox and the Unliberated Animals. [Notes] *Ethics* 88, no. 2 (January), 119–125.

Review of *The Limits of Altruism*, by Garrett Hardin. *Hastings Center Report* 8, no. 1 (February), 37–39.

Review of *Human Needs and Interests*, by ed. R. Fitzgerald. *Australasian Journal of Philosophy* 56, no. 1 (May).

Why The Whale Should Live. *Habitat* 6, no. 3 (June), 8–9.

Anglin on the Obligation to Create Extra People. [Notes] *Canadian Journal of Philosophy* 8, no. 3 (September), 583–85.

Is Racial Discrimination Arbitrary? *Philosophia* 8, nos. 2–3 (November), 185–203.

Unsanctifying Human Life. In *Ethical Issues Relating to Life and Death*, ed. J. Ladd (Oxford University Press).

Animal Experimentation. In *The Encyclopedia of Bioethics*, ed. W.T. Reich (New York: Macmillan).

Life: Value of Life. In *The Encyclopedia of Bioethics*, ed. W.T. Reich (New York: Macmillan).

Rights and the Market. In *Justice, and Economic Distribution*, by J. Arthur and W. Shaw (Prentice-Hall).

Famine, Affluence, and Morality, reprinted in: *Reason and Responsibility*, ed. J. Feinberg, 4th edition (Dickenson).

Animal Liberation. *New York Review of Books* (5th April, 1973), reprinted in: *Personal and Social Ethics*, ed. Vincent E. Barry (Wadsworth).

1979

Human Prospecting. *New York Review of Books* (22nd March), 30–32.

Forswearing Secrecy. *Nation* (5th May), 488–491.

Regan's Critique of Singer. [Notes] *Analysis* 39, no. 3 (June), 118–19.

Do Animals Have Equal Rights? *Animal Industry Today* 2 (July–August), 4–8.

Killing Humans and Killing Animals. *Inquiry* 22 (Summer), 145–156.

On Your Marx. *New York Review of Books* (20th December), 44–47.

Practical Ethics. Cambridge: Cambridge University Press.

Animals and Human Beings are Equals. *Animal Regulation Studies* 2 (1979–80), 165–174.

Not for Humans Only: The Place of Non-Humans in Environmental Issues. In *Ethics and Problems of the 21st Century*, eds. K.E. Goodpastor and K.M. Sayre (University of Notre Dame Press).

Animal Liberation. *New York Review of Books* (5th April, 1973), reprinted in: *Moral Problems*, ed. J. Rachels, 3rd edition (Harper and Row).

Animal Liberation. *New York Review of Books* (5th April, 1973), reprinted in: *Philosophy and Science*, ed. F. E. Mosedale (Prentice-Hall).

Famine, Affluence, and Morality, reprinted in: *Philosophy Politics and Society*, eds. P. Laslett and J. Fishkin, Fifth Series (Blackwell).

Famine, Affluence, and Morality, reprinted in: *Moral Problems*, ed. J. Rachels, 3rd edition (Harper and Row).

Famine, Affluence, and Morality, reprinted in: *Today's Moral Problems*, ed. Richard Wasserstrom, 2nd edition (Macmillan).

Bioethics and the Fetus, reprinted as: [Abridged] Fetal Research. In *Moral Problems*, ed. J. Rachels, 3rd edition.

The Case for Animal Liberation, reprinted in: [Dutch translation] *Dierproeven in de Moderne Samenleving*, ed. H. Smid. Deventer: Hermes.

Rights and the Market, reprinted in: *Ethical Theory and Business*, eds. T. Beauchamp and N. Bowie (Prentice-Hall).

1980

Review of *Doing Evil to Achieve Good*, by Paul Ramsey and Richard McCormick. *Hastings Center Report* 10, no. 1 (February), 42–44.

On Your Marx, reprinted in: [Portuguese translation] *O Estado*, Brazil: E.S. Paulo (3rd March).

Review of *Liberal Thinking*, by C.J. Puplick and R.J. Southey. *The Age* (21st June).

The Case for Prostitution. *The Age*, Melbourne (18th September).

Dictator Marx. *New York Review of Books* (25th September).

Revolution and Religion. *New York Review of Books* (6th November), 51–54.

Marx. Oxford: Oxford University Press.

Marx. New York: Hill and Wang.

With James Mason. *Animal Factories*. New York: Crown.

Advocacy, Objectivity, and the Draize Test. [Notes] *International Journal for the Study of Animal Problems* 1, 212–13.

Utilitarianism and Vegetarianism. *Philosophy and Public Affairs* 9, 325–337.

Animal Liberation. *The Connecticut Scholar*, Occasional Papers, no. 3, 70–88.

Review of *Refugees, Resources, Reunion*, by R. Birrell et al. *Migration Action* IV, no 3, 60–62.

Animals and the Value of Life. In *Matters of Life and Death*, ed. T. Regan. (Random House).

Preface to *Animal Rights*, by H.S. Salt (first published 1892) re-issued 1980, Society for Animal Rights (Clarks Summit), v–x.

Famine, Affluence, and Morality, reprinted in: *Philosophy Now*, eds. P. and Struhl, 3rd edition.

Famine, Affluence, and Morality, reprinted in: *Philosophy and Contemporary Issues*, eds. J. Burr and M. Goldinger (Macmillan).

Animals and Humans as Equals, reprinted in: [Polish translation] *Etyka* 18, 49–61.

1981

How the Bunny Lobby Terrorized Revlon. *The Age* (21st February).

Review of *The Panda's Thumb* by Stephen Gould. *Sydney Morning Herald* (2nd May).

Genes and Dominance. *The Age Monthly Review* 1, no. 1 (4th May).

With Yew-Kwang Ng. An Argument for Utilitarianism. *Canadian Journal of Philosophy* XI (June), 229–239.

Review of *The Evolution of Culture in Animals*, by John Tyler Banner. *Sydney Morning Herald* (11th July).

The Real Marx. *The Age Monthly Review* 1, no.4 (3rd August).

Marx and the Real World. *The Age Monthly Review* 1, no. 5 (September).

Conceptions and Misconceptions. *Times Literary Supplement* (October).

The Control of Cures. *The Age Monthly Review* 1, no. 7 (November).

Marx. [Italian translation] *Dall Oglio* (Milan).

The Expanding Circle: Ethics and Sociobiology. Farrar, Straus, and Giroux.

The Expanding Circle: Ethics and Sociobiology. Oxford University Press.

Reply to Dr. Harris. [Notes] *Philosophical Books* XXII, 198–200.

Review of *Violence for Equality*, by Ted Honderich. *Philosophical Quarterly* 31, 284–85.

Teaching about Human Rights. In *Teaching Human Rights,* ed. A. Erh-Soon Tay for the Australian National Commission for UNESCO (Canberra: Australian Government Publishing Service), 95–98.

Why Human Rights for Humans Only? In *Teaching Human Rights,* edited by A. Erh–Soon Tay for the Australian National Commission for UNESCO (Canberra: Australian Government Publishing Service), 179–182.

The Concept of Moral Standing. In *Ethics in Hard Times*, eds. A. Caplan and D. Callahan (New York: Plenum), 31–45.

Animal Liberation. *New York Review of Books* (5th April, 1973), reprinted in: *Environmental Ethics,* ed. K.S. Shrader-Frechette (Boxwood).

Altruism and Commerce: A Reply to Arrow, reprinted in: *Medicine and Moral Philosophy,* eds. M. Cohen, T. Nagel, and Scanlon (Princeton University Press).

Chapter 8 of *Practical Ethics*, 1st edition, reprinted in: [Abridged] *Morality and Moral Controversies,* ed. J. Arthur (Prentice-Hall).

Conceptions and Misconceptions, reprinted under the title: The Abortion Question. *The Age Monthly Review* 1, no. 8 (December 1981–January 1982).

1982

Can We Avoid Assigning Greater Value to Some Lives than to Others? *Community Health Studies,* supplementary issue (May), 39–44.

How Do We Decide? [Notes] *Hastings Center Report* 12, no. 3 (June), 9–11.

Review of *Karl Marx* by Allen Wood. *Australasian Journal of Philosophy* 60 (June), 191–92.

Preferences, Pleasure, and Happiness. *Times Literary Supplement* (27th August).

Dim Seer. *The Age Monthly Review* 2, no. 4 (August).

The Whitlam Experiment Revisted. *Sydney Morning Herald* (1st December).

Whales and The Japanese: A Lesson in Ethics. *The Age Monthly Review* 2, no. 8 (December).

Review of *Animals in Research*, ed. by D. Sperlinger; *Animal Rights and Human Morality*, by B. Rollin, and *Animal Suffering*, by M. Dawkins. *Quarterly Review of Biology* 57 (December), 481–82.

Animal Liberation: A New Ethics for Our Treatment of Animals. [German translation] *Befreiung der Tiere* (Munich: Hirthammer).

Marx. Italian Book Club edition, Milan: Club degli Editori.

The Expanding Circle: Ethics and Sociobiology. New York: New American Library.

Hegel. Oxford and New York: Oxford University Press.

With William Walters. *Test-Tube Babies: A Guide to Moral Questions, Present Techniques, and Future Possibilities.* Melbourne: Oxford University Press.

Ethics and Sociobiology. *Philosophy and Public Affairs* 11, 40–64.

The Oxford Vegetarians: A Personal Account. *International Journal for the Study of Animal Problems* 3, 6–9.

Animal Liberation and Changing the Role of the Modern Zoo. *Thylacinus (Journal of the Australasian Society of Zookeepers)* 7, no. 1, 26–30.

With Helga Khuse. The Moral Status of the Embryo. In *Test-Tube Babies,* eds. William Walters and Peter Singer (Melbourne: Oxford University Press), 57–67.

Contemporary Theories of Morality: A Secularist Perspective. In *Health Care in Crisis: A Bioethical Perspective,* ed. T.J. Connolly (Sydney: Laurdel Bioethics Foundation), 101–115.

Famine, Affluence, and Morality, reprinted in: *Social Ethics,* eds. T. Mappes and J. Zembaty, 2nd edition (McGraw-Hill).

Famine, Affluence, and Morality, reprinted in: *Philosophy: The Basic Issues,* eds. E.D. Klemko, A.D. Kline, and R. Hollinger (St. Martin's).

Famine, Affluence, and Morality, reprinted in: *Applied Ethics,* ed. Vincent Barry, 1st edition (Wadsworth).

Rights and The Market, reprinted under the title: [with minor alterations] Individual Rights and the Free Market, *Australia and the New Light,* ed. M. Sawyer (Sydney: Allen and Unwin).

Is Racial Discrimination Arbitrary?, reprinted in: *Social Ethics,* eds. T. Mappes and J. Zembaty, 2nd edition (McGraw-Hill).

The Right to Be Rich or Poor, reprinted in: *Reading Nozick,* ed. Jeffrey Paul (Oxford: Blackwell).

The Oxford Vegetarians: A Personal Account, published in: [Swedish translation] *Djurens Ratt!,* no. 6, 10–13.

1983

The Horizon Lecture: A Covenant for the Ark? *The Listener* (14th April), 11–14.

In Vitro Veritas. *The Age Monthly Review* 2, no. 12 (April).

Review of *Secrets,* by Sissela Bok. *Financial Review* (1st July).

Sanctity of Life or Quality of Life? [Notes] *Pediatrics* 72, 128–29.

Sanctity of Life or Quality of Life, reprinted in: *National Right to Life News* (18th August).

The Animal Liberation Movement. *Current Affairs Bulletin* 60, no. 3 (August), 15–21.

With H. Khuse and C. Singer. The Treatment of Newborn Infants with Major Handicaps: A Survey of Obstetricians and Paediatricians in Victoria. *Medical Journal of Australia* (17th September), 275–78.

The Politics of Procreation. *Australian Penthouse* (October), 156–57.

Thinking about Animals. *Habitat* 11 (October), 15–16.

Sanctity of Life or Quality of Life, reprinted in: *Human Life Review* (Fall).

Misleading Arguments on the Right to Die. *The Age* (15th December).

With Deane Wells. In Vitro Fertilisation: the Major Issues. *Journal of Medical Ethics* 9 (December), 192–95, 198–99.

Animal Liberation: A New Ethics for Our Treatment of Animals (London: Thorsons).

With James Mason. *Animal Factories.* [Japanese translation] Tokyo: Gendai Shokan.

With William Walters. *Test-Tube Babies: A Guide to Moral Questions, Present Techniques, and Future Possibilities.* [Japanese translation] Tokyo: Iwanami Shoten.

A Comment on the Animal Rights Debate. [Notes] *The International Journal of Applied Philosophy* 1, no. 3, 89–90.

With Y-K. Ng. Ng and Singer on Utilitarianism: A Reply. [Notes] *Canadian Journal of Philosophy* XIII, no. 2, 241–42.

Review of *The American Blood Supply,* by A. Drake, S.N. Finkelstein, and M. Sapolsky, and *Blood: Gift of Merchandise?* by P.J. Hagen. *Hastings Center Report* 13, no. 4, 48–50.

Review of *The Tangled Wing,* by Melvin Konner. *Quarterly Review of Biology* 58, 294–95.

Review of *Triage and Justice,* by G. Winslow. *Ethics* 94, 142–43.

The Ethics of Animal Use. In *World Animal Science* A1, eds. L. Peel and D.E. Tribe, *Domestication, Conservation, and Use of Animal Resources* (Amsterdam: Elsevier), 153–165.

Rights and the Market, reprinted in: *Moral Issues in Business,* ed. Vincent Barry, 2nd edition (Wadsworth).

Chapter 7 of *Practical Ethics,* 1st edition, reprinted in: [Abridged] *Ethical Issues in Modern Medicine,* eds. J. Arras and R. Hunt (Mayfield).

Is Racial Discrimination Arbitrary?, reprinted in: *Moral Issues,* ed. Jan Narveson (Toronto: Oxford University Press).

Moral Experts, reprinted in: *Contemporary Moral Issues,* ed. Wesley Cragg (Toronto: McGraw-Hill Ryerson).

Sanctity of Life or Quality of Life?, reprinted in: *Perinatal Press* 7, no. 8.

1984

All Animals Are Equal, reprinted in: [Swedish translation] *Brutus* 1 (January).

In Reply. [Notes] *Pediatrics* 73 (February), 261–63.

With Helga Kuhse. The Future of Baby Doe. *New York Review of Books* (1st March), 17–22.

Mind Over Manure: Changing Thoughts on Man and Animals. Review of *Man and the Natural World* by Keith Thomas and of *Animal Thought* by Stephen Walker. *The Age Monthly Review* (April), 17–18.

The Moral Status of Embryos: Response. [Notes] *Journal of Medical Ethics* 10, no. 2 (June), 80–81.

Ethics and Sociobiology, reprinted in: *Zygon* 19, no. 2 (June), 141–158.

Review of *The Case for Animal Rights*, by Tom Regan. *Quarterly Review of Biology* 59 (September), 306.

Predicting the Quality of Their Lives. Review of *Selective Treatment of Handicapped Newborns*, by Robert Weir. *New York Times Book Review* (30th September), 14–15.

Measure of Respect. Review of *Report of the Committee of Inquiry into Human Fertilisation and Embryology*, by Chairman Dame Mary Warnock. *Times Higher Education Supplement* (5th October), 20.

Sense and Sensibility in Animal Research. Review of *Man and Mouse*, by William Paton and *Of Models and Men*, by Andrew Rowan. *New Scientist* (25th October), 35–36.

Practical Ethics. [German translation] *Praktische Ethik* Stuttgart: Reclam.

Practical Ethics. [Spanish translation] *Etica Practica* Barcelona: Ariel.

With Deane Wells. *The Reproduction Revolution: New Ways of Making Babies.* Oxford: Oxford University Press.

Review of *Ethics and Animals*, by ed. H. Miller and W. Williams. *Quarterly Review of Biology* 59, 57–58.

Famine, Affluence, and Morality, reprinted in: *Philosophy and Contemporary Issues*, ed. Milton Goldinger, 4th edition (Macmillan).

Famine, Affluence, and Morality, reprinted in: *Reason at Work*, eds. S. Cahn, P. Kitcher and G. Sher (Harcourt Brace).

Famine, Affluence, and Morality, reprinted in: *Ethics: Theory and Practice*, eds. M. Velasquez and C. Rostankowski (Prentice-Hall).

Utility and the Survival Lottery, reprinted in: *Bioethics Reporter* 1, Pt. 1.

Chapter 1 of *Practical Ethics*, 1st edition, reprinted in: [Abridged] *Social and Political Ethics,* eds. G. Brodsky, J. Troyer and D. Vance (Prometheus).

Not for Humans Only, reprinted in: *Ethics: Theory and Practice*, eds. M. Velasquez and C. Rostankowski (Prentice-Hall).

Sanctity of Life or Quality of Life, reprinted in: *Death and Dying: Opposing Viewpoints*, eds. B. Szumski (Greenhaven).

1985

Ten Years of Animal Liberation: A Review of Ten Recent Books. *New York Review of Books* (17th January), 46–52.

With Helga Kuhse. Handicapped Babies: A Right to Life? *Nursing Mirror* (20th February), 17–20.

Technology and Procreation: How Far Should We Go? *Technology Review* 88, no. 2 (February–March), 22–30.

Neonatal Intensive Care: How Much, and Who Decides. [Notes] *Medical Journal of Australia* 142 (18th March), 335–36.

Animal Rights and Wrongs. *Times Higher Education Supplement* (29th March).

A Dog's Worse Enemy. Review of *Dominance and Affection: The Making of Pets, by Y-F Tuan. The New Republic* (3rd June), 4–42.

Making Laws about Making Babies. *Hastings Center Report* 15, no. 4 (August), 5–6.

The Code-Crackers Break with Morality. Review of *Broken Code: The Exploitation of DNA* by Marc Lappe. *New Scientist* (24th October), 50–51.

Ethics and Intensive Farming. *60 Days* (October), 7–9.

Technology and Procreation: How Far Should We Go?, reprinted under the title: [Italian translation] La Rivoluzione Riproduttira. *Prometeo* (Milan) 3, no. 12 (December).

Democracy and Disobedience. [Spanish translation] *Democracia y Desobediencia,* Barcelona: Editorial Ariel.

Animal Liberation: A New Ethics for Our Treatment of Animals. [Spanish translation] *Liberacion Animal,* A.L.E.C.A., Mexico: Lope de Vega.

With Deane Wells. *The Reproduction Revolution: New Ways of Making Babies.* Revised American edition, *Making Babies* (Scribner's).

With Deane Wells. *The Reproduction Revolution: New Ways of Making Babies.* [Dutch translation] *Het Nieuwe Nageslacht* (Baarn: Anthos).

With Helga Kuhse. *Should the Baby Live? The Problem of Handicapped Infants* (Oxford University Press).

In Defence of Animals (ed.). Blackwell.

The Ethics of the Reproduction Revolution. *Annals of the New York Academy of Sciences* 442, 588–594.

With Helga Kuhse. Ethics and the Handicapped Newborn Infant. *Social Research* 52, 505–542.

With Helga Kuhse. Resources and Hard Choices in Aged Care. *Proceedings of the 20th Annual Conference of the Australian Association of Gerontology,* 39–41.

The Animal Liberation Movement. Nottingham: Old Hammond Press, 20.

The Ethics of Animal Liberation: A Summary Statement. In *Animal-Human Relationships: Some Philosophers' Views* (West Sussex: RSCPA).

Arguments Against Markets: Two Cases from the Health Field. In *Medical Care and Markets,* eds. C.L. Buchanan and E.W. Prior (Sydney: Allen and Unwin), 2–19.

Foreword, to Daniel Dombrowski. In *Vegetarianism: The Philosophy Behind the Ethical Diet* (Wellingborough: Thorsons).

Animal Liberation. *New York Review of Books* (5th April, 1973), reprinted in: *Elements of Argument,* ed. A.T. Rottenberg (St. Martin's).

Animal Liberation. *New York Review of Books* (5th April, 1973), reprinted in: *People, Penguins and Plastic Trees,* eds. D. Vandeveer and C. Pierce (Wadsworth).

Famine, Affluence, and Morality, reprinted in: *Applied Ethics,* ed. Vincent Barry, 2nd edition (Wadsworth).

Famine, Affluence, and Morality, reprinted in: *Vice and Virtue in Everyday Life,* by C.H. Sommers (Harcourt Brace).

Famine, Affluence, and Morality, reprinted in: *International Ethics,* eds. C.R. Beitz, M. Cohen, T. Scanlon, and A.J. Simms (Princeton University Press).

All Animals Are Equal, reprinted in: *Contemporary Moral Philosophy,* ed. James White (West).

All Animals Are Equal, reprinted in: [Italian translation] *I diritti degli animali,* ed. S. Castignone (Bologna: Il Mulino).

Chapter 3 of *Animal Liberation*, reprinted in: [Abridged in Italian translation] *I diritti degli animali* (Bologna: Il Mulino).

Chapter 10 of *Practical Ethics*, 1st edition, reprinted in: [Abridged] *Vice and Virtue in Everyday Life,* ed. C.H. Sommers (Harcourt Brace).

Sanctity of Life or Quality of Life, reprinted in: *Terminating Life,* eds. G. McCoen and T. Boucher (Hudson).

Can We Avoid Assigning Greater Value to Some Lives than to Others?, reprinted in: *Moral Issues in Mental Retardation,* eds. R.S. Laura and A. Ashman (London: Croom Helm).

After Live Aid: How Much Is Enough? *The Age Monthly Review* (December 1985–January 1986).

1986

Technology and Procreation: How Far Should We Go?, reprinted: [Spanish translation] *El Pais,* Madrid (February).

The Will to Live. Review of *The Value of Life,* by John Harris, and *Death, Brain Death, and Ethics,* by David Lamb. *Times Higher Education Supplement* (18th April), 21.

Reductio ad Embryo. *The Age Monthly Review* (May).

Animal Liberation: A Personal View. *Between the Species* 2 (Summer), 148–154.

Animal Welfare and Scientific Inquiry. *Times Higher Education Supplement* (12th September).

Acting on Kant. *The Age Monthly Review* (October).

Embryo Report Is Just the Beginning of the Debate. *The Age* (17th November).

Ten Years of Animal Liberation, reprinted in: [Italian translation] *Communita* (Milan), no. 188 (December).

Hegel. [Portuguese translation] Lisbon: Dom Quixote.

With Helga Kuhse. *Should the Baby Live? The Problem of Handicapped Infants* (Oxford University Press).

In Defence of Animals (ed.). Harper and Row.

In Defence of Animals (ed.). [German translation] *Verteidigt der Tiere*, Vienna: Neff.

In Defence of Animals (ed.). [Dutch translation] *Dierenactiboek*, Baarn: Anthos.

In Defence of Animals (ed.). [Japanese translation] *Doubutsu no Kenri*, Tokyo: Gijutsu to ningen.

With Terry Carney. *Ethical and Legal Issues in Guardianship Options for Intellectually Disadvantaged People.* Human rights Commission Series, no. 2. Canberra: Australian Government Publishing Service.

Applied Ethics (ed.). Oxford University Press.

With Helga Khuse. The Ethics of Embryo Research. *Law, Medicine, and Health Care* 14, 133–38.

With Helga Khuse. For Sometimes Letting–and Helping–Die. *Law, Medicine, and Health Care* 14, 149–154.

Luv a Duck, I Just Can't Understand It. *The Age.*

Review of *Biophilia*, by Edward O. Wilson. *Biology and Philosophy* I, no. 3, 367–371.

Review of *Ethics of Dealing with Persons with Severe Handicaps: Toward a Research Agenda*, eds,. by P. Dokecki and R.M. Zaner. *AandNZ Journal of Developmental Disabilities* 12, 273–274.

Animals and the Value of Life. In *Matters of Life and Death,* ed. T. Regan, Revised edition (Random House).

Ethics. In *Encyclopaedia Britannica,* 1986 and subsequent printings, 627–648; [Abridged] *Encyclopaedia Britannica 1986 Book of the Year.*

Famine, Affluence, and Morality, reprinted in: *Introduction to Philosophy*, eds. J. Perry and M. Bratman (Oxford University Press).

All Animals Are Equal, reprinted in: *The Informed Argument,* ed. Robert K. Miller (Harcourt Brace).

Ethics, reprinted in: [Abridged with Japanese translation] *TBS-Britannica Yearbook* (Tokyo), 14–20.

1987

Animal Liberation or Animal Rights? *The Monist* 70 (January), 3–14.

Carrying the White Man's Burden. *The Age* (7th March).

The Vatican Viewpoint on IVF: Stop It, You Will Go Blind. *Sydney Morning Herald* (19th March).

The Dog in the Lifeboat: An Exchange. *New York Review of Books* (25th April), 57–58.

As the World's Numbers Rise, Our Aid Falls. *The Herald* (3rd June).

Which Babies Are Too Expensive to Treat? *Bioethics* 1, no. 3 (July), 275–283.

Public Life and Private Morality. *The Herald* (13th August).

A Question of Mice and Men. *The Herald* (14th October).

Animal Liberation: A New Ethics for Our Treatment of Animals. [Italian translation] *Liberazione Animali,* Rome: Lega Anti-Vivesezione.

In Defence of Animals (ed.). [Italian translation] *In Difesa degli Animali,* Rome: Lucarini.

With Lori Gruen. *Animal Liberation: A Graphic Guide.* London: Camden.

The Expanding Circle: A Reply to Munevar. [Notes] *Explorations in Knowledge* IX, no. 1, 51–54.

With C. De Garis, H. Kuhse, and V.Y.H. Yu. Attitudes of Australian Neonatal Paediatricians to the Treatment of Extremely Preterm Infants. *Australian Paediatric Journal* 23, 223–26.

With Helga Kuhse. Can the Law Cope with Our Increasing Ability to Preserve Life at Any Cost? In *Winds of Change: Papers from the 24th Australian Legal Convention* (Melbourne and Sydney: Law Council of Australia and The Law Book Company).

Creating Embryos. In *Ethical Issues at the Outset of Life,* eds. W.B. Weil and M. Benjamin (Blackwell), 43–62.

Hegel and Marx (a dialogue with Bryan Magee). In *The Great Philosophers,* ed. B. Magee (London: BBC Books), 190–208.

With Helga Kuhse. Ethical Issues Raised by Treatment of Extremely Preterm Infants. In *Prematurity,* eds. V.Y.H. Yu and E.C. Woods (Edinburgh: Churchill Livingstone), 257–273.

Life's Uncertain Voyage. In *Metaphysics and Morality: Essays in Honour of J.J.C. Smart,* eds. P Pettit, R. Sylvan and J. Norman (Blackwell), 154–172.

With Helga Kuhse. Ethical Issues in Reproductive Alternatives for Genetic Indications. In *Human Genetics,* eds. F. Vogel and K. Sperling (Berlin: Springer), 683–691.

Animal Liberation. *New York Review of Books* (5th April, 1973), reprinted in: *Morality in Practice,* ed. J. Sterba (Wadsworth).

Famine, Affluence, and Morality, reprinted in: *Social Ethics,* eds. T. Mappes and J. Zembaty, 3rd edition (McGraw-Hill).

Famine, Affluence, and Morality, reprinted in: *Ethics for Modern Life,* eds. R. Abelson and M.L. Friquenon, 3rd edition (St. Martin's).

Chapter 7 of *Practical Ethics,* 1st edition, reprinted in: [Abridged] *Intervention and Reflection: Basic Issues in Medical Ethics,* ed. R. Munson, 3rd edition (Wadsworth).

A Covenant for the Ark, reprinted in: *Life and Meaning: A Philosophical Reader,* ed. O. Hanfling (Blackwell).

Luv a Duck, I Just Can't Understand It, reprinted in: *Focus on Writing,* edited by Jill Thompson (Hawthorn: Martin Educational).

Can Bioethics Be Both Rigorous and Practical? *Reseaux* 53–54 (1987–1988), 121–130.

1988

With Renata Singer. How Many and Who? Australia's Refugee Policy. *The Age Monthly Review* (April), 18–21.

Australian Developments in Reproductive Technology. [Notes] *Hastings Center Report* 18, no. 2 (April–May), 4.

With Helga Kuhse. Doctors' Practices and Attitudes Regarding Voluntary Euthanasia. *Medical Journal of Australia* (20th June), 623–627.

Comment on Frey: Moral Standing, the Value of Lives, and Speciesism. [Notes] *Between the Species* 4, no. 3 (June), 202–03.

With Renata Singer. Migration Policy: Nasty, Brutish and Short-sighted. *The Age* (4th August).

With J. Mackenzie and H. Kuhse. Allocating Resources in Perinatal Medicine: A Proposal. *Australian Paediatric Journal* 24 (August), 235–39.

Why Anorexics Lose Their Right to Die. *The Herald* (9th September).

With Helga Kuhse. Survey Shows Australian Professionals Seek Change. *New South Wales Doctor* (20th September).

With E. Carl Wood. Whither Surrogacy? *The Medical Journal of Australia* (17th October), 426–29.

Do Blacks Need Extra Help? *The Herald* (15th November).

Natural Defence. Review of *Thinking about Nature*, by Andrew Brennan. *Times Higher Education Supplement* (14th December).

Defending My Right to Put Pin-Ups on My Walls. *The Herald* (16th December).

Animal Liberation: A New Ethics for Our Treatment of Animals. [Japanese translation] Tokyo: Gijutsu-to-Ningen.

With Thomas Regan. *Animal Rights and Human Obligations: An Anthology.* [Italian translation] Turin: Edizioni Gruppo Abele.

Practical Ethics. [Spanish translation] *Etica Practica* Barcelona: Ariel.

With Deane Wells. *The Reproduction Revolution: New Ways of Making Babies.* [Polish translation] *Dzieci z Probówki,* Warsaw: Wiedza Powszechna.

In Defence of Animals (ed.). [German translation] Frankfurt: Ullstein.

With Helga Kuhse. Resolving Arguments about the Sanctity of Life: A Response to Long. [Notes] *Journal of Medical Ethics* 14, 198–199.

With Helga Kuhse. Age and the Allocation of Medical Resources. *Journal of Medicine and Philosophy* 13, 101–116.

With Karen Dawson. IVF and the Argument from Potential. *Philosophy and Public Affairs* 17, 87–104.

Review of *Setting Limits: Medical Goals in an Aging Society,* by Daniel Callahan. *Bioethics* 2, no. 2, 151–169.

Reasoning towards Utilitarianism. In *Hare and Critics,* eds. D. Seanor and N. Fotion (Clarendon), 147–159.

Ethical Experts in a Democracy. In *Applied Ethics and Ethical Theory*, eds. D. Rosenthal and F. Shehadi (Salt Lake City: University of Utah Press), 149–161.

With Renata Singer. The Ethics of Refugee Policy. In *Open Borders? Closed Societies?*, ed. M. Gibney (Greenwood), 111–130.

Animal Liberation. *New York Review of Books* (5th April, 1973), reprinted in: [Japanese translation] *Bioethics,* eds. N. Iida and H. Kato (Tokyo).

Famine, Affluence, and Morality, reprinted in: *Reason at Work*, ed. George Sher, 2nd edition (Harcourt Brace).

Moral Experts, reprinted in: *Contemporary Moral Issues*, ed. Wesley Cragg, 2nd edition (Toronto: McGraw-Hill Ryerson).

1989

Your Freedom of Speech Is Under Threat. *The Herald* (24th January).

Review of *Vivisection in Historical Perspective*, by N. Rupke. Quadrant (January–February).

Unkind to Animals. *New York Review of Books* (2nd February), 36–38.

Absence of Malice. *The Animals' Voice* (February), 8–9.

With Pascal Kasimba. Through an IVF Glass Darkly. *The Age* (8th April).

Stutters Are Still Good for a Laugh. *The Herald* (3rd May).

Splicing Ethics with Genetics. Review of *Genethics*, by Suzuki and Knudtson. *The Herald* (5th May).

With Pacal Kasimba. Australian Commissions and Committees on Issues in Bioethics. *Journal of Medicine and Philosophy* 144, no. 4 (August), 403–424.

With Stephen Buckle and Karen Dawson. The Syngamy Debate: When Precisely Does a Human Life Begin? *Law, Medicine, and Health Care* 17, no. 2 (Summer), 174–181.

Experiments on Animals. [Notes] *British Medical Journal* 299 (18th November), 1238–39.

To Do or Not to Do? *Hastings Center Report* 19, no. 6 (November–December), 42–44.

With Thomas Regan. *Animal Rights and Human Obligations: An Anthology*, 2nd revised edition. Prentice-Hall.

Practical Ethics. [Italian translation] *Etica Pratica* Naples: Liguori.

Marx. [Japanese translation] Tokyo: Yushodo.

With Deane Wells. *The Reproduction Revolution: New Ways of Making Babies.* [Japanese translation] Kyoto: Koyo Shobo.

With Helga Kuhse. The Quality/Quantity-of-Life Distinction and Its Moral Importance for Nurses. *International Journal of Nursing Studies* 26, no. 3, 203–212.

Il Concetto di Morte tra Etica Filosofica e Medicina. *Politeia (Milan)* 5, no. 16, 4–13.

Interview with M. Mori. Bioetica: Dilucidazioni e Problemi (Bioethics: Elucidations and Problems). *Iride* 3 Rome, 167–181.

The Animal Liberation Movement. [Italian translation] *Il Movimento di Liberazione Animale,* Torino: Sonda.

Hegel and Marx (a dialogue with Bryan Magee). [Portuguese translation] (Presenca, Lisbon).

With Karen Dawson. Some Consequences of Regulating Reproductive Medicine in Australia. In *Procreation artificielle ou en sont l'ethique et le droit?*, ed. C. Byk (Lyon: Lacassagne), 185–192.

Interview with Robyn Williams. Animal Liberation? In *The Uncertainty Principle*, ed. Robyn Williams (Sydney: ABC Books), 139–150.

Il Dibattito Bioetico in Australia (The Bioethics Debate in Australia). In *Il Bambino Bionico,* eds. O. Polleggioni and M. Russo (Florence: La Nuova Italia), 139–143.

Geleitwort. [Introduction] In *Warum Vegetarier?,* by Helmut Kaplan (Frankfurt: Peter Lang), 7–10.

With Helga Kuhse. Should All Seriously Disabled Infants Live? In *Children, Parents and Politics,* ed. Geoffrey Scarre (Cambridge University Press), 168–181.

Extract from Chapter 2 of *Animal Liberation,* reprinted in: *Patterns for College Writing,* eds. L. Kirszner and Stephen Mandell, 4th edition (St. Martin's).

Practical Ethics, 1st edition reprinted in: [German translation] *Medizin und Ethik,* ed. H.M. Sass (Reclam).

Ten Years of Animal Liberation, reprinted in: [Abridged in Swedish translation] *Djurens Ratt!* 3.

Luv a Duck, I Just Can't Understand it, reprinted in: [Abridged in Swedish translation] *Djurens Ratt!* 3.

To Do or Not to Do, reprinted and published as: [Italian translation] Fare o non fare? *Ethica and Animali* 2, no. 2, 96–98.

1990

With Karen Dawson. Should Fertile People have Access to *in Vitro* Fertilisation? *British Medical Journal* 300 (20th January), 167–170.

Bioethics and Academic Freedom. *Bioethics* 4, no. 1 (January), 33–44.

Salt of the Earth. *New York Review of Books* (15th February), 41–42.

Review of *Reshaping Life: Key Issues in Genetic Engineering,* by G.J.V. Nossal and R.L. Coppel. *Medical Journal of Australia* 152 (5th March), 273–74.

To Do or Not to Do, reprinted in: *PETA News* (People for the Ethical Treatment of Animals, Washington, DC) (April).

With Karen Dawson. The Human Genome Project: For Better or for Worse? *Medical Journal of Australia* 152 (7th May), 484–86.

The Great Research Grant Caper. *The Age* (2nd July).

Experiments on Animals, reprinted in: *Bulletin of the Institute of Animal Technology* 26, 7 (July), 37–39.

New Attitudes Needed on Animal Testing. *New Scientist* (11th August), 4.

Green Rights. Review of *The Rights of Nature,* by Roderick Nash. *Sydney Morning Herald* (4th November).

Viewpoint: Animal Experimentation. *Scientific European* (December), 8–9.

Animal Liberation, 2nd edition. New York Review/Random House.

Animal Liberation, 2nd edition. London: Jonathan Cape.

Practical Ethics. [Swedish translation] *Praktisk Etik,* Stockholm: Thales.

With James Mason. *Animal Factories,* 2nd Revised edition. New York: Harmony.

With Helga Kuhse, Stephen Buckle, Karen Dawson, and Pascal Kasimba. *Embryo Experimentation.* Cambridge University Press.

The Significance of Animal Suffering. [Notes] *Behavioral and Brain Sciences* 13, 9–12.

Ethics and Animals. [Notes] *Behavioral and Brain Sciences* 13, 45–49.

With Yew-Kwang Ng. An Argument for Utilitarianism: A Defence. [Notes] *Australasian Journal of Philosophy* 68, no. 4, 448–454.

With Helga Kuhse. Viel Wind um Nichts (Much Ado about Nothing). [Notes] *Ethik und Sozialwissenschaften* 2, no. 3, 411–14.

With Helga Kuhse. Zwischen Leben entscheiden: Eine Verteidigung (Deciding between Lives: A Defence). *Analyse and Kritik* 12, 119–130.

The 'Singer-Affair' and Practical Ethics: A Response. *Analyse and Kritik* 12, 245–264.

Rats, Patients, and People: Issues in the Ethical Regulation of Research. [Annual Lecture 1989] Canberra: Academy of the Social Sciences in Australia, Australian National University, 27.

Introduction, to the *Catalogue of 100 Artists Against Animal Experimentation.* (Deutscher Brunswick St Gallery), 3–4.

When Do People Begin? In *Collaborating in Health Care: Proceedings of the 1989 Annual Conference on Bioethics,* eds. K. Andrews and M. Stainsby (Melbourne: St Vincent's Bioethics Centre), 21–25.

IVF and Australian Law. In *Philosophical Ethics in Reproductive Medicine,* eds. D. Bromham, M. Dalton and J. Jackson (Manchester: Manchester University Press), 31–47.

With Helga Kuhse. [Introduction] The Nature of Ethical Argument. In *Embryo Experimentation,* by Peter Singer, Helga Kuhse, Stephen Buckle, Karen Dawson and Pascal Kasimba (Cambridge University Press), 37–42.

With Helga Kuhse. Individuals, Humans, and Persons: The Issue of Moral Status. In *Embryo Experimentation,* by Peter Singer, Helga Kuhse, Stephen Buckle, Karen Dawson, and Pascal Kasimba (Cambridge University Press), 65–75.

With Karen Dawson. The New Genetics: Some Ethical Issues. In *Advances in Biotechnology: Proceedings of an International Conference* (Stockholm:

Swedish Council for Forestry and Agricultural Research and the Swedish Recombinant DNA Advisory Committee), 213–220.

Je Mehr Wir Fuer Andere Leben, Desto Zufriedener Leben Wir. In *Woran ich Glaube,* ed. K. Deschner (Guetersloh: Gerd Mohn), 267–271.

Famine, Affluence, and Morality, reprinted in: *Moral Theory and Practice,* ed. J. Rachels (Random House).

Reconsidering the Famine Relief Argument, reprinted in: *Why Food Aid? Department of Agricultural and Applied Economics and Center for International Food and Agricultural Policy,* ed. Vernon Ruttan (St. Paul, Minnesota: University of Minnesota).

All Animals Are Equal, reprinted in: [Abridged] *Political Theory and Animal Rights,* eds. Paul Clarke and Andrew Linzey (Pluto).

Extract from Chapter 2 of *Animal Liberation,* reprinted in: *Strategies of Argument,* ed. Stuart Hirschberg (New York: Macmillan).

With Karen Dawson. IVF Technology and the Argument from Potential, reprinted in: *Embryo Experimentation,* by Peter Singer, Helga Kuhse, Stephen Buckle, Karen Dawson, and Pascal Kasimba (Cambridge University Press).

With Stephen Buckle and Karen Dawson. The Syngamy Debate: When Precisely Does a Life Begin?, reprinted in: *Embryo Experimentation,* by Peter Singer, Helga Kuhse, Stephen Buckle, Karen Dawson, and Pascal Kasimba (Cambridge University Press).

Setting Limits: Medical Goals in an Aging Society [Review Essay] by Daniel Callahan, reprinted in: *A Good Old Age? The Paradox of Setting Limits,* eds. P. Homer and M. Holstein (Simon and Schuster), 170–181.

1991

Tutti Gli Animali Sono Uguali. *Cenobio* XL, no. 1 (Lugano and Varese), January–March, 5–11.

Review of *Humans and Other Animals,* by Barbara Noske. *Animal Liberation Magazine* (January–March), 30.

To Do or Not to Do, reprinted in: *Cenobio* XL, 1 (Lugano and Varese) (January–March), 77–82.

A Refutation of Ordinary Morality. A Review essay on *The Limits of Morality,* by S. Kagan. *Ethics* 101, no. 3 (April), 625–633.

Speciesism, Morality, and Biology. [Notes] *The Psychologist* 4, no. 5 (May), 199–200.

The Ethics of Patenting Life-Forms. *Intellectual Property Forum* 14 (May), 31–38.

Remember: Dogs and Cats Are People Too, You Know. *Sunday Age* (7th July).

On Being Silenced in Germany. *The New York Review of Books* (15th August), 36–42.

On Being Silenced in Germany, reprinted in: *Australian Jewish Democrat* 2, no. 3 (Summer), 23–26.

Review of *Factory Farming*, by Andrew Johnson. *Nature* 353 (17th October), 613–14.

Thinking about Suicide. *The Independent Monthly* (October), 16.

Über das Recht, Fragen zu stellen. *Zitty* 22, (Berlin), October, 18–19.

Interview with Terry Lane. The Philosopher and the Future. *21C* (Autumn), 43–47.

With Helga Kuhse. Prolonging Dying Is the Same as Prolonging Living: One More Response to Long. [Notes] *Journal of Medical Ethics* 17, no. 4 (December), 205–06.

Animal Liberation, 2nd edition. New York: Avon.

Animal Liberation, 2nd edition. London: Thorsons.

Animal Liberation, 2nd edition. [Italian translation] *Liberazione Animali*, Milan: Mondadori.

Animal Liberation, 2nd edition. [Finnish translation] *Oikeutta Eläimille*, Helsinki: Werner Söderström.

Practical Ethics. [Spanish translation] *Etica Practica*, Barcelona: Ariel.

Practical Ethics. [Japanese translation] *Jissen no Rinri*, Kyoto: Showa-do.

A Companion to Ethics (ed.). Oxford: Blackwell.

With Barbara Dover and Ingrid Newkirk. *Save the Animals!* Australian edition. North Ryde: Collins, Angus, and Robertson.

The Pervasiveness of Species Bias. [Notes] *Behavioral and Brain Sciences* 14, no. 4, 759–760.

A Philosopher among the Test-Tubes. *Meanjin* 50, 493–500.

Euthanasia and Academic Freedom in the German-Speaking World. *Kriterion* 1, no. 2, 8–10.

Applied Ethics in a Hostile Environment. *Theoria* LXVII, nos. 1–2, 111–114.

The Animal Liberation Movement. [French translation] *Le mouvement de liberation animale*, Lyon: Francoise Blanchon.

Introduction and Afterword. In *A Comparison to Ethics*, ed. P. Singer (Blackwell), v–vi, 543–545.

Research into Aging: Should It Be Guided by the Interests of Present Individuals, Future Individuals, or the Species? In *Life Span Extension: Consequences and Open Questions*, ed. Frederic C. Ludwig (New York: Springer), 132–145.

With Helga Kuhse. Bioethics and Education. In *Bioethics in Education*, ed. G. Rex Meyer, International Union of Biological Sciences, Commission for Biological Education, Erziehungswissenschaften Bd. 27 (Muenster: Lit Verlag), 60–67.

Environmental Values. In *The Environmental Challenge*, ed. Ian Marsh (Melbourne: Longman Cheshire), 3–24.

With C. Fehige and G. Meggle. Mir leuchtet nicht ein, wie man so Werte bewahren will. In *Zur Debatte ueber Euthanasie Suhrkamp*, eds. R. Hegselmann and R. Merkel (Frankfurt a. M.), 153–177.

Problems in the Legislative Regulation of Reproductive Technology: Learning from the Victorian Experience. In *The Australian Bioethics Association First Annual Conference: Bioethics and the Wider Community* (Melbourne), 273–76.

Democracy and Disobedience, pp. 84–92, reprinted in: *Civil Disobedience in Focus,* ed. H.A. Bedau (Routledge).

Animal Liberation. *New York Review of Books* (5th April, 1973), reprinted in: *Philosophy: The Quest for Truth,* ed. L.J. Pojman (Wadsworth).

Animal Liberation. *New York Review of Books* (5th April, 1973), reprinted in: *The Moral Life,* eds. Steven Luper-Foy and Curtis Brown (Harcourt Brace).

Famine, Affluence, and Morality, reprinted in: *The Moral Life,* eds. Steven Luper-Foy and Curtis Brown (Harcourt Brace).

All Animals Are Equal, reprinted in: [Abridged] *Moral Problems*, ed. Michael Palmer (Cambridge: Lutterworth).

Extract from Chapter 3 of *Animal Liberation,* reprinted in: *Writing with a Purpose,* ed. J. Trimmer, 10th edition (Houghton Miflin).

Practical Ethics, 1st edition, reprinted in: [German translation] *Weibliche Moral,* ed. G. Nunner–Winkler (Frankfurt: Campus).

Is Racial Discrimination Arbitrary?, reprinted in: *Contemporary Moral Problems*, ed. James White (West).

With Helga Kuhse. Chapter 2 of *Should the Baby Live?*, reprinted in: *Time as a Human Resource,* eds. E.J. McCullough and R.L. Calder (University of Calgary Press), 121–150.

To Do or Not to Do, reprinted in: *Animal Experimentation: The Moral Issues Prometheus,* eds. R. Baird and S. Rosenbaum (New York), 57–66.

The Significance of Animal Suffering, reprinted in: *Animal Experimentation: The Moral Issues Prometheus*, eds. R. Baird and S. Rosenbaum (New York).

Bioethics and Academic Freedom, reprinted in: [German translation] *Zur Debatte ueber Euthanasie Suhrkamp,* eds. R. Hegselmann and R. Merkel (Frankfurt a. M.), 312–326.

On Being Silenced in Germany, reprinted in: [German translation] *Suhrkamp Wissenschaft Neuerscheinungen* 2 (Halbjahr), 44–56.

1992

The Last Rights. *The Age* (6th March).

With Helga Kuhse. Euthanasia: A Survey of Nurses' Attitudes and Practices. *Australian Nurses Journal* 21, no. 8 (March), 21–22.

Greed is Stupid. *Australian Business Monthly* (March), 78–81.

Not What You Produce, But How Much You Spend. *Modern Times* (March), 16–17.

Bandit and Friends. *New York Review of Books* (9th April), 9–13.

That Dangerous Animal. *Modern Times* (April), 10–12.

Xenotransplantation and Speciesism. *Transplantation Proceedings* 24, no. 2 (April), 728–732.

It's All a Question of Ethics. *The Australian* (4th June), 6.

Can Free Trade Make You Happy? *Australian Business Monthly* (June), 98–100.

Bioethics at Monash University. *International Journal of Bioethics* 2, no. 3 (June/July), 111–15.

L'éthique appliquée. *Cahiers antispécistes lyonnais* 4 (July), 5–12.

On Being Silenced in Germany, reprinted as: Redeverbot in Deutschland, *Gaia* 11 (Summer), 25–27.

Animal Liberation: An Exchange. *New York Review of Books* (5th November), 60–61.

Has Capitalism Reached Its Limits? *Australian Business Monthly* (November), 112–13.

A Response to David DeGrazia. *Between the Species* 8, no. 1 (Winter), 51–53.

Animal Liberation, 2nd edition. [Swedish translation] *Djurens Frigörelse,* Stockholm: Nya Doxa.

Marx. Great Political Thinkers: Machiavelli, Hobbes, Mill and Marx, ed. K. Thomas (Oxford University Press).

A German Attack on Applied Ethics. *Journal of Applied Philosophy* 9, no. 1, 85–91.

A Question of Morality. *Australian Wildlife Calendar* (Hobart: The Wilderness Society).

With Helga Kuhse. Hard Choices: Ethical Questions Raised by the Birth of Handicapped Infants. In *Ethics on the Frontiers of Human Existence*, ed. Paul Badham (Paragon), 153–177.

Ontogeny of Pain and the Concept of Speciesism: A Comment. In *Animal Pain: Ethical and Scientific Perspectives*, eds. T. Kuchel, M. Rose, and J. Burrell. Australian Council on the Care of Animals in Research and Teaching (Glen Osmand), 74–76.

Embryo Experimentation and the Moral Status of the Embryo. In *Philosophy and Health Care*, eds. E. Matthews and M. Menlowe (Aldershot: Avebury), 81–91.

Foreword, to Lewis Gompertz, *Moral Inquiries on the Situation of Man and of Brutes* (Fontwell: Centaur), 11–15.

With Helga Kuhse. Allocating Health Care Resources and the Problem of the Value of Life. In *Death and the Value of Life*, ed. D. Cockburn (Lampeter: Trivium), 7–23.

Foreword, to Richard Ryder. In *Animal Welfare and the Environment* (London: Duckworth), vii–x.

Animal Liberation. *New York Review of Books* (5th April, 1973), reprinted in: *Writing Arguments,* eds. J. Ramage and J. Bean, 2nd edition (Macmillan).

Animal Liberation. *New York Review of Books* (5th April, 1973), reprinted in: *Ethical Issues,* ed. E. Soifer (Broadview).

Animal Liberation. *New York Review of Books* (5th April, 1973), reprinted in: *Personal Values,* ed. E. Gampel (Dubuque: Kendall-Hunt).

Famine, Affluence, and Morality, reprinted in: *Social Ethics*, eds. T. Mappes and J. Zembaty, 4th edition (McGraw-Hill).

Famine, Affluence, and Morality, reprinted in: *Reason and Responsibility*, ed. J. Feinberg, 5th edition (Dickenson).

Famine, Affluence, and Morality, reprinted in: *Ethics for Modern Life*, eds. R. Abelson and M.L. Friquenon, 4th edition (St. Martin's Press).

Famine, Affluence, and Morality, reprinted in: *Doing and Being: Introductory Readings in Moral Philosophy*, ed. J.G. Haber (Macmillan).

Famine, Affluence, and Morality, reprinted in: *A Community of Voices: Reading and Writing in College*, eds. T. Fulwiler and A. Biddle (Macmillan).

Famine, Affluence, and Morality, reprinted in: *Thirteen Questions in Ethics*, ed. L. Bowie (Harcourt Brace).

All Animals Are Equal, reprinted in: *Social Ethics*, eds. T. Mappes and J. Zembaty, 4th edition (McGraw-Hill).

All Animals Are Equal, reprinted in: *Critical Issues: Race and Gender in Applied Ethics*, ed. S. Gold (Wadsworth).

Chapter 4 of *Animal Liberation*, reprinted in: *Cooking, Eating, Thinking*, by D. Curtin and L. Heldke (Indiana University Press).

Chapter 8 of *Practical Ethics*, 1st edition, reprinted in: [Abridged] *Writing Arguments*, eds. J. Ramage and J. Bean (Macmillan).

Chapter 8 of *Practical Ethics*, 1st edition, reprinted in: [Abriged] *Ethical Issues*, ed. E. Soifer (Broadview).

Moral Experts, reprinted in: *Contemporary Moral Issues*, ed. Wesley Cragg, 3rd edition (Toronto: McGraw-Hill Ryerson).

Ethics and Sociobiology, reprinted in *Readings in Science and Religion*, ed. J.E. Hutchingson (Holt, Rinehart, and Winston).

Creating Embryos, reprinted in: *Social Ethics*, eds. T. Mappes and J. Zembaty, 4th edition (McGraw-Hill).

It's All a Question of Ethics, reprinted in: *Creating the Future*, eds. Dennis Gastin and Chris Mitchell (Sydney: Department of Industry, Technology and Commerce, and *The Australian*).

With Deane Wells. In Vitro Fertilisation: The Major Issues, reprinted in: [Italian translation] *Introduzione alla Bioetica*, eds. G. Ferranti and S. Maffetone (Naples: Liguori).

Environmental Values, reprinted in: [Italian translation] *La Madre*, eds. Laura Marchetti and Peter Zeller (Il Gioco, La Terra, Laterza, Bari).

1993

Be Radical: Let's Try Self-Reliance. *Australian Business Monthly* (January), 58–59.

The International Association of Bioethics. *Medical Journal of Australia* 158 (1st March), 298–99.

With Helga Kuhse. Holding Back on a Question of Life or Death. *The Australian* (7th May), 15.

Cultural Clash Sets Rite Against Reason. *The Australian* (9th June).

The Rights of Apes. *BBC Wildlife* (June), 28–32.

Review of *Bioethics in a Liberal Society,* by Max Charlesworth. *Australian Bookseller and Publisher* (June), 58.

Review of *Encyclopedia of Ethics,* by Lawrence C. Becker and Charlotte B. Becker. *Ethics* 103, no. 4 (July), 807–810.

Review of *Life's Dominion,* by Ronald Dworkin. *British Medical Journal* 307 (23rd October), 1077–78.

After the Horrors. Review of *Benzo Junkie,* by Beatrice Faust. *The Age* (30th October).

Animal Liberation. *Island* 54 (Autumn), 62–66.

The Great Ape Project and its Implications for Scientific and Biomedical Research. *Genetic Engineering News* (1st November).

Is There a God? *The Age* (24th December).

The Rights of Apes, reprinted under the title: The Great Ape Project. *ProAnimal* 4 (Israel: Rehovat), December, 6–8.

Animal Liberation, 2nd edition. [French translation] *La Libération Animale,* Paris: Grasset.

Practical Ethics, 2nd edition. Cambridge University Press.

Practical Ethics, 2nd edition. [Danish translation] *Praktisk Etik,* Copenhagen: Hans Reitzels Forlag.

With Helga Kuhse. *Should the Baby Live? The Problem of Handicapped Infants.* [German translation] *Müss dieses Kind am Leben Bleiben?,* Erlangen: Harald Fischer.

With Helga Kuhse, Stephen Buckle, Karen Dawson, and Pascal Kasimba. *Embryo Experimentation.* Updated paperback edition, Cambridge University Press.

A Companion to Ethics (ed.). Paperback edition, Blackwell.

With Paola Cavalieri. *The Great Ape Project: Equality Beyond Humanity.* London: Fourth Estate.

How Are We to Live? Ethics in an Age of Self-Interest. Melbourne: Text.

With Helga Kuhse. Voluntary Euthanasia and the Nurse: An Australian Survey. *International Journal of Nursing Studies* 30, no. 4, 311–322.

With Helga Kuhse. More on Euthanasia: A Response to Pauer-Studer. *The Monist* 76, no. 2, 158–174.

Animals and the Value of Life. In *Matters of Life and Death,* ed. T. Regan. Revised edition (McGraw-Hill).

Beyond Traditional Religion. In *Voices on the Threshold of Tomorrow,* eds. Georg Feuerstein and Trisha Lamb Feuerstein (Wheaton: Quest), 251–52.

With Edgar Dahl. Das gekreuzigte Tier. In *Die Lehre des Unheils: Fundamentalkritik am Christentum,* ed. Edgar Dahl (Hamburg: Carlsen), 280–289.

Animals, Ethics, and Experimentation. In *Animal Welfare Conference: Proceedings, Animal Ethics Unit,* ed. N.E. Johnston (Monash University), 1–8.

Animal Liberation. *New York Review of Books* (5th April, 1973), reprinted in: *Environmental Philosophy,* ed. M. Zimmerman (Prentice-Hall).

Famine, Affluence, and Morality, reprinted in: *Vice and Virtue of Everyday Life,* by C.H. Sommers, 3rd edition (Harcourt Brace).

Famine, Affluence, and Morality, reprinted in: *Issues and Images: An Argument Reader,* ed. William E. Rivers (Harcourt Brace).

Reconsidering the Famine Relief Argument, reprinted in: *Why Food Aid? Department of Agricultural and Applied Economics and Center for International Food and Agricultural Policy,* ed. Vernon Ruttan. Reissued by John Hopkins University Press.

Chapter 1 of *Animal Liberation,* reprinted as: [Abridged] *The PETA Guide to Animal Liberation* (Washington, DC: People for the Ethical Treatment of Animals).

1994

Review of *Monkey Business,* by Kathy Snow Guillermo., and *In the Name of Science,* by Barbara Orlans. *Nature* 367 (10th February), 523–24.

Review of *Essays on Henry Sidgwick,* ed. Bart Schultz. *Ethics* 104, no. 3 (April), 631–33.

Feminism and Vegetarianism: A Response. *Philosophy in the Contemporary World* 1, no. 3 (Fall), 36–39.

Address to Council. *RACS Bulletin* 14, no. 3 (November), 23–26.

The RACS Code and the Patient Who Asks for Help in Dying. *RACS Bulletin* 14, no. 3 (November), 29.

Democracy and Disobedience. Aldershot: Gregg.

Animal Liberation, 2nd edition. [Dutch translation] *Dierenbevrijding,* Breda: De Geus.

Practical Ethics, 2nd edition. [Portuguese (Brazil) translation] *Ética Prática* (Sao Paolo: Livraria Martins Fontes).

Practical Ethics, 2nd edition. [German translation] *Praktische Ethik,* Stuttgart: Reclam.

With Helga Kuhse. *Should the Baby Live? The Problem of Handicapped Infants.* Aldershot: Gregg.

With Paola Cavalieri. *The Great Ape Project: Equality Beyond Humanity.* Hardback edition, St. Martin's Press.

With Paola Cavalieri. *The Great Ape Project: Equality Beyond Humanity.* [German translation] *Menschenrechten für die Grossen Menschenaffen,* Munich: Peter Goldmann.

With Paola Cavalieri. *The Great Ape Project: Equality Beyond Humanity.* [Italian translation] *Il Progetto Grande Scimmia: Equalianza oltre i confini della species umana,* Rome: Theoria.

Ethics (ed.). Oxford University Press.

With Helga Kuhse. *Individuals, Humans, and Persons: Questions of Life and Death.* Sankt Augustin: Academia Verlag.

Rethinking Life and Death: The Collapse of Our Traditional Ethics. Melbourne: Text.

How to Argue with Egg Producers. [Notes] *Behavioral and Brain Sciences* 17, no. 4, 749.

Bioethics and the Limits of Tolerance. *The Journal of Medicine and Philosophy* 19, no. 2, 129–145.

With Helga Kuhse. Abortion and Contraception: The Moral Significance of Fertilization. In *The Beginning of Human Life,* eds. Fritz Beller and Robert F. Weir (Dordrecht: Kluwer), 145–161.

Life and Death Decision: The Need for a New Approach. In *Bioethics and Environmental Education,* ed. M. Rajaretnam (Singapore and Kuala Lumpur: UNESCO/Information and Resource Center/Institute for Policy Research), 81–83.

The Role of Ethics. In *Ethical Issues in Prenatal Diagnosis and the Termination of Pregnancy,* ed. J. McKie (Monash University: Centre for Human Bioethics), 1–7.

On the Nature of Bioethics. In *Individuals, Humans, Persons,* by Helga Kuhse and Peter Singer (Sankt Augustin: Academia), 21–32.

Late Termination and Selective Non-Treatment of Disabled Infants: Some Comparisons. In *Ethical Issues in Prenatal Diagnosis and the Termination of Pregnancy,* ed. John McKie (Monash University Centre for Human Bioethics), 71–79.

Australia's Core Values and the Next Thirty Years. In *Economic Planning Advisory Commission, Ambitions for Our Future: Australian Views,* Conference Report 3 (Canberra: Australian Government Publishing Service), 69–71.

New Assisted Reproductive Technology. In *Reproductive Technology: The Science, the Law, and the Social Issues,* ed. Karen Dawson (Melbourne: VCTA), 99–102.

Famine, Affluence, and Morality, reprinted in: *Environmental Ethics: A Reader,* ed. L. Pojman (Jones and Bartlett).

Famine, Affluence, and Morality, reprinted in: *Life and Death,* ed. L. Pojman (Jones and Bartlett).

All Animals Are Equal, reprinted in: *Environmental Ethics: A Reader,* ed. L. Pojman (Jones and Bartlett).

All Animals are Equal, reprinted in: *Life and Death,* ed. L. Pojman (Jones and Bartlett).

Pp. 7–10, 15–21, 269–271, of *Animal Liberation* (revised edition), reprinted in: *Taking Sides: Clashing Views on Controversial Moral Issues,* ed. Stephen Satris, 4th edition (Guildford: Dushkin).

Pp. 1–4, 8–9, of *Animal Liberation* (revised edition), reprinted in: *Environmental Law and Policy,* eds. Menell and Stewart (Little, Brown), 1–9.

Other passages from *Animal Liberation* (revised edition) have been reprinted in: *Ethics: Theory and Contemporary Issues,* ed. Barbara MacKinnon (Wadsworth).

Has Capitalism Reached Its Limits?, reprinted in: [Abridged] *Economics,* eds. John Jackson, Ron McIver and Campbell McConnell, 4th edition (Sydney: McGraw-Hill).

Is There a God?, reprinted in: *English Matters,* ed. Roslyn Guy (Wentworth Falls, NSW: Social Science Press).

1995

What Price a Human Life? *The Sunday Age* (8th January).

To Live Ethical Lives. *The Age* (16th January).

Brave New Territory. *The Sunday Age* (4th February).

Equality: Why It Matters. *Australian Business Monthly* (February), 36–39.

Menschenrechte für Menschenaffen. *Geo* (April), 176–79.

Is our Changing Definition of Death for the Better? *USA Today* (18th May), 15A.

Animal Acts. Review of *The Monkey Wars,* by Deborah Blum. *The Age* (27th May).

With Leslie Cannold and Helga Kuhse. William Godwin and the Defence of Impartialist Ethics. *Utilitas* 7, no.1 (May), 67–86.

Taking Note of the Quality of the Life that Chooses Death. *The Age* (7th June).

Late Termination and Selective Non-Treatment of Disabled Infants: Some Comparisons, reprinted in: *Bulletin of The Information Alliance of F.N.Q.,* Families of Disabled People Inc. (June).

Final Frontiers. *Times Higher Education Supplement* (18th August), 15.

With Alison Hutchinson. Xenotransplantation: Is It Ethically Defensible? *Xeno* 3, no. 4 (August), 58–60.

State Policy and the Sanctity of Human Life. In *Death and the State: Papers Presented to a Conference on Euthanasia at the Centre for Public Policy,* University of Melbourne (August), 23–24.

Animal Liberation: An Exchange. *New York Review of Books* (5th November, 1992) reprinted in: *Animal Husbandry* 49, no. 8, Japan: Yokendo Ltd (August), 852–56.

Is There a Universal Moral Sense? *Critical Review* 9, no. 3 (Summer), 325–339.

Killing Babies Isn't Always Wrong. *The Spectator* (16th September), 20–22.

Literature, Truth, and Argument, reprinted as: [Abridged] Fiction, Faction, Fact and Literature, *Sydney Morning Herald* (16th September), 33.

Extract from Literature, Truth, and Argument, reprinted as: The Two Helens in Intellectual Footy Match, *The Age* (19th September), 11.

With Helga Kuhse. Euthanasia: Kuhse and Singer Respond. [Notes] *Australian Nursing Journal* (September), 26.

Sentenced to Life. *The Sunday Age* (22nd October), 14.

The Legalisation of Voluntary Euthanasia in the Northern Territory. *Bioethics* 9, no. 5 (October), 419–424.

Abortion: A Woman's Right. *Beat* (1st November), 10.

Active Voluntary Euthanasia, Morality and the Law. *Journal of Law and Medicine* 3, no. 1 (November), 129–135.

Dangers of a Life Without Skyhooks. Review of *Darwin's Dangerous Idea,* by Daniel Dennett. *Sydney Morning Herald* (23rd December).

A Christmas Roast. *The Sunday Age* (24th December), 10.

Animal Liberation, 2nd edition. [Spanish translation] *Liberacion Animal,* Mexico.

Practical Ethics. [Spanish translation] *Etica Practica,* Barcelona: Ariel.

Practical Ethics. [Spanish translation] *Ética Práctica.* Cambridge University Press.

Hegel. [Czech translation] Prague: Odeon.

A Companion to Ethics (ed.). [Spanish translation] *Compendio de Etica,* Madrid: Alianza.

With Paola Cavalieri. *The Great Ape Project: Equality Beyond Humanity.* Paperback edition, St. Martin's.

How Are We to Live? Ethics in an Age of Self-Interest. London: Mandarin.

How Are We to Live? Ethics in an Age of Self-Interest. Prometheus.

How Are We to Live? Ethics in an Age of Self-Interest. [Japanese translation] Kyoto: Horitsu-bunka sha.

Rethinking Life and Death: The Collapse of Our Traditional Ethics. St. Martin's.

Rethinking Life and Death: The Collapse of Our Traditional Ethics. Oxford University Press.

Straw Men with Broken Legs: A Reply to Per Sandström. [Notes] *Journal of Medical Ethics* 21, no. 2, 89–90.

Die Ethik der Embryonenforschung. *Aufklärung und Kritik* (Sonderheft 1), 83–87.

With John McKie, Helga Kuhse, and Jeff Richardson. Double Jeopardy and the Use of QALYs in Health Care Allocation. *Journal of Medical Ethics* 21, no. 3, 144–150.

Is the Sanctity of Life Ethic Terminally Ill? *Bioethics* 9, nos. 3 and 4, 327–343.

With Erik Nord, Jeff Richardson, Andrew Street, and Helga Kuhse. Maximizing Health Benefits vs. Egalitarianism: An Australian Survey of Health Issues. *Social Science and Medicine* 41, no. 10, 1429–437.

With Paola Cavalieri. The Great Ape Project: Premises and Implications. *ATLA* 23, 626–631.

Coping with Global Change. *Critical and Creative Thinking* 3, no. 2, 1–12.

With Erik Nord, Jeff Richardson, Andrew Street, and Helga Kuhse. Who Cares About Cost? Does Economic Analysis Impose or Reflect Social Values? *Health Policy* 34, 79–94.

Literature, Truth, and Argument. *1995 New South Wales Premier's Literary Awards Address* (Sydney: NSW Ministry of Arts).

With Erik Nord, Jeff Richardson, Andrew Street, and Helga Kuhse. The Significance of Age and Duration of Effect in Social Evaluation of Health

Care. *Centre for Health Program Evaluation Working Paper 47* (Monash University and the University of Melbourne).

The Great Ape Project. In *Ape, Man, Apeman: Changing Views Since 1600*, eds. Raymond Corbey and Bert Theunissen (Department of Prehistory, Leiden University), 367–376.

Animal Research: Philosophical Issues. In *Encyclopedia of Bioethics* 1, ed. W.T. Reich (Macmillan and Simon and Schuster), 147–153.

With Helga Kuhse, John McKie, Erik Nord, and Jeff Richardson. Ethical Problems in Economic Evaluation of Health Care. In *Economic Evaluation in Australian Health Care*, eds. C. Selby Smith and M.F. Drummond (Canberra: Australian Government Publishing Service), 172–78.

Kirche und Embryonenforschung. In *Die Lehre des Unheils: Fundamentalkritik am Christentum*, ed. Edgar Dahl (Hamburg: Goldmann), 276–285.

Taking Sides on the Right to Die. In *The Last Right: Australians Take Sides on the Right to Die*, eds. Simon Chapman and Stephen Leeder (Melbourne: Mandarin), 142–44.

Abortion. In *A Companion to Philosophy*, ed. Ted Honderich (Oxford University Press), 2–3.

Animals. In *A Companion to Philosophy*, ed. Ted Honderich (Oxford University Press), 35–36.

Applied Ethics. In *A Companion to Philosophy*, ed. Ted Honderich (Oxford University Press), 42–43.

Dialectic. In *A Companion to Philosophy*, ed. Ted Honderich (Oxford University Press), 198.

Fertilization in Vitro. In *A Companion to Philosophy*, ed. Ted Honderich (Oxford University Press), 275.

Hegel. In *A Companion to Philosophy*, ed. Ted Honderich (Oxford University Press), 339–343.

Killing. In *A Companion to Philosophy*, ed. Ted Honderich (Oxford University Press), 445–46.

Owl of Minerva. In *A Companion to Philosophy*, ed. Ted Honderich (Oxford University Press), 638.

Vegetarianism. In *A Companion to Philosophy*, ed. Ted Honderich (Oxford University Press), 897.

World-Soul. In *A Companion to Philosophy*, ed. Ted Honderich (Oxford University Press), 919.

Animal Liberation. *New York Review of Books* (5th April, 1973), reprinted in: *Ethics for Modern Life,* by R. Abelson and M.L. Friquenon, 5th edition (St. Martin's).

Famine, Affluence, and Morality, reprinted in: *Ethics for Modern Life,* by R. Abelson and M.L. Friquenon, 5th edition (St. Martin's).

All Animals Are Equal, reprinted in: *Morality and Moral Controversies,* ed. J. Arthur, 4th edition (Prentice-Hall).

Chapter 8 of *Practical Ethics*, 1st edition, reprinted in: [Abriged] *Morality and Moral Controversies,* ed. J. Arthur 4th edition (Prentice-Hall).

Chapter 8 of *Practical Ethics*, 2nd edition, reprinted in: [Abridged] *Writing Arguments*, by J. Ramage and J. Bean, 3rd edition (Allyn and Bacon).

Creating Embryos, reprinted in: *Ethical Issues in Modern Medicine*, by J. Arras and B. Steinbock, 4th edition (New York: Mayfield).

Je Mehr Wir Fuer Andere Leben, Desto Zufriedener Leben Wir, reprinted in: *Die Lehre des Unheils: Fundamentalkritik am Christentum*, ed. Edgar Dahl (Hamburg: Goldmann).

Sidgwick and Reflective Equilibrium, reprinted in: *Meta-ethics*, ed. Michael Smith (Aldershot: Dartmouth).

1996

Review of *Dangerous Diagnostics*, by Dorothy Nelkin and Laurence Tancredi., *Lost Lullaby*, by Deborah Golden Alecson., and *Time to Go*, eds. Anne Hunsaker Hawkins and James O. Ballard. *Bioethics* 10, no. 1 (January), 88–89.

Coping with Global Change: The Need for Different Values. *Journal of Human Values* 2, no.1 (January–June), 37–48.

The Ethics of Commercialising Wild Animals. *Animals Today* 4, no. 1 (February–April), 20–23.

Meaning of Life. *Resurgence* (March–April), 14–15.

Unnatural Practices. *The Sunday Age* (7th April).

Ethics and the Limits of Scientific Freedom. *The Monist* 79, no. 2 (April), 218–229.

Dilemma von Leben und Tod. *Universitas* 51, no. 559 (May), 432–37.

Natural Classic. *BBC Wildlife* 14, no. 6 (June), 89.

The Great Ape Project, Animals. *Agenda* 16, no. 3 (July–August), 12–13.

Time to Bid Farewell to the Politics of Fear. *The Age* (10th October), A15.

Standing for the Greens. *Generation* 6, nos. 1 and 2 (October), 3–6.

With John McKie, Helga Kuhse, and Jeff Richardson. Allocating Healthcare by QALYs: The Relevance of Age. *Cambridge Quarterly of Healthcare Ethics* 5, no. 4 (Fall), 534–545.

Animal Liberation, 2nd edition. [Chinese translation] Taipei: Life Conservation Association.

Animal Liberation, 2nd edition. [German translation] *Befreiung der Tiere*, Hamburg: Rowohlt.

Practical Ethics, 2nd edition. [Swedish translation] *Praktisk Etik,* Stockholm: Thales.

Practical Ethics, 2nd edition. [Bengali translation] Dhaka: Bangla Academy.

Hegel. [Spanish translation] Mexico: Harla.

Hegel. [Polish translation] Warsaw: Michael Urbaƒski.

Hegel. [Romanian translation] Bucharest: Humanitas.

Hegel. [Japanese translation] Aoki Shoten.

With Paola Cavalieri. *The Great Ape Project: Equality Beyond Humanity.* [German translation] *Menschenrechten für die Grossen Menschenaffen,* Paperback edition, Munich: Goldmann.

How Are We to Live? Ethics in an Age of Self-Interest. [German translation] *Wie Sollen Wir Leben?,* Erlangen: Harald Fischer.

Rethinking Life and Death: The Collapse of Our Traditional Ethics. [Italian translation] *Ripensare la vita,* Milan: Il Saggiatore.

With Bob Brown. *The Greens.* Melbourne: Text Publishing.

Blind hostility: A Response to Russell and Nicoll. [Notes] *Proceedings of the Society for Experimental Biology and Medicine* 211, no. 2, 139–146.

With John McKie, Helga Kuhse and Jeff Richardson. Double Jeopardy, the Equal Value of Lives and the Veil of Ignorance: A Rejoinder to Harris. [Notes] *Journal of Medical Ethics* 22, no. 4, 204–08.

With John McKie, Helga Kuhse and Jeff Richardson. Another Peep Behind the Veil. [Notes] *Journal of Medical Ethics* 22, no. 4, 216–221.

With Leslie Cannold, Helga Kuhse, and Lori Gruen. What Is the Justice-Care Debate Really About? *Midwest Studies in Philosophy* XX, 357–377.

With Erik Nord, Jeff Richardson, Andrew Street, and Helga Kuhse. The Significance of Age and Duration of Effect in Social Evaluation of Health Care. *Health Care Analysis* 4, 103–111.

With Maurice Rickard and Helga Kuhse. Caring and Justice: A Study of Two Approaches to Health Care Ethics. *Nursing Ethics* 3, no. 3, 212–223.

O Naravi Bioetike (On the Nature of Bioethics). *Drustvena Istrazivanja* 5, nos. 3–4 (Zagreb), 523–532.

State Policy and the Sanctity of Human Life. In *Death and the State: Papers Presented to a Conference on Euthanasia at the Centre for Public Policy* (University of Melbourne Centre for Public Policy).

This I Believe. In *This I Believe,* ed. John Marsden (Sydney: Random House), 293–96.

Animal Liberation. *New York Review of Books* (5th April, 1973), reprinted in: *Animal Rights: The Changing Debate,* ed. Robert Garner (London: Macmillan).

Famine, Affluence, and Morality, reprinted in: *Western Philosophy: An Anthology,* ed. John Cottingham (Blackwell).

Extract from Chapter 2 of *Animal Liberation,* reprinted in: *Intervention and Reflection: Basic Issues in Medical Ethics,* eds. R. Munson, 5th edition (Wadsworth).

Chapter 3 of *Animal Liberation,* reprinted in: [Abridged] *Contemporary Moral Issues,* ed. Lawrence M. Hinman (Prentice-Hall).

Other Passages from *Animal Liberation* (revised edition), have been reprinted in: *Biomedical Ethics,* eds. Thomas Mappes and David De Grazia, 4th edition (McGraw-Hill).

Practical Ethics, 2nd edition, reprinted in: *Contemporary Moral Issues*, ed. Lawrence M. Hinman (Prentice-Hall).

Creating Embryos, reprinted in: *Biomedical Ethics*, eds. T. Mappes, and D. De Grazia, 4th edition (McGraw-Hill).

Animal Liberation or Animal Rights?, reprinted in: [Italian translation] *Etica Analitica*, eds. P. Donatelli and E. Lecaldano (Milan: Edizione Universitarie di Lettere Economia Diritto).

Zwischen Leben entscheiden: Eine Verteidigung, reprinted in: *Unterrichtsideen: Textarbeit im Philosophie–Unterricht*, by Norbert Diesenberg and Hans Gerhard Neugebauer (Stuttgart: Ernst Klett).

On Authenticity. *Australian Book Review*, no. 187 (December 1996–January 1997), 49.

1997

Humanismen Maste överskrida Gränserna. *Dagens Nyheter,* Sweden (9th February).

With Helga Kuhse, Maurice Rickard, Malcolm Clark and Peter Baume. End-of-Life Decisions in Australian Medical Practice. *Medical Journal of Australia* 166, no. 4 (17th February), pp. 191–96.

With Helga Kuhse and Peter Baume. Euthanasia: No Time for Hastened Conclusions. *The Australian* (24th February).

Angling for Equality of Consideration. *Times Higher Education Supplement* (28th February), 22.

Cloning the News. *The Republican* (4th April), 16.

With Helga Kuhse, Peter Baume and Malcolm Clark. "Muddled" Commentary on End-of-Life Study. *Australian Doctor* (18th April), 23.

The Drowning Child and the Expanding Circle. *New Internationalist* (April), 28–30.

Review of *Persons, Animals, and Fetuses*, by Mary Gore Forrester. *Bioethics* 11, no. 2 (April), 179–180.

The Ethics of Commercialising Wild Animals, reprinted in: [German translation] *Moma,* Zurich (April), 31–36.

Research Babies: Another Case of the Stolen Children. *Sydney Morning Herald* (11th June).

To Give or Not to Give? *Horizons* 6, no. 2 (Spring), 10–11.

Practical Ethics, 2nd edition. [French translation] *Questions d'éthique pratique*. Bayard Presse.

Hegel, included in full in: *German Philosophers: Kant, Hegel, Schopenhauer, Nietzsche*. Oxford University Press.

How Are We to Live? Ethics in an Age of Self-Interest. Oxford University Press.

How Are We to Live? Ethics in an Age of Self-Interest. [Swedish translation] Stockholm: Natur och Kultur.

How Are We to Live? Ethics in an Age of Self-Interest. [Spanish translation] *Etica para vivir major*, Barcelona: Editorial Ariel.

How Are We to Live? Ethics in an Age of Self-Interest. [Korean translation] Seoul: Sejong Books.

Rethinking Life and Death: The Collapse of Our Traditional Ethics. [Dutch translation] *Tussen Dood en Leven,* Utrecht: Jan van Arkel.

Rethinking Life and Death: The Collapse of Our Traditional Ethics. [Polish translation] *O "yciu i Êmierci,* Warsaw: Pa∫stwowy Instytut Wydawniczy.

Rethinking Life and Death: The Collapse of Our Traditional Ethics. [Spanish translation] *Repensar La Vida y La Muerte,* Barcelona: Paidos.

Neither Human nor Natural: Ethics and Feral Animals. *Reproduction, Fertility, and Developmen* 9, no. 1, 157–162.

With Helga Kuhse, Maurice Rickard, Leslie Cannold and Jessica van Dyk. Partial and Impartial Ethical Reasoning in Health Care Professionals. *Journal of Medical Ethics* 23, no. 4, 226–232.

How Are We to Live? In *After Politics: New Thinking for the Twenty-First Century,* ed. Geoff Mulgan (London: Fontana), 49–55.

With Helga Kuhse, John McKie, Jeff Richardson and Erik Nord. QALYs: Some Methodological and Ethical Issues. In *Bioethics Research: Policy, Methods and Strategies: Proceedings of a European Conference,* eds. S. Gindro, R. Bracalenti, and E. Mordini (Directorate-General XII: European Commission), 83–92.

All Animals Are Equal, reprinted in: *Contemporary Moral Philosophy,* ed. James White (West).

All Animals Are Equal, reprinted in: [German translation] *Naturethik,* ed. Angelika Krebs (Suhrkamp).

Chapter 7 of *Practical Ethics,* 2nd edition, reprinted in: *Contemporary Moral Philosophy,* ed. James White (West).

Practical Ethics, 2nd edition, reprinted in: *Contemporary Moral Philosophy,* ed. James White (West).

Is Racial Discrimination Arbitrary?, reprinted in: *Contemporary Moral Philosophy,* ed. James White (West).

Animal Liberation (from Island), reprinted in: [Swedish translation] *Djur and Människor,* ed. Lisa Gälmark (Nora: Nya Doxa).

Ethics and the Limits of Scientific Freedom, reprinted in: [Italian translation] *Oltre le due Culture,* ed. Magda Talamo (Soveria Manelli: Rubbettino), 69–83.

IVF and the Argument from Potentiality, reprinted in: [Spanish translation] *Analisi Filosofico* XVII, no. 2, 171–188.

1998

Individuals, Humans, and Persons: The Issue of Moral Status, and The Syngamy Debate: When Precisely does a Life Begin?, have been reprinted in: [Italian translation] *Le Scienze Quaderni* 100 (February), 36–41 and 50–55.

The Great Ape Project. *Biologist* 45, no. 2 (April), 87–88.

Evolutionary Workers' Party. *Times Higher Education Supplement* (15th May), 15, 17.

With Helga Kuhse, Peter Singer, Peter Baume, and Malcolm Clark. Medical End-of-Life Decisions: Australia and the Netherlands. *Mature Medicine Canada* 1, no. 3 (May–June), 37–38.

Darwin for the Left. *Prospect* (June), 26–30.

A Conception to Come to Terms With. *The Sunday Age* (26th July), 15.

With Hartmut Kuhlmann. Die alte Ethik bröckelt. *Universitas* 53 (July), 665–680.

The Poet and the Engineer. Review of *The Art of Moral Protest*, by James Jasper. *Times Higher Education Supplement* (7th August).

Should an Environmentalist Eat Meat? *Renew* 64 (July–September), 44–46.

A Darwinian Left, reprinted as: [Italian translation] Ciao Darwin, Benvenuto a Sinistra, *Reset*, no. 51 (Novembre–Dicembre), 66–76.

Animal Liberation, 2nd edition. [Croatian translation] Zagreb: Ibis Grafika.

Practical Ethics. [Korean translation] Seoul: Chul-hak.

A Companion to Ethics (ed.). [Polish translation] *Przewodnik po etyce*, Warsaw: Wydawnictwo Ksi?¿ka i Wiedza.

With Paola Cavalieri. *The Great Ape Project: Equality Beyond Humanity.* [Spanish translation] *El Proyecto 'Gran Simio'* Madrid: Trotta Sociedad Anonima Editorial.

Rethinking Life and Death: The Collapse of Our Traditional Ethics. [German translation] *Leben und Tod*, Erlangen: Harald Fischer.

With John McKie, Jeff Richardson and Helga Kuhse. *The Allocation of Health Care Resources: An Ethical Evaluation of the 'QALY' Approach*. Aldershot: Ashgate.

With Helga Kuhse. *A Companion to Bioethics*. Blackwell.

Ethics into Action: Henry Spira and the Animal Rights Movement. Rowman and Littlefield.

With Helga Kuhse and Maurice Rickard. Reconciling Impartial Morality and a Feminist Ethic of Care. *Journal of Value Inquiry* 32, 451–463.

Zur Natur der Bioethik. *Der Blaue Reiter*, no. 7, 101–06.

On Comparing the Value of Human and Non–Human Life. In *Applied Ethics in a Troubled World*, eds. Edgar Morscher, Otto Neumaier, and Peter Simons (Dordrecht: Kluwer), 93–104.

Possible Preferences. In *Preferences*, eds. Christoph Fehige and Ulla Wessels (Berlin: Walter de Gruyter), 383–398.

A Vegetarian Philosophy. In *Consuming Passions: Food in the Age of Anxiety*, by Sian Griffiths and Jennifer Wallace (Manchester University Press), 71–80.

Utilitarianism. In *Encyclopedia of Animal Rights and Animal Welfare*, by Marc Bekoff (Greenwood), 343–44.

Foreword. In *A Theory of the Good and the Right*, by Richard B. Brandt (Prometheus).

All Animals Are Equal, reprinted in: *Classic Works in Medical Ethics,* ed. Gregory Pence (McGraw-Hill), 231–243.

All Animals Are Equal, reprinted in: *Environmental Philosophy,* eds. Michael Zimmerman et al, 2nd edition (Simon and Schuster).

Practical Ethics, 2nd edition, reprinted in: *Social and Personal Ethics*, by William H. Shaw, 3rd edition (Wadsworth).

Not for Humans Only, reprinted in: *Social and Personal Ethics*, by William H. Shaw, 3rd edition (Wadsworth).

Extracts, from *Making Babies,* reprinted in: *Classic Works in Medical Ethics*, ed. Gregory Pence (McGraw-Hill), 83–91.

On the Nature of Bioethics, published as: [German translation] Zur Natur der Bioethik, *der blaue Reiter* 7, 101–06.

1999

An Ethical Storm. *The Age* (19th February), 15.

Should We Breach the Species Barrier and Grant Rights to the Apes? *Prospect* (May), 17–19.

Rights for Chimps. *The Guardian* (29th July), 19.

Sense and Sentience. *The Guardian* (21st August), 24.

The Singer Solution to World Poverty. *New York Times Sunday Magazine* (5th September), 60–63.

Sense and Sentience, reprinted as: The Origin of the Specious, *The Age* (19th September), 23.

The Singer Solution to World Poverty, reprinted as: [Abridged] The Cost of a Moral Life, *The Age* (25th September), 4.

A New Ethic for Living and Dying. *Daily News*, New York (7th October), 57.

Not Right: American Apathy Influences Health Policy. *Daily Princetonian* (19th October).

Beastly Behaviour. *The Age* (23rd October), 56–57.

Response from Dr. Peter Singer. *Yeshiva University Commentator* (23rd November), 5.

A More Civilised World, but Only Just? *Sydney Morning Herald*, Good Weekend Millennium edition (27th November), 19–21.

Animal Liberation, 2nd edition. [Spanish translation] Spain: Trotta Sociedad Anonima Editorial.

Animal Liberation, 2nd edition. [Hebrew translation] Or-Am.

Animal Liberation, 2nd edition. [Korean translation] Seoul: In Gan Sa Rang.

Marx. [Dutch translation] Rotterdam: Lemniscaat.

The Expanding Circle: Ethics and Sociobiology. [Korean translation] Seoul: In Gan Sa Rang.

With Helga Kuhse. Individuals, Humans and Persons: Questions of Life and Death. [German translation] Individuen, Menschen, Personen. Sankt Augustin: Academia Verlag.

Ethics into Action: Henry Spira and the Animal Rights Movement. Melbourne: Melbourne University Press.

With Helga Kuhse. *Bioethics: An Anthology.* Blackwell.

A Darwinian Left. Weidenfeld and Nicolson.

With Arlene Klotzko. Learning from Henry Spira. *Cambridge Quarterly of Healthcare Ethics* 8, no. 1, 3–6.

Ética Más Allá de los Límites de la Especie. *Teorema* XVIII, no. 3, 5–16.

A Response. In *Singer and His Critics,* ed. Dale Jamieson (Blackwell), 269–335.

Reflections. In *The Lives of Animals,* ed. Amy Gutman (Princeton University Press), 85–91.

Some Issues of Morality. In *The Decameron Project,* eds. Richard Kowalski and Michael Coe (Monash University), 72–78.

Ethics Across the Species Boundary. In *Global Ethics and Environment,* ed. Nicholas Low (Routledge), 146–157.

Chapter 4 of *Ethics into Action: Henry Spira and the Animal Rights Movement,* reprinted as: Henry Spira's Search for Common Ground, *Cambridge Quarterly of Healthcare Ethics* 8, no. 1, 9–22.

All Animals Are Equal, reprinted in: *Ethical Vegetarianism: From Pythagoras to Peter Singer,* by Kerry Walters and Lisa Portness (State University of New York Press).

All Animals Are Equal, reprinted in: [French translation] *Anthologie Historique et Critique de L'utilitarisme,* ed. Catherine Audard (Presse Universitaires de France).

Literature, Truth, and Argument, reprinted in: *Writers on Writing,* ed. Neil James (Rushcutters Bay, NSW: Halstead Press), 115–125.

Ethics Beyond the Species Barrier. *Earth Matters* (Winter 1999–2000), 28–29.

2000

Stem Cells and Immortal Souls. *Free Inquiry* 20, no. 2 (Spring), 9.

The Freest Nation in the World? *Free Inquiry* 20, no. 3 (Summer), 16.

Everyday Ethics: Racial Slurs; Donating for Dollars. *The Prince Magazine* (A Supplement to *The Daily Princetonian*) (25th September).

Everyday Ethics: Cheating; Investment Banking. *The Prince Magazine* (A Supplement to *The Daily Princetonian*) (9th October).

Everyday Ethics: Sexual Ethics; Charity Balls. *The Prince Magazine* (A Supplement to *The Daily Princetonian*) (23rd October).

How Are Your Morals? *Economist* (Special edition: The World in 2001) (December), 76.

Animal Liberation, 2nd edition. [Portuguese translation] *Libertação Animal*, Oporto: Via Óptima.

Practical Ethics, 2nd edition. [Portuguese translation] *Ética Prática*, Lisbon: Gradiva.

Marx. Reissued as: *Marx: A Very Short Introduction*. Oxford University Press.

Marx. [Persian translation] Teheran: Tarh-e-No.

Hegel. [Persian translation] Teheran: Tarh-e-No.

Hegel. [Dutch translation] Rotterdam: Lemniscaat.

A Darwinian Left. Yale University Press.

A Darwinian Left. [Italian translation] *Una sinistra darwinia*, Turin: Edizioni di Comunita.

A Darwinian Left. [Spanish translation] *Una izquierda Darwiniana*, Barcelona: Crítica.

A Darwinian Left. [Greek translation] Athens.

Writings on an Ethical Life. New York: Ecco.

Morte Cerebrale ed Etica Della Sacralita Della Vita. [Notes] *Bioetica* 8, no. 1, 31–49.

With Paula Casal. El "Proyecto Gran Simio" y el Concepto de Persona. *Laguna* 7, 333–347.

Einkauksbummel im Supermarkt der Gene ('Shopping in the Genetic Supermarket'). *Zeitschrift fuer Kultur Austausch* 50, no. 3 (Stuttgart), 39–40.

Review of *Darwinian Dominion*, by Lewis Petrinovich. *British Journal for the Philosophy of Science* 51, 495–98.

Embryos and Animals: Can We Justify Their Use in Research and Treatment? In *Ethical Dilemmas in Neurology*, eds. Adam Zeman and Linda Emmanuel (London: Saunders).

A Utilitarian Approach to Ethics and to Animals. In *Bioethics and the Use of Laboratory Animals*, eds. A. Lanny Kraus and David Renquist (Dubuque: Benoit), 57–64.

Extending Ethics Beyond Our Own Species. In *Bioethics and Biolaw* I, eds. Peter Kemp et al, *Judgement of Life* (Copenhagen: Rhodos International Science and Art Publishers, and Centre for Ethics and Law), 133–142.

Animal Liberation. *New York Review of Books* (5th April, 1973), reprinted in: *Moral Reasoning*, eds. Richard Fox and Joseph DeMarco (Harcourt Brace).

Famine, Affluence, and Morality, reprinted in: *International Relations: Critical Concepts in Political Science* 5, ed. Andrew Linklater (Routledge), 1902–912.

Practical Ethics, 2nd edition, reprinted in: *Taking Sides,* by Stephen Satris, 7th edition (Dushkin/McGraw-Hill).

The Singer Solution to World Poverty, reprinted in: *The Best American Essays 2000*, ed. Alan Lightman (Houghton Miflin), 140–46.

The Human Genome and the Genetic Supermarket. *Free Inquiry* 21, no. 1 (Winter 2000–2001), 7–8.

2001

Princeton Is One of the World's Wealthiest Universities . . . So Why Won't It Pay Its Workers Better Wages? *Daily Princetonian* (12th January).

The Right to Protest. *The Independent on Sunday*, London (21st January), 18.

Let the Doctor Clone Humans—If He Can. *The Age*, Melbourne (5th February), 15.

Everyday Ethics: Grades, Preceptors, and Ethics. *The Prince Magazine* (A Supplement to *The Daily Princetonian*) (12th February).

Fair Pay, Fair Play. *Princeton Alumni Weekly* (21st February), 13.

Dream of a World Where People Come Before Power. *Times Higher Education Supplement* (23rd February), 17.

A Bouyant Market for Ethics. *Financial Times* (12th March).

Everyday Ethics: Giving to Princeton University. *The Prince Magazine* (A Supplement to *The Daily Princetonian*) (12th March), 3.

Heavy Petting. Review of *Dearest Pet*, by Midas Dekkers. *Nerve.com* (March).

Everyday Ethics: The Ethics of Wining and Dining Professors and Killing Abortion-Providers. *The Prince Magazine* (A Supplement to *The Daily Princetonian*) (16th April), 3.

What Comes First: Americans or Ethics? *Dagens Nyheter*, Stockholm (30th April).

Heavy Petting. Review of *Dearest Pet*, by Midas Dekkers. *Prospect* (April), 12–13.

Humanity's Giant Step into a Moral Minefield. *The Age* (30th May), 1, 15.

Animal Rights: A Dialogue with Richard Posner. *Slate* (11th–14th June).

Standing By, Again. *Free Inquiry* (Spring), 10–11.

Ethical Lives. *The Sydney Papers* 13, no. 4 (Spring), 61–65.

Changing Ethics in Life and Death Decision Making. *Society* 38, no. 5 (July–August), 9–15.

Animal Liberation Revisited. *Sydney Morning Herald*, Spectrum section (18th–19th August), 7.

The Year of the Clone. *Free Inquiry* 21, no. 3 (Summer), 12–13.

Darwin for the Left, reprinted as: [German translation] Der neue Mensch ist am Ende, *Die Weltwoche* (20th September).

The Secret to Beating Fundamentalism. *The Age* (11th October).

First Things First? How Far Should a Leader Go? *Free Inquiry* 21, 4 (Fall), 13–14.

Who Deserves the 9/11 Cash Pile? *Slate* (12th December).

Animal Liberation, 2nd edition. [with a new preface] New York: Ecco.

Animal Liberation, 2nd edition. [Czech translation] *Osvobození Zvírat*, Prague: Práh.

Practical Ethics. 2nd edition. [Serbian translation] Belgrade: Signature.

Hegel. Reissued as: *Hegel: A Very Short Introduction*. Oxford University Press.

With Paola Cavalieri. *The Great Ape Project: Equality Beyond Humanity.* [Japanese translation] Kyoto: Showado.

Rethinking Life and Death: The Collapse of Our Traditional Ethics. [Japanese translation] Showa-Do.

Ethics into Action: Henry Spira and the Animal Rights Movement. [German translation] Henry Spira und die Tierrechtsbewegung, Erlangen: Harald Fischer Verlag.

A Darwinian Left. [Dutch translation] *Darwin voor links*, Amsterdam: Boom.

Writings on an Ethical Life. London: Fourth Estate.

Writings on an Ethical Life. [Dutch translation] *Een ethisch leven*, Utrecht: Het Spectrum.

Writings on an Ethical Life. [Italian translation] *Il vita come dovrebbe*, Milan: Il Saggiatore.

Unsanctifying Human Life: Essays on Ethics, edited by Helga Kuhse. Oxford: Blackwell.

Response to Mark Kuczewski. [Notes] *American Journal of Bioethics* 1, no 3, 55–56.

With Peter Ratiu. The Ethics and Economics of Heroic Surgery. *Hastings Center Report* 31, no. 2, 47–48.

With Paula Casal. Grandes Simios, Personas y Animales. Respuesta a los Criticos. *Laguna* 9, 173–186.

Animals. In *A Companion to Environmental Philosophy*, ed. Dale Jamieson (Blackwell), 416–425.

Cloning Humans and Cloning Animals. In *The Cloning Sourcebook*, ed. Arlene Klotzko (Oxford University Press), 160–68.

With Paola Cavalieri. Apes, Persons, and Bioethics. In *All Apes Great and Small: African Apes* 1, eds. Birute Galdikas, Nancy Briggs, Lori Sheeran, Gary Shapiro, and Jane Goodall (Kluwer/Plenum), 283–291.

All Animals Are Equal, reprinted in: *Biomedical Ethics*, eds. Thomas Mappes and David DeGrazia (McGraw Hill).

With Helga Kuhse. Chapter 4 of *Should the Baby Live?*, reprinted in: *Bioethics*, ed. John Harris (Oxford University Press), 42–61.

Where the President's Ethics Lecture Went Wrong. *Free Inquiry* 22, no. 1 (Winter 2001–2002), 23–24.

2002

Might or Right. *New Internationalist* 342 (January–February), 26–27.

My Better Nature. *Sydney Morning Herald*, Spectrum section (2nd March), 4–5.

Why We Should Ignore the Catholic Church on Stem Cells. *The Age* (29th March), 9.

Join Rally in Trenton to Protect Farm Animals. *The Princeton Packet* (12th April).

Review of *Death Talk*, by Margaret Somerville. *Canadian Medical Association Journal* 166, no. 8 (16th April), 1070–71.

The One Percent Solution. Syndicated, available at www.projectsyndicate.org in English, Spanish, Russian, French, German, Czech, Chinese, and Arabic (June).

Freedom and the Right to Die. *Free Inquiry* 22, no. 2 (Spring), 16–17.

Ms B and Diane Pretty: A Commentary. [Notes] *Journal of Medical Ethics* 28, no. 4 (August), 234–35.

Christians, Riches, and Camels. *Free Inquiry* 22, no. 3 (Summer), 9–12.

Navigating the Ethics of Globalization. *Chronicle of Higher Education* (11th October), B7–10.

Our Priorities Have to be Trans-Global. *Canberra Times* (15th November), 23.

The Debate of the Century: A Response. [Notes] *Crux* 2, no. 3 (Autumn), 3, 6.

Review of *Great Apes and Humans: The Ethics of Coexistence*, ed. by Benjamin Beck, et al. *Quarterly Review of Biology* 77, no.4 (December), 485.

Animal Liberation, 2nd edition. [Norwegian translation] Oslo: Spartacus.

Practical Ethics. 2nd edition. [Swedish translation] *Praktisk Etik*, Stockholm: Thales.

A Darwinian Left. [French translation] *Une gauche Darwinienne*, Paris: Cassini.

Writings on an Ethical Life. [Portuguese (Brazil) translation] Rio de Janeiro: Ediouro Publicacoes.

Writings on an Ethical Life. [Spanish translation] *Una vida ética: Escritos*, Madrid: Taurus.

One World: The Ethics of Globalization. Yale University Press.

One World: The Ethics of Globalization. Melbourne: Text.

Poverty, Facts, and Political Philosophies: Response to "More than Charity." [Notes] *Ethics and International Affairs* 16, no. 1, 121–24.

Achieving the Best Outcome: Final Rejoinder. [Notes] *Ethics and International Affairs* 16, no. 1, 127–28.

De Compras por el Supermercado Genético. *Isegoria* 27, 19–40.

R.M. Hare's Achievements in Moral Philosophy. *Utilitas* 14, no. 3, 309–317.

Gimpy Cat. In *The Good, the Bad, and the Difference*, by Randy Cohen (Doubleday), 245–46.

Unus Multorum. In *Nothing Makes You Free*, ed. Melvin Bukiet (Norton), 338–349.

El Pan que Retienes le Pernece al Hambriento. In *Etica y Desarrollo*, ed. Bernardo Kliksberg (Buenos Aires: Editorial El Ateneo), 149–162.

Preface to Clare Druce and Philip Lymbery. *Outlawed in Europe: How America Is Falling Behind Europe in Farm Animal Welfare* (New York: Archimedian Press), i–iii.

Famine, Affluence, and Morality, reprinted in: *Ethics*, eds. Steven Cahn and Peter Markie (Oxford University Press).

Famine, Affluence, and Morality, reprinted in: *Ethics in Practice*, by Hugh LaFollette, 2nd edition (Blackwell).

All Animals Are Equal, reprinted in: *Ethics in Practice*, by Hugh LaFollette, 2nd edition (Blackwell).

Chapter 1 of *Animal Liberation*, reprinted as: [Abridged] *The PETA Guide to Animal Liberation, Everyday Ethics*, ed. David Benatar (McGraw-Hill).

Practical Ethics, 2nd edition, reprinted in: *Everyday Ethics*, ed. David Benatar (McGraw-Hill).

How Reliable Are Our Moral Intuitions? *Free Inquiry* 23, no. 1 (Winter 2002–2003), 19–20.

2003

Impatience, A Bad Reason to Wage War. *The Age* (5th February), 15.

How Many Lives Is This War Worth? *Los Angeles Times* (27th March).

The Ties that Bind. *Los Angeles Times* (28th April).

Animal Liberation at 30. *New York Review of Books* L, no. 8 (15th May), 23–26.

Some Are More Equal. *The Guardian* (19th May), 17.

The Ties that Bind, reprinted in: *Minneapolis Star-Tribune* and *Philadelphia Inquirer* (May).

With Karen Dawn. There Should Be No Room for Cruelty to Livestock. *Los Angeles Times* (8th June), M5.

The Ethics of Belief. *Free Inquiry* 23, no. 2 (Spring), 10–12.

Trivially Honest, Morally False. *Moscow Times* (1st August).

Thinking about the Dead. *Free Inquiry* 23, no. 3 (Summer), 22–23.

With Karen Dawn. Back at the Ranch: A Horror Story. *Los Angeles Times* (1st December) Pt. 1, 11.

One World: A Response to My Critics. [Notes] *Analyse and Kritik* 25, no. 2 (December), 285–293.

Practical Ethics. 2nd edition. [Polish translation] *Etyka praktyczna*, Warsaw: Wydawnictwo Ksià"ka i Wiedza.

Marx. [Portuguese translation] Sao Paolo: Edicoes Loyola.

With Paola Cavalieri. *The Great Ape Project: Equality Beyond Humanity*. [French translation] *Le Projet Grands Singes*, Nantes: One Voice.

Rethinking Life and Death: The Collapse of Our Traditional Ethics. [Korean translation] Seoul: Cheolhak-Gua-Hyunsil.

A Darwinian Left. [Japanese translation] Tokyo: Shinchosa.

One World: Ethics and Globalization. [Spanish translation] *Un Solo Mundo, La ética de la Globalización*, Barcelona: Paidós.

One World: Ethics and Globalization. [Italian translation] *One World: L'etica della globalizzazione*, Turin: Einaudi.

One World: Ethics and Globalization. [Dutch translation] *Een Wereld: Ethiek in een tijd van globalisering*, Rotterdam: Lemniscaat.

One World: Ethics and Globalization. [Swedish translation] *En Värld*, Stockholm: Thales.

One World: Ethics and Globalization. [Chinese translation] Taipei: Discourse/Business Weekly Publications.

One World: Ethics and Globalization. [Korean translation] Seoul: Acanet.

Pushing Time Away: My Grandfather and the Tragedy of Jewish Vienna. New York: Ecco.

Pushing Time Away: My Grandfather and the Tragedy of Jewish Vienna, Melbourne: HarperCollins.

Voluntary Euthanasia: A Utilitarian Perspective. *Bioethics* 17, nos. 5–6, 526–541.

How Can We Prevent Crimes Against Humanity? In *Human Rights, Human Wrongs: The Oxford Amnesty Lectures 2001,* ed. Nicholas Owen (Oxford University Press), 92–137.

Foreword. In *The Great Ape Project Census: Recognition for the Uncounted* (Portland: Great Ape Project Books), 1–4.

One World: The Ethics of Globalisation. In *The Impact of Global Movements in the Twenty-First Century: The Proceedings of the Conference to Launch the Monash Institute for the Study of Global Movements,* by Felicity Rawlings-Sanaei and Andrew Fernando (Melbourne), 26–30.

Heavy Petting, reprinted in: [French translation] *Cahiers Antispécistes,* no. 22 (Fevrier), 13–17.

The Drowning Child and the Expanding Circle, reprinted in: *Raging Against the Machine,* ed. Chris Brazier (Oxford: New Internationalist Publications).

2004

With Karen Dawn. When Slaughter Makes Sense. *Newsday* (8th February), A30.

Killing Animals for Art. *The Art Newspaper,* no. 144 (February), 22.

An Ethic of Responsibility. *Free Inquiry* 24, no. 2 (February–March), 16–17.

Bush's Meandering Moral Compass. *Los Angeles Times* (25th March), B13.

Adventures of the White Coat People. Review of *Opening Skinner's Box,* by Lauren Slater. *New York Times Book Review* (28th March), 6.

The Ethics of George Bush: Good, Bad, or Irrelevant? *The Times Higher Education Supplement* (14th May), 19.

The Harm that Religion Does. *Free Inquiry* 24, no. 3 (June–July), 17, 58.

With Karen Dawn. Echoes of Abu Ghraib in Chicken Slaughterhouse. *Los Angeles Times* (25th July), M5.

Humans Are Sentient Too. *The Guardian* (30th July), 21.

A Bit Rich. *The Sunday Age* (22nd August), 15.

The Pope Moves Backward on Terminal Care. *Free Inquiry* 24, no. 5 (August–September), 19–20.

Taking Humanism Beyond Speciesism. *Free Inquiry* 24, no. 6 (October–November), 19–21.

Por Que Sou Vegetariano. *Veja,* Brazil (24th November), 118.

Ethic Cleansing. *The Bulletin* (15th December), 39–42.

With Renata Singer. Rootless, Voteless, but Happily Floating. *The Age* (26th December).

Stem Cell Research: The Fallacy in Bush's Position. *New Jersey Medicine* 101, no. 12 (December), 15–17.

Animal Liberation, 2nd edition. [Polish translation] *Wyzwolenie zwierzàt*, Warsaw: Pa∫stwowy Instytut Wydawniczy.

Animal Liberation, 2nd edition. [Portuguese (Brazil) translation] *Libertação Animal*, Rio de Janeiro: Lugano Editora.

Rethinking Life and Death: The Collapse of Our Traditional Ethics. [Slovenian translation] *Razmislimo znova o Ïivljenju in smrti*, Ljubljana: Studia Humanitatis.

One World: Ethics and Globalization, 2nd edition. Yale University Press.

One World: Ethics and Globalization. Hyderabad: Oxford Longman.

One World: Ethics and Globalization. [Portuguese translation] *Um Só Mundo*, Lisbon: Gradiva.

One World: Ethics and Globalization. [Portuguese translation] Sao Paulo: Livraria Martins Fontes.

Pushing Time Away: My Grandfather and the Tragedy of Jewish Vienna. London: Granta.

The President of Good and Evil: The Ethics of George W. Bush. New York: Dutton.

The President of Good and Evil: The Ethics of George W. Bush. London: Granta.

The President of Good and Evil: The Ethics of George W. Bush. Melbourne: Text.

The President of Good and Evil: The Ethics of George W. Bush. [With a new introduction] U.S. paperback edition. New York: Plume.

The President of Good and Evil: The Ethics of George W. Bush. [Dutch translation] Rotterdam: Lemniscaat.

The President of Good and Evil: The Ethics of George W. Bush. [Japanese translation] Kyoto: Showado.

The President of Good and Evil: The Ethics of George W. Bush. [German translation] Erlangen: Harald Fischer Verlag.

The President of Good and Evil: The Ethics of George W. Bush. [Spanish translation] *El presidente del Bien y del Mal*, Barcelona: Tusquets Editores.

The President of Good and Evil: The Ethics of George W. Bush. [Catalan translation] *El president del bé i el mal*, Lleida: Pagès Editors.

Comment Vivre Avec Les Animaux. (A French translation of three essays on Animal Liberation), Paris: Les Empêcheurs de penser en rond/Le Seuil.

With Tom Gregg. *How Ethical Is Australia? An Examination of Australia's Record as a Global* Citizen. Melbourne: Black.

Fazendo Compras no Supermercado Genético. ('Shopping at the Genetic Supermarket'), *Impulso* 15, no. 36, 13–23.

Ethics Beyond Species and Beyond Instincts: A Response to Richard Posner. In *Animal Rights: Current Debates and New Directions,* eds. Cass Sunstein and Martha Nussbaum (Oxford University Press), 78–92.

Preface to the 2nd edition. In *One World,* by Peter Singer, 2nd edition (Yale University Press), ix–xix.

Outsiders: Our Obligations to Those Beyond Our Borders. In *The Ethics of Assistance,* ed. Deen Chatterjee (Cambridge University Press), 11–32.

Famine, Affluence, and Morality, published in: [Swedish translation] *Vad är moraliskt rätt? Texter I normativ etik,* ed. Henrik Ahlenius (Stockholm: Thales), 149–160.

Passages from *Animal Liberation* (Revised edition), have been reprinted in: *Food for Thought,* by Steve Sapontzis (Prometheus), 108–117.

Chapter 6 of *Practical Ethics,* 2nd edition, reprinted in: [German translation] *Geschichte der Philosophie in Text und Darstellung: Gegenwart,* ed. P. Stekeler-Weithofer (Reclam).

Ethics Across the Species Boundary, reprinted in: [Spanish translation] *Los derechos de los animales,* ed. Marta Tafalla (Barcelona: Idea Books).

The Reproduction Revolution (An Extract entitled 'Genetic Engineering: Goals and Controls'), reprinted in: *Should Parents be Licensed?,* ed. Peg Tittle (Prometheus).

Writings on An Ethical Life (An Extract entitled 'Four Ethical Principles') reprinted in: *The Truth About the World,* ed. James Rachels (McGraw-Hill).

2005

Catastrophe: Apocalypse When? Review of *Catastrophe: Risk and Response,* by Richard Posner. *New York Times Book Review* (2nd January).

Obituary of Paul Edwards. Philosopher Insisted on Clarity and Rigour. *The Age* (14th January).

Chapter 6 of *Ethics into Action,* reprinted as: [French translation] Henry Spira. Faire avancer le schmilblic, *Les Cahiers antispécistes,* no. 24 (January), 11–26.

Law Reform, or DIY Suicide. *Free Inquiry* 25, no. 2 (February–March), 19–20.

Pulling Back the Curtain on the Mercy Killing of Newborns. *Los Angeles Times* (11th March).

Ethics for One World/Etica Para un Solo Mundo. *CONfines,* no. 1 (June), 9–18, 19–29.

Eating Ethically. *Free Inquiry* 25, no. 4 (June–July), 18–19.

Making Our Own Decisions about Death. Competency Should be Paramount. *Free Inquiry* 25, no. 5 (August–September), 36–38.

Se la Vita Non Vale La Vita. *L'espresso* (15th September), 101–04.

The Sanctity of Life. *Foreign Policy* (September–October), 40–41.

Ethics and Intuitions. *Journal of Ethics* 9, no. 3–4 (October), 331–352.

Chapter 3 of *One World,* translated reprinted as: [French translation] L'Organisation Mondiale du Commerce: Un Obstacle au Progrès de la Protédes Animaux? *Les Cahiers antispécistes,* no. 25 (October), 7–19.

La Sacralidad de la Vida. *Foreign Policy,* Edicion Espanola (October–November), 24–25.

Who Pays for Bird Flu? Syndicated, available at www.projectsyndicate.org in English, Spanish, Russian, French, German, Czech, Chinese, and Arabic (November).

Ethics and Disability: A Reply to Koch. [Notes] *Journal of Disability Policy Studies* 16, no. 2 (Fall), 130–33.

Revolutionary Ethics of Embryo Research. Syndicated, available at www.projectsyndicate.org in English, Spanish, Russian, French, German, Czech, Chinese, and Arabic (December).

Animal Liberation, 2nd edition. [Chinese (simplified characters) translation] Qingdao: Qingdao Publishing House.

Animal Liberation, 2nd edition. [Turkish translation] *Hayvan Özgürleflmesi*, Çemberlitas: Ayrinti Yayinlari.

Practical Ethics, 2nd edition. [Chinese (simplified characters) translation] Beijing: Oriental Press.

One World: Ethics and Globalization. [Japanese translation] Toyko: Showa-do.

One World: Ethics and Globalization. [Chinese (simplified characters) translation] Beijing: Oriental Press.

Pushing Time Away: My Grandfather and the Tragedy of Jewish Vienna, [German translation] *Mein Grossvater: die Tragödie der Juden von Wien*, Hamburg: Europa-Verlag.

Pushing Time Away: My Grandfather and the Tragedy of Jewish Vienna, [Italian translation] *Ciò Che Ci Unisce Non Ha Tempo*, Milan: Il Saggiatore.

With Renata Singer. *The Moral of the Story: An Anthology of Ethics Through Literature*. Oxford: Blackwell.

In Defense of Animals. The Second Wave. ed. Blackwell.

Intuitions, Heuristics, and Utilitarianism. [Notes] *Behavioral and Brain Sciences* 28, no. 4, 560–61.

Beach Philosophy. *Rusty's Byron Guide* Immersion, 20–23.

Ethics. [In Chinese] In *The Map of Contemporary British and American Philosophy*, ed. Kang Ouyang (Dangdai Yingmei Zhexue Ditu), 274–298.

Famine, Affluence, and Morality, published in: *Ethical Health Care*, eds. Patricia Illingworth and Wendy Parmet (Prentice-Hall).

All Animals Are Equal, reprinted in: [Hungarian translation] *Környezet és etika. Szöveggyıjtemény*, eds. Lányi András, Jávor Benedek (Budapest: L'Harmattan), 39–56.

Eating Ethically, reprinted in: *Melbourne University Magazine*, 12–13.

Poverty, Facts, and Political Philosophies, and One More Try, have been reprinted as: Poverty, Facts, and Political Philosophies: A Debate with Andrew Kuper, *Global Responsibilities: Who Must Deliver on Human Rights*, ed. Andrew Kuper (Routledge), 173–181.

Je Mehr Wir Für Andere Leben, Desto Zufriedener Leben Wir, reprinted in: *Bruchen wir Gott? Moderne Texte zur Religionskritik*, ed. Edgr Dahl (Stuttgart: S.Hirzel Verlag), 158–161.

Shopping at the Genetic Supermarket, reprinted in: [Spanish translation] *Los Desafios Eticos de la Genetica Humana*, eds. Florencia Luna and Eduardo Rivera Lopez (Mexico: Universidad Nacional Autonoma de Mexico), 131–146.

Rights of Apes, reprinted in: *Thinking Allowed: The Best of Prospect, 1995–2005*, ed. David Goodhart (London: Atlantic).

With Marc Hauser. Morality Without Religion. *Free Inquiry* (December 2005–January 2006), 18–19.

2006

With Paul Shapiro. Seeking a More Ethical Egg. *The Times*, Trenton, NJ (28th January), A11.

With Helga Kuhse. 1980–2005: Bioethics Then and Now. *Monash Bioethics Review* 25, no. 1 (January), 9–14.

Godless Morality. Syndicated, available at www.projectsyndicate.org in English, Spanish, Russian, French, German, Czech, Chinese, and Arabic (January).

Fear and Freedom on the Internet. Syndicated, available at www.projectsyndicate.org in English, Spanish, Russian, French, German, Czech, Chinese, and Arabic (January).

30 Years of Animal Liberation, reprinted as: [German translation] Dreissig Jahre Tierbefreiung, *Emma* (January–February), 76–78.

Will We Let Jill Carroll Be Killed? *Los Angeles Times* (15th February), 13.

Devaluing Life. Syndicated, available at www.projectsyndicate.org in English, Spanish, Russian, French, German, Czech, Chinese, and Arabic (February).

Free Speech, Muhammad and the Holocaust. Syndicated, available at www.projectsyndicate.org in English, Spanish, Russian, French, German, Czech, Chinese, and Arabic (March).

Review of *The Evolution of Morality*, by Richard Joyce. [Online] *Notre Dame Philosophical Reviews* (18th April).

People in Greenhouses Should Turn Up the Heat. *Sydney Morning Herald* (28th April).

Why Pay More for Fairness? Syndicated, available at www.projectsyndicate.org in English, Spanish, Russian, French, German, Czech, Chinese, and Arabic (April).

Why the Korean Stem-Cell Controversy Matters. *Free Inquiry* (April–May), 25–26.

The Protests Must Go On. [Online comment] *Guardian* (19th May).

The Great Ape Debate. Syndicated, available at www.projectsyndicate.org in English, Spanish, Russian, French, German, Czech, Chinese, and Arabic (May).

The Ethics of Eating. Syndicated, available at www.projectsyndicate.org in English, Spanish, Russian, French, German, Czech, Chinese, and Arabic (June).

The Freedom to Ridicule Religion—and Deny the Holocaust. *Free Inquiry* 26, no. 4 (June–July), 21–22.

Happiness, Money, and Giving It Away. Syndicated, available at www.project-syndicate.org in English, Spanish, Russian, French, German, Czech, Chinese, and Arabic (July).

Symposium: Jihad, McWorld, Modernity: Public Intellectuals Debate "The Clash of Civilizations." *Salmagundi*, no. 150–51 (Spring–Summer), 85–213.

With Jim Mason. Can You Do Good by Eating Well? *Greater Good* III, no. 1 (Spring–Summer), 10–15.

The Great Ape Project, reprinted in: [French translation] *Mouvements*, nos. 45–46 (May–August), 22–35.

Will the Polluters Pay for Climate Change? Syndicated, available at www.projectsyndicate.org in English, Spanish, Russian, French, German, Czech, Chinese, and Arabic (August).

Expanding the Circle. *Free Inquiry* 26, no. 5 (August-September), 23–25.

With Agata Sagan. Choose Life. *The Bulletin* (5th September).

Soll Sterbehilfe Erlaubt Werden? *Die Ganze Woche*, Vienna, no. 37 (13th September).

With Bruce Friedrich. The Longest Journey Begins with a Single Step: Promoting Animal Rights by Promoting Reform. *Satya* (September), 12–13.

The Mixed Blessing of Genetic Code? Syndicated, available at www.project-syndicate.org in English, Spanish, Russian, French, German, Czech, Chinese, and Arabic (September).

Look Your Dinner in the Eye. *New Scientist* (7th October), 22.

Homosexuality Is Not Immoral. Syndicated, available at www.projectsyndicate.org in English, Spanish, Russian, French, German, Czech, Chinese, and Arabic (October).

What Greater Motivation? *Free Inquiry* (October–November), 17–18.

Madonna and Child. Syndicated, available at www.projectsyndicate.org in English, Spanish, Russian, French, German, Czech, Chinese, and Arabic (November).

What Should a Billionaire Give—and What Should You? *New York Times Magazine* (17th December), 58–63, 80, 83, 87.

Questions for Peter Singer. [Web Exclusive] *New York Times Magazine* (24th December).

Pigs, Calves, and American Democracy. Syndicated, available at www.project-syndicate.org in English, Spanish, Russian, French, German, Czech, Chinese, and Arabic (December).

Marx. [Greek translation] Athens: Polytropon.

Hegel. [Greek translation] Athens: Polytropon.

With Helga Kuhse. *Bioethics. An Anthology*, 2nd edition. Blackwell.

One World: Ethics and Globalization. [Polish translation] Warsaw: Ksià"ka i Wiedza.

One World: Ethics and Globalization. [Slovakian translation] Bratislava: VSSS.

With Jim Mason. *The Way We Eat: Why Our Food Choices Matter*. New York: Rodale.

With Jim Mason. *The Way We Eat: Why Our Food Choices Matter*. Melbourne: Text.

With Jim Mason. *The Way We Eat: Why Our Food Choices Matter*. London: Random House.

Ethics and Climate Change: A Commntary on MacCracken, Toman and Gardiner. [Notes] *Environmental Values* 15, 415–422.

Foreword. [Notes] *CleanFood Organic* I, no. 3, 7.

Foreword: Shopping at the Genetic Supermarket. In *The Ethics of Inheritable Genetic Modification*, eds. John Rasko, Gabrielle O'Sullivan, and Rachel Ankeny (Cambridge University Press), xiii–xxxi.

The Ethical Responsibilities of Writers Addressing Political Issues. In *Making Waves: 10 Years of the Byron Bay Writers Festival*, eds. Marele Day, Susan Bradley Smith, and Fay Knight (University of Queensland Press), 155–162.

Morality, Reason, and the Rights of Animals. In *Primates and Philosophers*, by Frans de Waal, Edited by Stephen Macedo and Josiah Ober (Princeton University Press), 140–158.

Éthique Appliquée. In *Le Dictionnaire des Sciences Humaines*, eds. Sylvie Mesure and Patrick Savidan (Presses Universitaires de France), 398–401.

Moral Experts, reprinted in: *The Philosophy of Expertise*, eds. Evan Selinger and Robert Crease (Columbia University Press), 187–89.

2007

Early Births Fade to Grey. *The Australian* (3rd January).

A Convenient Truth. *The New York Times* (26th January).

A Victory for McActivism. [Online comment] *Guardian* (29th January).

The Right to Die. Syndicated, available at www.projectsyndicate.org in English, Spanish, Russian, French, German, Czech, Chinese, and Arabic (January).

America the Hypocritical. Syndicated, available at www.projectsyndicate.org in English, Spanish, Russian, French, German, Czech, Chinese, and Arabic (February).

Can You Be Too Rich? *Los Angeles Times* (18th March).

Should We Trust Our Moral Intuitions? Syndicated, available at www.project-syndicate.org in English, Spanish, Russian, French, German, Czech, Chinese, and Arabic (March).

No Smile Limit. Syndicated, available at www.projectsyndicate.org in English, Spanish, Russian, French, German, Czech, Chinese, and Arabic (April).

With Agata Sagan. The Moral Status of Stem Cells. *Metaphilosophy* 38, no. 2–3 (April), 264–284.

A Private Affair? Syndicated, available at www.projectsyndicate.org in English, Spanish, Russian, French, German, Czech, Chinese, and Arabic (May).

With Ruth Chadwick, Helga Kuhse, Willem A. Landman, and Udo Schüklenk. *The Bioethics Reader: Editors' Choice*. Oxford: Blackwell.

With Laura Grabel and Lori Gruen. *Stem Cell Research: The Ethical Issues*. Blackwell.

Practical Ethics, 2nd edition. [Kurdish translation].

Practical Ethics, 2nd edition. [Hebrew translation] Jerusalem: Magnes Press.

Marx. [Spanish translation] Mexico: Harla.

Marx. [Chinese translation] *Great Political Thinkers*, Hong Kong: Oxford University Press.

Hegel. Brazil: Edicoes Loyola.

Hegel. [Turkish translation] Altin Kitaplar.

A Companion to Ethics. [Chinese translation] Beijing: The Commercial Press.

A Companion to Ethics. [Turkish translation] Yapi Yayinlari.

A Companion to Ethics. [Korean translation] Chulhak-Kwa-Hyunsil.

A Companion to Ethics. [Serbian translation] Izdavacka Knjizarnica Zorana Stojanovica.

A Companion to Ethics. [Romanian translation] Bucharest: Polirom.

With Helga Kuhse. *A Companion to Bioethics.* [Korean translation] Seoul: In Gan Sa Rang.

Ethics into Action: Henry Spira and the Animal Rights Movement. [Chinese translation] Taiwan: Persimmon Cultural Enterprise.

A Darwinian Left. [Korean edition] Seoul: E–Um.

Writings on an Ethical Life. [Portuguese translation] Lisbon: Dom Quixote.

2008

Unsanctifying Human Life: Essays on Ethics, edited by Helga Kuhse. [Spanish translation] Ediciones Catedra.

Unsanctifying Human Life: Essays on Ethics, edited by Helga Kuhse. [Japanese translation] Koyo Shobo.

One World: Ethics and Globalization. [Croatian translation] Zagreb: Ibis Grafika.

The President of Good and Evil: The Ethics of George W. Bush. [Italian translation] Il Saggiatore.

With Jim Mason. *The Way We Eat: Why Our Food Choices Matter.* [Portuguese translation] Lisbon: Dom Quixote.

With Jim Mason. *The Way We Eat: Why Our Food Choices Matter.* [Portuguese (Brazil) translation] Elsevier.

With Jim Mason. *The Way We Eat: Why Our Food Choices Matter.* [Italian translation] Il Saggiatore.

Living Ethically in the Twenty-First Century: Contemporary Society and Practical Ethics. Tenth Dasan Memorial Lectures in Philosophy. Seoul: Chulhakkwahyunsilsa, Seoul. In Korean and English.

The Way We Eat: Why Our Food Choices Matter. [Korean translation] Seoul: Woongjin Think Big.

Foreword to Marian Stamp Dawkins and Roland Bonney, *The Future of Animal Farming* (Blackwell), vii–ix.

Preface to Jean-Baptiste Jeangène Vilmer, *Éthique Animale* (Paris: Presses Universitaires de France), 1–3.

Preface to A. Asai and T. Yamauchi, *Reading Singer: Practical Ethics in the Global Age,* (in Japanese; Tokyo: Showado), i–ii.

Worshipping at the Temple of Diana. *Free Inquiry* (December 2007–January 2008), 22–23.

Putting Practice into Ethics. Review of *Experiments in Ethics* by Kwame Anthony Appiah. *New York Sun* (January 16th).

Hypocrisy on the High Seas? Syndicated, available at www.projectsyndicate.org in English, Spanish, Russian, French, German, Czech, Chinese, and Arabic (January).

Holding Charities Accountable? Syndicated, available at www.projectsyndicate.org in English, Spanish, Russian, French, German, Czech, Chinese, and Arabic (February).

Should We Discuss Race and Intelligence? *Free Inquiry* (February–March).

No Diseases for Old Men. Syndicated, available at www.projectsyndicate.org in English, Spanish, Russian, French, German, Czech, Chinese, and Arabic (March).

We Put It There, So Let's Go First in Cleaning Up. *The Age* (April 3rd).

Is There Moral Progress? Syndicated, available at www.projectsyndicate.org in English, Spanish, Russian, French, German, Czech, Chinese, and Arabic (April).

Whales: The Sacred Cows of the Sea? *Free Inquiry* (April–May 2008), 18–19.

The God of Suffering? Syndicated, available at www.projectsyndicate.org in English, Spanish, Russian, French, German, Czech, Chinese and Arabic (May).

Blatant Benevolence. Syndicated, available at www.projectsyndicate.org in English, Spanish, Russian, French, German, Czech, Chinese, and Arabic (June).

Withh Geoff Russell and Barry Brook. The Missing Link in the Garnaut Report. *The Age* (July 10th).

When Is It Time to Let Go? *Free Inquiry* (June–July), 18–19.

The Rights of Apes—and Humans. Syndicated, available at www.projectsyndicate.org in English, Spanish, Russian, French, German, Czech, Chinese, and Arabic (July).

The Hidden Costs of Money. Syndicated, available at www.projectsyndicate.org in English, Spanish, Russian, French, German, Czech, Chinese, and Arabic (August).

Harriet Johnson: A Tribute. *New Mobility* (August), 17–18.

Tuberculosis or Hair Loss? Refocusing Medical Research. Syndicated, available at www.projectsyndicate.org in English, Spanish, Russian, French, German, Czech, Chinese, and Arabic (September).

Right, Wrong, and Green. Review of Dale Jamieson, *Ethics and the Environment*. *Times Literary Supplement* (September 10th).

What McCain and Obama Ignore. Syndicated, available at www.projectsyndicate.org in English, Spanish, Russian, French, German, Czech, Chinese, and Arabic (October).

God and Suffering, Again. *Free Inquiry* (October–November), 19–20.

Obama's Global Ethical Challenges. Syndicated, available at www.projectsyndicate.org in English, Spanish, Russian, French, German, Czech, Chinese, and Arabic (November).

The Rights of Animals. *Newsweek* (November 19th).

The Tragic Cost of Being Unscientific. Syndicated, available at www.projectsyndicate.org in English, Spanish, Russian, French, German, Czech, Chinese, and Arabic (December).

Happy Nevertheless. Obituary for Harriet McBryde Johnson. *New York Times* (December 24th).

The Hidden Costs of Money. *Free Inquiry* (December 2008–January 2009).

2009

With Paola Cavalieri. Reply to Îiïek: On Îiïek and Animals. *International Journal of Baudrillard Studies* 6:1 (January).

Thirty Years of 'Test-Tube' Babies. Syndicated, available at www.projectsyndicate.org in English, Spanish, Russian, French, German, Czech, Chinese, and Arabic (January).

Capitalism's New Clothes. Syndicated, available at www.projectsyndicate.org in English, Spanish, Russian, French, German, Czech, Chinese, and Arabic (February).

The Science Behind Our Generosity. How Psychology Affects What We Give Charities. *Newsweek* (March 9th).

America's Shame: When Are We Going to Do Something about Global Poverty? *Chronicle of Higher Education* 55:27 (March 13th), B6–B10.

The Life You Can Save: Acting Now to End World Poverty. New York: Random House.

Help the World's Poor, even During This Great Recession. *Daily News* (March 10th).

Thirty Years of 'Test-Tube' Babies. *Free Inquiry* (April–May).

Index

by Kathleen League

act consequentialism, 268, 288. *See also* act utilitarianism
  options in, 293
act/omission distinction, 472–73
actions, moral degrees in, 273
act utilitarianism (AU), 176–77, 275
  critique of, 437, 439
Adams, Douglas, 54
  A Hitchhiker's Guide to the Galaxy, 54
Adler, Alfred, 2, 59, 61
Adorno, Theodor, 399
Aid as Obstacle, 235
aid programs, critiques of, 234–37
Alexander, John, 4
altruism, 38
altruistically focused life, 275–76
animal liberation movement, phases of, 164–65
animals
  and humans, comparative value of, 105–112
  moral standing of
    as experiential subjects, 108–09, 111
    and pain, 107, 109
    using lives of, question of, 107–08
animal treatment, as human question, 91
Anstötz, Christoph, 48, 54, 419
antislavery movement, in Britain, 256–57
Applied Ethics, 46
Aristotle, 465, 482
  Nicomachean Ethics, 481
Arthur, Leonard, 43

assisted suicide, xvii, xx, 200
Aung San Sun Kyi, 335
Austin, J.L., 4
Australian Greens, 58–59
availability cascades, 255
Ayer, A.J., 9, 21, 347, 381
Aziz, Tipu, 124

Bailey, Ronald, 219
Barro, Robert, 345
Barry, Brian
  Political Argument, 24
Batavia, Andrew, 200
Batson, Daniel, 245
Bayles, Michael, 30
Beauchamp, Tom L., 400
behavior, situational influences on, 243–49
Bekoff, Marc, 54
The Bell Curve, 214
beneficence, iterative versus aggregative approach, 270–71
Bentham, Jeremy, 6, 37, 349, 455, 460, 491, 501, 502
Berlin, Isaiah, 9, 336
Bill and Melinda Gates Foundation, 490
Binmore, Ken, 469
bioethics, 34, 213, 220
  hostility to, in Germany, 52
  international association of, 52
  reactions to, 399–400
  and sanctity of life doctrine, 397–98
  stories in, 215
Bioethics (journal), 47

bioethics debates, as dualistic, 397–98
blameworthiness
    and consequentialism, 291–92
    and moral code, 290–91
Boesky, Ivan, 56
Bogart, John B., 499, 503
Bono, 337
Boonin, David, 139, 145, 155
Boyce-Gibson, Sandy, 4
Brandt, Richard, 176, 179, 388
Broad, C.D., 21
Brown, Bob, 58, 59
Brown, Louise, 36
Bruno, Giordano, 78
Buckle, Stephen, 46, 151
Buffett, Warren, 325, 490
Bundy, Ted, xix, 369, 383
Burger King, 187
Bush, George W., 70, 71, 101, 334, 398,
    472
Butler, Joseph, 385

Cain (Biblical), 474
Callahan, Dan, 36
capitalism, and growth, 307–08
Caplan, Art, 36
cardinal utilitarianism, zero discount
    rates in, 303–05
Carney, Terry, 46
Carruthers, Peter, 105
Cavalieri, Paola, 53–55
Center for Human Values, 62, 84,
    99
Centre for Human Bioethics, 40, 45–46,
    53
channel factors, in behavior, 245
Childress, James F., 400
The Chimpanzee Project, 54
chimpanzees, 53–54
    basic rights for, 53–54
Chomsky, Noam, 70
Cialdini, Robert, 254
Cincinnatus, 340
Clark, Stephen, 19, 54
Clarke, Richard, 71
Clarkson, Thomas, 257
Clinton, Bill, 188

Close Encounters of the Third Kind
    (film), 92
Coetzee, J.M.
    Elizabeth Costello, 62
    The Lives of Animals, 62
Cohen, G.A., 10
Coleman, Diane, 170, 220
collective action, logic of, 344–45
communitarians, 347
A Companion to Ethics, 46
Compassion in World Farming, 24
Condemned to Repeat?, 235
consequentialism, rights in, 436–37
contractualism, 280, 415
Cooper-Dowda, Rus, 219
Cowen, Tyler, 207, 208, 303
Crisp, Roger, 56
Crowe, Russell, 183n38
Cullity, Garrett, 235, 270–76, 285
    The Moral Demands of Affluence, 390

Dahmer, Jeffrey, xix
The Dark Sides of Virtue, 235
Darley, John, 245, 246
Darwin, Charles, 354
Dawkins, Marion Stamp, 129, 191
Dawkins, Richard, 54
Dawson, Karen, 46
Dean, John, 71
Deaton, Angus, 328
Declaration on Great Apes, 55
demi-vegetarianism, 166n9
Descartes, René, 74
development agencies, and legal reform,
    341–42
Diamond, Jared, 54
Diamond, Renata. See Singer, Renata
Dickens, Charles, 470, 491
disability movement, in Germany, 401
disabled persons
    happiness of, 170
    medical prejudice against, 217–18
    public reaction to, 197
    silencing of, 219–220
    value of, 203
Doe, Baby Jane, 216–17
Doe, Indiana Baby, 216

Dostoevsky, Fyodor
  Crime and Punishment, xviii
Dover, Barbara, 47
Draize test, 164, 175n23
Drake, Stephen, xxii
Dworkin, Ronald, 11
Dwyer, John, 3

Easterbrook, Gregg, 69
economic growth, utilitarian argument
    for, 306, 312
Eichmann, Adolf, 348–49
Ellis, Brian, 27, 29
Embryo Experimentation, 46, 150–51
embryos, question of moral status of,
    412–14
Emma (magazine), 50
emotivism, 13
empathy/sympathy distinction, 469–470
Epicurus, 486
Equiano, 257
*Ethical and Legal Issues in
    Guardianship Options for
    Intellectually Disadvantaged People*,
    46
ethical egoism, 387
ethical intuitions, 362, 373, 378–79
Ethical Issues in Life and Death, 34
Etica e Animali (magazine), 53–54
Euclid, 482
eugenics movement, 213–14
Evans, Gareth, 9

Falwell, Jerry, 332
Famine Crimes, 235
Fast Pain Relief thought experiment, 441
Ferdinand, Franz, 70
fertilization, and beginning of life,
    150–51
Flannigan, Matthew, 157
Fletcher, Joseph, 135
food pyramid, 165
Foot, Philippa, 9
Forbes, Steve, 64
foreign aid, 338–39
    and policy goals, 338–39
    U.S. government budget for, 321

Fouts, Deborah, 54
Fouts, Roger, 54
Francione, Gary, 54
Franken, Al, 71
Freud, Sigmund, 2, 60, 61, 211
    "Dreams in Folklore," 59
Frey, Ray, 97
Friends of Animals, 39
fundamental attribution error, 247

Gadamer, Hans-Georg, 399
Gandhi, Mohandas K., 28
Gates, Bill, 322, 469, 490
Gates, Melinda, 490
Geldorf, Bob, 337
Genovese, Kitty, 244, 248, 255
Gensler, Harry J., 207, 208, 211
    "Peter Singer: Moral Hero or Nazi?"
    163
Gilgamesh, 347
Gill, Carol, 200
giving behavior, effecting change in,
    252–55
Gladiator (film), 183n38
Glass, Carol, 224
Glass, David, 217, 223–24
Glaucon, 486, 496
global poverty, 238
Glover, Jonathan, 12, 15, 86
    Causing Death and Saving Lives,
    12
Godlovitch, Roslind, 24
    Animals, Men, and Morals, 16, 19,
    25–26
Godlovitch, Stanley, 16, 19, 24, 25
golden rule, 486
Goldstein, Noah, 254
Goodall, Jane, 54
Grandin, Temple, 129
Great Ape Project, 54–55
The Great Ape Project, 54
greatest good, question of, 345–46
Gregg, Tom, 72
Gribble, Diana, 56, 57
Griffin, James, 12
Griskevicius, Vladas, 254
Gruen, Lori, 45

Animal Liberation: A Graphic Guide, 46
Gutmann, Amy, 62
Gyges, 496

Haiseldon, Harry, 214
Hall, James, 219
Hampshire, Stuart, 9
Halpern, Dan, 65, 69, 71
Hare, R.M., 9, 13–15, 22–23, 49, 177, 289, 381, 382, 389, 391, 392, 456, 480, 485, 486, 487, 495
  Ethics, 421
  Freedom and Reason, 13–14
  The Language of Morals, 13
  universalizability in, 13–14
Hare and Critics, 382
Harman, Gil, 62
harming/not-helping distinction, 477–78
Harris, John, 16, 25, 115, 116, 406
Harrison, Helen
  Premature Baby Book, 44
Harrison, Ruth
  Animal Machines, 16, 26
Hart, H.L.A., 9, 20, 33
  The Concept of Law, 11
Hastings Center, 36–37
Hawke, Bob, 58
Hawking, Stephen, 171
hedonistic utilitarianism, 211, 396
Hegel, G.W.F., 10, 37, 399
  Phenomenology of Spirit, 11
Heidegger, Martin, 399
"helping behavior," experiments in, 244–49
Helpman, E., 310
Hensel, Abigail, 161
Hensel, Brittany, 161
Heyward, Michael, 57
Hick, John, 171
Hinduism, 501
Hirsch, Fred, 250
Hochschild, Adam, 256–58
  Bury the Chains, 256
Hodgson, D.H.
  Consequences of Utilitarianism, 20

Hoerster, Norbert, 398
hospital thought experiment, 435
Howard, John, 72
Human, Alan, 20
human/animal distinction, questions about, xviii–xix
human behavior, explaining, xix
humanism, 77–78
humanitarian assistance, critics of, 234–37
human needs, variations in, 249–250
humans, importance of, question of, 78–84
human prejudice, and aliens, 94–95
human rights, 134
human values, 81
Hume, David, 360, 382, 384–85, 410, 454, 459, 482, 483, 485, 496
  A Treatise of Human Nature, 384
Husserl, Edmund, 399
Hutcheson, Francis, 385
Hyppolite, 10
Hun Sen, 342

In Defence of Animals, 46, 47
In Defense of Animals: The Second Wave, 71
Independence Day (film), 92, 95
"indicators of humanhood" (Fletcher), 135
infanticide, 183. *See also* Singer, Peter: on infanticide
informational cascades, 255
institutional utility, and trust, 438–39
International Association of Bioethics, 52
intervention in state sovereignty, justifying, 335
intuitionism, 5
  and revisionary ethics, 377
  and utilitarianism, 377
investment, utilitarian argument for, 305–06
in-vitro fertilization (IVF), controversy over, 40
Irenaeus, 171
Irwin, Bill, 171n16

Jackson, Frank, 29, 32
Jamieson, Dale, 45, 54, 68, 236
Jefferson, Thomas, 501, 502
Jellyby, Mrs., 470, 491
Jesus, 37
Johnson, Harriet McBryde, xxii, 189, 223
justice, 440
  and equality, 204

Kagan, Shelly, 233
Kahnemann, Daniel, 327
Kant, Immanuel, 336, 348–49, 399, 410, 411
  on autonomy, 136
Kasimba, Pascal, 46
Kateb, George, 61, 62
Kennan, George, 338
Kernot, Cheryl, 59
Keshen, Richard, 15–16, 18, 19, 24
Kevorkian, Jack, xx, 215
killing and letting-die, utilitarian views on, 181–83
Kravinsky, Zell, 443
Kroy, Moshe, 30
Kuhse, Helga, 40, 41, 43–47, 52, 53, 63, 398
  Should the Baby Live?, 44
Kuper, Andrew, 235, 236
Kuran, Timur, 255

Ladd, John, 34
Latané, Bibb
  The Unresponsive Bystander, 246
Lebenshilfe, 419
Lecky, W.E.H., 37
Lewis, Alan, 20
Lewis, David, 62
libertarians, 231
Linzey, Andrew, 19
Locke, John, 454
Lockean natural rights theory, 285–86
Lorber, John, 43, 44
Lords of Poverty, 234
Lukacs, György, 399
Luther, Martin, 78, 90

Mackie, John, 9, 20, 23, 421
Maclean, Anne, 405, 407–09, 421
  The Elimination of Morality, 421
Maple Leaf Foods, 187
Maren, Michael, 235
Martini, Carlo Maria, 160
Marx, Karl, 10, 37, 63, 266, 354, 399, 486
Mason, Jim
  Animal Factories, 39, 72
  The Ethics of What We Eat, 72, 125, 127, 188
McCloskey, H.J., 4–6, 8, 29, 31
McDowell, John, 9
McGinn, Colin, 54
McKee, John, 63
McMahan, Jeff, 160–61
  The Ethics of Killing, 160
McPhee, Hilary, 56
meat-eating
  arguments against, 165–67
  goal of reducing, suggestions for, 166–67
  increase in, 165
meat market, expansion of, 121
Meggle, Georg, 48, 49
Mendelssohn, Felix, 146
Mengele, Josef, 401
meta-ethics, 359
Miles, Lynn White, 54
Milgram experiments, 248
Mill, John Stuart, 32, 33, 57, 50–51, 157, 295, 432–33, 436, 460, 471
  On Liberty, 50
Miller, David, 446
Miller, Richard, 277, 279–285
Millgram, Elijah, 442n20
minimizing suffering, question of relative importance of, 441–42
Monkeys, Rats, and Me: Animal Testing (documentary), 124
Monro, D.H., 494
Montaigne, Michel de, 78
Moore, G.E., 13
moral community, of experiential subjects, 108–09
moral intuitions, 287

morality
  common-sense, 292
  and cultural context, 240–41
  ethical egoism, 387
  as guide, 479, 481
  Humean, 388
  and ideal observers, 484
  impartial, 388
  negative priority in, 471–72, 486
  objectively rational, 387
  options in, 292–93
  as overriding, 478
  as rational, 480–83
  rational choice, 388
  scope of, 408–09
  and special status of humans, 411
  and species membership, 412–13
  universal view in, 485–86
  validity of, 408–09
  versus matters of taste, 483–84
moral obligation. *See also* Singer, Peter:
      on moral obligation
  coherent moderate doctrines, 284–85
  common-sense view of, 276
  as indeterminate, 239–240
  and influences on behavior, 238–39,
      241–42
  and partial ideas of greatest good,
      337
  and personal projects, 274–75
  and poverty, 237–38, 256
  principle of moderate beneficence,
      284–85
  question of, 231
  of rich to poor, 336–37
The Moral of the Story, 71
moral philosophy
  naturalists, 22
  non-cognitivists, 22
  on publicity, 242
moral theory, maplike nature of,
      446–450, 453, 459
moral thinking
  critical level, 289, 456
  intuitive level, 289, 456
Morgenthau, Hans J., 338
Moses (Biblical), 183
Mynott, Jeremy, 30

Nader, Ralph
  Unsafe at Any Speed, 32
Napoleon Bonaparte, 2
Narveson, Jan, 12
Nasar, Sylvia
  A Beautiful Mind, 69
national development
  ambiguity of, 339–340
  and infrastructure, 340
  and subsidies, 344–45
  and trade, 344
  and women's equality, 343
Newkirk, Ingrid
  Save the Animals!, 47
Nicolas of Cusa, 78
Nietzsche, Friedrich, 80, 98, 399
Nisbett, Richard E., 245
non-cognitivism
  critique of, 368
  on ethical intuitions, 374–75
Not Dead Yet, xxii, 64, 170n14, 197,
      200, 215, 220
Nozick, Robert, 91, 101, 440, 470
"Nutrition Facts" box, suggestions for,
      166–67

objective list view, 115
Odysseus, 294
Oklahoma Study, 218
Olivieri, René, 47
Olson, Harry, 214
Oppenheim, David, 2, 59
Organ Harvesting thought experiment,
      363
Orwell, George, 500, 503
Otteson, James, 295
Oxfam, 19, 320
Oxfam America, 65, 264

pain, as moral-bearing characteristic,
      104–05
Papa Doc, 342
Parfit, Derek, 12, 15, 21, 30, 115, 263,
      303
Passmore, John, 31
Patterson, Francine, 54

Paul, G.A., 9
Pearson, John, 216
Pence, Gregory, 217
    Classic Cases in Medical Ethics, 216
People for the Ethical Treatment of
    Animals, 47
personhood
    question of emergence of, 169–170
    versus human being, as moral
        category, 86–87
persons, definition of, 85, 135
Persson, Ingmar, 54
Peters, Michael, 19
Petrarch, 78
Plamenatz, John, 9, 10
Plato, 78
    Republic, 4, 496
Pogge, Thomas, 325
Poirot, Hercule, xviii
positional goods, 250–51
Posner, Richard, 378
preference utilitarianism, 168, 211–12,
        402
    critique of, 172–76, 192
    principle of equal consideration of
        interests, 372, 374, 391, 402–05,
        421
Principle of Nearby Rescue, 281–83
Principle of Sacrifice, 267–68, 270, 275,
        276, 290, 293
    as counterproductive, 288
Principle of Sympathy, 277–79, 281
professional fund-raisers, 443
Project Syndicate, 66
Protagoras, 78
protest, question of effectiveness of, 120

QALY approach, 63, 112–13, 129
    problems of, 113–19
Quinton, Anthony, 9

Rachels, James, 26, 54, 471
Radical Philosophy Association, 24
Ramsey, Frank, 80
Rand, Ayn
    Atlas Shrugged, 30

Rationalism, 77
rationalist intuitionism, 361–62
    and reason for action, 370–71
Rationalist Society, 6
Ratzinger, Joseph, 398
Rawls, John, 174, 330, 440, 453
    on rules of thumb, 437
    A Theory of Justice, 23–24
Reason (magazine), 219
Reed, Candice, 39
Reeve, Andrew, 20
Reeve, Christopher, 207
Regan, Tom, 28, 54
reputational cascades, 255
Revlon animal experiments, protests
        against, 164–65
Rice, Condoleeza, 188
Rice, Vernon, 6
Richardson, Jeff, 63
Risse, Mathias, 236
Ritter, Joachim, 399
Robbins, Kathy, 69, 71
The Road to Hell, 234
Roberts, Peter, 25
Rollins, Bernard, 54
Roosevelt, Franklin D., 171
Ross, Lee, 245
Ross, W.D., 5
Rousseau, Jean-Jacques, 331, 338, 347,
        354, 355
rule utilitarianism (RU), 176–77, 179
Russell, Bertrand, 64
    A Free Man's Worship, 80
    History of Western Philosophy, 3
Ryan, Alan, 264
Ryder, Richard, 19

Sachs, Jeffrey
    The End of Poverty, 266
Sachs, Oliver, 129
sanctity of life doctrine, 134, 147, 168,
        411–12. *See also* Singer, Peter:
        on sanctity of life doctrine
    counterexamples to, 134
    critique of, 410
Sapontzis, Stephen, 54
Save the Children, 235

Savulescu, Julian, 46
Schiavo, Terri, xvii, 220, 225
Schuklenk, Udo, 46
Schwarzer, Alice, 50
Sea Shepherd Society, 442
Seiling, Eleanor, 27
selective focus, in moral psychology,
       442
Sen, Amartya, 344
Serebrinsky, Julia, 69–70
Severe Demand, 271–72, 275
Shaftesbury, Lord, 385
Shah of Iran, 306
Shallow Pond analogy, 231, 267, 281,
       287, 373, 374, 505
Shapiro, Harold, 64
Sidgwick, Henry, 12, 174, 241, 242,
       260, 262–63, 372, 373, 376,
       391–92, 460, 467,468, 486, 487,
       488
    The Methods of Ethics, 262, 392, 488,
       490
    on utilitarianism, 262–63
Silvers, Robert, 25–26
Singer, Joan, 1, 2, 61
Singer, Marion, 30
Singer, Peter
    on abortion, xvi, 7, 133, 135, 158,
       172, 404
       and argument from potential,
          425–26
       and future-of-value arguments,
          158–160
    on absolutism, 124
    on act/omission distinction, 472
       and potentiality, 148–49
    and act utilitarianism (AU), 178, 179,
       181, 182, 455–56, 459
    "All Animals Are Equal," 349
    *The Allocation of Health Care
       Resources*, 63
    on altruism, 38
    on animal experimentation, xxi, 27,
       123–25, 209
    Animal Factories, 39, 72
    Animal Liberation, 26, 27, 34, 56, 58,
       73, 100, 101, 105, 106, 111, 112,
       123–26, 461, 500, 504, 505

    economy of argument in, 104, 119
       limits of, 107
    on animal liberation, xviii, xxi, 25–26
    on animal preferences, 191
    and animal rights, xviii, 106, 123
    *Animal Rights and Human
       Obligations*, 28
    on animal suffering, 461
       magnitude of, 128
    and applied ethics, 73, 453
    on autonomy, 136–37
    on behavior, influencing, 264–65
    on bioethics, and medical profession,
       224
    on brain-death, xvii, 57, 215, 221–22
    on capitalist market economy, and
       poverty, 324–25
    cardinal utility in, 303
    childhood of, 2
    on Christianity, 3, 6–7
    on civil disobedience, 15
    on common-sense morality, 295–96
    A Companion to Ethics, 46
    on conscientious omnivores, 127–28
    consequentialism of, xviii
    on consumer society, 444
    on consumption, and happiness, 312
    on conventional morality, 367
    critiques of
       abstraction in, 347
       on act/omission distinction,
          473–74
       on autonomy, 137
       on best consequences, 347
       on coercion, 332
       on consequences, 335
       as dangerous, 220, 500
       on disabilities, 195, 198, 201–02,
          204–05, 499–500, 502
       as disregarding, 501–03
       on effectiveness, 332
       on equality principle, 406, 408,
          409, 416, 464–67
       on ethics, 348–350, 368–370
       on greatest good, 333, 338
       on helping animals, 474–75
       on helping others, 474–75
       on humanitarian aid, 235–36, 238

on impartiality, 406
on infanticide, 167, 169–171,
    197–200
on international justice, 415–16
on intuitions, 375–76
on meta-ethics, 359, 363, 370
on morality
    and foundations, 467
    and ideal observers, 484–85
    as not overriding, 465, 466, 475,
        478
    and rationality, 466–67, 483, 484
on moral obligation, 233–34, 241,
    269–271, 277–78, 281,
    287–290, 332, 336–37,
    474–78
    to animals, 476, 478–80
    denial of options in, 292
    of rich to poor, 344, 443–45,
        476–78, 485
on mother's Alzheimer's, 218–19
as non-cognitivist, 368
on partiality, 334
as preference utilitarian, 172–76,
    367–68
on redistribution, 302
stories in, 215, 217–19
tensions in, 373–74
on universe's point of view, 467–69,
    475
utilitarianism of, 164
on war, 472
on wrongness of killing, 141, 148
on cruelty to animals, reduction in,
    187
A Darwinian Left, 39, 63, 324, 354
Dasan Memorial Lectures, 72–73
on democracy, and legitimacy, 355
on development institutions, 341
on disabilities, 121
    and quality of life, 206–07
on disability representatives, 225
on disabled infants, 42–43, 189
on Down syndrome, 215–16, 222–23
as eclectic, 331
on economic growth, 307
    negative effects of, 323, 326
education of, 2–15

Embryo Experimentation, 46, 150–51
on embryo experimentation, 149–150
Ethical and Legal Issues in
    Guardianship Options for
    Intellectually Disadvantaged
    People, 46
on ethical standing, and suffering, 349
on ethics, 356, 360
    biological basis of, 37–38
    as important, 464
    as nonobjective, 359–360, 370
    as universalizable, 464
"Ethics and Intuitions," 39, 73, 394
ethics in, xv, 362–63
    and positivism, 347–48
    as very demanding, 368–69
Ethics into Action, 60–61
"The Ethics of Life" monthly column,
    66
The Ethics of What We Eat, 72, 125,
    127, 188
on euthanasia, xvii, xx, 143, 209
on evil, 6–7
The Expanding Circle, 37, 39, 381,
    382, 424
on exporting bads, 461–62
on factory farming, 126–28
"Famine, Affluence, and Morality"
    21–22, 229, 231, 233, 234, 238,
    264, 297–98, 332, 429, 505
on future generations, 323–24
on globalization, 67–68, 307
on greatest good, bringing about,
    344
on group-specific principles, 423
Hegel, 37
How Are We to Live?, 56, 327, 331,
    333, 337, 338, 347–48, 351, 354,
    497
How Ethical Is Australia?, 72
on human/animal distinction, 461
on human nature, 354
on human rights, 123
on impartiality, 351, 353
importance of, xv
In Defence of Animals, 46, 47
In Defense of Animals: The Second
    Wave, 71

at Princeton, 64, 66–67, 187
principle of equal consideration of
    interests, 397, 402, 421–24,
    463–64
on Principle of Sacrifice, 288–90, 295
prominence of, 103–05
protests against, 48–51, 167, 186,
    419–420
    in Germany, context of, 398–402
Pushing Time Away, 2, 70
on reason, 355
on redistribution, 320–22
The Reproduction Revolution, 41
Rethinking Life and Death, 58, 215,
    221–23, 505
revisionary ethics of, 363, 364
on right-to-life issues, 86, 139, 154,
    168, 212
as rule utilitarian (RU), 177–81
on rule utilitarianism, 456
on sanctity of life doctrine, xviii, 34,
    86, 134–35, 153, 193–94, 397,
    404, 410, 422, 426
on self-interest, 56, 312, 356
Should the Baby Live?, 44, 45, 51,
    139, 140, 148
on slogans, 209
on speciesism, 34, 53, 84, 97, 99–101,
    123, 210, 402, 403, 410, 416, 425
student activities of, 6–7
on subsidies, 324
on suffering, xvi, xviii, 349
on torture, 261
on two-level utilitarianism, 456–57
Uehiro Lectures, 72–73
on universalizability, 383, 421–22
on universe's point of view, 98
"Unsanctifying Human Life," 34
on utilitarianism, 422, 455–57
    and bad consequences, 491
    and burdened nondemocratic states,
    355
    and family and friends, 294
    ideal observer in, 98
    two-levels, 456–57
utilitarianism of, 98–99, 106, 138,
    168, 177–181, 182, 192–93,
    329–331

on utility, interpersonal comparisons
    of, 128–29
on utility of others, as motivation,
    489–90
and vegetarianism, 16–18, 120, 121,
    125–27
The Way We Eat, 72
on wealth, and happiness, 326–28
on Western civilization, 459
Writings on an Ethical Life, 65, 74
Singer, Renata (Diamond), 7, 10, 16–17,
    58, 61, 62, 71–72
    The Moral of the Story, 71
Singer, Ruth, 26
Singer: A Dangerous Mind
    (documentary), 224
"Singer Affair," 48, 52
Singerites, lack of, 105, 106
Singer Principle (SP), 429–430, 461,
    462
    consequences of, in strategic world,
    433–34
    critique of, 453
    and exporting bads, 452
    and species equality, 431–32
    symmetry problem, 430–31
situationism, 243–44, 252
    experiments in, 244–49
Smart, J.J.C., 29, 456
Smith, Adam, 250, 331, 340, 347, 354,
    454
Smithfield Foods, 187
social psychology, experiments in,
    244–49
sociobiology, 36
Socrates, xxi, 436, 496
speciesism, 104, 413
    and aliens, 92–93
    defense of, 93
Spira, Henry, 28, 60, 164–65, 167, 301,
    440
Star Wars (film), 92
Steigleder, Klaus, 408, 409
Stevenson, C.L., 13, 381
    Ethics and Language, 5
Stirner, Max, 92
Stone, Jim, 150
Strawson, P.F., 9

subsidies, problems of, 344–45
suffering, justifications of, xxii
suicide, physician-assisted, xvii, xx, 200
Sunstein, Cass, 255
Swan, John, 35, 40
Swinburne, Richard, 189
Swindal, James, 169
Swindells, John, 60
sympathy, as not rational, 470

Ten, Chin Liew, 32
Test-Tube Babies, 41
Thomas, J.L.H., 11
Thomson, Judith Jarvis, 2886
  "A Defense of Abortion," 230
Tighe, Margaret, 64
Tocqueville, Alexis de, 258
Tooley, Michael, 85, 139, 141, 151
Tooley-Singer theory, 139, 141, 150, 151
  critique of, 141
  and ideal desires, 143–45
  revisions of, 141–44
Townsend, Aubrey, 32, 33
Tragic Commons thought experiment,
  433
Transparency International, 356
trolley thought experiment, 434–35,
  439–440
Trounson, Alan, 40
Tucker, Robert
  Philosophy and Myth in Karl Marx,
  10

Unger, Peter, 233, 390, 444, 478
  Living High and Letting Die, 371, 391
UNICEF, 65, 67, 264, 320
United Action for Animals, 27
United States Agency for International
  Development (USAID), 338
utilitarianism, 32–33, 234. *See also* act
  utilitarianism; cardinal
  utilitarianism; hedonistic
  utilitarianism; preference
  utilitarianism; rule utilitarianism.
  and agent/institution distinction, 458
  and animals, 89, 460

and applied ethics, 396
and bioethics, 395–98
classical, 168, 396
critique of, 5–6, 105–06, 333–35, 346
  harm caused by, 470–71
  sympathy in, 470
and democracy, 335
and economic growth, 306–312, 317
and exporting bads, 440
on human prejudice, 88
Ideal Observer (IO) in, 87–89
and legal moralism, 33
and moral obligation, 241–42
and no-harm principle, 397
and optimizing constraints, 436–38
and personal projects, 275
and public/private distinction, 262–63
and redistribution, 310–11, 317
rule of practice versus rule of thumb,
  437
and self-interest, 336
on suffering, 89, 301
two-levels, 456–57
as very demanding, 301–02
and welfare state, 310–11
and wrongness of killing persons,
  137
utility, as subjective, 468

value, respecting versus promoting,
  434–35
value of life, quality of life view,
  109–111
vegetarianism. *See also* Singer, Peter:
  and vegetarianism
  as not causally effective, 120–22
  as protest, 120

Waller, Louis, 40
Walters, Bill, 34–36, 40–41
Walzer, Michael, 70
Washington, George, 340
Watson, Paul, 442, 443
wealth, and happiness, 313–16
Webb, Beatrice, 63
Webb, Sidney, 63

well-being, relativity of, 249–252
Wells, Deane, 41–42
　The Reproduction Revolution, 41–42
Wells, H.G.
　War of the Worlds, 92
Wikler, Dan, 52
Williams, Bernard, 263, 274, 335
Wilson, E.O., 38
　Sociobiology, 36
Wittgenstein, Ludwig
　Philosophical Investigations, 4
Wood, Carl, 40
Wood, David, 19
World Bank, 338–342, 356

World Trade Organization, protests
　against, 67–68
wrongness of killing
　desire account of, 139, 147, 150
　future of value account of, 145–150,
　　152
　potentiality theory of, 147
　Tooley-Singer account of, 141

Young, Robert, 29, 30

Zachary, R.B., 44